**DATE DUE**

| | | | |
|---|---|---|---|
| | | | |
| | | | |
| | | | |
| | | | |
| | | | |
| | | | |
| | | | |
| | | | |
| | | | |
| | | | |
| | | | |

# MERCHANT OF DREAMS

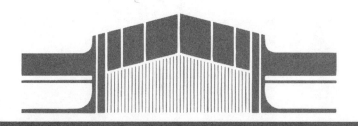

# MERCHANT OF DREAMS

## Louis B. Mayer, M.G.M., and the Secret Hollywood

## BY CHARLES HIGHAM

DONALD I. FINE, INC.

*New York*

Library of Congress Cataloging-in-Publication Data
Higham, Charles
Merchant of dreams : Louis B. Mayer, M.G.M., and the secret Hollywood / by
Charles Higham.
p. cm.
Includes bibliographical references and index.
ISBN 1-55611-345-5
1. Mayer, Louis B. (Louis Burt), 1885–1957. 2. Metro-Goldwyn-Mayer. 3. Motion
picture producers and directors—United States—Biography. I. Title.
PN1998.3.M397H54   1992
791.43′0232′092—dc20
[B]     92-54463
CIP

Manufactured in the United States of America

10   9   8   7   6   5   4   3   2   1

Designed by Irving Perkins Associates

*To the one who knows who it is for*

# CONTENTS

# PROLOGUE

On May 2, 1970, over three thousand people crowded Metro-Goldwyn-Mayer's sound stage 27 for the greatest auction in Hollywood history. They watched, enthralled, as the first selection of 11,855 colored slides was flashed before them; a world was being sold. There were imitation trains, ships, and airplanes; chariots; half a dozen kinds of Victorian carriages and cabs; royal coaches; Rolls Royces; Düsenbergs; vintage hot rods. You could buy *Show Boat*'s *Cotton Blossom*; galleys from *Ben-Hur*; the Stanley Steamer from *Summer Holiday*; the train from *The Harvey Girls*; a grand piano from *Camille*; a copy of the *Mayflower* from *Plymouth Adventure*; ball gowns; wedding dresses; white-tie-and-tails suits; shoes; stuffed birds and animals; family portraits; weapons, from clubs and bows and arrows to .38 revolvers and modern rifles. Of all the nostalgic items, the most touching were Judy Garland's ruby slippers from *The Wizard of Oz*: somebody bought them for $15,000, only to hear doubts raised as to whether they were authentic. How could anyone be sure, in a make-believe world?

I was at the auction; it was a painful spectacle, of a Hollywood being eaten away by the acids of terror and greed. Terror that all of this vast mass of close to twelve thousand items might never be used again; greed on the part of the new owners, who cared nothing for preserving what might fetch a profit. Nine years earlier, almost to the day, I had made my first visit to M.G.M., when, already, a sense of panic had begun to set in. I was taken care of by Howard Strickling, the genial and deeply secretive head of publicity, who had the grave and sensible air of a gentleman farmer, and by Robert Vogel, the quick, bright, witty and wiry head of the foreign division. As we went into the big old art deco commissary, with its beige walls and tubular steel furnishings, Vogel introduced me to Douglas Shearer, Norma's brother, head of the sound department and influential studio honcho. Told, loudly, my name, Shearer cupped his hand to his ear and said, "Eh? What's that?" Later, one of the studio's leading color cinematographers congratulated me on my green jacket. It was blue.

At that moment, I fell in love with Hollywood. It was Looking Glass Land, where nothing made sense, where fantasy reigned, where everything was the opposite of what it seemed. Like the poet in Cocteau's *Orphée*, who put his hands through a mirror that dissolved like water and found himself in the Underworld, I walked into a mysterious and secret universe, a universe that was created from the fantasies of the immigrant Jewish studio chiefs. They had dreamed of perfect ladies and gentlemen in perfect settings; of moral standards sustained in adversity; of infinitely wise parents; of the glories of the Flag. And of them all, I learned once again, Louis B. Mayer was the leader, the greatest merchant of all the vivid dreams.

He was profoundly sentimental; his favorite composers were Rachmaninoff and Tchaikovsky; his favorite painter was Grandma Moses. Although he made exceptions for Marie Dressler and Wallace Beery, he, for the most part, insisted on perfection in his stars. If they had flaws, such as Garbo's broad shoulders and great height, Clark Gable's jug ears and false teeth, Norma Shearer's eye cast—then these would be concealed through skillful direction, lighting, makeup; the one mode that must never be encouraged at M.G.M. was realism.

Mayer believed that actors did not know what was good for themselves; he controlled them to the point of personally putting saccharine in their coffee to keep their weight down, telling them what they could eat for breakfast, lunch and dinner, whom they could marry, whether it was time to have a baby or not, how to obtain an abortionist if a picture was at stake; he was as stern and loving to them as he was to his own daughters. He actually addressed them as his children; when the great star Robert Taylor sought a raise, he treated him like any seven-year-old begging for money to buy a toy train. Leaving the office disappointed, Taylor told a friend, "I didn't get the raise, but I gained a father."

He made everyone who worked for him feel that they were members of a royal family. They traveled first-class on planes, ships and trains; they stayed in good hotels; if they ran short of money, they were advanced cash for expensive clothes, houses and cars, and could pay back in installments from their salaries.

No man without jacket and tie would be received, no woman not perfectly tailored walked into Mayer's huge white office; but, until the advent of the blacklist era after World War II, he allowed for a wide range of political opinion. He nourished Communists and fascists alike;

if they could do a good job, and didn't blow up the studio, they were all right with him, as, in a magnificent stand before the House Committee in 1947, he made abundantly clear. Nor did he cancel an actress's contract because she wouldn't sleep with him; and, until their behavior became publicly scandalous, he protected his gay stars as well. Twice he covered up acts of manslaughter, one of them by Clark Gable, the other by John Huston. An executive was found who went to prison to protect Gable's reputation; the district attorney was paid off and Huston sent overseas.

Mayer was in love with many famous women, including Jean Howard, Ad (mother of Budd) Schulberg, Grace Moore, Ann Miller, Eleanor Powell, Ginny Simms and Jeanette MacDonald. He conducted his affairs with all of the courtly gallantry of one of his WASP movie heroes, with flowers, champagne, mothers brought along as chaperones, discreet rhumbas and tangos in nightclubs protected from the press.

Often portrayed as a stupid ogre, most notably in a brilliant caricature by Michael Lerner in the recent film *Barton Fink*, Mayer was, in fact, an inspired and culturally aware executive who made the most beautifully crafted of Hollywood films. He carried, well into the twentieth century, the great theatrical traditions he had respected as a boy: the traditions of those giants of the stage, David Belasco, Charles Frohman and Florenz Ziegfeld, of sumptuously presented, morally instructive dramas or glowing musicals. He succeeded largely because of his unique capacity to select the right producers, directors, writers and performers for a particular enterprise, and then giving them autonomy.

Mayer wasn't perfect; he could be manipulative, despotic, cruel, unforgiving. But that he was not the monster portrayed in such celebrated works as Lillian Ross's *Picture* can be shown by the unswerving love to be found, even today, in his surviving movie and personal family members. I hope that, in following the chronicle of a man who, without looks, money or background, rose to become the highest-paid individual in America and whose almost unbearably overcrowded life would have destroyed most men long before he succumbed, I shall succeed in proving my point.

A note is necessary on the book's form. Although this is, in essence and by definition, a biography of a great man, it is also the biography of a great studio. Thus, I have often digressed to include the lives of the stars whose careers Mayer guided, and also the political, business and production of M.G.M., much of it drawn from hitherto sealed government files. It became especially important to extend the book's range when covering the period of World War II, as the complex dealings with potential or actual enemy governments became crucial; and thereafter, when the Truman and Eisenhower administrations effectively wrecked the studio system. But always the story returns to Mayer, the genius whose dream turned into a horrifying nightmare.

# 1885–1907

LAZAR MEIR WAS BORN in 1885 in the small, lumber-producing town of Dymer (the Russian spelling; the Ukrainian spelling at the time was Dumier), which was situated some twenty-five miles north-northwest of Kiev, in the rich, rolling land of the Ukraine. With patriotic whimsicality, Mayer always referred to his birthdate as July 4, even taking the risk of giving that date in his Declaration of Intention and Petition for Naturalization for American citizenship, which he made at the District Court of Massachusetts, in Boston, on February 11, 1911.[1]

Lazar's father, Jacob, who is believed to have been of Austro-Hungarian origin, was about thirty-five when the boy was born. Jacob was tiny, scarcely over five feet four inches, thin, with a bristling beard, exuding, despite his narrow shoulders and pinched chest, a fierce strength. He was known for his outbursts of violent rage, yet he could also be a wise, loving and guiding parent. He was a gifted linguist and a student of the Torah and the Talmud, who could find parallels, for the rest of his life, in the sacred texts for most problems, and could deal with those problems accordingly. His granddaughter, Irene Mayer Holt, says that he was too proud to earn a living, compelling his wife, the gentle and appealing Sarah Meltzer, to support him as best she could. Affectionately known as Chaya, Sarah was an Austro-Hungarian girl of higher class. She and Jacob were married through a broker in 1874.

Their elder daughter, Yetta, was born in 1878. She was a bright, clever, scholarly child, who inherited her father's yearning for religious knowledge. But she was forbidden by him to study the sacred writings; her sharpest memory in later life was reading the Torah in secret, when her father and mother were fast asleep in the next room. In those days of

---

[1] The name Meir has been determined from documents filed by Louis B. Mayer's father on his entry to the United States in 1921. Louis would give his birthplace variously as "Russia-Poland," Vilnius, Minsk and Omsk, according to his mood; his daughter Irene, in her memoirs, mentioned "Kovno-Vilnius," all presumably intended to throw potential biographers off the trail.

poor midwifery and inadequate hygiene, it is not surprising that Sarah gave birth to a number of stillborn children, possibly as many as six, before her second girl, Ida, was born in October 1883. Ida shared her elder sister's strength, determination and courage, and would also set about learning as much as she could in the dark hours of the Russian nights.

Aside from the harsh despotism of their father, the three children, Yetta, Ida and Lazar, suffered in their earliest years from a state of terror. It was the time of the pogroms, the mass murders of Jews.

It will probably never be known when the Mayer family patriarch made the decision to seek freedom in Great Britain. All that is certain is that they managed to make their way to England in 1886; they stayed there for almost a year. But Jacob Mayer was unable to succeed in any field and went to Ireland, hoping to find employment, while his wife, Yetta, Ida and Lazar sailed separately across the Atlantic. Unsuccessful, Jacob followed. In one version, that of Irene Mayer Selznick, they got off the ship in St. John, New Brunswick, Canada, and in another, that of Irene Mayer Holt, Yetta's daughter, they went directly to New York. Records of the time are incomplete and scattered; St. John immigrant files were burned long ago, and there is no trace of the family on any New York City passenger arrival list between 1885 and 1890. In his U.S. immigration documents, signed in 1921, Jacob Mayer stated that he was resident in Long Island from 1887 to 1892.

A fourth child, the bad seed, Rubin, later known as Rudolph, was born on April 17, 1889, in New York City, and a fifth, Gershon, later known as Jerry, was born in Brooklyn, almost exactly two years later, on April 16, 1891.

It is generally accepted that Jacob Mayer worked as a peddler during those years, selling bottles, old tin cans and other scrap off a cart.

Struggling and unhappy, the family, with the exception of Yetta, moved to St. John, New Brunswick, in 1892. There has been much speculation about the reason for the move. Mayer's niece, Mitzi Fielding, revealed that Jacob Mayer had gotten into a fight in circumstances unknown and almost succeeded in killing his opponent. The man was so severely injured that there might have been a question of attempted manslaughter and the family had to escape the police immediately. Flight across the border to Canada was not difficult in those days. The reason for choosing St. John was a practical one.

The town, which the family may have remembered from their ship's stopover in the late 1880s, offered many opportunities, most of them unavailable in New York, for happy Jewish settlement. Jews had arrived there from as early as 1760; the first settlers were British, led by the

tobacconist Soloman Hart. Prosperous, forward looking, the Jewish merchants not only brought a strong cultural influence to the community but were accepted at once by the British, and by the Scandinavian immigrants who dominated the town. Their children were happily admitted to Protestant and Catholic schools, and there is no evidence that they suffered from ill treatment. Yet there were only about eight families resident in the district when the Mayers arrived from New York. The Fernhill Jewish Cemetery had been in existence for only two years; previously, the Harts, Isaacses and other merchants had chosen to bury their dead in faraway Boston.

In those days, St. John was a town of wooden, neatly kept houses, well-swept streets and sparkling, clean sea air, with magnificent views from its stony peninsula across the Bay of Fundy. It was Canada's most popular winter port, since its waters in that season were free of ice, and the ships from Europe could sail unencumbered to safe harbor. The soil around St. John was rich and fruitful, the steam trains roared in from all over the continent, and the fisheries, with their hundreds of mostly Scandinavian employees, thrived in all seasons.

Larger than nearby Fredericton, St. John was the most bustling, brisk and energetic city in all of the sturdy pro-British state of New Brunswick. The massive Victorian edifices, the Roman Catholic Cathedral, Wiggins' Orphan Asylum, the Masonic and Odd Fellows Hall, the YMCA and Town Hall, stood foursquare against the stinging winds off the Atlantic.

In 1894, Yetta, who was barely sixteen, had met and fallen in love with Abraham Rieder, a young and handsome, if physically frail, languages teacher who had lately immigrated from Germany, where he had been a lecturer at the University of Berlin. Yetta obtained work as a clerk in Manhattan, in order not to be separated from Rieder, to whom she became engaged in about 1899.

The Mayers moved first to a small house, 425 Main Street, in Portland, in the northern part of the town, then, in 1899, to 28 Acadia Street, only a few blocks away. A single photograph survives of the neighborhood at the time the family lived there. It shows houses of bleached or beige clapboard, built tight together, without an inch of space between, their doors painted a drab brown, their roofs russet and pointed, decorated with fancy eaves. Shops have white canvas awnings flapping in the wind. A brown tram clangs down the center of Main Street; a Mayerish peddler is seen, his cart drawn by a poor dray horse on loose reins, a white, crumpled hat on his head, a blue coat hung on his shoulders; in the distance, against fluffy, cottonish cumulus and a washed-out blue-green northern sky, there is the thin, narrow spire of a church.

Pedestrians are sparse: a few men in suits tightly buttoned against the wind, wearing bowler hats. The subdued colors of the scene, the tight-and-no-prying closeness of the houses with windows as narrow as fortress slits evoke an atmosphere of propriety, but the glittering, pure air makes this architectural rectitude both pleasing and picturesque.

Such was the world the Mayers entered, far removed from the squalor of Manhattan. It is easy to picture them: dwarfish, furious, high-powered, learned Jacob, no doubt grumbling about his plight as a mere peddler as he drives his cart down the hard, newly asphalted streets; round, plump-faced Sarah, weary but determined to keep her home immaculate and glossy with constant dusting, boiling the unsold remnants of the chickens she sold to make a soup, the taste of which would remain with her children for the rest of their lives; womanly, bustling Ida, a big girl at sixteen; Lazar, now known as Louis, his eyes sharp as diamonds, sturdy, muscular, inheriting his mother's square, stocky build, already foxy enough to take on anyone; and the good-looking Rubin (Rudolph), the baby, Gershon (Jerry), no doubt bawling vigorously away.

Among the numerous legends handed down about the Mayers was one that the brood was ill-treated, pelted by the local children with anything that would move. But the surviving reliable account from that period, obtained from Mrs. Emma MacCready of St. John, whose mother-in-law, Alice Maud Wilson, was Mayer's English literature teacher, corrects this view. Mrs. MacCready remembers that Louis began as a student in 1895 in the fifth grade at the Winter Street School, with Lizzie G. Corbet as head teacher. There were thirteen Jewish children in the class, a remarkable number considering there were only thirty boys and girls in all. They were all happy together, and nobody objected when the Jewish children, gifted scholars and effective athletes, rapidly moved into the front rows of desks, reserved for the best and brightest. "The Mayers were known as very thrifty, clean and decent people," Mrs. MacCready says. "There was no shame attached to the fact that their father picked up bones and bottles and tins, and in fact the children helped out as much as they could."

So, far from being attacked on their walks to school, the Mayer children formed close friendships among gentiles. Louis would walk with his best Jewish friends, Ben Guss, a tough kid who later became a prominent Canadian judge, and Nathan (Nate) Freedman. A third boy was Walter Golding, whose father ran the local Imperial Theater. Louis had his first taste of the glories of theatrical performance when Walter would let him in for a dime. There, in the scented plush interior, amid the gilt and gingerbread, Louis saw a world of fantasy opening up in the proscenium, an escape from the reality of poverty.

As long as he lived, Louis Mayer would never forget Miss Wilson reading to him from the magic pages of *Robinson Crusoe* and *The Swiss Family Robinson*. He developed an energetic treble, singing in the Protestant church choir as well as in the synagogue (so eclectic was the ecumenicism of St. John) with his friend Bill Roberts, later a pioneer of pasteurized milk and wrapped bread.

So absolute was the lack of prejudice in St. John that, when the more snobbish Jewish families began to restrict poor people's attendance at the synagogue, Jacob Mayer joined with both Protestant and Catholic businessmen to build a new one. The contrast with New York City scarcely needs stressing.

Sarah Mayer raised her children with religious precepts. Many years later, Louis remembered her taking him and his older brother to a picnic ground in a mountain area. She told them she wanted to teach them a lesson:

> She said to my brother, "Yell, yell 'God bless you,' " and he did. The echo came back with, of course, the same words. She told me to do the same, and, naturally, the echo repeated me. The third time, she told us to shout, "Go to hell!" and we heard the words reverberating, "Go to hell!" After we had absorbed this, mother said, "You see, what you put out in life, you get back."

Mayer told the famous journalist Adela Rogers St. Johns, years later:

> There was a little hotel in St. John. With a dining room. I used to walk by and stare in, seeing the little tables in the windows with silver candlesticks, and electric candles in pink shades. I would stand on the curb and say, "Someday I'm going to get in there and sit at a table and order an expensive meal." But when I finally had the money and went back to St. John, the restaurant was gone. That, Adela, is the definition of the tragedy of success.

Jacob Mayer obtained Canadian citizenship on June 26, 1895, in Fredericton; in 1896, the family traveled to Manhattan to attend the wedding of Yetta and Abraham Rieder. By December 1897, Louis was in the seventh grade at the Winter Street School. The next record we have is of his Bar Mitzvah in St. John in 1898. A picture survives, taken in a photographer's quasi-Oriental studio. The thirteen-year-old Louis is wearing a fancy, high-crowned hat, no doubt borrowed for the occasion, a tallith, or prayer shawl, draped over his already strong shoulders, a white bow tie affixed firmly to a staid wing collar, a prayer book gripped tightly in his right hand, his middle finger marking a particular passage.

The boy's coat is woolen, buttoned up tightly; he wears an expensive watch fob, dark gray knickerbockers and long woolen socks with firmly laced leather boots polished to a fault. The face we see is keen, sharp, open; the eyes are level, extremely bright and acute, staring straight ahead, challenging the world; the ears are large and stand out distinctly. Next to him is a sadly faded rubber plant in an earthenware pot, standing on what appears to be an Indian table; so powerful is the personality expressed in the picture, one is scarcely aware of the decor. Here is a young boy, on the edge of manhood, who is not handsome but is attractive, strong, determined, tough but sensitive, and very sure of himself. Only the hands seem old: they are wrinkled like an old working man's.

With the usual moviemaker's penchant for invention, Louis B. Mayer told his daughters, both of whom repeated the story ad infinitum, thus bamboozling successive chroniclers, that he was busy traveling in his school years all over Canada, appearing at auctions to buy bridges for his father, who is supposed by 1898 to have been prominent in the scrap and salvage industry. Irene Mayer Selznick wrote in her book *A Private View*, "A thin little boy in short pants could be safely ignored by other buyers, and hardly suspected of being able to pay cash." She described vividly his mother's terror for his personal safety, her tears as she sewed money into the waistband of his pants. There is no truth in these tales. At that time, as we know, Louis was at the Winter Street School; Elm Street School only went to grade six; he continued to the St. John High School until 1902. By 1899, Jacob Mayer was in the dry goods business, with a store on Main Street, his home still at humble 28 Acadia. He had progressed scarcely at all from the family's arrival seven years earlier, and certainly couldn't have bought a wooden footbridge, much less a steel structure.

The family befriended the former peddler and clerk, now junk and dry goods dealer, Isaac Komiensky and his wife, Leah, who lived over their store at 688 Main Street, with Isaac's brother David. There is no evidence of any competition between the Mayer and Komiensky businesses. Instead, the two families would help each other if a family member was sick, and Leah Komiensky and Sarah Mayer would exchange laundry duties. In 1900, the Komienskys were more prosperous than the Mayers. Their son Louis, a clerk now in his parents' store, had been in his younger years the best-dressed boy at Elm Street School. Twenty-five-year-old Louis Komiensky was attractive, if hampered by poor health and inherited fragility of physique, and he was very much drawn to Ida, who was seventeen in 1900. Ida was in love with another man and wanted him to marry her, but Jacob Mayer insisted she wed into the Komiensky family because of their associated businesses. This harsh decision was agonizing for her, and she never got over her love for the jilted man for the rest of her life. Though they had nothing in common except an interest in music, and certainly were not mutually attracted, the couple began to see each other regularly, with the blessings of both sets of parents.

On September 2, 1902, the Mayers and Komienskys celebrated the loveless, convenient union of Louis and Ida, the religious ceremony conducted by Rabbi Wolensky at the Carleton Street Synagogue, followed by a reception at the York Street Theatre rooms. The marriage would prove to be a disaster: Ida was vivacious, dynamic, full of life; Louis remained a chronic invalid, pallid, painfully thin, hobbling about on a cane. Ida tried to make the best she could of the marriage, and there would be three children, Ruth, Jack and Mitzi; but there could be no physical, mental or emotional satisfaction for her in the relationship. Louis, who was deeply fond of his sister, must have felt the reality of her situation.

That same year, Jacob Mayer, more successful but restless as always, set up a scrap iron business at 705 Main Street, later at 74 Smythe Street, while Sarah ran the dry goods store on her own and Ida joined her, as a clerk. Soon afterward, in 1902, Yetta and Abraham arrived from Manhattan and moved in with the Mayers. They soon started up Rubin and Rieder, Ladies' and Gentlemen's Clothing, at 675 Main Street, a store they maintained for several years. On June 8, 1903, Louis and Ida's first child, Ruth, was born.

The tradition in those days called for young men to marry at the same age as their sisters. It was felt that the lusts of youth must be satisfied in a comfortable and respectable relationship sanctified by religion. Affairs with young girls were unthinkable, not only on moral grounds but because of the practical fact that contraceptives were virtually unknown. A wife must be found for young Louis, and as soon as possible. According to Irene Selznick, Mayer learned through an aunt of his mother's in Chicago that Margaret, the daughter of the Boston kosher butcher, rabbi and cantor Hyman Shenberg, was looking for a bride. Others recall that a marriage broker from Boston traveled to St. John, on instruction from the Shenbergs, looking for a likely husband for the attractive young girl. It is possible that both versions of the story are true; when young Jewish men and women needed to be married, it was commonplace for messages to be passed from community to community, informing the grapevine that a match was called for. Louis saw Margaret's picture; she was plump, dark-eyed, with curly, dark brown hair and beautiful pale skin. He was excited; he was probably still more so by the prospect of returning to America.

Louis was well equipped for the future. He had graduated in 1902 at seventeen from St. John High School; his graduation was celebrated at Miss Wilson's house at 35 Union Street. He was fit from years of playing baseball in St. John; his mind was fine-honed, geared to money, hard work and success. It was no problem crossing the border between Canada and the United States in those days; there were no strict immigration laws, nor did officials board the train as he crossed on January 3, 1904, on his way to Boston.

Louis boarded in a lodging house at 17 Rochester Street, across from the Shenberg apartment on the second floor of No. 14. Eighteen-year-old Louis and twenty-one-year-old Margaret immediately hit it off, and Victor, Margaret's brother, became a close friend. Like Margaret, Victor worked as a bookkeeper.

It was decided to waste no time in arranging the marriage. Because of the need to seem to be of equal age to Margaret, Louis falsely entered the application for the license as, "Born July 4, 1882." The nuptials took place, with Rabbi Abram Shershevsky officiating in place of the absent Rabbi Aaron H. Chaimowitz, and with the Mayers present, along with the Shenbergs, at the 15 Emerald Street First Orthodox Synagogue on June 14, 1904. The reception was held at the Leverett Street Hall on nearby Scollay Square. Mildred Nesselroth, of Portland, Oregon, recalls the occasion:

> I was the youngest flower girl. I helped to carry the veil, which was of the most exquisite lace! The Reverend Shenberg spared no money to make this a memorable occasion! I believe they used up all their savings! Afterwards, the finest kosher food was served, and everyone was happy. You never saw such a fancy occasion—they might all have been millionaires!

The couple's home was a short trolley ride from the synagogue, a single room in a brick row lodging house owned by Clarence Poor, at 7 Rollins Street, in the congested working-class neighborhood of the extreme south end of Boston. It was arguably the shortest and most depressing thoroughfare in the city. Just one block in length between Washington and Harrison streets, consisting largely of ugly and overcrowded tenements, Rollins Street was filled with the dust and deafening clatter of the building crews, who were constructing the city's first elevated railroad in those months. The din of pneumatic drills, the grinding of cranes, the blasting, filled the air in that suffocating humid summer, one of the worst in years.

It was not an auspicious location for a new marriage, and Louis had an inauspicious job: he bought and sold cotton waste, fluff from the cotton mills rolled into balls and used to clean or lubricate factory machinery or employed for packing or as bedding for workers, both male and female, who were compelled to sleep in the corners of factories. It was in these circumstances that, much to the elation of the Mayer and Shenberg families, the couple's first child, the fragile, pretty Edith, was born, on August 13, 1905. Soon afterward, Louis gave up the cotton waste business and moved his family to Brooklyn. The Mayers lived at 101 Russell Street, Greenpoint, where Louis began to thrive selling junk. A second child, Irene, was born there (apparently following a stillbirth the previous year) on April 2, 1907.

## CHAPTER TWO

# 1907–1914

NINETEEN HUNDRED AND SEVEN was a year of panic and bank failures in the United States. Running his meager business in Brooklyn proved unsatisfactory, and Mayer began to cast about for other opportunities. He had gotten wind of the newfangled motion pictures, which were beginning to sweep the country. For a nickel, the poor could enjoy a certain privilege of the rich: though they could not see the idols of the stage at close quarters because of the dollar or two-dollar cost of orchestra seats, they could observe them on the screen. Moreover, the immigrant with a poor command of English could follow the romantic, melodramatic or comic situations without the need of dialogue. Though the titles that interlarded the scenes might not always be accessible, the gist of the drama could easily be understood because of the new and expressive methods of acting that the screen was developing.

Over forty-five years later, in an address to the Screen Producers' Guild on November 19, 1952, Mayer recalled a meeting with the Boston pioneer exhibitor Joseph Mack. From Mack, Mayer learned of a disused burlesque house that was for sale at 8 Essex Street, at Washington Square, in Haverhill, a town situated at the northern border of Essex County, Massachusetts, on the north bank of the Merrimack River. He traveled to Haverhill to investigate the theater. The 600 seats it contained were of moldering plush; the walls were thick with grime, and the floor was covered in a noisome blend of old, dried tobacco juice, solidified spit and sawdust. Named The Gem, the burlesque house was commonly known in Haverhill as The Germ.

Mayer decided to buy the property, which was available for a mere $600 down payment. His sisters, Yetta and Ida, managed to provide the money; the unhappily married Ida and her ailing husband Louis by that time were, like the Mayers, running a successful dry goods and junk business in Portland, St. John. They had three children, Ruth, Jack and

Mitzi. Yetta had moved with her equally sickly husband, Abraham, to Montreal, where, to support him, and their children Ruth and Henry, she started up another dry goods store, which rapidly flourished.

Mayer moved his family from Brooklyn to Haverhill in August 1907. They first stayed in a drab, four-story wooden lodging house at 21 Temple Street; Louis needed every penny to fix up the theater. He renamed it the Orpheum and began engaging cheap labor to fix it up. Big, burly John H. Flynn, popularly known as "Bodger," a former policeman, was hired as doorman, bouncer, usher and flashlight detective, who would seek out any rowdies or excessively amorous couples in the theater. Money was so tight that Flynn often had to go without his wages.

Mayer hired a slick, fast-talking youth of fifteen, Mosie Schlafman, to head up a team of neighborhood boys who, for a few cents a day, would run from school, Central High on Ninth Street, to sweep the floor, polish the arms of the seats, scrub down the walls and repaint them and restore broken exit signs. Mayer's brothers, Rudolph, age eighteen, and Jerry, age fifteen, came down by train from St. John, where they had been helping out in the family's business, to assist Flynn and Schlafman in the exhausting cleanup operation. Victor Shenberg arrived from Boston to act as projectionist and boarded with the Mayers.

Haverhill was a pleasant town. It was a center of boot, shoe, slipper and hat manufacturing, gristmills and sawmills, its brown monotony of brick and stone relieved by four lakes, known locally as ponds, that acted as reservoirs and sources of power, recreation spots and skating rinks.

It is easy to imagine the young Mayer setting out in the morning from his lodging house by streetcar for the Orpheum, or to various offices where he was raising money, tightly buttoned into his dark gray suit, pince-nez balanced on his prominent nose, his eyes piercing and dark, his stomach already beginning to swell a little under his watch-chained waistcoat, his shoes immaculately polished.

His voice was impressively deep by now: warm, throaty, like (the description is his grandson Daniel Selznick's) "very dark maple syrup." He could fascinate people with it; he could convince all but the most skeptical. He seldom (contrary to the testimony of his enemies) would slip grammatically or use foul language; but when he wrote letters, he had not the patience to trouble himself with punctuation. So driving and urgent was his pace that he couldn't pause to consider a correct use of a colon or semicolon.

In addition to her household chores, Margaret continued as a bookkeeper, based on her early training, and became the accountant and ticket seller at the theater. Somehow, she managed still to take care of the children, and even an addition to the family circle, Ruth Komiensky, elder daughter of Louis and Ida, who came to stay because her mother could not afford to maintain her. Ruth would never forget her aunt Margaret's extraordinary kindness, the fact that she would be so generous that she would give away anything she could, and taught her children to surrender their dolls to others less fortunate.

The greatest pain Mayer suffered at the time was undoubtedly the separation from his mother and the fact that he never could find the time to visit with her, and that she seemed reluctant to visit with him. She must have been too busy running her dry goods business to find the time to get away. But Jacob Mayer did arrive (described in an article in the Boston *Herald* on November 6 as "a quaint little man with a twinkle in his eye and an appraising manner") to inspect the building.

On November 28, 1907, Thanksgiving Day, the Orpheum Theater opened. It offered moving pictures by the Miles Brothers, film of a bouncing ball that would excite the audience into a group sing, and various vaudeville acts. In his first advertisement for the theater, the young proprietor announced that he was offering "clean, wholesome, healthy amusement, continuous hourly shows, no waits, no delays, laugh hearty, come and laugh, the best bill, the biggest bill, the longest show . . . such is to be the policy of Haverhill's home of refined amusement." Orchestra seats were ten cents, children would be admitted for five cents, and the program would be changed Sunday and Thursday in the "best ventilated and best equipped moving picture theater in the city." The following day the Haverhill *Evening Gazette* reported the occasion:

> Throughout the day, a large number of patrons attended, welcoming [the] change and assuring the new management of a generous support in its new field . . . The program will be frequently changed as the new reels are received, and it is planned to conduct the theater along the same lines as those practiced in the best houses . . . in the country.

In addition to movies, Mayer also offered legitimate and vaudeville performances. The first feature motion picture shown at the Orpheum, on December 24, was Pathé's two-reel *The Passion Play*, the story of Christ's final days, which earned him substantial profits in the Christmas season. It was accompanied by two sets of colored religious slides, and an organist played sacred music on a Hammond organ—the instrument being an expensive item for Mayer's limited budget. Nobody in New England had dared show a picture of that length before. Mayer was so concerned about the program running too long that he took over the projection himself, speeding up the film with a hand crank, thus squeezing in an extra show. Despite the heavy price of fifteen and twenty-five cents for the best seats, when a nickel was the most people expected to pay, the audience was large and thrilled to Mayer's vivid lecture on the death of Christ. *The Passion Play* was followed by *Bluebeard*, a grisly story of mass murder that had the audience screaming in delighted terror. Mayer learned from the outset that sanctity and violence were among the essential staples of film success.

Already beginning to accumulate some capital, Mayer hired Hattie Platz Kelley's all-woman orchestra to provide a serious tone. The women played violins and wore white shirtwaists, black skirts and laced-up shoes. At 7 P.M. on September 3, 1908, after a week's remodeling, he reopened the theater as the New Orpheum, with the same orchestra and Miss Sanborne, popular Haverhill Sunday afternoon park band concert singer, performing the entr'actes. The first picture shown was *The Dreyfus Affair*, with, among the supporting films, *A Jewel of a Servant*, *Just Like a Woman*, *I Can't Read English* and *Dan Casey Joins the Lodge*.

At this time, the Mayers moved to a pleasant cottage across the river to the south, at 8 Merrimack Street, Bradford, renumbered 2 the following year. It says much for Mayer's extreme tightness with money that it took him all this time to take his family out of a lodging house in a depressing neighborhood to a home where there was a yard that his children could play in.

Mayer had reason to be in a good temper in those years. His wife was devoted, unwavering in her support for his vigorous ego; his children (Edie, delicate and feminine, and Irene, already showing signs of being a tomboy), the apples of his eye; his theater, spectacularly thriving.

Always restless and ambitious, Mayer had larger dreams. The former Lillian Tall, now eighty-eight and living in Johannesburg, South Africa, remembers Mayer coming into the home of her father, Samuel, and her mother in Roxbury, Massachusetts, and to the home of their neighbors, Mr. and Mrs. Saul Brener. He was often present playing pinochle in the evenings, and was seeking money to develop his interests in the nickelodeon business. Mrs. Tall recalls that the Breners and other local business people refused to back him, called him "Crazy Louis," and he went away empty-handed. They saw no future in moving pictures. Saul Brener's son, Leonard, now a Boston stockbroker, confirms the story.

In 1910, when he was twenty-five, Mayer cast about for a bigger theater. He heard that the Eagle Hotel, popular with visiting salesmen, was up for sale for $30,000 by its owners, the Holihan brothers of Lawrence, Massachusetts. He had not sufficient money to put down a payment; every cent he had was tied up in the New Orpheum. With manic energy, he invaded offices, clubs, synagogues and meeting halls, looking for backers. He formed a partnership with the young and boisterous

Colman Levin, an up-and-coming rug merchant from Boston, who had opened a local branch of his business. He also raised money from an equally thriving young coal merchant, George C. Elliott, and from Charles Howard Poor, who may have been related to his former Boston landlord. Poor was an attorney with Poor and Abbott; as a major figure of the local water board, he could undoubtedly assist with water connections. Mayer often went hunting and fishing with Poor and Levin and their wives.

The syndicate bought the Eagle, razed it to the ground, and announced that the new theater, to be called the Colonial, would cost $125,000. The transaction was completed on May 25, 1910. Then Mayer and his partners suddenly decided not to go ahead and sold the land at a profit to a business group for a commercial block, proceeding instead to build in a different location at 185 Merrimack Street, across the bridge from the Mayer house. The street frontage, on the corner of Emerson Street, was eighty-seven feet. Walter Coulson of Lawrence, Massachusetts, who owned the building, known as the Sargent property, was a partner in the enterprise, and Rudolph Mayer invested his small savings in it. The contract was drawn up by Bernard Berenson, a distinguished member of the Boston bar and cousin of the famous aesthete.

Building what would soon be called the Colonial Theater was a tremendous task. It was put together in a mere nine months from the commencement of the building on March 11, 1911. Mayer can only have felt intense pride as the handsome interior emerged. There was a ninety-five-foot-long lobby, hung with pictures of the stars, leading to a rich marble staircase carpeted in red. The lobby walls were lined with finest rosewood with frescoes of country scenes. Floors were thickly carpeted. To the right of the entrance was a carving in stone of a lion in its den; to the left was an imposing oil painting of Louis B. Mayer himself: the first touch of showmanship in his life.

Given his temperament, it takes no feat of the imagination to see that young Louis B. Mayer was involved at every moment of the work. He wanted to create the most beautiful building in Haverhill, and certainly he achieved the most handsome of theaters. At last, the thirty-six-foot proscenium arch was completed, and the 1,500 seats with their rich red plush were firmly installed. Mayer's daughters would never forget him rushing home night after night to announce, with immense enthusiasm, his joy in his creation.

It proved impossible to open the Colonial Theater on Thanksgiving, so the date of December 11 was settled on. Mayer outlined a policy of showing movies with vaudeville at twenty-five cents a seat top prices. He began with three days of William Morrow and his company of players, the mimic J. Walter McKay and the Milano Singing Duo, as well as Miles Brothers films. Opening night was a big occasion. Mayer, his wife, his children, his powerful business friends and their families were present. The fashionable crowd, in black or white tie or evening gowns, walked through an archway of five hundred electric light bulbs into the rosewood lobby, talking excitedly.

As the audience was seated, the thirty-piece orchestra, conducted by Edwin F. Hoyt, struck up the Colonial March, written especially by the local composer Will E. Brown. Films were shown, then Mayor Edwin H. Moulton walked up to the stage to the strains of "Hail to the Chief." Moulton introduced the theater backer George W. Cummings's daughter Patricia, who formally opened the theater in a nicely worded speech and spilled freshly cut roses from a large solid gold cornucopia all over the stage. To applause, she called for "this theater's true creator, our family's beloved friend, Louis B. Mayer," to step up. Fifteen hundred people stood cheering as Mayer, flushing with pleasure, squeezing his wife's hand, stood up and ran to the stage.

He was deeply moved, and gave an excellent speech, saying, with absolute truth, "The Colonial Theater is the zenith of my ambitions." He described the hard work put in by the building team under contractor John Roche, the sacrifice and struggle it had taken to build his dream theater. When he finished, on the verge of tears, the audience became hysterical. This small, unhandsome, nervous young man was the epitome of the immigrant who had made good, and, in those happy provincial days, there was little jealousy or hatred in Haverhill toward him, only a feeling that he represented the American dream come true.

Another excitement followed: On March 9, 1912, Louis "Bert" Mayer, who would later change his invented middle name to Burt and then to Burrill, was granted citizenship of the United States in Boston. Bernard Berenson, attorney, made the arrangements; in filling out his application forms, Mayer had to renounce King George V and the British Empire, surrendering all loyalty to Canada. It is doubtful if he felt a twinge of regret; he was already passionately fond of America and overjoyed at the opportunity it had granted him.

He had another reason to be in Boston at the time. After many weeks of negotiation, he had managed to sign Henry Russell's distinguished Boston Opera Company for the Colonial Theater, bringing grand opera to Haverhill for the first time. On March 21, 1912, the company presented, under Mayer's management, *Madame Butterfly*; the Puccini opera had been premiered eight years earlier at La Scala in Milan. The star was Alice Nielsen, Tennesseean prima donna from the Metropolitan Opera, who had performed with Caruso, Melba and Destinn. The reviews were ecstatic, and even the Boston papers took note of the occasion.

The Colonial was an instant success. The policy of combining live and film performance paid off handsomely. Mayer's two daughters at grade school were popular and bursting with pride. He was exceedingly thrifty still, saving relentlessly on his profits. He also saved money by installing his brother Jerry as temporary manager of the New Orpheum, while Victor Shenberg continued as projectionist at the Colonial.

During 1912, Mayer had achieved sufficient reputation to be able to show such stars as George M. Cohan in *Forty-five Minutes from Broadway* and Laurette Taylor in *Peg O' My Heart*.He toured more operas to Haverhill. He was fond of music and enjoyed nothing more than singing opera arias whenever he could.

He began traveling to Boston and New York to build up his theater interests. In April 1912, the theatrical impresario Henry B. Harris had been drowned in the sinking of the *Titanic*, and Harris's manager, Ben Stern, was seeking new opportunities. Mayer formed a partnership with him; they would together present plays in cities of New England. He also formed a partnership with an unrelated namesake, Adolph Mayer, and, starting in December 1912, toured the tragedienne Nance O'Neil, starting in Portland, Maine, in the play *The Fires of St. John,* by Hermann Sudermann, first performed by her at the Daly's Theatre on November 28, 1904. A gifted actress with a big following, she was rumored to be the lover of alleged murderess Lizzie Borden.

Soon, Mayer was able to afford a handsome, three-story house at 27 Hamilton Avenue, which still stands in 1992. He bought a third house of entertainment, calling it the Scenic Temple.

At the end of 1912, Mayer converted the New Orpheum into a legitimate theater, where he ran his own stock company, starring Frank E. Elliott and Valarie Valaire. Among the plays he showed were *Alias Jimmy Valentine, The White Sister,* and *The Rosary.* All three of these would become M.G.M. productions in later years. He leased the Academy of Music, brought in by train the Boston Symphony Orchestra, snapped up the Bijou movie theater and ran a musical revue starring the later-famous Eddie Dowling.

By now, Mayer was wearying of Haverhill. His constant visits to Boston and New York City had further inflamed his ambitions. He did not quite dare to move to Manhattan, but he took a step up by selling his house on Hamilton Avenue, only a year after moving into it, and took his family to the pleasant Boston suburb of Brookline (population 27,000), where he found a comfortable row house at 501 Boylston Street. It cost him $2,500. Standing on the corner of Warren Street, it was, as it remains today, a pleasant, semi-classical 1903 white brick building of three stories, consisting of no less than fourteen rooms. The Brookline reservoir could be seen from the third floor: it had the appearance of a handsome lake, surrounded by trees. For his children, who were now of school age, it was close to the nineteenth-century John D. Runkle School on wealthy Druce Street, near the prosperous district of Buckminster Road. He made the move in August 1913, hiring the vigorous William E. Ferber to run the Colonial and New Orpheum theaters for him.

There were tensions in his household, based partly on the fact that he was so often absent from home. A father's presence was needed for girls ages eight and six, and Margaret perhaps overreacted by being strict with the children.

Edith Mayer said later, "In those days, there was a theory, 'Spare the rod and spoil the child.' Mother was *very* severe; father loved to spoil us, but he also believed you must be 'seen and not heard.'" According to Irene Mayer, Edie was the center of all the attention; Edith insisted that Irene was by far the more demanding and self-centered. The sisters were locked in sibling rivalry. Irene hated Edith's expertise in "artistic" matters, her self-pity and her crying fits; Edith resented Irene's briskness, toughness and comparative athleticism.

If Margaret was excessively strict, then Louis was excessively protective and possessive. The home became increasingly claustrophobic, filled with that form of stress which often underlies deep mutual affection.

In 1913, Ida, Louis's elder sister, divorced Louis Komiensky. They were to remain friendly for the rest of their lives, happier together, like so many people, when they were no longer married. Komiensky acted as manager and caretaker for property Ida owned near St. John, and corresponded with her for years about it.

Soon after the Mayers settled in Brookline, they were given shocking news. Louis's mother, Sarah, whom he had scarcely seen since 1904, had been suffering from cholecystitis, a disease of the gall bladder. Mayer must have been torn between the exhausting commitments of his burgeoning career and a desire to make the journey to St. John to be with her. On October 13, Mayer, unable to obtain a reservation on the overcrowded trains, threw caution to the winds and hired a private railroad car to take him and his family to St. John. At the same time, Rudolph, who was living in Montreal, and Jerry, who, after marrying the beautiful Rheba Gilinsky in New York in 1902, had also moved there, arrived with their recently widowed sister Yetta and her five children, Henry, Ruth, Joseph, Irene and Mendel.

Mayer brought with him his own doctor, William F. Ferrin of Boston.

He managed to hire the celebrated Montreal surgeon Dr. Pierre Gareau, who had operated recently on the Duchess of Connaught, and summoned him to his mother's bedside.

Gall bladder operations were straightforward, even in those days, but surgery had been left till very late. The operation was successful, but, complications set in following and the best efforts of doctors Gareau and Ferrin and their associate, Dr. A. F. Emory, failed.

Late on the afternoon of October 14, 1913, almost all of her family at her bedside, Sarah Mayer, sixty-one, passed away in her private room at the General Public Hospital. Ida's daughter Ruth remembers, almost seventy-seven years later, the dying woman saying to everyone in Yiddish, "I shall be crossing a great sea. And I shall never come back." The children held each other's hands and cried as they walked home. Devastated at the house at 724 Main Street, the Mayers were flooded with phone calls and telegrams of sympathy, and the living room was filled from end to end with floral tributes. Mayer sobbed like a child. The grave marker was placed in front of an iron fence, before a small hillock covered in scrub. Mayer ordered the inscription in Yiddish under the Star of David to read: "Here lies Sarah, the wife of Rabbi [sic] Jacob Mayer. Let her soul rest in peace." Under the inscribed name, birth and death dates, the words appeared in English, "Rest In Peace O Mother; Sleep Within Our Hearts." And then, under the main plinth of black granite, the single name "MAYER" was inscribed, and underneath that again a rough, uncarved stone.

Mayer never got over the shock. For the rest of his life, wherever he traveled, he kept a picture of his mother in his wallet, and in whichever home or office he occupied, a painting or tintype of her could be found.

## CHAPTER THREE

# 1914–1917

Work, CONSTANT WORK was the Puritan solution for grief, and the young Louis B. Mayer worked desperately hard in the first months of 1914. He was determined to build himself up as a motion picture distributor, taking on all comers. In April, in partnership with George C. Elliott and Charles Howard Poor, with offices in New York, Boston, 162 Tremont Street and Haverhill, he founded the American Feature Film Corporation.

Mayer had learned of the great success of a hard-driving young former cornet player and theatrical producer, Jesse L. Lasky, whose company, the Lasky Feature Play Company, had, with Cecil B. DeMille, begun production of motion pictures in California. Their first feature was the western *The Squaw Man*. Mayer was present at its premier screening, held on February 17 at the Longacre Building on West Forty-eighth Street. He was at once enthralled; he saw the commercial possibilities of the picture from the first frame.

There was no resisting the picture, and the audience of editors, journalists, exhibitors, distributors and a smattering of rival "plants" went wild. They jumped to their feet; they cheered as Sam Goldfish, later Goldwyn, one of the movie's progenitors, stood tall and rangy on the stage, flashing his famous ear-to-ear shark's grin and introducing the powerfully built, athletic Cecil B. DeMille and the slighter, ecstatic Jesse L. Lasky. Mayer offered $4,000 if his American Feature Film Corporation could have the New England rights. According to Goldwyn's biographer A. Scott Berg, Goldwyn spent a lifetime blaming Mayer for failing to pay back more than the $1,000 original guarantee; but this is improbable because Lasky let Mayer have more product, and far more than $4,000 was involved in that deal.

*The Squaw Man* was a great advance on previous attempts at westerns, and glowed with the sunshine and fresh air of the artistically unexplored territories west of the Rockies. New Englanders thrilled to the story of an Indian squaw fatally in love with a white man, driven at last to suicide. The American Feature Film Corporation expertly advertised the production and its successors, netting substantial sums of money in the process. But Mayer was still impatient: this essentially local operation was not enough for his consuming ambition. That August he abandoned his partners and, setting up an apartment on Riverside Drive in New York, where he spent longer and longer periods away from his family, he formed a friendship with the high-powered newspaper man turned film distributor Walter Hoff Seeley, whose thrust toward personal aggrandizement considerably surpassed his moral propriety. Mayer's meetings with Seeley, at the popular Claridge Hotel on Sixth Avenue between Forty-third and Forty-fourth streets, were joined by yet another dynamo of the burgeoning industry. The dapper, sleek-haired Al Lichtman, also in his twenties, a former circus roustabout and acrobat, monologist on the vaudeville stage and famous prankster, sported fancy Panama hats, sharp suitings and spats. He had been squeezed out of the Jesse L. Lasky Feature Play Company by Adolph Zukor when Paramount Pictures Corporation was founded. Understandably furious, he wanted to join any organization that would undermine the influence of Paramount in the New England states.

The three men agreed on the basic principles of the new corporation, which would be called Alco, based on Lichtman's first name. Paramount was trying to create a theater monopoly; therefore Lichtman and Seeley, with Mayer's support in New England, would set up a powerful circuit of their own, distributing pictures by various companies including All-Star, Popular Plays and Players, and B. A. Rolfe. Seeley wanted to place his theaters in cities that had more than 200,000 population; each theater owner would give exclusive territorial rights to a particular movie of quality, whose script and casting and all other credits would be approved by Seeley and Lichtman. The movies would be shown for only one week in each place.

This was a stunt rather than a genuine policy. One week of any successful picture in a city would not be sufficient to help toward recouping its costs. This was not only a stunt but a heist: local distributors were forced to pay Seeley for the territorial rights to their areas in advance, without any guarantees of what pictures would be made—that is, what they would be paying for. Thus, Seeley would accumulate a great deal of money on the basis of promises, and would then siphon the money off into other companies. He eventually declared himself bankrupt, paying everyone a mere forty cents on the dollar. This was a not unfamiliar device in those brutal days of the early film industry.

Seeley issued a false prospectus that claimed the company had a working capital of $132,000, free of liabilities, whereas in fact it had only $40,000, much of that figure made up of promissory notes of highly questionable origin. It seems that Seeley signed several of the notes himself, and by October he had diverted much of the $1.5 million obtained from the distributors into a deliberately collapsed and now allegedly defunct company called Atsco. Of this million and a half dollars, a large proportion was cash investment from unwitting individual shareholders. Seeley's false prospectuses and rash promises not only lured the normally canny and skeptical Louis B. Mayer, but also the exceedingly shrewd thirty-seven-year-old multimillionaire Richard Rowland of Pittsburgh, who had a large film exchange in Pennsylvania. Rowland had inherited a carbon lamp business from his father earlier in the century, which he sold for a cool $7 million by the time he was thirty. Balding, fair, strongly built, with a cold Nordic face, he was a formidable presence at the Claridge Hotel meetings. As Mayer and Rowland and Lichtman sat listening to Seeley's high-powered promises, they appear to have been totally bamboozled, on fire with the thought of getting even richer, faster.

Becoming a Mason was considered desirable among up-and-coming businessmen, and it is not surprising that, on September 15, 1914, Mayer became a third-degree Mason at the St. Cecile Lodge No. 568 at Masonic Hall, 7 West Twenty-third Street, New York. Other members included Al Jolson, D. W. Griffith, the comic John Bunny, and the prominent actor Raymond Hitchcock. Mayer's registration record shows that he had dropped "Bert" as his middle name and was now calling himself Louis Burrill Mayer.

By now, the Alco Film Company, its deals to release the movies of various companies firmly sealed up, had established offices in the Heidelberg Building, located in an island between Broadway and Sixth Avenue, opposite the Knickerbocker Building on Times Square. An exciting scene greeted Mayer each evening as darkness fell. A flood of electric light swept along Broadway, both sides of which were crammed with dance palaces, pleasure gardens, cabarets and nightclubs. But there was little time to enjoy the pleasures they offered. By October 1914, Alco was struggling for survival. Walter Hoff Seeley was draining off the reserves into separate companies, all of which had been set up to avoid the newfangled income tax. Lichtman, who was so absentminded that he was caricatured in a show business magazine asking where his car was, while eight others honked around him, simply let the business slip through his hands; he never kept a proper check on Seeley, and failed to produce evidence that he had ordered a sufficient number of good-quality motion pictures to fill the theaters in the chain.

By all accounts, the partners quarreled violently, and by November, Alco, despite eleven pictures in release, was insolvent. Lichtman fled back to Paramount. Later, he would make his peace with Mayer and would work with him during his great career. On November 21, the company's treasurer, St. Louis distributor William Sievers, brought suit against Seeley on behalf of all the stockholders, saying he had no money to distribute anything.

That same day, Judge Learned Hand put Alco into receivership in the Federal District Court of New York. Mayer and Rowland, stuck with large quantities of worthless stock and with nothing to put into their theaters, appeared in court to testify. Undaunted, Seeley paid off everyone with borrowed money, thus escaping bankruptcy, transferred all of his holdings into different places, and then, by a series of complex maneuvers, managed to dissolve Alco without actually going to prison.

Somehow, as the bailiffs moved in, not only on Alco but on its associated All-Star Feature Corporation, and seized All-Star's thirteen completed films, literally carrying the office furniture down the stairs into the street, Mayer and Rowland managed to avoid financial ruin. With great skill, Mayer latched onto Rowland, who did not find him entirely compatible, and formed the Metro Pictures Corporation. Richard Rowland would be president, Louis B. Mayer, secretary. The offices were set up six floors below those being vacated by Alco in the same Times Square building. There was a series of meetings at the Claridge Hotel; other partners were Joe Engel, another associate of Jesse L. Lasky pushed out of the Paramount merger, and George Grumbacher, who had a powerful theater exchange in the western states. Mayer suggested bringing in, as company lawyer, the dapper thirty-two-year-old J. Robert Rubin, who had been assistant to the district attorney of New York City and had acted as official receiver and later counsel for the bankrupt Alco. Rubin had many useful local government connections that would undoubtedly prove valuable in the future. The bustling, fast-talking Harry L. Reichenbach was hired as publicist and immediately began concocting extravagant stories about the partners.

These tough, determined men were of one mind: they would not be swallowed up by Paramount or the other conglomerates, Mutual and Universal. They would enter into partnership with producers, controlling what pictures would be made; among those who joined their distribution organization were Columbia, Quality Pictures Corporation, Popular Plays and Players, Dyreda and Rolfe. They would also obtain their own studio and put their own stars into orbit. Rowland's millions provided the essential cash flow, and Louis B. Mayer and the other partners invested to the limit.

It was an exciting venture, ambitious and inspired by great energy. Full incorporation occurred on March 5, 1915. Meanwhile, Mayer had discovered that his fellow Mason, D. W. Griffith, had created a masterpiece in his new motion picture *The Birth of a Nation*. He was determined to be its sole distributor in New England. The film portrayed the Ku Klux Klan as avenging angels, treated blacks patronizingly and exhibited a simpleminded view of the issues of the Civil War. But it was a triumph of cinematic construction and execution, and it promised to make colossal sums of money.

Just seven days after Metro was formed, the trade papers reviewed the picture in terms which could only be encouraging to any exhibitor. Mayer contacted the film's backers and made an across-the-board deal for regional distribution. With the lawyer David Stoneman, his old friend the rug merchant Colman Levin, jewelers and paper-bag manufacturers, and even his secretary, who gave her life savings of $1,000, he scraped up part of the money by selling (he told Lillian Gish years later) or pawning everything he owned, including Margaret's jewelry, cleaning out his savings and borrowing from his brothers and sister. He made a down payment of $20,000 on a $50,000 guarantee against a remittance of ten percent of the net profits received from local bookings. It took chutzpah to embark on this venture; there were threats of demonstrations against the picture in New England, but Mayer knew that this controversy would further enhance people's desire to see it. He was busy dealing with the NAACP, headed in Boston by Moorfield Storey, which was bombarding virtually every home and office in the city with pamphlets condemning the picture. He traveled restlessly between his home in Brookline, his new offices at 60 Church Street in Boston, his apartment at Riverside Drive and his offices on Times Square, trying to deal with a hundred matters at once.

Mayer made at least $500,000 on the film. By late summer of 1915, several stars were under contract to Metro, most notably Quality Pictures' Francis X. Bushman, who had begun his career as a sculptor's model. In March 1912, *Motion Picture Story* magazine had named Bushman, then twenty-eight, the most popular screen actor in America. Vain, extravagant, this Adonis rejoiced in driving hand-tooled touring cars with gold door handles, his monogram inscribed in gold plates on the doors. He owned Bush Manor, a thirty-room mansion on 115 acres of gardens in Maryland. He had racing stables, kennels and a large collection of birds.

Another Metro star of 1915 was thirteen-year-old Mary Miles Minter, the Shirley Temple of her day, who captivated audiences with her huge, pale blue eyes and golden curls. Ruled by a monster stage mother, willful, temperamental and spoiled, she would one day be the center of a famous murder case.

Metro Pictures Corporation also offered the movies of Olga Petrova, star of *The Vampire*, *The Heart of a Painted Woman*, and *My Madonna*. Harry Reichenbach cooked up a story that she was a Russian noblewoman, born in Warsaw and driven into exile due to some obscure family scandal. Actually, she was Muriel Harding, a middle-class British woman, who was about as exotic as shepherd's pie. She was photographed, not in her simple home on Long Island, but languishing on tiger skins or against silk cushions, discreetly draped, one white hand languidly raising a sinful glass of wine, as she awaited the arrival of the fatally weak husband of an unsuspecting bride.

The Metro studios were set up at 1 West Sixty-first Street; Mayer would go there from his new suite of offices at 2 West Forty-fifth. His daughter Edith remembered that he would walk the sixteen blocks at breakneck speed, ignoring traffic signals and leaving any companion who was unfortunate enough to accompany him totally exhausted.

Placed above a garage, the Metro studio was reached by arguably the most insecure Otis elevator in Manhattan. Once Mayer arrived on the second floor, he was greeted by a cacophony of music, saws and drills, banging doors and stage actresses playing scenes at the tops of their lungs. Among those he met was Ethel Barrymore, the great star of Broadway, who had condescended to appear in pictures because of the exorbitant sum she was being paid. Witty, adorable, she was strikingly beautiful, with huge, liquid, dreamy eyes, pure white skin and masses of brown-gold hair arranged à la concierge. She made an unforgettable impression on the young exhibitor. And, although it is not recorded, it is likely that he also met her brother Lionel, a feisty, dynamic, hammy presence in Metro pictures.

Nineteen sixteen was a good year for Mayer and for Metro. Within a few months, on Richard Rowland's initial investment of $400,000, augmented by his partners' savings, Metro was on its way to over $1.5 million in profits. In July, *The Moving Picture World* threw its hat in the air: "Metro is the miracle-working institution of the industry." The same magazine announced, improbably, that there was only one movie theater the whole length of Broadway that was not showing a Metro picture. Seventy were released in a mere twelve months: an astonishing figure even by the grind house standards of the day.

But even this triumph was insufficient to satisfy Mayer. He wanted to be a film producer. He persuaded Richard Rowland and his partners to allow him to make, for the Quality Pictures Corporation, which Metro handled, a chapter play entitled *The Great Secret*, starring Francis X. Bushman. At first, Bushman was contemptuous of the idea of making a serial, which he felt would undermine his position as a major star. But there was no stopping Mayer in his determination, and he convinced Bushman that the serial would in fact enhance his already enormous popularity. He offered him over $2,000 a week, or fifty times that in present-day money, to undertake the venture. Mayer still further reassured him by hiring as director Christy Cabanne, a tough, twenty-seven-year-old protégé of D. W. Griffith. Cabanne was noted for his fashionable, very "French" waxed mustache and tireless ability to work. So convinced was Mayer that the project would succeed, he invested heavily in it himself. The serial began production on October 14, 1916.

*The Great Secret* was shot at Quality Pictures studios in Cliffside, New Jersey. It was a familiar brew: a sinister plot contrived by a mysterious foreign villain that is thwarted by the frequently stripped hero, who rescues from a fate worse than death Bushman's favorite costar, the beautiful Beverly Bayne.

During the shooting, uncomfortable facts came to light; and, despite every effort of Harry Reichenbach, it began to leak that Bushman, married and the father of five children, was involved in an overheated romance with Miss Bayne. Even his marriage itself, though eminently respectable, had been concealed because it was feared that Bushman's female audience would set aside their romantic fantasies and abandon him if they learned the truth. If he were found to be an adulterer, it could literally end his career.

Perhaps because the rumors were too strong, perhaps because *The Great Secret* was clumsily produced and directed, the serial flopped. Even when it was in release, Bushman, much to Mayer's chagrin, announced that he would be divorcing his wife; he was quoted as saying that one of his reasons was she had become enormously fat. A year later, he would make matters worse by costarring with Miss Bayne in a film entitled *Their Compact*, in which Bushman played a man ridding himself of a despotic and vicious wife, finding true love with a maidenly Beverly Bayne. In retaliation, Josephine Bushman announced that her husband had been a wife beater and had injured his children. Mayer detested Bushman from that moment on.

But the thrill of producing was in Mayer's blood. He would not be content with being an exhibitor again. He would pursue, and fiercely, the sixth most successful motion picture star in America, twenty-two-year-old Anita Stewart. He had learned through the grapevine that Miss Stewart was annoyed with her studio, Vitagraph, with its bosses, J. Stuart

Blackton and Albert E. Smith, and with working conditions at their studios in Flatbush.

Dark-haired, sultry-eyed, and voluptuous Anita Stewart was typical of the new breed of motion picture stars. She was petulant, girlish, spoiled; she was earning over $127,000 for batches of four pictures at a time, worth millions in 1992 money, and she was saving most of it, living frugally with her mother in a large but unfashionable apartment in Brooklyn.

Born Anna Marie Stewart on February 7, 1895, she was fortunate enough to be the sister-in-law of the prominent director Ralph Ince, who plucked her out of high school to appear in several Vitagraph pictures. She made a considerable splash in *The Goddess*, a fifteen-part serial about a desert island brat corrupted by civilization; as a "primitive" child of nature, she was close to naked.

When she did not get her way, she would stage imaginary typhoid attacks or nervous breakdowns; she would disappear until her salary was adjusted. She liked beaded black satin dresses, dancing all night, cocktails and perfumed cigarettes; she composed songs, banged away at a concert grand piano and trilled to unsuspecting guests in a rather insecure lyric soprano.

She pretended to be English, was observed running barefoot through the rain along the Brooklyn streets and kept up a secret: a steamy love affair with the slight, smooth actor Rudolph Cameron. Although she was married to him by early 1917, she pretended she would never marry anyone. To add to her self-fostered legend, she declared her love instead for a dashing youth who, much to the delight of her publicist, went off to France, sent her love poems and was killed in a crash flying for the Lafayette Escadrille.

Legend has it that Mayer was introduced to her by a fan, a hunchbacked dwarf, from whom he would buy newspapers at a stand near the Knickerbocker Hotel. He chose the right moment: Miss Stewart was having one of her familiar nervous breakdowns and was presently in Atlantic City to take the sea air. After netting his fortune from his distribution of *The Birth of a Nation* (allegedly, he had fiddled the books), he was firmly placed to make her a substantial offer. His first meetings with her were successful; he knew that the way to an actress's heart was often through her mother. He sent roses, flowers and even jewelry to Mrs. Stewart, visiting her so frequently that gossips might have been forgiven for suspecting a romance. When, still not getting the salary she wanted from Vitagraph, Anita Stewart decided to have another "nervous breakdown" in May, he visited her several times at a Stamford, Connecticut, sanitarium. Prompted by Mayer, she wrote to Albert E.

Smith, president of Vitagraph, announcing that she wished to sever relations with the company. Mayer promised her that she would have her own Anita Stewart Productions as a corporate, tax-saving arrangement, and that she would have her choice of subjects, with Rudolph Cameron as a director. This was an astonishing example of raiding a company for a star. Immediately, Mayer ran headlong into the fury of Albert E. Smith and a protracted and stormy litigation.

## CHAPTER FOUR

# 1917–1918

AMERICA WAS AT WAR that summer of 1917. The doughboys were marching through the streets to loud brass fanfares as they prepared to leave for France and the muddy hell of the trenches, family Victrolas emitted a stream of patriotic songs, and the draft, for which, at thirty-two, Louis B. Mayer was then too old, was snatching up the fit and the strong. The country was afire with pride, as Mayer was committed to a war of his own. He was determined to break Anita Stewart's contract with the fierce Albert E. Smith. By August, it was beginning to be obvious to Richard Rowland, who always regarded the feisty young exhibitor with suspicion, that Mayer wasn't going to be capturing Anita Stewart for Metro, but for himself and for his newly revamped film exchange, set up with his friend Nathan Gordon, the Gordon-Mayer Company of Boston. And this despite the fact that Mayer had no studio, no production company and no national distribution deal. Chutzpah could scarcely go further. It seems probable that Mayer led Miss Stewart to believe that her pictures would be made by Metro.

Early in September, the chips were down. Miss Stewart's tantrums and absences and meetings with Mayer had finally exhausted what was left of Smith's patience. Unable to reason with the temperamental star, he had New York Supreme Court Justice George D. Mullen, coaxed by the influential Vitagraph lawyer Daniel H. Coakley, hand down a temporary restraining order preventing Anita Stewart from working for any person or corporation until she completed two more pictures. Her contract would be concluded in January 1918, but she would be required to work for twenty-six more weeks to make up for time lost by her unwarranted absences from the studio.

Mayer immediately hired his favorite lawyers, Dunbar, Nutter and McLennan of New York, and Bernard and Arthur Berenson of Boston, to fight the case. Evidently stimulated by his defiance and flattery, Miss

Stewart illegally signed a contract with Mayer to work for him for a year with options. Richard Rowland got wind of this, but before he could fire Mayer, Mayer resigned as secretary of Metro, effective October 12, 1917. Two days later, he had signed up with Lewis J. Selznick's Select Pictures Corporation at 69 Church Street, Boston. Selznick was another expert in star stealing: forming his company in April 1916, he had snatched the popular Clara Kimball Young from the World Film Corporation and, according to her husband, bedded her in the bargain. Select was fifty percent owned by Adolph Zukor by the time Mayer became its New England distributor, but that meant nothing. Much as he hated Zukor, he was like any other businessman: when money was to be made, the look of anybody's face was unimportant. Select was doing well that fall. They released the movies of Constance and Norma Talmadge, Alice Brady and—a hint of Mayer's future—William Randolph Hearst's beautiful blond mistress, Marion Davies.

While the decision on the court battle with Vitagraph was postponed after several stormy hearings, Mayer was also in court with a battery of Berensons to fight Metro itself, which had filed suit against him for campaigning to wreck the Metro organization by intimidating its employees, compelling them to leave Metro for Select and using "fraudulent misrepresentations" to get them to do so. On October 25, Justice James Wait of the Superior Court of Boston granted a restraining order, preventing Mayer from making any further offers to Metro's employees.

In November, the draft regulations called for any able-bodied male under thirty-nine to enlist. An exhaustive search of Boston and New York records shows that the hard-pressed Mayer failed to file a card. Since he was fiercely patriotic, this dereliction can only be put down to the extreme pressure of his situation. Every day, he was fighting the temporary restraining order against Miss Stewart.

His character underwent a change in those difficult months. He became subject to fainting spells brought on, according to his daughter Irene, by low blood pressure. These spells, coming on occasionally in the middle of a conference, appear also to have been the result of nervous tension and stress. Mayer's enemies always claimed that the spells were induced theatrically, in order to excite sympathy when he was beginning to lose a battle.

He had become an intermittent hysteric: often charming, possessed of immense vitality, so that few could resist him, he would suddenly change from extreme enthusiasm and voluble pan-Slavic exclamativeness to profound depression. On the surface, he may have looked just like millions of other well-buttoned and burnished young businessmen, but he was, in his heart, a very different kind of animal. He searched always for the best in people and in life. And he knew which organizations to belong to: he was already an honorary Hibernian and, as we know, a Mason. In politics, he was a dyed-in-the-wool Republican; he was following the career of the up-and-coming Calvin Coolidge, and would later be a devotee of Herbert Hoover.

His brothers were doing well in Montreal. Rudolph had become a dandy, at twenty-eight the president of the Dominion Iron and Wrecking Company, the Norwood, Tanton and Sharon Street Railway Company, the Consolidated Brass Foundries Company and the Standard Steel Company. Jerry was his partner in everything; the pair had removed and dismantled railways in Nova Scotia, ships in St. John and the Quebec Bridge, over 37,000 tons of steel. They had pioneered the use of sophisticated canalons, resembling buoys, with clamps that raised ships from the ocean floor. In 1917, when a French munitions ship collided with a hospital supplies ship in Halifax harbor and a subsequent explosion killed over one thousand, Jerry had worked heroically to rescue the Mayer business and save scores of lives. Now, Rudolph lived like a potentate: he had a magnificent home at 210 Peel Street, collected antiques, smoked expensive cigars, maintained an exotic mistress named Vera Caveny and had a chauffeur-driven Isotta-Fraschini town car. He quite overshadowed Jerry, who lived more modestly. By 1917, the brothers had turned over most of their business to manufacturing shells for Japan's ill-fated campaign against German bases in China.

News of the sisters, Yetta and Ida, was not as good. Yetta was working very long hours in her dry goods store in Montreal to support her children. On May 22, 1917, Ida had hastily married the dull, rather unattractive Julius Meyers, a deputy sealer for the Boston Department of Weights and Measures. Meyers had been a confirmed bachelor and had no understanding of children, disliking Ruth, Jack and Mitzi as much as they disliked him; the quarrels were lacerating and terrible. This must have been disturbing to Louis, who was obsessed with the idea of family unity; one divorce was a very serious matter indeed, and the prospect of a second was shattering for the whole family. Despite the miserable nature of the marriage, it dragged on for years, and on December 23, 1921, a child would be born of it: Lazarus Herzl, later known as Leonard, who would die tragically young.

Mayer's battle with Metro and Vitagraph continued. He clashed with Lewis J. Selznick, of whose lifestyle he disapproved: Mayer despised Selznick's gambling, drinking, and womanizing and his neglect of his wife and two sons, Myron and David.

According to Irene Selznick, her father brought much of his anger home, and fought with his wife and daughters. The girls, now on the verge of womanhood, were obsessed with movie stars, battling over movie magazines and photographs and dreaming of stage careers. At their new row house at 74 Pleasant Street, Brookline, they spent their preteen years in a spin of make-believe, fending off parental squabbles and working hard and successfully to move ahead at their girls' school. Severe though he may have been, Mayer was proud of both of them: pretty, tearful, tempestuous Edie and severe, frowning, serious, tomboy-ish Irene.

During a Supreme Court of New York hearing on the Vitagraph case on January 15, Mayer suffered a shock: Sam Seabury, tough counsel for Vitagraph, rudely asked Anita Stewart on the witness stand the question, "Are you single?," a truthful reply to which might wreck her future, since the sexual fantasies of millions of males would be dampened severely. "I prefer not to answer," the blushing star replied, even before her attorney, Moses Molevinsky, could raise an objection. Judge Collahan insisted she reply; she was compelled to point to Rudolph Cameron, who was in court posing as a mere bystander. "Why did you not reveal the wedding?" Seabury demanded to know. "Because of business reasons and my illness," Miss Stewart replied.

Mayer and Anita Stewart lost the case. It was a landmark legal decision, affecting stars' contracts for at least a decade to come. He also lost the Metro case. Many would have despaired at that moment, but not Mayer. He decided simply to wait out the twenty-six weeks left on Miss Stewart's Vitagraph contract, and began looking for stories for her in magazines. He also went to Richard Rowland and, with astonishing nerve, announced that he could deliver Anita Stewart! Still more surprisingly, Rowland believed him, and Mayer resumed his position as head of Metro's New England exchange in February 1918, just three weeks after Metro's final decision against him was handed down.

Mayer, of course, had no intention of letting Rowland, or anyone else, have Anita Stewart. At the same time, he had moved yet again, buying another row house for $2,500 at 1199 Beacon Street in Boston, his best address to date, situated on the very edge of a fashionable district. He was busy negotiating with J. D. Williams's First National Exhibitors' Circuit, Inc., of which his partner Nathan H. Gordon's Empire Theater Co. of Boston was a founding exhibitor, and which was already making substantial sums of money by obtaining films directly from stars and directors, to become the distributors of his own Anita Stewart Productions. He again assumed control of the American Feature Film Company, abandoned Lewis J. Selznick once he had secured promises from First National and coolly moved his offices from 69 to 60 Church Street to start up his new business.

Anita Stewart began shooting the first of her two final Vitagraph pictures, *The Mind the Paint Girl,* directed by Wilfrid North, at the end of April 1918 (it was released in 1920). A stroke of good fortune for Mayer occurred: after only a few days of work, North, his cameramen and several crew members were driving from location in New England to the Vitagraph Studios in Flatbush when they collided with a car. For weeks North was unable to work, and when he resumed, his direction visibly deteriorated.

With charming effrontery, Mayer went to Albert E. Smith and made him an offer: he would agree to finish the picture and take the second one off Smith's hands if Smith would release Miss Stewart two months ahead of schedule and allow him to make his first picture with her immediately. To sweeten the offer, he would pay the sum of $40,000 in cash. Smith crumbled; Vitagraph had severe financial problems and there was obviously no way to oppose such determination. The deal was struck.

Meanwhile, Mayer had found a serial story, "Virtuous Wives," in William Randolph Hearst's *Cosmopolitan* magazine. He felt it would be perfect for Anita Stewart. It was the story of Amy Forrester, a decent housewife lured into a corrupt social set; her flirtatious society girlfriend, determined to bed the housewife's husband, encourages the foolish girl into extramarital flirtations, then lies to the absent husband about his wife's imaginary adulteries. In the end, the virtuous Amy recaptures her husband and disposes of the wicked female deceiver.

It was just the kind of story that would appeal to Mayer, but it was slightly tactless as a choice since he and Anita Stewart had been linked by the gossips, and she was known to be an incorrigible flirt. When she read the story, she was not happy about going ahead with it, and there was a $1 million offer being dangled before her by the much aggrieved Lewis J. Selznick and Adolph Zukor. But she was a woman of her word, and her contract with Mayer was ironclad. She was also very fond of him, dazzled, no doubt, by his remarkable confidence and promises for her future, and she agreed to go ahead.

He assured her of the best presentation. He hired as costar the half-British, elegantly handsome Conway Tearle. As writer and director, he hired no less than George Loane Tucker, who had made a sensation five years earlier with his picture *Traffic in Souls,* which Tucker both cowrote and directed, and which revealed all of the horrifying details of white slave traffic. Banned in several countries, this succès de scandale earned Tucker a busy career.

Tucker had recently returned to New York, and no doubt Mayer felt, because he was a stern disciplinarian, as well as a handsome, athletic and attractive man, he would be perfect for handling his temperamental star. At the same time, Mayer signed the contract with First National, and, displaying his customary sense of humor, leased part of Vitagraph's Flatbush studio in which to make *Virtuous Wives*.

Mayer evidently sensed that Anita Stewart would be at her best if she had a strong rival in the movie. It was necessary to find a vivid actress for the part of Irma Delabarre, the wicked society woman who tries to destroy a happy marriage. He settled on the thirty-two-year-old Hedda Hopper. In later years, Miss Hopper would become one of the most powerful columnists in America. She was spry as a fox, with sharp features, and made of finest steel. Her determination surpassed her talent, which was distinctly minor; but she had great charm, style and presence on stage and screen. A malicious gossip, pretty but poisonous, Miss Hopper was ideal for *Virtuous Wives*. But Anita Stewart had to approve her: the Mayer contract gave her the right to interview every woman in her pictures, in case they should upstage her by being too attractive. Miss Hopper cunningly turned up at the interview at Flatbush dressed in the cheapest clothes she could find, and with an unappealing hair style. Miss Stewart was delighted. "You're perfect!" she exclaimed, quite ignoring the fact that the role of society bitch called for an expensive wardrobe.

Once Miss Hopper was signed, she went to the well-known couturiere Lady Duff Gordon of the House of Lucile and blew her entire salary, $5,000, on exquisite, very feminine clothes. She turned up for work on location at a rented mansion in Huntington, Long Island, magnificently dressed in a lilac and mauve chiffon tea gown. Miss Stewart was clad in a dull, dark blue taffeta dress. The furious Miss Stewart, right in front of Mayer, turned to George Loane Tucker and said, "She isn't dressed properly!" Miss Hopper replied that Lady Duff Gordon of Lucile had personally designed the gown. "I don't like it!" Anita Stewart snapped. Tucker demanded that Miss Stewart continue with the scene, but she walked off in a rage and refused to work for three days. Mayer at last managed to force her to obey the terms of her contract. But there were fights between the actresses from morning to night; Mayer authorized Tucker to increase Miss Hopper's role in the movie, virtually reducing Miss Stewart to a supporting player.

Shooting continued in summer heat on Long Island and at the Flatbush studios, Miss Hopper paying the price of her vanity by suffering in her heavy, opulent gowns, while Miss Stewart's more sensible and subdued clothes were designed to combat the weather.

The difficult picture finished, Mayer was confronted with another problem: a Spanish influenza epidemic was sweeping the eastern states, hundreds were dying in New York and New England, and he feared for his star and his unit. He began preliminary work on his next movie, *In Old Kentucky*, a reliable chestnut that foreshadowed his *National Velvet* decades later, about a girl who rides her favorite horse to success, disguised as a jockey in the Kentucky Derby. Scenes were shot at the Louisville racetrack and George Loane Tucker was starting to rehearse with Miss Stewart when suddenly Mayer canceled production, deciding to shoot it in California instead, fired Tucker and cast around for appropriate studio space in Los Angeles.

With his customary speed, he found the ideal solution. The visionary and peripatetic William N. Selig, a former magician and minstrel show operator, familiarly known as the Colonel, had been active at the outset of motion pictures, one of those who saw their vast potential as early as 1896. In April 1908, the Colonel had shot the first feature film completed in Los Angeles, *The Heart of a Race Tout*, for the most part at the Santa Anita racetrack.

Moving to Edendale, also favored by the comedy producer Mack Sennett, he had made a series of pictures; he produced *Hunting Big Game in Africa* in 1909, a fake version of ex-president Theodore Roosevelt's African expedition, at his Lincoln Park Zoo in Chicago. In 1911, he opened up the Selig Jungle Zoo, opposite Eastlake Park on Los Angeles's Mission Road, with over three hundred animals and birds, and, by 1916, he had moved from his studio on Alessandro Road to the zoo location, renaming Eastlake Park Lincoln Park, after his Chicago property, informing the Los Angeles authorities that he wished to honor the memory of President Lincoln.

In 1918, when Mayer started negotiating with Selig, the Selig Company was almost out of business. This was the ideal time for Mayer to strike a deal, and he got the studio for a very reasonable price. He signed the contract in late October, and by the second week of November, just after the armistice brought World War I to an end, he left for the West Coast with Margaret by the Twentieth Century Limited from New York. He put their two daughters in the care of a housekeeper. After a traditional stopover at the Blackstone Hotel in Chicago, where he met with the Selig executives, Mayer and his wife proceeded, with a new friend, Martin Quigley, who would later become the publisher of motion picture trade papers, by the Santa Fe Railroad to their destination.

In those days, there was no dining car on the train. At selected stops, to allow for a change of crews, the provision of water and coal and wheel inspections, the passengers would alight and enjoy fine meals at the excellent Harvey House restaurants, owned by Chicago's Fred Harvey, who had a unique franchise arrangement with the Santa Fe. It was an uncomfortable trip; the ventilation system blew out clouds of cindery smoke into the carriages, making everyone choke and forcing repeated cleanup visits to the bathroom. But it was a picturesque journey, through mountains and deserts and plains, a spectacle of the America that Louis B. Mayer loved so deeply. And ahead for this thirty-three-year-old was a new world to conquer: California.

CHAPTER FIVE

# 1918–1920

THE MAYERS STEPPED OUT of the train at the Southern Pacific Railroad Station and were met by a delegation that included First National executives Anita Stewart and Rudolph Cameron; that famous couple had arrived on a previous train. As the Mayers made their way to Hollywood, where the First National office had rented them a small house at Franklin Avenue and Ivar, about a mile east of La Brea, they saw an ugly, sprawling boom town, with gas stations and squat office buildings surrounded by large empty tracts overgrown with sun-browned grass, looming telegraph poles and cracked sidewalks.

The scent of orange blossoms blended with the stench of burning film. Palm trees slanted under a harsh blue sky. Houses were mostly of hastily constructed clapboard or brick and stucco, either imitations of New England structures with sun porches and steps, California craftsman–style bungalows or vaguely "Spanish" cottages and villas, with tiled roofs the color of recently dried blood.

Los Angeles was one of the most vigorously developing cities in the nation. At the turn of the century, it had boasted less than 135,000 people: a sleepy provincial town located between the desert and the sea. Now the population had grown to a million, bank deposits were in the hundreds of millions and the city was known as "the Mecca of America," or, improbably, "the Paris of California."

For all of its new prosperity, there was an aching sense of emptiness for easterners when they arrived in this uncultured wilderness. Mayer was far too busy to fret over such considerations. His first task was to inspect the Selig Studio, whose space he had rented sight unseen.

The Selig Polyscope complex was 700 by 600 feet in diameter, shaped like a wedge. At the north end were offices, each one occupying a space no more than 14 feet long and 3 feet wide, in temporary wooden structures. There were outside septic tanks; nearby, there was a dressing room only 7 feet long, and a 20-foot administration office at the northeast corner. The film vaults of fireproof concrete and a property stage were situated north of two closed stages and one that was open to the sky. A single star dressing room to house Anita Stewart was placed slightly to the southwest, and was only 12 feet long.

Flanking the structures to the west were a bear cage, an aviary and an elephant cage next to the star dressing room. Anita Stewart had only to look out her window to see a gray trumpeting beast looming before her. Beyond that were more cages, a constant flurry and cackle of every manner of parrot and other bird; the monkeys were always escaping and getting into the cutting rooms, playing with the long, snaking coils of celluloid.

Mayer checked into his modest clapboard office. He had been given only a very small staff and had to hire immediately. Going downtown to the offices of his newly appointed lawyers, Edwin J. and Joseph Loeb, at Loewenthal, Loeb and Walker (later Loeb, Walker and Loeb) at the Haas Building at 219 West Seventh Street, he was impressed by their smart young secretary, Florence Browning, and charmed them into letting him hire her. He put on typists, a camera crew, electricians, grips and a team of carpenters, made arrangements with the authorities for gas and electricity and worked closely with First National's local office to set up the proper distribution channels.

He worked day and night, in a constant turmoil, firing off letters to all and sundry as Florence Browning scribbled away in shorthand. He would again plunge into depression or become overexcited, collapse in fainting fits; then he was cheered by many visits to the home of Edwin J. Loeb, increasingly a close friend, at Loeb's comfortable house at 815 South Kingsley Drive, south of Wilshire.

He conferred with Anita Stewart, who, with Rudolph Cameron, had rented for six months, from Cecil B. DeMille, the house next door to DeMille's in elegant Laughlin Park, just a short drive from Mayer's modest home. It was a movie-star mansion, a contrast to the humble wooden residence in which the Mayers lived. Terrified of failure and bankruptcy, as he later admitted to his daughter Irene and to such friends as Hedda Hopper, Mayer resisted the temptation to live more lavishly. He had to start work immediately; First National was screaming for product, and his own impulsive nature would not let him rest. He concluded negotiations, begun before he left Boston, to hire thirty-six-year-old Lois Weber, who was at her peak as the most successful woman director in America.

Lois Weber was noted for her commitment to moral issues. Her *Where Are My Children?* attacked abortion and called for birth control at a time when those subjects were taboo in America; she denounced capital punishment in *The People vs. John Doe,* and anti-Semitism in *The Jew's Christmas,* and she took on the Church and the Senate in *Hypocrites.*

Under contract to Universal, she made the early vehicles of the pretty, china doll–like, seventeen-year-old Mildred Harris, mindless entertainments all; Miss Harris had married Charlie Chaplin shortly before Mayer arrived in Hollywood. Now Miss Weber was preparing to move out of Universal. To support her independent venture, she arranged to be subleased to Mayer for certain Anita Stewart movies. Even while she worked for Mayer, her Universal pictures were being released in a steady stream across the nation.

Lois Weber was dark-haired, her face stopped short of physical beauty because of a broken nose. She had a strong personality, expansive and dynamic. Her husband and codirector, Phillips Smalley, was milder mannered, with an oval, rather moony face, large, reflective brown eyes and a gentlemanly air. Despite his constant emphasis on cost and profits, Mayer managed to hit it off with the more artistically inclined Smalley. Work began almost at once on a picture, *A Midnight Romance,* another idealistic portrait of women close to the producer's heart.

In *A Midnight Romance* Miss Stewart played the maid Marie, a survivor of a torpedoed ship, who falls in love with the wealthy Roger Sloan, played by Jack Holt. It turns out that Marie is a Russian princess, a refugee from communism. Much of the movie was shot at beaches south of Los Angeles, and it was completed during the Christmas season. While it was in postproduction, Mayer needed another director to make the next Stewart film. He settled on Marshall (Mickey) Neilan.

Neilan was twenty-seven at the time. A native Californian, Neilan was a former child actor with dusty blond-brown hair, an open, handsome, freckled face and a powerful, broad, muscular physique. His flashing smile and impish charm made him irresistible to women. He was addicted to the bottle, frequently disappearing off his pictures into bars or brothels. He was also addicted to practical jokes: a typical jape of which he was fond was to walk up and down a Pullman car corridor, imitate a black porter and announce a meal at the wrong time, a fire, an imminent collision or a derailment; he would laugh as heartily as a child at the resulting excitement. He spent all the money he earned and more. His life was a succession of debts, threats, sudden fierce affairs—he had an insatiable sex drive—followed by recriminations, miserable separations and new romances.

He left school at eleven to work as a messenger, became a railway office boy, blacksmith's helper, mechanic, dishwasher, automobile salesman, fruit picker and actor. He rose steadily as an actor, then a director, proving to be an expert with performers, handling Mary Pickford skill-fully in the hit pictures *Rebecca of Sunnybrook Farm, Stella Maris* and *Daddy Longlegs*, in which he also appeared as a performer.

Neilan and Mayer clashed from the beginning. It is just possible that Mayer thought, observing the sweet, romantic sentimentality of the Pickford pictures, that Neilan was a decent, well-mannered citizen; he may have disregarded the stories about his adulteries (Neilan had married the actress Gertrude Bambrick in 1914), love of liquor and gambling. This proved to be a disaster for Mayer. As they started work on his first Anita Stewart picture, *Her Kingdom of Dreams*, at the beginning of January 1919, another tale of a seemingly underprivileged girl caught up in the life of the wealthy, Neilan ordered Mayer off his set, refused to be on time, ignored all budgetary restrictions, flirted with the star in front of her husband and sometimes could not be extracted from his rooms at the Los Angeles Athletic Club downtown or from the thriving bordellos nearby. The picture dragged on over schedule while Mayer became frenzied and frustrated. But First National could not wait for product; Mayer dared not risk firing the recalcitrant director.

At last, *Her Kingdom of Dreams* was finished, and Mayer turned to *Mary Regan*, his next Lois Weber production. Unhappy with *Her Kingdom of Dreams*, he released *Mary Regan* four months earlier.

As if he were not busy enough, Mayer was in New York that winter, bringing with him a print of *A Midnight Romance*. He went to Boston, where Edith, his elder daughter, was recovering from influenza; he decided he must move the children to Los Angeles in September.

He was back in New York again in April, following final scenes of *Mary Regan* shot in Chicago. He conferred with First National executives on *In Old Kentucky*, which Marshall Neilan would direct; Alfred E. Green, as Neilan's assistant, selected locations in Louisville and built streets and cabins at the Selig Zoo, while Neilan did some pick-up shots on *Her Kingdom of Dreams*. *In Old Kentucky* started shooting in June, with Mayer, Neilan and Anita Stewart, in Louisville. The star had spent months between other assignments and the shooting of two pictures learning to ride, as Mayer wanted to avoid a double in the scenes in which the young girl disguised as a jockey wins the Derby on her beloved horse. In Louisville, Mayer announced that he had signed Mildred Harris to a long-term contract; but she was still under contract to Universal. Universal's boss, Carl Laemmle, was furious. His lawyers took steps to prevent the dizzy blond star from making the change. Mayer hired a fast-talking character named Benny Zeidman, whom he would shortly appoint vice president and general manager, to approach Universal with a lucrative deal for Miss Harris's services, subleasing her to

Mayer for several pictures. Since Lois Weber was already under his control, and she was felt to be the only director able to handle Miss Harris successfully, he was able to bring off this new and daring coup.

Mildred Harris was a ruthless, self-indulgent, spoiled charmer who had tricked Charlie Chaplin into marriage by pretending she was going to have a baby. Now she was genuinely pregnant, but her second child was stillborn shortly after she made the deal with Mayer. Chaplin was insanely jealous of their relationship; he was convinced Mayer was having an affair with his wife.

A Midnight Romance became a great success, commercially if not critically, and so did Her Kingdom of Dreams and Mary Regan. On September 11, 1919, Mayer's contract with Mildred Harris was at last concluded, the arrangements expertly attended to by J. Robert Rubin, the suave and polished lawyer who had just left Metro and would remain Mayer's staunch friend and ally for decades to come. Nine days after the signing, Mayer left for New York to confer with First National executives on plans for Mildred Harris's pictures.

The Mayers brought their children to New York, an exciting privilege for twelve- and thirteen-year-olds. Margaret took the girls to see the Broadway shows, while Mayer went to Boston to dissolve his theatrical interests, separate from his partner Nathan H. Gordon and sell 1199 Beacon Street. He was delayed interminably, and as a result the girls were late for school in Los Angeles, arriving on November 1. They had to enter the Hollywood School for Girls several weeks after the beginning of the term. Edith remembered years later that this was annoying, that she and her sister Irene were shocked by the humble residence on Franklin Avenue. They were scarcely consoled by being exhibited like two prize dolls to Anita Stewart, who had now moved from Laughlin Park to a sumptuous hillside home.

Meantime, shooting had begun on Mildred Harris's first picture, The Inferior Sex. She starred with Milton Sills in yet another drama of a saintly heroine involved in the corrupt world of high finance. Winter rains that December of 1919 brought the Los Angeles River into flood, and Mission Road was under water, the cutting rooms drenched and all of the negative of the movie destroyed. While the picture was being reshot under the lean and sharp-featured, thirty-three-year-old John M. Stahl, a New York director who had his own independent unit at the Selig Zoo, Mayer insisted on starting another picture, Polly of the Storm Country. The subject matter called for a good deal of rain, conveniently discovered by merely stepping outside the door of the studio stage. Yet another picture, *The Fighting Shepherdess*, starring Anita Stewart and directed by Edward José, was completed by January 17.

Meanwhile, *In Old Kentucky* was breaking all records despite below-zero weather conditions and blizzards in the East and Midwest. Theater fronts and lobbies were turned into imitation racetracks, with *In Old Kentucky* handicap races played with wooden horses. Next to the box offices temporary betting clubs with blackboards indicating the entries and odds were set up, with chalkers changing figures from time to time. Orchestra seats were renamed grandstands, balcony chairs were called bleachers and seven-foot white picket fences divided the lobbies, with ushers dressed as jockeys and multicolored pennants hanging overhead. Harry Reichenbach and his fellow publicist Eddie Hesser worked round the clock to carry out Mayer's inspired publicity campaigns.

Despite the excitement of his burgeoning career, Mayer had his share of problems. His daughters were snubbed by old-money girls at school; his brothers, Rudolph and Jerry, were wiped out when the end of World War I cut out their Japanese armaments market (they had turned over too much of their operation to making shells for Japan in that country's war against Germany in China, Manchuria and the Northern Pacific), and were seeking money from him;[1] and Charlie Chaplin was a constant thorn in Mayer's side.

High-strung, neurotic, obsessive, Chaplin had little time for tough businessmen like Mayer, and the fact that Chaplin also was under contract to First National made no difference. Chaplin had exhausted the nubile charms of his wife, Mildred Harris, and discovered he was married to a greedy and unscrupulous fool. One night, Mayer came to the house for discussions with his star; Chaplin, maddened with jealousy, and aggravated by the logo "Chaplin-Mayer Productions," hid in the conservatory to spy on them. Mayer evidently heard a sound, as he kept the conversation strictly to business. He had been invited to dinner and a tête-à-tête, but left before the meal was served.

In April, there was a party at the Alexandria Hotel at which both Mayer and Chaplin were present. Everyone was excited and tense; several interpreted Mildred Harris's glances at Mayer as being romantic, and notes were exchanged between the two men. Chaplin snapped. He asked Mayer to step outside. While the crowd poured into the lobby to watch, they clashed in a fistfight. Mayer was heavier and taller, but Chaplin was agile and deft. The fight ended as quickly as it began. Darting around Mayer, Chaplin tripped on a painter's scaffolding and fell, knocking himself out.

[1] Jerry started out for Japan in December 1918 to save the situation, but the influenza epidemic in San Francisco was so severe that it forced him to take his pregnant wife back to Montreal.

## CHAPTER SIX

# 1920–1922

OUR HERO IS, at the outset of the 1920s, thirty-five years old; his eyes are sharper and more fiercely intent than ever, owlish behind pince-nez. His body has thickened somewhat; he is as neatly attired as always, immaculately groomed, manicured, his shoes brightly polished. He still talks in a nonstop stream of hyperbole; his passion for making pictures, money and seeing a better America, his addiction to his children's welfare, are fiercer than ever. He has become a hypochondriac, haunted by his mother's painful death. He is terrified of illness, of being cut off prematurely. He frets over food and drink; he fears contagion; he fusses over his elder daughter Edie's uncertain health and high-strung, fragile temperament.

Prohibition is the law of the land. Since he drinks in moderation, this is not a problem; however, he has to consider the First National salesmen and office executives from the east, and soon the studio will engage an effective bootlegger and pimp, Frank Orsatti.

In 1920, the Mayer life was one of constant conflict; even after Marshall Neilan walked out of the studio in the fall of 1919, the heavy-drinking director had managed to provoke Mayer's wrath by insulting anyone who would listen. Even now, from his roost at the Los Angeles Athletic Club, Neilan could be heard attacking those who praised Mayer's handling of *In Old Kentucky* with such words as, "Does a man who merely complains about the cost of chairs have a right to be called a film maker?"

Director John M. Stahl, now numero uno at Selig Polyscope, was also a formidable adversary. Stahl found it difficult to deal with Mayer's constant cost cutting; in turn, Mayer was often irritated by Stahl's deliberate, slow, meticulous approach. But Mayer respected Stahl, his essential good taste, command of film rhythm and control of actors.

In March 1920, a month before the fracas with Chaplin at the Alexandria Hotel, Mayer completed the rebuilding of the Selig Studio. An elaborate gate, opening onto a driveway, and a facade that was an imitation of the renaissance chateau of Chenonceau added an air of spurious grandeur to the humble Mission Road location; a $100,000 administration building also was added. Given her temperament, Mildred Harris cannot have been pleased that, despite the fact that she had a new and fancier dressing room, it was still half the size of Anita Stewart's. The press was having a field day that spring with her mercenary dealings with Chaplin over their divorce. She hated him so much that she even used her influence with J. D. Williams, chairman of First National, to have him threaten to attach all of Chaplin's pictures, including the recently completed *The Kid* with Jackie Coogan, unless Chaplin increased the $100,000 he had already agreed to pay her. By August of that year, Chaplin would be forced to hide the film in a vault in Salt Lake City to escape Williams's detectives, and later would deposit it in New York, where he had to disguise himself as a woman to evade Williams's men as he slipped through the lobby of the Ritz Hotel.

Miss Harris was temperamental and aggravating during the shooting of *The Woman in His House,* a new picture directed by Stahl. Mayer had had enough of her; despite the successful preview of the picture and generally good reviews and audience response, he brought her contract to an end with one more film, *Habit,* directed by Edwin Carewe. She would soon fall into bankruptcy through her extravagance; Mayer would have to break apart Chaplin-Mayer Productions in litigation and attach her few assets in order to retrieve money owed to him on promissory notes. He was also having difficulties with Anita Stewart; but he would hang on to her as long as he could, as she was still in the top ten of box office stars: seventh now, just behind Elsie Ferguson.

Picture after picture was making money, despite press criticism of Mayer's weak stories. He was forced to have a team in New York searching every magazine as it came out for serial stories. So fierce were the continuing demands for product from First National, he would snap up anything that looked remotely satisfactory and hand it out to a passel of women writers. Lois Weber had left him; she had set up in her independent production company. He needed to obtain other craftswomen who could tap into the needs of the female audience. Within a year, he would find the writers Bess Meredyth and Frances Marion, of whom more later.

On September 7, Mayer left by train for Chicago and New York with his wife and daughters, John Stahl and his wife, and one of his team of writers, Madge Tyrone. This was followed by a trip to Boston. It was not a comfortable visit. In Boston, Irene was endlessly complaining about such matters as her hat being too small for her; she rejected the most innocent inquiries from her former schoolfriends concerning Hollywood gossip. Mayer was busy in both Manhattan and New England, conferring with his various partners; in Boston, he hobnobbed with his former partner Nathan Gordon, who still distributed First National product under the New England franchise, and with Colman Levin, who put the family up at his house.

Back in Hollywood, having surrendered the Franklin Avenue bungalow his daughters hated, Mayer moved his family into the rambling and unfashionable Hollywood Hotel on Hollywood and Highland.

"Irene was horrified when she found we were going to live in the Hollywood Hotel," Edie recalled. "We used to pass it often in walks from Mrs. Willet's Hollywood School for Girls. We considered it definitely déclassé"! Yet in fact it was not as déclassé as it looked; New Yorkers often preferred it, because they could more easily reach the studios without having to come all the way from downtown. One guest who was firmly installed there would later be associated with Mayer: the British Elinor Glyn, one of the most popular novelists of the hour, fascinated the Mayer family as she drifted through the lobby in a cloud of chiffon, with purple lipstick and fingernails, her hair elaborately coiffed, wearing a succession of picture hats and swathed in multicolored silk scarves. Her books featured torrid, sexually driven heroines, seeking handsome, rich and powerful men whom they could enslave.

While Margaret Mayer did her embroidery in the hotel suite and the girls ogled the stars who condescended to pass through the lobby, Mayer was as absent as ever, shooting pictures on location. In mid-January 1921, he was at Truckee, in the California Sierras, shooting the Anita Stewart vehicle The Tornado, later retitled The Yellow Typhoon (in which she played twins). The company found themselves in the teeth of a blizzard, housed in ramshackle wooden accommodations and practically frozen solid as they battled the snow. They shifted to Santa Rosa Island off the Northern California coast in heavy rain and wind for more dramatic scenes. During the editing of this harrowingly difficult production in April, Mayer was told by his doctors that Edie, who was increasingly thin and pale and miserable, was found to have tuberculosis.

According to Irene Mayer, her father overreacted as always where illness was concerned; the terror of his mother's death evidently overwhelmed him, and he ran everywhere, looking for advice. It was obvious that Edie could not remain in a hotel; there was fear at that time that even a cough could spread TB, and the unfortunate girl was put in an isolation tent, food brought to her by masked nurses, her mother and sister forbidden to kiss her. It was felt that the mountains were good for consumption, so Edie was packed off to Big Bear, where it was extremely cold and damp. Naturally, her condition worsened. So that she could be fully isolated when he moved her back to Los Angeles, Mayer rented a large house on Sunset Boulevard, near North Crescent Heights. Her sister Irene was repeatedly x-rayed, a dangerous way of investigating her lungs. It is hard to believe Irene's story that she was made to sleep out on the balcony of the house, even when it rained; it is doubtful if she could have survived such unthinking treatment without getting pneumonia. Understandably, Edie clashed with her father over this treatment; so he packed her off to the fashionable Mission Inn at Riverside, which at least offered a dry, healthy climate.

Mayer's father, Jacob, now seventy-one, who had been staying with Rudolph in Montreal, arrived for what would turn out to be a permanent visit. Jacob brought word of Ida, who was still in Boston, unhappily married to Julius Meyers and pregnant with her fourth child. Jacob Mayer proved to be a formidable presence in the house on Sunset Boulevard; he dazzled his nieces with his extraordinary learning. He would constantly cite the Talmud whenever anybody came to him with a problem. Two stars who sat at his feet, seeking advice, were Mabel Normand and Mary Miles Minter, who would soon need more than verbal help: they were involved with the ill-fated director William Desmond Taylor.

That same month, the Mayers, along with the whole of Hollywood, were dismayed by an appalling scandal. Protective as he was of his daughters, Mayer could not keep the sordid details from them. At the St. Francis Hotel in San Francisco, the popular comedian Fatty Arbuckle was entertaining a group of friends, the director Lowell Sherman, and three pretty girls, including the Mayers' near neighbor on Franklin Avenue, Virginia Rappé. It was stated, probably falsely, that Arbuckle, in a drunken frenzy, had raped Miss Rappé with a Coca-Cola bottle, which broke inside her; she died four days later of peritonitis.

The scandal drew the fire of virtually every public puritan in America. There had been widespread talk of orgiastic parties in Hollywood, the proliferation of brothels and speakeasies and the widespread use of drugs. It was hinted that certain stars were addicts, including Mabel Normand, who was supposed to keep cocaine bags in her hair curlers.

The picture was absurdly overpainted. Ostentation and vulgarity were in most cases the worst of Hollywood's sins, and, with rare exceptions, like the handsome hero Wallace Reid, who was heavily addicted, the inhabitants were too tired at night after working twelve to fourteen hours a day at the studios to enjoy anything more stimulating than charades, dumb crambo or pinochle. The incident increased Mayer's desire to make sure that his pictures could not be subject to moral criticism. Another, more practical concern was that various states were threatening the industry commercially by severe local censorship.

The Presbyterian Church and its Temperance and Moral Welfare Board were foremost in criticizing scenes of heavy kissing, drinking and cigarette smoking in movies. Well before the Arbuckle scandal various state legislatures were busy passing bills that would render transporting immoral pictures a felony; theater licenses were being revoked when their owners showed "hot" movies; and the licentiousness of certain scripts was being rapidly cut out by nervous producers, afraid of seeing whole market areas closed up. The cleanup campaigns, combined with Mayer's own nervous feeling about sex itself, led to his rigorously instructing each and every writer on his staff that they must not turn in anything that would not be entirely acceptable to his wife, who thenceforth read everything before it went through to production.

Mayer's brother Jerry arrived in November from Montreal with his wife, Rheba, and their baby son, Gerald. They found a small wooden cottage at 5156 Franklin Avenue, just a few blocks east of Mayer's original house. They brought word of Rudolph and much detail of the sad collapse of the Dominion Iron and Wrecking Company, and its associated companies. Rudolph was still living in perilous grandeur with his mistress and butler. It appeared he was always about to make or lose a million and had no intention of moving to Hollywood. Jerry became plant manager of the Selig Studios.

Soon afterward, Mayer moved Edie from the Mission Inn to the Desert Inn in Palm Springs. She still had to occupy a bungalow on the grounds, as it was feared that, should she enter the hotel, she would infect the other inhabitants. She was accompanied by a warm, good-natured nurse, Peggy Syme.

Meanwhile, other matters were afoot. On September 7, 1921, at a meeting at the Congress Hotel in Chicago, Robert Lieber, who had supplanted J. D. Williams as president of First National, which still distributed the Mayer product, Mayer's old associate at Alco, the charmingly absentminded Al Lichtman, and Oscar Price, president of Associated Pictures, signed a contract that enormously enhanced the power of the organization. This meant that Lichtman, as Associated's general manager, was back with Mayer again, sure cause for rejoicing. Yet Associated was about to suffer a blow: Charlie Chaplin, who detested Robert Lieber and Mayer's old friend, Nathan Gordon, of the Associated New England Circuit, decided to desert the organization. He had never forgiven the company for threatening to attach *The Kid*. No doubt to Mayer's chagrin, Chaplin formed the Screen Artists Guild on December 17, 1921, made up of the studio bosses who wished to dispose of the costly Wall Street middlemen, releasing their pictures directly to the theater chains.

Mayer ostracized this organization, which was subscribed to at a Biltmore Hotel luncheon by the prominent film makers Thomas H. Ince (Ralph's brother), Mack Sennett, Buster Keaton and, most notably, Joseph M. Schenck, who composed and read a proclamation signed by forty stars. It cannot have pleased Mayer that Anita Stewart turned up at the meeting to give the Guild full support, though he could have extracted some amusement from the fact that among those who attended and signed the paper was Jackie Coogan, age seven.

Also at that time, Mayer added an important new scenario writer to his list: the aforementioned thirty-year-old Bess Meredyth, who later married the director Michael Curtiz. This strong and independent woman was typical of those in whom Mayer placed his faith; his respect for women, and his understanding of the importance of elevating them to the top of the film industry, was remarkable. Miss Meredyth was unhappily married to the actor Wilfred Lucas. She had begun as a dollar-a-story journalist in her hometown of Buffalo, New York, had acted on Broadway, had written and directed early *Tarzan* pictures and had acted in a picture with her husband in Australia. Mayer took a chance on this tiny, pretty, extremely outgoing and very determined young lady and hired her to write several pictures, including *The Dangerous Age*, *One Clear Call* and *Rose O' the Sea*. It was typical of him at once to see talent in people, then to give that talent an astonishingly free reign.

Another writer who interested him at the time was the remarkable thirty-two-year-old Frances Marion. With her gypsyish good looks, dark eyes and hair, and strong, bony features, she was something to behold. A gifted constructionist with an acute sense of what the female audience wanted to see, and possessed of a great sense of humor, she had written the successes *Rebecca of Sunnybrook Farm* and *Stella Maris* for Mary Pickford. They were, of course, directed by Mayer's enemy, Marshall Neilan. She also had acted in *Little Lord Fauntleroy* and directed *Just Around the Corner*. It is remarkable that, given her success and growing wealth, Miss Marion was prepared to even consider the still second-level Louis B. Mayer as an employer; but apparently she had temporarily tired of Mary Pickford, and Neilan was obviously on the way down. She agreed, perhaps only from curiosity, when Mayer called her to the studio to talk to her.

She would never forget the encounter. She drove through the imitation sixteenth-century gate, parking her car among a cluster of automobiles, including Mayer's humble Ford. She made her way into his office, furnished with leather and plywood chairs. She saw a figure that to her resembled Humpty Dumpty, a neckless head attached to the shoulders of a stevedore with a body that seemed to go straight down to the floor without a single contour.

She coolly advised Mayer that, if he wished to employ her, she must have $1,000 a week. His eyes suddenly went completely dead, like those in a wax doll. She repeated the sum. He took off his glasses and wiped them. He told her that, the business matter aside, whatever she wrote must be acceptable to his daughters: the scripts must be innocent of any hint of depravity; they must be family pictures. He gave her the script of James Forbes's Broadway play *The Famous Mrs. Fair*, which he saw as a vehicle for the popular comic opera singer Myrtle Stedman. "I expect a damn good script for the lousy price I'm paying you," Mayer said. Miss Marion was not impressed. "I'll do my best," she snapped as she walked out.

Miss Marion had rushed the script out at record speed; she wrote no less than seven that year. Mayer submitted the screenplay to his wife, who instantly approved it and told him the story. Reduced to tears as she spoke, he knew he was onto a winner. Mayer called Miss Marion and told her he was accepting the material. "How about a check?" she asked. "You'll find it when you get home," he replied, "and with a bonus."[1] She recalled in 1970: "This seemed satisfactory. I was about to leave when suddenly this unnerving little man moved around the desk. Then, quite suddenly, he grabbed me and began pinching my behind! This was scarcely what I was looking for, and I made my way out of the office in about half a second. I decided then and there to take my work elsewhere from that moment on!"

At the time, Florence Browning left Mayer's employ and was replaced by a new and very attractive secretary, Margaret Bennett, who passed on vivid reminiscences to her namesake and niece, Margaret Kruse. Miss Bennett liked Mayer, and he paid her surprisingly well, but there was a price attached: not sex (though, she claimed, he chased her several times around the desk) but consolation. He would call her at two or three in the morning, say he was nervous and unable to sleep, and she would drive from her home on Franklin to his own, pick him up in her car and drive him around. What Margaret Mayer must have made of this can only be speculated on.

Mayer would pour out his troubles to her, and she would give him what advice she could. She felt she acted as a kind of tranquilizer for his several neuroses. Sometimes, they would stop off at a roadside, all-night stand to have a cup of coffee. She noted that Mayer was by no means a

[1] It turned out to be a signed photograph.

saint in his personal behavior: he would pursue and bed young women very casually, mostly the young new girls who applied for work.

At the beginning of December, Mayer moved his family from sinful Sunset Boulevard to the leafy, safely residential Los Feliz district. He bought for $10,000, on a $1,000 deposit and seven percent interest, a modest, two-story dwelling at 1834 North Kenmore, just south of Franklin Avenue. The house had bay windows and a front lawn running down to an earthquake-cracked sidewalk. Edie was still at the Mission Inn, but there would be plenty of room for her when she returned.

Mayer was busy all through Christmas 1921 shooting *One Clear Call*, his most important picture to date. Written by Bess Meredyth, directed by John M. Stahl, starring Henry B. Walthall and Claire Windsor, it was the affecting story of a gambler in the Deep South, who, given only a few weeks to live, reforms himself after narrowly escaping a lynching by the vigilante Night Riders. Mayer was also busy with *Rose O' the Sea*, starring Anita Stewart and (for once) her underemployed husband, Rudolph Cameron.

That winter the appointment of Will H. Hays preoccupied the entire film industry. With great skill, and not a little cunning, Hollywood's leaders knew that a sure way of squelching the increasingly threatening local censorship boards would be to hire a prominent Republican to head up a Producers' and Distributors' Organization that could quash the local boards' decisions at the federal level. Hays was the ideal choice. As chairman of the Republican National Committee, he had been a committed and effective instrument in the election of President Warren G. Harding in 1920. He had waged war on mail fraud and had lobbied successfully for the burgeoning air-mail services. He was expert at addressing Boy Scout rallies, was a continual presence at the White House and was known to be fascinated by movies.

In appearance Hays was an uninspiring figure: short, spindly, he resembled the skinny boy in the weight-lifting advertisements who had sand kicked on him by lifeguards. His face was as narrow and jug-eared as a bat's. He spoke in a thin drawl, redolent of his Hoosier origins. There was nothing about his presence to suggest a commanding, virile authority; he was to all appearances a wimp. Yet he possessed a fierce and steely spirit. And whatever his looks, he would be the perfect instrument for saving the industry. Not only could he effectively overrule the local boards, but, as postmaster general, he could instruct his successor should he leave that post and could assist greatly in alleviating the heavy costs of film shipments, furthering the cause of distribution by extending airmail services across the nation. In addition, he would have the ear of the president at all times. The public would be satisfied of the industry's good intentions by appointing this impeccable family man to be its crusading captain.

Meetings were held with Hays in New York. By the outset of 1922 he was already making the appropriate arrangements to resign his government post and take up his new position. This occurred on March 4; he at once set about defeating the congressional resolution that called for federal investigation of the industry. Mayer publicly declared his enthusiasm for Hays's appointment. Hays was attacked in the House of Representatives, but it was hard to impugn his integrity. On March 16, in his first public appearance as head of all movies, Hays said he would give the country good and clean pictures. Shortly thereafter, the American Association of Advertising Agencies announced that his first job would be to establish the highest possible motion picture standards.

On February 5, 1922, Mayer and his wife, with Irene, drove down to the Desert Inn at Palm Springs to visit with Edie. In those days, Palm Springs was a rambling wooden village with dirt roads, scattered prefabricated structures, humble stores and cowboys galloping in, surrounded by clouds of dust. The Desert Inn was the only building that had electricity. Edie was much recovered; she had gained twenty pounds in the fine desert air, and she rushed out, looking plump and healthy, as her parents frantically honked their auto horn and ran in to embrace her. They were delighted to find that she was well enough to be moved back, with her nurse, Peggy Syme, to Kenmore Avenue. She was bubbling over with stories of a handsome British actor, Herbert Rawlinson, who played the ukulele and took Edie and Peggy up Palm Canyon in his roadster. She cannot have confided in her father what occurred during the ride, but amusingly suggested some harmless hanky-panky to her cousin Ruth Komiensky in Boston.

With *Rose O' the Sea* and *One Clear Call* wrapped up in March, Mayer signed another young and vigorous director, Reginald Barker. He also hired J. G. Hawks in the unusual combined role as writer and overall production manager, and he made a surprising deal with Metro Pictures to release some of his First National films through that organization. This was especially odd, since First National was, as we know, more powerful than ever, and Metro was still headed by Richard Rowland, Mayer's old enemy. Evidently, Rowland desperately needed more commercial product; he had overpaid heavily for the rights to several books, including Vicente Blasco Ibañez's *Four Horsemen of the Apocalypse*, a vehicle for Rudolph Valentino. As it turned out, Rowland would leave Metro for First National that December.

In April, Mayer made another major move. Al Lichtman had formed a working partnership with Benjamin P. Schulberg, a sharp, humorous, lively thirty-year-old producer who had been a reporter and editor in New York. Like Lichtman, he had worked for Adolph Zukor and Jesse L. Lasky as a publicist. In 1920, Schulberg had formed Preferred Pictures Inc., and produced dramas of much energy and little merit starring the buxom Katherine MacDonald. Schulberg rented space from Mayer at Mission Road. By arrangement with First National, Preferred would now meld with Louis B. Mayer Productions, starting with the movie *Rich Men's Wives*.

In June, Mayer was in New York to buy rights to plays. He gave one of his very rare interviews to the *Moving Picture World*'s T. S. da Ponte, saying that Will Hays's appointment was the best thing that had happened to the industry to date. He praised Adolph Zukor, for whom, he said, he had "no particular love" (a rare case of an understatement), for backing up Will Hays by dropping his own Fatty Arbuckle pictures at a loss of $2 million. He said he was happy to be a member of the Motion Pictures Producers and Distributors Association under Hays, stating that he had never been censored, but kept his pictures clean, and that if Will Hays slapped him on the wrist, metaphorically speaking, telling him he could not show a particular picture, he would be perfectly willing to abide by the decision. He spoke of his credo: Writers were of first importance, actors were secondary. Yet actors must be well paid: a black woman playing a maid in one movie he had made recently was getting $100 a day. He mentioned that *In Old Kentucky* had cleared a million dollars, at a cost of only $240,000 to produce. In a veiled reference to Mildred Harris, he spoke of great stars falling by the wayside.

Next, Mayer hired director Fred Niblo. With his strong good looks, huge pearl tie pins, expensive silk ties, handmade suits and dashing, forceful manner, the forty-eight-year-old Niblo was probably Mayer's favorite filmmaker: *The Mark of Zorro* and *The Three Musketeers* were triumphs of the action picture. Niblo was an autocrat, dominant and sarcastic in his humor; in private a charmer, he was at work fierce and unbending.

Niblo was a workaholic and plunged directly into preparing two pictures for Mayer: *Captain Applejack* and *The Famous Mrs. Fair*, the latter from Frances Marion's screenplay. On August 5, 1922, Mayer was in San Francisco, investigating the possibility of shooting movies there, setting up a separate studio with a separate management, but the day he arrived, the notorious Pacific fog rolled in, and he knew at once why the bay city would never be a movie capital.

He gave a rare interview to George C. Warren of the San Francisco

*Chronicle* on August 6. Referring to the plot of his recently completed *The Dangerous Age*, and, incidentally, to his own life, he spoke revealingly:

> A young man of twenty [Mayer was eighteen when he got married] wants to marry or get a sweetheart. What he really needs is a mother; somebody to mother him. And he usually gets a wife who does that until he is forty [he was thirty-seven when he gave the interview]. Then he thinks he wants younger society. He is afraid to go with men and women of his own age, because people will think he is old, so he goes with the young ones. But he finds he isn't as young as he imagined he was, and he is glad to go back to the woman who "mothers" him . . .

Nothing could be more accurate as an account of his life with Margaret.

## CHAPTER SEVEN

# 1922-1923

MAYER'S LAWYER, Edwin J. Loeb, had told him, earlier that year, of another client, twenty-three-year-old Irving Thalberg. Loeb was convinced that Thalberg was going to quit as vice president in charge of production at Carl Laemmle's Universal Pictures Corporation. Thalberg was irritated by the fact that Laemmle was trying to force him to marry Laemmle's good-natured but lantern-jawed daughter, Rosabelle.

Years before, when Thalberg had worked as a secretarial assistant for Laemmle in New York City, he had become infatuated with Rosabelle. Unimpressed by his pale face and feeble physique, Rosabelle had refused him point-blank when he had suggested taking her to a dance at the Biltmore Hotel. Now that he was a big wheel, she was attracted to his power; she even had her father intercede with William Thalberg, Irving's parent, to make a match. But by now, Thalberg had his eye on a star: Constance Talmadge, sister-in-law of Joe Schenck.

Thalberg was irritated by the fact that Laemmle's brothers-in-law, who had no talent, were in charge of making second-rate knockabout comedies at the studio, which he was forced to approve. The stingy Laemmle was paying him only $450 a week. He had already approached Cecil B. DeMille for a job and been turned down because DeMille's executive board did not approve of him. This was shortsighted: Thalberg was, at that tender age, already a legend. He had advanced Universal's commercial and critical success through a brief but brilliant career; in particular, he was noted for his development of, and clashes with, a number of important directors, of whom the most notable was Erich von Stroheim.

He had advanced the career of Lon Chaney and was just completing one of Chaney's best films, *The Hunchback of Notre Dame,* from the novel by Victor Hugo. He emphasized good taste, meticulous period detail in historical films and the classical dramaturgy of struggle. He

followed Carl Laemmle's example in encouraging temperamental directors, giving them license, then would act censoriously when they took
the law into their own hands. He was both patron and scourge, encour-
ager and controller. He wanted everything: prestige pictures made by
directors of quality, box office success and obedience.

Thalberg never secured a proper schedule or budget for Erich von
Stroheim on the latter's *Foolish Wives*. He allowed the movie to drift on
for thirteen months, permitted the director to shoot only at night and
gave him a free hand in casting. But he was rapidly forced to the conclusion that von Stroheim was abusing these unique privileges: the director
drove one actress into hysterics and almost burned two performers to
death when he set fire to a tower. After indulging him to the limit,
Thalberg panicked, took von Stroheim's lights away so he could not
shoot and closed down the picture until von Stroheim obeyed his com-
mands.

When Mayer met Thalberg at Edwin Loeb's home, the young man
made an immediate impression on him: a cool, delicately authoritative
Jewish Prince who kept all but a gilded handful of friends at arm's distance. To those few friends, he could be playful, charming and boyishly
relaxed. He took an almost childlike pleasure in riding in his enormous
white Cadillac convertible with the top down driven by a black chauffeur who would refer to himself as "a fly in a milk bottle." Thalberg was
five foot six and 122 pounds. He had black, wavy hair that resisted the
most careful plastering down with oil and was worn without a part; a
high, pale, intellectual forehead; large, dark, reflective eyes that missed
nothing; a tip-tilted, shiny nose; and a mouth set firmly in a look of
quiet determination. Thalberg was extremely slight, his bones like a
bird's; a well-shaped collarbone gave a good set to his shoulders, but his
limbs were pale and slender, as muscleless as a girl's. He had a bluish,
transparent pallor, the result of chronic insomnia and an early bout with
rheumatic fever. The disease had weakened his heart, and his formidable
mother, Henrietta, never hesitated to point out that "the boy is delicate," "He may not live," "You mustn't argue with him," and—the coup
de grace—"Irving must be given exactly what he wants." She would
appear at frequent intervals, ordering him off a dance floor or tennis
court, summoning him home from a party to their house at 446 South
Norton Avenue in the Larchmont district, treating him like a sickly
child. She overlooked his stubborn will and steely, irresistible psychological strength. She used his condition; everyone in Hollywood, knowing
he would die young, made the appropriate responses: he assumed the
glum respectability of a member of a doomed species.

Evenings at the Thalbergs' were odd. William Thalberg was prominent in real estate, but at home Henrietta treated him with contempt. She wandered about the house, with her hair hopelessly tangled, a dressing gown drawn loosely about her as she swore at her husband, who was stiff-backed, correct and heel-clickingly German but was completely a victim of his imposing Alsatian spouse. Irving's sister Sylvia was, by contrast, very good-natured and high-spirited. No one who visited the Thalbergs ever forgot the comic melodrama of those evenings.

Thalberg's manners were smooth and impeccable. He would sit at his desk, or more often stand, very tightly wound, staring at his visitor with an intent, concentrated gaze, hands clenched on the desk, knuckles white as almonds, papers and books piled about him, expressing sympathetic interest, a hint of danger if certain borderlines of conversation were crossed, a carefully precise emphasis in a soft, subdued voice on important matters and a hint of impatience with trivial ones, and, all the time, a sense of formal, controlling power.

He was not to be crossed. He had a fiery temper, surprising in one so frail, and so complete a certainty in his own judgment that he could strike fear. He was an insomniac workaholic, conscious every moment of the passage of time, which was his enemy. He would try to relieve his nervousness by insistent habits: he constantly nibbled away at apples, dates or candy for instant energy, or would flick a twenty-dollar gold coin in the air while he was talking, sometimes watching it clatter on his desk, spin a gold watch on its chain, pace about with his hands clasped tightly behind his back, jingling money or keys in his pocket, or thrum his nervous, white, fragile fingers on the desk or jig his knee up and down.

The alliance with Thalberg found a stronger foundation, held secret by all concerned. In January 1923, Mayer formed the Louis B. Mayer Real Estate Company, with, as partners, Irving and William Thalberg and the businessmen Melvil Hall, A. B. McGrillis, and J. B. Rhodes. On March 29, they made their first major purchase, 625 valuable acres of land north of Cumberland Drive and west of the Baldry Mountains in Valinda, near West Covina. This hidden partnership would continue for many years, giving a special complexion to Mayer's familial relationship with the Thalbergs.

Mayer saw more and more of Thalberg in the winter of 1923. He brought him home to North Kenmore to meet Margaret, Edie and Irene. He felt that Thalberg was the son he had never had, but he warned his daughters that they must never date or marry Thalberg; again, he was treating the young executive like a fragile china doll. And he was concerned about the dynasty.

Like Laemmle, he misunderstood Thalberg's nature. Instead of going to bed early and pampering himself, Thalberg ran around with three high-powered companions, visiting speakeasies at all hours. One of these, the playwright John Colton, was a homosexual; the others, the director Jack Conway and the powerful leading man and future star John Gilbert, were aggressively heterosexual.

After much negotiation, Mayer signed Thalberg, in February 1923, to a contract as vice president in charge of production for a salary of $600 a week, plus a share of the profits. Mayer was rushed off his feet at weekends, hobnobbing with his partner B. P. Shulberg, Shulberg's wife, Adeline, and their blond, eight-year-old son known as Budd. He and Margaret exchanged weekend brunches at their home with the Shulbergs, who were now living at 525 South Lorraine Boulevard, north of Wilshire, having just moved six blocks west from Gramercy Place. Somehow, during those busy days, Mayer would find time to visit with his real estate partners William and Henrietta Thalberg at their new home at 689 South Bronson, a stone's throw from the Schulbergs, to discuss Irving's future and how best his health should be protected.

Mayer's weeks were even more crowded than his weekends. He was among the most important independent film makers in Hollywood that year; in early March, the Rialto Theater in Manhattan was ablaze with lights, announcing boldly: LOUIS B. MAYER PRESENTS *HEARTS AFLAME*: THE BLAZING BIG TIMBER DRAMA . . . BOOK IT AND WATCH YOUR BOX OFFICE RECORDS GO UP IN SMOKE. The rugged backwoods adventure was his biggest hit to date.

Most prominent among replacements for Anita Stewart, who drifted away after refusing to renew her contract, was the tempestuous Barbara La Marr. Then twenty-seven, gorgeous and overripe, with dark hair and enormous, liquid, heavy-lidded violet eyes, she had had a stormy personal life and three marriages. At the time Mayer hired her, she was getting $250,000 a picture, and she was in love with one of Mayer's writers, Paul Bern.

Bern, who would play an important role in Mayer's life and would feature in a notorious incident nine years later, was one of Mayer's trusted allies, but he never warmed to him on a personal level. Mayer was convinced Bern was bisexual; furthermore, it was an open secret that he suffered from a handicap: through some hormonal imbalance, he had developed unusually small genitals, which gave him a severe inferiority complex, even though he was apparently capable of performing intercourse. It is probable that he suffered from recurring (but not absolute) impotence. His relationship with Miss La Marr was a constant subject of discussion at the studio. Leatrice Joy, a movie star friend of Bern, remembered years later that Bern was in anguish over her. One night, Miss La Marr had promised to turn up at a party at which Miss Joy and Mayer's writer friend Carey Wilson were present, and when she did not, Bern flung the orchid corsage and diamond bracelet contained in it into bushes at the back of his hillside home. The guests searched for the bracelet for hours before giving up. On another occasion when she jilted him, Carey Wilson found Bern kneeling face down at a flushing toilet, in an absurd effort to drown himself.

In view of her private life, it is astonishing that Mayer worked with Barbara La Marr. But he did, on movie after movie. In May 1923, shortly after adopting a young boy, she married the western actor Jack Dougherty. It turned out that she had not been divorced from her previous husband and now teetered on the edge of bigamy charges, which Edwin Loeb had to go to great lengths to suppress. But she was enormously popular, and Mayer had to stretch a point to keep her working.

Mayer was more comfortable with a new acquisition, Norma Shearer. With the constant possibility of Barbara La Marr's pictures being banned, it was essential he groom an actress with an impeccable reputation. He asked the New York agent Edward Small, who had brought John M. Stahl to him, to find someone suitable. Small, who worked hard for his clients, recommended Miss Shearer. She was Canadian, of Scottish-English parentage; this fact would help in exploiting her in the valuable British market. She had sold sheet music, worked in a department store and been rejected for the Ziegfeld Follies because she had thick legs, irregular teeth and a cast in one eye. But at nineteen she was possessed of a stubborn will and determination that refused to recognize even physical obstacles. She obtained work as an extra, finally securing a modest featured role in a picture called *The Stealers*. Despite her eye problem, she became a model, most notably in the Springfield Tire advertisements. Irving Thalberg had noticed her in *The Stealers*, observing a quality of quiet, subdued intensity in her playing. With his instinct for star quality, he saw great success for her in the future.

When she arrived at the Selig Studios, Norma Shearer made an immediate, and not entirely favorable, impression on Mayer. Admittedly, she was petite, as actresses were supposed to be in those days, she had excellent posture, and, apart from her eye problem, which she was already working carefully to control, she had good looks: an oval, pale face, good bones and a certain presence. But her figure was still heavy and she had a haughty air, as though she were already a big star. She not only mistook Irving Thalberg for a secretary, she treated him like one. And although Mayer retained a deep respect for all mothers, Mrs. Shearer gave him some pause: she was the show-biz mom incarnate.

Mayer did not realize that Norma Shearer's hauteur was a mask for extreme insecurity. Not only was she self-conscious about her eye, but she also disliked what she felt to be her thin, high-pitched voice. She was consoled by the fact she was in silent pictures, but she was afraid of the effect the voice's particular timbre might have on others.

She did have the advantage of being "pure," seemingly virginal (the macho director Victor Fleming would soon take care of that) and determined to work. Mayer and Thalberg conferred, and decided to give her a full-scale screen test. It was not successful: she was poorly dressed, her eye crossed alarmingly in the camera and her nose in profile appeared to be broken. Mayer decided she would have to go back to New York. She begged for a second chance, and, with great generosity, the two executives gave her one.

For the second test, directed by John M. Stahl, Miss Shearer bought an expensive evening gown; she began parading about like a little girl in her first party dress as the camera was set up. But then Stahl told her that she was trying to look a lady, and that she wasn't one. Hypersensitive, she began to cry. When he asked her to act out the scene, which involved a display of tears, there were none left. She managed still a third test, walking down a flight of stairs, carefully following Stahl's instructions not to look down at her feet. Stahl, however, felt she wasn't up to the leading role in the picture for which he had thought of her, *The Wanters*. He gave her the consolation prize of a small part.

The moment she was seen in rushes, her quality emerged. For all of her visual disadvantages, there was something quietly cool, still and concentrated about her that caught the attention. Mayer decided to build her quickly; it was a courageous decision, based on very little, but characteristic of him. He cast her in *Pleasure Mad*, directed by Reginald Barker, who at once was irritated by her. Barker complained to Mayer and Thalberg, who ordered her to learn her business and behave. She did. She steeled herself and succeeded in giving a good performance. But the public didn't cotton to her immediately, and she was loaned out to several other studios in order to give her more experience and the Mayer company some extra profits.

This encouragement of a seemingly inadequate and not overwhelmingly attractive actress was typical of Mayer, who took gambles on people and backed them to the limit. That spring of 1923, when Shearer was starting out, Thalberg was on his first assignment: *The Shooting of Dan McGrew*, starring Barbara La Marr, who was in the usual trouble with the law. The picture was shot in the Sierras, and Mayer had to go up there to check on everything because Thalberg's heart might be affected by the altitude. Back in Hollywood, Mayer was busy seeking a merger between his company, Warner Brothers, and the Al Lichtman–

B. P. Shulberg outfit. He was unhappy with Metro Pictures, which was in financial difficulties, and in June, he was in New York, trying to improve matters, at the Metro annual sales convention at the Hotel Astor. The meeting was presided over by Marcus Loew, head of Loew's Inc., which owned Metro. In this year of important new meetings, Mayer's encounter with Loew was of extraordinary significance.

Worth $35 million in 1923, Marcus Loew had receding, thin hair, a bulbous forehead, large, staring eyes like those of a ventriloquist's doll, and an enormous walrus mustache that only served to emphasize a receding chin. His tiny body was meager, his shoulders sloping, his voice soft and subdued. Like Thalberg, he was handicapped by rheumatic fever as a child; he knew that his heart condition would give him only a chance at old age. Now fifty-three, he had devoured theater after theater, building new and imposing palaces. He was so intense a workaholic that when he ate his meals he would spread out the financial pages of the newspaper under his plate and would have reports on box office takings piled around him.

Born in a shack on the Lower East Side, over which he would one day build a magnificent theater, Loew never forgot his humble origins, and was the most generous of executives: he had over two hundred unemployed theater men on his personal payroll; he fought stock raiders to protect his shareholders; he gave millions in secret to charity. He was more beloved than anybody in the business. Mayer was captivated by him and by his attractive wife and magnificent home, Pembroke, at Glen Cove, on the Long Island Sound.

Mayer did not warm to Nicholas Schenck, Marcus Loew's general manager in charge of the theater chain. Schenck had just replaced his brother Joseph in that capacity.

According to their signed immigration registration records, Nicholas Schenck was born in Russia on November 15, 1880, Joseph on December 25, 1876. They arrived in New York, Joe following Nicholas, in 1892. They had begun life as errand boys, working for a drugstore in the Bowery; within a year, they were running the drugstore together, and a year after that had begun opening stores of their own. Nicholas was a fan of the popular singer Eva Tanguay, known as the "I Don't Care Girl." She lent him money to start a chain of such shops.

At weekends, shortly after the turn of the century, the two boys would swim at Fort George. There, they invested in a primitive amusement park, calling it Paradise Park, and they built the largest ferris wheel in the Northeast. In 1908, they shifted across the Hudson River and bought a controlling interest in the popular Palisades Amusement Park. They met Marcus Loew, who took an interest in one of their attractions, a replica of a railroad car past whose windows moved a cyclorama of American urban and rural scenes. From there, the brothers moved to link up with Loew, and, showing considerable expertise, came to the forefront of his Consolidated Theater Enterprises.

The brothers were very different. Mayer warmed to Joe, who became a close, lifelong friend. A genial pirate with a deceptively mild Slavic face, Joe was flashy, enterprising and always slightly crooked. Nicholas strongly resembled him but with harder, pebble-cold eyes peering through large horn-rim spectacles, he was shrewd, detached, endlessly alert for the main chance. He no more responded to Mayer than Mayer responded to him. Although he recognized Mayer's ability from the outset, he found Mayer too fierce, emotional, intense and hysterical for his icy tastes. They would never, in a lifetime of extraordinary and powerful association, get used to each other.

On the night of June 6, 1923, Mayer shot his bankroll and invited all of the Metro conventioneers to a gala evening at Coney Island; two nights later, he threw a stag dinner at the Astor, and showed his latest pictures.

In September, Mayer was busy supervising Fred Niblo's *Thy Name Is Woman*, written by Bess Meredyth and starring Barbara La Marr. Her costar was Ramon Novarro. The handsome twenty-four-year-old had become the idol of millions of women when he stripped down to a loincloth in the South Sea drama *Where the Pavement Ends;* the historical swashbuckler *Scaramouche* made him a big star. When Mayer engaged him, he had returned from shooting that film in Nice, at the Victorine Studio, for Rex Ingram.

Mexican-born Novarro was known to his fellow workers, and, of course, to Mayer, as a homosexual. His effeminacy carefully concealed, he was a passionately sincere and committed actor with a total involvement in the parts he played. He was simple, sweet-natured, generous, self-indulgent in his private life; his concern, which must have touched Mayer, was to give his mother and five sisters a home in Los Angeles, and he at last installed them in a Victorian mansion on West Adams Street. Mayer was apparently prepared to endure anything in view of Novarro's huge popularity: it was a great coup to have obtained his services.

In late November 1923, while visiting New York, Mayer accepted an invitation from the New York *Times* to write an article entitled "Thrills in Films"; it appeared on December 3. He spoke of "the thrill" as the one element in pictures that had weathered all changes; that thrills in a picture could be a measure of its box office success. He added a characteristic comment:

George Ade [the humorist] says that while the highbrows may sniff at good old heart-touching hokum on the screen, the American public could not keep house without it . . .

Mayer mentioned the spectacular gathering and wild night ride of the Ku Klux Klan in *The Birth of a Nation* that had so excited him in his youth and had helped to make him rich. He described recent pictures he had made, in which the crews had battled 80-foot waves off the Massa-chusetts coast and the Grand Banks of Newfoundland, or had fought with 600-pound swordfish; of a cameraman suspended in a steel cage over the raging Seymour Canyon Rapids; of a scene with a female star caught in the path of a train that switched tracks at the last minute; if the appropriate switch hadn't worked, she would have been killed. Vivid and lively, this was an expert piece of journalism.

## CHAPTER EIGHT

# 1923-1924

THE NEXT TWELVE MONTHS would prove to be the most extraordinary of Louis B. Mayer's young life. The first of a series of momentous events occurred when, in November 1923, the Metro Pictures Corporation, in the wake of Richard Rowland's departure, ran into still more difficulties. The vast amounts the company had spent on certain best-selling books exhausted its coffers, and Rudolph Valentino, its chief asset, decided not to renew his contract. Marcus Loew began seriously considering closing down the company for good. The tycoon was vacationing in West Palm Beach when, on December 26, he met with Frank J. (Joe) Godsol, chairman of the Goldwyn Pictures Corporation, who had kicked Samuel Goldwyn out for poor commercial performance the previous year. Godsol suggested to Loew that Goldwyn, itself in trouble, be melded with Metro, under Marcus Loew's overall governorship.

Loew warmed rapidly to the idea. Not only could he add two new chains to his already massive empire, but he could obtain control of the world's largest movie house, the magnificent Capitol Theater in New York, of which Goldwyn Inc. owned fifty percent. By combining two lame production companies, he could revitalize them under strong leadership, and he could compete effectively with First National. The question was: Who in Hollywood would be sufficiently experienced and strong to take over the vast combine?

Mayer's friend and ally, the polished Loew's, Inc. lawyer J. Robert Rubin, suggested Mayer. Marcus Loew knew Rubin to be a man of sound judgment and listened carefully. Rubin made sure he was on the train with Loew when Loew came out to California at the end of the year. Rubin had certain bases for his persuasions: Mayer had built a neat little group of stars and directors under difficult and pressing conditions. He was known as a tough but sympathetic autocrat, who had a strong sense of family where his employees were concerned. Rubin drove Loew out to

Mission Road, where Loew saw *Thy Name Is Woman* and *Women Who Give* being shot, and shook hands with Ramon Novarro and Barbara La Marr. Loew was impressed with the tight, tidy operation and told Rubin so.

With amazing swiftness, Loew set about achieving the amalgamation of the two companies. He hired Mayer almost immediately at $1,500 a week; Irving Thalberg would receive $650. Mayer would receive thirteen percent of twenty percent of the net profits, Rubin would get five percent and Thalberg two percent. They would also have a share of performers' salaries; should any of them resign or be forced out, they would be entitled to retain their percentages of the profits in perpetuity. The decision was made to take over the elaborate Goldwyn Studios at Culver City. It ran behind fences and Corinthian columns along Washington Boulevard for 800 feet, and along the private Ince Way for 450 feet. Long wooden dressing rooms built in two stories ran almost the entire length of the Washington Boulevard side of the studio; next to them, at the corner of Ince, stood the modest wooden administration building, and behind that the wardrobe building. Supplies, carpentry shops and a planing mill, a garage and a foundry occupied the front of Ince Way. Inside, just behind them, were the cutting and projection rooms, a restaurant with a sun porch, a paint shop, a locker room and a lumber shed; nearby was a swimming pool that could be whipped up by wind machines into wild waves.

Right down the middle of the studio were offices, the art department and property room, storage and drapery rooms; on either side of this central artery were the sound stages, seven in all, topped by wood-truss roofs. Scattered in the open spaces were frame outdoor sets of streets of foreign cities. Except for the fireproof film department housing the nitrate stock, the entire studio was highly flammable.

By special arrangement with Joe Godsol, Mayer was installed in a small bungalow office at the studio as early as January 5, 1924. That same week, he was pleased to receive a letter from an admirer of his, a new friend, whom he had met in New York, the energetic secretary of commerce, Herbert Hoover. Hoover was a man after his own heart: a Quaker from the Iowa heartland who believed in hard work, Puritan ideals, devotion to home and parents.

The sudden move to the Goldwyn Studios, with the merger still by no means near conclusion, presented problems. Mayer had had to leave Mission Road very abruptly, with three pictures uncompleted and two more in the cutting room. He had to commute constantly to deal with still more pressing matters. He was compelled to leave B. P. Schulberg in the lurch, with half the studio on his hands. He had to dump Richard Rowland, as well as First National, by somehow wriggling out of his long-term contract. He would have to contend with Sam Goldwyn, who retained a substantial holding in the company that had disposed of him. And, no longer his own boss, he would be working for the dreaded Nicholas Schenck.

On January 10, 1924, Mayer took a train to Manhattan for further meetings with Loew and Schenck at the Heidelberg Building, which held so many memories. He signed over his contracts and his lease at Mission Road, with Colonel Selig's authorization, for approximately $76,500, and sewed up the petty clauses in the new financial agreement. He moved into a financial and operational no-man's-land, as merger negotiations began dragging so slowly that he must have feared the entire matter would fall apart and he would be left with nothing. He cautioned his family not to make any premature announcements of his new glory.

Mayer wooed the tough and ambitious Harry Rapf away from Warner Brothers, in part by including him in his real estate consortium, with Irving Thalberg, Douglas Fairbanks and Mary Pickford. The Denver-born son of a prosperous tailor, Rapf was forty-three years old. He had begun his career in vaudeville and had become a talent manager, handling many well-known artists, after his small popularity as a performer ran out. He joined the Warner brothers, who also came out of vaudeville, and became well known in the industry as the producer of the *Rin Tin Tin* pictures. He was feisty, hard-working and nobody's fool; and he had a sharp eye for merit in a performer. He originally attracted Mayer's, and, particularly, Thalberg's attention, because he had actually been ahead of them in spotting the values of Norma Shearer. When they had loaned her out to Warner's, he had cast her in interesting roles, leading them to see her potential as a star.

In March, Mayer went on waiting for news of the merger. Argument followed argument; then, on March 25, Marcus Loew finally took over Joe Godsol's $750,000 worth of Goldwyn stock and copper magnate William Braden's $450,000 worth, while offering William Randolph Hearst, the newspaper tycoon and chairman of Cosmopolitan Productions, a large share of the new company in return for his massive holdings, estimated by *Variety* as much as fifty percent. The contract called for Goldwyn's thirty-one exchanges to be melded with Metro's twenty-one. The deal, as indicated earlier, included the Capitol Theater. In addition, Metro-Goldwyn would take over the epic *Ben-Hur*, which was about to start shooting in Rome.

The agreement required one signature that would finally close it. That signature was Sam Goldwyn's; he owned about $500,000 in stock.

Goldwyn held up the negotiations, demanding a shorter payoff period and higher rates of guaranteed interest, until Marcus Loew finally lost patience and asked Goldwyn's lawyers, Stanchfield and Levy, what the movie mogul would need to get out of his hair. They replied that Goldwyn wanted a cool million. Loew paid it: now the way was clear. The Goldwyn company thus came in with $20 million in assets, Metro with $3.1 million, Mayer with $500,000, all combined with Loew's $26 million. With other assets added, the combined authorized stock was worth $65 million. Marcus Loew became president of Metro-Goldwyn, Louis B. Mayer vice president in charge of production, with Irving Thalberg as assistant vice president. Joe Godsol was temporarily named to the board but, due to a tubercular condition, soon left and moved to Florida, thence to Switzerland. Major Edward Bowes, former vice president of Goldwyn and general manager of the Capitol Theater, Messmore Kendall, president of Moredall Realty Corporation, which owned fifty percent of the Capitol, and William Braden were also on the directorial board; unofficially, so, too, was William Randolph Hearst.

As always in the picture industry, the theater chains were greedy monsters, hungry for product. Marcus Loew may have been a decent, considerate and genial man, but he knew his days on earth were numbered and he wanted to make a splash in the world with his new combine. Mayer would be obliged, with Thalberg, to produce no less than fifteen new pictures in twelve months; he would have to monitor the progress of the remaining movies made under his own banner; he would have to blend staffs from three competitive companies; he would have to increase those staffs, already in the hundreds, into the thousands. Thalberg, in consultation with him, would have to have teams of writers working round the clock to produce scripts on schedules of less than a month, select the directors for them, engage the appropriate stars and set the whole vast machinery in motion with no time to spare.

The challenge excited Mayer. Suddenly, he would become king of the Hollywood castle. He relaxed sufficiently to celebrate with his family, but, to the chagrin of his ambitious daughters, made no plans to move into any of the fashionable districts. His home on North Kenmore remained dwarfed by the DeMille estate, less than a quarter of a mile away.

The question arose of designing a trademark. Mayer was given the task of selecting it. He decided to carry over the lion's head, framed in an inscribed circlet, and stamped with the words *Ars Gratia Artis* ("Art for Art's Sake") used by Samuel Goldwyn. Howard Dietz, who would continue as head of publicity from the Goldwyn organization, had drawn up the logo in 1921. He had found his inspiration in the lion motif of the cover of his alma mater, Columbia University's humorous journal *The Jester*. *Ars Gratia Artis* was a favorite slogan blackboarded by his classics professor. The lion that modeled for the artist's likeness was originally brought from the Sudan in 1917 by the owner of a Pennsylvania animal farm. Three years later, Mayer replaced the pictured lion with footage of a real one roaring; it was, appropriately, an alumnus of the Selig Zoo. Three separate lions were recorded to create the three-part lion roar when talkies came in.

By April 26, 1924, Mayer had pulled together a celebratory opening of the Metro-Goldwyn-Mayer Studio, with Fred Niblo as master of ceremonies. The party was held on the front lawn, below a dais hung with the Stars and Stripes and a large, hastily done portrait of Marcus Loew. Ten Army and ten Navy airplanes roared in formation overhead, dropping roses and wreaths of spring flowers. Three hundred naval personnel, resplendent in white uniforms, were headed by Admiral S. S. Robinson and the commander of the Pacific Fleet. Among the stars present were John Gilbert, Ramon Novarro, Antonio Moreno, Barbara La Marr and Lon Chaney. A spic-and-span Navy band blared out popular songs, and Niblo read congratulatory telegrams from President Coolidge, Herbert Hoover, Marcus Loeb, Will Hays and (surprisingly) Jack and Harry Warner of Warner Brothers. Abraham Lehr, vice president of Goldwyn, handed over an enormous gold key to Mayer, who replied:

> I hope that it is given me to live up to this great trust. It has been my argument and practice that each picture should teach a lesson, should have a reason for existence. With seventeen of the greatest directors in the industry calling this great institution their home, I feel that this aim will be carried out . . . This is a great moment for me. I accept this solemn trust and pledge the best that I have to give.

He had not written the speech: it had been put together for him by a publicist, Pete Smith, and the star Conrad Nagel had taught him how to deliver it. He meant every word of it. The word "home" was his lodestone. He wanted those who worked at M.G.M. to feel that it *was* their home, and that he was their stern but loving father.

There were two interruptions to the ceremony. The first was amusing: Will Rogers, the corn-pone comedian, rode in on the back of a horse with the words "Sorry I'm late, folks! I forgot my chewing gum and had to ride home to get it!" He added, "I know why this show was a half hour late in starting. Marcus Loew's check hadn't been certified." Rogers leaned from the saddle to present smaller replicas of the studio keys to Irving Thalberg and to Harry Rapf.

The second interruption was less appealing. The ever-obstreperous Marshall Neilan, furious that, as a Godsol director, he would now have to work for the hated Mayer, assembled his cast and crew for a film in progress, *Tess of the D'Urbervilles*, and noisily walked out. Mayer was enraged. Yet, ever mindful of the necessity to avoid scandal and conflict in his team, he chose not to reprimand Neilan, but rather to continue to use him as best he could.

Among the important employees with whom Mayer made it his business to be acquainted were some of the important new people inherited from other companies. Preeminent among these was the brilliant, thirty-one-year-old Irish artist Cedric Gibbons, who had begun his career with Thomas Edison at the age of twenty-two, and had been with Joe Godsol, and, before that, with Samuel Goldwyn, for the past five years. Mayer was impressed with his sketches, recognizing, with his customary instinct for talent, the striking abilities of this attractive young man. The tough and wiry young Joseph J. Cohn, known as J. J., brought from Godsol's operation as production manager, was a great asset; he had worked vigorously on the Italian locations of *Ben-Hur* and on Erich von Stroheim's *Greed*. By contrast, Mayer was not impressed with the director Rex Ingram, who had made arrangements with Godsol to set up his own Victorine Studio at Nice on the French Riviera, where he would be working independently of any control. Mayer had found Ingram's film *The Four Horsemen of the Apocalypse* static and excessively picturesque for all of its critical and commercial success. Ingram's *The Prisoner of Zenda* and *Scaramouche* had also left Mayer cold. He was annoyed that Ingram's new picture, *The Arab*, now being cut, was held back from him, and he demanded to see the uncut version. He disliked it as much as he had disliked the other Ingram films, and Ingram's feelings for him were, of course, mutual. Mayer insisted that the rushes be sent by cargo ship from Nice to Los Angeles, no matter how long this would take.

Mayer also had meetings with Buster Keaton, a twenty-eight-year-old Kansan, son of vaudevillians, who had begun life as the Human Mop. Keaton was under special contract to Joe Schenck, his pictures to be released now through Metro-Goldwyn. He did not actually join the studio until 1926. His solemn face was internationally renowned; he had achieved an extraordinary degree of autonomy in the industry through creating several works of genius: *The Electric House*, about an inventor who becomes entrapped in his own house full of gadgets; *Three Ages*, in which he appeared in the Stone Age, ancient Rome and modern times; *Our Hospitality*, about the clash of the Hatfields and the McCoys; and

*Sherlock Junior,* in which, as a movie projectionist, he entered into the actual screen and joined the characters in a photoplay. Wisely, Mayer and Thalberg allowed him to continue with his independent company, based on his box office results and his extraordinary réclame among international critics.

Mayer also began negotiations with William Randolph Hearst to continue the association of Hearst's Cosmopolitan Pictures Corporation, now severed from Godsol. It was understood that Hearst would have his own semi-independent unit at the studio, that budgets would be set by mutual agreement on his movies, and that Hearst would continue to control the selection of stories and artistic contributions. Marion Davies, Hearst's mistress, would be the star of most of these films, which would be budgeted to surround her with the best of everything. Mayer liked her: the blond, huge-eyed actress was adorable, sweet-natured, generous to a fault. The only problem she presented, in view of the Hays office watchdogs of the industry, was that she was involved in an affair with Mayer's old enemy, Charlie Chaplin. Her stand-in, Vera Burnett, notes that, whenever Hearst was said to be arriving at the studio, Chaplin, as farcically as in any of his movies, would have to hide his small frame in a closet or under the couch.

A continuing presence at the studio in those early days at Culver City was Elinor Glyn. She brought several new properties to M.G.M., and was in conference with Mayer at her suite at the Hollywood Hotel, where she would exhaust him by reciting the entire plots in minute detail. Yet she was so famous that even he could not refuse her invitations. She would receive him lying on a tiger skin, an elaborate hat of blue tulle perched on her head, her body indiscreetly draped in flowing silk. She wore exotic perfume, which tended to make him feel unwell. He rapidly passed her on to Thalberg, who barely tolerated her affectations.

A more important difficulty was presented by one of Mayer's bêtes noirs, Erich von Stroheim. Von Stroheim represented everything Mayer detested: he was haughty, harsh and vain. The fact that Mayer had to inherit him from Godsol was almost as infuriating as inheriting Ingram. However, he couldn't argue with one thing: von Stroheim was an enormous popular success; his movies' unsentimental tone and far from subtle emphasis on sex, corruption and vice excited audiences the world over. Seeing a von Stroheim picture was the equivalent of reading a forbidden book under the bed covers; the moralists might grumble, but the public ate it all up.

Irving Thalberg, of course, shared Mayer's horror. After his struggles with von Stroheim at Universal, he now had to confront this fabled monster again. But at least he had Mayer standing beside him.

In *Greed,* based on a novel by Frank Norris, von Stroheim had sought to invoke life itself. He adhered carefully to the novel's story of human beings trapped in their own desires and compulsions and shot the picture largely in San Francisco, partly in Death Valley, insisting on un-glamorous lighting, correct light sources and no more than street makeup for the female players. With a disregard of marketing require-ments, he shot from March to October 1923, producing a picture that lasted approximately nine and a half hours. It would have had to be shown on three or four successive days, an unthinkable projection. By March 18, working round the clock, von Stroheim had managed to reduce the film to twenty-two reels, or three hours and forty minutes.

When Mayer and Thalberg first ran the picture, it was about three and a half hours. They were appalled. In particular, Mayer must have been shocked by the fact that a subplot involved a hideous junkman, a gross parody of the sort of person his father was. Suffering as he did from dental problems, Mayer could not have been pleased by the fact that in the crucial scene, the dentist who is the central figure of the picture orders the extraction of several teeth belonging to a female patient. Quite apart from these personal considerations, he was dismayed by the brutal, antipathetic and stark revelation of obsession with money; in one sequence, the dental patient, now married to the dentist, undresses, gets into bed and fondles gold coins in a highly suggestive manner.

As if von Stroheim had not upset Mayer sufficiently, he made a fatal mistake in shipping the picture to New York behind Mayer's back to have it edited by Rex Ingram, who was visiting Manhattan for consulta-tions with Nicholas Schenck in connection with his studio in Nice. Ingram cut the picture down to 180 minutes, and returned the cans by train with a telegram: IF YOU CUT ONE MORE FOOT I'LL NEVER SPEAK TO YOU AGAIN. Incredibly, von Stroheim was unaware that Mayer despised In-gram more than any other director. He showed Mayer the telegram. Mayer exploded. He said he didn't give a damn about Rex Ingram or von Stroheim, the picture would be a total loss to the company anyway, and it was immediately to be cut to ten reels, or 100 minutes, to render it exhibitable. Mayer and Thalberg gave the movie to the title writer Jo-seph Farnham, telling him to make the story comprehensible by the frequent use of title cards, and to cut it to the acceptable length.

Several of these titles, most notably "Let's go over and sit on the sewer," helped to provoke the gales of laughter that would greet the picture on its first trade and press screenings at the end of the year. Disgusted with the whole affair, Mayer refused to talk to von Stroheim,

but, unfortunately for him, the unbreakable contract with Godsol called
for the arrogant director to make a version of *The Merry Widow* right
afterward. Franz Lehár's celebrated operetta, with its story of a millionairess caught up in a Ruritanian kingdom was one of Mayer's favorites;
he could only guess at what von Stroheim would do with this lighthearted diversion. Nothing Mayer could do could stop him, and there
was no indication that Nicholas Schenck would buy out von Stroheim's
contract.

One of Thalberg's first tasks at M.G.M. was to prepare a vehicle for
Lon Chaney, who was free-lancing at the time. This great star, then just
over forty, was the son of deaf-mute parents, and had learned of necessity the art of pantomime. Obscure and recessive, respectable and subdued, Chaney was devoted to his work, which involved extreme and
bizarre roles. He had played a legless criminal, with his legs bound
tightly behind him, a hunchback, with forty pounds of rubber attached
to his back, and Fagin, the hook-nosed king of the thieves, in *Oliver
Twist*. The public loved this man of a thousand faces, and Mayer admired him.

Mayer was also looking for a vehicle for his protégé, Norma Shearer.
He hired Carey Wilson, then thirty-five, to write for Chaney and
Shearer a script based on Leonid Andreyev's stage play, *He Who Gets
Slapped*. It was the story of a tragic circus clown to be played by Chaney;
Norma Shearer would portray a bareback rider. To direct the picture,
Mayer hired the sensitive and gifted Swedish director Victor Sjöström,
and he assigned Irving Thalberg to take personal charge of the produc-
tion. The deal was concluded in May, and filming started on a circus set
designed by Cedric Gibbons in June.

One of the heaviest burdens Mayer had to shoulder in those first
taxing weeks at Culver City was the romantic leading man John Gilbert,
soon to become the studio's chief financial asset. The actor had everything: only twenty-four, he was already rich and successful; he had striking dark looks, with thick, wavy black hair, glowing eyes, a virile mustache and a clean-cut jaw line. His physique was perfectly proportioned,
muscular but graceful as a champion swimmer's. He was alive and laughing, adorable and daring; few women could resist him. Yet he was tortured and self-destructive. He had already begun the downward course of
alcoholism. Unable to resist any attractive woman, he was constantly
unfaithful to his pregnant wife, the beautiful and intelligent star Leatrice
Joy. His behavior infuriated Mayer.

By contrast, the more tolerant and sophisticated Irving Thalberg had
a soft spot for Gilbert and would play tennis with him on Sunday after-
noons. Thalberg tried to reassure Mayer that Gilbert would mend his

ways. The publicist Pete Smith was asked to spin a cocoon of falsehoods around Gilbert, portraying him as a loving husband and saintly prospective father. Few in the film industry were convinced; the public swallowed everything.

Gilbert was cast with Aileen Pringle in Elinor Glyn's nonsensical farrago *His Hour*, which King Vidor, who despised such romantic material, was forced to direct. Gilbert broke his promise to Mayer and Thalberg to behave decently during the picture, and, unable to extract the slightest interest from Miss Pringle, instead launched an affair with the married actress Laurette Taylor. Mayer hated Gilbert more than ever.

Miss Glyn's behavior was equally irritating. She shocked the casting director, and Thalberg, by insisting on inspecting all male members of the cast in an unladylike manner. She insisted that if any male wore tights in the picture, he must not be permitted to wear a jockstrap. "I do not believe in interfering with nature," she said. According to the M.G.M. writer Lenore Coffee, "It was said that on the days of these tests [there was] a lamentable shortage of knockwursts [in the commissary]." They had been used to stuff into trousers to pass Miss Glyn's feverish inspection.

Mayer dispatched Marshall Neilan, no doubt to their mutual relief, to England to work location shots for *Tess of the D'Urbervilles*; asked Reginald Barker to make preparations to shoot Robert W. Service's story *The Trail of '98*, which would involve two thousand extras repeating the thrills of the Yukon gold rush (it would not be made until several years later); arranged the release of *Women Who Give*, a held-over picture from the Selig Studio; supervised the cutting of John M. Stahl's *Husbands and Lovers*, also shot at Selig; watched keenly as the young Texas honcho King Vidor shot *His Hour* and *Way of a Centaur*; and above all concerned himself with the biggest production of all, *Ben-Hur*.

General Lew Wallace's flamboyant best-seller expertly combined steamy descriptions of male and female characters and a heavy undercurrent of violence and eroticism with battles of a Roman galley with a pirate ship, conflicts between broad-chested warriors in armor, the corruption of the Roman Empire and the birth and crucifixion of Jesus Christ. There could be no argument with the potential commercial success of such a concoction in the movies, despite the colossal sums paid for it by a combine that included the stubby, chaw-spitting tycoon Abe Erlanger and the shrill genius of the musical theater, Florenz Ziegfeld, both of whom would share fifty percent of the gross proceeds.

Problems had arisen with the production in Rome from the beginning. Joe Godsol had made a disastrous choice of scenarist, star and

director. The script was written by the tiny, plump, gypsyish June
Mathis, whose script for Rex Ingram's *Four Horsemen of the Apocalypse*
had propelled her to the top of the industry. She had talked Abe
Erlanger into letting her put together the ingredients of *Ben-Hur*. Her
lover was George Walsh, brother of the director Raoul Walsh, an actor
of feeble talent if grand physique whom she personally selected to play
the title role. Opposite him, she cast Mayer's hated Francis X. Bushman.
As director, she chose a mild, alcoholic Englishman, Charles Brabin,
whose chief claim to fame was that he was married to the screen vamp
Theda Bara.

Mayer was dismayed by the news from Italy. Brabin was proving incompetent, and when, at last, still photographs arrived before the daily
rushes, Mayer hit the ceiling. The costumes were too large, hanging on
the two leading men; the photography, by John T. Boyle, was murky and
diffuse; the replicas of the Roman galleys looked absurdly small when
seen against the Mediterranean backgrounds. By the beginning of May,
it was obvious the situation was critical. Although he was not connected
to the studio, Joe Schenck, brother of Loew's right-hand man Nicholas,
and now chairman of United Artists, was asked by Marcus Loew to give
his advice. Mayer, Schenck, Irving Thalberg and Harry Rapf held a
meeting at Culver City on May 1. They agreed that June Mathis must be
dismissed from Rome; that Walsh (whom she had now dumped as her
lover in favor of the better-looking Silvio Balboni) was unacceptable;
that Brabin must be removed; and that Fred Niblo, as the sternest and
most commanding director on the Metro-Goldwyn lot, must be dispatched at once to take over absolute control of the picture. J. Robert
Rubin was to go with him, and, if needed, Rapf must follow.

Mayer sent over to Niblo June Mathis's telephone book–sized script,
with its 1,700 scenes, designed to last a staggering 250 minutes. Niblo
agreed that it was impossible. At the outset of June, Mayer ordered
production on *Ben-Hur* temporarily suspended. Later that month, he
took the train to New York with Ramon Novarro, hired to replace
George Walsh, Carey Wilson, Bess Meredyth (these two trusted writers
would rework the screenplay even on the express, and on the ship across
the Atlantic), J. Robert and Reba Rubin, Fred Niblo and his wife (the
Australian star Enid Bennett), and others. He saw them off on the
*Leviathan*, crowding their suites with flowers, wishing them the best and
promising them his full and unqualified support. The crossing was a
pleasure for all. With his customary democratic charm, Marcus Loew
invited Bess Meredyth, the Wilsons, and the Rubins to cocktails and
dinner night after night. He continued to take care of them in France
and Italy, where he had the disagreeable task of firing Mathis, Brabin

and Walsh; he kept Bushman on, simply because it would have been difficult to replace him. The Mayer team arrived in a thunderstorm. Bess Meredyth, Carey Wilson and Marcus Loew toasted Mayer every night with champagne, complained about how awful the Brabin footage was and agreed that Mayer would share their opinion.

Mayer was in touch with Niblo constantly during those weeks. Harsh and brutal, Niblo proved to be ideal for the task. Carey Wilson and Bess Meredyth came up with an excellent script, powerful, expertly constructed and suspenseful. They enhanced Wallace's romantic and passionate account of a young man struggling against his anti-Semitic childhood friend, played by Bushman, a theme with which Mayer could identify strongly. In order to ensure that Niblo adhered to his commandments, Mayer dispatched to Rome a trusted if temperamental associate, Alexander Aronson, head of Metro-Goldwyn's newly formed Paris office. Aronson disliked Niblo from the beginning, but proved to be a useful correspondent and controller. Harry Edington, as production manager, represented Metro-Goldwyn on the set, and Mayer constantly cabled him, urging him to act as a check to Niblo, while he urged Niblo to act as a check to Edington. He had learned much from having Irving Thalberg as his own master of checks and balances, finding arguments and restrictions of policy and execution invariably valuable.

On July 15, 1924, Niblo reported to Mayer that some two hundred reels of Ben-Hur shot by Charles Brabin would have to be destroyed. Niblo was also worried about getting a good cameraman; he wanted von Stroheim's man, Ben Reynolds, but Reynolds wasn't available. At last, Thalberg managed to supply three expert craftsmen, most notably Karl Struss. By August, it was obvious that Ben-Hur was going to cost at least $3 million.

In mid-July, during a heat wave, Mayer decided to break his rule of only showing his daughters enlightened and upbeat entertainment, and subjected them to the ten-reel cut of Greed. Even in this reduced version, they found the masterwork exhausting and overlong.

Von Stroheim became convinced that Mayer was going to replace him as director of The Merry Widow with the amiable Robert Z. Leonard, husband of the movie's star, Mae Murray. Though this would have been contractually impossible and would have resulted in a lawsuit, von Stroheim by now was in the grip of paranoia. He barged into Mayer's office and demanded to know: was it true that Leonard would replace him? There was a violent argument, resulting in Mayer striking von Stroheim firmly in the face. The German's brash swagger was not accompanied by physical courage, and he simply walked out. He announced to anyone who would listen that he would swear out a warrant for Mayer's arrest on a charge of assault and battery; then he calmed down quickly and went back to work on the script.

Mayer clashed with the director Monta Bell, a discovery of Harry Rapf, who had been lured away from Warner Brothers. Mayer was unhappy with the young former newspaperman, finding him something of an upstart, and was greatly annoyed by the fact that Bell had started an affair with Norma Shearer, who had recently been dumped by Victor Fleming. Mayer stalled Bell's *The Snob* week after week, and Bell clashed with him, announcing that he had offers from other studios. Again, the combatants simmered down, and Bell went back to work preparing the picture, which started shooting in September.

In the midst of all this tension and stress, with cables crossing the Atlantic day after day, Mayer's sister Ida arrived from Boston in the third week of July with her daughters Ruth and Mitzi. Jack, Ida's only son, had been with Mayer for some time, working as an assistant at Mission Road and then at Culver City. Ida's second husband, Julius Meyers, had sued her for desertion but was not granted the divorce; he was still trying as late as 1931. Mayer did everything to make his relatives comfortable, but Irene resented them. They found a modest house on South Serrano Avenue, later moving to a better address on South Tremaine, south of Wilshire.

At the same time, Margaret Mayer's parents, Hyman and Rachel Shenberg, arrived from Boston; they settled into a house at 1408 Normandie Avenue. In 1927, Shenberg would become the rabbi of Congregation Kneset Israel.

Mayer was distressed at the beginning of August when he heard of the death of President Warren G. Harding, apparently from food poisoning; there were whispers of murder or suicide, and the matter was buried swiftly. It was clear that Vice President Calvin Coolidge would take over, which would give greater strength to Mayer's close friend and ally, Herbert Hoover. Three weeks later, Hoover was in Hollywood, and Mayer gave him a full-scale tour of the studio.

John Gilbert continued to be a nuisance. Leatrice Joy had discovered a telegram from Gilbert's lover, Laurette Taylor, thanking him for a gift of roses. Gilbert begged Leatrice to return to him, and she hesitantly agreed, only to find him drunk on the floor of their house. She filed for divorce; three weeks later, her daughter was born. Mayer could have killed Gilbert; there was no way to suppress such vile publicity. A headline in *Variety* read LIQUOR IN BULK MADE LEATRICE JOY'S LIFE SAD.

On August 12, Marcus Loew returned to New York aboard the *Leviathan*, advising Mayer by telegram of the very poor quality of Charles Brabin's work on *Ben-Hur*. The same day, Rene Guissart, Technicolor cameraman, and J. A. Ball, of the Technicolor Corporation, sailed on the *Berengaria* for Cherbourg and Rome to shoot the color sequences.

On August 30, Charles Brabin sued Metro-Goldwyn for $583,000 in damages, charging that he was entitled to $500,000 for loss of prestige alone. He was awarded $33,000.

Heartbroken at her dismissal, June Mathis did not even sue. After writing for Colleen Moore, her career began to slide; two proposed pictures with Rudolph Valentino fell through because Valentino's wife suspected her of having an affair with the star. On July 26, 1927, she was watching Jean Bart's *The Squall,* starring Blanche Yurka and Dorothy Stickney, at New York's 48th Street Playhouse, when she suddenly exclaimed to her mother, who was sitting beside her, "I'm dying! I'm dying!" Rushed to the lobby, she was dead before the ambulance could arrive; she had been dieting too severely and her heart had given out.

In the midst of the court case with Brabin, Mayer had pleasant news: on September 11, Sir William Jury, noted British head of Imperial Pictures Ltd., formed Jury-Metro-Goldwyn Ltd. in London. Mayer had enjoyed Sir William's visit the previous February, and happily accepted Jury's invitation to see the British studios. Mayer had made arrangements to leave for Italy to survey *Ben-Hur* in progress, and left for New York with Margaret, Edith and Irene on September 13. Mayer told Thalberg as he went ahead with the travel plans, "If I weren't going to Europe now, I would take care of that bastard Jack Gilbert personally. Either you straighten the son of a bitch out before I get back, or I'll deck him myself!" Just before his departure, Mayer had cabled Herbert Hoover in Washington, D.C., to say that he would like to spend a day with him and talk over the upcoming presidential campaign. Hoover replied that he would be glad to see Mayer any time on twenty-four hours' notice.

The Mayers arrived in Washington on September 17 aboard the Broadway Limited. They were only able to stay until that evening. Hoover made them welcome, and arranged for an important meeting with Mayer's friend John Lewis of the Interstate Commerce Commission. It was a pleasant day, followed by several more in New York, meeting with Marcus Loew and Nicholas Schenck. But there was disturbing news from Hollywood: on September 16, William Randolph Hearst ordered all the film made on Marion Davies's first M.G.M. picture, *Zander the Great,* being shot at Culver City, to be scrapped; he fired Clarence Badger, the director, and every player except Miss Davies, and hired George Hill to replace Badger. This was a costly matter.

There was an incessant series of setbacks on *Ben-Hur,* detailed in a lengthy report from Leon Dominian, American consul in Rome, to the

U.S. secretary of state dated September 26. There was constant interference from the fascist authorities and from the labor organizations under their control. One disabled war veteran had to be employed for every nine fit men. Even the insane, including a suspected rapist, were imposed upon the company. Once a scene was finished, all workers must be kept on for the rest of the day at full salary whether they were needed or not. When Harry Edington refused to use certain men, there was a twenty-four-hour strike. Edington contracted with a firm to build the Roman war galleys; when it became clear that the contractor was in financial difficulties, Edington had to take over. Despite rushed work, the galleys were not ready. When it came time to settle accounts, Edington deducted money for the delay. The contractor sued; three fascist officials arrived at the studio and demanded full payment at once—or else they would seize the cameras and generators. Edington had to yield.

A riot occurred between the fascists and the Socialist party's unauthorized workmen. The fascists charged in and took over the picture. It took the American ambassador to resolve the problem.

While Mayer and his family were still in New York, staying at the Astor Hotel, Herbert Hoover wrote letters to Henry C. MacLean, commercial attaché of the U.S. embassy in Rome, J. F. Butler, acting commercial attaché of the U.S. embassy in Paris, and Hugh G. Butler, acting commercial attaché of the U.S. embassy in London. The letters, mailed on September 24 from the Department of Commerce, sought every possible help for Mayer, who was described as "a very special friend." Hoover requested the Secretary of State to make sure that formal letters of introduction would be sent by him to the appropriate ambassadors. ("His company is engaged in making some extensive films in Europe. He is not the kind that will cause them any trouble unless he is in urgent need of assistance.") Mayer was even granted the rare privilege of traveling by diplomatic passport.

This was possible because he had obtained an extremely important contact in Washington, D.C., a woman who was to become a lifelong friend and supporter. Thirty-five-year-old Mabel Walker Willebrandt, known as "the First Lady in Law," was the assistant attorney general. Dark, not beautiful, but striking and fiercely intelligent, this remarkable woman was born in a homestead cabin in Woodsdale, Kansas, in 1889. She learned to read at her mother's knee and did not enter formal schooling until she was thirteen. She was admitted to the California bar in 1915. She began her career in Los Angeles, where, oddly enough, Mayer does not appear to have run into her. During World War I, she was head of the Legal Advisory Board for draft cases, rapidly obtaining great fame in legal circles and securing her post in the Department of Justice under the Harding administration.

Mrs. Willebrandt exuded enormous energy, passionate commitment to justice and great strength. She would address her interlocutors with formidable intensity, crushing her opponents; in a world of men, she was a lone wolf, following her instincts with total commitment. She was a keen supporter of Prohibition and was fascinated by the motion picture industry. Mayer, always impressed and influenced by powerful women, would never cease to seek her guidance in everything.

For once, Mayer shot the bankroll (it must have been Metro-Goldwyn's), and he and his family sailed on the *Majestic*, occupying the Imperial Suite, on September 28. He was not well on the crossing. His teeth were aching; he had neglected them for years, and abscesses had formed in the roots, draining toxicity into his bloodstream. He was irritable, tired and restless; when Irene and Edie went on moonlight deck walks with male passengers, he became furious and confined them to their cabin. Mayer was out of sorts in Cherbourg, terrified that his daughters would bring in some item that could be considered contraband. Once in Paris, at the Ritz, he was equally put out, no doubt in part by his wife and daughters' extravagant (and quite understandable) shopping sprees. He insisted that they list every single purchase, so as to be sure that when they returned to America they would not be disgraced by failing to file the appropriate customs forms.

He was unable to eat on the Simplon-Orient Express; Irene Selznick put this down to his annoyance at being given a set menu, but, of course, he would be accustomed to this when traveling across the United States. The real reason must have been that he was in so much misery from his teeth that he lost all appetite for food.

Although he should have gone to a dentist, he dragged his family to Livorno, where Fred Niblo was busy shooting a battle scene between prison galley and pirate boat on Leghorn Bay. It was a thrilling spectacle, observed by Mayer in a choppy sea from a movie crew launch. The principal galley, with its three tiers of oars, manned by 150 stalwart rowers, was 250 feet from prow to stern and could carry 2,000 men, including the movie employees. Mayer saw it rammed by the other galley, sinking in flames; the men jumped overboard into the sea. The decks were on fire; the heat was intense; many who could not swim clung to the rudders like flies on lumps of sugar until the boat submerged. Several were rescued by the assistant director Buddy Gillespie. An estimated three men were drowned.

The sequence involved twenty-eight cameras, some on the battling vessels, some on the decks of other boats, and more on floats, insecurely placed on sixty-foot wooden towers that tossed in the wind.

The Mayers traveled from the Palace Hotel in Livorno with Niblo, Gillespie and members of the company by the Rome Express to the capital. Mayer's discomfort was increasing by the hour. But he insisted on inspecting the offices of Metro-Goldwyn at 149 via Quattro Novembre; the spacious Cine Studios on the via Veio; the fifty-foot set of the Joppa Gate, built near an ancient aqueduct; the Roman Circus, designed for the chariot race that would be the major set piece of the film, and no less than a quarter of a mile long on each side; and numerous other important sets. He spent hours with Niblo in an overcrowded office built inside the Joppa Gate itself, commuting from a large, gloomy apartment on the via Sistina. Niblo and all the other M.G.M. employees were housed at the Excelsior.

Suddenly, on October 18, 1924, Mayer collapsed. He was in excruciating pain; fortunately, his (and the studio's) physician, Dr. Edward B. Jones, had arrived from Hollywood. Dr. Jones rushed Mayer to a dentist, who immediately determined the cause of the swelling in the jaw, the inability to swallow and the excruciating agony. Almost all of Mayer's teeth were abscessed, and the gums were drastically inflamed. The local dentist removed four teeth immediately, reducing (as Carey Wilson telegrammed Irving Thalberg at Culver City) Mayer to a mental and physical wreck. It was feared that the infection had become generalized and that Mayer might not live.

As Mayer tossed and turned in his hotel bed, it was decided to remove more teeth, until finally there were none left. On October 20, Mayer summoned enough strength to cable J. Robert Rubin in New York, telling Rubin to make sure that Irving Thalberg or Harry Rapf, preferably the latter, came to Rome immediately. Carey Wilson cabled Thalberg that Mayer must be sent home at once; Wilson would get him as far as Paris, where he could meet with Thalberg.

Wilson proved a tower of strength, but Mayer's condition worsened, and Thalberg cabled back that he was "naturally paralyzed with fear" over Mayer's illness. He did not agree that Mayer should be shipped to Paris, but instead sent to a health resort to recover. Thalberg demanded that Dr. Jones keep him informed on Mayer's physical condition day by day.

For another week, as tooth after tooth was extracted, Mayer fought stubbornly against death. Aided by Carey Wilson and Bess Meredyth, insisting Niblo continue shooting, but fretting over the quality of his work, he at last rallied; this was remarkable, since death from toxemia following tooth abscesses was not infrequent in those days, some twenty years before antibiotics.[1] Dr. Jones continued to urge Thalberg to have Mayer shipped home, but Thalberg was certain Mayer could not undertake the journey. Alexander Aronson of the Paris branch returned to Rome to take charge of everything, which he did, with great expertise.

By mid-November, Mayer had recovered fully. He made plans to travel to Berlin, and thence to London, returning to America in December. His reasons for going to Berlin were threefold: he would confirm arrangements for the consolidated German head office of Metro-Goldwyn, as well as deals that would be made with the UFA Studios; he wanted to talk to the Swedish director Mauritz Stiller, whose movie *The Saga of Gösta Bjerling* he had seen in Hollywood; and he wanted to find a suitable actress to play the Virgin Mary in *Ben-Hur*.

Both disturbing and exciting news came from the United States. The disturbing news was that Thomas Ince, a director Mayer much admired, had fallen ill aboard William Randolph Hearst's yacht and had died shortly after in a California hospital. The official cause of death was heart failure, but rumors began to leak back to Rome that Hearst had fired at Charlie Chaplin when he found him in a bunk with Marion Davies, the bullet had passed through the bulkhead and killed Ince on the other side. There was no truth to the story, but it would certainly have distressed Mayer, who was always mindful of the danger of scandal, and whose association with Hearst and Davies had only been firmed up four months earlier.

The good news was that Calvin Coolidge was firmly elected to presidential office by the American public: the results were very cheering and meant that Mayer's influence through Herbert Hoover would continue at the top of government.

Mayer and his family got on the train for Germany on November 21. He had managed to supervise the editing of the rushes of the galley sequence, and Carey Wilson informed Thalberg that Lewis had accomplished wonders with it.

Mayer arrived in Berlin on November 26, checked into the Adlon Hotel and arranged to meet with Mauritz Stiller, who made a disconcerting impression, talking to Mayer partly in Yiddish, partly through a translator. Stiller was a tall, rawboned man, ungainly and awkward; he had a certain heaviness of approach that must have aggravated Mayer. It is also likely that Mayer had heard rumors of Stiller's homosexual proclivities.

Stiller suggested that Mayer might wish to take another look at *The Saga of Gösta Bjerling,* which had just opened a tremendous success in

---

[1] Lewis Warner, twenty-five-year-old son of Harry Warner, of Warner Brothers, died six years later of that very cause.

Berlin. Stiller was pushing his bisexual protégé, nineteen-year-old Greta Garbo, for a Hollywood career; she played an important role in the movie as a newlywed countess. Mayer agreed to see the picture again with his daughters. Although it was excessively long and not very exciting, Miss Garbo made an impression: she had a sensitivity, delicacy and subtlety that made the rest of the cast seem heavy and obvious; there was a spiritual radiance in her face that may have suggested to Mayer she could possibly play the Virgin. Mayer told his daughters he was sure he could make a star of this virtually unknown girl. But she had a contract to make a movie in the next few weeks: *Joyless Street,* to be directed by Georg Wilhelm Pabst.

Mayer returned to the Adlon from a screening room; there, he met Stiller in his suite. He found Stiller no more congenial than at the first meeting, but he discussed signing him to a contract. Stiller yielded to Mayer's request that Miss Garbo should lose weight.

As Margaret, Irene and Edith Mayer went into the elevator, having lingered in the Adlon lobby to allow Mayer to meet with Stiller in private, Miss Garbo in a black taffeta hat walked in after them. They all went up to the suite together. In front of Miss Garbo, whom he was careful not to treat with too much deference lest she should get starry ideas and ask for too much money, Mayer repeated his insistence that she slim down. She nodded her assent.

Greta Garbo appeared to be a simple, unsophisticated girl. Acting for her was a way of obtaining money and independence, though she had been trained briefly at the Stockholm Royal Academy of Dramatic Arts. She was excessively nervous, insecure and hypersensitive; she was also earthily sensual, practical and had a brain like an adding machine. She worshipped Stiller, who had brought out the best in her, but she was not physically attracted to him. He was involved with a handsome young man, the actor Einar Hanson, who was about to costar with her in *Joyless Street.* Stiller did not discourage rumors that he was having an affair with Miss Garbo; he needed to cover the uncomfortable truth.

## CHAPTER NINE

# 1924–1925

BEFORE LEAVING BERLIN, Mayer made a verbal agreement with Stiller and Garbo, agreeing to supply them with first-class steamer and railroad passage from Berlin to Culver City. Furthermore, the studio would supply free of charge the clothes Miss Garbo would play in. It is likely, given her native canniness, that Miss Garbo added this sentence herself. Later, the studio tried to have her pay for her modern wardrobe, but this was scratched out of the contract. She would sign the letter of agreement with Loew's Major Edward Bowes on January 30, 1925. The exact details of her salary ($400 a week with options for four years at $600, $750, $1,000 and $1,250 a week) would follow. She was not to arrive in America before April 15, and would submit a statement of the cost of the passage, which would be refunded immediately. She was to report, with Stiller, to the New York office on arrival.

While in Berlin, Mayer saw a number of German pictures, which impressed him with their artistry. Mayer left for London on November 25. He was feted by Sir William Jury of Jury-Metro-Goldwyn at 14 Tower Street. The next night Sir William welcomed Mayer to a magnificent banquet at the Trocadero. Before a large audience of English movie people, Mayer gave a long and impassioned speech. He began by saying that pictures were bigger than individuals, and those who had failed in producing, distributing or exhibiting had failed because they had taken themselves too seriously. His next remarks stretched credulity to the limit: "Successes only come from humility. What little success I have been able to achieve I regard with humility and thankfulness in that I have become useful to our great industry." Apparently, he succeeded in fooling his audience, who clapped at his remark.

He dared to criticize the British movie people by saying that England had not done its duty in the matter of local production. Much more thought would have to be given to the work if the United Kingdom was not to be left behind in the movie industry race. ("The procession moves on, and if you stand still it goes by you.") Expressing his disappointment that the largest local studio was only 40 by 90 feet, he pointed out that each of the sound stages at M.G.M. was 150 by 250 feet. He mentioned the $1.5 million spent on *Ben-Hur* and that the picture would finally cost $5 million.

There was a masochistic ovation at the end of the speech. Many present were delighted that Mayer had obtained American rights to distribute one of the most ambitious movies ever made in England, Herbert Wilcox's *Chu-Chin-Chow*, from the stage success that had run over five years at His Majesty's Theater in London. Following the banquet, Mayer and his family did a lengthy tour of England in a Rolls Royce supplied by Sir William.

The Mayers sailed on the *Aquitania*, arriving in New York on December 10. While crossing the Atlantic, Mayer received a telegram from Mauritz Stiller, saying that "the reindeer girl," his nickname for Garbo, was, he felt, wrong for the Virgin Mary and was ten years older than her official age. His reason for making this false announcement may have been a fear that Mayer would feature her in this special cameo and then not use her again. In a good humor, Mayer gave a vivid interview to the press in Manhattan; the reporters boarded the vessel by launch. He told them that Hollywood would have to look to its laurels in view of the great advancement in the quality of German productions. On board, he had met the French director Georges de Vilmorin, who had with him the picture *The Miracle of the Wolves*, set in the time of Charles the Bold of Burgundy and Louis XI; Mayer said he was deeply impressed with it. Then he went on to describe the episode at Leghorn when the Roman galleys sank.[1]

During Mayer's absence, Edgar J. Mannix arrived in Hollywood to join the executive staff. Born in 1891, in Fort Lee, New Jersey, Eddie Mannix dropped out of Hackensack High School to work as a ticket seller at the Palisades Park, the Schenck brothers' amusement facility. Muscular, bullish, he worked his way up to the bookkeeping department, where he was said to be a master of all kinds of financial juggling and chicanery. When questions began to be asked by local authorities about his two sets of books, he was given the job of bouncer instead. It was said that he could punch out five rowdies at one time.

He was general manager of Palisades Park until 1916, when he became supervisor on the director Allan Dwan's picture *The Inner Woman*, starring the notorious Evelyn Nesbit Thaw. Three years later, he was

[1] Bess Meredyth had managed to smuggle the controversial footage of the sinking, which showed men actually drowning, to Paris in her luggage on the train, for secret shipment to Los Angeles.

manager of Joe Schenck's New York studio, in charge of Norma and Constance Talmadge pictures. Mayer had always admired him and arranged for him to come into the Hollywood operation as comptroller, later studio manager, and assistant to Irving Thalberg. Mannix was an irrepressible vulgar presence, but somehow this human pit bull attracted respect. He was a very able handler of labor and other problems at Culver City.

Back in Hollywood, Mayer had more than his share of problems. *Zander the Great*, under the replacement director George Hill, was limping along; and there was trouble involving the shooting of Maurice Tourneur's *Never the Twain Shall Meet*, starring Anita Stewart. Hearst was threatening to pull Davies and Cosmopolitan Pictures out of the M.G.M. partnership.

Worse, *The Merry Widow*, as directed by Erich von Stroheim, was in difficulties. Irving Thalberg had forced John Gilbert on the director, who made no bones about his loathing of the star. The other leading player, the flamboyant Mae Murray, was heading rapidly for a divorce and was also at odds with von Stroheim.

The director had his own cameramen, but Miss Murray refused to work with either one, and had introduced Mae Marsh's brother, Oliver T. Marsh, as her personal cinematographer. The rows were constant and violent. Miss Murray would stamp her foot and call him a "filthy Hun." In turn, von Stroheim insulted her, mocked her, tore away at her artificial gestures. Exasperated by the party scene suggesting a violent orgy, and another sequence in which an old man seemingly masturbated in a shoe closet, she screamed at Thalberg, "This is filth! Kissing people's bottoms and kissing feet!"

Although Mayer's reaction to the footage he saw has not been recorded, there is no question that he must have been beyond exasperation. Certainly, he was appalled to find that, once again, von Stroheim would only work at night and refused to pay the extras any overtime. On Thalberg's orders, J. J. Cohn, the project's production manager, sabotaged von Stroheim repeatedly by cutting off the electricity at midnight. Thalberg took off to New York, with the picture still in production, on January 12, leaving Mayer in charge of everything for six unpleasant weeks.

Meantime, troublesome news arrived in Rome throughout late December and into January. Severe rain held up the schedule; the morale of the company ran low; Carey Wilson was temperamental and emotional; Aronson kept urging Mayer to remove Niblo, whom he described as hated by the cast and the technicians, but Mayer refused. What he had seen of the rushes was satisfactory, and perhaps having two other directors, including Christy Cabanne, would push him into getting faster results.

But by Christmas, Mayer was much worried over the slow progress and was cabling Niblo to speed everything up, using all of his resourcefulness to get results. By December 26, a crisis had been reached. Niblo refused to have a schedule drawn up for him, would not give more than thirty percent of the work to the other directors and did as many as sixty takes of a leper colony scene. Aronson urged Mayer again to remove Niblo, and Carey Wilson confirmed this ill feeling. But Mayer stood firm with Niblo, repeatedly encouraging him in his messages.

Some publicity was stimulated by the fact that Benito Mussolini several times visited the set. In those days, this was considered, in Hollywood, to be a mark of distinction.

Further trouble occurred at the outset of the new year. Ramon Novarro, always miserable and introverted, suddenly rebelled against Niblo's needling. He left without warning for Nice to see his friend and former director Rex Ingram, announcing that he intended taking a two-month vacation. Under threat of discipline, he soon returned. Carey Wilson's baby daughter was stricken with pneumonia; his wife collapsed from nervous strain; and then Harry Edington, production manager, fell down a flight of stairs.

Francis X. Bushman was demanding $3,000 immediately to pay off his ex-wife, Beverly Bayne, or he would walk off the picture and go to Egypt. Mayer cabled back to Aronson that if Bushman quit he would be finished forever in the theatrical world. He did walk off, and he was finished—after Ben-Hur and one other contracted picture, The Masked Bride.[2] At last, Mayer lost patience and, on January 24, cabled Niblo to come home, leaving Cabanne to shoot extra sequences. Only the galley sequence finally seemed satisfactory, as, at the end of January, Niblo and his cast returned to New York.

On February 6, 1925, the reels of the galley sequence left the Cine Studios in Rome by steamship from Naples; three days later, Mayer authorized Aronson to destroy all of the Brabin footage. Then, on February 19, a storm in Rome blew down part of the Joppa Gate and smashed the executive offices.

As late as March 20, Christy Cabanne was still shooting secondary footage and planning to ship plaster molds for the Circus Maximus sets to be reconstructed in Hollywood. This plan was canceled and the molds were dumped into the sea. Finally, Niblo began repreparing at Culver City.

[2] With a remarkable lack of vindictiveness, Mayer hired Bushman's son, Francis, Jr., as an actor in several pictures after that.

*The Merry Widow* continued. During a sequence being shot in Griffith Park, Mae Murray refused to obey von Stroheim's instructions. Von Stroheim shouted, "Who do you think you are?" and Miss Murray replied, "Queen of M.G.M.!" Shooting was closed down for the rest of the day while Mayer tried to pacify director and star. During a re-creation of the Merry Widow Waltz, involving 350 extras, von Stroheim had the impertinence to show Miss Murray dance steps, when she had already been a very successful dancer. She tossed her headdress, made of peacock feathers, on the studio floor and stamped on it.

Following another violent fight, Miss Murray ran off the set into her dressing room and threw off her gown. The phone rang; her costar John Gilbert was on the line. He said he was leaving for South America immediately and would never work at the studio again. She yelled out to her maid to see where Gilbert was. Told that he was in the parking lot, getting into his car, she ran headlong from the building in her underwear, her bird-of-paradise headdress flying in the wind, and screamed at him not to leave. Admonished by a studio policeman, she ignored his orders to desist and pulled Gilbert bodily back into her dressing room. She forced him to agree to continue; he would do so only if von Stroheim was fired. Both stars made their way into Mayer's office; he was delighted to agree with their decision.

Mayer immediately fired the director and replaced him with Monta Bell. But when Bell mounted the crane to shoot the sequence, there was a scream from everyone of "We want von Stroheim!" The crew struck and would not work for Bell. Mayer arrived furiously on the set and shouted at everyone. When a member of the crew lashed out at Mayer, Eddie Mannix struck the assailant to the ground.

Mayer was forced to rehire von Stroheim. Soon after the picture was finished, on March 9, 1925, Mayer threw the director out of the studio for good. Thalberg had been absent in the east until February 14, thus missing most of the shenanigans. Mae Murray took off with twenty-six steamer trunks to Paris, where, in May, she divorced Robert Leonard.

Pleasanter news for Mayer was that of the forty top box office pictures of the previous year, M.G.M. had produced ten. He was seized by an overwhelming feeling that Niblo's footage in Rome was, with the exception of the galley sequence, unacceptable; even the great scene at the Joppa Gate, involving 30,000 people, and the bits and pieces of the chariot race with six black and six white chariot horses, were unusable. Millions had gone down the drain. Arrangements began to build a complete replica of the Circus Maximus in Hollywood.

Mayer hired Joseph von Sternberg to direct *The Exquisite Sinner*, the story of a young Frenchman escaping the conventions of society, with

Mayer's friend Conrad Nagel and René Adorée. Mayer hated the direction, and so did Thalberg. They fired von Sternberg and hired the mediocre Phil Rosen to redirect it, with lamentable results.

There was a big event on March 17, when the great, thirty-two-year-old, Russian-born French artist and decorator Erté (Romain de Tirtoff) arrived from France via New York to work at the studio. Mayer celebrated his arrival with an elaborate luncheon at the Beverly Hills Hotel. Mayer was extremely generous to Erté. He gave him a present of an expensive Packard automobile; he gave him a grand tour of the studio; and he assigned him to design Tod Browning's film *The Mystic*, starring the British actress Aileen Pringle. Mayer arranged for Erté to stage a fashion show for the Friends of the Council of Jewish Women at the Ambassador Hotel on April 13, with Norma Shearer, Miss Pringle, and the stars Carmel Myers (of *Ben-Hur*; Erté designed a costume for her in the picture), Eleanor Boardman and Pauline Starke modeling Erté's clothes. Mayer authorized Erté to design a masked ballet for *Dance Madness*, a display of black-and-white-clothed figures prancing in a fast Charleston. Erté did a cubist dressing room for *A Little Bit of Broadway* (renamed *Pretty Ladies*) and costumes and masks in art deco designs for *Time, the Comedian*. Despite the fact that Erté was, to say the least, outré, Mayer was fascinated by him. Erté turned up at the studio in rose and gray crepe de chine or crimson and black brocaded coats and gold pants, or in gray suits with red stripes; his twenty pairs of shoes ranged from gold-embroidered slippers to handmade soft calf oxfords.

Mayer went to the extraordinary length of having the artist's studio in Sèvres, France, photographed and copied, brick by brick, at Culver City. Even the exact green and black colors of the walls and furniture were mirrored, and the furniture was a replica of Erté's own designs. Mayer found Erté a splendid house in Beachwood Canyon because the artist loved solitary walks.

Erté described the studio at the time: "Royal facades without palaces; sumptuous interiors without walls; kings and queens in full regalia eating sandwiches in a cafeteria with beggars in rags."

Mayer became a father to the pale, slight, exquisitely groomed young man. Where talent like Erté's was concerned, Mayer could be considerate and thoughtful; he was far from being the monster of legend.

Not everything at the studio was decorous at this time. One incident, on March 8, involved a lunchtime quarrel between Marshall Neilan and his wife, Blanche Sweet, in the M.G.M. commissary, the Plantation Cafe. Without warning, Miss Sweet socked Neilan in the jaw. He socked her back. Before Mayer or anyone else in the commissary could do anything, a tourist who took objection to Neilan's action smashed the

director in the jaw. The waiters grabbed Neilan before he could retali-
ate. Police arrived. The Plantation Cafe dissolved into a brawl; chairs
and tables were smashed, and broken glasses lay everywhere.

A few days later, Marion Davies's bungalow at the United Artists'
Studios was moved to M.G.M. The $20,000 luxury building with a
sunken bathtub and rich carpets and curtains was cut in half and drawn
by truck on moving platforms.

That same week, on March 24, Marion Davies threw an expensive
housewarming party for 300 guests at her $125,000 home at 1700 Lex-
ington Drive, Beverly Hills. Mayer and his wife and daughters mingled
happily with the throng.

There was trouble that month in consummating a new contract between M.G.M. and William Randolph Hearst for Marion Davies pictures. It was felt that the movies were costing too much, and that the
actress's enormous salary of $10,000 a week was infuriating Mayer's less-
well-paid stars. It was only when Nicholas Schenck arrived from New
York that the matter was solved. Miss Davies was granted the privilege of
two salaries: one from M.G.M. and one from Hearst's Cosmopolitan
Pictures. Cosmopolitan would divide profits with M.G.M., but Miss Davies would only profit from her majority shareholding in Cosmopolitan.
Hearst fired his motion picture staff, except for three executives, and
closed down his New York operation.

On March 31, no doubt to Mayer's relief, the troublesome Marshall
Neilan at last quit M.G.M. for good. By mid-April, ten units were working at Culver City. Monta Bell was shooting *Pretty Ladies*, with a complete re-creation of the New Amsterdam Theater in New York on the
lot for a replica of the Ziegfeld Follies. Venice, California, then a western
version of Coney Island, was taken over for the shooting of *The Rebellious Girl*.

April 14 was a day of celebration. Twenty-eight-year-old Lillian Gish,
arguably the greatest screen actress of her day, was given a lavish welcome at the studio. Mayer arranged for her to be greeted with flags and
multicolored bunting; he and the other executives, Thalberg, Harry
Rapf, Eddie Mannix and a new addition, thirty-year-old supervisor Hunt
Stromberg, personally welcomed her. Her contract called for a total of
$800,000 to be paid to her. She would have the right to select directors,
stories and script writers; if she disapproved of costumes, she was permitted to reject them.

Such an arrangement was unique in Louis B. Mayer's career, but, quite
apart from Lillian Gish's enormous power at the box office, he had never
forgotten the fact that *The Birth of a Nation*, in which she had so admirably starred, had been the foundation of his personal fortune. Indeed,

when she had visited Los Angeles the previous winter for the West Coast premiere of her film *Romola,* Mayer greeted her at the station with a reminder that she had played a crucial role in putting him on the motion picture map.

She was much troubled at the time; an unscrupulous lawyer, Charles H. Duell, was suing her, claiming he had an exclusive contract for her services. On April 2, Judge Julian W. Mack of the Superior Court of New York had dismissed Duell's claims following a harrowing court hearing, and had him arrested on a charge of perjury. The next few months would be marked by further hearings, which would seriously affect Miss Gish's sense of well-being. But, made of finest steel under her delicate Victorian surface, Miss Gish, at last, would triumph.

On April 16, Mayer left for New York with little Jackie Coogan for the studio's first annual sales convention, cabling Herbert Hoover that he would be proceeding to Washington. Just before leaving, Mayer had a major row with Fred Niblo, who objected to Betty Bronson's performance as the Virgin Mary in *Ben-Hur,* and said that unless she went, he would. He announced that she was "a gambling, frolicking little girl, incompetent to properly express the role of compassionate tenderness which was expected of the Madonna." Mayer lost patience with Niblo and wrote to Nicholas Schenck, saying that he might have to remove the director permanently. He didn't fire Niblo, but he forced the director to accept Miss Bronson.

Even as Mayer was on the train, Reginald Barker, Mayer's old friend and colleague, walked out, objecting to Mayer's and Thalberg's interference with his movies and their editing. Mayer was riding his directors hard, insisting that Thalberg allow nothing to go through without extensive alteration, reshooting and cutting, to obtain what he felt to be the best results.

The first birthday celebrations of Metro-Goldwyn at the Pennsylvania Hotel in Manhattan were riotous and spectacular. Mayer glowed with pride as, for two hours without a break, he addressed hundreds of exhibitors seated in the Grand Ballroom with enthusiastic prophecies of future success.

Mayer had a painful contretemps with his daughter Edie that month. She longed to be a singer and dancer on the musical stage; from her earliest girlhood, she had been fascinated by the Broadway shows to which her parents had taken her. Mayer had allowed her to be trained by a professional singer. Now, during a trip to New York with her mother, she auditioned for a show and was approved. She proudly took the letter of acceptance to her father, who asked her how she proposed getting back to Manhattan. She replied that she would, of course, make the journey again by train. He asked her how she proposed to raise the fare. She responded that naturally he would give it to her.

He refused. It may be that Mayer wanted to protect her from the morally dissolute atmosphere of Broadway. He said to her, "You're the best goddamned actress of them all. You need that talent for living. It would be wasted on the stage." "Why did you let me take all those singing lessons?" she asked. "Because it kept you busy," he replied. "It gave you something to do when I wouldn't let you go to college." Sixty years later, Edie broke down again as she recalled the incident. And she added a footnote: "I enrolled at Wellesley. I was accepted. And he wouldn't let me go there. I felt it wasn't worth living anymore. He also stopped Irene in her desire to go to Bryn Mawr."

At that time, Mayer and Thalberg approved a public relations movie, "Inside the M.G.M. Studios," which, in titles, introduced the audience to "The Shadow Land of Make-Believe." The camera roamed across well-cropped lawns and enormous stages, through forty-three acres and forty-five buildings, and along three miles of streets. The main gate was shown, well guarded by police. The camera tracked along the colonnade of Corinthian columns that fronted the building; showed sound stage 14 being built; introduced the studio's story department, led by Mrs. M. F. Lee; and closed up on Carey Wilson, looking understandably haggard after the ordeals of Rome, and other writers, including Waldemar Young, Jane Murfin and Frederic and Fay Hatton, all looking bedraggled, no doubt after all-night writing sessions. The all-female typing pool was shown convulsed in giggles. A line of directors stood, self-conscious before the cameras; only a coolly detached Josef von Sternberg, sleek-haired and mustachioed, leaning on a black enameled cane, and a magisterial Erich von Stroheim, in what appears to be a large motoring cap, seemed to be composed. The dressing rooms on two levels of the long wooden building looked remarkably drab, the men's on the lower level, the upstairs section patroled by a restrictive matron. Not shown was a sign that read: "The gentlemen may not ascend to the ladies' rooms." Like most such notices, it was seldom heeded.

The wardrobe mistress, Mrs. E. F. Chapman, appeared, with a staff of over sixty. Erté was shown dressing newcomer Lucille Le Sueur, soon to be known as Joan Crawford. The viewers saw a strong-looking J. J. Cohn; Cedric Gibbons, with dark, curly hair, smoking nervously; construction manager C. F. Wilhelm; numerous workers responding to the silent toot-toot of a whistle; Louis Kalb, whose electrical plant could power some eight thousand homes; a mild Tod Browning rehearsing a splendiferous crowd scene for The Mystic; a thirty-piece orchestra used to provide mood music for the stars; a dance school; fireproof vaults that contained forty million feet of film; and glimpses of Elinor Glyn, Conrad Nagel and the screen writer Rupert Hughes in the overcrowded Plantation Cafe.

Mayer was shown hunched over his dictaphone, a plain, dark wall his only background. Thalberg, in a natty, light gray three-piece suit, and Harry Rapf, with his anteater's nose, acted up a storm for the cameras as they issued silent instructions.

A pressing issue that June was securing permission to allow a new Ramon Novarro vehicle, *The Midshipman,* to be shot at the U.S. Naval Academy at Annapolis. On June 1, Mayer cabled Secretary of Commerce Herbert Hoover (who had recently visited the studio), urging him to arrange for President Calvin Coolidge to allow Novarro to be present when diplomas were handed out at an official graduation ceremony.

Hoover cabled back on June 2, SETTLED YOUR MATTER I BELIEVE SATISFACTORILY THIS MORNING. Hoover had gotten the president and the secretary of the navy on the telephone, and the arrangement was made.

That June, King Vidor's *The Big Parade* was filmed in and around Los Angeles, with the cooperation of the Army and the Marine Corps. Second-unit shots were taken at Fort Sam Houston in Texas, with 10,000 men of the Ninth Infantry, the Second Engineers, the Twelfth Field Artillery, the Fifteenth Field Artillery, and the Second Signal Corps, as well as six truck units enlisted for Metro-Goldwyn through Generals Malone and Bishop. Vidor had embarked upon the picture, written by the young Laurence Stallings, who had lost a leg in the trenches in World War I, with remarkable energy. He had persuaded a reluctant John Gilbert to eschew all stage makeup and allow his fingernails to grow long and dirty. He cast Renée Adorée as a French farm girl. Using hundreds of reels of film obtained from the U.S. Army Signal Corps, he had meticulously recreated the horror of the front line.

Vidor followed the dictates of Stallings' screenplay in arranging for John Gilbert's leg to be strapped behind him for those sequences in which the character he played was shown to have had a leg shot off. Mayer, who had not troubled to read the screenplay, was appalled when Vidor explained this to him, suggesting that Gilbert should only limp. He was very uneasy about a romantic idol being shown as a handicapped person. But, as so often before and after, Irving Thalberg went behind his back and got Nicholas Schenck's permission to follow the script to the letter. Mayer also hated the fact that Gilbert's character lacked heroic stature, but rather reflected the uncertainties, awkwardnesses and innocent discomforts of an average young American of those days faced with the brutal reality of killing other men. Again, Vidor went to Thalberg; again, Mayer was overruled.

Not only was Thalberg undermining Mayer, he was also plotting with Nicholas Schenck against the director. He had promised Vidor, a friend with whom he played tennis on Sundays, twenty-five percent of the profits of the picture, but he failed to meet that promise. As a result, Vidor lost at least a million dollars. How he managed to forgive Thalberg he was unable to explain when interviewed on the subject forty years later.

Mayer did give Vidor permission to launch the movie with spectacular sound effects at the screenings, which seemed to reach toward the forthcoming era of talkies. In addition to the customary full orchestra playing martial or romantic themes at the big-city screenings, Vidor arranged for bass drummers beating away behind the screen as the four thousand actual enlisted servicemen marched in a scene that itself had been directed to a metronome. Vidor also arranged for eighteen Army buglers to stand next to the drummers, sounding reveille and taps. Recordings of explosions were played.

Mayer insisted on opening and closing scenes emphasizing the central figure's mother; Thalberg again went behind Mayer's back and cut out the sequences, and several more, to make room for song-and-dance stage shows. He even hired Vidor's bête noire, the dreaded editor Joseph Farnham, to make these cuts. Vidor defied him; when he found out what had taken place, he scoured the editing rooms at M.G.M. to rescue his lost footage, forcing the irritated Thalberg to accept a new cut in which almost the entire masterpiece was preserved.

*The Big Parade* would turn out to be a colossal hit, earning over $15 million and making John Gilbert a major star. A matinee idol of this calibre had seldom been seen covered in mud, drenched in rain; the results were justly praised by critics. Mayer played a crucial role in the film's success: he took it to New York, persuading the executives there, including the skeptical Nicholas Schenck, that the movie must be handled with the utmost commitment by Metro-Goldwyn.


On July 7, Greta Garbo and Mauritz Stiller arrived aboard the Swedish vessel *Drottningholm* in New York. Garbo and Stiller had filled the months since Mayer's meeting with them in Berlin making G. W. Pabst's story of the postwar depression in Germany, *Joyless Street*, and had made an abortive trip to Istanbul.

Perhaps because of the pressure of his working schedule, Mayer had not prepared a suitable vehicle for Miss Garbo, and may have had qualms at this stage because of her uncertain command of English. Stiller also remained defiantly unable to speak the language, which would be a major problem in handling motion picture crews. Whatever the truth, Mayer did not advise Thalberg to have anything ready for the Swedish actress, who, with her companions from Stockholm, spent two months doing nothing except posing for photographs, one of which appeared in *Vanity Fair*.

When Mayer returned to Hollywood in September, he decided that he dare not risk using Stiller for Miss Garbo's first picture, but instead must have a reliable American handle her. Mindful of the success of film versions of works by Vicente Blasco Ibañez, he settled on the novel *The Torrent*, the story of a poor farm girl who emerges as an opera star in Spain. He chose the contract writer Dorothy Farnum to undertake the adaptation. Opposite Garbo, Mayer would cast Ricardo Cortez. Once again, as in *The Saga of Gösta Bjerling*, Garbo would be playing a Latin. Although she complained that Mayer did not make proper use of her, this casting against type proved his and Thalberg's conviction that her abilities as an actress could rise above anything.

Shortly before Miss Garbo arrived in Hollywood, Lillian Gish was hard at work on King Vidor's next picture, *La Bohème*, based more on the stories by Henri Murger than on Puccini's popular opera. There was trouble from the beginning. Miss Gish, who had selected Vidor as her director after seeing *The Big Parade*, insisted on principles of work that were quite foreign to the director. When she announced that she expected to rehearse the film in full, Vidor, puzzled, since he was not directing a stage play, mocked up some scenery with Cedric Gibbons for her to act against. She looked at it aghast and announced that she would only rehearse out of doors, on the studio lawn. With tourists, actors and personnel watching in astonishment, she mimed her way through the scenes, playing to invisible props, including a dressing table, a truckle bed, a window and a wall. Vidor was bewildered; he couldn't understand what she was doing. Finally, he talked her into working indoors.

Mayer and Thalberg backed him in this. They also supported him when he argued with her about the sort of portrait lighting she wanted, with long, static close-ups. Miss Gish also demanded the use of panchromatic film, which had never been handled by the studio before. She objected to Erté's calico dresses for the impoverished heroine Mimi, insisting on using old, worn silk and running up the clothes herself at home. She clashed with Cedric Gibbons, demanding a sordid attic in place of the lavish house he had wanted for Mimi. The worst problem was John Gilbert, cast as Mimi's lover in the picture. He began writing her love letters; he tried to kiss her behind the scenes, when she declined to allow kissing sequences in the film. Mayer overrode her decision; he added kissing scenes later. Locked in her court struggle with Duell, who was claiming to be her fiancé, Miss Gish did not want a scandal and refused to date Gilbert. To make matters more complicated, King Vidor also tried to seduce her, but she was unattainable always.

Mayer was fascinated by Miss Gish's devotion to her work. She made no complaint when, in one sequence, actors playing Paris street revelers tossed her over their heads like a rag doll. In order to give complete realism to her death scene, she starved herself for three days. She stuffed cotton in her mouth to give the impression of puffy, unhealthy cheeks; when she passed away, she seemed already to be a ghost. Mayer, who never applauded at a preview, wept and clapped and embraced Miss Gish when he saw the finished film in the screening room. Until the advent of Marie Dressler, she was his favorite actress: the embodiment of his dream of innocent, ideal womanhood.

Miss Gish was among the stars present on October 1, 1925, to see the long-delayed shooting of the *Ben-Hur* chariot race. For days before, J. J. Cohn and Eddie Mannix had tested the course by driving their own chariots around, almost turning them over as they negotiated the curves. Not only did virtually every player on the M.G.M. lot dress up in Roman costume to join the throng on the Cedric Gibbons set, but Douglas Fairbanks, Mary Pickford, Mrs. Fred Niblo (Enid Bennett) and John and Lionel Barrymore were there.

Some forty-two cameras were placed around the arena, and Mayer put up a prize for all of the drivers. When the crowd of three thousand was assembled, Irving Thalberg told J. J. Cohn he didn't think there were enough people present. Cohn disagreed, thinking that Thalberg was being fussy, but went out into the street, plucked three hundred people off the sidewalk, offered them extras' wages and hurriedly dressed them, ushering them out into the benches.

A fog rolled in from the Pacific Ocean, and Thalberg announced that it must be blown out with wind machines. Cohn was obliged to point out that there was no way to blow fog back into the Pacific, but Thalberg was adamant, and wind machines were brought in to at least keep the fog away from the arena. Another problem emerged when three thousand box lunches failed to arrive. Thalberg insisted that the race not begin until the lunches came.

Cohn realized that extras waving angrily for their lunch would seem at a long distance only to indicate their excitement in the race. He defied his boss, and also Mayer, and risked his job by ordering the chariots out before the lunches came in. The result was that caterers actually walked through the crowd with hats on, serving the lunches; fortunately, they were so far distant that the audience could not see them.

Twelve chariots drawn by forty-eight horses drew out into the midday sunshine. The thousands of imitation Romans, Jews, Egyptians and Assyrians in the crowd stood and cheered as Fred Niblo relayed his orders through the public address system; Army and Navy signal flags controlled by a U.S. Army sergeant under chief cameraman Percy Hilburn semaphored the chariot drivers. Thirteen thousand feet of telephone wire connected the different camera teams; overhead, a biplane flew in, a team coordinating the aerial shots. As the screenwriters dictated, Novarro as Ben-Hur was crowded into ninth position at the takeoff, and Francis X. Bushman was launched in fourth position. Lap after lap was performed according to the dictates of the screenplay. Mayer and Thalberg watched excitedly as the chariots careered around the track; a horseshoe came loose from one of the horses, spun out into the audience and almost hit some extras. Two chariots went over, one on top of another, in a spectacular pileup that, according to one version, killed a driver; J. J. Cohn says that nobody was even injured. Francis X. Bushman claimed that five horses were killed; J. J. Cohn denies it.

Both Bushman and Novarro handled their horses magnificently; there was no chance for doubles. The results were thrilling: one of the finest action sequences on the screen to date. B. Reeves Eason, the special second-unit director in charge of the race, made his reputation overnight. Mayer and Thalberg were delighted by the rushes.

As Ben-Hur at last went into editing, Mayer was involved in a major matter. Marcus Loew had decided to merge M.G.M. with United Artists under Joe Schenck, which would, in effect, bring the Schenck brothers together in a business union and would amalgamate Metro with the most powerful and effective independent moviemaking organization in Hollywood. The venture may have looked good on paper, but it was in many ways ill-advised, because of the fact that the hated Charlie Chaplin was a partner, with Douglas Fairbanks and Mary Pickford, in UA.

Chaplin had little to gain and much to lose from the arrangement. He had a handsome twenty percent of his own pictures, he would lose the autonomy he enjoyed, he would have Mayer on his back and he would face a future that might involve conflict and hostility. He stalled by saying that he would have to consult with his lawyer, Nathan Burkan, before he could move ahead. Then he began raising difficulties with his partners. At the same time, exhibitors the world over began to protest that the blending of the companies would amount to a motion picture trust.

At the end of November, Chaplin finally vetoed the merger; it would, he told *Variety*, be in essence "a club" for Metro-Goldwyn "to force exhibitors into line, using block booking as a means to foist its film junk on the exhibiting market." Douglas Fairbanks was furious with Chaplin over this: he called him a "kicker." "Fairbanks is a jumper!" Chaplin said in reply, meaning that Fairbanks had wanted to jump over him to make the deal. The merger fell apart in the first week of December.

Mayer was having his problems on the domestic front as well. He had decided to buy a tract of real estate at Santa Monica Beach; there, he would build his first house, in keeping with his status as a leader of the motion picture industry. On November 17, 1925, he sold 1834 North Kenmore for $20,000 to Hugh C. and Josephine W. Pritchard. The mortgage called for interest payments of six percent over a twenty-five-year period, arranged through the Pacific-Southwest Trust and Savings Bank. No sooner had the Pritchards signed the necessary papers than they failed to meet the payments, and much of the following year would be absorbed in the unpleasant process of attaching the property. Temporarily, the Mayers moved into a rented house in Fremont Place while the complicated procedure of obtaining the Santa Monica land, which had already been mortgaged once, went ahead.

*The Big Parade* opened to big business that winter in New York and other cities. William Fox of the Fox Studios grumbled that the picture would take away commercial value from his picture *What Price Glory*, cowritten by Laurence Stallings, which was in the works. Mayer brushed the complaint aside, rejoicing that he was first with his own picture. He announced, on December 15, that the unprecedented price of $11 a ticket would be charged for the *Ben-Hur* premiere in Manhattan. A last-minute battle was taking place over the screenplay credits, Carey Wilson demanding, with Bess Meredyth, that he receive a full panel, June Mathis grumbling in the wings and flourishing her original contract; separating the contestants and giving them proper weight on the screen proved to be a major problem.

That December, while M.G.M.'s sales force was in high gear for the opening of *Ben-Hur*, work began on Greta Garbo's *The Torrent*. She objected to Stiller not directing her; she had little rapport with Monta Bell, who was continuing his affair with Norma Shearer and seemed indifferent to Garbo's sensitivity. She was homesick, missing the dedication of the Stockholm film crews and the cottage industry atmosphere of Swedish picture making. The emphasis on time and money, the humdrum if craftsmanlike approach of Bell, the six-day working schedules and the testy impatience of Mayer and Thalberg, all grated on her. She longed to return to Sweden; the presence of visitors on the set exasperated her, and she insisted on their removal. She seemed to have little rapport with Ricardo Cortez.

Sad and restless, if animated by occasional bursts of humor, empty and lost, Garbo became so complete a creature of the screen that she lost some special essence of herself. Those who met her found her in every way ordinary; a reason at the beginning for Howard Dietz in New York and Pete Smith in Hollywood to create a publicity machine for her that would limit the number of interviews she gave and would build around her an aura of impenetrable mystery. But once the camera turned, and she was seen in the rushes, she blossomed. Mayer and Thalberg were astonished and ordered Dorothy Farnum to write a second vehicle for her, supplied by William Randolph Hearst's Cosmopolitan Pictures: *The Temptress*, also based on a novel by Vicente Blasco Ibañez.

## Chapter Ten

# 1925-1926

Even up to the last days before the world premiere of *Ben-Hur* in New York City, at the George M. Cohan Theater, changes were being made in the picture. In spite of the custodianship of Will Hays, religious pressure groups were objecting to the announcement that Christ would be represented on the screen, if only by the use of a merciful arm stretching out, and by the evocation of His Nativity. Perhaps because of the stress Irving Thalberg was stricken with a heart attack at the end of November. This was a matter of agonizing concern to Mayer, and indeed it was not immediately certain that Thalberg would recover. It was obvious that he had taken on far too much work, and that he must at once have a vacation; he refused. The problem was exacerbated by the fact that Harry Rapf had to make a trip to Europe to confirm the appointment of Alexander Aronson, formerly head of the Paris office, as general manager of all M.G.M. interests in Europe.

On December 21, Thalberg was slowly recovering at his home on South Bronson in Los Angeles, still cutting *Quo Vadis* from his bed, the film projected onto the wall or the ceiling, quite in defiance of doctor's orders. Calvin Coolidge, his wife and their son, John, saw *The Big Parade* in the East Room of the White House, the first time any president had seen a motion picture there. Mayer was unable to be present because of the pressing problems occasioned by Thalberg's illness. Jack Connolly of the Will Hays Organization arranged the evening in connection with special M.G.M. representative William A. Orr. By now, M.G.M. was fourteen pictures behind schedule.

That same month, Mayer joined with Carl Laemmle and Famous Players–Lasky in coordinating a major deal with the Berlin-based UFA to make motion pictures together; jointly, M.G.M. and Famous Players advanced UFA $4 million in exchange for distribution of UFA films.

This was a huge step forward in the internationalizing of Marcus Loew's empire.

The premiere of *Ben-Hur* on December 30, 1925, was an overwhelming success. The picture is still magnificent today. The antiracist theme, interlaced with the story of Christ, retains its emotional impact. And Fred Niblo's direction still resounds with just the right degree of barbaric physicality. A sexual undercurrent, vibrant and continuous, gives the succession of images of the ancient world their emotional power. The attack of the pirate fleet, the scenes in the galleys, Ben-Hur's journey through the desert when the hand of Christ is seen giving mercy and succor, and, above all, the chariot race, thrillingly staged from first shot to last, are portions of the tapestry of the masterwork. Contrasted with Francis X. Bushman's meaningless posturings, Ramon Novarro plays throughout with an impassioned sincerity that easily overcomes any technical deficiencies in his performance. He was, and is, the spirit of youth, and his physical beauty, the result of his months of intensive training, remains very striking.

The audience cheered repeatedly throughout the screening, and at the end rose to their feet in a standing ovation. John Stahl rushed to the telephone to call Mayer and the ailing Thalberg at home, telling them excitedly of the audience's response.

The reviews were extremely enthusiastic. The movie, following upon the great success of *The Big Parade*, put M.G.M. firmly ahead of any other studio in Hollywood. It confirmed Marcus Loew's faith in Louis B. Mayer; it put Fred Niblo, whose career, after all, Mayer had most surely developed, in the forefront of directors.

When Marcus Loew visited Culver City at the outset of the new year, immediately following the premiere, Thalberg rallied, and Loew was overwhelming in his compliments. On New Year's Day, Mayer gave an interview to *The Moving Picture World*, unhesitatingly comparing himself with Benvenuto Cellini, who "started carving gold with the crudest of tools—and then explain[ed] in his naive way his joy when he finally saved enough for the purchase of the finest tools obtainable—not because they merely gave him private ownership and saved him time—but because they actually enabled him to do greater things."

As he made the comparison, the chief executive puffed at his cigar and looked out proudly as a tractor, hauling a dynamo and gas engine, chugged past his window, hundreds of workers milled through the maze of asphalt lanes and others poured into the sound stages. He gave a rat-a-tat description of the vast holdings of period furniture imitated in a factory that would "make Grand Rapids jealous"—copies of statuary, including the thirty-foot-high athletes presented in the Circus Maximus chariot race of *Ben-Hur*; modern furnishings, covered in gold leaf, and the complete recreation of parts of New York in Marion Davies's *Lights of Old Broadway*. He talked of the lumber mills, the best on the West Coast, with planers, hand saws, lathes, joiners; rolling stock; a paint shop with 125 men, from marblers and grainers to sign writers and scenic artists, able to run up a castle if needed in less than a week. He knew the statistics: a hundred thousand pounds of dry colors, ten thousand gallons of shellac, fifteen to twenty thousand gallons of paint and a thousand gallons of oil and varnishes. It could fairly be said that if a light was left on in a broom closet, Louis B. Mayer knew about it. When he gave the exact number of kilowatts in a motor generator, it was certain he was on target.

It was just as well, because he decided to turn over the construction of a new house on a block of land bought at 625 Ocean Front, Santa Monica, on the tract known as Rancho San Vicente, to art director Cedric Gibbons and to the M.G.M. building, electrical and carpentry shops. The lot, oddly enough, neighbored that of his much-hated enemy, Samuel Goldwyn. On the other side was the house of Jesse L. Lasky; Goldwyn always accused Mayer of advising Lasky's sister Blanche not to marry Goldwyn. The cost of the dwelling was $28,000, and the design was Mediterranean Spanish, with a dark red tiled roof, a white stone front, a large, curving living room with windows facing the ocean, and wrought iron balconies onto which French windows opened; the swimming pool was decorated with white sun umbrellas. A sandstone cliff rose behind the house, subject to crumbling, or worse, during earthquakes and floods. A line of palms stood, regular as sentinels, on the road above, against the deep blue skies of a still smogless coast.

The house was built on thirty-foot pilings to secure it against being swept away in a tidal wave. The walls were a foot thick, to ensure coolness in the height of summer. Mayer's den had a heavy, Spanish antique desk and on the window sill behind it a model of a Spanish galleon, without sails. The curtains throughout the house were of satin or chintz, and the carpets were richly woven; the furnishings were Spanish, with tapestries of coats of arms on the walls and heavy oak beams in the ceilings. The house had thirteen onyx-and-marble bathrooms, far more than were required by the four bedrooms.

Work was completed, according to the existing records, in an incredible six weeks, by April 18, 1926. Mayer's wife and daughters were overjoyed with the results, and looking forward to a much expanded social life in the future. The girls spent inordinate amounts of time at the beach, burning themselves to a crisp. They remained as different as ever: Edie romantic, dazed with daydreams of the stars, flirtatious, af-

flicted with bouts of self-pity, casting glances at attractive men everywhere, dressed in the height of fashion; Irene, forced to share a room
with her sister despite the larger accommodations, still severe, hard and
masculinely tailored. Mayer reminded his daughters that they must
watch every penny, despite his newly acquired wealth, granting $100 a
month to Edie and $75 a month to Irene, on condition they saved $25 a
month each. He warned them constantly that if they married poor men,
they would need to be extremely careful.

Mayer would still drive recklessly. Mindful of his influence (and he
was already very close to the district attorney, Asa Keyes), police would
look the other way. When he did, by chance, receive an occasional
ticket, it was promptly canceled. He was beginning to exert his influence
in other ways, too: he was quietly up to his eyes in local politics, and was
beginning to become involved with the questionable operations of the
Julian Petroleum Corporation, of which more later.

He and William and Irving Thalberg, partners in the Melvil Hall
Corporation, real estate operators, were locked almost constantly in litigation. On January 14, 1926, they obtained 625 acres in Glendale, for a
price of $171,875, and were sued promptly by a Blanche Teigeler for not
having paid her for negotiating the sale. The case was settled out of
court.

At the same time, Mayer joined with a curious assortment of figures,
including his wife, Irving Thalberg, Harry Rapf, Joe and Norma Talmadge Schenck, Douglas Fairbanks and Mary Pickford, in the top-secret
Title Guarantee and Trust Company, buying and selling vast amounts of
real estate in and around Los Angeles, some of the transactions amounting to as much as $500,000 at a clip.

Mayer was getting rich in land as well as from the unadvertised personal share he had in the contracts of individual players, including Lon
Chaney, Ricardo Cortez, Eleanor Boardman, Norma Shearer and even,
surprisingly, the hated John Gilbert. He was well past his third million
by the spring of 1926, when his house was completed. Thalberg was in
New York for several weeks, with King Vidor and Gilbert, in February
and March, leaving Mayer with a crushing work load which he shoul-
dered with his customary determination. He even found time to go to
San Francisco on March 12 for the opening of the picture The Barrier,
which meant a good deal to him. It starred Lionel Barrymore, who would
remain a lifelong friend and ally, and whom he had never forgotten from
the early days at the Metro Studios in New York. The neurotic and
unstable Barrymore, already suffering from the first indications of the
painful arthritis that would finally cripple him, fascinated Mayer to a
degree that many found inexplicable. Mayer had a strong stake in the

career of the film's director, George Hill, a no less unstable and driven individual, who would be doomed to a tragic early death.

Mayer, with his family, was in an unusually buoyant mood on the San Francisco visit. As always, he received a rapturous reception there, and a mob of firemen greeted him off the train. He had become interested in the fire fighters and was an honorary fire chief. He considered himself a patron of these courageous men and secured the support of the local authorities (the Los Angeles equivalents had been giving him a hard time) to make *The Fire Brigade*, a mélange of melodrama involving burning buildings and last-minute escapes down fire ladders. Mayer developed yet another career: that of the thirty-five-year-old, rugged, rangy, hard-drinking director W. S. Van Dyke, who would become known as "One-Take Woody" because of the extreme speed with which he made motion pictures. He sent Van Dyke to the wilds of Northern California to shoot two pictures back to back, *War Paint* and *Winners of the Wilderness*, the latter starring the up-and-coming Joan Crawford.

Mayer had begun a policy similar to that of running a baseball team: he had his minor league and major league, raising junior players to the top through careful grooming, not letting them go too far too fast. He was both coach and father to his players. They treated him as a confessor, pouring their hearts out to him in a way they never did to the more cool and detached Irving Thalberg. He responded with intense emotionalism, crying with them or laughing with them; he had a deep understanding of the peculiarly egomaniacal, insecure, childlike, hypersensitive and slightly daffy characters of actors and actresses.

Mayer was in many ways still a young boy at heart, for all his ruthless capacity to weed out weak sisters from the studio operation, and his temperamental inability to deal with unreliability, bad temper and bad manners. Because his emotions were open and untrammeled he could reach out to the hearts of his performers, and they could reach out to him. Actors like John Gilbert and Mae Murray were the prodigal children. Lillian Gish, of course, satisfied him, though she had less rapport with him than with Irving Thalberg, because of his well-lettered sensibility and middle-brow intellect. Following *La Bohème*, she had wanted to start immediately with a version of Nathaniel Hawthorne's controversial novel *The Scarlet Letter*, the story of a minister who commits adultery with a beautiful woman. Mayer informed her that the book was blacklisted by members of organizations protective of public decency. Miss Gish, with her customary boldness, wrote to each and every organization he named, insisting that this classic work should be brought to the screen. They responded immediately, telling Miss Gish that they trusted her to handle the material. Mayer at once agreed, and allowed

Miss Gish to import from Sweden Lars Hanson, who had costarred with
Garbo in *The Saga of Gösta Bjerling,* for the leading role opposite her.
Mayer agreed with Miss Gish that Victor Sjöström should direct the
film.

Just before the picture ended, Miss Gish's mother suffered a stroke in
London. Mayer was moved to tears, remembering his mother's final illness and the desperate rush he had had to get to Canada in time. He
agreed that Miss Gish should go, and the picture was completed in
seventy-two hours of nonstop shooting. So tight was the schedule that
Miss Gish had to catch the train, after an all-night shoot, still dressed as
Hester Prynne. It is typical of Mayer's extraordinary consideration for
this great star that he insisted on seeing her off, with Thalberg and Harry
Rapf, at the Pasadena station. Her mother recovered, and Miss Gish
returned. Her protracted lawsuit with Charles Duell continued; Duell
blackmailed Miss Gish and threatened her life, but she still managed to
do pickup shots. When *The Scarlet Letter* opened in August, it was an
immediate success, one of the finest pictures M.G.M. ever made.

Mayer introduced a new custom: on March 23, he announced he was
throwing open the M.G.M. gates to trainee writers and directors who
would be given one picture to prove themselves, at low salaries, and, if
they made good, would be awarded yearlong contracts. He rejoiced in
the success of *Beverly of Graustark,* Marion Davies's lavish new production, which opened triumphantly at the Capitol in New York, in March;
and at the beginning of April, he signed the great director Clarence
Brown, another man destined to be a lifelong friend, a decent and gentle
Tennesseean whose love of the land and of human beings gave an intense warmth and brilliance to his best motion pictures.

That same month, after a wait of several weeks, Garbo began work on
*The Temptress,* the writing of which had occupied Dorothy Farnum since
December. With much reluctance, for he still found the man tiresome
and the business of communicating with him through a translator irritating, Mayer, at Miss Garbo's urgent behest, agreed to have Mauritz Stiller
direct the film. There was some idea of casting John Gilbert with her; he
was, whatever Mayer thought of him, still enormously popular. But
when approached to discuss the movie, Gilbert announced that he had a
much better idea in mind. Wearily, Mayer agreed to listen to it. Gilbert
strode into Mayer's office accompanied by Thalberg and Eddie Mannix.
Gilbert said he would like to appear in a version of *The Widow in the Bye
Street,* a poem by the British poet laureate John Masefield. Gilbert began
to tell the tale of a working-class widow and her son living in the
English midlands; the boy was devoted to his mother, but he fell into the

hands of a prostitute who took his virginity. The boy killed the woman's lover and was sent to the gallows.

Mayer didn't like the idea. Grimacing, with that cold glare that could cast terror into the stoniest human being, he snapped, "A nice boy falling in love with a whore? What kind of movie would that make?"

Gilbert cited several classics, including two that Mayer would later make as films: *Anna Christie* by Eugene O'Neill, and Alexandre Dumas's *Camille*. Both had been made, with some success, previously. Mayer shouted, "Only you, you bastard, would allow a whore to enter a story about a beloved mother and her young boy!" Gilbert replied, "What's wrong with that? My mother was a whore!" Mayer screamed, "You should have your balls cut off for making such a remark!" Then he leaped up and struck Gilbert on the jaw. Gilbert got to his feet and said, "Even with no balls I'd be a better man than you!" Mayer flew at him, but Mannix, the former bouncer, wrestled Mayer into submission. Red-faced, Mayer flailed his arms about, shouting, "He's a bad apple! I hate the bastard . . . He doesn't love his mother!" Few who saw it would ever forget the intensity of Mayer's rage. Yet a dollar was a dollar, and he rushed Gilbert into a new King Vidor picture, *Bardelys the Magnificent,* while Antonio Moreno was cast with Garbo in *The Temptress*.

Mayer left for New York City on April 16, with Daver Gershon, Metro-Goldwyn district manager, and Mayer's favorite, the publicist Pete Smith. They played pinochle all the way to New York, where the second annual M.G.M. convention was held at the Hotel Pennsylvania. It was even more successful than the first, with much discussion of the fact that *The Merry Widow*, for all of the problems with von Stroheim, had run for seven months at the Embassy Theater in New York, and that *Ben-Hur, The Big Parade, La Bohème* and Rex Ingram's *Mare Nostrum*, based on the story of Mata Hari, were all running on Broadway at top prices—two dollars—an unrivaled record in the industry.

In Mayer's absence, he was advised by Thalberg that *The Temptress* was in serious trouble. It is incredible that Dorothy Farnum's script had been passed for production, since it represented everything that Mayer disliked in movies. It was overt in its eroticism, and Stiller was insufficiently controlled by Thalberg. The story opens at an elaborate masked ball in Paris, at which a disconsolate Garbo, rejecting a wealthy banker's advances, runs into a crowd of merrymakers, several men lewdly embracing her. She is rescued by Antonio Moreno's Argentinean engineer, who makes her remove her flesh-tinted mask. Garbo's expression when the mask is removed was the most openly erotic ever seen in an American film. She actually looks aroused, and Stiller makes no secret of their coupling in a park, symbolized rather crudely by a shooting star, followed by figures of a columbine and harlequin, exhausted under the trees.

The heroine is shown married to a decadent French marquis, who, in his very first scene, enjoys the charms of a nubile chambermaid. At a dinner party, given by the rejected banker, the director explores under the table, showing the guests shedding their shoes, feet caressing feet in a daring parallel of sexual intercourse. At the height of the occasion, the host, announcing that the girl has ruined him, pours arsenic into his wine and drinks it in front of the horrified guests, the wine glass exploding in his hand and cutting it to pieces, the blood dripping in front of the spectators as he falls dead.

In another sequence, two half-naked men, muscles gleaming in the light, lash each other to a bloody pulp with whips. It is fortunate that Mayer was absent during the rushes, which must have reduced even the sophisticated Thalberg to desperation. Stiller was fired on the grounds that he was too slow. On May 3, 1926, Fred Niblo took over, but amazingly these audacious sequences were retained. The same day Stiller left M.G.M. in despair, and Garbo had to brace herself to cooperate with Niblo, Mayer was greeted by a standing ovation at a salesmen's banquet at the Hotel Pennsylvania ballroom, following a two-hour speech of impassioned eloquence ("He got right to the boys and they admitted it," *Variety* said).

An addendum of that season was Howard Strickling, who came in as publicist Pete Smith's assistant. Smooth, secretive, infinitely capable, he would remain for a lifetime the guardian of M.G.M.'s status, the preserver of standards and Mayer's intimate friend.

Strickling was almost twenty-nine years old at the time. Like so many of Mayer's best friends, he was a Southerner, born in St. Mary's, West Virginia, on August 25, 1897. His parents, who were in the grocery and poultry business, had moved when he was a boy to the Gardena and Ontario districts of Los Angeles County. He began his life as a newspaper sportswriter, then became an office boy at the Metro Company in 1919, moving over to the Goldwyn operation in the mid-1920s. After the merger of the studios in 1924, he traveled to Nice to work for Rex Ingram at the Victorine Studios, returning to join Mayer, no doubt with many stories of Ingram's hatred.

Tall and ruggedly built, with a deeply secretive face, Strickling was essentially a country man, with a country man's quietness, discipline and calmness. Away from the studio, his main interests were gardening in his yard, raising chickens and turkeys and helping his parents out, a fact which instantly endeared him to Mayer. In 1934, Strickling would take

over as head of publicity, when Pete Smith became head of the production of short featurettes.

Back in Hollywood in June, following a successful visit to Washington, D.C., where the secretary of the navy received him at a luncheon at
the Hotel Mayflower and thanked him for making *The Midshipman*,
Mayer had to face up to the final showing of *The Temptress*. Perhaps he,
who never had a strong sense of irony, noted the fact that the picture
concerned the very kind of whore he had objected to in the *Widow in the
Bye Street* project. A further irony was that he had no alternative but to
cast Gilbert with Garbo in a picture to start production immediately,
*Flesh and the Devil*. Thalberg and the director Clarence Brown had convinced him that the combination of the two performers would be box
office dynamite, but none of them could possibly have guessed what
would eventuate: the love affair of the decade.

The two stars first met at rehearsals, she responding to Gilbert's greeting of "Hello, Greta," with an icy, "My name is Miss Garbo." Gilbert
was furious, since he was by far the bigger star, earning $10,000 a week
against her $1,000, but there was something about her that fascinated
him. When Clarence Brown introduced them properly, they were
strongly attracted: within a night or two they were in bed.

Whatever misgivings Mayer may have had over this situation, he was
never less than shrewd and he must have realized how this passionate
relationship would enhance the intensity of the production. Pete Smith
was ordered to publicize the affair to the limit. Garbo resisted strongly,
but her efforts were useless, and Gilbert hugely enjoyed the nonsensical
campaign that M.G.M. embarked upon.

The fans climbed trees and ladders to peer through the windows of the
Gilbert house on Tower Road, high up in Beverly Hills, to try to see the
massive eight-foot African mahogany bed Gilbert had bought or stolen
from the set of *Monte Cristo*, where the glamorous couple spent their
perfumed nights. The fans listened enthralled as symphonic music
floated through the grounds from Hollywood's most expensive public
address system, and they sought in vain to discover the couple stretched
naked by the pool.

Garbo daringly moved into the house in mid-production, and the
studio did not discourage her; anyone who thought that M.G.M. was
puritanical would have to think again by August 1926. Garbo's guest
room was a conceit of Gilbert's: it was a copy of Cedric Gibbons's set, in
*The Merry Widow*, of a bedroom in the form of a monk's cell, the bed
narrow and unaccommodating, accompanied by an ebony crucifix hanging on the wall and a small altar with prayer books. It is doubtful
whether Garbo spent much time in it until the decorator Harold Grieve

converted it into a lady's bedroom of the time of Louis XVI, as suffocatingly rich as any room in an expensive bordello, a riot of white, gold and blue.

On the set, Garbo and her lover made no secret of their affair, and Clarence Brown encouraged passionate kissing, some of it open-mouthed, in *Flesh and the Devil*, which defied every principle of the heavily censored American film. They could hardly keep their hands off each other, even in the sequences that didn't call for caresses. To enhance one romantic moment, the cinematographer William Daniels put a tiny bulb in Gilbert's hand, controlled by a rheostat, which glowingly lit up Garbo's face as Gilbert put a match to her cigarette. When he put one cigarette in his mouth and then placed it in hers, the phallic parallel was all too obvious.

Like *The Temptress, Flesh and the Devil* was a revolutionary effort and turned out to be a major sensation. Even Mayer was forced to admit that Gilbert was unrivaled as a romantic leading man in the picture. But there was a tragic underpinning to this glamorous real-life tale of stars in love. It turned out that Garbo had to have no less than eight abortions; the studio was on its mettle constantly to conceal these.

In those days of insufficient contraception, it became necessary for the studio to retain an abortionist, sharing the substantial costs with other studios, and a constant stream of female stars went in and out of the clinic for the next two or three decades. In addition, according to Gilbert's daughter, Leatrice Gilbert Junior, a brothel was maintained for visiting salesmen at a remote canyon location. One visitor there noticed Irving Thalberg, no doubt protective of his health, sitting in the lobby reading a newspaper.

Another controversy had blown up at the end of May, when Eugene V. Brewster, publisher of *Motion Picture* magazine, *Motion Picture Classic* and *Movie Monthly*, allegedly made a deal with M.G.M. in which a girlfriend of his would be given a Metro contract in return for his turning over his publications to support of the studio, and a promise that not a single M.G.M. movie would ever be panned by him. *Variety* published a letter by Brewster, dated April 15, 1926, confirming the arrangement. As a result, the deal was canceled, with embarrassment on all sides. Mayer and Thalberg came to the edge of disgrace over this; Pete Smith somehow managed to shield them from widespread accusations of bribery.

There was also yet another argument involving Lillian Gish, who demanded that Norman Kerry should act opposite her in her new film, *Annie Laurie*. Mayer wanted an unknown youth called Peter Norris, just out of the University of Southern California, to play the role. Miss Gish was adamant that she would accept no one but Kerry, and she complained about the script, despite the fact that she herself had approved it. Finally, she won her point, and Kerry was cast. But the film was a failure, and she would never discuss it afterward. More successful was Joan Crawford's first major vehicle, *The Taxi Dancer*, in which she played a ten-cents-a-dance girl, in a whirligig of cocktails, seductions and separations. With her huge eyes, big gash of a mouth and sturdy shoulders, the tiny Miss Crawford made a strong impression. She herself scarcely represented Mayer's ideal of womanhood: it was claimed she had appeared in soft-porn pictures as a girl, and that she had risen in her career up a ladder of beds. He disbelieved such stories, building her carefully to what he was convinced would be major stardom.

Through the year, he continued to be locked in lawsuits. He was forced to issue a summons on July 16 to Hugh C. Pritchard, who had bought 1834 North Kenmore from him, because Pritchard had failed to keep up payments on the house. The result of the protracted and unpleasant lawsuit was that Pritchard, who had moved to Des Moines, Iowa, had to surrender the house to the Mayers on September 26, 1926, following Loeb, Walker and Loeb's move to foreclose.

Garbo presented the usual number of headaches during the making of *Flesh and the Devil*. On August 4, 1926, Mayer was compelled to send her a note at her hotel, the Miramar in Santa Monica, calling on her to report at 4:30 P.M. that afternoon at Irving Thalberg's office to receive instructions. Should she miss the note, she was to report at ten o'clock the following morning. If she failed to comply with the demand, particularly in view of the attitude displayed by her hitherto and her general insubordination, she would be held in breach of contract. Any and all action would be taken to protect the company's interests. Mayer continued, charging her with repeating certain scenes (in terms of her interpretation) and insisting on being dressed in a manner he had not authorized. She was told she must play the part as instructed and accept clothes assigned to her or she would be stripped of her salary.

The following day, she sent her secretary, who told Thalberg that Miss Garbo was too ill to respond. This was, of course, nonsense, and he stopped her pay. Eight days later, he dismissed her. She did return finally, but again was an absentee.

Mayer was busy that week attending the ceremonial opening of Marion Davies's new, $25,000 bungalow, a fourteen-room two-story house built in the Spanish style under the supervision of Cedric Gibbons. It was built in three sections, so that it could be moved anywhere. Lavishly furnished, it was moved years later to Warner Brothers, then in part to Beverly Hills, becoming the home of the actress, singer and dancer Ann Miller.

On September 8, Garbo again proved to be a major irritation. That day had been fixed for a double marriage: King Vidor was to marry the enchanting actress Eleanor Boardman and John Gilbert would marry Garbo at the same time. The location of the wedding was Marion Davies's home in Beverly Hills. The guests arrived, led by Mayer, Irving Thalberg, Hunt Stromberg, Harry Rapf and Eddie Mannix, and their wives. Mayer's decision to attend the hated Gilbert's nuptials was clearly due to the fact that he saw the public relations opportunities, and, in fact, he posed, placed modestly at the lower right side of an extraordinary group, for the studio and press cameras.

After some delay, the justice of the peace arrived. There was no sign of Garbo. Gilbert paced up and down, becoming more and more hysterical. King Vidor and Miss Boardman tried to stall, placing phone calls and ordering more photographs. But everyone was becoming extremely restless, and the JP had another appointment. Gilbert's face went dark. Garbo had stood him up two years before, fleeing down the steps of City Hall just as they were about to be wed.

Mayer lost patience. Forgetting his usual rule about bad language in the presence of women, he gripped Gilbert by the shoulder and glared at him, saying, "Why do you have to wait to marry her? Why don't you just go on fucking her and forget about the wedding?"

John Gilbert snapped. He seized Mayer by the neck and tried to strangle him. Before anyone could stop him, he hurled Mayer into the marble bathroom. Mayer's glasses fell to the floor and broke. Eddie Mannix ran in and dragged Gilbert loose. He threw Gilbert into the living room. Mayer could still feel the imprint of Gilbert's fingers on his throat. A few moments later, he would have been dead. He managed to climb to his feet. He screamed, "You're through! I'll destroy you if it costs me one million dollars!" Gilbert lashed back. "It will cost you a million— millions!" he yelled. "I just signed a new contract with Nicholas Schenck!" It took the combined efforts of Mannix, Rapf and Stromberg to control Mayer at that moment. His loathing of Schenck had deepened; Schenck's increasing power over Marcus Loew grated on him. The statement was true. Gilbert did have a new contract, signed over Mayer's head, guaranteeing him a million for his next three pictures.

Somehow, the photographers and all other bystanders were either talked or bribed into not releasing the story. Thalberg told Gilbert, "Just keep your nose clean and Louis can't touch you." Mayer correctly saw this as a form of betrayal. Incredibly, Garbo continued to live at the

Gilbert house, but was confined to the guest room and the kitchen. Gilbert was disgusted with her, and it was several months before they returned to their physical affair.

The episode was typical, as Mayer had learned from her intransigent behavior during her picture making, of Garbo's skittish, self-centered and cruel nature. For all of her magic on the screen, she remained opaque, unsympathetic and unfeeling in private. All she needed to have done was to have told Gilbert that she could never commit herself to any man; that would have made her point without damaging permanently Gilbert's fragile ego. Much as Mayer hated Gilbert, we can see from Mayer's memoranda to Garbo that he hated her equally or even more. And it was a supreme irony that he would soon be basking in public acclaim when *Flesh and the Devil* broke records all over the world, and that Gilbert went straight into another picture, *The Show*, directed by Tod Browning, which Gilbert had very much wanted to make. It had been scheduled before *Flesh and the Devil*.

In October, Mayer was preoccupied with attending, as honorary member and patron, the International Convention of Fire Chiefs in New Orleans. Twenty-five percent of the profits of *The Fire Brigade* would be given to the Fire Chiefs' Association. Mayer arranged for the renting of an entire train known as the Louis B. Mayer Special, decorated with banners; he entertained aboard fire chiefs and delegates and their families from all of California and Washington State. Mayer could not persuade Secretary of Commerce Herbert Hoover to break his political tour itinerary, switching from Louisville to New Orleans to attend the celebrations. He telegraphed Hoover on October 16, begging him to respond to him aboard the Sunset Limited, and obsessively giving the time of every station stop from El Paso to Houston. But Hoover could not attend.

A further annoyance was that Universal did, in fact, battle with him in New Orleans, stealing some of his thunder and relentlessly pushing the outdated and worthless *The Still Alarm*. It would be reasonable to deduce that he came back to Los Angeles crowned with the laurels of the fire chiefs but not in the very best of tempers.

There was more trouble with Garbo on November 4. She was supposed to appear in a film entitled *Diamond Handcuffs*, later renamed *Women Love Diamonds*, in which she would appear with Douglas Fairbanks, Jr. It was the story of a girl who discovers she is an illegitimate child. It was a tactless suggestion that she should make the movie: Garbo had fears of her own illegitimacy, she hated children and her successive abortions showed her horror of bearing a child out of wedlock.

She behaved with her usual skittishness. Instead of saying that she emphatically would not make the film, going to Mayer as a father figure and explaining her very personal reasons, she agreed to make it and then failed to report to wardrobe at 2 P.M. on November 4. She again failed to report at ten o'clock the next morning. She was told that unless she reported to work immediately she would be dismissed; that there were no film vehicles suitable for her now, and that she would be left idle because of her attitude and disobedience. She then demanded $5,000 a week, $4,000 more than she was getting, to return to the studio. Mayer angrily refused. He tried to loan her out to several other studios, but no one would have her. The fight continued for weeks, and Pauline Starke took over in *Women Love Diamonds*. In the midst of this, Mayer was horrified to learn that Gilbert had suggested Garbo's salary increase. Mayer was so distraught that he would literally shake with anger at dinner with his family at night. On one occasion, he snarled at his wife and daughters, "The son of a bitch is inciting that damned Swede and it's going to cost us a fortune." He decided to have Garbo deported. She announced, defiantly, that she would now marry Gilbert and Mayer would no longer be able to toss her out of the country because she would be an American.

Yet, in the last analysis, money meant everything, and Mayer could not deny the overwhelming box office response to *Flesh and the Devil*. There was no alternative: he had to make peace with Gilbert. When Marcus Loew visited the studio on November 15, he was informed by the watchman that Mr. Gilbert had ordered two people off the set already that day and that he would not agree to Loew bringing in his personal friends from New York. Even Loew, *el supremo*, had to yield: *The Big Parade* had just passed $1 million in profits after its first year at the Astor in New York. This was a record.

On December 20, Garbo made peace with Mayer and was offered and accepted a new contract, to be concluded on January 1, 1927, which would call for $2,500 a week for one year, $4,000 for the following year, $5,000 for the year after that, and $6,000 for 1931 to 1932. She would appear in a film entitled *Love*, based on Tolstoy's *Anna Karenina*, a name that was felt to be too difficult for most Americans to pronounce.

On Christmas Eve, following the traditional studio party, almost everybody left, leaving Norma Shearer behind. She had been visiting the powder room and didn't hear the honking of the last automobile to depart. She was in her dressing room, about to call a taxi, when her phone rang. It was Irving Thalberg on the line. He wished her the best of the season. This was very unusual for him, and she was intrigued.

A few days later, his secretary called and asked if she would accompany him to a premiere at Grauman's Egyptian Theater. Again, this was unheard of: for the head of the studio to invite any star would spark gossip. But she agreed. Picked up from her home by chauffeured car, she was taken to Thalberg's house. From there they went, not to the premiere but to the Cocoanut Grove, where they danced the hours away. In the morning, Miss Shearer recalled, a bouquet of roses arrived at her door, dozens of them, and on a small ivory card were inscribed the words: YES SIR! She knew it was from Thalberg: "Yes Sir, That's My Baby" had been their frequent request from the Cocoanut Grove band the previous night. Captivated, she agreed to date Thalberg regularly, and their romance was the talk of the town. But, according to the custom of the day, Miss Shearer's mother accompanied them everywhere as a chaperone. Very correct, despite her fling with Victor Fleming, Miss Shearer was uneasy concerning any adverse comments concerning her throwing herself at the boss.

Both she and Thalberg were present at a New Year's Eve party at Mayer's beach house at the end of 1926. One of the guests was David O. Selznick, an up-and-coming young executive at M.G.M. whose father, Lewis J. Selznick, it will be recalled, had been in severe conflict with Mayer in the early years in Boston. Selznick was high-powered, his apparent lack of sex appeal—he had a rather plain, toothily grinning face and an out-of-shape figure—compensated for by his brilliance and charisma. Harry Rapf, for whom Selznick was working, was undoubtedly trying to advance his own position by encouraging a match with a Mayer daughter. Edith said later, "I got one look at that zebra, and I said to Irene, 'You can have him.'" Irene wasn't interested either, but that would soon change.

Others at the party, the first such lavish event Mayer held, were his nephew Jack Cummings, who was doing well at the studio as an assistant; Ruth, Jack's sister, who was emerging as an excellent title writer, most recently on *La Bohème*, and Mitzi, Jack's other sister, who would soon become a magazine writer; along with their imposing mother, Ida. Rudolph Mayer was still in Montreal, making and losing fortunes; Jerry was still in the doghouse. Yetta, Louis's elder sister, also remained in Montreal, running her dry goods store and raising her brood of five; her eldest sons were going successfully into law and politics. Jacob Mayer was as energetic as ever, though nearing eighty, an antic, high-strung presence always.

Another guest at the party was Motley H. Flint, a powerful banker who had played a crucial role in the financing and development of Warner Brothers. An intimate of Mayer's friend and land partner Joe Schenck, Flint had recently, and unfortunately, become close to Mayer. Flint was associated with C. C. Young, newly elected governor of California, as a partner in the Julian Petroleum Corporation, which was, at the time, involved in the illegal issuing of some five million shares of spurious stock and was forming stock pools, bunches of shares taken off the normal market and traded in by individuals in order to increase their value in the eyes of the public. With uncustomary indiscretion, Mayer entered the Motley Flint pools in September, the agreement signed for joint ownership by corporations of questionable value. Members of the first Motley Flint pool, designed to run for forty-five days, earned nineteen percent on their investment; their number included the respectable Judge W. R. Hervey and such prominent figures of the Los Angeles business world as Joe Toplitzky, Alvin H. Frank, Albert Lane and Benjamin Platt. The second pool, equally well backed, also included Mayer, as did a third, in which his own lawyer, Mendel Silberberg, later to become a Hoover Committee man, was dominant. Yet another in the pool was Harry M. Haldeman, head of the Better American Federation of Los Angeles and grandfather of the prominent figure in the Watergate affair. Mayer finally owned 1,075 shares, valued at approximately $50,000.

For Mayer to become part of a group that was overissuing stock seems incredible in view of his normal caution, but possibly the temptation of quick money (though he had millions already) proved impossible to resist. His supporters feel that he was duped into the arrangement, though this seems unlikely in view of his shrewdness and grasp of financial affairs. At all events, this unwise move would plunge him into severe difficulties in the year to come.

CHAPTER ELEVEN

# 1927-1928

THE MAJOR CHALLENGE of the new year for Mayer was to find vehicles for Garbo and Gilbert that would ensure immediate results at the box office. Mayer's threat to destroy Gilbert's career could only seem hollow in view of the fact that he remained by far the most commercial male star in the business. Thalberg cast Gilbert opposite Joan Crawford in *Twelve Miles Out*, a story about bootlegging. The picture was quite successful.

There were always problems. Director Monta Bell charged Mayer with restraining him from working, following a quarrel over a circus picture he was supposed to have made. Mayer was involved in litigation with Mr. and Mrs. J. Gamble Carson, to whom he had loaned, through a third party, Alvin Asher, $65,000 against a promissory note, including mortgage on a large property near his house in Santa Monica. He would only succeed in seizing the property in late 1928.

He had one distraction. At a meeting at his beach house in January, he, with a group that included Fred Niblo, Conrad Nagel and another close friend, Fred W. Beetson, decided to form an Academy of Motion Picture Arts and Sciences, made up of 275 leading figures of the business, who would pay a $100 initiation fee each. Douglas Fairbanks would be president; each member would be able to vote for another member to receive an award, the nature of which would not be determined for some time, for his achievements. At least initially, the awards would be restricted to those in the category of director, leading player (male and female) and, perhaps, cameraman and art director. Mayer became obsessed with this new idea.

On February 26, Garbo failed to appear for work on the film *Love*; her salary was once more cut off. She was absent for over a week, and then wrote to Mayer saying she had not been instructed to appear at M.G.M. She took off with Gilbert to Santa Ana, promising to marry him there, but at the altar she changed her mind and turned him down. She drove off in the white Rolls Royce Gilbert had given her and refused to return it. Furiously, Mayer responded that she had deliberately delayed mailing her letter and told her to report on March 6 to Thalberg. Correspondence between Mayer and Garbo shows that she had never in fact signed her new four-year contract and that she would not sign it. She informed Mayer and M.G.M. lawyer J. Robert Rubin in New York, by telegram and letter, that the contract called for three roles a year, which would cause her to have a nervous breakdown; she had been promised that she would not have to work excessively, and that M.G.M. completely failed to understand her or consider her in any way. She continued to be absent from the picture, until it became obvious that it could not be continued. Furthermore, the rushes were appalling, and Mayer threw up his hands and canceled the film. He was faced with the choice of scrapping everything and starting again, letting the movie go, and sacking Garbo before she could marry Gilbert, or trying to set it up again with a new director and male star. He settled on the latter, further evidence that practical considerations overruled his personal feelings. He chose Edmund Goulding, a close British-born friend of Garbo's, to take over the direction, burned the existing footage and, with amazing self-control, appointed Gilbert in place of Ricardo Cortez as Garbo's costar. He supplied the best cameraman available, Garbo's favorite, William Daniels, and ordered Cedric Gibbons to build even more lavish sets.

On May 11, 1927, Mayer headed up five hundred figures of the film industry at a banquet at the Biltmore Hotel in downtown Los Angeles to announce the granting of a state charter for the Academy of Motion Picture Arts and Sciences. Mayer's speech was inspirational, impassioned and lengthy; all of his extraordinary eloquence, aided, no doubt, by the writing skills of Pete Smith, poured out in an address that had the audience on its feet applauding. Troubled as he was, tortured by daily problems with his impossible stars, Mayer remained as deeply in love with motion pictures as ever, and there were few in that room who failed to respond to his enthusiasm.

On June 3, work was again suspended on *Love*, because of Garbo's misbehavior. Garbo, Stiller and Dr. and Mrs. Gustav Bjorkman, close friends, were at dinner with Einar Hanson and Hanson's new roommate. Apparently, a quarrel took place, no doubt based on the fractured relationship between Stiller and his separated companion. After the guests left, Hanson, visibly disturbed, flew out of the door and jumped into his car. Accompanied by his dog, an Airedale, he drove recklessly along the Coast Highway. Drunk, he crossed the yellow dividing line and, swerving to avoid a head-on collision with an approaching vehicle, spun off the road and struck a sand layer. His car somersaulted twice, landing upside-down on the beach, pinning him underneath. The dog's frantic barking summoned three passersby, who found him already dying. His chest was crushed. Driven to the Martin Sanitarium, he died four hours later. He was only twenty-nine. This was another shattering blow for Garbo, who adored him, and Stiller, who never recovered.

Mayer was further embroiled in financial affairs. Discovering that the Julian Petroleum Company, whose improper stock pool he had joined, needed funds, he had committed the further error of lending it some $35,000, along with several of his business acquaintances, allegedly to bail it out of potential bankruptcy. But in fact he had loaned the money at an interest rate of more than twelve percent.

On June 27, he was charged by District Attorney Asa Keyes with conspiracy to violate the usury law, a felony. A warrant was issued for his arrest, calling him to answer the indictment and to be delivered into the custody of the sheriff to the magistrate's office, where he would be required to provide the sum of $10,000 in bail. The arrest order was issued based on his hearing before the grand jury.

He appeared and paid the bail; the trial would be in September. Now John Gilbert wound up in prison. Following a two-day break that came after Einar Hanson's death, he drove to Garbo's hotel in Santa Monica and, when she declined to see him, climbed up a drainpipe to her window. Mauritz Stiller told him to leave, as he was upsetting the star. Stiller threw him from the second-floor balcony onto the lawn. Gilbert wasn't injured, but screamed, "The son of a bitch tried to kill me!" He was jailed for drunkenness and breaking and entering. Mayer had him released. Gilbert soon after found that he had a flaring appendix, but refused to have it operated on and came on the set holding an ice bag to his abdomen. The insanity continued for several days, until at last he consented to an appendectomy and *Love* closed down for another three weeks while he went into surgery and recovered.

In spite of everything, *Love* was an acceptable modern dress version of Tolstoy and was incandescent with the passion of its leading players. Goulding had allowed Gilbert to supervise the direction of some of the scenes of youthful desire, which were among the most inflammatory ever seen on the screen. The eroticism of the movie astonished everyone who saw it. Mayer's state of mind as he watched the rushes can only be imagined. His detestation of Garbo and Gilbert must have been mingled with a sense that the picture would be another sensation; and every day there was the thought that he might soon face ruin and even jail in the Julian Petroleum affair, no matter how carefully the matter was soft-pedaled. And soft-pedaled it was, his name buried in the back columns of tiny print—and not only by the Hearst newspapers.

The evenings at his house at Ocean Front, Santa Monica, were often stressful. There was the constant fretting of a Victorian father over his children's future romantic plans. Unable to bring himself to discuss what would be required of them on their wedding nights, he had given them Havelock Ellis's heavy volumes on human sexuality, which they found virtually unreadable.

Mayer presided over the highly fraught dinners, restlessly going over the merits of the ideal males whom he envisaged as his daughters' partners. These paragons would be handsome, clean-cut, athletic, college educated, preferably in the movie business, medicine or law, and would (a touch of the improbable) be virgins. The girls had daydreams of their own: Edie's fantasy man was a painter, a composer or a sculptor, and would be pale, blond and slender, an artist to his fingertips; Irene had a more realistic objective: her man would be a former football player, stocky, stolid, stalwart, with a good job and prospects of inherited money. Mayer insisted that he look over any males his girls would want to date; above all, he decided that neither daughter should date either of Lewis Selznick's boys, David and Myron. The hated Selznick of Boston days had now lost his fortune, much of it squandered on his mistress, Clara Kimball Young, the motion picture star. His family had been forced to leave their lavish, fourteen-room apartment in New York and settle in a humble two-roomer.

Irene, Edie recalled later, was exasperated by her father's controlling attitude and deliberately set about pursuing David O. Selznick—far from her dream beau. With her customary acute instinct, she saw that he had a future: she was impressed by his wit, command of anecdotes, inventive mind and force of character; his lack of physical beauty meant nothing to her.

Mayer was not only quarreling with his daughters (and with Margaret, who took Irene's side in the Selznick matter), he was also at loggerheads with William Randolph Hearst. Hearst wanted the humorist George Ade to adapt his own Broadway hit of 1907, "The Varsity Girl," as Marion Davies's next picture. Mayer was opposed to this, and was furious that Thalberg joined with Hearst in opposing him, and finally overruling him. But Mayer managed to install his own director: Sam Wood instead of Sidney Franklin.

Mayer was also not comfortable with King Vidor's The Crowd, a harshly realistic story of a young couple struggling in a big city. As so often before, the project had been pushed through without Mayer's approval and involved a complex conspiracy between Vidor, the producer

Sarah Mayer, circa 1890.
(*Courtesy of Irene Mayer Holt*)

Jacob Mayer, circa 1890.
(*Courtesy of Irene Mayer Holt*)

Sarah Mayer with her brood, circa 1890. *(Courtesy of Mrs. Sol Fielding)*

Louis B. Mayer, on the occasion of his bar mitzvah, age thirteen, April, 1898. (*Jewish Historical Society of St. John*)

Young Mayer. (*Courtesy of Irene Mayer Holt*)

First site of Louis B. Mayer Productions at 3800 Mission Road in North Los Angeles, circa 1920. (*Marc Wanamaker: The Bison Archives*)

Mayer (left) with Anita Stewart, one of the most popular motion picture stars of the 1920s, and director Mickey Neilan, on location for *Her Kingdom of Dreams*, 1919. (*Marc Wanamaker: The Bison Archives*)

Mayer (in boater) and Joe Engel at the Mission Road studios, circa 1920. (*Marc Wanamaker: The Bison Archives*)

The Mayer daughters: Edith (left) and Irene in the early 1920s. (*Marc Wanamaker: The Bison Archives*)

Margaret Mayer, 1922. (*Marc Wanamaker: The Bison Archives*)

Margaret with her daughters: Irene (left) and Edith, 1922. (*Marc Wanamaker: The Bison Archives*)

Irene Mayer in the garden of the house on North Kenmore, 1924. (*Marc Wanamaker: The Bison Archives*)

Jacob Mayer with the Talmud, 1924. (*Marc Wanamaker: The Bison Archives*)

Mayer, 1924. (*Marc Wanamaker: The Bison Archives*)

Mayer with Secretary of Commerce Herbert Hoover on a tour of the studios, August 1924. (*Marc Wanamaker: The Bison Archives*)

Mayer family and associates on the Rome set of *Ben Hur*, 1924; from left: Irene, Margaret, unknown man, Fred Niblo, Carey Wilson, Mayer, Edith, Bess Meredyth. (*Marc Wanamaker: The Bison Archives*)

Mayer and Irving Thalberg welcoming Lillian Gish, April 1925. (*Marc Wanamaker: The Bison Archives*)

Edith Mayer, circa 1925, at the time her
father cut short her performing ambitions.
*(Marc Wanamaker: The Bison Archives)*

Mayer at M.G.M., circa 1925. *(Marc Wanamaker: The Bison Archives)*

Hunt Stromberg, Thalberg and Nicholas Schenck. Throughout much of the summer, Vidor was shooting the picture, costarring a former extra named James Murray and Vidor's wife, Eleanor Boardman, on the top of the New York Telephone Building, in Battery Park, on the South Ferry, on the elevated railroad, on a Staten Island steamer, in Times Square and on Broadway, in Trinity Church yard, and on bridges in Buffalo, near Niagara Falls and Pittsburgh. Mayer disliked the rushes, and Thalberg set about cutting scene after scene, much to the director's fury; Thalberg even deferred a delayed European trip again and again to complete the work.

Mayer was determined that David O. Selznick would be booted out of M.G.M., which he had joined on October 4, 1926, as a reader. Selznick had been promoted to manager of the writers' department and associate producer of two pictures. He was the protégé of Harry Rapf, initiating a long career of writing memoranda, peppering even Mayer with detailed notes. Mayer's annoyance could scarcely be calculated.

And in that week, Mayer was faced with the unpleasant prospect of his rearraignment two days later. In a last-minute move to stave off disaster, he induced his friend Asa Keyes, the district attorney, to let him pay back $53,709.05 to the court, earned from his usurious loans to Julian. He was again driven downtown by the sheriff on June 14 and compelled to appear before Judge Stephens, along with his disgraced colleague, Motley Flint, and ten others.

As he stood with the alleged coconspirators in the somber, brown-painted Hall of Justice, he was again informed that he would be required to go before the judge for arraignment in September. He returned to continue his day's work.

In that same week, in a move that even Mayer may not have suspected, Irving Thalberg made the decision to marry Norma Shearer. Despite wooing Miss Shearer with evenings out, dancing, champagne, diamonds and furs, Thalberg seemed to regard the match as a corporate merger. Disappointed because he was unable to consummate his long and obsessive interest in Constance Talmadge, he apparently felt that the time had come to satisfy Norma Shearer's desires. There is no doubt that Miss Shearer, despite her dalliances with Victor Fleming and Monta Bell, had Thalberg as her target from the beginning. Marrying the boss would put her firmly at the top of the Hollywood heap, not to mention the fact that she would soon be elevated in terms of her own income.[1] There was nothing romantic about the couple's decision to marry. Thalberg summoned her to his office and took out a tray of engagement

[1] Thalberg had Marcus Loew pay her a salary of $10,000 a week as a wedding present.

rings. She selected the most expensive one. The wedding date was set for September 29, six days after Mayer was due in court again.

Mayer cannot have been consoled by the fact that the Julian scandal escalated that July. Hundreds of shareholders, duped by the artificial manipulation of stock values by the members of the Motley Flint pool, were wiped out; the director Andrew Stone recalls that his father was paid off with a check for a million dollars that could never be cashed.

Mayer was busy again, wheeling and dealing in land; with Irving Thalberg, Harry Rapf, Joe Schenck, Douglas Fairbanks and Mary Pickford, and the recently appointed M.G.M. producers Bernard Hyman and John W. Considine, he bought and sold tracts at Playa del Rey, on the Pacific Ocean, south of Santa Monica. Simultaneously, he, Joe Schenck and Motley Flint joined hands to assist in the preliminary stages of Herbert Hoover's 1928 nomination for president.

Mayer had other concerns. There were setbacks during the shooting of Victor Sjöström's *The Wind* in 120 degrees of heat in the Mojave Desert. Mayer was unable to visit the site; he sent Irving Thalberg in his place. Playing a pioneer woman, the star, Lillian Gish, was shown with the force of nine airplane propellers driving sand in her face and hair; Thalberg cruelly added sawdust. He insisted on smoke pots, the cinders of which burned off Miss Gish's eyelashes and scarred her hands. Herself a perfectionist, the actress put up with everything.

Mayer did not like the movie when he saw the daily rushes, predicting doom for it and for the star. He turned out to be correct commercially, because the movie was too depressing, but he was shortsighted artistically, because *The Wind* turned out to be one of the masterpieces of the screen.

Mayer presided over an occasion at the studio on July 28. Nicholas Longworth, Speaker of the U.S. House of Representatives, who was staying with Mayer at the beach house, joined him for a luncheon at Culver City. Virtually every director on the lot was present, along with Hearst, Eddie Mannix, Hunt Stromberg, Harry Rapf, Marion Davies and the actress Sally O'Neill. Marion Davies's favorite musicians, used to move her to tears or laughter on the set, provided Strauss waltzes.

The pressure at the studio was constant. Mayer set up a newsreel unit; he opened thirty radio stations in a special circuit similar to the recently established CBS; he was exasperated by the rushes of *Rose Marie*, based on the operetta by Rudolph Friml, after two weeks of locations in the Rockies, and by the fact that the director, William Nigh, was charged with assault after beating up a man in a bar. He fired Nigh, hired Edmund Goulding, rejected Goulding's version, replaced Renée Adorée with Joan Crawford and assigned Lucien Hubbard to write and direct.

He took off to New York for three weeks in August, there to be assuaged by Marcus Loew with a contract that would bring him $800,000 a year, the highest salary paid to anyone in the film industry and the equivalent of some $16 million a year in 1991.

At the time, Mayer had authorized and pushed through *The Callahans and the Murphys*, starring Marie Dressler, directed by the brilliant George Hill, one of Mayer's favorites, and written by Hill's wife, Frances Marion. Somehow, despite his honorary position with the Hibernians, he had not taken note of the fact that this tale of feuding slum families portrayed the Irish-immigrant population of New York City as violent, brutal and uncivilized. When the picture opened at the Lexington Theater in Manhattan, the largely Hibernian audience screamed with rage and beat and tore at the screen with their bare hands. Police were called in, aiming hoses at the crowd and ruining many of the seats. Not even Hearst could protect Mayer as the Irish-controlled pressure groups called for Mayer's dismissal from the industry and the permanent blacklisting of M.G.M. Mayer and Loew were compelled to yield and have the movie withdrawn.

Mayer adored Marie Dressler; of all the performers at the studio, he liked her the best. Plain, in her late fifties, the former Canadian music hall artist and star of *Tillie's Punctured Romance* and other comedies was yet another of his mother figures, uncertain in health but possessed of great feistiness, good humor and charm. He was determined to build her as a motion picture star, seeing the warmth and strength within her that, he believed, the public would respond to. He was convinced that sexual attractiveness and physical beauty were not essential to stardom. This showed a good deal of maturity on his part. Like Lewis Stone and Lionel Barrymore, Miss Dressler became one of his very few actor friends, and he learned much from her earthy but morally elevated wisdom. She had her oddities: she seemed to think Mussolini was desirable, and fascism a good idea, but this was a fairly harmless example of political naiveté. He always gave her first billing; toward the end of her life, he would refer to her as "the equal in my life of my own mother," the ultimate compliment.

Back in Hollywood, Mayer was yet again bothered by John Gilbert, who had managed to incorporate elements of his rejected story, *The Widow in the Bye Street*, as part of Alice Duer Miller's script for *Man, Woman and Sin*. Thalberg had assisted Gilbert in the conspiracy, and Mayer felt compelled to watch, day after day, the hated tale being shot. Thalberg had insisted on casting the magnificent Jeanne Eagels, the great Broadway actress, as Gilbert's costar. Mayer objected because she was sleeping with Gilbert despite the fact that she was married to the sporting idol Ted Coy, and he was appalled to find that she was a heroin addict, her eyes so sensitive to sunlight that she could only work between nightfall and dawn. Her absences from the set were so frequent, her tantrums so extreme, her language so foul, that Mayer fired her just before shooting ended, using a double for her in several scenes.

Then came a severe blow. On September 5, 1927, the beloved Marcus Loew died of heart disease at his home at Glen Cove, Long Island. He had been ill for some time; he had had to be carried into board meetings in New York on a stretcher. Mayer burst into tears when he heard the news; he and Joe Schenck tried to charter a plane to fly them via Salt Lake City to the funeral, but weather conditions prohibited the trip.

Mayer announced that the studio would be closed for one day; all other studios would be shut down for ten minutes of silent prayer. Five thousand, five hundred mourners attended the solemn obsequies at Glen Cove. Mayer joined Rabbi Magnin and ministers of several denominations at the memorial service at M.G.M. Loew left $35 million, divided among his family. He had forgotten to name the thousands who depended on his private charity; no provision was made for them, and they were left destitute.

On September 15, 1927, Nicholas Schenck was appointed president of Loew's Inc. and M.G.M. for Marcus Loew's unexpired term of office. This was distressing for Mayer. He and Schenck still had little in common; Joe Schenck had many differences with his brother; and Mayer dreaded, with some foresight, years of difficulties ahead. In effect, Nicholas Schenck had been in charge during Marcus Loew's declining years, approving Thalberg projects again and again over Mayer's head, but now he would be unhampered by Loew's affection for Mayer. And Schenck would be watching, with the concentration of a vulture, Mayer's upcoming trial for usury.

In mid-September, Mayer and publicist Pete Smith launched a stunt to fly a live lion, symbolizing the M.G.M. trademark, from Culver City Airport to New York. The cage was made of glass. The plane was put together by the B. F. Mahoney Corporation of San Diego, which had built Charles Lindbergh's *Spirit of St. Louis*; the two aircraft were virtually identical. The lion would be taken from the plane at Roosevelt Field, New York, and paraded through the lobbies of the Loew's theaters accompanied by a beautiful blond trainer equipped with a golden chain.

The stunt backfired. The plane came down in bad weather in a crash landing in Arizona. Mayer urged his close friend Ida Koverman, Herbert Hoover's California campaign secretary, to do what she could. She arranged for forty U.S. Navy search planes to be commandeered at San Diego's North Island Naval Base. When no authority was received from the Department of the Navy for them to proceed, Hoover pulled a string. The extensive hunt made more headlines than the disappearance of the plane itself. There was talk of the lion getting loose, roaming about mountain communities and snapping up babies from their cradles, or terrorizing Boy Scouts and mountaineers; this was all worth about $1 million in free flackery. But at last, these stories were disproved, and Mayer cabled Hoover that both pilot and lion were found safe near Roosevelt Lake on Apache Ranch country, Arizona.

On September 20, Mayer joined with his executive staff, stars and directors at Marion Davies's celebratory breakfast for Charles Lindbergh at the studio. William Randolph Hearst was present as beautiful young girls, in scanty clothing, danced and joined in basketball on an improvised stage. Actors playing soldiers on the set of a new war picture formed an impromptu honor guard for America's hero.

Just two days afterward, Mayer was driven downtown to the Hall of Justice for final arraignment for trial before Judge Stephens. His appearance lasted only a few minutes. He had returned the $53,709.05 in alleged illegal gains, and District Attorney Asa Keyes called for the dismissal of the complaint. A statement made by the receivers of the Julian Petroleum Company was read in court. It stated, "Mr. Mayer's action in returning money he received on his loan has had a salutary and beneficial effect upon other persons involved in the same situation. The return of the money at that time was particularly advantageous for us because of the critical condition of our finances."

The judge, based on this note and the Keyes recommendation, dismissed the case against Mayer. He supported the district attorney's assertion that the papers signed by Mayer in connection with the transactions set out in the indictments showed that they had been prepared by Motley Flint and that Mayer had been duped. Judge Stephens confirmed that Mayer was induced to enter into the transactions by the same method that millions of shares of worthless stock were sold to the public. No mention was made of Mayer's membership in the Julian share pool.

Whatever the truth, whether he was guilty or innocent, Mayer could not have been sent for trial based on the evidence available. He issued a statement to the press:

Naturally, I am very happy over the dismissal of the charge against me. Personally, I never had any doubt as to the outcome. I am told that the dismissal is based upon a thorough investigation by the District Attorney and concurred in by the court in which my complete innocence was established.

Ida Koverman showed her devotion to Mayer by telegraphing Herbert Hoover on September 23 that he should send a letter to Mayer congratulating her friend on his acquittal. Hoover responded at once.

One day after his acquittal, Mayer celebrated by appearing at the Mayfair Ball, a spectacular regular event at the Biltmore Hotel ballroom in downtown Los Angeles. He was in the Conrad Nagel party (Nagel was still instructing him on perfect diction) with Margaret, Edie and Irene; significantly, John Gilbert was at the rival Irving Thalberg table, with Norma Shearer, who had just finished the movie *After Midnight*, Harry and Tina Rapf, Marion Davies, the Jack Conways, Clarence Brown, the director Eddie Sutherland and his wife, the mysterious Louise Brooks.

Then, on September 29, the wedding of Irving Thalberg and Norma Shearer took place at Marion Davies's Beverly Hills home. It was presided over by Rabbi Magnin. As the Hearst columnist Louella Parsons gushed to her readers, the bride looked radiant. Her elder brother, Douglas Shearer, gave her away; she was estranged from her father, who was living in Canada. Marion Davies was matron of honor, Edie and Irene Mayer were attendants. A photograph shows the group lined up, Mayer grim-faced and bespectacled just behind Thalberg's sister Sylvia. Several of the women are carrying enormous bouquets of flowers. There was an awkward mishap: a wind blew the bride's wedding veil into a large rosebush and it took the efforts of several Hollywood celebrities to disentangle it.

Thalberg was having difficulties editing King Vidor's *The Crowd*. As a result, the couple had to make do with a honeymoon at the Del Monte Lodge in Monterey. Mayer and Thalberg had another major headache: Lillian Gish's latest picture, *Annie Laurie*, was flopping everywhere and might have to be recut and revamped for its opening in New York. And there were problems with Hearst, who was bombarding the two executives with criticisms of Marion Davies's recent films *The Red Mill* and *Tillie the Toiler*, attacking the slapstick scenes in the latter picture, feeling that "the star" was humiliated.

As Mayer left for New York on September 30 for conferences with Nicholas Schenck, Hearst hailed him with telegrams aboard the *Santa Fe Chief*, apologizing for his previous angry complaints. Mayer and his wife and daughters, all of whom were on the train, responded with a conciliatory wire to their "Uncle William." One of the reasons Mayer was whisking his daughters off to New York was to quash Irene's clandestine romance with David Selznick.

On October 3, 1927, Mayer delivered an impassioned address at the Motion Picture Trade Conference in New York, attacking immorality in pictures, citing a long list of forbidden subjects; he was upset by the response of pressure groups to certain of his pictures, and was trying to overcome moralistic criticism of those pictures that Thalberg had forced through with Loew's and Schenck's collusion.

On October 5, while Mayer was still at the Astor Hotel, a big event took place in Manhattan. The Warner brothers launched *The Jazz Singer* at their Warner Theater. It was the first film of quality to break the barrier of silence. Al Jolson galvanized the audience to a standing ovation as he sang "Mammy" and the Kol Nidre. Jolson's words, "You ain't heard nothin' yet!" thrilled the public that night and would thrill millions in the months to come. Although there is no record of Mayer seeing the picture, we cannot doubt that he rushed to it. So far, he had resisted talkies as an idea: he and Thalberg loved the fact that silent films crossed all language barriers, providing an international language of mime; there was no question that talkies would present huge problems not only technically, but in the matter of foreign distribution. He and Thalberg had been put off by the derisive laughter that greeted an early halfhearted experiment in sound, with Norma Shearer and Lew Cody in the film *A Slave of Passion.* The stars had recorded their lines at the M.G.M. radio station; these were fed through to the special preview theater, with disastrous results. Shearer was heard booming with Lew Cody's solid baritone, and Cody was heard uttering his words in Shearer's high-pitched voice.

Leaving his family in New York, where they were to spend the Christmas holidays, Mayer returned to Los Angeles on November 8, 1927. He and Thalberg conferred on how quickly they could begin constructing sound stages at Culver City and which studios they could use in the meantime to make part-talkies. They would begin by introducing a word or two here and there and some sound effects, and see how audiences would respond. At the same time, Mayer heard bad news about the completion of Clarence Brown's re-creation of the Klondike gold rush, *The Trail of '98.* On location in Colorado, three men had drowned in the Rio Grande, and another was killed when the director's gunshot, used to summon the extras, triggered off an avalanche. The picture was not protected by insurance; four deaths (some said six) on location were a devastating mark against the studio, and it took all of Mayer's influence to prevent the story from getting into the papers and the picture being banned.

Mayer continued to be exasperated by Irene's interest in David Selznick, even after he managed to dislodge the hated swain from the studio at the beginning of 1928.

Selznick struck back by going to work, first as script supervisor, then as supervisor, and finally as associate producer and executive assistant, to Mayer's deadly enemy B. P. Schulberg at Paramount, a move that also meant he would now be working for the even more dreaded Adolph Zukor. None of Selznick's pictures for Paramount did him much credit: they included the embarrassing *Chinatown Nights*, the fatal talkie debut of King Vidor's former wife, Florence Vidor; the clumsy Nancy Carroll vehicle *The Dance of Life*; and a pathetic attempt at an adventure story, *The Four Feathers*. Mayer's disdain for Selznick now knew no bounds. For Irene to marry the son of his most vigorous opponent constituted outright betrayal. He fought constantly to break the affair; she took this behavior as irrational, and, even when she came to write her memoirs decades later, still failed to provide particulars of that element of treachery that made his activity understandable.

David O. Selznick was a dynamo at Paramount. He would call up his film editors at 4 A.M. after he had let them go at three; he would drag his secretaries from their beds to take down long, anguished or excitable notes; he would walk into the office, bleary-eyed from sleeplessness, with four-foot sheets of shelf paper completely covered from end to end in a manic scrawl.

But although everyone he worked for found him ruthless, incessantly demanding, they bathed in the flames that burned them; they found the hell they were in with him glamorous, stimulating and almost ridiculously exciting. Mayer must have known that it was useless trying to stop him from marrying Irene. But he tried anyway.

At the same time, Garbo, after many misgivings, renewed her contract. She agreed to make the tropical melodrama *White Orchids*, but balked at the idea of it being called *Heat*. The idea of being advertised as Greta Garbo in *Heat* had her in convulsions of laughter for years. *White Orchids* was restored as the title.

At 1 A.M. on February 15, 1928, the Thalbergs took off on their delayed honeymoon to Europe. Mayer was at the platform along with a galaxy of studio executives, John Gilbert and King Vidor, to see them off on the train. Six days later, the couple sailed on the *Mauritania* from New York. From Spain, Algiers, the south of France, Naples and Rome, they went on to Egypt and Berlin. They wound up in the spa at Bad Nauheim, Germany, where Thalberg, his frail body immersed in bubbling brown mud, said he felt better. There was another reason for being there: William Thalberg was born nearby, and his family greeted the couple warmly. They went on to Paris and offered Maurice Chevalier a contract. But Mayer was not impressed with his test (it was later stated wrongly that Chevalier had refused to make the test), and Paramount got the star instead. The couple traveled on to London to meet with Sir William Jury of the M.G.M. outfit there. They kept in touch with Mayer with a constant stream of cables. He was as worried about Thalberg's health as Thalberg had been worried about his during the making of *Ben-Hur*. But Thalberg returned refreshed and energized from the trip.

In those early months of 1928, Mayer was preoccupied with problems on the exotic melodrama *White Shadows in the South Seas*. He and Thalberg had contracted Robert Flaherty, the great documentary film-maker, to shoot the picture, a picturesque and sentimental story of Tahi-tian romance. Thalberg and producer Hunt Stromberg had quarreled with Flaherty's associate director, W. S. Van Dyke, who had little or no poetic sense and wanted to turn the movie into a tits-and-ass concoc-tion. Flaherty went off the picture. The shooting in Tahiti was so tor-menting that even the tough Van Dyke faltered, peppering Mayer with complaints about the humidity, the centipedes, the land crabs, the winged cockroaches and the scorpions that made this legendary paradise more closely resemble hell.

But Mayer and Thalberg were pleased with the rushes that came at thirty-day intervals into San Pedro, the port of Los Angeles, by tramp steamer. The movie was ravishingly photographed and, more impor-tantly from the box office point of view, extremely sexy; Pete Smith cooked up a romance between the half-naked stars, Monte Blue and Raquel Torres. Mayer ordered a startling effect: in the midst of a silent sequence, a noiseless sea washing against a beach, Monte Blue was heard whistling in imitation of bird song. Even more eerily, he uttered the one word, "Hello!"—an effect that was to rivet audiences all over the world. Most important, Mayer ordered from the Bronx Zoo a recording of a particularly vocal lion, whose penetrating roars would match the photo-graph of the Selig Zoo lion sitting in the M.G.M. trademark.

Mayer ordered a series of talkie vaudeville shorts that winter, similar to the knockabout mini-plays that he had once presented in Haverhill. The former press agent Nick Grinde went to New York on Mayer's behalf to shoot several of these one- and two-reelers, with sound on disc, at a studio specially arranged by Metro. Grinde was faced with problems: when comedy teams blew their lines, the laborious records had to be spun again. Dogs failed to bark on cue in a performing-dog act. During the recording of a female opera star, unnerving clicks were heard in the control room; the technicians looked at each other: they worked out that the noise came from her false teeth, which had to be taped in. It was impossible for singers to be anything less than perfect; no coughing or clearing of the throat was permitted.

Meanwhile, back in Hollywood, panic set in: each individual player would have to be handled separately. The M.G.M. star William Haines recalled something of the terror that seized Mayer and Thalberg as they began to embark gingerly on the new era. "The outbreak of sound at Metro was like the discovery of clap in a nunnery," Haines told this author in 1970. Haines remembered that Mayer hired a voice coach named Oliver Hinsdell, "a dreadful old fool," to train him in "pear-shaped tones." Hinsdell insisted that Haines pose almost naked as a Greek god, uttering lines from classical dramas, despite the fact that the star had a rather chunky figure quite lacking in ideal proportions and had a nasal twang. Hinsdell made him recite a speech from *Romeo and Juliet*. Haines threw up his hands in despair. Hinsdell screeched at him that he was "lip lazy!" Haines struck back with, "That's the first time I've ever had a complaint!" The remark may have gotten back to Mayer, because soon after that he warned Haines that if his homosexuality were to become known to any columnist he would be dismissed from the studio on the spot.

Mayer was fearful that Garbo, who was difficult enough already and still the object of his hatred, would have too strong a Swedish accent to be accepted by the public. He maintained that she must be kept in silent films as long as possible. Furthermore, she must give no interviews, since not only was she dangerously outspoken, but people might say she would not record properly. Ramon Novarro could also be destroyed if it were shown that his voice was not only markedly Mexican but overtly effeminate; Gilbert's pleasant, light tenor would seem insubstantial emerging from his strong face. Norma Shearer was still under the rigid command of actress Constance Collier; Buster Keaton, who was coming under the control of Thalberg and Mannix for his new picture *The Cameraman*, must be kept as a silent mime . . . would he be able to play talkie comedy?

Mayer flattered the newly powerful engineers, who would control the quality of sound, at an Academy of Motion Picture Arts and Sciences dinner in their honor on April 17, saying they were far more important than producers and actors.

He strengthened his writing team, realizing that soon his title writers, including his gifted niece Ruth Cummings, would be turning over their talents to talkie scripts. He realized he would soon have to hire playwrights from Broadway, and would have to begin purchasing as many suitable plays from Broadway as possible. He argued with Frances Marion, who said that films must use natural sound, the wind in the trees and grass, someone playing scales in a neighborhood street, the sound of rain, of a mower growling across a lawn. Mayer felt that talkies should be like stage plays, with little or no use of extraneous noise, which might interfere with the actors' words.

Mayer's interest in sound brought him to the door of the engineer J. Roy Pomeroy, who, at Paramount, had successfully worked on synchronization of sound and image, his system supported by the powerful firm of General Electric. Mayer also linked up with RCA, and prepared a satisfactory blending of image and talk in a specially prepared, in-house-only version of *Flesh and the Devil*, using other voices for Garbo and Gilbert. Thalberg embarked upon a bold venture: he would reshoot the last two reels of a recently completed silent thriller, *Alias Jimmy Valentine*, starring William Haines, Lionel Barrymore and Leila Hyams, with sound. Since work had not advanced on the new M.G.M. talkie stage, Mayer was compelled to bring about an alliance with his old enemy Adolph Zukor in order to shoot those reels at Paramount.

Making the final scenes was an ordeal for all concerned. Haines and Leila Hyams found the experience unendurable. They had to work all night, because Paramount was shooting talkies in the daytime. The players had to sit at small tables with a microphone hidden in a plant or vase or telephone; they could scarcely move an inch, or their voices would fade. Chalk marks permitted only a quarter of a step. The walls of the sound stage were ten feet thick, designed to block out external sounds such as those made by airplanes or automobiles. Because the walls were not tested acoustically, they reverberated with echoes, bumps and an unpleasant feedback. Eddie Mannix had an inspiration: he hired Verne Knudson, an expert in stage management, to make holes in the sound-stage floors, which killed the echoes.

The heat was so intense on the sound stage that sweating ruined the players' makeup. The cameraman had to sit in a box that resembled a telephone booth, without ventilation and about 130 degrees inside. It was double soundproofed by the application of a quilted cover, through a hole in which could be seen a glass panel, with the unfortunate cameraman's face pressed against it. Even strong men fainted in these conditions.

Norma Shearer's brother Douglas was made head of the sound department, for want of anyone else who could undertake the job. When audiences saw *Alias Jimmy Valentine*, they sat restlessly through several reels of silent movie, only to be startled out of their wits by the sudden booming voices of the actors.

## CHAPTER TWELVE

# 1928–1930

THE BIG EVENT of the summer of 1928 was Cecil B. DeMille's joining the studio in partnership with Louis B. Mayer and by special arrangement with Nicholas Schenck. From his splendiferous previous offices, an exact replica of Mount Vernon, DeMille was welcomed by Mayer at a celebration in August. Mayer had built for him a special bungalow, more elaborate than his own (William Randolph Hearst frequently complained that Mayer's quarters were far too modest for a man in his position, and Mayer would soon commission Cedric Gibbons to design him a handsome office).

Work on the Culver City sound stage continued. The Cosmopolitan Studios in New York were turned over to full talkie production. With some unease, Mayer and Thalberg decided to launch their first all-talkie picture, *The Broadway Melody*, about two ambitious sisters heading for the Great White Way. The script was rushed together, and Bessie Love and Anita Page were cast. A leading man had to be found at once. Mayer went to New York to look over the possibilities. Benjamin Thau, a notoriously womanizing booker for Loew's Theaters' live acts, came up with the idea of the energetic young Charles King, who had recently had a hit in *On the Deck*. Mayer met with King, heard him sing, and not only hired him but also took on Thau, whom he made casting director. From then on, Thau's casting couch was the busiest in Hollywood.

Mayer was in Kansas City in July, attending the Republican Convention and addressing the delegates with a powerful speech in support of Hoover. Carried away by enthusiasm, he promised to deliver the motion picture industry to the Republican party, a statement which infuriated Nicholas Schenck, a Democrat. New York Mayor Jimmy Walker, in San Francisco on July 24, stated that no such promise could properly be made. The same day, Mayer and Pete Smith flew into that city to greet the presidential candidate on his arrival from New York.

It was becoming clear that Mayer was getting rather too embroiled in party politics. He was leaving studio responsibility to Irving Thalberg, whose health remained insecure. Harry Rapf was spending much time in New York City, where he was supervising short subjects and seeking Broadway actors who might be useful in the new medium.

Ironically, when Herbert Hoover came to Stanford in August, partly to celebrate his birthday and partly to raise more funds and support in that area, much of it from former fellow alumni of the university, Mayer was stricken with a mysterious viral malady that kept him in bed and made it impossible for him to be present either then or at the Los Angeles City Hall welcoming ceremonies on August 17. He showered Hoover with telegrams and letters. Hoover was so anxious about his condition that, unable to visit with him because of his crowded schedule, he cabled Mayer, expressing his concern and urging him to report further progress. Ida Koverman was especially disappointed that Mayer could not be present; she kept Mayer informed day by day of the enthusiastic crowds that greeted Hoover everywhere.

M.G.M. pictures, in keeping with others, and as approved by Mayer, were released in both silent and sound versions that month and for some time thereafter. On September 18, a new picture, The Bellamy Trial, began shooting under the direction of Monta Bell. It was virtually a sustained courtroom scene from beginning to end; only a portion of it was rendered audible. Western Electric supplied the equipment, for a sound-stage building that was 70 by 100 feet, with thick walls and built-in earthquake protections. To accommodate the increasing numbers of employees, the Plantation House Cafe was pulled down and replaced by a new commissary, designed by Cedric Gibbons in the art deco mode. By September 26, no fewer than twenty-six sound shorts were ready for fall release. And by October 3, the Cosmopolitan Studio in New York, with its excellent sound stages, was completed, a forty-piece studio orchestra was hired under the direction of David Mendoza of the Capitol Theater, and the production of The Broadway Melody was already started in Hollywood.

That movie was shot at night, in conditions of overpowering heat, at the Culver City facility. To this day, Anita Page remembers the ordeal; again, because no extraneous sounds could enter and soundproofing was not properly understood, the set had to be sealed against the outside world. This meant that she and fellow actress Bessie Love often fainted from the suffocating closeness and had to be revived with smelling salts. Moreover, it had proved impossible to find a sufficient number of gorgeous chorus girls for the dance scenes, and a motley collection of plump, poorly trained young women carried out embarrassingly awkward routines. Only the brash charm of the two leading ladies and a certain freshness in the direction of Harry Beaumont made the movie tolerable. But its very existence as only the second full-length screen musical (the first was a pathetic effort, made at Universal in 1928, called *The Melody of Love)* caused a sensation. Mayer, Thalberg and the other executives were delighted with the contribution of lyricist Arthur Freed; he would later become the greatest producer of M.G.M. musicals.

Torn between his commitments at Culver City and his passionate desire to see Hoover in the White House, Mayer risked a recurrence of his illness by wearing himself out preparing a campaign speech to greet the Republican leader in Beverly Hills in October. He had a radio hookup in his office at all times, listening to every speech Hoover gave and bubbling over to Ida Koverman and Hoover's other aides every time he heard a single word. Perhaps because he was so rushed, and because Thalberg was always so persuasive, he scrawled out with great misgivings permission for King Vidor to make an all-black movie, the first in history, to be entitled *Hallelujah.* This was a most daring decision.

In the meantime, Mayer had to face the challenge of introducing John Gilbert to talkies. He authorized his old friend Lionel Barrymore to guide Gilbert in his sound debut. He and Thalberg chose *Redemption* for Gilbert, a version of the novel *The Living Corpse,* by Tolstoy, to be adapted by the reliable Dorothy Farnum, with dialogue by Edwin Justus Mayer. Mayer, always tending to overlook weaknesses in those he admired, seemed not to have noted the fact that Barrymore was a morphine addict, using the drug to kill the constant pain of arthritis. He was certain that Barrymore would guide Gilbert effectively through the dangerous shoals of talkie stardom.

The picture would start production in a few weeks, after the conclusion of *The Broadway Melody* and *The Bellamy Trial,* which was being shot in the daytime. Although it has been theorized that Mayer set out to destroy Gilbert by choosing Barrymore, there is no evidence to this effect. Much as he hated Gilbert, he was protecting an asset; and anyway, the final decisions had to be made by Nicholas Schenck. What is true is that Gilbert, so impressive in silent films, would soon show that his acting ability was essentially that of a mime and could not survive in the equivalent of theatrical performance.

While *The Broadway Melody* continued shooting and King Vidor made headlines combing through Chicago, Harlem and Memphis, casting unknowns for vital roles in *Hallelujah,* Mayer was more and more devoting his time to political affairs. Throughout the final stages of the election, he was in an ecstatic mood; but then, something happened that must have given him very severe qualms.

The dynamic assistant district attorney, Buron Fitts, became convinced that his boss, Los Angeles DA Asa Keyes, had been bribed to
throw out the Julian Petroleum case. No saint himself, Fitts saw not only
headlines in exposing Keyes, but also, of course, the chance to succeed
him as district attorney. He hired a team of private detectives to worm
their way into offices throughout the city and piece together a sinister
jigsaw puzzle of intrigue that would expose Keyes. He found a star witness in Milton Pike, a tailor's assistant, who conveniently kept a diary,
in May and June of 1928, which provided evidence of money being
passed through the medium of a clothing store. By late October, the
matter was before a grand jury, and by November 1, that same grand jury
charged Keyes with willful and corrupt behavior.

There can be no calculating the effect of this news on Mayer. He can
only have been advised by his counsel, Edwin Loeb, that he would be
rearrested and retried, because Fitts would put high on his agenda of
potential prosecutions those prominent individuals whom Keyes had so
spectacularly excused. He was sure he was on the verge of seeing his
good friend Herbert Hoover take up residence in the White House, for
the early polls were highly encouraging. He was beginning to think he
would take an ambassadorship or a high post in government; he was
launched into the talking picture era; his income as movie executive was
the highest of any in the industry; the Academy Awards, his dream
child, were even now fully mooted, and the first ceremony would take
place in just a few weeks. And now, once again, the ground could be cut
from underneath his feet and he could be ruined.

But he was as tough as ever as he harangued club after club, business
meeting after business meeting, with his Republican convictions. His
telegrams to Hoover still jump off the page over forty years later; when
Hoover was swept to victory by an overwhelming majority in November,
there was no containing him.

Throughout and beyond the time of Hoover's entry into the White
House, the Julian case continued. Normally secret transcripts of grand
jury hearings were released by special arrangement of Buron Fitts and
appeared in the newspapers; all of them were damaging to anybody who
had escaped prosecution at an earlier stage.

And now Mayer had another matter to deal with. Mayer's longtime
enemy Adolph Zukor got wind of the fact that Mrs. Marcus Loew
wanted to dispose of 400,000 shares of stock, which, in effect, gave her
control of Loew's Inc.; her price was $50 million. He opened negotia-
tions. Harry Warner, who ran the business end of Warner Brothers in
Manhattan, also wanted to buy that controlling interest. But William
Fox, head of the Fox Film Corporation, was even hungrier; he saw the

enormous potential of Loew's in the talking-picture era, and he knew he could get Nicholas Schenck's ear. To raise the money, he approached the powerful firm of Halsey, Stuart, and Company, which was deeply involved, as investment bankers, in motion picture theaters. He also approached, equally successfully, AT&T, which wanted to snatch Loew's shares from Warner Brothers, with which it was arguing. Other money came from the Bankers' Securities Company of Philadelphia, on whose board Fox sat as a director; Fox Theaters Corporation floated shares to the tune of $16 million.

With great duplicity, Schenck had a series of secret meetings with William Fox and Fox's chief lieutenant, the production chief Winfield Sheehan, who for years, before he joined Fox, had been a shady go-between of former police commissioner Waldo and the madams running the Manhattan brothels. Sheehan had also managed to obtain powerful Mafia connections and had been present at the shooting of the gambling czar Herman Rosenthal, in which he may or may not have been involved.

Mayer did not get wind of the negotiations between Schenck (who repeatedly lied to the press that nothing was going on) and Fox. He could do little to stop Schenck signing John Gilbert to a new $250,000 salary for each of six pictures to be made at the rate of two a year, a contract entered into, at least in part, because Schenck was determined that United Artists would not succeed in a vigorous attempt to steal Gilbert from M.G.M.

Schenck acted with continuing duplicity at the time. He paid off Irving Thalberg to the tune of $250,000, with additional gifts to Eddie Mannix and other studio executives, in return for their promising not to tell Mayer what he was doing, and he even managed to keep the facts from Mayer's perennial friend and supporter, J. Robert Rubin.

And now, with more than an inkling that the Julian case would turn out to be disastrous for him, Mayer began to plunge back into studio affairs in the late fall of 1928.

He had had to leave much of the control of King Vidor's all-black *Hallelujah* to Irving Thalberg, and indeed it may be said that the subject matter of crime, revivalism and struggle in the Deep South was still unappealing to him. But he had to confer with Thalberg on the numerous complications faced by Vidor on location, even when he was on one of his numerous visits to Washington, D.C. The shooting near Memphis was dogged by storms, the male star Daniel Haynes was plagued by illness, and the last-minute replacement of Vidor's discovery Honey Brown by Nina Mae McKinney was not entirely satisfactory.

In August, Mayer had authorized W. S. Van Dyke to return to the

South Seas to make *The Pagan*, a companion piece to *White Shadows of the South Seas*, with Renée Adorée and Ramon Novarro, whose singing voice was heard by audiences for the first time. He was in touch with Tahiti, through all of his commitments in Washington, and was greatly concerned by news that the actor Donald Crisp was almost taken by a shark at a beach on location.

He agreed with Irving Thalberg on Van Dyke's next project. This was a bold venture indeed: *Trader Horn*, based on the South African journalist Ethelreda Lewis's best-seller about the famous ivory trader Aloysius Horn. Among other things, the story describes Horn's encounter with a missionary's daughter, who had become the white goddess of an African tribe.

Mayer and Thalberg commissioned a team of writers to adapt the book; it became the story of Horn and his Spanish friend Little Peru, who traveled 14,000 miles from Uganda to the Belgian Congo on their journey of adventure. Originally, Thalberg offered the parts of Horn and the great white goddess to Wallace Beery and the New York showgirl Mary Nolan, known on the stage as Imogene Wilson, whose antics had kept the columnists busy for a decade. But Beery did not relish the idea of shooting in Africa, and Mary Nolan was discovered to be a drug addict and too ill to accept the role.

Thalberg, with Mayer's approval, now offered the part of Trader Horn to the leathery, tough Harry Carey. Carey was appalled, because Horn went around in a beard that reached to his knees. But he desperately needed the money, and he was forced to accept the job for a mere $600 a week. His only condition was that he should not wear a beard and that his wife, Olive, should join him, playing the part of a missionary. Irving Thalberg agreed that they could take their two children, who would be housed in Nairobi.

The handsome and athletic Duncan Renaldo, who had been successful in *The Bridge of San Luis Rey*, was cast as Little Peru. He would work also on the production end, since he had been Robert Flaherty's assistant on the classics *Nanook of the North* and *Moana*.

Now came the difficult problem of casting the white goddess. A talent search went on for an unknown. The selection finally fell on twenty-four-year-old Edwina Booth, named for the great American stage star Edwin Booth. Her real name was Constance Woodruff.

Miss Booth was delicately beautiful, extremely fair, with sensitive skin; she had never been well. Raised by her doctor father, a Mormon, in Provo and Salt Lake City, she had acquired the disease hypoglycemia, which caused general weakness and fainting spells. Her schooling limited by her condition, she found her escape in movies and movie magazines.

Her father encouraged her in her dreams of stardom. She came to Hollywood, worked as an extra and bit player and studied with the actress Lucille LaVerne. She appeared successfully on the stage in Los Angeles in the play *Sunup* and as Regina in Ibsen's *Ghosts*. She had considerable talent, but, due to her condition, she had to rest between scenes on the stage and was always in danger of passing out before the audience.

Her father, intoxicated by boyhood dreams of a romantic Africa, pushed her into the role of the white goddess against her wishes. Incredibly for a doctor, he seems not to have realized that exposure to the tropical sun and grueling conditions on location could possibly prove fatal to her. Why he did not make it a condition of her contract that he should accompany her is almost inexplicable, but he may have assumed that M.G.M. would dispatch a full first-aid and medical team with the unit.

Miss Booth was forced into the picture, because her father, in collusion with M.G.M., announced her as first choice in the Los Angeles *Examiner* before she had agreed. She was distraught at the prospect; her father's failure to grasp what would be involved if she undertook the trip led her into a disaster that could have wrecked the reputation of the studio and of Louis B. Mayer himself.

Neither Mayer nor Thalberg made anything like the proper preparations for *Trader Horn*. The script was written with no research to speak of and with insufficient consultation with Aloysius Horn. The idea of an African epic suggested commercial potential at a time when the public was fascinated by stories of jungle adventure. Rashly, foolishly, everyone rushed into the film. The cameraman Clyde De Vinna was sent ahead to prepare the groundwork; the team would sail for Africa in March.

November 1928 brought another distressing matter. From Stockholm came word that Mauritz Stiller, still only in his forties, had died of pleurisy. The news was brought to Greta Garbo while she was on a set; she collapsed, and the picture was closed down for the rest of the day. She left for Sweden the moment the shooting was completed, threatening never to return.

While in New York in January, Mayer renewed his intimate friendship with Mabel Walker Willebrandt. He boldly accompanied her—without his wife—to a showing of the popular new Broadway musical *Rio Rita*, a fact that touched Mrs. Willebrandt deeply. She would certainly do anything for him; by now, she had become official representative of M.G.M., handling numerous taxation problems for the studio in Washington. She told Mayer that she had ambitions to be a judge. Although he supported her in her ambition, he urged her to retain her position, as she was only just beginning to exercise full-scale influence in his adopted state.

All through the new year of 1929, Mayer had to endure daily reports on the malfeasances of Asa Keyes, whose trial began on January 7, while the intrigues of Nicholas Schenck and William Fox continued apace. On January 8, Lon Chaney upset Mayer and Thalberg by announcing that he would not appear in talking pictures; he refused to turn up in promotional shorts in which other stars were featured. He would finally yield and make one talkie, a remake of his own *The Unholy Three*, but died soon after.

Mayer wasted little time in making the best use of his considerable influence with the incoming President Hoover. He began recommending new appointees, in one case a friend as a potential ambassador, in another case a person he could rely on as head of internal revenue in California. He pulled strings in every direction, not always successfully. Mayer did play a particular role in the appointment of Herbert Hoover, Jr., as head of the radio department of Western Air Express. Ida Koverman continued as go-between, urging Hoover's secretary, Lawrence Richey, in a letter dated January 28, to invite Mayer to Florida:

> This is another small boy—new at the game and used to a great deal of attention. I know he would strut around like a proud pigeon. And you must not forget that the people closely allied with him and with whom he is intimately associated are inclined to sort of "rub it in" that his efforts are now a thing of the past and he himself more or less in the discard.

This last sentence shows that Ida Koverman knew a great deal. She knew, or suspected, that powerful forces were at work to dislodge Mayer.

Lionel Barrymore, in the grip of morphine, was clumsily directing Ruth Chatterton in *Madame X*, starting on January 23. Microphones were going dead, rushes were badly scratched; the construction department had laid the floor incorrectly for sound use and it had to be drilled out and changed. Barrymore was constantly late on the set, so that the assistant director had to rehearse the actors without him. Some of the shooting took place between 7:00 P.M. and 6:40 A.M., which caused the star, Ruth Chatterton, and the actor Raymond Hackett to collapse from overwork.

Simultaneously, in the daytime, *The Trial of Mary Dugan* was being completed; it starred Norma Shearer and was directed by its author, Bayard Veiller. Thalberg hated the idea of her playing the part of a chorus girl accused of murder. She insisted. Finally, he said that, if she would agree to do the whole thing as a stage play on the set of the courtroom before Mayer and all of the executives, with the actors Raymond Hackett and H. B. Warner, and if her performance matched up to theirs, he would let her go ahead. Petrified, she conferred extensively with Veiller, and, after two weeks of preparation, the performance was given. It was greeted with warm applause, and she got the part. The scene in which, in a slip, a gun in her hand, she gave a bloodcurdling scream won a particularly loud burst of applause.

Norma Shearer began to shoot the picture. She was exceedingly nervous about her voice and terrified that the long takes occasioned by shooting the trial scene that lasted almost the entire length of the picture would expose the serious flaw in her left eye. Veiller had to fight hard to control her severe tension; yet, he and others recalled, she worked fiercely, at all hours of the night, dedicated so completely to work that she almost wore herself out.

In late January, Mayer was busy contacting Lawrence Richey, President Hoover's secretary, to lay the diplomatic groundwork for *Trader Horn*. The secretaries of state and commerce were asked to send letters to appropriate Belgian and British officials to ensure the company's complete support in the length and breadth of Africa. Yet still Thalberg made no provision for a medical unit.

At the same time, Mayer was approached by President Hoover about becoming ambassador to Turkey. Mayer stated that he was too busy to accept this honor. The offer was blown up out of all proportion in the press.

*The Broadway Melody* opened at Grauman's Chinese Theater on February 1, 1929. The William Morris Agency had booked in fourteen singing and dancing acts to precede the movie. A huge crowd was outside, illuminated by sweeping searchlights. As the Mayers arrived, followed by the Thalbergs and one famous director or star after another, the columnist Louella Parsons, already a star of radio, gurgled lavish praise as she dragged the seemingly reluctant Louis B. to the microphone; the interviews were relayed around the block. Once the audience was settled in its seats, the curtains parted on George Gershwin playing "Rhapsody in Blue" with the Chinese Symphony Orchestra, the Ada Broadbent Dancers whirling around in tributes to the spirits of jazz and terpsichore, Edith Murray and her Torrid Ensemble performing a number entitled "Hot (Positively!)" and the composer/conductor Dmitri Tiomkin directing the stage finale, the movie's stars descending Cedric

Gibbons's specially designed white staircase in elaborate costumes span-
gled with hundreds of sequins. The picture was greeted with a standing
ovation, and was followed with a lavish party hosted by Mayer and
Thalberg across the street at the Blossom Room of the Hollywood Roosevelt Hotel.

As if Mayer had not enough on his hands, he was involved in the final
preparations for the first Academy Awards. In February, the Central
Board of Judges had met, with Mayer as supervisor of the voting. Mayer
was much opposed to the Artistic Quality of Production award to King
Vidor's *The Crowd.* He even sat up all night quarreling with the judges
over the decision and begging them to choose F. W. Murnau's romantic
movie, *Sunrise,* instead. Ironically, *Sunrise* was produced at Fox by Winfield Sheehan, Mayer's mortal enemy and potential boss.

At dawn on February 16, the judges gave in to Mayer's pleas. The Best
Actor award would go to Emil Jannings for two pictures; Mayer ensured
that Chaplin would fail to get the main award for his film *The Circus;*
*The Jazz Singer* would receive a special award.

Mayer received disturbing news from Sweden that week. Greta Garbo
was embroiled in a major scandal: she had had an affair with Prince
Sigurd, Duke of Upland, the handsome twenty-three-year-old son of
Crown Prince Gustav. The royal family disapproved of the match, one
of the reasons being that Garbo was not only an actress, but was also
romantically interested in socially prominent Countess Wachtmeister,
who was related to the family. In order to break the match, the Swedish
royals announced that Prince Sigurd would marry Crown Princess Juli-
ana of the Netherlands, but this was simply a device. Garbo sailed back
to New York in a very bad temper.

The Asa Keyes prosecution continued. The result was that Keyes was
sent to the county jail, and from there to San Quentin. A gunman tried
to murder Jacob Berman, also known as Jack Bennett, the state's star
witness. Buron Fitts began plans to have Mayer rearrested, following a
series of interrogations of his former boss.

*Madame X* ran into serious problems in March. The script called for a
camera and microphone to move simultaneously; a desperate Eddie
Mannix had to improvise a fishing rod, on which he hung the mike.
Eight men had to move the camera box, under the direction of Barrymore in the monitor room, where he was listening to all the lines. On
the floor, Willard Mack, author of the screenplay, was fighting with Ruth
Chatterton, who could not deal with the heat and lack of air. But,
experienced actress as she was, she managed to turn on real tears during
the sequence in which she stood at the witness stand in the courtroom
and broke down, and even allowed her mascara to run down her cheeks.

Mayer's and Thalberg's hunger for new voices was partially assuaged by the handsome, twenty-five-year-old Robert Montgomery, whom Nicholas Schenck hired away from his brother Joe. Montgomery was pale, slender, soft, making him unsuitable for movies that involved swimming pool or beach scenes in which he would have to display his physique. An impeccable lounge lizard, he looked perfect in white tie and tails, and he was so poised and smooth that he suggested sex without brutality to millions of women. Paradoxically, he had that essential ingredient in male stardom: an occasional suggestion of vulnerability; he looked as though he needed to be mothered. Norma Shearer described him perfectly: "A naughty boy who has just swallowed a canary and isn't going to tell."

Montgomery was born in Beacon, New York, in 1904, attended fashionable private schools and was slated for Princeton. His father's early death following financial ruin sent him to work at sixteen as a blue-collar employee, toiling as railroad and ship's deckhand and garage mechanic before he worked his way up the Broadway ladder from walk-on to juvenile lead in society comedies and melodramas. His journey to the top in pictures would be astonishingly swift, starting with *So This Is College*, and the maddening part was that he let everyone know he was terrific. His cold, distant and somewhat insulting behavior, the result of going too far, too fast, made him the most unpopular man at M.G.M.

Montgomery was stubborn and determined and kept a careful record of the box office results on every picture he made. When he asked for a salary raise after six months, Mayer refused it. Montgomery reminded him that Nicholas Schenck had promised him an increase if he made good. Mayer screamed, "You're a goddamned liar!" Montgomery replied, "If you were a younger man, I'd deck you here and now!" Mayer threw him out of the office, but soon after gave him a bonus. He didn't like Montgomery, though, as an ardent Republican and supporter of Hoover, he was politically impeccable in Mayer's eyes. If anything, Montgomery was further to the right than he was.

That winter, Mayer had a violent clash with his daughter Irene. She came home at a quarter to two in the morning after a date with David Selznick, and he, guessing where she had been, hid in the shadows of the staircase, awaiting the ring of the doorbell. As she walked up the stairs, he sprung out with terrifying swiftness and confronted her. He screamed at her in rage, and she, her sister Edie recalled, fought back. The quarrel rang through the house, bringing Margaret from her bedroom. Irene insisted that she would not stop seeing Selznick. Mayer told her he would only tolerate this if she would agree to date other men; he was praying that an eligible young bachelor would attract her and she would desist from seeing the hated David. She said she would think about it. He whisked his whole family off to New York on February 25. They would attend the inaugural ball in Washington.

On March 4, with the Mayers in New York, the New York *Times* announced that William Fox had acquired control of Loew's by buying up 400,000 preferred shares for $50 million, with the permission of the U.S. attorney general and with the aid of a $15 million loan from Western Electric. The *Times* did not mention that he had also acquired through Fox Theaters 260,900 shares on the open market for $23 million. Mayer discovered that Irving Thalberg had betrayed him by securing the silencing settlement of $250,000, and that Mannix and others had also acted treacherously. Both Arthur M. Loew and Fox himself confirmed the deal. The combined assets of the two companies would exceed $225 million. Loew stated that the shares held by his mother, his brother and himself were sold for cash and that Fox had bought all of Nicholas Schenck's private shareholdings in exchange for cash and Fox stock.

Nicholas Schenck, under new arrangement, would remain as president, with David Bernstein as vice president and treasurer. This was news to Mayer. Another shock was that Fox was with President Hoover, discussing the deal, and Hoover had not mentioned it to Mayer. Fox had poured a fortune, equivalent to Mayer's, into the Hoover campaign, and Fox's Movietone News had turned over its whole operation to supporting the new president—as, indeed, had the Hearst-Mayer newsreels.

Mayer's fury knew no bounds. Irving Thalberg immediately headed east, abandoning control of Marion Davies's new film and first talkie, *Marianne*, which had run into censorship troubles and the continual latenesses of the star.

That week, Mayer was mollified considerably by being invited to the White House. He, Margaret and Irene were the first house guests of President Hoover following his inauguration. This was a great privilege, never to be forgotten.

Soon after, the *Trader Horn* company was on the way to Le Havre aboard the *Majestic*, sailing from New York on March 29, with a dazzling passenger list that included Cecil Beaton, Noël Coward, Otto Kahn and Antonio Moreno. They went from Le Havre to Paris by boat train, and from there to Genoa, Italy, sailing on April 13 on the SS *Ussukama* for Mombasa. Foolishly, W. S. Van Dyke exposed Edwina Booth to direct sunlight on the boat deck, hoping to acclimatize her. She was severely affected by sunburn; that night, she rose without warning from the dinner table and fainted. She suffered third-degree burns and tossed and turned all night, carefully tended by Olive Carey. Mayer was not informed until the vessel arrived in Mombasa on May 1.

From then on, Edwina Booth suffered from recurring attacks of hysteria and insomnia; she complained constantly of blinding headaches. Dr. Tom Clark, a Mombasa physician who had no special knowledge of tropical diseases, was attached to the unit but could only supply cascara (a laxative), bicarbonate of soda and quinine whenever she or other cast members took ill. Despite frequent requests by cable, Irving Thalberg failed to assign a special first-aid and mobile ambulance unit. His behavior in the entire matter was appalling. He had been told, Olive Carey testified later, that if the company stayed one more day past six months, M.G.M. would be charged $100,000 extra duty on the movie equipment, and he was afraid that any protracted medical treatment, or shipment of Miss Booth to Mombasa, would slow down the production and bring about these additional charges.

Dr. Clark did manage to fly in some morphine to Murchison Falls when the company was shooting there. Edwina Booth screamed in frenzy all night long, keeping the company awake. She was torn to pieces by thorns, the wounds festering in minutes, and was plagued by ticks, because of her skimpy clothing.

The nightmarish journey went on, Mayer kept informed by shortwave radio, since obviously no telegrams could be sent from the heart of the jungle. Duncan Renaldo recalled that there was one moment of relief when the crackling radio informed the movie company that Admiral Byrd had successfully reached the South Pole. But there were few other pleasures on the journey. However, touched by pity as well as by physical attraction, Renaldo did fall in love with Edwina Booth.

Throughout March and April, the discussion of the Fox-Loew merger was the hubbub of New York and Hollywood. Would Mayer, Thalberg and J. Robert Rubin remain in office, or would their three-year contract be suspended? How could Mayer suppress his anger that Schenck had made a personal profit of about $10 million through Fox's acquisition of the stock? How would the Warner brothers deal with the fact that Schenck had promised them control of Loew's, thereby increasing the value of the stock, and then had snatched it from under their noses at the last minute?

For weeks, Mayer, Thalberg (keeping his role in the matter secret) and Rubin were in conference over the matter, angrily blaming Arthur Loew for betraying his father's cause by surrendering to the lure of $50 million and berating Nicholas Schenck for his traitorous behavior. What strings could they pull in Washington to rectify the situation? Mysterious telegrams in the Hoover files at West Branch, Iowa, suggest that Mayer was in touch with the president in an effort to retrieve the situation. He was back in Hollywood in April, fretting that Hearst's high-ranking Arthur Brisbane of the New York *Evening Journal* might have played a role in the merger. He was wrong.

That month, the ever-troublesome Garbo was making *The Single Standard* with Nils Asther, directed by John S. Robertson. It was being shot without sound. Mayer was still concerned that Garbo's Swedish accent would not be accepted by the public. Not only was she continuously late on the set, but she behaved in a manner that proved unacceptable. When Asther kissed her passionately in a scene, she was annoyed; she had wanted John Gilbert to play the role, even though he was about to become engaged to Ina Claire. Asther was homosexual. As he boldly embraced her, Miss Garbo broke free and said, to the roaring delight of the crew, "Don't kiss me so hard! I'm not one of your sailors!" Asther was mortified.

The Academy Awards ceremony was held on May 19 at the Blossom Room of the Hollywood Roosevelt Hotel. Douglas Fairbanks and the director William C. deMille, brother of Cecil (who preferred to spell his name with a capital D), were the hosts, and all awards were presented by Fairbanks.

The dinner was preceded by an hour of dancing; Louis and Margaret Mayer were most frequently on the floor, followed in second position by Irene (who defiantly fox-trotted with David Selznick) and Edie. The room was lit by Chinese lanterns, and each table was decorated with candles and candy replicas of the newly designed gold statuette. The Best Actor, Emil Jannings, was absent in Berlin, but Janet Gaynor was sweetly present to accept the Best Actress award. It was certainly cause for surprise when Mayer, despite his role in preventing the picture from getting the main award, accepted an honorable-mention scroll for *The Crowd*. The occasion was pleasant but lacking in real glamour; few people felt that the ceremony would become an institution.

Just over two weeks later, Mayer and Margaret celebrated their twenty-fifth wedding anniversary at Santa Monica and were delighted to receive a telegram from Mr. and Mrs. Herbert Hoover, warmly expressing their fond good wishes. It was a great occasion; despite the fact that Margaret Mayer never felt comfortable in the film industry world, their marriage still worked, unrocked, as yet, by scandal.

Was Mayer faithful to his wife at the time? There is great controversy about this among those who knew him. Maurice Rapf, son of Harry Rapf, is convinced that Mayer took advantage of his access to beautiful young women who began flooding into the studio as potential chorus-line members and extras. So is John Gilbert's daughter, Leatrice. Mil-

dred Knopf, who later married the producer Edwin H. Knopf and was a
friend for forty years of Margaret Mayer, says that Margaret never ceased
to weep to her over Mayer's promiscuity. Friends and supporters like J. J.
Cohn, Samuel Marx and Robert Vogel, who joined the studio at the
beginning of 1930, loyally insist otherwise. But Mayer's secretary, Margaret Bennett, was still closest to him on a day-to-day basis and categori-
cally stated to her niece that Mayer enjoyed the favors of many young
women. And it is hard to believe that Mayer could have been living like
a monk. No amount of willpower or devotion to the memory of his late
mother could have compensated for the pleasures that awaited him
around every corner of the studio.

There was more treachery in his circle that June. William Randolph
Hearst was negotiating behind his back, first to move the Hearst Metrotone newsreels from M.G.M. to Warner Brothers, and second to carry
off to the rival operation in Burbank his entire Cosmopolitan Productions unit and Marion Davies herself. He pointed out to the negotiator,
E. B. Hatrick, of his New York office, that the films *Our Dancing Daughters* and *Broadway Melody* had some investment from the Cosmopolitan
outfit. It seems from Hearst's correspondence that he was panicking at
the time, convinced that the actual or potential merger with Fox was
putting him out of the picture business. Hearst's excuse for this secret
maneuvering was that he could not bring himself to tell Mayer what he
was up to because he was too fond of him. This is impossible to believe.

He even began negotiating with Fox itself behind the scenes, offering
to meld by buying a quarter interest in the Fox-Case Corporation, the
talkies company, and Fox's Movietone News.

While all this finagling was going on, Mayer only finding out about it
by reading the movie trade papers, Mayer's daughters were going ahead
willfully with their marital plans. Edie had fallen in love with the amusing and attractive twenty-seven-year-old movie executive William
Goetz. Mayer had moved her, because she was suffering from bronchitis,
from the chilly night winds of the Pacific that swept the beach house to
the confines of a bungalow at the Ambassador Hotel. One night, at 10
P.M., after returning from a movie premiere, Edie walked into the lobby
and accidentally bumped into Goetz. He drew back, looked her up and
down, and suggested she join him for dancing and cocktails at the Cocoanut Grove nightclub at the hotel. She glanced at her watch and said
to herself, she remembered decades later, "Why not?" They tangoed and
fox-trotted until 4 A.M., then raced across the street for breakfast at the
Brown Derby. Goetz made her laugh almost continuously until dawn; he
had the most sparkling wit Edie had known.

She told her father she had decided to date Goetz regularly. Mayer knew enough about him to feel confident in agreeing, but said, characteristically, "You can go out with him every other night!" She had to laugh, and followed his edict. After a few pleasant evenings, she told Mayer she wanted to marry the man. She had armed herself with a virtual encyclopedia of details about him, revealing that he was running the big star Corinne Griffith's movie company; one of his brothers was a treasurer of Paramount, another the head of the Consolidated Film Laboratory. She also delivered a punchline: he was devoted to his mother. That did it: Mayer followed up with a detailed investigation through industry sources and did not find the gentleman wanting.

The next procedure was to have Edie invite Goetz for dinner so he could look him over. Mayer smiled as the dapper young man walked in, very well dressed in a handmade suit, with a pearl pin in his tie. He was cleverly respectful to Mayer, asking about Mayer's dead mother. Then, at dinner, he began telling humorous anecdotes, which Mayer didn't respond to. Everybody else was in peals of merriment, but Mayer, who usually only laughed at slapstick movie comedies, was not sufficiently sophisticated to see the point of these rather cynical tales. After Goetz left, Mayer said to Edie, "Okay, he's a nice man. But what's with all these jokes?" "What does it matter? I'm going to marry him, not you!" Edie replied. Mayer threw up his hands and told her to do what she wanted.

Goetz's brothers Harry and Ben paid for the engagement ring. After some argument, Mayer yielded to the arrangement and presented Edie with a diamond bracelet; later, he would add an ermine coat and a Cadillac. But he was devastated when Irene accepted David Selznick's proposal, even though Selznick was doing quite well at Paramount. For months, the young women were busy planning their trousseaus, the homes they would live in and their honeymoon trips.

Mayer was in New York in June. At the suggestion of Colonel Claudius Huston, treasurer of the Republican National Committee, Mayer agreed to see William Fox in an effort to reach some basis of agreement in the continuing and upsetting process toward the merger. For some weeks he had been in close touch with Mabel Walker Willebrandt, now an assistant attorney general at the Justice Department, making efforts, by citing the Sherman Antitrust Act, to have the entire Fox operation declared illegal. Mayer stormed into Fox's offices. After a peremptory handshake, he announced how appalled he was that, after all he had done to build up M.G.M. as the greatest film-producing company in the world, he had been shafted, without a penny to show for it, and felt his position was virtually untenable. He said he had, and would, use every legal remedy to stop the consolidation. Fox replied, "If you can't stop it legally, why try to do it illegally?" Mayer screamed with rage. Finally, Fox said, as calmly as he could, that, to ensure Mayer's support, Mayer and J. Robert Rubin would receive a total of $2 million once the merger was completed; in addition, Fox promised Mayer an entirely new contract that would ensure his future at an equitable rate of payment. Mayer replied that he was interested, but how could he get the attorney general to change back what he had already set in motion—namely, the shattering of the agreements? Fox later testified under oath, at a 1934 U.S. Senate inquiry into the motion picture business, that Mayer did promise to cause the record to be changed from a restriction to a consent, with the words, "This is not going to be easy, but I will try it, and I think I will be able to accomplish it." Fox added in 1934: "When I learned that a man had the power to go into the Department of Justice and change the record I was rather ashamed to be a citizen of this nation." As it turned out, Fox made a thorough investigation later and informed his official biographer, Upton Sinclair, that business man Harley M. Clarke, who was involved in the takeover, had effected the alteration when Mayer proved unable to do so.

Hearst's surreptitious arrangements with Warner broke loose that June, and Mayer outsmarted Jack Warner in securing Hearst's contract for another two years. Marion Davies's hesitations about shifting studios also had something to do with the collapse of the arrangements.

On June 3, 1929, Joan Crawford married Douglas Fairbanks, Jr., in New York. Mayer did not attend, though he was visiting the city. The wedding was felt to be advantageous to the studio: there had been much adverse publicity attached to Miss Crawford, who had been named in two divorce suits as alienating the husbands' affections, and was said, probably unfairly, to be among the most sexually available of the female M.G.M. stars. The Fairbankses were Hollywood royalty, and Mayer was still in partnership in the real estate trust with Douglas Fairbanks, Sr. The match was also a great advantage to Miss Crawford because of the real estate connection.

At the same time as Mayer was in New York, he and Thalberg were in touch with W. S. Van Dyke on location in Mombasa, Kenya, British East Africa, where *Trader Horn* was starting production. Van Dyke sent a series of articles to the New York *Times*, carefully polished and rewritten by publicist Howard Dietz, describing only the colorful and adventurous aspects of the trip and hiding the personal tragedy of Edwina Booth.

Fox continued his shady dealings, again with William Randolph Hearst. He met frequently with E. B. Hatrick in New York City, urging Hearst to blend with him, to combine the Hearst and Fox Movietone newsreels and (again) buy a twenty-five percent interest in Fox-Case.

The price of this was now set at $1.25 million. While these negotiations were going on, and while Mayer was doing his best to reverse the wheels in Washington, an extraordinary incident took place. At 10 A.M. on July 17, Fox and a friend of his, Jacob L. Rubenstein, were being driven in a Rolls Royce by Fox's chauffeur, Joe Boyes, from Fox's home in Wood-mere, Long Island, to the Lakeville Golf and Country Club, where they would meet with Adolph Zukor and Nicholas Schenck. The presence of these individuals indicates that Fox was still playing an elaborate game, very much behind Mayer's back, and may have intended to sell M.G.M. to a Zukor–Schenck consortium.

As the Rolls Royce reached the corner of Roslyn and Old Westbury roads, a car driven by Dorothy Kane headed for the intersection. Joe Boyes tried to cut in front of the Kane sedan. The Rolls spun around and crashed onto its left side, while the Kane automobile remained upright. Boyes was killed instantly, his head crushed under the car. Fox and Rubenstein were injured. When police arrived, Dorothy Kane and her sisters, who accompanied her, were screaming hysterically and it was some time before they were brought under control.

Fox and Rubenstein were rushed to Nassau Hospital and were given blood transfusions. There is no record of Mayer visiting Fox at the time; instead, he made two visits with President Hoover in ten days and also met with Mabel Walker Willebrandt. There are no minutes surviving of these encounters, but there can be no doubt that Mayer was determined that, whatever happened as a result of the accident, he would not lose his promised money. Back in New York, he decided that he would give the hated David O. Selznick an engagement present, presumably as a publicity device. He summoned Selznick to the Warwick Hotel and showed him a large box of male jewelry; he asked Selznick to choose what he wanted. Selznick selected a set of gold studs and links. But this gesture did nothing to ease his dislike of Mayer, and Mayer continued to detest the thought of him marrying his daughter. (Back in Los Angeles, Irene was busy trying to cure her stammer with an expert at UCLA.)

On his return, Mayer attended the shooting of Garbo's last silent film, *The Kiss*, directed by Jacques Feyder; she appeared with an understand-ably nervous young Lew Ayres. There was concern at the studio that Garbo's recent lesbian activity would leak to the press. But the fears were groundless; such matters were never discussed publicly in those days.

Mayer liked Feyder and Feyder's wife, the brilliant French actress Françoise Rosay. Even Garbo seemed to behave better now, and enjoyed speaking French and German with her director—a process that left Lew Ayres out in the cold.

* * *

A "sound school" was set up at M.G.M. in August, with young men coming from all over the United States to attend. Once they completed the postgraduate course in sound to film transmission, they would be dispatched to instruct Loew's theater managers and projectionists in how to present talkies.

There were always the big social occasions to take care of. Herbert Hoover's friend, Ambassador Davila of Chile, was the first of a series of notables given an elaborate luncheon at Culver City that August.

And during all of these events, the John Gilbert headaches increased considerably. Earlier that year, the star had married the brilliant stage actress Ina Claire, and Mayer had followed his previous plan in assigning Lionel Barrymore to direct him in *Redemption*. Gilbert could not manage the stage technique necessary for a talking-picture player. He tended to deliver his dialogue in the manner of old stock company melodrama stars, rolling his r's excessively. Barrymore was unable to do anything with him; Fred Niblo was brought in by Thalberg to replace Barrymore and managed to provide some spirited sequences, particularly at the opening when Gilbert rides into a gypsy camp on a white horse. But there was no alternative: Mayer and Thalberg agreed that the picture's release would have to be delayed. In a desperate effort to satisfy the public demand to hear Gilbert speaking, they rushed him into a second picture, *His Glorious Night*.

Incredibly, despite his now obvious ineptitude, Mayer refused to consider anybody except Lionel Barrymore to handle this second vehicle. It was one of the most serious mistakes of his life; presumably, his frequent visits to the East Coast and his many distractions simply resulted in this fatal across-the-board executive decision. Barrymore lost control of the movie and it became a rush job, finished in only thirteen days to satisfy the exhibitors and given none of the usual weight and care of a Metro picture.

Mayer was back in New York in August, when he showed the compilation movie, *The Hollywood Review of 1929*, to the M.G.M. salesmen. It was an ambitious, extraordinarily clumsy effort; it ran 11,000 feet, or 110 minutes, and was boiled down from three million feet of film. Originally, ninety songs were performed; twenty were finally chosen. Among the stars were John Gilbert and Norma Shearer in a scene from *Romeo and Juliet*, Marion Davies, Joan Crawford, Buster Keaton, Marie Dressler, Jack Benny and the Albertina Rasch Ballet. Miss Crawford's attempts at singing and dancing were embarrassing, and so was Conrad Nagel's singing debut, parodying Charles King in *Broadway Melody*. Yet the public was soon mesmerized by what appeared to be a succession of failed auditions by amateurs. The opening at the Astor Theater on August 14 was elaborate; twenty-six girls sang and danced on top of the electric sign with its eight-foot letters.

After the premiere, Mayer moved on to Washington. In September he and Margaret spent a weekend at the White House, entertained by the president, and attended a dinner in their honor at the Chilean embassy. That same week, Edwin M. Stanton of Plandome, Long Island, led other Loew's shareholders in filing suit against Nicholas Schenck, Arthur M. Loew and David Bernstein of Loew's, charging that the three defendants had made an excessive profit through the sale, to Fox, of their shareholdings in the organization. They stated that the sale had been made at $125 a share when the market price was $84, an illegal operation; Stanton disclosed that others involved with Loew's were caught up in the deal, including David Sarnoff of RCA, Joseph Schenck and, surprisingly, Harry M. Warner, who apparently was benefiting from the deal despite the fact that he was supposedly opposing it. Fortunately for the reputations of several of the major defendants, the case was settled out of court.

On September 18, 1929, former British Chancellor of the Exchequer Winston Churchill, then in the political wilderness, visited the studio with his son Randolph. Mayer and Hearst presided over the lunchtime banquet held on a sound stage, and featuring a twenty-piece orchestra and twenty-five M.G.M. stars headed by Charles King in a miniature musical. Among the guests were Marion Davies, Joan Crawford, Douglas Fairbanks, Jr., Ramon Novarro and Anita Page.

Then, in October, the stock market suddenly collapsed. Mayer had invested the bulk of his money in the aforementioned Title Guaranty and Trust and had very little Loew's stock. Irving Thalberg was involved in shares; ironically, his duplicity in the matter of the Fox–Loew's deal cost him a fortune, since he had purchased at a special price a large piece of preferred stock that was now heavily reduced in value. It had dropped from $64\frac{1}{4}$ to $49\frac{5}{8}$; within a year, Loew's would sink to as little as 16.

The crash severely affected Fox; his 660,900 shares of stock in Loew's, for which he had paid more than $73 million, lost fifty percent of their value overnight. He hung on grimly to the shares despite everything; he sold $20 million worth of other stock and drained his personal fortune in order not to sacrifice his holding. By November, Mayer's and Thalberg's future was still uncertain as Fox hung on precariously to his majority interest. When Samuel Marx, the young editor of a small magazine in Manhattan, was approached by Thalberg to run the story department in Hollywood, Thalberg was obliged to tell him that he should not resign from his position, only take a leave of absence, as Thalberg himself wasn't sure if he would be able to continue. Thalberg told Marx that if Fox's henchman, the shady Winfield Sheehan, should even set foot on the M.G.M. lot, Thalberg would walk out at once.

After a series of immensely complicated negotiations, arguments, conflicts, reunions and separations, Fox was slowly but surely eased out of his controlling interest in Loew's. The collapse of the national economy had weakened him so severely that he could not sustain his position or pay off his colossal debts to his backers, who ruthlessly closed in on him. Mayer and J. Robert Rubin received the equivalent of the promised William Fox payoff from Schenck himself so that they would assist in acing Fox out of his position of strength.

Irving Thalberg did not inform Norma Shearer, his wife, of his own thirty pieces of silver, namely, $250,000. Evidently, Thalberg was afraid of her determining the nature of the windfall and demanding it be included in their community property arrangements.

There were other headaches. *His Glorious Night* was laughed off the screen as Gilbert squeakily uttered the words, "I love you! I love you! I love you!" Gilbert's inability to give a "stage" performance was painfully obvious; what was to be done about his future? *Redemption* would be released in 1930, simply in order to satisfy still faithful fans, but there was little hope that it would save Gilbert's career. The emphasis was on musicals: in *Untamed,* Joan Crawford was heard singing "Chant of the Jungle." Ramon Novarro starred in *Devil May Care,* an operetta that all too clearly exposed his effeminacy. But Mayer kept him on, impressed by his pleasant light tenor singing voice.

Still the shooting of *Trader Horn* dragged on, till October 1929. The filming had covered 14,000 miles; the company concluding work in November in the Belgian Congo, where pygmies took part in several scenes.

Edwina Booth, who had never recovered from her early sunstroke, contracted a form of pernicious anemia. She was also stricken by a mysterious ailment, probably bilharziasis, a sickness caused by a parasite that dwells in the liver.

With no medical attention, living under primitive conditions in jungle regions with no proper drinking water or food, she almost died. But she managed to develop her own language, a sort of imitation African dialect, and her own costume of grass; she actually succeeded in running up a tree trunk, which only locals could normally do, faced a charging rhino that killed one of the extras, and experienced a lion jumping over her.

The voyage back to New York was painful for Miss Booth; she had to be brought to Los Angeles, in hospital conditions, by train. According to members of her family, a madman threatened to scar her with vitriol, and her life was in constant danger from William Randolph Hearst, who had financed the picture and feared that she might reveal what had taken place in Africa.

The costar of the film, Mutya Omoolu, with other Africans in the cast, was brought to Hollywood. Refusing to stay in hotels, because they were appalled at the idea of human waste flowing through pipes, the blacks were put up in tents and on the set of a modern straw village in the back lot. According to Duncan Renaldo, Eddie Mannix pimped for them, arranging for prostitutes. Renaldo said that he and some young male members of the crew would crawl in silently on hands and knees to watch the visitors copulating.

While the *Trader Horn* shooting was nearing its end, Greta Garbo was making her sound debut in *Anna Christie*. She scarcely ever behaved properly, even though she liked the director, Clarence Brown. Several scenes were shot in Venice, California, only a short distance from her hotel at Santa Monica; still she would arrive as much as fifty-five minutes behind schedule. She behaved better on a German version, directed by Jacques Feyder. Perhaps because of her admiration for Feyder, her greater ease at speaking in German and her feelings for her costar, Lars Hanson, she gave a far finer performance than she did in the Brown version.

During the shooting, Mayer made a very important decision. He offered Ida Koverman a position, which was, in effect, that of executive assistant; she would occupy the office next to his, both recently completed by Cedric Gibbons and furnished in white. She would be far more than a secretary, and perhaps could be considered the most important person in the studio next to Mayer and Thalberg. Like the great editor Margaret Booth and Mayer's team of favorite writers, led by Frances Marion and Bess Meredyth,[1] she was expected to help keep his finger on the pulse of feminine taste. Despite their various ages, the women were all sisters or mothers to him. He remained a man who placed women first in his life, for all that he was a man's man, still fond of pinochle and poker, still capable of bawling out writers or salesmen, still the very picture of bullish aggression.

---

[1] He had also kept on his niece, Ruth Cummings, and added to the roster her sister Mitzi and Irving Thalberg's sister, Sylvia.

## CHAPTER THIRTEEN

# 1930–1931

So HERE MAYER IS, at the outset of a new decade, the time of the Depression, of bread lines and suicides, of great businesses laid in ruins. M.G.M. is weathering the crisis; the talkie craze is saving the studio from financial destruction, and indeed an unrivaled $15 million in profits will be earned that year.

But Mayer is still deeply troubled. His temper has progressively worsened; his relationship with Thalberg is increasingly unhappy; he is maddened by the thought that Thalberg has again and again crossed him with Nicholas Schenck, and that Thalberg has benefited from the crushing of William Fox. The Julian affair still hangs over him, along with the possibility that he will be sent to prison. And he remains distressed by his bigger stars. He has reached a point with Garbo (as, indeed, has Irving Thalberg) that he cannot bring himself to speak to her directly, but instead must send her notes through intermediaries, instructing her what to do. Impeccably inconsiderate, Garbo succeeded in torturing everyone she came in contact with. She was unable to give of herself, and even when acting in pictures, she made love more convincingly to the camera than to her leading men. Her fabled beauty and hypnotic presence pulled her through one hastily assembled screenplay after another. Casting was a constant nightmare for Mayer and Thalberg in those early talkie days. Even with the number of stars they had under contract, there were never enough. The hated Adolph Zukor had to be asked for the heavy-lidded, amusingly vampiric Kay Francis to fill the title role in *Passion Flower*, a typical romantic invention about a rich woman bedding her chauffeur; Ruth Chatterton was brought back again from Broadway to moon about with huge, sad eyes, proscenium technique and liquid vowels in *Lady of Scandal;* the ladylike Kay Johnson was imported for Cecil B. DeMille as a genteel addendum to the payroll. Basil Rathbone, with his knife-sharp profile and icy, haughty demeanor, was a considerable asset, and there was a constant search for rugged leading men, since William Haines, Nils Asther and Ramon Novarro lacked the necessary qualities.

Although he cannot be said to have been the instrument of John Gilbert's destruction, there is evidence from statements made by his daughters that Mayer privately relished Gilbert's downfall. Any prodigal son or daughter would only be the object of his wrath; he was brutal when it came to a star failing to rise to the challenge of sound. He was greatly irritated by Norma Shearer. Her highfalutin airs distracted him; even her huge personal triumph in *The Trial of Mary Dugan* could not quell his annoyance with her. According to one of Mayer's nieces, Miss Shearer would, typically, order clothes from Bullock's Wilshire on approval, keep the wardrobe department up all night copying the clothes, then return the originals as unsuitable. Nobody dared point out that she was being photographed at social events in the very clothes whose designs she had declared unacceptable.

The writing team, controlled more by Thalberg than Mayer, was beginning to grasp the requirements of the new talkie medium. They understood that they must tailor the scripts very carefully for the stars' own personalities, making sure that they would not speak in a manner foreign to their normal forms of address. As much as in silent films, sincerity in a performer was vital; there was no longer the protection of delicately artistic cutting, of fluid, untrammeled photography.

A recent addition to the studio was proving to be very successful. Adrian Adolph Greenberg, known only by his first name, was twenty-seven years old. He was a graduate of the Parson's School of Design in New York and, at a mere twenty-two years of age, had done the lustrous Russian wardrobe for *The Eagle*, costarring Rudolph Valentino and Vilma Banky, thereby upstaging Mrs. Valentino, Natacha Rambova, who customarily took care of all her husband's movie costumes.

Mayer and Thalberg had noted Adrian's contribution to film after film, and, in 1928, had granted him the supreme honor of designing Garbo's clothes for the picture *A Woman of Affairs*. By 1930, Adrian was her personal couturier. Intense, driven, crouch-shouldered from hours of working over his designs, Adrian became the reigning figure of the wardrobe department, keeping armies of seamstresses busy round the clock. His taste ran to the extreme: the clothes he made, marvels of ruffles and furbelows, of huge collars and sweeping, embroidered skirts, were as much trademarks of the M.G.M. grand style for the next decade as Cedric Gibbons's paneled walls, richly gold-leafed doors and sumptuous white furnishings.

Another recent studio employee, destined to be equally significant, was the composer and arranger Herbert Stothart. While still in his early twenties, he had composed the operetta *Rose Marie* with Rudolf Friml; its success on Broadway and elsewhere propelled him to the top. At the outset at Culver City, he worked chiefly for DeMille; his Ballet Electrique for DeMille's *Madam Satan* was an accomplished pastiche. In the next few years, he would emerge as the studio's leading creator of dramatic scores and prominent arranger of operettas and musicals. In contrast to the resounding strains of Max Steiner or Erich Wolfgang Korngold at Warner Brothers, he provided subtle, restrained, if somewhat anemic accompaniments to the action. He would eventually provide the delicately sinister refrain for *The Picture of Dorian Gray*, and would skillfully rearrange Frederick Delius's Florida music (an inspired choice of his own) for *The Yearling*.

The Foreign Department, always ramshackle, was firmed up in 1930 as Culver Export Corporation, with Arthur, the tall, elegantly slender, trimly mustached and sportive twin son of Marcus Loew, in charge.[1] The smart young New Yorker Robert Vogel, taking over the Hollywood end, found that to impress overseas interests, there had to be a Hollywood box number, as Culver City meant nothing. Arthur Loew hated Mayer, Vogel states; he felt that he should have inherited the studio from his father. Furthermore, Loew was married to Adolph Zukor's daughter, a link that Mayer found threatening.

Under Arthur Loew was the high-voltage livewire L. L. ("Laudy") Lawrence, who was in charge of European sales. It became a major challenge to make all M.G.M. pictures in a variety of foreign languages.

With the advent of talkies, the story department inevitably grew. The tall, broad-shouldered, warmly genial Samuel Marx, hired by Irving Thalberg, applied his considerable skills as story editor to building up the division. He reported that 400 properties a week, or 20,000 a year, came in for analysis, discussion and, in most cases, rejection. Forty writers were under contract by mid-1930. Nathalie Bucknall, described by Marx as "a solidly built Russian woman reliably reported to have ridden with the Cossacks," was in charge of research. Marx was firmly settled in by the spring of 1930.

In January 1930, Thalberg was fretting over the assembled footage of *Trader Horn*. Although Margaret Booth had worked heroically to rescue it, it was no more than a travelogue, and Thalberg sent it back to the cutting room for more work. Sam Marx hired the writer Cyril Hume to

[1] His sensitive brother David was vice president in charge of Loew's multimillion-dollar real estate holdings; David later became a distinguished producer (*The Southerner; The Moon and Sixpence*).

put together a new continuity and to enhance the story line. That same month, Hearst closed the Fox sound newsreel deal, receiving in return 15,000 shares of preferred stock in Fox and twenty-five percent of the common stock, with Hearst's E. B. Hatrick on the board. Yet Hearst continued to keep Marion Davies firmly at M.G.M., somehow contriving to pacify Mayer and Thalberg over these questionable arrangements with their archenemy. Also in January, Mayer and Thalberg entered upon contracts for five years each.

In February, Buster Keaton, unable to adapt to talkies, left the studio, and so did Renée Adorée, whose French accent was not considered appealing.

On February 20, the Mayers announced their daughter Edith's engagement to William Goetz. Mayer was, as we have seen, resigned to the match; there was still the dreaded thought of Irene's forthcoming wedding.

Mayer made an important addition to the staff. Fifty-two-year-old Kate Corbaley became his chief storyteller; she was chosen for her ability to relate a plot suspensefully and colorfully to save him the time of reading a screenplay. Although she was matronly, white-haired and plump, with a rather plain face, she actually had a colorful background herself. She had been born on a ship at sea and had, at a time when women were generally restricted to writing romantic stories, put together vivid action and adventure tales that formed the bases for Harry Carey westerns. Deserted by her husband, she had raised four daughters, then had entered into a mysterious intimate friendship, or perhaps liaison, with the writer Florence Ryerson, a Paramount contractee, whom she would later arrange to be brought over to M.G.M. to write the excellent Lionel Barrymore vehicle, *This Side of Heaven*. When Florence Ryerson's husband, who had vanished to the South Seas, returned to claim her, Mrs. Ryerson rejected him in favor of Kate Corbaley.

Late in February, Mayer suffered a shock: his friend, the bootlegger and pimp—and turning actors' agent—Frank Orsatti, whose father, Morris Orsatti, had recently been sentenced to twenty years' imprisonment for attempting to bribe a federal agent, was himself indicted for income tax evasion, a charge to which he pleaded guilty. Mayer pulled every string to get him off; Orsatti escaped prison by paying a large sum to the tax commissioner whom Mayer had recently had appointed through Hoover.

At this time, the ever-reliable Frances Marion completed her script for a prison picture, *The Big House*. Mayer and Thalberg sent her to San Quentin, where Asa Keyes was about to be incarcerated. Ida Koverman made the arrangements with Warden James Holohan. Miss Marion, whose husband, George Hill, would direct the film, ran a gauntlet of angry or mocking stares as she noted certain characters as bases for her story: a vicious, beef-slashing butcher would be an ideal part for Wallace Beery; a handsome young man in death row could be a model for Robert Montgomery (a muscular double had to be used for him in a scene at the beginning when he was strip searched). As for the warden, he was pure Lewis Stone. Cedric Gibbons embarked on a magnificent prison set to match the vividness of Frances Marion's concept.

At the beginning of March, Mayer was locked in a dispute with the actor Charles Bickford, who was independently wealthy through owning gas stations, whaling boats and markets. Bickford declined to work at night on the movie *The Sea Bat*; Mayer ordered him to report to work at 8:00 P.M. on March 10, but he refused to appear and the picture had to close down for several days. Bickford offered $100,000 to buy back his contract; Mayer finally bullied him into returning to work.

In mid-March, a mentally disturbed prison hospital parolee sent death threats to Mayer; the man was sent to jail.

By this time, Mayer had a piece of the bootleg action on the lot— despite the fact that he was a teetotaler. When Frank Orsatti became an agent, Mayer set up a man to supply liquor; that man was the only one allowed on the lot. When Prohibition ended, Mayer was in partnership with him in a liquor business around the corner next to a drugstore. Mayer also had a special deal with Western Union. The studio had its own telegraph office and Mayer's spies knew what went through the system; anything critical of the studio or dubious in content went to him. Lou Reynolds, head of the telegraph room, was fired eventually because he knew too much.

He also had a split of the commissary take: everyone had to eat his chicken soup. But he supplied the food at very reduced prices (lots were drawn at the tables to see who would pay the bill). He benefited, too, from the European antique-buying trips of Edwin B. Willis, assistant to Cedric Gibbons. Willis and Mayer shared an antiques business on Santa Monica Boulevard; the stars bought their furniture there. According to the assistant director Wallace Worsley, "The furniture went out the M.G.M. back door."

On March 19, William Goetz and Edith Mayer were married at a lavish ceremony at the Biltmore Hotel in downtown Los Angeles. Irene was furious when she found out that Mayer had ordered Adrian to design her sister's exquisite wedding dress and long veil. "She screamed and railed about it," Edie said. Goetz family members and guests arrived drunk by private car on the Santa Fe Chief. Mayer spent a fortune on the wedding and subsequent dinner dance. The ceremonies took place at

8:00 P.M. in a room that was turned into a bower of spring flowers; multicolored wax candles and ceiling and wall lights bathed the salon in rainbow tints. Edith was stunning in Adrian's white satin, with long sleeves and a royal train; her veil was made of duchesse and rose point lace. Irene, forcing a smile, in yellow tulle, carrying a bouquet of yellow roses, was maid of honor. The bridesmaids were Marion Davies, Corinne Griffith (for whom William Goetz was still working), Bessie Love and the actresses May McAvoy and Carmel Myers; they were dressed in turquoise blue crepe and carried bouquets of pink camellias.

The ushers were the producer Walter Morosco, David O. Selznick, Mayer's nephew Jack Cummings, Eddie Mannix and the directors William A. Seiter and Edwin L. Marin. Goetz's brother Ben was best man. The ceremony was performed by Rabbi Edgar Magnin.

Of all the lavish gifts, Edie's favorite came from President Hoover. He had sent her a magnificent silver tureen which had sat at the center of the dinner table when she and her parents had been at the White House for the first dinner after the inauguration. Unfortunately, an embarrassed note appeared the next day, stating that the president had no business to have sent her the present at all, since White House furniture is the property of the nation. Wailing loudly, Edie had to send it back.

Immediately after the wedding, David Selznick decided on the date of his marriage to Irene, without even being engaged to her officially. B. P. Schulberg had granted him vacation leave starting April 29, and that was the date he settled on. Courageously, he and Irene walked into Mayer's office at the studio and informed him of their decision. Mayer was furious that he had not been asked if the date would suit him: a stickler for protocol, he believed that the father of the bride should be given a choice of dates so that he could make the necessary arrangements. This seems to have been reasonable, in view of his crowded schedule and the fact that he was due to face the old usury charges at any time and might wind up in prison. Irene made no mention of this crucial fact in her memoirs.

If Irene is to be believed, Selznick behaved abjectly at the meeting, answering Mayer's cries of anger with complaints that he needed to experience sexual fulfillment. Mayer rightly found this tasteless. Selznick slammed out; Irene stayed behind, fiercely arguing with her father, possessed of a spirit as strong as his. Then, apparently seeming to lose, she fainted.

She returned home to force her unhappy mother to confront Mayer, then impatiently announced to Selznick that she was giving up the marriage. He begged her to change her mind. Despite Irene's protestations in her book, only Mayer emerges from this entire story with any credit.

Just nineteen days later, after the Goetzes returned from their honeymoon, Mayer was again arrested on the old usury charges and, with Motley Flint and eighteen other defendants, made to stand before the judge in Superior Court. With the able counsel of a new lawyer, Jerry Geisler, he had worked hard for weeks to figure a way of avoiding the results of the grand jury's latest indictment. He cited the law of double jeopardy; that he had already been arraigned, that the charges against him had been dismissed, that conspiracy and usury had not been established in his case, and that he should therefore be set free. Jerry Geisler, who would later have a colorful career as protector-lawyer for big Hollywood stars, made sure that Mayer was let off again. According to some sources, his friends at the U.S. attorney general's department in Washington brought to bear their necessary influence; it is hard not to believe that Mabel Walker Willebrandt was the chief string-puller in the matter.

Mayer was faced with another agony. His cantankerous but respected father, Jacob, was ailing. At the time Mayer was rearrested, he lay in the Glendale Sanitarium with the advanced symptoms of chronic myocarditis. Attempting, with his usual stubbornness, to get out of his hospital bed when he had been ordered not to, he fell to the floor and broke his left femur. Irritable with the nurses, fretful when his family visited him, the old man passed away on April 18, 1930. He had resolutely refused to accept money from his son and left a mere $10,107.05, divided between the various members of his family and Jewish charitable institutions. Upon his grave in the Beth Israel Cemetery, Mayer placed the inscription, in Yiddish, "A wonderful man, exceptionally versed in learning experience through the Talmud, and greatly beloved."

Yetta Mayer was unable to leave her ladies' clothing store in Montreal for the occasion; Jerry, having long reconciled with his brother, was working as location manager, and was present with his wife, Rheba. Rudolph Mayer was in town for the funeral. He had abandoned his Canadian mistress Vera Caveny and had moved to Florida, where he had gotten rich selling worthless swampland to unsuspecting speculators. In the wake of the Florida land crash of 1925, he himself had been ruined through equally ill-advised investments. In 1927, he was in Mexico, where he outsmarted himself again in a series of real estate deals. Still dressed in the height of fashion, sporting a new mistress and smoking Havana cigars, he dazzled everyone; then he disappeared again. He would return to California following a Boston arrest in 1934, as attractive, glamorous and dangerous as ever.

The quarrels between Mayer and Irene continued even after her engagement to Selznick. So desperate was the situation that, within days of the wedding, Irene announced to Selznick she couldn't go ahead. He pleaded, begging her not to leave him; harsh and strong though she was, she could not resist his pleas, and the engagement was patched up. Edie recalled that Selznick and Irene urged her to protest to Mayer that he must give them a marriage as elaborate as her own. She claimed that she did intercede; Irene wrote in her memoirs that Edie refused to do anything for her. Whatever the truth, Mayer decided not to stage a spectacle such as that which had occurred at the Biltmore; he would have the wedding at the beach house instead. When Hoover suggested that the Selznicks should come to Washington and visit the White House, he could scarcely decline; it must have gone against the grain that his future son-in-law would be received by the president.

The Selznick nuptials took place at the beach house at 8:30 P.M. on April 29; the official reason for the modesty of the occasion was Jacob Mayer's recent death. Irene had arranged to be dressed in the same design as her sister: she even carried the same bouquet of white orchids, another act of defiance.

Edie was matron of honor. The bridesmaids were Janet Gaynor; Marjorie Daw, wife of Selznick's brother Myron; Mayer's niece Mitzi; and a friend, Marjorie Straus, who would soon marry Mayer's nephew Jack Cummings. All were dressed in yellow. Myron Selznick was best man; the ushers were B. P. Schulberg (!), William Goetz, Paul Bern and the writer Oliver H. P. Garrett. Schulberg's presence is astonishing: it can only be put down to Lewis Selznick's hatred of Mayer.

In her autobiography, Irene wrote bitterly of the inclusion of her father's relatives, a particularly inexcusable attitude since she had chosen Mitzi Cummings as a bridesmaid. She left with her husband for an awkward honeymoon in Santa Barbara. It was a disaster; Irene went out for an early morning walk on the beach, wondering if she hadn't made a major mistake. On the train to New York and Washington, their luggage left behind because of a mishap, the couple quarreled noisily, smashing up furniture.

The Selznicks traveled on to the White House and from there went on their honeymoon voyage to France and England.

With that extraordinary juxtaposition of dates which marked Louis B. Mayer's career, the same day the hated marriage took place, a Superior Court of New York hearing on William Fox resulted in Fox's having to give up his company and yield control of Loew's, Inc., to the dangerous Winfield Sheehan's chosen man, Harley M. Clarke, president of General Theaters Equipment Company and the Utilities, Power and Light Company. For $100 million, Clarke bought out Fox and his 660,900 shares of Loew's.

One night after the wedding, the second Academy Awards banquet was held at the Cocoanut Grove, with all awards presented by the Academy president, William deMille. *Broadway Melody* was Best Picture, and Mayer accepted the statuette for it; Cedric Gibbons won for *The Bridge of San Luis Rey* and Clyde De Vinna for *White Shadows in the South Seas*. Mary Pickford won for *Coquette* and Warner Baxter for *In Old Arizona*.

There was much discussion about the fairness of the awards, and Mayer and other members of the board of judges were accused of favoritism. It was decided that in the future less influence must be exercised on the decisions.

Star divorces were always a headache for Mayer, who struggled to maintain a front of propriety at the studio. Yet again, John Gilbert proved an irritation: he was threatening to kill Ina Claire, during a series of violent quarrels, and Miss Claire walked out on him, went back to him, then walked out again.

The problems with *Trader Horn* continued. Mayer and Thalberg had ordered W. S. Van Dyke to reshoot much of the picture in Mexico. But Edwina Booth was too ill to work consistently; she had never recovered from the sicknesses contracted in Africa. To avoid unfriendly publicity, Mayer, with great shrewdness, offered her the use of a house owned by himself and the Thalbergs as part of their Playa del Rey real estate development. This would keep her from prying photographers.

Thalberg decreed that there must be a sequence in *Trader Horn* in which lions would fight over a recent kill. The animal trainers in Mexico informed the studio production team that no such fight could possibly take place: there was no way to make the creatures battle with each other. Somebody decided on a solution. They slaughtered a horse, and the lions, excited by the smell of blood, tore at each other violently.

When David and Irene Selznick returned from their European honeymoon, they went to live with Mayer's archenemy, David's father, Lewis. Still more irritatingly, they rented Marshall Neilan's Beverly Hills house and gave a party for Adolph Zukor, which they forced Mayer to attend. In self-defense, he gave them the use of a house in one of his Santa Monica estates owned with the Thalberg-Rapf-Fairbanks-Pickford Title Guaranty Trust.

That summer, King Vidor embarked on the most ambitious M.G.M. picture of the year, the pioneer talkie western *Billy the Kid*. For years, Vidor had tried to get Thalberg to consent to the project; at last, Thalberg yielded when Mayer suggested using the former Alabama football star Johnny Mack Brown in the title role. Mayer was convinced that

Brown had tremendous potential, whereas Vidor saw him only as a star athlete whose chief acting ability consisted of riding backwards on a horse. He wanted the young James Cagney.

Mayer insisted that Wallace Beery be cast as Pat Garrett. Again, Vidor opposed; Beery was too domineering, he felt. Helen Hayes was supposed to play the female lead, but Mayer ruled her out on the grounds that she was insufficiently attractive, and Thalberg agreed with the decision. She was replaced by Kay Johnson, who had just appeared in DeMille's *Madam Satan*. (That picture was a disaster, and Mayer terminated DeMille's contract after one more picture, a remake of *The Squaw Man*.)

Boldly, Mayer and Thalberg authorized Vidor to shoot *Billy the Kid* in the revolutionary 70mm format; a regular 35mm version would also be made. The locations in the Grand Canyon, Zion National Park and an area near Monument Valley were impressive in the large-screen format, and Mayer and Thalberg were delighted by the rushes. In the San Fernando Valley, Vidor built a studio street and a full-scale county courthouse, front and back. Later sequences were shot at Gallup, New Mexico. One day, when Mayer was on the set, he had a big thrill: his childhood idol, the great cowboy star William S. Hart, arrived, carrying Billy the Kid's original revolver; Mayer entertained him to a lavish luncheon in the newly finished commissary. *Billy the Kid* was the first Vidor picture that Mayer unequivocally liked. He had always loved westerns, but paradoxically he would make very few in the genre in the years to come. The difficulties of shooting on location with cumbersome talkie equipment inhibited him and Thalberg from making any major commitments.

On July 14, 1930, Mayer received another shock. His close friend and associate in the Julian affair, banker Motley Flint, was testifying in court before Judge Collier. David O. Selznick was suing Flint's former bank and, by extension, Flint for $250,000 that remained unaccounted for. As Flint stepped down from the witness stand, Frank Keaton, a real estate broker ruined by the oil men, fired across Mrs. Lewis Selznick's shoulder and shot Flint dead; the Selznicks were both spattered with blood. Judge Collier himself leaped down from the bench and pulled the gun from the killer's hand. Keaton escaped hanging because of doubts about his sanity.

Toward the end of August, Mayer was appalled to learn that Lon Chaney, only forty-seven years old, had cancer of the throat. The first signs of trouble had come during his only talkie, the remake of *The Unholy Three*, when, as he was imitating a parrot cry, a blood vessel had burst in his throat. It turned out that a tiny gypsum imitation snowflake, blown by a wind machine, had lodged in his throat during one scene and had set up an irritation that caused the growth. On August 27, Chaney died; Mayer was unable to attend the funeral, as he was in New York.

September brought a high honor for Mayer: he was selected as vice chairman of the Republican State Central Committee and received many congratulations, the first of which came from President Hoover, the second from Judge Leon R. Yankwich of the Superior Court of Los Angeles.

The following week, Mayer attended a big Republican rally at Dreamland Rink. At the luncheon, Mayer spoke warmly of the film industry's future. The masses needed escape from their plight; with millions on the bread line, M.G.M. led the other studios in supplying glamorous, make-believe stories that took the audience into a world of luxury, where they could forget their own discomforts in observing the problems and stresses of the rich. Garbo wore sumptuous clothes in *Romance,* in which, yet again, she was improbably cast as an Italian; Ramon Navarro appeared in a film whose title would have brought laughs in a later era: *In Gay Madrid.* Norma Shearer starred in *The Divorcee,* a story of society wives and their affairs, which would win her an Oscar; Marion Davies charmingly portrayed the title character of *The Floradora Girl,* which vividly evoked the gay nineties in the theater world.

Two performers emerged very strongly that fall. Joan Crawford had emerged as a huge-eyed, jazz-mad flapper, memorably sexy and driven by a manic energy. Cruder than Shearer, without the elegant, remote, mysterious quality of Garbo, she had a disturbing earthiness and electricity. At last talkies released her, because her voice, tense, deep and challenging, added immeasurably to her presence on the screen. In *Dance, Fools, Dance,* a story of a young woman joining a newspaper's city desk after her family is smashed in the 1929 crash, she made a vivid, startling impression. And with her in the cast was an equally charismatic presence. Clark Gable, though not yet launched on a major career, was far more robust and masculine than any other M.G.M. male performer. With Gilbert sinking rapidly, there was a desperate need for a virile and heroic leading man.

Born in Cadiz, Ohio, just after the turn of the century, Gable had worked as a laborer, a stock company actor, a movie extra and a roustabout before he finally had successes on the stage in *Madame X* and *Chicago.* He married an older woman, Josephine Dillon, who pushed his career successfully; appearing in *Machinal* in New York City in 1928, he was described by one reviewer as "vigorous and brutally masculine." His presence was irresistible; his strong, forceful stance, his dimpled, boyish smile, his muscular shoulders and chest, his air of sexual self-confidence proved irresistible to almost every woman he met. Together, he and

Crawford were dynamite: they created an erotic tension that had audiences flocking to the picture.

They were involved in an intense sexual relationship during the shooting. This presented yet another headache for Mayer. Miss Crawford was married to Douglas Fairbanks, Jr., while Gable had dumped Josephine Dillon and was married now to Ria Langham, a wealthy Texas divorcée of great sophistication and charm. Gable and Crawford had to indulge in an astonishing succession of lies in order to hide their liaison. Later, Miss Crawford made no secret of her fascination with Gable, saying, "He was the most exciting actor of them all . . . he had balls . . . his nearness in *Dance, Fools, Dance* had such impact, my knees buckled. If he hadn't been holding me by the shoulders, I would have dropped to the floor." She added, "I don't believe any woman is telling the truth if she ever worked with Gable if she says she did not feel twinges of a sexual urge beyond belief."

Douglas Fairbanks, Jr., has confirmed the relationship. No inkling could appear in the columns, but Mayer and Thalberg knew a good thing when they were onto it. They immediately began preparations for further costarring vehicles.

Mayer traveled to Washington in January 1931 for yet another stay at the White House, then continued to New York for meetings with Nicholas Schenck, returning in time for a new scandal that embroiled the studio.

Edwina Booth was again threatened with murder just before *Trader Horn* had its lavish premiere in Hollywood. Mayer had to arrange for her to be accompanied to the occasion by Whitey Hendry, who doubled as Chief of Police of both Culver City and M.G.M. Just as *Trader Horn* opened in Hollywood, and in New York at the beginning of February, Suzette Renaldo, who had been divorced by her husband the previous year, was in court, suing Edwina Booth for alienation of her husband's affections and for having an affair with him during the shooting of the picture. Suzette also charged that Miss Booth had been involved in a plot to kidnap their four-and-a-half-year-old son "by hook or by crook" unless she dropped the alienation suit. She stated that Miss Booth had sent her a box of chocolates. When she ate one, she became violently ill. Mrs. Kate L. Wagner, Suzette Renaldo's neighbor, said under oath: "There was a knock on my door. I opened it and Mrs. Renaldo fell into my arms. She cried, 'God save me! That woman has poisoned me!' I put her in bed. When she woke, she said, 'This is where that Booth woman and my husband slept together!' "

Two psychiatrists said on the witness stand that Mrs. Renaldo suffered from "mental disturbances," and she lost the case. Later, her appeal

against the divorce was ruled out by the court. In that hearing, Miss
Booth gave testimony in a wheelchair.

There was no way the matter could be kept out of the papers, and
indeed public curiosity was so enhanced by it that when *Trader Horn*
opened, its huge success was increased.

Incredibly, Edwina Booth rallied sufficiently to make a picture, *The
Midnight Patrol,* directed by Mayer's old employee Christy Cabanne. She
played second female lead to Mary Nolan, who had originally been
chosen for her role in *Trader Horn.* She had to be carried on a stretcher
to the set of this and another picture, *Trapped in Tijuana.* She had to go
to England later on for treatments, and from there to France. For years
afterward, she had to stay in dark rooms, unable to endure sunlight. The
studio finally settled with her for less than $45,000, the amount of the
original insurance policy. According to her brother, Booth Woodruff, a
shyster lawyer hired by Metro tried to terrorize her into accepting
$17,000 in full settlement, but the family protected her.

Yet another problem involved *The Phantom of Paris,* in which the
British actress Edna Best starred with John Gilbert. The first day she was
called for work, she was not in her dressing room. Two hours later, the
director, John F. Robertson, received a telegram from her from Needles,
California, begging forgiveness and saying that she was on her way to
New York to rejoin her husband, the actor Herbert Marshall. She was
hastily replaced by Leila Hyams.

Leaving Thalberg to handle these crises, Mayer lingered on in the
east. He saw *Private Lives,* the Noël Coward comedy, at the Selwyn
Theater in New York, starring Gertrude Lawrence and the author; in
conference with the producer-director Sidney Franklin, he decided to
buy it for Norma Shearer. Robert Montgomery was later cast in the
Coward role. Mayer had meetings with Arthur Loew, discussing extensive setting up of foreign productions in Europe, in place of the foreign
versions being shot in Hollywood.

He returned to Los Angeles for meetings at the Academy of Motion
Pictures Arts and Sciences; he intended developing the Academy
Awards as a major social event. He tried to patch up his differences with
his daughters. Because of the peculiar relationship between the Fox Corporation and M.G.M., he had been able to obtain a job for William
Goetz at Fox, somehow swallowing the fact that Goetz would be working
with Winfield Sheehan. When Corinne Griffith's company collapsed
following her failure in talkies, it was necessary, if only for publicity
reasons, that Goetz be found a job. Mayer perhaps feared charges of
nepotism if he hired Goetz himself; or he may have been influenced by
the fact that Goetz was an unregenerate Democrat and could not be

relied upon to supply either personal or financial support in the upcoming election. Many studio employees would soon be required to contribute one day's salary each to the Republican campaign—a heavy burden for those with small wages.

A major clash took place between Mayer and industry writers at a meeting of the Academy on March 25, 1931. Academy President William deMille, aware of the conflicts between writers, directors and producers, had rashly opened a series of "squawk forums," in which members were encouraged to speak their minds. No sooner had Mayer walked in than he was hailed with abuse by several writers under contract to the studio. They charged him with giving them unsuitable pictures, forcing them to work in competition with each other on scripts and never being allowed into production conferences. They stated that directors would often rewrite them, and that many movies were reconstructed over their heads. Mayer screamed, "As long as we put up the money we're entitled to final say! The only test of art is financial success! And you writers aren't like playwrights—you get paid every week whether you work or not!" Every writer in the room booed him, and William deMille clashed with him also. He left in a fury; soon after, several M.G.M. writers were fired or suffered heavy pay cuts.

In April, Mayer signed a newcomer, twenty-four-year-old Robert Young, whom he saw at the Pasadena Playhouse. Slight, insecure, nervous, hating his own face on the screen, Young was seized by an inferiority complex in the face of the big stars he was working with. He was already showing signs of alcoholism, but Mayer nursed him along like a son.

A topic of the studio gossip mill was Joan Crawford's jealous outbursts against Norma Shearer. She hated Miss Shearer, complaining that her only virtue was she was "screwing the boss." Miss Crawford was arguably the more talented of the two, more exciting and impressive on the screen. Crawford's agent forced her salary up to $2,000 a week; it was still $8,000 a week less than Mrs. Thalberg's.

In April, a two-month hearing began in New York Supreme Court before Justice Cotillo. Minority stockholders of Loew's, Inc., were suing Nicholas Schenck, Arthur Loew and their partner David Bernstein for profiteering secretly in the merger deal of 1929. Edwin Stanton and Fred Warren, holders of 600 shares of common stock, represented the group. During the hearing, the truth of Irving Thalberg's duplicity in accepting $250,000 for his silence was exposed.[2] In addition, it was revealed that Leopold Friedman, Loew's counsel, was paid $200,000; Eddie Mannix

[2] He also received $75,000 in a final settlement paid by Schenck to Mayer, to hide his previous involvement.

was paid $50,000; the director Edgar Selwyn, $10,000; Supervisor Felix
Feist, $10,000; Marvin Schenck, nephew of Nicholas Schenck, $10,000;
Howard Dietz, $10,000; and several others, $10,000. Fortunately for
them, the Thalbergs were in Europe during the hearing, leaving Mayer
in full charge of the studio.

He was back on the firing line in May. It was charged by independent
film exchanges on the nineteenth of the month that, whereas other
studio pictures were severely censored, M.G.M. productions were allowed through without a cut. Particularly singled out was *The Secret Six*
which exposed brutal conditions in the meat industry. Even though
Wallace Beery was shown cruelly slaughtering a steer in the opening
reel, and wholesale corruption in the city of Chicago was exposed, nothing was done about the picture. Mayer remained silent; he knew that
Will Hays would continue to overrule local censorship boards. At the
same time, to cover himself, Mayer, who had just become head of the
Motion Picture Producers Association, smartly supported a fully outlined
motion picture Code, designed to restrict overt sexuality and violence in
the movies. But it was not fully implemented until 1934.

An event of June 6 was the signing of eight-year-old Jackie Cooper, a
gifted child actor and a sensation in Paramount's *Skippy*, to a contract.
Mabel Cooper, his mother, appeared with Mayer at the Superior Courthouse downtown to make the necessary arrangements via Loeb, Walker
and Loeb. Cooper was cast in Harry Rapf's production of King Vidor's
*The Champ*, the story of a relationship between a prizefighter and a little
boy, with Wallace Beery cast in the title role. Beery, who had made an
impression in *The Big House* and *The Secret Six*, was being carefully
groomed by Mayer for stardom. The forty-four-year-old Kansan's pug-
ugly face, ungainly 250-pound wrestler's physique and crinkly, boyish
grin fascinated audiences. This dangerous charmer, who ignored most
dialogue he was given, ill-treated Jackie Cooper and improvised everything to the despair of his supervisor and director, had started his life on
a railroad section gang and a circus elephant trainer. A stage transvestite, he couldn't resist dressing up in evening gowns and feathered hats
at the slightest provocation. He was brutal to women; he bloodily raped
his first wife, Gloria Swanson, on their wedding night and ill-treated her
henceforth; he was no kinder to his present wife, Rita Beery.

Beery was a handful in 1931. He was a reckless flyer whose inept
piloting of his own hand-tooled monoplane often landed him in mountains and deserts, from which he had to be rescued. Mayer retained a soft
spot for him perhaps because, in April, Beery, learning that his mother
was dying of pneumonia, had flown his aircraft through stormy weather,
which forced him to make a pancake landing in St. Louis, to be at her

bedside in New York. That kind of devotion overcame all Mayer's objections.

The shooting of The Champ went smoothly. But that could not be said of the new Crawford vehicle with Johnny Mack Brown, Torch Song, about the love of a Salvation Army woman for a ne'er-do-well. The movie was a disaster; Mack Brown was fired and it was reshot as Laughing Sinners, with Clark Gable taking over. Miss Crawford's next picture, This Modern Age, involved a change of directors and an equal amount of reshooting. This made the high-strung actress nervous; she complained that because of the changes she had had to cancel going to Europe with her husband and the Thalbergs. There was no basis for the complaint: if she had gone, she would have been separated from Gable.

An incident occurred on June 6. Mayer was friendly with Douglas Shearer, Norma's brother and chief sound recording engineer at the studio, who after much work had improved the quality of the studio sound tracks and had worked miracles with difficult voices like his sister's and John Gilbert's. Shearer was enjoying an adulterous affair, and he foolishly told his wife, Marion, about it. That afternoon, Marion went to the Venice amusement pier, walked up to a shooting gallery where pistols with actual bullets were in use, picked up one of the guns, placed it against her right temple, then put it down and fired three rounds at the targets. Immediately after that, she set the pistol between her eyes and blew her brains out. The publicity department's official reason for the suicide was that she was grieving over her mother's death.

Three days later, a columnist revealed that Clark Gable's marriage to Ria Langham was illegal, and that they should be remarried at once. On June 13, Gable applied for the marriage license under the pseudonym William C. Gable. When reporters asked him about it, he said, unwisely, that William was his brother and would be marrying Ria in his place. Mayer dispatched M.G.M. publicist Joe Sherman to the Santa Ana Courthouse on the nineteenth, to fight off the reporters at the wedding. Ria panicked, begged the reporters to leave, then fled the scene by automobile in hysterical tears. Gable was distraught; furious at his refusal to cooperate with them, the pressmen dug up Josephine Dillon, who was only too ready to complain about everything Gable had done to her. On August 2, she wrote Mayer a long, tortuous letter, demanding money, indeed a permanent income, to keep Gable's disgrace out of the newspapers. In desperation, Mayer paid her off, but canceled the payments just under a year later, at the same time Gable suspended alimony and reaped a whirlwind in terms of adverse publicity.

That week, during the shooting of Susan Lenox, Her Fall and Rise, with Gable, Garbo was introduced by the writer and actress Salka

Viertel to the Spanish beauty Mercedes de Acosta, an artist, author and dilettante with numerous friends in high society and literary circles. She fell in love with Garbo at first sight, and Garbo with her. She listened while Garbo grumbled endlessly about the misery of making *Susan Lenox*, in which she felt she was giving her worst performance to date. Garbo had asked for Gable, but was unable to relate to him. He in turn found her boring, and was irritated by the fact that her salary was over $9,000 larger than his.

Garbo walked off the picture six times, using numerous excuses; the real reason was that she spent days and steamy nights with Miss de Acosta. Mayer demanded that she return to work, which she did, with great reluctance. The moment the shooting was over, she took off with Mercedes, somehow evading the press and finding a secret location on an island in Silver Lake in the Sierra Nevadas. For six weeks, the couple swam naked, undertook mountain climbs bare to the waist and fished for mountain trout. Miss de Acosta wrote in her memoirs, *Here Lies the Heart*, "I would see [Greta] above me, her face and body outlined against the sky, looking like some radiant, elemental, glorious god and goddess melted into one . . . six weeks that seemed only six minutes . . ."

On July 1, 1931, Margaret Mayer was sworn in to the Board of Supervisors of the County Juvenile Probation Committee, supervising the work of county probation officers in the handling, correction and placing of juvenile court wards.

It was just as well that she was busy, because Mayer was in love with the popular singing star Grace Moore. He signed her to a high-priced contract and personally supervised the two pictures in which she appeared for him, *A Lady's Morals*, an amusing version of the life of the Swedish singer Jenny Lind, and *New Moon*, from the operetta by Sigmund Romberg. Mayer was captivated by Miss Moore's looks, wit and energetic charm, and when she told him that she admired Edie's voice, he was stuck; he couldn't refuse when she offered to teach Edie free of charge. Edie went to the Mayer house glowing with excitement, her latest brief demonstration approved by her teacher. Mayer was delighted, and admitted he had been wrong. Even though he could not approve of her having a career on the stage, he saw no reason why she should not give the occasional recital, perhaps for charity. More or less content with this parental decision, she went back to her own house. William Goetz was out. When he returned, she was seated at the piano, trilling prettily through a scale. "What is this all about?" Goetz asked irritably. She told him of Miss Moore's and her father's decision. Goetz exploded. He told his wife she had no business to have any such ambition. How had she managed to keep the secret of her lessons from him so long? She closed the piano lid for good and never sang a note again.

Later that month, James A. FitzPatrick launched the first of his handsomely made, but heavy-handed, series of travelogues, with thirteen expertly done mini-features evoking the sights and sounds of his recent world cruise. They were destined to become the laughing stock of critics but were perennially popular with the public.

The Thalbergs returned on July 31. Irving was in uncertain health, his marriage, despite the prolonged second honeymoon, in great difficulties. Norma Shearer was a demanding and temperamental wife; he found the burdens of a loveless relationship a strain both mentally and physically. He and Mayer were busy in the first weeks of August confirming a deal with Warner Brothers, whereby M.G.M. would release many of its products through Warner theaters. There was much heated discussion over the share of distribution fees.

On August 4, 1931, Ina Claire was at last granted a divorce from John Gilbert. His latest picture, *Way of a Sailor*, had been held up for weeks because the all-important Capitol Theater in New York was fully booked. When at last it emerged, it flopped dismally. Gilbert was still making $10,000 a week; Mayer and Thalberg looked desperately for properties to justify his salary, hoping against hope that *The Phantom of Paris* would succeed. That hope was dashed.

Another of Mayer's burdens was William Haines. According to the rumor mill, Haines was caught by police in the downtown Los Angeles YMCA making love to a sailor, and in Pershing Square picking up a hustler. It took all of Mayer's influence with District Attorney Buron Fitts to bury the matter. Mayer announced that Haines would be released from his contract, but the unsuspecting public (women found Haines attractively boyish) protested loudly, and Haines's contract was renewed for another year. He was not fired until 1934 in a cleanup operation, following the dismissal of Nils Asther and followed by the removal of Ramon Novarro.

A new vehicle had to be found for Garbo. Much against his policy of never imitating another studio's films, Mayer consented to her appearing as the star of *Mata Hari*, the story of the alleged World War I secret agent, despite the fact that Marlene Dietrich had appeared in a version of the same story, *Dishonored*, at Paramount.

Garbo moved to a house next door to Mercedes de Acosta; even she did not quite dare to live with her. Mercedes de Acosta shared her home with a "beard": Irving Thalberg's gay friend John Colton, the author of the play *Rain*. But the Garbos, as she and de Acosta were known, did not help the disguise by going out together to parties dressed in match-

ing slacks. A photograph appeared in the paper with the caption GARBO
IN PANTS. Underneath the caption was printed this commentary:

> Innocent bystanders gasped in amazement to see Mercedes de Acosta and
> Greta Garbo striding swiftly along Hollywood Boulevard dressed in men's
> clothes.

On September 29, Edie announced she was expecting her first child;
the baby, born eight months later, was a girl, Barbara. The same day,
Mayer left for New York; he had meetings with Schenck on the outcome
of the minority stockholders' lawsuit against Loew's, Inc. The conclusion
in the judgment was that the majority shares would, due to the retirement and incompetence of William Fox, be handled by a special committee, including a former attorney general, selected by the court. This
was an ideal arrangement for M.G.M.: it would reduce the influence and
power of Winfield Sheehan and would, in effect, mean that, while all
the benefits of the alliance continued, the jurisdictional committee
would prove to be supportive to Schenck's wishes. The arrangement can
only be put down to Mayer's influence at the presidential level.

Mayer's relationship with William Randolph Hearst continued; but
Hearst remained disloyal to his friend and colleague, yet again negotiating with Warner Brothers to take Marion Davies's contract there.
Louella Parsons, his chief columnist, played a peculiarly devious role in
the negotiations, begging Hearst in her secret memoranda not to reveal
anything to Mayer; she needed Mayer as a source of stories.

On October 12, 1931, after testing a number of male athletes and
contract players, all of them in loincloths, Mayer and Thalberg settled
on the twenty-seven-year-old champion swimmer Johnny Weissmuller
for the title role in *Tarzan the Ape Man*, the first of a series of movies
based on the popular novels of Edgar Rice Burroughs. Weissmuller was
handsomely proportioned, powerfully built and rangy; his charm was
considerable. He would not be expected to utter more than grunts or
loud yodels as he swung from tree to tree. His Jane would be the genteel
Irish actress Maureen O'Sullivan; jungle footage from *Trader Horn* would
be used as background.

Mayer left for Washington on October 26 for lunch at the White
House, continuing to New York and Chicago; he returned for prepara-
tions for the Academy Awards in November. He was pleased that Marie
Dressler was nominated for *Min and Bill*, in which she costarred with
Wallace Beery, and Norma Shearer for *A Free Soul*. Lionel Barrymore,
still one of his favorites, was also nominated for *A Free Soul*, and Jackie
Cooper, terrific now in *The Champ*, for *Skippy*.

By contrast, Thalberg decided to go ahead that month with Tod Browning's *Freaks*, a movie involving grotesquely deformed human beings, including a man consisting only of a head and torso, a pinhead, and Siamese twins. It was a project Mayer detested from the first moment and would turn out to be a failure at the box office, with preview audiences running out into the street.[3]

The Academy Awards banquet took place on November 10. It was a tremendous occasion for Mayer: among the guests were Vice President Charles Curtis; Curtis's sister, the socialite Dolly Gann; James Rolph, the governor of California; Mabel Walker Willebrandt, Will Hays and Navy and Army leaders. Vice President Curtis, Rolph and Willebrandt exhausted the audience with lengthy tributes to Mayer, whom Mrs. Willebrandt called "the liaison officer of the motion picture industry . . . in its contacts with the national capital," and added, "he is beloved in the halls of Congress." *Variety* rudely commented, "The laudation for Mayer struck many [as] funny in view of Will Hays's presence and his hired position as the so-called liaison between the industry and legislative and nationally political matters."

The audience was ecstatic when Marie Dressler won the Best Actress award for *Min and Bill*. She was arguably the most beloved star in Hollywood; she moved many when she burst into tears during her acceptance speech. Lionel Barrymore was warmly received when he took his Best Actor statuette for *A Free Soul*. It was a double triumph for the studio and for its chiefs.

But the occasion had a depressing aftermath. Although M.G.M. was well into profits for 1931 and was ahead of the industry in every way, it became obvious that audiences were deserting motion pictures in quantity, and Mayer was compelled to meet with such long-term enemies as Adolph Zukor and Winfield Sheehan to discuss how best to deal with the situation. On November 15, at a summit meeting at the Hollywood offices of Will Hays, it was decided that salary cuts, up to twenty-five percent, would go into effect for many employees. At the same time, a pattern of actors' walkouts, followed by tough negotiations by their agents and sudden increases, drained the studio's coffers. On December 3, Clark Gable, who was excellent in the censor-defying *Possessed*, with Joan Crawford, and *Hell Divers*, with Wallace Beery, walked off the set during the second day of *Polly of the Circus*, costarring Marion Davies.[4] Mayer called Minna Wallace, Gable's agent, and Gable to his office, staying up until 2:00 A.M. the next morning, demanding that he yield.

[3] It was embarked on as competition for Universal's hugely successful *Frankenstein*, starring Boris Karloff and directed by James Whale.
[4] Producer Bernard Hyman later applied the idea to the Spencer Tracy character in *San Francisco*.

Hearst walked in and said to Mayer, "Tell the bastard I'll buy him the best car going—a ten-thousand-dollar Rolls. Anything he wants!"

Gable said he wouldn't move until he got $1,000 a week instead of $650. Mayer replied that if Gable didn't return to work the following day, he would never work in Hollywood again. Minna Wallace ran out and called her boss, Ruth Collier, vice president of the Agents and Manufacturers Association. Collier spoke to Gable, who did return to work and, after many arguments, achieved a two-year contract of $2,000 a week, starting January 22, 1932. He was worth at least $10,000; as a draw card for women, he was second to none at the studio. But even he dared not ask for too much: he knew Mayer would dump him without a tremor if he went any further. And the studio could expose his affair with Joan Crawford through the columns and give his wife Ria a chance to take half of their community property in a divorce.

Mayer twisted Jean Harlow's arm. Scenes of her recent crime picture, *Beast of the City*, with an unprecedented introduction by President Hoover, whom Mayer had talked into supplying some vibrant critiques of city hoodlerism, didn't work, and she refused to return from a stage appearance in Pittsburgh. When she insisted on holding to her deal with Warner's Theaters, Mayer threatened her with blacklisting and she came back at once.

Christmas 1931 brought its share of excitement: a madman threatened to kill Mayer and blow up the studio unless Mayer paid him $10,000. Mayer notified D.A. Buron Fitts. A package of fake dollar bills was mailed to a box number. When the extortionist arrived, the police were waiting. He went to jail.

On Christmas Eve, the studio was the scene of an astonishing orgy, which soon became an annual event. While Mayer drove home to the beach house and Irving Thalberg took off to dinner with Norma Shearer, Eddie Mannix and Benny Thau spread it around that any man and woman could have as much booze as they wanted, and that they could choose a partner who appealed to them and make love against desks, on the floor, against the walls, anywhere they wanted.

A stranger wandering about in those sacred corridors of the executive building would have been able to see naked or partly dressed couples of all ages frenziedly copulating—even on Irving Thalberg's desk (Mayer kept his office locked). Some vigorous clerks serviced two or three women in succession. If this incident had leaked, it would have been the end of M.G.M.

While Garbo was in *Mata Hari* that December, Mercedes de Acosta was writing a screenplay: *Desperate*. Garbo was excited by it and sent Miss de Acosta to Mayer and Thalberg. They were horrified: Garbo would play a man. Thalberg screamed, "Do you want to put all America and the women's clubs against that woman? You must be out of your fucking mind!" When the author returned crestfallen to her light of love, Garbo said cheerfully, "I have a better idea. I'll play the title role in *The Picture of Dorian Gray*."

By year's end, Garbo was hard at work on *Grand Hotel*, with an all-star cast including Wallace Beery, John Barrymore, Lionel Barrymore and Joan Crawford, who gave her best performance to date. The first days were marked by quarrels between Edmund Goulding as director and Paul Bern, who was currently dating Jean Harlow, as supervisor. Irving Thalberg fired Bern and took over the production, with strong results. Although the story was depressing, with many characters doomed by fate, the electricity of the performers overcame everything. Garbo played the part of the Russian ballet star Grusenskaya with extraordinary skill. Her scenes with John Barrymore as the fading Baron Von Geiger had great poignancy; for once, she was up against an equal, and the competition brought out the best in her.

## CHAPTER FOURTEEN

# 1932–1933

With $12 MILLION IN PROFITS, M.G.M. had done magnificently in 1931 and was far ahead of any other studio. Mayer and Thalberg could look back with pleasure on a year in which Alfred Lunt and Lynn Fontanne had appeared in *The Guardsman*, Robert Montgomery and Norma Shearer had made *Private Lives*, Marion Davies had given a sparkling performance in *Five and Ten* (a version of the Barbara Hutton story) and Clark Gable had made a vigorous impression in *Sporting Blood*. However, the steadily slipping careers of John Gilbert, William Haines, Ramon Novarro and Buster Keaton were burdens.

Another was Mayer's brother Jerry, who had continued as location manager. Mayer had frequently quarreled with Jerry, and now matters came to a head: Jerry criticized Mayer's association with Frank Orsatti, feeling that Mayer should have nothing to do with such a hoodlum, and Mayer fired his brother, who then set up a small agency, ironically representing two M.G.M. performers, Nils Asther and Anita Page, both of whom took a considerable risk in joining him. Neither star lasted much longer.

The new year of 1932 brought the fourth annual January 1 brunch party held at the Mayers' beach house. It was obligatory by now for any and every M.G.M. supervisor and director of importance to appear; the top stars were also expected to put in an appearance. As usual, this led to tensions and complications: Joan Crawford was present with Douglas Fairbanks, Jr., while her extramarital love, Clark Gable, was there with his angry and jealous wife Ria; while Chester Morris, soon to be appearing with Jean Harlow in *Red-Headed Woman*, flirted openly with her in front of her fiancé Paul Bern; the casting director Benjamin Thau, whose couch had become notorious, was under suspicion from several husbands. Only the plain and aging Marie Dressler, who was already suffering from the first symptoms of cancer, sailed above scandal. John Gilbert, William Haynes, Ramon Novarro and Nils Asther were conspicuous by their absence.

The studio set up its own brothel north of Sunset Strip. Visiting exhibitors and overseas representatives were always accommodated by the madam, the popular and beautiful Billie Bennett, whose girls were always doubles of the stars. One M.G.M. veteran recalls that when a Mexican executive arrived it was understood that he wanted to bed a blond movie-star actress—any actress. Since it was impossible to orga-nize a guaranteed night of sex, Billie Bennett arranged for a very pretty girl, the dyed-blond double of Jean Harlow, to become her for the night. Billie told the M.G.M. veteran: "It's all set up. But remember: when he goes down on her, he's going to wind up with a mouth full of peroxide!"

Billie Bennett was generous. When an actor was in trouble, or an executive was desperate for money, she would always take care of them, with generous loans. Irving Thalberg would stop by to watch in the lobby or to play the piano.

In the early months of 1932, Anita Loos was hard at work on *Red-Headed Woman*, which began shooting in March. This was the most audacious picture Mayer had approved to date; it was openly defiant of the very motion picture code that he had helped to introduce, another example of the double standard by which he operated. Harlow would play a tough, baby-faced redhead who seduces and marries a hapless, small-town businessman, Chester Morris, then ditches him for a coal magnate. Unpunished at the end, she is last seen dating a white-bearded French politician, receiving a cup for the winning horse at Longchamps and cuckolding her husband with the chauffeur, Charles Boyer. The picture launched Harlow as a major star, but it cast a blight over the studio's reputation with women's clubs and religious pressure groups. Mayer had reason to regret having authorized this movie.

He traveled with Margaret to Washington in late May for yet another dinner at the White House. He was guest of honor at a luncheon hosted by the indispensable Mabel Walker Willebrandt, who was stepping down to take up a private law practice in Los Angeles and Washington; Vice President Curtis was at the party. Mayer gave one of his rare press conferences at the Mayflower Hotel, saying that Congress should legalize beer, and that he supported sales taxes. He was fighting the wind. The public was disillusioned with Hoover, convinced he was doing nothing about the Depression and the armies of the unemployed, and was even shafting the war veterans. It would take a steel-clad optimist like Mayer to see much hope for Hoover's being returned in the fall election.

Even his relationship with the President had become shaky, despite his diligent attention, sometimes at the cost of his devotion to the studio, to his duties as vice chairman of the Republican Committee of California. He found that Hoover did not approve his desire to legalize beer, nor did he see in the President even a minimum of patience for Mayer's other friend and ally, William Randolph Hearst. Always correct morally, Hoover found the Hearst newspaper editorials increasingly offensive and sensational. When Mayer asked Hoover to meet with Hearst at the White House to discuss their differences, Hoover refused. Hearst would soon transfer his alliance to Franklin D. Roosevelt, throwing the power of his newspapers behind the Democratic candidate.

Mayer continued to Chicago for the Republican National Convention, while bulletins reached him from Culver City on Clark Gable's pneumonia in Palm Springs, Garbo's latest complaints over money and threat to return to Sweden, and the banning of *Red-Headed Woman* in England, Australia and New Zealand. Mayer approved in absentia a publicity campaign in which *Red-Headed Woman* was promoted in combination with Lux Soap; few were convinced that the picture was anything but dirty. But Harlow was a sensation with the public, and Nicholas Schenck bought her contract from Howard Hughes for $30,000. Mayer, who regarded her as a slut, cannot have been overjoyed by the news, nor by the reports that appeared in *Variety* that month that Thalberg was going ahead with a project Mayer disliked: *Soviet Union*, of all things a sympathetic account of life in the USSR, to be directed on location by George Hill, with Wallace Beery as the star.

While Mayer was in Chicago, his lawyers, Loeb, Walker and Loeb, were involved in fighting another real estate lawsuit, against the Hollywood Recreation Company, which had reneged on mortgage payments on a bowling alley and billiard hall Mayer owned on Western Avenue.

In Chicago, the delegates' voting moved away from Mayer's friend, Charles Curtis, and toward General Edward Martin, as the vice presidential candidate. A Pennsylvania delegate told Mayer that it needed only a few extra votes to ensure Curtis's position; Mayer, who was about to leave for the train, rushed back to the Delegates' Section and pleaded his friend's cause with intense passion to the Pennsylvanians. They voted for Curtis.

The Mayers returned to Hollywood to bad news. On June 7, the First National Bank of Beverly Hills closed its doors permanently, wiping out Greta Garbo's $1 million in savings (she somehow managed to get through a back entrance with Mercedes de Acosta and rescue some bonds in a safe deposit box).

Mercedes de Acosta wired President Hoover on June 16:

Please forgive me for bothering you at this moment when you have so much on and so much is at stake. As you no doubt know, the First National Bank of Beverly Hills closed last week in which the film star Greta Garbo had all her money. I consider much grave dishonesty surrounds her. She is a child and incapable of taking care of herself. I have wired the Swedish ambassador Mr. Böström to protect her and hope you will communicate and advise him. I hope you will personally attend to this matter and thank you very much.

It isn't surprising to note that there was no response from the White House.

Mayer instantly used Garbo's misfortune to force her to sign a new contract, for $12,000 a week, making her the highest-paid star at the studio.

Charles Laughton, doyen of the British stage, was giving a performance of startling excellence in the murder thriller *Payment Deferred*. The picture was notable for the introduction at M.G.M. of the handsome young Ray Milland. *Rasputin and the Empress* was also shooting; it had been hastily written by Charles MacArthur: a version of the story of the czar and czarina of Russia, and Rasputin's influence over them, leading up to their assassination in 1919. Cedric Gibbons recreated the slightly dingy atmosphere of the royal palaces, and cinematographer William Daniels gave the picture the look of period daguerreotypes. The three Barrymores, Ethel, John and Lionel, were in conflict throughout the picture, fighting for scenes. The picture would soon plunge the studio into one of the most celebrated court cases of the decade.

On another sound stage, Tallulah Bankhead was starring in *Faithless*, as a society trollop on the make. She despised Mayer, Thalberg and the studio, regarded the job as slumming and acted with a throwaway laziness that paradoxically turned out to work perfectly for the role.

Mayer attended the wedding of Jean Harlow and Paul Bern on July 2, 1932. Mayer can only have been puzzled by the relationship. His physician, still Dr. Edward Jones, was also Bern's own and undoubtedly had told him that Bern had an inferiority complex because he was underdeveloped sexually. Mayer may also have suspected that the gentle, civilized and tender-minded, but neurotic and hysterical Bern was a repressed homosexual. He cannot have forgotten that incident in the late 1920s when Bern reacted so violently to his rejection by Barbara La Marr that he threw an expensive diamond bracelet he had intended to give her into some bushes, and was rescued by Carey Wilson from a feeble effort at suicide. Mayer must have noted that Bern was grief-stricken over the death of an intimate friend, the handsome Joseph

Jackson, who had been swept away and drowned in a riptide while both men were swimming at Malibu that May. It cannot have been pleasant for Mayer to have to greet John Gilbert, who was best man, or note, as Irene Selznick did, how Harlow flung her body at C. V. Whitney, of the Whitney millions, right in front of her new husband.[1]

Adela Rogers St. Johns, the Hearst columnist, was a close friend of Miss Harlow's. To the present author, she confirmed Paul Bern's suicide attempt over Barbara La Marr. She also stated that Jean Harlow knew that Bern was sexually ambivalent and preferred this because she could be protected from men who weren't appealing to her and wouldn't have to commit herself emotionally to those who were. Quite the opposite of her mindless screen image, she was well read and was starved for intellectual companionship with such rough-and-tough lovers as Clark Gable. She could read poetry and appreciate music with Paul Bern; they would have something to talk about, something in common. But Bern, Miss St. Johns said, had insane fits of jealousy. In front of Adela, he accused Harlow of having sex with a cab driver who had picked her up when her limousine broke down. His feelings can only have been exacerbated if he could give no satisfaction to his wife in bed.

That same July, for the first time in his life, Mayer became involved in a serious love affair outside of his marriage. Though passion had long since burned out at home, it is a reasonable guess that Margaret had at least provided a safety valve for Mayer's extreme tensions. But now he met a woman who in many ways resembled her physically. The difference was that, unlike the increasingly vague Margaret, who would be in and out of sanitariums during the next few years, she was exciting and gifted: Adeline, known as Ad, the wife of B. P. Schulberg.

Ad Schulberg had long been a secret friend of the Mayers, behind her husband's back. She had, of course, known them from the old Mission Road days, when they exchanged visits, and before Mayer developed his horror of her husband, and her husband of him. Ad Schulberg had been devastated by her husband's prolonged and spectacular affair with the dewy-eyed but steely Paramount star Sylvia Sidney.

Following an ugly, argument-ridden separation, Ad started up her own agency, taking in as partner the handsome Charles Feldman. On July 18, 1932, they opened offices in the Taft Building on Hollywood Boulevard with a spectacular party for over a hundred guests; Mayer was conspicuous by his absence. Among those present were Edie Goetz (without her husband), Edward G. Robinson, Nancy Carroll, Mary Duncan and Boots Mallory. Displaying a peculiar lack of tact, Ad Schulberg took on John

---

[1] In her memoirs, *Kiss Hollywood Goodbye*, Anita Loos stated that, while attending a football game, Harlow pointed to a husky member of a team and said to Bern, "Daddy, buy me that!"

Gilbert as a client; later, she would add Charles Boyer, Gene Raymond and Bess Meredyth. Mayer encouraged her because he wanted her to compete with Myron Selznick, brother of David, and with Phil Berg, who were making excessive demands for their clients. However, it is odd that he does not seem to have considered that she might prove to be a successful rival of his beloved friend Frank Orsatti; also, that she would be in competition with his brother Jerry.

Ad, in her late thirties, not beautiful but charismatic and vital, paid several visits to Mayer at his office during those weeks. One afternoon, he led her to a couch, set her down on it and, to her astonishment, embraced her, caressing her shoulders, then her breasts. He said he had loved her for all the years he had known her but had kept his feelings bottled up. He began to cry, an infallible technique when he wanted something, and sank to his knees before her, a rather clumsy and over-weight Romeo to her plain-featured Juliet. "You can't do this to Marga-ret!" Ad exclaimed. "She's going insane," Mayer replied, according to Ad's son, Budd Schulberg. "We don't sleep together anymore. And I will build your agency to the heights! King Louis and Queen Adeline can rule Hollywood!"

Now began a hidden sexual relationship that, if it had leaked, could have wrecked Mayer's image and would have reduced to nonsense his condemnation of his own stars' adulteries. It must have been painful to him to realize that he wasn't the paragon he had painted himself: that he was a man, after all, his desires satisfied by a brilliant woman whom he had always coveted.

In the midst of this liaison, Garbo, after negotiating a salary raise to $12,500 a week, making her the highest-paid star of the studio, took off on a dramatic expedition to New York on her way to Sweden, where she would spend several months before starting her next picture. Aban-doning discretion, she embarked with Mercedes de Acosta in the same Santa Fe Chief drawing room from San Bernardino to Chicago, and then by the Twentieth Century Limited to New York, where she led a wild goose chase of reporters from the 126th Street Station in Harlem to the Hotel Gramatan in Bronxville. She eluded a thousand fans at the North German Lloyd Pier, racing up a second-class gangway to the SS *Bremen* after kissing her female paramour an audacious goodbye on the lips. She snubbed the society passengers, who responded by refusing to quit the boat deck when she was playing shuffleboard, so that she went to the officers' decks to play and ate with them in the mess. No sooner had she reached Stockholm than she resumed an earlier love affair with the vigorous Countess Wachtmeister. There was nothing Mayer could do about these shenanigans.

He had much to put up with on the home front: the tantrums and tears of Joan Crawford, who was complaining to the press that she had been unfairly charged with imitating Garbo in *Grand Hotel* and took off to Europe with Douglas Fairbanks, Jr., dividing herself permanently from Clark Gable; the U.S. Post Office, which blocked the reinstatement of fast night airmail service from Southern California, which Congress had approved; and B. P. Schulberg, who, aggrieved by Mayer's relationship with Ad, was found out to be secretly negotiating with Garbo for a deal to make pictures in England. He fought with Jackie Cooper's mother, Mabel, who kept her son off the set until the boy received a spectacular bonus for a national personal-appearance tour. He allowed Howard Strickling to announce, on July 19, that M.G.M. would now go "all out for sex."

In support of his new policy, he set in motion two pictures, to be shot in September, both of which broke every rule of the Code. The first of these was *The Mask of Fu Manchu*, in which Boris Karloff and a sexually overheated Myrna Loy kidnap a male beauty (Charles Starrett) in China and subject him to strippings, pawings and whippings in a mélange of eroticism that might have given pause to the Marquis de Sade; and *Kongo*, directed by Lenore Coffee's husband, William Cowen, in which Walter Huston, as a crippled white slave trader, tortures young women to compensate for his sexual impotence. The tempestuous Lupe Velez, playing a slave, was having an affair with Winfield Sheehan, who kept turning up on the set, only to be asked to leave. Mayer had bragged that no picture made at his studio would be unsuitable for viewing by his daughters; perhaps by now he had obtained a shrewd grasp of what those rebellious women could tolerate. This included, in *Kongo*, a scene in which Walter Huston began to twist Lupe Velez's tongue with a length of wire.

Mayer was busier than ever, involved now with the Olympic Games as a Committee member. The Games started on July 30, calling for his full attention. But at the beginning of August, the Games still in progress, he left for the notification ceremonies in Washington, significantly without Margaret; instead, he took with him Frank Orsatti, who represented everything the President was battling in terms of crime, bootlegging and widespread procuring of women, and whom Hoover's namesake, J. Edgar, was fighting to put out of business. Mayer succeeded in getting Orsatti into the White House; how he brought this off remains a mystery.

In his absence, John Gilbert married Virginia Bruce on August 10. Miss Bruce, transformed from her filthy *Kongo* slave's rags, emerged at the ceremony in a black-and-white Adrian wedding dress. Irving

Thalberg was best man, and the witnesses included Norma Shearer, who was given two hours off from making *Smilin' Through*. Lupe Velez made a scene at the ceremony, crying loudly, and saying to an astonished Lenore Coffee, "Jack told Virginia, 'If you're still a virgin by this coming Saturday, I'll marry you!' "

Mayer's visit to Washington was again uncomfortable. He met with Will Hays, who, aggrieved by Mayer's effrontery in approving a series of objectionable scripts, refused to let him make a version of the sensational stage play *Lulu Belle*, with Jean Harlow.

Back in Hollywood, Mayer overruled Thalberg and would not allow John Gilbert to appear in *Red Dust*, a story of a Cochin China planter in love with two women; he cast Clark Gable instead, with Harlow, Gene Raymond and Mary Astor.

On August 4, Irene Mayer Selznick gave birth to a seven-pound boy, Jeffrey, in a hospital in Santa Monica. Mayer was still in Washington and didn't come to the coast to see the baby, but from that moment, he softened in his attitude to David Selznick. Still irritated by Irving Thalberg, whom he felt was plunging the studio into an impossible position with Will Hays, he began to realize that blood was thicker than water, that he and his old enemy Lewis J. Selznick were grandfathers of the same child, and that Selznick was having an impressive record at RKO. Soon *King Kong* and *A Bill of Divorcement* would establish Selznick as a producer of considerable skill; the latter movie would introduce the radiant new star Katharine Hepburn. Mayer began to speak warmly and considerately to Selznick; he started to lay plans to bring Selznick into M.G.M. to supplant Thalberg. Sixteen days after Irene had her child, Mayer was at another wedding: Douglas Shearer married for the second time: one of Sam Marx's readers, Ann Lee Cunningham.

On the morning of Labor Day, September 5, the Mayers were awakened at the beach house by the ring of a telephone. They were told that Paul Bern was dead of a gunshot wound. According to the late Samuel Marx, Mayer's thought was that Jean Harlow had killed him. It was known at the studio, Marx says, that the couple had quarreled. Jean could not persuade Bern to invest in a gold mine owned by her stepfather, Marino Bello. She was planning to hand over control of their house to Bello, who was acting as her business manager, and Bern hated Bello, who was a thug and a bully and was himself having an affair with Harlow.

Marx stated that Mayer was driven to Bern's house. An informant told Marx that Hendry Mayer had arranged with Police Chief Whitey Hendry to put one of the two guns in the house, a .38 pistol, in the dead man's hand and ordered the body moved in front of a mirror in the dressing room in order to make the death look like suicide—to protect Jean Harlow. But there is no evidence, circumstantial or primary, to support such a statement.

Indeed, it is impossible to believe that Mayer would risk his career by thus making himself an accessory to a killing. To have dragged the body to another place would have left bloodstains on the carpet. In those days, no chemical solution existed which could remove stains instantly, and it is extremely improbable that Hendry would have carried a cleaning fluid with him. Furthermore, the position of the gun in the dead man's hand was such as to make it difficult to believe that it could have been placed there. The arm was twisted under the back of the corpse, and the finger was clenched tight on the trigger. The bullet had entered the right temple at point-blank range, leaving burns on the inside of the skull and in the brain tissue. Once Hendry saw such a wound, he, as a policeman, would instantly have told Mayer that Bern had committed suicide. There would have been nothing to indicate murder, since to kill someone by pressing the nozzle of a gun to the right of that person's head and then firing was an extremely rare method of homicide.

There is also no evidence that Mayer was in the house at all that morning. According to various sources, Mayer is supposed to have found a suicide note on the bedroom mantelpiece and put it in his pocket, only to be told by Howard Strickling to return it to its proper place. Again, this story has no documentable basis in fact. The note was not scribbled on a piece of paper and placed on the mantelpiece, but was inscribed on the thirteenth page of a green, morocco-bound combined diary and visitors' book, in which, among others, Gary Cooper and his lover, Lupe Velez, had inscribed greetings. The last entry was "Paul Carey."[2] The book may have been too large to put in Mayer's pocket. Its existence was confirmed repeatedly, including in testimony given by two detectives at the Homicide Division, and was obtained for thorough inspection by a reporter for the Los Angeles *Examiner*.

Marx asserted that Mayer bribed Jean Harlow's personal staff, the district attorney and just about everybody else, including, presumably, the six jury authorities who confirmed the autopsy report, to say that this was death by suicide. In view of the reputations of the autopsy physicians and the coroner, this charge is unacceptable. In addition, Mayer could never have been sure that someone would not crack and reveal the truth, thereby finishing his career and ruining the studio. In an interview with this author in 1971, Howard Strickling said that he be-

---

[2] Or was it "Paul—Carey"; from Carey Wilson? Or Cary Grant?

lieved the suicide note to have been forged. But again, he had no sub-stantive evidence upon which to base his statement.

The entry in the guest book read:

Dearest dear,
    Unfortu[n]ately this is the only way to make good the frightful wrong I have done you and to wipe out my abject humiliation. I love you. Paul. You understand that last night was only a comedy . . .

Irving Thalberg is known to have gone to Paul Bern's house at about 11:30 A.M., accompanied by David Selznick. Thalberg stated under oath at the inquest that he did not go upstairs but accepted the word of Bern's servants that Bern was dead. Thalberg attempted to call the police but had some difficulty in reaching the right number. Indeed, in his dis-tressed state, it was quite possible he called the wrong numbers and hung up irritably when put through to the wrong extension. He finally reached the West Los Angeles precinct at 2:15 P.M., and fifteen minutes later Detective Lieutenants Joe Whitehead and Frank Condaffer were on the scene. They found two guns, a .38 Colt automatic lying on the dressing table in the mirrored dressing room and a second .38 Colt in the dead man's hand. Only one bullet had been discharged from it. There was so much oil on the gun handle that fingerprints could not be dusted off. The body was stiff in rigor mortis. It took an effort for Whitehead to pry the gun loose from the fingers.

The corpse was taken to the offices of Dr. Frank R. Webb, autopsy surgeon, who determined the position of the gun, the bullet's entry and the fact that it exited the head and had been flattened against the wall.

That afternoon, Mayer went to see Harlow at her parents' house on Club View Drive. She pushed past him in a state of hysteria, screaming, "I must go to Paul! He needs me!" and ran to a balcony. She tried to throw herself off. Mayer grabbed her and pulled her back just in time. He struck her and threw her into the bedroom, to calm her down; a doctor arrived to sedate her.

By nightfall, reporters were mobbing both the Bern house and the Bello house. Mayer was still at the Bello house that evening, with How-ard Strickling, his and Jean Harlow's attorney, Mendel Silberberg, and her other lawyer, Oscar O. Cummins. Mayer told Silberberg to make it a priority to find Bern's will.

The newspaper stories the following morning said that suicide was the finding of the autopsy surgeon. Nobody questioned the authenticity of the suicide note, and, what was more, a telegram reached Mayer from Dr. Edward Jones from Honolulu, where he was vacationing, saying:

UNDERSTAND SUICIDE MOTIVE. WILL RETURN AT ONCE IF NEEDED. Mayer called him and the result was that Jones went aboard a ship within hours and sailed to Los Angeles. Bern's friend, the writer Lawrence Stallings, and others, officially stated that Bern had talked of suicide with them.

According to Marx, Mayer's next move was to ensure the support of his executive staff. He held a summit meeting in the M.G.M. executive bungalow, telling Irving Thalberg, Benjamin Thau, Harry Rapf, Hunt Stromberg, Albert Lewin and Marx that Bern did the right thing when he shot himself. Of course, Mayer added, everyone present knew that Bern was homosexual and impotent with women. Albert Lewin denied this; Mayer was furious when Thalberg agreed with Lewin. Mayer walked over to Thalberg and stood over him, threatening to kill him if he didn't admit the truth. Thalberg yielded. Hunt Stromberg, the supervisor on *Red Dust*, which was in production, said he knew for a fact that Bern was "a fairy."

Mayer announced that he would find a substitute for the star of *Red Dust*, that Jean Harlow could not continue. He was in his office, calling Nicholas Schenck in New York, who had already left for the coast, saying he was going to hire Tallulah Bankhead, whose performance he had liked in *Faithless*. Miss Bankhead wrote in her memoirs that she was in his outer office at that moment. She was furious at being kept waiting and threatened to leave unless he saw her at once. Ida Koverman told her to go in. Mayer offered her $2,500 a week to take over. "That's half of what you paid me for *Faithless!*" Tallulah drawled. She hated him, and didn't care whether he hired her or not. "But you were on loan-out!" he said. "Now, Paramount has dropped your contract!" With his world falling apart, Mayer began haggling with Tallulah over money. She told him she wouldn't take advantage of Jean Harlow's plight, then advised him that several men on his payroll were also sexually dubious. Mayer pleaded; he began to move around the desk, telling her that he would now enact the "suicide" scene. He began to pick up an imaginary gun, which he then aimed at his head, until she stopped him in his tracks. He threw her out.

Now that he could find no alternative player for *Red Dust*, he ordered scenes in which Harlow's presence would not be required to be shot immediately. The script was reconstructed to allow her to be written out of the story for a longer period than hitherto. It was obvious she would be unable to work for several days.

Mayer made a statement to the press later that afternoon:

Bern's demeanor during the week before he killed himself changed entirely. I called it to Irving Thalberg's attention. Mr. Thalberg told me that

Bern needed a rest and should be sent away for a few days. I thought this strange, for he had only returned some days before from a short vacation.

I had never seen him act so strangely before. He had the queerest look about his eyes and appeared to me to have something preying on his mind. In fact, during this period, he had "words" with one of the boys on the lot, and if you knew Mr. Bern you would realize this was unusual for him. I deeply sympathize with Miss Harlow.

On September 7, Mayer was waiting at the Bello home with Mendel Silberberg and members of his staff when Paul Bern's brother Henry drove up, following a flight through stormy weather from the East Coast. Henry Bern, in a short and awkward conference with a swarm of reporters gathered on the driveway, stated that, as some newspapers had reported, Paul had maintained in New York a common-law wife, Dorothy Millette. It seemed that she had moved to San Francisco, and that Paul Bern had been giving her an income. What did this mean?

Kept secret from the public, and not mentioned in the press at the time, on September 6 a grand jury met to interrogate Harlow and others. Bypassing Buron Fitts, whom the foreman had just indicted, they hired a suite for the purpose at the Ambassador Hotel. Harlow made a statement; no sooner had she completed it, and it had been placed in a file, than it was abstracted and was never seen again. Two years and two months later, when there was a new grand jury hearing on sums received by Buron Fitts during the investigation, that statement was still missing.

The inquest took place next day, September 8. Mendel Silberberg had lodged an objection with Buron Fitts to having it at all, but Fitts could do nothing to stop it. Mayer was able to keep Jean Harlow out of the hearing on medical grounds.

It was held in a crowded, uncomfortably hot room crammed with high wicker chairs at the offices of Price and Daniel, morticians, on Sawtelle Avenue in Culver City. Mayer, his face frozen, his eyes expressionless behind heavy horn-rims, strode in, followed by a visibly shattered Irving Thalberg, who sat, shoulders hunched, through the proceedings.

Six jurors were present. Marino Bello was the first witness. He referred to Bern's moments of melancholy; that he had in his house innumerable bottles of pills. The houseman, John Herman Carmichael, said that Bern's parting conversation with Harlow, when she went to her parents' house that weekend, was affectionate and warm. He described finding the bedroom in disorder; Bern had spent the day in bed and many books were scattered about. Carmichael's wife, Winifred, the housekeeper, stated simply that she could give no reason for a suicide motive. Irving Thalberg was shown the visitors' book containing the suicide note and confirmed that the writing was Bern's. He said that Bern had mentioned suicide as a possibility.

Studio business manager Martin Greenwood again confirmed the authenticity of Bern's handwriting. The gardener, Clifton Davis, and Bern's chauffeur, "Slickum" Garrison, supported each other's statements. Garrison said that Bern had often talked of suicide, took a great deal of medication and was being treated by Dr. Edward Jones.

Detective Lieutenant Whitehead gave his description of finding the body and confirmed that the visitors' book was on the bedroom table. Detective Lieutenant Condaffer testified to the large number of bottles of pills in the room. Coroner Nance asked autopsy surgeon Frank Webb whether Bern's nervous state could have affected his marital situation. Webb stated that neurasthenia, or a nervous condition, could cause "incompetence"—that is, impotence—and that condition could cause melancholia. He found that the sexual organs were developed normally but were undersized; he could not confirm that their condition (of itself) would indicate "impotency." The jury, composed of well-respected physicians and a dentist, were entirely in order in reaching a verdict of suicide. Indeed, there was no evidence to suggest anything else.

The funeral took place the next day, at the flower-bedecked Grace Chapel at Inglewood Park Cemetery, south of Los Angeles, at 2 P.M. More than a thousand people milled outside the building. Mayer was there, with his executive staff, as Marino Bello assisted Jean Harlow, weeping in a black veil and widow's weeds, down the path. One by one, Paul Bern's friends and associates filed past the coffin to pay their last respects. Mayer's nerves cannot have been helped by Friederike Marcus, Bern's sister, screaming, "He's gone! Where have they taken him?" And she kept on yelling the words even though she was looking directly at the body. Conrad Nagel said in his funeral oration (and how Mayer must have warmed once again to that old and gallant friend):

> He suffered a tinge of melancholia, so we must feel that Paul was taken from us by an illness, and not really by an act of self-destruction on his part. Had a strange noise interrupted his chain of thought, had someone just knocked on his door, the illness would have passed over for the time being, and Paul would not have done what he did.

While the harrowing ceremonies went on, it was discovered that Dorothy Millette, Bern's common-law wife, had made her way from the Plaza Hotel in San Francisco to the *Delta King*, a Sacramento River ferry, and drowned herself on the night of Bern's death. Though the body had not yet been found, witnesses described her on board and told of her wandering on the deck in the early morning hours.

The search for Bern's will continued. Mayer summoned Bern's secretary, Irene Harrison, to his office, and the distraught woman announced that she had placed the will in Bern's safety deposit box at the Bank of America in Culver City. But when Mendel Silberberg accompanied her there, the will was missing. All that was found in it were two or three pieces of paper indicating a connection to Dorothy Millette.

Mayer gave chutzpah a new meaning on September 10, when he gave a dinner party for Governor Frank Merriam of California to meet Mr. and Mrs. Will Hays at his house. He telegraphed the invitation to Merriam at the last minute, obviously wanting to make sure that he had support at the highest level. It says much for his influence that Merriam accepted.

Jean Harlow returned to work on September 12. She had begged Thalberg to send her back, because, if she didn't do something immediately, she was sure she would go insane. He instructed the director, Victor Fleming, to shoot, out of schedule, an episode in which she would take a shower in a primitive, hastily improvised rain barrel; the splashing of the water would disguise her puffy face and bleary eyes. But when she emerged from the water, she looked so ill that the sequence had to be shot again. Compelled to go through a sequence of slangy, sexy dialogue with Clark Gable, she collapsed and had to be carried off the set.

Also on September 12, Irene Harrison stated that the suicide note was definitely not in Bern's handwriting, as the letter *P* in Paul was incorrectly formed. Later, she reversed her statement. She, at last, found the will in her own safety deposit box. It made clear that Bern had revised the terms, replacing previous life insurance policies made out in favor of Dorothy Millette to a new policy naming his wife (that is, Marino Bello, her manager) as sole beneficiary. This must have been a problem for Mayer: if Harlow had persuaded Bern to make a change, that would add to the theory that she had killed Bern. With ingenuity, Mendel Silberberg changed the whole thing around so that Bern had been thinking of his wife when he made the alteration. He wanted to be sure she would be the beneficiary when he shot himself. Samuel Marx stated that Bern would have read the policy carefully, and would have seen the clause in which it was stated that suicide would invalidate the policy. But did he?

On September 13, a Japanese fisherman and his son found Dorothy Millette's body, partly decomposed, floating face-down in a tributary of the Sacramento River known as the Georgiana Slough. From that moment, little was heard of the case. California authorities sued Jean Harlow for moneys allegedly due to Dorothy Millette and her surviving relatives, but had to wait four years until they obtained a modest settlement.

In November 1934, the case was reanalyzed by the auditors for the grand jury, according to Samuel Marx and Joyce Vanderveen, authors of the book *Deadly Illusions: Jean Harlow and the Murder of Paul Bern* (Random House, 1990). Unfortunately, Miss Vanderveen, who has examined the documents, has declined either to make them available or to name the official figure in the Los Angeles Archives from whom she obtained them; the officers of the grand jury and the Hall of Records have not been able to trace them. Much discussion, the authors state, followed the discovery that Jean Harlow's original statement to the grand jury was not available to this new jury. Clifton Davis, who had previously asserted his conviction of suicide, now said that he was certain from the outset it was murder. Was he, the authors asked, protecting some unknown killer? It was revealed that Winifred Carmichael, the housekeeper, had seen a "mysterious woman" arriving in a car; she was obviously flustered, and when shown a picture of Dorothy Millette, asserted that that woman was she. Yet how she could have remembered the face so clearly, and of a stranger, is open to question.

Marx believes that Dorothy Millette murdered Bern. He and Joyce Vanderveen state that Miss Millette came to the house that night, swam with Bern in the pool, stood behind him and fired a bullet point-blank into his right temple. The problem with this theory, and one must respect the authors' four years of exhaustive research and Samuel Marx's unique and intimate knowledge of all the principals, is that there remains no documentary evidence to support it.

Even if Mrs. Carmichael actually did see Dorothy Millette at the house that night, it still does not prove the theory that she went into the pool, had a drink with Bern, made her way into the house, pressed herself against him, fired into his temple from behind while he stood passively watching her in his mirror, placed the gun on the floor and left.

What, then, are we left with? Still suicide. There is a significant item in Paul Bern's probate file. On November 22, 1932, the Dora Ingram Book Shop of 10349 Washington Boulevard, Culver City, claimed against the estate for an unpaid bill for books supplied. Among the books sold to Bern in July and August were *The Worship of the Generative Powers* by Thomas Wright, published by the Dilettante Society of London in a limited edition, an illustrated work filled with reproductions of the male organ; *A Discourse on the Worship of Priapus* by Richard Knight, issued by the same publisher, and of an almost identical character; *The*

*Biological Tragedy of Woman* by A. Nemilov, which dealt with, among other things, the fact that women were dependent upon men for sexual fulfillment; and *The Glands Relating to Personality* by Louis Berman, published by Macmillan, which dealt with hormonal disturbances that could result in sexual problems. From this reading list, it would not be difficult to deduce what was troubling Paul Bern.

There was that episode years earlier, confirmed by John Gilbert in an interview with the press on September 6, 1932, in which Bern had tried to kill himself because Barbara La Marr had not agreed to marry him. Many reliable friends testified to his melancholia; the inquest had confirmed that he had smaller genitalia than would be found in a normal male. Sally Rand, the fan dancer, testified to an acquaintance, the Los Angeles film journalist and critic Kevin Thomas, that Bern had a successful affair with her; so did others. But a man suffering from recurring impotence caused by an inferiority complex could have a satisfactory relationship with one woman and a failed one with another who was less sympathetic and supportive.

Thalberg was so distressed by the matter that he discussed leaving the studio. On September 18, Anita Loos wrote to her friend Cecil Beaton in London, referring to another inconvenient subject: the bisexual Edmund Goulding, in the wake of his great success with *Grand Hotel*, had begun to indulge a voyeuristic taste for orgies. As a result of the latest one, several women had been injured in a manner that recalled the ugly circumstances of the Fatty Arbuckle affair. Thalberg asked him to leave town, and he obeyed; he did not return until the matter had blown over and the necessary arrangements had been made with District Attorney Buron Fitts. In London, Goulding would soon be in trouble again.

Nicholas Schenck arrived in Los Angeles on September 20. There was a stormy meeting at the Biltmore Hotel, at which Thalberg said that unless he received an enormous salary increase he would quit; the stress and misery of his life were, he said, too severe to bear. Nicholas Schenck threatened him with blacklisting; Thalberg dismissed the threat with a laugh. Joe Schenck, on behalf of his brother, replaced the threat with a bribe: Thalberg would be given 100,000 shares of Loew's preferred stock at half-price to stay on. Thalberg agreed. Mayer received 80,000 shares, also at that reduction.

In October, Mayer was in the midst of a political controversy. He was charged by Democratic leaders in California with threatening staff members with dismissal if they did not vote for Herbert Hoover in the upcoming election. Incensed, he made one of his rare radio broadcasts on October 28, saying:

This charge is nothing but tommyrot. It is obviously made for the purpose
of stirring up resentment and prejudice. If there is one thing no American
can be forced to do, that is his marking of a ballot in an election.

That week, Mayer was smarting at William Randolph Hearst's
$25,000 gift to Joseph Kennedy to pay for propaganda for Franklin D.
Roosevelt.

In October, after many delays, Mayer, Thalberg, Howard Strickling,
Hal Roach and Howard Dietz embarked on a unique publicity stunt to
enhance the studio's reputation as not only a place where adventure
pictures were made, but where men were men and adventurers themselves were likely to be on the payroll. Knowing that the dashing Arthur
Loew was a daredevil pilot, they decided to send him on an M.G.M.-
sponsored expedition across two-thirds of the world, ostensibly to visit
Loew's foreign enterprises, an adventure sufficient to have challenged
the courage of a Clark Gable or a Wallace Beery. Gable was appearing at
the time in George Hill's hair-raising *Hell Divers*, a story of Navy fliers.

As copilot to the feisty U.S. Reserve Flying Corps Captain Jim Dickson, Loew would make the epic journey in Hal Roach's *Spirit of Fun*, a
Lockheed 9/A187, equipped with a Wasp 450-HP engine, with a camera
to be used, among other things, for pioneer aerial shots of Mount Everest. Originally, the *Spirit of Fun* was to have been shipped to Europe,
then flown from London via Paris and Rome to Cairo, before continuing
lap by lap to India, Tibet, the Dutch East Indies and Australia. But Loew
didn't keep to this plan; he infuriated the State Department by constantly changing the itinerary, even when important embassies and con-
sulates had been put on alert to take care of the fliers as they arrived in
each country. It was very similar to the incompetence displayed in the
matter of *Trader Horn*.

Finally, after still further meaningless changes, the *Spirit of Fun* was
sent by cargo vessel to Sydney, Australia, whence the fliers took off on
October 28. Among much ballyhoo, trailing banners proclaiming
M.G.M., Roach Productions and Loew's, Inc., the plane flew perilously
in changeable weather conditions to Java, Sumatra, Hong Kong, Shanghai and Calcutta. Bypassing Everest because of severe thunderstorms,
Dickson and Loew next hopped to Johannesburg in seven and a half
days.

On the morning of November 17, the *Spirit of Fun* touched down at
Victoria Falls. Major Patrick Cochran, of the local Aircraft Operating
Company, warned Dickson not to fly from the airstrip until it had been
steamrolled, but he was impatient and decided to continue the journey.
Cochran then said that the severe heat that morning would create fur-

ther problems for the takeoff and a tire might burst. Again, Dickson waved away his cautions.

Dickson and Loew boarded the plane in a good temper, looking forward to continuing on to Egypt. The *Spirit of Fun* rose and dipped suddenly, its right wing striking a tree. Dickson tried to straighten it, and at that moment it struck another tree. The plane turned upside down and crashed. It was too late for Dickson to break free. Caught in the collapsed fuselage, his head was almost completely severed from his body. He died instantly; he was only thirty-two years old. His wife gave birth the next day.

Arthur Loew had a miraculous escape, clambering out uninjured to rescue a passenger, Joe Rosthal, who was hanging head-down, caught in a tree branch.

Somehow, the combined forces of M.G.M. and Loew's kept this ghastly incident out of the papers for several weeks, until people started asking what had happened to the expedition. An official board of inquiry determined that the accident was Dickson's fault: he had disregarded Major Cochran's advice, and had not made full use of the length of the runway.

On October 29, Mayer had Ida Koverman cable presidential secretary Lawrence Richey at the White House, calling for the president to telegraph a greeting to the five thousand people gathered at a Republican rally in San Diego. Mayer had the pleasure of reading the telegram to the crowd. But he was doomed to disappointment in November, when forty-two out of forty-eight states went against Hoover: a grievous blow to Mayer.

Meanwhile, the conflicts with Thalberg had become more serious. Thalberg had annoyed his supervisors, now called associate producers, telling them they would either have to "hit the nail on the head" in terms of cutting thousands from their budgets, or quit. This was not the sort of policy Mayer wanted: he disliked Thalberg's belligerence, even if he approved of his economizing. He began to prepare to replace Thalberg. Over Thalberg's authority, he personally read and rushed through fourteen important scripts, including the second Tarzan picture, *Tarzan and His Mate*, which he would allow Cedric Gibbons to direct.

Mayer can only have been exceedingly annoyed by word of the troublesome Garbo in Paris. She was reported attending, in a black wig and glasses, a notorious lesbian nightclub with the Countess Wachtmeister, who danced with women in male costume while Garbo swapped drinks with others at the bar.

Mayer wrote to David Selznick, offering him the job of vice president in charge of production at M.G.M., a direct act of betrayal of Thalberg, but Selznick declined. Mayer may have been troubled by the fact that Thalberg was conducting an extramarital affair with a female member of his personal staff.

Samuel Marx describes a scene in which screenwriter F. Hugh Herbert received a knock on his door very early one morning; he was astonished to see Irving Thalberg standing there. Thalberg looked flustered and asked if he could come in. Later, Herbert worked it out that Thalberg had rung the wrong doorbell. Thalberg's mistress was living next door.

The Academy Awards were held on November 18, at the Fiesta Room of the Ambassador Hotel. Mayer seemed to be in good spirits, enjoying one dance after another with Helen Hayes, leaving his wife at the table. He was pleased to accept the Best Picture award for *Grand Hotel*. But he was disturbed because Marie Dressler sent a message saying she was still too ill in New York to attend. She was deeper in the grip of cancer.

There was a fuss over the voting: Fredric March was the winner for *Dr. Jekyll and Mr. Hyde*, but in those days there was a rule that if a player was one vote short of the winner, there was a tie. Mayer demanded a recount, which resulted in the discovery that Wallace Beery was one vote short for *The Champ*. It was claimed afterward that Mayer knew more than he should have: that he had had access to the secret ballot and had arranged for Hedda Hopper, his old friend from the Selig Zoo days, to place a casting vote.

On November 22, Mayer appointed Benjamin Thau, former casting director, as his personal assistant; Thau's reputation for bedding nubile actresses did not abate. Mayer's fascination with Thau is hard to understand: Thau was a cold, detached man, who spoke in an almost inaudible whisper. His pallor, rather mousy, dull features and unimpressive physique did not suggest executive power and authority. But apparently Mayer felt that Thau was indispensable in handling "talent," in dealing with recalcitrant employees.

One major matter that concerned Mayer and Thau was that of Duncan Renaldo, the handsome star of *Trader Horn*, whom Mayer always thought was Mexican. Renaldo stood trial in Los Angeles on November 22 in U.S. District Court for having allegedly made a false statement that he was an American citizen when he obtained a passport to go to Africa in March 1929. He had stated at the time that he was born in Camden, New Jersey. His unhappy wife, Suzette, had informed authorities that he was in fact born Vasili Dumitri Coghieanas in Romania, and had come to the United States in 1921 as a stoker on a French freighter, obtaining at the time a sixty-day permit that he had illegally extended. He was found guilty in January 1933, and was sent to prison. Renaldo also lost a prolonged custody battle over his son, Edwin; the child had made a number of dramatic appearances in court in the previous two years, including, in one instance, punching both Renaldo's attorney and Renaldo himself. This entire matter was seriously embarrassing to Mayer, who, in this instance, did not step in to protect his star.

Trouble, as always in Mayer's life, followed trouble: Rudolph, his questionable brother, was charged on December 12, in Baltimore, with having illegally offered and sold stock in Maryland, promising his investors certain rights in a film company that would make twenty-six short features instructing viewers in how to play contract bridge. The shorts would be introduced by the local expert, Mrs. J. Ralph Emery; Mrs. Emery wrote a column on bridge for the Baltimore *Post*.

A Mrs. Blanche K. Rosenstein was the largest shareholder, with $7,000 in the company. She was to supply costumes for the performers in what would be a series of comic or dramatic incidents, with bridge games as the climaxes. Mayer obtained support from others on the basis that he was a Mayer. Loew's posted notices all over Baltimore advising people not to have anything to do with Rudolph Mayer. The U.S. attorney general's cease-and-desist order was categorical, and fraud was charged. Rudolph disobeyed the appropriate injunction and, the following year, a warrant would be issued for his arrest.

The pressure at M.G.M. built rapidly in December. At a meeting on December 15, Mayer and Thalberg, with Harry Rapf, Eddie Mannix, Hunt Stromberg and Bernie Hyman, pressed their staffs to the limit to wring every drop out of every dollar spent. The result was that several pictures released in 1933 lacked the customary M.G.M. glamorous look; among them were *The Chaser*, *Tugboat Annie*, *Another Language* and *The Stranger's Return*. Gary Cooper was fired off Joan Crawford's new picture *Turn About*. He had wanted a bonus of $25,000. Nicholas Schenck had offered him $13,000; he had agreed on $20,000. When he suddenly had an attack of flu on the first day of shooting, the excuse was used that he was in breach of contract, thus saving the studio the $20,000. Cooper went back to Paramount; several months later, the picture was turned into *Dancing Lady*, with Clark Gable.

The last thing Mayer wanted in that time of cost-cutting was a major lawsuit. And that is exactly what he had to face in December 1932. The engineer of the matter was the high-powered lawyer Fannie Holtzmann, who had handled Ina Claire's divorce from John Gilbert. She had noted from reviews and magazine articles the story of *Rasputin and the Empress*, and proposed to M.G.M.'s New York publicity chief Howard Dietz a lawsuit in which the Prince and Princess Youssoupoff, then living in Paris, and portrayed in the picture by John Barrymore and Diana Wynyard under fictitious names, would sue, claiming that they had been defamed; Dietz would then arrange for Nicholas Schenck to make a $10,000 out-of-court settlement, and the resulting publicity would ensure that the picture would be a tremendous hit.

When Howard Dietz declined this suggestion, Miss Holtzmann announced that she would arrange a lawsuit anyway, and M.G.M. would be grateful. She was wrong. Many years later, when Dietz published his memoirs, *Dancing in the Dark*, which mentioned this episode, Miss Holtzmann sued him for libel and the book was withdrawn.

That November, Hearst started to make *Gabriel Over the White House* for Cosmopolitan Pictures. Directed by Gregory La Cava, the film shows Walter Huston as a weak president, easygoing and subject to pressure. Following a near-fatal car crash, he is visited by the angel Gabriel, who compels him to use strong-arm methods. Walter Wanger was appointed producer; the script was cowritten by Mayer's friend Carey Wilson. Because this was a Cosmopolitan movie, Mayer was not consulted on any aspect of it.

Mayer was appalled when he saw the picture's rough cut in January. Its implication that President Hoover had not taken a sufficiently powerful stand on crime was anathema to Mayer, because he knew it was false; he had, after all, persuaded Hoover to provide the special written introduction to the M.G.M. crime film *Beast of the City*, in which Hoover directly attacked the weakness of the public in dealing with criminal activities. Nor had Mayer forgotten the visit to Washington during which Hoover had ordered the National Guard and police out to hose down the protesters outside the White House. Mayer intervened seriously for the first time over Thalberg in the cutting of the picture.

Exactly what took place between him and Hearst over this matter is uncertain, but a surviving Hearst memorandum shows Hearst's annoyance at certain last-minute changes Mayer made. Mayer switched the scene of the unemployed Army marchers from Washington to Baltimore; claiming that Hoover wanted the alteration, he staged an important scene at sea in which the president informs foreign leaders of the dangers of approaching war while on a presidential yacht instead of a battleship; he cut and altered a presidential speech to Congress (this no longer tallied with Hearst editorials in support of Roosevelt); he played down a court-martial scene because he felt it was too critical of Hoover.

Hearst brought up some big guns in support of his arguments, including, of all people, George Bernard Shaw. But Mayer was adamant that he would protect Hoover. At the same time, Mayer was shrewdly looking forward to March, when the new president would take up residence in the White House. He knew that he would have to trim his sails to the wind; Nicholas Schenck was a Democrat and could never be trusted not to remove him if he should too seriously displease the new administration in Washington. Mayer also had to consider how he might influence that administration, sustaining his present power despite his disaffection with Roosevelt. Nineteen thirty-three certainly did not offer a smoother passage than 1932.

On December 24, weighed down by his responsibilities and the constant pressure from Nicholas Schenck to cut the budgets on M.G.M. pictures, Irving Thalberg collapsed with another heart attack. It was immediately described as a bout of influenza in the press. It was obvious that Mayer would have to act swiftly.

He kept up pressure on David and Irene Selznick about joining M.G.M. Selznick wavered, while Irene begged him not to consider the offer. Selznick was finally convinced on January 24, when his father died of a brain hemorrhage after a long struggle with diabetes. With his expiring breath, Lewis J. told his son to go with Mayer ("Blood is thicker than water"). Selznick was moved by the statement and had several meetings with Mayer to discuss his joining the studio. Ben B. Kahane of RKO tried to hang on to Selznick by offering him a free hand with twenty new productions and a salary of $2,500 a week, plus ten percent of net profits. Mayer countered by offering Selznick an equal degree of autonomy, and $4,000 a week. Irene saw this as a paternalistic device to bind Selznick to the company. She raged to no avail.

Mayer had a series of stormy meetings with his executive staff, telling them that they must stop being prima donnas; that they must desist from petty jealousies and feuds; that they must stop coming in toward noon, and must arrive at 9 A.M. or before, as he did; that they mustn't waste time talking about parties and bridge games and dames; that writers were to be prisoners of their offices and not go off the lot when they felt like it; everyone left exhausted. He fired supervisors Bernie Fineman and Ralph Graves, packed supervisor Albert Lewin off to Europe for a vacation and hired Walter Wanger as associate producer.

At the same time, he pulled a last-minute string at the White House before Hoover left it, securing Garbo a new labor permit. He decided that Wanger would produce Garbo's next picture, *Queen Christina*, which he had snatched from the hands of B. P. Schulberg, and would shoot it on her return from Stockholm that summer.

On February 5, after much further agonizing, David Selznick at last officially resigned from RKO and moved into John Gilbert's converted dressing bungalow at Culver City. Gilbert was in Europe, his marriage to Virginia Bruce already on the rocks; he was firmly on his way out of M.G.M. and soon would be through in pictures. Selznick, on the verge of a nervous breakdown, his chronic logorrhea draining him, had to

commute daily to the RKO studios, where he was supervising the editing
on *Christopher Strong*, with Katharine Hepburn.

The Selznick contract called for no less than six and no more than
ten motion pictures; it gave Selznick complete charge over his pictures,
subject only to the control and direction of Louis B. Mayer or his appointee—a somewhat bleakly humorous contradiction in terms. Selznick
would have the right to terminate if Mayer left the studio.

He would, as promised, receive $4,000 a week. He was thus only
nominally free to complete his pictures as he chose. That same week,
RKO offered him absolute autonomy, but he rashly turned down the
offer.

As his first M.G.M. picture, Selznick would make *Dinner at Eight*,
from a play by George S. Kaufman and Edna Ferber; Nicholas Schenck
had bought it from his brother Joe. Mayer's favorite writer, Frances Marion, was hired to adapt it, along with the gifted Herman L. Mankiewicz
and Donald Ogden Stewart. Through a stroke of luck, almost all the top
M.G.M. stars were available, provided that the picture was made in less
than thirty days. Selznick was able to cast John Barrymore, Marie
Dressler, Jean Harlow, Billie Burke and Lee Tracy in important roles. To
direct the movie, Selznick hired George Cukor, who had ably handled
for him Katharine Hepburn's Hollywood debut film, *A Bill of Divorcement*. Mayer disliked Cukor from the beginning; Cukor was a homosexual, and Mayer already had enough of the breed on his hands. But there
was nothing he could do about Selznick's choice. And Cukor brought
the brilliant picture in on a record twenty-four-day schedule and budget:
$387,000.[3]

Mayer met with Thalberg several times at Thalberg's beach house in
middle and late February. Thalberg had determined the plot to negotiate
with Selznick behind his back, and felt angry and betrayed. Had he not
been emotionally and mentally disturbed at the time, he would surely
have thought the matter through: that Nicholas Schenck would never
allow Selznick to usurp him totally. In the custom of the time, Mayer
and Thalberg exchanged letters. On February 23, Mayer reassured
Thalberg that he would go on loving him to the end, and had never
intended him any harm. Thalberg responded with artificial sympathy,
his long letter showing a deep-seated fear that his days at the studio were
numbered. The Thalbergs decided they would sail to Europe, where
Thalberg could take the cure at Bad Nauheim in Germany.

On February 27, the eve of their departure, Mayer drove to the beach
house, and an armed truce was achieved. But Norma Shearer did not

[3] It made $3 million.

trust Mayer, and there was a degree of underlying tension during the encounter.

Next day, the Thalbergs sailed on the SS *California*, via the Panama Canal, accompanied by Helen Hayes and her husband, Charles MacArthur. This was an annoyance because Miss Hayes had to postpone shooting her new picture, *Another Language*, until May.

On March 10, Mayer had an unpleasant shock. He was discussing policy matters with other movie leaders in the Hollywood Roosevelt Hotel when the building began to shake violently and he was thrown into a chair. The Long Beach earthquake had struck. It says much for him that his first thought was for his daughter Irene, who was living at the Beverly Wilshire Hotel. Since all the telephones were cut off by the force of the quake, he dropped everything and drove helter-skelter to the hotel, where he found her out in the street carrying baby Jeffrey. Bits of buildings were falling down, and he berated her for not protecting herself inside the hotel, which was not heavily damaged. He made no effort to help Edie.

The next day, President Roosevelt ordered all American banks closed for several days. Mayer summoned every worker on the lot to a sound-stage meeting. To cheers, he announced that every salary would be paid in full, the money wired from the New York office from cash acquired by the last-minute selling of Treasury notes deposited by Nicholas Schenck at the Federal Reserve Bank. The cash was flown out by a private airplane and driven into the studio by armored cars accompanied by a full-scale police escort. When it arrived on March 11, a 400-foot-long line formed at the cashier's office; nobody went away empty-handed. The gesture enhanced Mayer's popularity among his employees.

On March 13, in the wake of their approval of his shunting in wages by armored car, ungrateful stagehands announced that they would strike. The studios were closed throughout Hollywood. Mayer was forced to sit down with Jack Warner, Harry Cohn of Columbia, Carl Laemmle, Jr., of Universal, and even Winfield Sheehan of Fox, in order to go over the matter. They agreed that the cause of the deadlock in negotiations with the union was that those who earned $50 or less a week could not, with the cost of living, afford to take a cut; therefore, their wages would remain intact. Those earning above that figure would agree not to argue with some minor adjustments. The Academy of Motion Picture Arts and Sciences was divided in the matter: the president, Mayer's old friend Conrad Nagel, resigned, feeling that the workers were being wronged. The strike was called off; Mayer's action in unlocking the bank closure for the benefit of his employees proved to be a swaying factor in the last-minute negotiations.

Having taken care of the rank and file, Mayer compensated by calling for a fifty percent temporary salary cut for directors, actors and writers. He called an emergency meeting in the executive projection room. He had been so distressed by the continuing crises that, for the first time (so far as is known) in his life, he neglected to shave. When he saw several of his stars and others lined up in rows, he temporarily froze. Lionel Barrymore broke in with warm words of reassurance. There was silence. Then Ernest Vajda, studio contract writer, grumbled that if the studio was doing so well, why should he have his salary cut? Mayer turned to stone. Barrymore interjected again: "Mr. Vajda is like a man who stops for a manicure when he's being driven to the guillotine." Everybody laughed. The Australian-born actress May Robson volunteered, as the oldest individual present, to accept her cut. A moment later, Freddie Bartholomew, the youngest, aged eight, piped up with an enthusiastic agreement. His mother, sitting next to him, looked understandably displeased. The result was that the cuts were made; but after six weeks, Mayer restored the salaries in full.

Early in March, Stephen Early, aide to President Roosevelt, called Will Hays, insisting that certain changes be made in *Gabriel Over the White House*. Nicholas Schenck assured him, in a letter to the White House dated March 11, 1933, that many telephone conversations had taken place between Los Angeles and New York, that all bookings of the picture were delayed and that the studio was at work developing new ideas, suggestions and eliminations. Before *Gabriel* was released it would be free from all objectionable features.

That same month, Mayer appointed Eddie Mannix in full charge of all operations at the studio, working in cooperation with Benjamin Thau. Mayer took a personal hand in the first movie made under his exclusive management, *When Ladies Meet*, costarring Ann Harding and Robert Montgomery. He also dealt through telegrams and letters with the intrepid W. S. Van Dyke, who, after more than seven months, was still shooting the protracted *Eskimo* in the Arctic circle. And he pressed Garbo to respond to his generosity in arranging her working visa and come back from Stockholm for *Queen Christina*. She did not respond to his letters, but he learned indirectly that the intolerable star had booked passage for Los Angeles in April.

Through the early weeks of that month, Mayer was involved in a complex and questionable operation that caused him to clash repeatedly with Irene. He continued to be aggrieved with Winfield Sheehan and the Fox Corporation, in the wake of the skullduggery of the previous years, and decided to embark on a venture which would eventually unseat Sheehan. This, despite the fact that the Film Securities Corporation, into which the government had placed the Fox controlling interest in Loew's, was aggressively active, making him, technically at least, still a Fox employee.

Mayer had secret meetings with Darryl F. Zanuck, the fast-talking, polo-playing and womanizing chief production executive at Warner Brothers. He convinced Zanuck that he should leave that studio and instead join Joe Schenck in a newly formed company called 20th Century Pictures, which Nicholas Schenck and Mayer would finance under the table with Joe. Joe Schenck would, in defiance of the Sherman Anti-Monopolies Act, remain chairman of United Artists, which would guarantee to distribute 20th Century Pictures product to its theaters. William Goetz would become vice president of 20th Century, thus locking the company, via Edie Goetz, into Mayer's own empire.

He decided to involve the Selznicks as well: he offered Irene a substantial share in the new company and would lend her a large sum of money on a promissory note; he offered Selznick the same opportunity. Irene turned him down, since she didn't want to be in debt to him, but agreed to accept a substantial shareholding as a free gift. When he balked at this, she, with characteristic chutzpah, replied that he could get an income tax reduction for an outright gift of money. David would not agree to the dubious deal. As a result, Irene alone joined the Goetzes, and 20th Century Pictures, designed to oppose and finally break the Fox Company, became essentially a Schenck–Mayer operation.

In those weeks, Fannie Holtzmann was working hard on the Youssoupoff lawsuit. Letters and telegrams were exchanged; J. Robert Rubin, at Loew's, Inc. in New York, made it clear there were no possible grounds for such a case. The matter dragged on unresolved.

On March 25, Mayer sent an impassioned plea to Stephen Early at the White House, beseeching him to allow the picture *Service*, about a British department store, to be retitled *Looking Forward*, to conform to the president's New Deal speeches. Permission was granted.

There were disruptions in Mayer's family of stars. Joan Crawford and Douglas Fairbanks, Jr., separated. Fairbanks was no longer able to tolerate her continuing relationship with Clark Gable, but apparently, in meetings with Mayer, was persuaded not to name Gable a corespondent. Such a scandal would be bad for the studio; instead, it was agreed that Miss Crawford would simply claim that the couple "could not get along." To make matters more complicated, a chemical engineer named Jorgen Dietz named Fairbanks in a $50,000 alienation of affection suit, charging him with having an affair with Mrs. Solveig Dietz, scenario writer. Fairbanks didn't know the woman. Years later, Miss Crawford stated that Mayer was sympathetic to her, proving to be a surrogate father as she told him of her tense and difficult situation, torn between two of the most handsome men in Hollywood.

On April 22, a Saturday, Mayer woke up feeling ill. He decided to take the day off, even while several pictures were shooting, and went to the Hillcrest Country Club to play golf with Nicholas Schenck, who was visiting. He was nearing the third tee when he suddenly fainted. He was carried into the club building, to which his doctor, Edward B. Jones, was summoned, and no evidence of actual illness was shown. Hearst, despite the fact that he was not happy with the interferences with *Gabriel Over the White House*, and was still negotiating for Marion Davies to join Warner Brothers, sent Mayer a note, urging him to sign William Goetz as head of production:

> You must certainly realize that you cannot get along, with a golf course coming up and hitting you in the face, and other things of that kind happening, without very vital injury to your self, and further injury to your precious company—which you think of as more important than yourself.

Hearst pointed out that one man, Thalberg, could not do half of what Mayer had to do without breaking down and going abroad: "The next time the golf course will come up and knock your blooming head off."

Two days later, Hearst wired Mayer, apologizing for the harshness of his note, and Mayer responded with affection, writing, "I know our friendship will go on until the end of time." He yielded to pressure from everyone and set sail for Honolulu aboard the Matson Line's *Malolo* on the 24th, returning by the same vessel a week later. He was accompanied on the trip by Ricardo Cortez and an old friend, the agent Major John Zanft, who was engaged to the fashion designer Hattie Carnegie. As general manager of the Fox Theaters, Zanft had played a crucial role in wresting Fox Studios from their owner; Mayer had rewarded him by giving him the position of agent to Marie Dressler. He needed no other client.

## CHAPTER FIFTEEN

# 1933-1934

THE REST DID MAYER GOOD; he was able to fulfill a long-held promise and visit with Herbert Hoover, who was now at Stanford University. Hoover came to San Francisco to greet him off the ship. Hearst was first in with a scribbled note of greeting:

> Welcome home Hoola Hoola. How ya feelin! Have a little poi on papa. Did you like the beach at Waikiki and the wiggly dancers? . . .

Meanwhile, the Thalbergs were making a royal progress in Europe. Nervously telegraphing the decorator Harold Grieve, who was redoing their house at Santa Monica, they traveled to London, where Prime Minister Stanley Baldwin had them to tea at 10 Downing Street, then to Bad Nauheim, where their old friend Dr. Franz Groedels operated on Thalberg for infected tonsils. Dr. Groedels was fearful of doing the operation since, if Thalberg died, he would be accused by the rest of the world of killing a famous Jew. That might brand him as a Nazi. After Thalberg recovered, the couple went on to visit with the German side of the family, then continued to Paris, where they learned, to their horror, that art director Cedric Gibbons had put eight-foot ceilings in their beach house in California. These had to be raised four feet.

They were at the Hotel du Cap at Eden Roc, Antibes, when they ran into Jeanette MacDonald, who was on vacation, following a successful concert tour, with her mother as chaperone, and Bob Ritchie, her handsome booking agent and loving admirer. Thalberg wanted to sign Miss MacDonald to a contract; he had always regretted losing Maurice Chevalier to Paramount in 1928, and had noted the huge success of the Chevalier–MacDonald musicals at that studio.

The Thalbergs joined Miss MacDonald and her party in the middle of a rainstorm for dinner at St. Paul de Vence in the mountains above

Antibes. Miss MacDonald enchanted them both with her humor, but they were less enchanted with her amazing ability to strike a deal. The dinner wound up with Thalberg weakly agreeing to a colossal contract. Then the entire party was entertained by Lord Louis Mountbatten on his yacht.

The visit to Europe was darkened by news that Mayer had appointed Eddie Mannix in charge of production. Thalberg was almost suicidal. Mayer must have been in a state of considerable torment, wondering how he would deal with Thalberg upon Thalberg's return.

Mayer wasted no time in plunging back into a very heavy work load. Helen Hayes had returned ahead of the Thalbergs and by May was giving a vivid performance in *Another Language*, as a newlywed bride dealing with her husband's capricious, stupid and possessive family. Surprisingly, the picture featured a monster parent, the very antithesis of Mayer's conception of motherhood. It was certainly a supreme irony that *Another Language* should kick off Mayer's career as direct head of production.

Mayer's fondness for Marie Dressler continued during that exhausting spring. She was on her way to shooting *Tugboat Annie* with Wallace Beery in Seattle, under the able direction of Mervyn LeRoy and production skills of Harry Rapf, when she spotted from the window of her chauffeur-driven limousine a small, pretty cottage, saying to Howard Strickling, who accompanied her, that she would love to own it. Mayer immediately offered its owners twice what it was worth to vacate, and they did so; he had it moved to Santa Barbara for her to live in. He knew she had only a short time to live; her suffering from cancer was agonizing for him, and he wanted her to be as happy as possible. She gave one of her finest performances in the picture, which became one of M.G.M.'s biggest successes to date.

It is surprising that Mayer encouraged and developed several pictures that defied the Motion Picture Code and contained aggressively frank discussions of sex. He passed for production *Penthouse*, a gangster picture starring Myrna Loy, in which the conversation frequently dealt with the immoral behavior of a call girl ("She'll come to dinner; and she won't give you an argument if you ask her to stay to breakfast."). The Hollywood satire *Bombshell*, starring Jean Harlow and Lee Tracy, was equally crude, and there were all manner of heavy innuendos in *Should Ladies Behave?*, a comedy about three women in love with the same man. In *The Barbarian*, Myrna Loy was seen, seemingly naked, in a tropical bath.

Part of the problem was that Mayer was still not used to reading screenplays and relied upon Kate Corbaley to tell him stories. It is possible that she shaded the highly charged sexual elements in the tales she spun for him; that he left it to the producers to take care of the actual productions and only saw the results of the studio's handiwork at the stage of final cut. It is astonishing that, given the nature of the movies made under his aegis, he did not intervene more strongly. The likelihood is that his shrewd sense of box office overcame his moral concerns, and perhaps his continuing affair with Ad Schulberg, who was sophisticated and enlightened, had an influence on him.

Normally, Mayer's and Selznick's relationship with the White House remained excellent in 1934. But they overstepped the mark in April when they sought permission to make a picture entitled *The Corpse on the White House Lawn*. Presidential aide Stephen Early advised them that "no one here would consider it [amusing] to see the White House and its lawns used as a background for a story involving a murder, a fight and the burning of the Executive Mansion." The idea was dropped immediately.

Jean Harlow continued misbehaving in June. Mayer had sent her to Chicago to open Hollywood-at-the-Fair, an exhibition of Hollywood artifacts, to which some two thousand people were invited, and at which Miss Harlow would appear as mistress of ceremonies. She failed to turn up, infuriating the guests and several hundred gate crashers, who booed when her absence was announced. After several further outcries, an electrical short caused all the lights to blow out, and everyone went home.

In July, Jack Warner accused Mayer of obtaining exclusive rights to entertain twenty state governors who were scheduled to attend a convention in Sacramento. The peevish Warner, realizing that he had been upstaged, and not for the first time, refused to entertain eighty-five Army and Navy fliers who had arrived for the National Air Race, saying, "Give them to Mayer." Mayer was delighted to receive them—yet more proof that his was the only studio in Hollywood that really mattered in high places.

Maureen O'Sullivan recalls an extraordinary meeting with Louis B. Mayer at the time. Summoned to his office, she walked in nervously, and he told her to sit down. He said, as though to an erring child, "You're not being a good daughter, Maureen. You're not writing home often enough. I have a letter here from your father. He complains that he does not hear from you sufficiently. You see these pictures? These are my lovely daughters. They're not like you. They take care of their father. They're in contact all the time. You? You don't write letters, and I want you to write." "I thought this was very sweet," Miss O'Sullivan says. She wrote.

An irritation of that summer was David O. Selznick. *Dinner at Eight* was a magnificent picture and would reap substantial profits, but Selznick faltered with *Meet the Baron*, a feeble comedy starring Jack Pearl and Jimmy Durante, and his gambling was a constant nuisance. At the Clover Club, Selznick played roulette obsessively into the small hours, losing almost all of his salary and much of his investment in 20th Century Pictures. Joe Schenck won $103,000 from him at a single session of gin rummy. According to Edie Goetz, part of Selznick's compulsion was to get away from home, where Irene was a hard taskmistress, berating him continuously for his sloppiness, demanding that he take more care of his appearance. She angered him by reminding him of his responsibilities to her and to their son.

Toothily smiling, cheerful for the cameras, this brilliant and gifted producer was, in person, as tortured and neurotic as ever. He felt prostituted by his position at M.G.M., frustrated in his insistences on buying new properties. The staff, Samuel Marx says, and with the notable exception of J. J. Cohn, made life difficult for him. They all longed for Thalberg to return; they disliked Selznick's obtaining of choice stars and directors. He was obstructed by everyone when he planned to make Robert Hichens's *The Garden of Allah* for Garbo, and John Galsworthy's *The Forsyte Saga* for John and Lionel Barrymore. Cutting an ill-conceived and ill-fated aviation drama, *Night Flight*, began in April. At the same time, Selznick had started work on the cumbersome *Dancing Lady* with Fred Astaire, in which he had wickedly cast Franchot Tone, who was still having an affair with Joan Crawford, with Clark Gable, whom she had left for Tone, and Crawford herself. The story called for an angry, bitter rivalry between the men for Crawford. A similarly outrageous penchant for using real events to give spark to screen drama came next year, when Selznick made *Reckless* and had Franchot Tone, as Jean Harlow's husband, actually shoot himself. Anything went—taste, lives, people's feelings—when money was to be made.

Two days into production, Clark Gable was due on the set from a bear-hunting expedition with Marino Bello, when the same problem that had afflicted Mayer in Rome struck him down. Gable had long neglected his teeth, and now a major infection invaded his gums, the result of very advanced pyorrhea. Mayer was afraid he might die; Dr. Edward B. Jones again came to the rescue and called for multiple extractions. Almost every tooth in his head came out, and he was fitted with porcelain dentures.[1] Gable was laid off, but he came in for a difficult day's work on July 30 and was applauded by the crew. His system was badly undermined, however, and he came down with an inflamed gall

---

[1] When Claudette Colbert kissed him very hard several years later in *Boom Town*, she broke them.

bladder and had to be operated on on August 1. Mayer was determined not to replace Gable; the rushes were disappointing, and it was clear only Gable could save the picture. Mayer called Nicholas Schenck and the picture was closed down until August 29, but Gable collapsed again, and again the picture was delayed.

Throughout the summer, Thalberg, concerned that he might be replaced by Selznick, kept in touch. He, Norma Shearer and Irving, Jr., returned to New York on the *Majestic*, arriving on July 18, only to be met with a suit from a Dr. W. C. McKee for unpaid medical services. They did not come directly to Los Angeles, but instead went to stay with Nicholas and Pansy Schenck, making sure of their position when they returned to the studio. Schenck approved Thalberg's plan to make for Jeanette MacDonald *I Married an Angel*, by Richard Rodgers and Lorenz Hart, who were under contract to M.G.M. to write screen originals.

Mayer became infatuated with Jeanette MacDonald from the first moment he met her. He was always mesmerized by "ladies," women of great style, presence and reserve. Her puritanism, her look of being an unassailable virgin, were irresistible to him. She was so cautious in her emotional life that no one was entirely sure whether the booking agent who still constantly accompanied her, Bob Ritchie, was actually sleeping with her. To this day, some of her admirers feel that she simply used Ritchie as an escort to avoid any possible commitment with a man; she was seemingly devoted to her career and afraid that an emotional involvement could distract her and upset her in her upward course.

Samuel Marx, among others, takes a different view, saying that she and Ritchie were very deeply involved and, in fact, he witnessed them living together. Certainly, she had no room in her heart for Mayer, and this was undoubtedly painful for him.

Miss MacDonald was a lyric soprano with a wide vocal range, E above high C, close to three octaves. She was more willful about her personal appearance than Mayer and Thalberg were used to. She detested false eyelashes and heavy makeup, and refused both. She wouldn't have her fine hair dressed by the studio cosmetologists, but instead opted for wigs.

After Rodgers and Hart had written *I Married an Angel*, sets were being designed and a possible male lead was being considered, the picture had to be canceled because the Hays office decided that the concept would be offensive to religious groups. Instead, Mayer and Thalberg decided to cast Miss MacDonald in the charming *The Cat and the Fiddle*, with Ramon Novarro.

Meanwhile, Norma Shearer had discovered Stefan Zweig's biography of Marie Antoinette and had decided that she would undertake it as a project. Mayer approved the idea. Unfortunately, Marion Davies had also felt that she might play Marie Antoinette, and this would soon prove to be a headache. It was decided that Edmund Goulding would first direct Miss Shearer in a society drama, *Riptide*, which would start shooting that fall.

Mayer arrived with Howard Strickling in New York on August 8. Another passenger on the train was his long-term lawyer, Edwin Loeb. They did not speak for the entire journey; they had clashed severely because Loeb was trying to abstract Thalberg from M.G.M. and have him set up his own independent company.

Mayer moved into the Schenck house; meetings took place between all parties on the studio's future. It was settled that Thalberg, to protect his health, would produce only a handful of pictures a year. He would have a separate executive bungalow and his own special unit, as well as an open choice of stars, producers and directors. What Mayer did not know was that Nicholas Schenck was plotting to replace him with Selznick. Irene was visiting New York at the time and came to stay over a weekend. She crept into Mayer's room in the early hours of one morning and wakened him, telling him of the plot against him. What followed is unknown, but it is safe to say that Mayer told Nicholas Schenck he had gotten wind of the plot, and the scheme to unseat him was summarily dropped.

Back in Hollywood, Mayer, who preceded the Thalbergs by one day on the train and returned to the station on August 19 to greet them on their arrival, ushered them into their new and handsome executive bungalow. Thalberg appeared at the Hillcrest Country Club, whose membership was exclusively Jewish, the following day. Samuel Marx recalled his impassioned warning of the danger to all Jews throughout the world as the forces of Nazism arose. Within the week, *Riptide* was embarked upon; *Eskimo* was finished at last. The great epic of the Arctic Circle turned out to be striking and impressive. Daringly, Mayer and Thalberg had made the decision not to dub the Eskimos, but to allow them to speak in their own language, with subtitles interlarded in the action. Such harrowing sequences as the hero's desperate journey across the pack ice in which all except one sleigh dog have to be killed excited audiences in that time, when adventure pictures of the wild and largely unexplored parts of the world were the rage, providing glorious escape from the Depression.

A great excitement of those weeks was the shooting of *The Prizefighter and the Lady*, one of the finest pictures of the Thalberg-less regime, and an indication of the influence not only of Mayer but of the former bouncer, the tough Irishman Eddie Mannix. It was typical of the slam-bang, dynamic, down-to-earth picture making that Mayer would increasingly favor and that was far removed from the sleek, cultivated, smooth, somewhat bloodless Thalberg productions. Directing this story by two tough writers, John Lee Mahin and John Meehan, W. S. Van Dyke, scarcely recovered from his Arctic trip, ably blended champion boxers— Max Baer as the egotistical, promiscuous, primitive hero, Primo Carnera and Jack Dempsey—with such polished players as the rapidly rising Myrna Loy and the impeccably dapper Otto Krueger. The final bout at Madison Square Garden, recreated amazingly on the sound stage, was a ripsnorter, with Nicholas Schenck among the spectators announced as present at ringside, and the massive Kate Smith, described as occupying "Seats 1, 2 and 3."

The authors, under Mayer's instruction, built the central role of the nightclub singer for Miss Loy with considerable skill, tailoring it so carefully to her personality, cool and detached on the surface, vulnerable and romantic underneath, in order to make her into a star.

During the shooting, Clark Gable, not well, still sleeping with Jean Harlow and hankering for Joan Crawford, tried to seduce Miss Loy; but she was having an affair with a producer, Arthur Hornblow, whom she would later marry. When Gable grabbed her, she threw him into some bushes. He consoled himself with the actress Elizabeth Allan. There was a constant merry-go-round of musical beds at the studio in those days. Mayer himself was strongly attracted to an actress whom he authorized to be cast in *The Prizefighter and the Lady:* Jean Howard, of whom more later.

*The Cat and the Fiddle*, starring Jeanette MacDonald and Ramon Novarro, whose homosexuality now irritated Mayer beyond endurance, was put together by the writers Samuel and Bella Spewack, from the work of Jerome Kern.[2] Apparently, it was at this time that Mayer at last lost control and proposed to Miss MacDonald that they should enter into a physical relationship. According to the MacDonald authority Tessa Williams, "Miss MacDonald said, as he made his advance, in a very off-putting, but sweet and polite, manner, 'Oh, Mr. Mayer, I had no idea! Really, I'm quite surprised!' " That effectively dampened Mayer's ardor, but he didn't cease to yearn for the star. Samuel Marx mentioned that on one occasion, when he needed to see Mayer on urgent business, Miss MacDonald swept past him, saying that what she had to attend to would simply take "half an hour." Marx believes to this day that the half hour was spent in lovemaking, but Tessa Williams denies this absolutely.

[2] Directed by William K. Howard, it would turn out to be an original and inventive movie, the most daring and progressive made at M.G.M. in the talkie period to that date, giving the Paramount Lubitsch and Mamoulian masterpieces of the musical, also starring Miss MacDonald, quite a run for their money.

"Jeanette MacDonald was a prude," she says, "a puritan. She didn't believe in illicit sex. And she didn't need to curry favor with the boss. She had it all! And she couldn't possibly have found Mayer attractive."

The biggest news of that August was Garbo's starting work on Walter Wanger's *Queen Christina*, directed by Rouben Mamoulian. For once, the temperamental star seemed determined to behave and to give of her best. Samuel Marx remembered her pacing up and down outside his office, repeatedly going over her lines and movements for the camera. Before that, she had bragged of studying her lines only on the actual day of work. Her lover, Salka Viertel, had worked hard on the script, along with Mercedes de Acosta, who did not receive credit, and Garbo herself had contributed many ideas, including playing much of the role in male attire. But the difficulties accompanying all Garbo productions returned to plague this one and greatly irritated Walter Wanger, the producer Mayer had assigned to it. The young Laurence Olivier proved to be inadequate at tests and rehearsals, and was fired, at Garbo's insistence. She went to see Mayer, demanding, to his annoyance, that John Gilbert be pulled back from exile and disgrace to take over the leading role.

Mayer exploded. He would not tolerate Gilbert returning to the studio. Garbo listened to him to the end, then announced that unless Gilbert were allowed to work with her, she would depart for Sweden at once. With money expended on sets and costumes, and with no other actress at the studio capable of playing the role, Mayer was forced to give in.

No sooner had work begun, than Gilbert fell apart. Terrified by the challenge of once more playing with the woman he had loved, and who had so ill-treated him in the past, anxious to live up to what the critics and public would expect of him, he announced he had influenza and disappeared. It would have been possible to shoot around him, but Garbo decided she would be ill as well and went home, refusing to answer the telephone or respond to messages at her front door. Mayer became more and more hysterical, screaming at everyone. The director recalled, in an interview many years later, that Mayer at one stage fell to the floor, sobbing and tearing at the carpet with his fingers, so absolute was his frustration.

Mayer summoned Walter Wanger to his office to demand a finishing date. Wanger replied he had no idea, and the picture would end when it would. He also stated that he had no idea what the final cost would be. Mayer lost control completely. He flew at Wanger, seized him by the throat, punched him and flung him to the floor, starting to strangle him. Wanger fought loose, struck Mayer hard in the face, struggled to his feet and ran out. From that moment on, Wanger refused to talk to either Mayer or Thalberg and made plans to leave the studio for good.

At last, the difficult stars returned to work. But then the oversexed Garbo found even the scholarly Mamoulian, in his round Harold Lloyd spectacles, irresistible and abandoned her prominent female companions to spend weekends with him.

Mayer had an impossible Joan Crawford on his hands. On October 21, 1933, she stormed into his office and demanded an increase from $3,500 a week to $4,500 or she would not continue work on the picture *Today We Live*. He told her, probably in more colorful language, to get lost. She did; she disappeared from the shooting on the following Monday, and could not be found. Finally, she settled for $4,000 and completed some final shots.

Clark Gable was irritated at the publicity surrounding the Mayer–Crawford fight because he was getting only $2,500 a week. He complained that he was suffering from adhesions following the gall bladder operation, and he was annoyed that Mayer was lending him to Columbia Pictures, considered the Siberia of the industry, to make a picture entitled *Overland Bus* (later, *It Happened One Night*). He began to drink heavily, partly because of the fact that Miss Crawford had dumped him in favor of the handsome young Franchot Tone. While driving drunk down to Sunset Boulevard from the Hollywood Hills, he rounded a bend too sharply and struck a pedestrian, killing her instantly. Mayer acted immediately; he laid him off salary for ninety days, canceled a proposed picture, cut his salary in half for all future movies and told him to lie low until it was time to make the Columbia movie. Somebody would have to say they were driving the car, since the press would get onto the fact if the court dockets were burned. The dead woman's family was howling for blood.

Mayer went over the list of his executive staff to find the one he could definitely spare. He selected an executive I will call Mark Pine and summoned him to the office. He told Pine that, whatever happened, the studio must not be damaged or destroyed by the exposure of its leading male star to charges of manslaughter; that Pine had an opportunity to save everyone's neck. Pine would be offered a guarantee of life employment at M.G.M., and an income stretching to death, if he would take the rap for Gable, plead guilty to a manslaughter charge, saying that he was with Gable at the wheel, and, by prearrangement with Buron Fitts, would go to prison for a limited time. He accepted; Gable went to Palm Springs and Pine served a twelve-month term. No inkling of the matter ever reached print.

At the same time, Gable was continuing an affair with Jean Harlow, as well as with Joan Crawford. Miss Harlow was involved with the cine-matographer Harold Rosson, to whom she had become strongly attracted when he provided a sympathetic shoulder to cry on following Paul Bern's death. Rosson was supposed to shoot Selznick's next picture, *Viva Villa*, in Mexico in the late fall, and the couple would spend their hon-eymoon in Mexico City. Mayer was anxious to engineer a quick mar-riage, and in particular to mask Harlow's relationship with Gable, which could only be dangerous if exposed by the press.

So he allowed Rosson to back out of *Viva Villa* and replaced him, with Selznick's approval, with James Wong Howe. On October 20, with Mayer's blessing, Harlow and Rosson eloped to Yuma, Arizona, where they were wed. They planned to honeymoon in Honolulu. But the fact that this was an arranged marriage was all too painfully clear when the couple returned to stay in separate rooms of a suite at the Château Marmont prior to the voyage. The hotel had been the trysting place of Gable and Harlow for months, as was testified by the receptionist in an interview years later.

The receptionist described Miss Harlow rushing downstairs on the following morning, black and blue, severely bruised from head to foot. She was rushed to the hospital. When the staff went into the suite, they found that the Murphy bed in the living room had been used; the latch was on between the two rooms.

The marriage continued. The couple put on a performance, entertain-ing, receiving friends, who brought gifts, giving interviews in which they expressed their love for each other. They had another fight, and Miss Harlow collapsed with what was described as a severe attack of appendi-citis, but may have been the result of another beating. On October 15, she was rushed to the Good Samaritan Hospital and operated on by Dr. Sidney Burnap. She recovered, but the long-delayed honeymoon to Ho-nolulu was canceled. She refused to appear in a picture entitled *Living in a Big Way*, complaining that her salary was only $1,500 a week. She was put on suspension. By November, she had begun quarreling with Rosson again; there were ugly scenes at the Château Marmont. It was evident that Rosson was no longer keeping his side of the bargain, and that she would not give up Clark Gable. Her affair with Gable recommenced, and soon Rosson moved to the Hollywood Athletic Club, haven of rejected husbands, and Gable moved into the Château Marmont.

In an extraordinary coincidence, yet another fatal accident occurred. On September 25, John Huston, son of Walter Huston and a promising writer in whose welfare Mayer took a strong interest, ran over a woman while driving on Sunset Boulevard and killed her instantly. He claimed that he was sober. Walter Huston was still one of Mayer's favorite actors and worked on and off at the studio. There was no way that this episode could be kept out of the papers: John Huston was a nobody, and Mayer could not again pull strings. It was announced on September 26 that a grand jury had been called to determine whether John Huston was guilty of manslaughter or murder. Walter went to see the hard-pressed Mayer; he begged him to see that William Randolph Hearst's all-important newspaper chain, and in particular the powerful columnist Louella Parsons, should underplay the matter. Mayer would, of course, have less influence over the other newspapers. Mayer is believed to have invested $400,000 to suppress the matter.

Huston escaped the charges, and it was arranged that he would leave the country and go to England for an indefinite period—the same prescription applied for Edmund Goulding.

On October 8, 1933, Mayer and Darryl F. Zanuck, the former as a silent partner, in view of the peculiar connection between the two studios, flung a 20th Century Pictures party at the Vendome, Hollywood's most fashionable night spot. To cover Mayer's involvement, the William Goetzes were officially listed as cohosts. It was the most colorful and amusing social event in the history of the movie community up to that time. The entire restaurant was converted into Chuck Connor's saloon, a re-creation, down to the last detail, of New York Mayor Connor's Chinatown resort of the late 1890s. At the height of the revels, one dazzling group rolled up in a coach-and-four. Among the passengers were Hal Roach, dressed as a French sailor, and his wife as a Paris dance-hall girl; Louella Parsons as Lillian Russell in diamonds and feathers, with her husband as Diamond Jim Brady; Sally Eilers as a Salvation Army girl, with her husband, the writer Harry Joe Brown, as a Bowery policeman with a helmet and a dancing mustache; and Jesse L. Lasky and his wife as a German brewer couple. Mayer was dressed as a Bowery blade in a square-top bowler and four-buttoned coat, with his wife as a society matron. Kay Francis and Mrs. Richard Barthelmess led the square dance, in which Mayer enthusiastically joined.

On November 9, Selznick and Thalberg took up occupancy of two handsome bungalows that Mayer had ordered for them; Selznick had constantly grumbled about living in John Gilbert's converted dressing room. Selznick had Ben Hecht and Charles MacArthur under contract; when Mayer came in to inspect his son-in-law's new quarters, he was horrified to see Hecht dictating to a secretary who was wearing nothing but lipstick and nail polish. Making his way past this spectacle, he entered the office. The walls were lined from end to end with pictures of men and women having various forms of sex. He stormed out in a fury; the secretary was fired. Such antics in a man married to his own daugh-

ter appalled Mayer; he never could get used to the freewheeling life of
the time.

On November 19, Mayer received unsettling news from his trouble-
shooter, Don Eddy, who was attached to the *Viva Villa* unit in Mexico
City. Lee Tracy, playing the camp-following American reporter Johnny
Sykes in the story, got drunk, stripped off his clothes and appeared on
the balcony of the Hotel Regis, swearing in a disgusting manner at the
military cadets marching on parade below and urinating on them. Police
stormed the hotel and marched him in handcuffs to police headquarters,
where Major Juan Viera, chief of the Bureau of Investigation and Public
Safety, held him in his office all night. Next day, Viera allowed Tracy to
go to the hotel to have breakfast. Under Mayer's orders, Eddy and Wallace Beery pleaded with Ambassador Josephus Daniels to resolve the
matter and save M.G.M.'s good name. It was finally agreed that Mayer
and Tracy would make public apologies and Tracy would pay a fine and
be allowed to leave the country voluntarily, rather than be deported.
Tracy never paid the fine and never worked at M.G.M. again.

Wallace Beery flew back in his own plane via El Paso; other cast
members came home by train. There could be no question of any further
shooting taking place in Mexico. Mayer hired Stuart Erwin to replace
Tracy, and Jack Conway took over for Howard Hawks as director. Some
footage was lost in a mysterious airplane crash. Beery demanded, and
got, a considerable increase in salary to soothe his annoyance at having
to play the part all over again.

Another annoyance of that November was the behavior of Franchot
Tone and Joan Crawford. It was always a rule that stars who were in love
would never be seen to be cohabiting; but the rebellious pair shared a
bedroom on the Santa Fe Chief for Chicago on November 10, boldly
granting an interview with the press as they stepped aboard. They had
not yet announced plans to marry, which was scarcely surprising, since
Miss Crawford had still not received her interlocutory divorce decree
from Douglas Fairbanks, Jr., and would not do so until the following
spring.

One of Mayer's favorite contracted actresses, Maureen O'Sullivan,
Jane in the *Tarzan* series, was in the news in a way that did not appeal to
Mayer. Her fiancé, John Farrow, a talented writer who would later become a prominent director, was in trouble with the law for making false
statements in his application for registration as an alien. Born in Australia, which had a limited quota, he had pretended to be born in England.
He had been arrested the previous January and was still fighting extradi-
tion. Mayer brought his influence to bear on Mabel Walker Willebrandt,
and by the beginning of January 1934, Mayer was able to hand Miss

O'Sullivan a welcome New Year's gift: Farrow would be granted American citizenship.

That same January brought increased struggles with Jean Harlow, whose demands for salary increases Mayer opposed. She was locked in a fight with the administrators of Sacramento County, who were denying her her share of Paul Bern's estate on the ground that Dorothy Millette was actually married to him. The case would drag on for years, until it was dismissed in Miss Harlow's favor. Then, on January 6, the matter of Rudolph Mayer's fraud in Baltimore reemerged. A new warrant was issued for his arrest. Rudolph fled to Hollywood, with two sheriffs following him, and Mayer sheltered him; he got him a job as gofer with J. J. Cohn. Three weeks later, Rudolph failed to turn up for work, and when Cohn asked what had become of him, Mayer announced that Rudolph had left for China. State Department documents show that Mayer actually aided and abetted his brother by swearing out affidavits that allowed him to obtain a passport; without confirmation of date and place of birth, Rudolph could never have left the country. Again, Buron Fitts must have been bribed, since to assist in the departure from the country of a wanted criminal was in itself a criminal offense on Mayer's part.

Garbo attracted much unwanted publicity yet again. She departed with Rouben Mamoulian by car for Arizona, under the pseudonyms Mary Jones and Robert Brown. They checked into the same suite at the El Tovar Hotel at the Grand Canyon, and into separate rooms at the Holbrook Hotel in Holbrook. According to Mamoulian, in an interview with this author in 1971, Garbo had promised to marry him; but he should have learned his lesson from her behavior toward John Gilbert.[3] When they reached Yuma, she repeated an earlier action involving Gilbert and drove off in his car, just when they were about to arrive at the home of the local magistrate. Mamoulian chased her in a taxicab, and the pair returned to Hollywood together.

In the midst of all these goings-on, Mayer had to sustain his public performance as a pillar of propriety. He turned up in San Francisco on January 11, in his role of chairman of the Republican State Central Committee, to which he had been promoted from vice chairman the year before, to be honored by the Shriners at the Islam Temple of the Mystic Shrine at a Palace Hotel ceremonial luncheon. He was accompanied by Buron Fitts, Mendel Silberberg, Major John Zanft, and Howard Strickling. Governor of California James Rolph, Jr., and San Francisco Mayor Angelo J. Rossi led the crowd in greeting. Mayer showed that he did not adhere to Jewish teachings by speaking to the predominantly

---

[3] Who was now involved in an exotic affair with Princess Liliuokolani of Hawaii.

Roman Catholic group of "following the Lord Jesus Christ's teachings
. . . good will to men on earth . . ." He received honorary life membership in the Temple, the highest honor the Shriners could bestow.

Mayer returned to settle his differences with Jean Harlow and force
her back to the studio on a compromise salary of $3,000 a week. She
would begin almost at once on *The Girl from Missouri*; it would turn out
to be a squalid, ugly movie, beginning with the man in whom the anti-
heroine is interested shooting himself Paul Bern-ishly. It was another
story of a heartless gold digger, teasing men sexually in return for marriage, jewels and furs; it would lead to enormous problems with the Hays
office and was a big mistake to have been made at all. Lacking the wit of
*Red-Headed Woman*, it was a tired replay of a well-worn theme, in which
everyone looked understandably jaded and Miss Harlow played with a
quite unusual degree of nervous tension.

There were constant meetings that winter on the matter of the Motion Picture Code; there were numerous conversations about the role of
each executive at M.G.M., with Selznick, Walter Wanger, Hunt
Stromberg and Harry Rapf all grumbling about the fact that Mayer had
put inordinate amounts of power into the hands of Eddie Mannix, who
was supposed to approve, along with Mayer, every project. They were
aggravated by the fact that excessive amounts of time and money had
been put into the Norma Shearer vehicle, *Riptide*, and *The Cat and the
Fiddle*, on which the director, William K. Howard, had lavished close to
a million dollars, while other pictures were being starved of funds. A
movie starring Gable and MacDonald, *The Duchess of Delmonico*, was
planned, then scrapped. Nicholas Schenck arrived at the end of February to try to sort everything out. Mayer stayed at the bedside of his
mother-in-law, who was grievously ill, and was unable to meet Schenck
off the ship at Caliente.

In the spring, the *Youssoupoff v.* M.G.M. case was causing much annoyance at the executive level in London. The basis of the suit had
changed: the distinguished Sir Patrick Hastings, K.C., acting for the
plaintiff, brought up the issue that the film showed the princess being
raped by Rasputin. In those days, British law stated that any such assertion amounted to defamation, even though the victim was innocent.
The defending counsel, Sir William Jowitt, handled the case rather
clumsily, and eventually M.G.M. lost. Fanny Holtzmann, who had initiated the matter, wound up with a considerable sum of her own, and the
studio had to pay £25,000 ($125,000) to the princess, a fortune in those
days. From that moment, motion pictures dealing with biographical subjects, and many others besides, featured a statement that there could be

no question of anybody portrayed in them resembling any person living or dead.

Mayer's affair with Ad Schulberg had fizzled out. He was attracted to the beautiful thirty-one-year-old, Maine-born actress Esther Ralston, and was considering putting her under contract. She was a client of Frank Orsatti, whom he always tried to help. Down on her luck, not very successful in talkies, Miss Ralston agreed to accept a lowly $750 a week, and Mayer announced that she would appear in a picture with Clark Gable. He arranged for photographs to be taken of her, reporters talked to her about her reviving career and she was invited to a party at Jean Harlow's parents' house. On another occasion, Mayer took a bold step: although he was still much married to Margaret, he would take Miss Ralston to a preview. But several others were in the party to conceal his interest in her. After the performance, the group continued to the Colony Club. Everyone stared at Esther; they knew Mayer was interested in having an affair with her. Mayer lost his usual caution and, evidently feeling protected by the Hollywood community, started caressing Miss Ralston and passing his arm around her shoulders. Suddenly, she recalled later, he said to her, "Let's leave now." Miss Ralston panicked; when he was distracted, she whispered to Randolph Scott and his date, Claire Trevor, that they should get into her car. When her chauffeur opened the door, Mayer, to his horror, saw Scott and Trevor. His face went pale with anger. Miss Ralston's chauffeur dropped him off at his house.

Next morning, Mayer summoned her to his office and screamed at her, "Think you're pretty smart, eh? Think you fooled me? Let me tell you, I can have any woman on this lot—Joan Crawford and . . ." Miss Ralston stood up and replied, "Perhaps you can—any woman but Esther Ralston!" Mayer paced up and down, threatening her with blacklisting and telling her she wouldn't work at the studio. She didn't. Six months later, she sought the role of a nightclub singer in the Joan Crawford vehicle *Sadie McKee*. Clarence Brown decided he would have her in the picture. Yet again, Mayer showed a lack of vengefulness. He allowed Miss Ralston to play the part, then loaned her out to Universal for a series of movies.

At the same time, Mayer had become more fascinated by the gorgeous, sophisticated and intelligent Jean Howard, whom he had noticed in *The Prizefighter and the Lady*. She had been born Ernestine Hill in Groveton, Texas, in 1910, the daughter of an investment broker. Florenz Ziegfeld had discovered her in the late 1920s; he considered her a perfect showgirl. Goldie Clough, Ziegfeld's legendary girl Friday, remembered her extraordinary charm, toughness, strength and ambition. Ziegfeld cast her in a tiny role, under the name Ernestine Mahoney, in the picture *Whoopee*, which he coproduced with Samuel Goldwyn, starring Eddie Cantor.

She returned to New York to appear in the *Follies* of 1931, parading in magnificent clothes through several scenes which featured the legendary Ethel Borden, who became an intimate friend. Ethel Borden was the daughter of the luminous Daisy Hurst, who later became ambassador to Norway. Ethel Borden introduced Jean Howard to a brilliant circle that included Cole Porter and Noël Coward; the latter wrote the introduction to Miss Borden's novel, published by Horace Liveright, *Romantic—I Call It*. As a gimmick, Ziegfeld showed off this society lioness as a hostess at pre-Prohibition and Prohibition party scenes in the spectacular 1931 revue, with Jean Howard as a partygoer; he presented Miss Borden as Texas Guinan, raucous nightclub queen of the era, with Howard as one of her nightclub hostesses. The two women were the talk of New York.

Jean Howard was not so much an actress as a presence: smart, knowledgeable, worldly-wise even at that young age. Mayer clearly saw star quality, or at least its potential, in her test, and she appeared, briefly but strikingly, in a jumble called *Broadway to Hollywood*. She comes across as a fly-by-night party girl in *The Prizefighter and the Lady* with a certain cool smartness that suggests that she would lack the warmth and identifiability that would take her further up the ladder.

In the wake of his defeat by Esther Ralston, Mayer apparently saw acquiring Jean Howard as a badge of honor. He was not immune to the requirement in Hollywood that every male worthy of the name should be seen with a drop-dead beauty at the various enclosed meeting places which the press could be relied upon not to invade. But he still had to bear in mind the danger of public scandal and the possibility that Margaret might divorce him and take half of his money and property—and possibly a handsome slice of his share of the studio as well.

Mayer sent a note to Jean Howard's dressing room and asked her to come to his office, where Ida Koverman ushered her in. He treated her like a father; at a later meeting he said to her that if she needed the attentions of a doctor or dentist, he would take care of it. Mayer felt that the only way to secure Jean Howard as a date was to arrange it through Ethel Borden; he knew that Miss Borden had ambitions to be a screenwriter, and he decided to use the head of the story department, Samuel Marx, as the go-between. Marx, with Mayer's authorization, put Miss Borden under contract.

He not only used Ethel Borden as an entrée to Jean Howard, but as a chaperone to avoid Margaret proceeding with a divorce and the columnists making something of the relationship. Evening after evening, Mayer, with Jean Howard and Ethel Borden as a third, went to nightclubs together, but Mayer never moved directly into any kind of proposition. Meanwhile, Miss Howard felt little attraction to Mayer; she was being pursued by Charles Feldman, the handsome agent and partner of Mayer's mistress, Ad Schulberg, who represented Ethel Borden. To make matters even more complicated, Feldman was also in love with, and strongly considering marrying, the Mexican actress Raquel Torres, costar of *White Shadows in the South Seas*. Renée Torres, presently Mrs. Edward Ashley, remembers that her sister was devastated by Feldman's interest in Miss Howard.

As this unsatisfactory matter dragged on, there was much to-do at the studio about the May wedding of Mayer's friend and favorite writer Carey Wilson, whom Mayer had all but forgiven for *Gabriel Over the White House*. Wilson had fallen in love with the beautiful actress Carmelita Geraghty; they were about to be wed, when the first Mrs. Wilson announced through her attorney that her marriage to him was still valid, and that the divorce decree was not final. She said that the only way she would agree not to block the marriage was if she received a large sum of money. Wilson charged into Mayer's office, absolutely desperate, and Mayer, who had been loaning him out to several other studios, was at first reluctant. But Wilson's anguish was so extreme that Mayer crumbled and loaned him $10,000 on the spot, as an advance against his fee for the next picture he would write for the studio. Two days later, Mayer assigned him to *Sequoia*, the simpleminded story of a deer and a mountain lion that was entirely unsuited to his talents but that would get him out of the financial hole.

Mayer was preoccupied with corporate matters at the time; through his interest in 20th Century Pictures, he and his partners snapped up, in collusion with Joe Schenck, an interest in Schenck's United Artists, then began a raid on Fox Pictures to oust Winfield Sheehan. A merger without the knowledge or approval of the Loew's stockholders would take place the following year.

There were the usual number of stresses with William Randolph Hearst; Thalberg had embarked on *The Barretts of Wimpole Street*, directed by Sidney Franklin, an ambitious version of Rudolf Besier's stage play about the clash between the poet Robert Browning and the sinister, incestuous Dr. Barrett over Barrett's poet daughter. Hearst had wanted Marion Davies to appear as Elizabeth Barrett Browning, but Thalberg, loyalty to his wife aside, knew that only Norma Shearer, of the studio's contracted stars, could play the part. Indeed, she turned out to give an impressive performance, sensitive but stubborn, authentically Victorian; her best work to date.

As a consolation prize for losing *The Barretts of Wimpole Street*, Marion Davies was cast in a preposterous Civil War story, *Operator Thirteen*, in which she appeared in blackface as a maid; the first version was so bad that the movie had to be almost entirely reshot. Although Hearst liked the picture, allegedly more than any other movie she had made, he was now completing his secret deal, several years in the works, with Jack Warner.

Another event of that spring of 1934 was Mayer's decision to bring back Clark Gable from exile and disgrace. Gable's performance in *It Happened One Night* at Columbia had added to his sensational popularity. When he stripped off his shirt in one scene and revealed that he was naked underneath it, female audiences went wild, and undershirt sales collapsed. Determined to show Mayer his stupidity in letting him go, Gable gave the best performance of his career. The February opening of the picture was tremendous. Mayer decided to put Gable into a hospital picture, *Men in White*, with Myrna Loy. Gable was still involved with Elizabeth Allan, cast as a nurse.

Also at this time Mayer, along with Joe Schenck, Irving Thalberg and Edwin Loeb, was held liable for $78,000 on defaulted bonds of the Southern California Realty Corporation, under a judgment handed down by Superior Court Judge L. R. Yankwich; the suit was filed by the bondholders in San Diego.

In June, David O. Selznick returned to Los Angeles, with Irene, from a two-month trip to England to scout locations for *David Copperfield.* As that film went on the drawing board, Selznick filled the time by making *Manhattan Melodrama*, the picture the notorious John Dillinger saw the day he was shot. Mayer took a special interest in the filming of *The Merry Widow*, directed by Ernst Lubitsch and starring his beloved Jeanette MacDonald and Maurice Chevalier. Lubitsch, to Mayer and Thalberg's annoyance, was constantly playing practical jokes on his cast. There was one sequence in which Miss MacDonald had to walk across an enormous set, singing; she reached an ornamental mantelpiece and saw, lying on it, a clipping from *The Hollywood Reporter*, announcing that the British singing star Evelyn Laye had been signed by the studio as a threat to her. She froze in the middle of a musical phrase and ran off the set in tears. Lubitsch doubled up with laughter.

On June 15, Harold Rosson, whom Mayer had wanted for a new picture, was stricken with polio and was paralyzed in the arms and shoulders. Reporters invaded the Los Angeles Orthopedic Hospital, brutally interviewing him while he was suspended from a platform by a cable and lowered into a pool. Jean Harlow didn't relent in her determination to divorce him. She was still seeing Clark Gable.

In mid-June, Mayer learned, via Mabel Walker Willebrandt, that efforts were being made by the Baltimore police to extradite his brother Rudolph from Shanghai and bring him to justice. With the increasing emphasis on purity and decency in Hollywood and Mayer's delicate position as head of the Motion Picture Producers Association, it was more than ever essential that this unpleasant matter be buried. Mrs. Willebrandt proved to be as effective as ever; she went to see the attorney general and pleaded with him to drop the charges on condition that the $30,000 owed to the cheated widow, Mrs. Blanche K. Rosenstein, would be repaid. Mayer was forced to produce the money himself. But soon, Rudolph would be on the verge of prison again.

Nineteen thirty-four saw the addition to the M.G.M. roster of stars like the gifted thirty-four-year-old Spencer Tracy, who had impressed Mayer in Michael Curtiz's magnificent Warner Brothers picture 20,000 Years in Sing-Sing, in which he played a convict sentenced to the electric chair for a crime he hadn't committed. Tracy, on the surface calm, sturdy and reliable, was in fact a tormented human being. He was a devout Roman Catholic driven by his sexual urges into a promiscuity he could not religiously excuse or emotionally suppress. His tortured mental state, since he knew that adultery could be punishable by hell (and he was deeply fond of his wife), drove him to alcoholism; but his addiction to the bottle failed to suppress his torment. He was a classic malcontent, finding life difficult even down to the smallest particulars, easily irritated with everything. He was the cause of many problems and a frequent absentee from the Fox Studios, where his fellow Irishman, production chief Winfield Sheehan, repeatedly threatened him with dismissal. Now that M.G.M. had a special relationship with the amalgamated 20th Century-Fox, Mayer, who had borrowed Tracy the previous year for the part of a congenital liar in The Show-Off, was easily able to buy out Tracy's contract through William Goetz's influence. Tracy proved adept in a lighthearted comedy, Whipsaw, in which he was costarred with Myrna Loy; his sturdy, man's man charm and smooth manners on screen were again quite in contrast with his own self.

Mayer was supportive of Tracy through one drinking bout and emotional crisis after another, until at last the magic presence in Tracy's life of Katharine Hepburn proved beneficial, if by no means curative.

As if he hadn't enough on his hands, Mayer, with Thalberg, had to deal with a colossal headache involving the preparatory work on a movie that was to become one of the most ambitious in the studio's history, a picture in which William Randolph Hearst had an unadvertised personal and financial interest. For several months during 1933, Frances Marion, who had recently separated from George Hill, had labored diligently on an adaptation of Pearl S. Buck's Pulitzer Prize–winning novel of Chinese farm life, *The Good Earth*, which Hill was to direct. Working closely with the Chinese consul general in Los Angeles, she had carefully eliminated those elements in the book that were considered offensive to the Chinese government, including mentions of banditry, opium, squalid conditions and superstitions.

She was surprised to find that Miss Buck was far from a heroine in China and in fact was held in such disfavor that, were she to set foot in Shanghai, she might not come back alive.

Once this emerged, Mayer and Thalberg were placed in a peculiar position. If they were to go ahead, without risking an international incident and grave disfavor from Chinese pressure groups, they must make a deal with the Chinese directly. Also, it would be desirable to shoot as much as possible of the backgrounds in China itself. George Hill, who was not in the best of health, suffering from the effects of syphilis, and his associate, the ill-tempered, dynamic location manager Frank Messinger, left for Shanghai by ship in February. No sooner had they arrived in Nanking than they ran into difficulties.

The genial Willys R. Peck, U.S. consul general in that city, was compelled to inform the two men that they had many obstacles facing them. Not only did they have to overcome the intense local anti–Pearl Buck feelings, but they also had to carve through a maze of government red tape. Although they hired a translator for their first meetings with the Film Commission, it was impossible to reach common ground. In desperation, Hill asked Peck what could be done. As a last-ditch effort, Peck arranged for Hill and Messinger to meet with General Chiang Kai-shek in Shanghai, based on the belief that the general was deeply Westernized. They managed to persuade him that if the picture were not made in China, no other Western movie ever would be. The general arranged for the high-powered Major General Theodore Tu, director of physical education at the Nationalist Central Military Academy of Nanking, who had Hollywood ambitions, to be appointed special adviser to the M.G.M. unit. Following the meeting, George Hill returned by ship to California. He was not well enough to do any more work, and had shot nothing.

Frank Messinger stayed on with a scratch camera crew. Frustrated by Chinese coolness and detachment, maddened by the restrictions imposed in the use of men and matériel by the existence of China's conflicts with Japan in the northern territories, Messinger proved hopelessly provincial and incapable of dealing with the situation. He arranged for expensive and difficult shots of an armored car, protected by soldiers with rifles, on the Peiping–Suiyan Railroad, then intemperately canceled the sequence after General Tu had pulled every string to make it possible. Tu instantly lost face in the eyes of the military commanders he had asked to grant this favor, and he shouted with anger at Messinger.

The last straw came when Tu went to extraordinary trouble to obtain the two crack cadet buglers of Tsinanfu Barracks. Messinger kept them waiting for hours for the correct light in the sky and the angle he wanted, and then, without warning, fired them and decided on two lesser buglers. The dismissed instrumentalists were infuriated, and Tu put his foot down; no more of this behavior would be tolerated.

On July 22, virtually empty-handed, Frank Messinger returned with the irritated General Tu to Los Angeles, without even bothering to meet certain obligations to the Chinese government to let them see the footage that had been shot or to grant them the privilege of making special documentary films of the Aviation School at Hanchow, for use by the Film Commission in its training branch.

Mayer and Thalberg were in despair. Hill and Messinger had effectively damaged U.S.–China relations; they had embarrassed the hardpressed Consul General Peck, four months had gone by for a script that now would prove unworkable and seven months had expired uselessly during the visit to China. Now it would take months more to rework the screenplay a third time. Like the muddle over *Trader Horn*, this was another example of Thalberg's inability to manage overseas assignments.

Ethel Borden was kept busy in order to secure the continuing presence in Mayer's life of Jean Howard. As Garbo finished pickup shots on her new movie, *The Painted Veil*, with her costar and lover George Brent, Mayer informed her that Ethel Borden would be writing for her the story of the novelist George Sand, a subject that appealed enormously to the star. With Eve Greene, Miss Borden put together an intriguing screenplay, which called for Garbo to spend much of the movie in trousers.

Mayer decided to go to Europe in July; for appearances' sake, he would be accompanied by Margaret. The intention was to follow up on Selznick's visit to Britain and to lay the foundation for an M.G.M. studio operation, making films in or near London. He would also go to Paris to catch up with his European operation.

Before he left for New York on July 10, he suggested to Jean Howard and Ethel Borden that they should join him in France in August. According to Jean Howard, she decided she would do this, because she had become disaffected with Charles Feldman; according to Raquel Torres' sister, Renée Ashley, Feldman again intended to marry Raquel. "He was never in love with Jean Howard," Mrs. Ashley says.

Margaret Mayer was ill during the Atlantic crossing and in London, from a condition officially described as pneumonia but in fact cancer of the uterus. That malady was never mentioned in the press in those days. During a meeting with his London executive, Ben Goetz, brother of William, Mayer was saddened to learn of the death, on July 28, of Marie Dressler. At their last encounter at her home in Santa Barbara, the pain and misery of her condition had driven her to scream at him in anger and turn her face to the wall when he lovingly took her by the hand and promised her she would soon be well and that he had new parts for her. He also learned of the suicide by gunshot, on August 10, of George Hill. Hill had never recovered from his disastrous misadventure in China earlier in the year. J. J. Cohn states that he was suffering from paresis, the final stage of syphilis, and was told that he would soon become hopelessly ill. His death was a considerable shock to Mayer; later, Frank Messinger also killed himself. These were two in a long chain of suicides at the studio, which would include Pete Smith and the costume designer Irene.

Mayer was plagued by word that Jean Harlow's recent vehicle, *The Girl from Missouri*, had run into severe censorship problems and had been cut to ribbons in various states. Sequences had to be reshot and the studio was drubbed by Will Hays for allowing the picture to have been made in the first place.

Mayer moved on to Paris after ten days in London. While there, he hired a number of skillful musical figures, including the witty, Polish Bronislau Kaper and the very gifted and charming Austrian Walter Jurmann. Their songs were the rage of Europe, and Mayer never ceased to be enchanted by their work. He secured their services for several years, but they were not able to leave immediately. Later, they created the music for the unforgettable song "San Francisco."

Margaret Mayer was ill, delirious; her emotional mood was bad, as she knew of her husband's love for another woman. She flew to Paris after Mayer, with the royal physician Lord Horder accompanying her, and was admitted to the American Hospital at Neuilly, where she underwent a radical hysterectomy some weeks later. The operation was not only difficult but psychologically disastrous. Mayer traveled to Le Havre with Howard Strickling for a week to greet Jean Howard and Ethel Borden off their ship. Also aboard the vessel was the private detective he had hired to follow Miss Howard and Charles Feldman. Aboard the boat-train, Mayer told Miss Howard, according to her, that Margaret had agreed to divorce him.

Miss Howard says that Mayer offered her $5 million if she would marry him. She says that he never stopped talking all the way to Paris. He had booked her into the same hotel he was staying in, the George V.

Miss Howard remembers saying to Ethel Borden in their suite, "Mayer wants to marry me." Miss Borden replied, "Why not just marry him for two years—you'll make some money." At that moment, Mayer had Strickling summon the two women to his own suite. He had received the complete detective report on her. When Jean Howard walked in, she saw him, she says, in a hysterical state. He was screaming at her, "How could you do this to me? How could you possibly do this to me?" And he waved the report at her. He filled a glass with whiskey, swallowed it, then moved toward the window and began to climb out of it. Jean Howard, Ethel Borden and Howard Strickling rushed at him and grabbed him. In the struggle, Strickling broke his thumb. Strickling flung Mayer into the bedroom and told Miss Borden to summon the hotel physician.

Next day, Mayer was his usual self. Jean Howard reminded him that she, Ethel Borden and he were all invited to Cole and Linda Porter's house for lunch. He suggested they talk the whole thing out. The lunch went forward comfortably; Jean said that she and Ethel were flying to London that afternoon. Mayer offered to drive Jean to the airport, with Ethel in another chauffeur-driven studio limousine. During the drive, Mayer sobbed, promising never to mention what had occurred again, begging her not to leave, declaring himself a fool, saying he was hopelessly in love with her. He knelt before her, begging like a child. She was forced to tell him that she had telephoned Feldman in Hollywood and said she was returning to him. He was in despair when she and Ethel flew off.

Mayer was taking the cure at the Richmond Park Hotel, Carlsbad, Germany, while Margaret, suffering from delusional and depressive symptoms, remained at the American Hospital in Paris. On August 25 he received the news that Jean Howard and Charles Feldman had eloped.

A frequently repeated falsehood is that, aggrieved by Feldman's marriage to Miss Howard, Mayer blacklisted Feldman, barred him from the M.G.M. lot and severely affected his career. Even if he had been tempted to undertake such drastic action, Mayer would not have been able to do so (it is likely that he would not receive Feldman at the studio in person). Not only was Ad Schulberg still an intimate friend of Mayer's, but her agency (with Charles Feldman) represented Norma Shearer, as well as Mayer's nephew Jack Cummings. The Charles Feldman collection of papers, housed at the American Film Institute in Los Angeles, shows an uninterrupted flow of correspondence and telephone calls between Noll Gurney, Laura Wilck and other Schulberg–Feldman agency representatives and the studio, both during the rest of that year and for subsequent years.

In London, Mayer learned that Upton Sinclair, the inexhaustible liberal muckraker whose *The Wet Parade* Thalberg had made over Mayer's disapproval, was about to run for governor of California. Sinclair had long expressed a desire to introduce crippling state taxes on the industry and compel the studios to revise their feudal attitude toward their lesser employees.

Sinclair had as his slogan END POVERTY IN CALIFORNIA, known as EPIC for short. On September 7, 1933, he had registered at the Beverly Hills City Hall as a Democrat, changing his designation from that of Socialist. He promised to eliminate mass unemployment, abolish sales tax and drop all taxes on homes valued under $3,000. He would introduce $50-a-month pensions for widows, the sick and the needy. His newspaper, *End Poverty*, was widely circulated. He promised to unseat and replace Mayer's close friend Governor Frank F. Merriam, who, he felt, was little short of a fascist demagogue, indifferent to the concerns of the underprivileged.

While these ominous events took place, Mayer gave a series of pep talks to the representatives of the British film industry at luncheons at the Savoy Hotel, where he was staying, and at the Trocadero; but Margaret Mayer's postoperative mental condition was so appalling that a third luncheon was canceled on September 8. She rallied sufficiently to accompany him back to Paris three days later, but was taken to the American Hospital at Neuilly following a relapse. She and Mayer were cheered by a telegram from Hollywood announcing that Edie Mayer Goetz had given birth to her second daughter, Judy.

Soon the word would be worse than ever on Upton Sinclair. By the beginning of October, the Democratic nomination for the governorship firmly in his pocket, he had begun to make serious threats. Joe Schenck actually flew to Florida to investigate the state's potential as a moviemaking center, stating that he would set up a studio in Miami, which would benefit Florida to the tune of $150 million a year. Jack Warner and Harry Cohn, of Columbia Pictures, supported Joe Schenck; Nicholas Schenck in New York began to make similar noises. Only Carl Laemmle, Jr., at Universal, stated that Sinclair's election would make no difference to him. Ex-President Hoover had urgent meetings with Ida Koverman in Hollywood, dragging her back from vacation; producer Hal Roach also announced his imminent departure if the worst should happen. In Germany, William Randolph Hearst trumpeted that he would come back immediately to destroy Sinclair, who was "an unbalanced and unscrupulous political speculator." Hearst was meeting with Nazi leaders, including Hitler, with whom Mayer had asked him to intercede on behalf of the Jews. There was talk of studio employees being forced to give contributions, even as much as a single day's salary, to assist Frank Merriam in his campaign.

Irving Thalberg sent the director Felix Feist around the state filming out-of-work hobos, who expressed their admiration for Sinclair, and more respectable and employed people supporting the cause of Merriam. These interviews would be included in newsreels released by M.G.M. under their regular logo.

Margaret remained in the American Hospital while Mayer sailed for New York on the *Paris*, arriving on October 30. He gave a press conference on board, announcing his grave concern at Sinclair's political position and the danger to the movie business in the future. Asked by reporters whether he would support Joe Schenck's leadership in withdrawing the movie industry from California if Sinclair were elected, Mayer said, "That is something to be considered seriously, if and when the time comes."

A satirical pamphlet was published, its origin unknown, and priced at five cents a copy, entitled "Letters to Louie from Frank." It was exceedingly scurrilous and contained an invented series of letters from Frank Merriam to Mayer that suggested all manner of corruption and indifference to the problems of the underprivileged.

Felix Feist continued with his interviews for Metrotone News. Greg Mitchell, authority on the 1934 election, wrote:

> [The] shorts, based on an innocuous inquiring reporter format, had an enormous effect. Well-dressed couples, and prim, elderly ladies invariably endorsed Merriam. Disheveled, wild-eyed citizens with thick accents stood up for Sinclair. One man observed that Sinclair was "the author of the Russian government, and it worked out very well there, and it should do so here."

Only three Metrotone newsreels have survived. With the exception of the third, they are less relentlessly biased and schematic than Mitchell suggests; possibly Upton Sinclair's campaign publicist exaggerated their prejudices and political slanting. Headed California Election News Nos. 1 and 2, each is introduced by a rousing version of "California, Here I Come." In the first of these newsreels, the commentator speaks over a map of the state. "Ladies and gentlemen, I am the inquiring cameraman," he says. "All day I travel the highways and byways" (shots of workers, a man standing next to a large barrel). "I knock on doors, visit homes, all to get views . . . They are not actors . . . I don't rehearse them . . . I am impartial."

A working man, lean and hard, in coveralls, says he has chosen Sinclair even though some of Sinclair's opinions are rather radical; he is evidently a worker in an orange grove, and peels an orange as he speaks. Another man says he is going to vote for Merriam. He also lunches on oranges. A black man says he will vote for Sinclair and is willing to take a chance. Another black man says he will vote for Merriam. He speaks of Sinclair's socialistic ideas and that Sinclair should not be governor. An old lady speaks for Merriam. A farm worker says he's going to vote for Sinclair. A white-collar worker is seen saying he will vote for Merriam. A fat man says he will vote for third party candidate Raymond Haight. A pleasant, decent-looking housewife says she will vote for Sinclair.

In the second newsreel, the "inquiring cameraman" again says he tries to be as impartial as possible. A housewife says she will vote for Merriam because Sinclair has described the school system as "rotten." A man in a bow tie speaks up for Merriam. He says, "I have a job and want to keep it." Then a well-dressed woman speaks up for Upton Sinclair, saying she believes in his policies. In one scene, there is a violent conflict between Merriam supporters and Sinclair. At the end, the inquiring cameraman says, "It doesn't matter how you register your vote, Republican or Democrat. You can cast your vote on November 6 for any man or any party you want to." Just before this book went to press, the third newsreel surfaced, which has been described as far more inflammatory and slanted against Sinclair.

The Hearst newspapers ran pictures of hobos in support of Sinclair; these were drawn from a Warner Brothers picture, *Wild Boys of the Road*. The campaign grew dirtier every day, until at last Sinclair clearly was slipping. Actually, it was doubtful, given the conservative, wealthy dominant class of California and the public's intrinsic dislike of socialism, that Sinclair would have been elected, even without the vast influences brought to bear against him. On November 3, the magazine *Literary Digest* took a poll, showing that Sinclair was the choice of only 25.72 percent of the electorate. There is some suggestion that the poll may have been inaccurate (*Literary Digest* often was), but it had the effect of shifting the betting odds and encouraging Sinclair's enemies. On Election Day, Sinclair received 875,5377 votes, Raymond Haight got 320,519 and Merriam garnered 1,138,620. Mayer and the other movie executives could breathe again.

## CHAPTER SIXTEEN

# 1934-1936

ON NOVEMBER 1, 1934, William Randolph Hearst, following his five years of secret finagling, at last showed his hand and informed Mayer (who already knew) that he had concluded a deal with Warner Brothers effective January 1. Warners would make two Marion Davies pictures and four separate Cosmopolitan productions during the first twelve-month period. The Hearst Metrotone Newsreel would continue to be made by M.G.M., the contract extending to its full length of five more years.

In addition to Hearst's fretfulness that Miss Davies had been denied *The Barretts of Wimpole Street*, he was aggrieved by Mayer's and Thalberg's refusal to allow her to appear in the title role of *Marie Antoinette* or even to consider her for George Bernard Shaw's *St. Joan*, on which the studio had taken an option. The latter play was, in fact, never turned into an M.G.M. motion picture.

Despite his personal fondness for Hearst and Marion Davies (and he had generously overlooked Hearst's duplicity in the matter over the years), Mayer, it is safe to say, was glad to see them go. Marion Davies was no longer top box office, and had not been for at least half a decade; if they had not left, Nicholas Schenck would undoubtedly have found a way to make them go. Norma Shearer must have been delighted that her would-be usurper was out of the picture.

*David Copperfield* was still shooting, its complex script by Howard Estabrook calling for an extraordinary variety of settings and performances. So heavy was the burden on George Cukor that individual sequences were shot by the director Leontine Sagan and by John Waters, Cukor's special assistant, while still other episodes were handled by a master of montage, Slavko Vorkapich. Charles Laughton proved impossible; after two days of work as Micawber, he had disliked his performance at the rushes and had asked to be replaced. Selznick let him go, putting in W. C. Fields. The result was one of the finest performances of that year.

Nineteen thirty-five began with an even heavier work load for Mayer. Again in contradiction of his image as a family filmmaker, he was in charge of *Vampires of Prague*, later renamed *Mark of the Vampire*, an all-out horror film. He was in touch with Tahiti for the shooting of *Typee*, later renamed *Last of the Pagans*, written by John Farrow, a highly erotic chronicle of romance in the South Seas. The troubled Edmund Goulding was about to start on *The Flame Within*, which would turn out to be one of the most remarkable movies made by the studio, a penetrating study of psychological disturbance in the New York social set, brilliantly played by the still underrated Maureen O'Sullivan, Ann Harding and Herbert Marshall.

None of these pictures was controlled by Irving Thalberg or David Selznick. The latter was hard at work on preproduction on *Anna Karenina*, with Garbo. Much to Mayer's annoyance, Erich von Stroheim was brought in as technical adviser on life in nineteenth-century Russia; he knew nothing about it. The Austrian-American was dumped.

In the midst of this grinding toil (Mayer was starting to show his hand in the dramatic emphases of these productions, guided by his trusted team, most especially the Thalberg protégé Bernard Hyman and the excellent Hunt Stromberg), Mayer was plagued by Robert Montgomery, who had headed up the newly formed and belligerent Screen Actors Guild. Like many men in his position, Mayer dreaded the formation of a union which could hold the studio to ransom; he had no more respect than any other studio head for the selfishness, manic ambition and temperamental behavior of most movie stars, despite the fact that he was still, secretly, taking a piece of most of their earnings. When, on January 21, the American Federation of Labor announced to Frank Gillmore of Equity that the Hollywood actors were welcome as members, Mayer went berserk. He and Thalberg exchanged a series of tense notes; it is clear they would fight the union to the last ditch.

Among the important pictures in production that winter of 1934–1935 was *Naughty Marietta*, a special favorite of Mayer's; it was based on an operetta by Victor Herbert and Rida Johnson Young, adapted by the ever-reliable John Lee Mahin, Frances Goodrich and Albert Hackett. The stars were Nelson Eddy and Jeanette MacDonald. Mayer was still infatuated with Miss MacDonald; ruthlessly, he dispatched Bob Ritchie to Europe as a talent scout, hoping to shatter her romantic interest in the handsome junior executive. He had allowed Ritchie to use the studio switchboard as a private answering service, and various empty offices as they became available, to give the illusion of his having an official position at M.G.M., all to please Miss MacDonald.

Yet, once again, Mayer showed that he was capable of rising above annoyance and resentment in the interests of the studio and of a performer's commercial and artistic value. He liked Miss MacDonald's style; he had been captivated by her stylish performance in *The Cat and the Fiddle* and by her arch, charming simperings in *The Merry Widow*. Miss MacDonald had not been pleased by the idea of *Naughty Marietta*, finding the role of the romantic Princess Marie de la Bonfain somewhat tiresome. A persistent rumor, inflated lately into history, was that Mayer got on his knees and sang the Kol Nidre (or, in some versions, Victor Herbert's song from the film, "Ah, Sweet Mystery of Life") in order to show her how the part should be performed. There is no truth in this. But he did talk her into it.

The ideal choice for her costar would have been the handsome and athletic Allan Jones. Mayer sent talent scout Al Altman to Boston, where Jones was on tour for the Shubert brothers. Altman asked Jones if he would do a test. Jones agreed, provided the test was done on a Sunday and in secrecy. There were two years left on his Shubert contract.

Jones arrived on time, wearing the period costumes with flair and singing so splendidly that Mayer was overcome. He realized he had a great new star on his hands. He instructed the film's producer, Hunt Stromberg, to sign Jones at once. But the Shuberts stepped in and demanded, via an instant lawsuit, $50,000 for Jones's contract. Phone calls went back and forth. Finally, it came to the point that Jones would have to pay the Shuberts $50,000 to avoid being taken to court. Jones borrowed the money from a St. Louis shoe executive; he drove to the St. Louis airport with the authorization for the bank draft, only to learn that, because Stromberg couldn't reach him on the telephone at that moment, Nelson Eddy had been cast.

Thirty-three-year-old Eddy had not an ounce of Allan Jones's magnetism, physical presence or star quality. He was fighting a weight problem, and his bland and sheepish demeanor and cherubic, expressionless face were drawbacks. He was known as "The Singing Capon." The reason Eddy got his big break was Ida Koverman. She had seen him at a concert in Los Angeles in 1933, his vigorous voice, much his strongest asset, earning him eighteen encores. Mayer had used him in minor appearances in *Broadway to Hollywood*, *Dancing Lady* and *Student Tour*.

Eddy was cantankerous, often charming, sometimes witty. (In 1965, he told the present author, when asked what he thought of Herbert Stothart, the reigning studio composer and arranger, "The guy couldn't arrange a dinner party in an automat.") He was pedantic, literal-minded, boring; Jeanette MacDonald was sweetly intelligent and sharp. Yet to-gether they created a chemistry that made *Naughty Marietta* and its musical successors overwhelmingly popular with the public. Mayer was prepared to put up with Eddy's complaints in order to bring off a success-ful picture; Hunt Stromberg and the director, W. S. Van Dyke, expertly conveyed the operetta's melodic froufrou. Such songs as "Ah, Sweet Mystery of Life," "Tramp, Tramp, Tramp" and "'Neath the Southern Moon" captured Mayer's heart. More than a thousand actors and extras were used in the movie, which would later win an Oscar for Douglas Shearer for the soundtrack. The picture was important from every point of view, not only because it launched Mayer's career as a production genius apart from Thalberg, but because it revived a genre that had faltered and failed in the early talkies.

An unhappier association of that winter was Mayer's with the Marx Brothers. Irving Thalberg was captivated by them; he adored the lecher-ous, forward-sloping, woman-chasing, cigar-crunching Groucho; the ever-silent, curly-headed, bottom-pinching Harpo; and Chico, who played the piano with his thumb and forefinger. Their younger brothers, Zeppo and Gummo, became talent agents. In their early Paramount pictures, they were ferociously anarchistic, exploding one convention after the other. They had begun to slip badly; their masterpiece, *Duck Soup*, had proved far too sophisticated and surrealistic for the public, and Paramount had dropped them. Thalberg was convinced they should be put under contract; Mayer was appalled at the idea. He found them un-American, their screen personalities oversexed. The last thing he wanted, now that he was in charge of all production, was to have such creatures on the payroll.

That February of 1935, Thalberg began to have a script written for the brothers, which would parody Mayer's favorite art form: *A Night at the Opera*. No less than six writers were given the job, the most celebrated of whom was George S. Kaufman; Bert Kalmar and Harry Ruby added uncredited material. Thalberg sent the Marxes off on an extensive road tour to test the various gags on live audiences; this was a unique device, and paid off, since some of the more off-color or heavily satirical gags were dropped following silence from an audience. Several of the Marxes' ideas were offensive to Mayer. They wanted to poke their heads through the laurel wreath of the M.G.M. logo and issue roars one, two and three in place of the familiar lion. Mayer ruled out the irreverent suggestion.

While the brothers continued their lengthy tour, Mayer had other work on his hands. He had the heavyweight task of supervising, along with the again-ailing Thalberg, who was nominally in charge of the production, preparations for *Mutiny on the Bounty*, based on the rousing

Mayer in the doorway of the Santa Monica beach house designed by Cedric Gibbons, circa 1926. (*Marc Wanamaker: The Bison Archives*)

The Mayer women at the Santa Monica beach house, circa 1926; from left: Irene, Margaret, Edith. (*Marc Wanamaker: The Bison Archives*)

Mayer with newly signed director Herbert Brown in 1925; from left: Edith, Margaret, Mayer, Renee Adoree, Brown, Irene and Ruth Roland. (*Marc Wanamaker: The Bison Archives*)

Greta Garbo and John Gilbert, circa 1926. (*Culver Pictures*)

Mayer and family en route to New York, 1925; from left: Irene, Mayer, Margaret, Edith. (*Marc Wanamaker: The Bison Archives*)

An M.G.M. gathering; from left: Paul Bern, Mayer, Aileen Pringle, H. L. Mencken, Norma Shearer, Thalberg, Harry Rapf. *(Marc Wanamaker: The Bison Archives)*

While William Randolph Hearst plotted to move his mistress Marion Davies from M.G.M., she posed with Mayer, October 1928; from left: Mayer, Davies, Norma Shearer, Thalberg. *(Marc Wanamaker: The Bison Archives)*

Mayer with director Cecil B. DeMille, who joined the studio in 1928. *(Marc Wanamaker: The Bison Archives)*

Former president Calvin Coolidge on a visit to the M.G.M. Studios; from left: Will H. Hays, Coolidge, Mrs. Coolidge, Mary Pickford and Mayer, circa 1930. *(Marc Wanamaker: The Bison Archives)*

Edwina Booth, whose health was ruined during filming of the epic *Trader Horn* in Africa, 1928. *(Marc Wanamaker: The Bison Archives)*

Mayer and William Randolph Hearst presided over a September 18, 1929 luncheon honoring Winston Churchill, then in the political wilderness. Held on the M.G.M. sound stage, it featured a twenty piece orchestra and twenty-five M.G.M. stars in a miniature musical. From left: Hearst, Churchill, Mayer, Fred Niblo, Randolph Churchill. *(Marc Wanamaker: The Bison Archives)*

Mayer with key M.G.M. figures, from left: Mayer, Harry Rapf, Hunt Stromberg, Thalberg and John Gilbert, circa 1928. *(Marc Wanamaker: The Bison Archives)*

Joseph M. Schenck, circa 1929. *(Marc Wanamaker: The Bison Archives)*

Director W. S. Van Dyke with Clyde de Vinna at the camera, May 16, 1930. (*Marc Wanamaker: The Bison Archives*)

Wallace Beery, a stage transvestite who couldn't resist dressing up in evening gowns and feathered hats, circa 1931. (*The Howard Strickling Collection*)

Edith Goetz was married to producer William Goetz, in a gown designed by Adrian, March 19, 1930. *(The Howard Strickling Collection)*

fictionalized account written by Charles Nordhoff and James Norman Hall. Months had been spent preparing an exact replica of the vessel aboard which the rebellious Fletcher Christian had summoned officers and crew to eject Captain Bligh. The ship had to be tested in all kinds of still and stormy waters off Catalina Island. Clark Gable, selected by Mayer for the role of Christian, did not want to make the picture; he would have to shave off his mustache, since any facial decoration would have been forbidden by eighteenth-century naval regulations, and he would not train with a voice coach to adopt a convincing British accent. Mayer, always uneasy about making the *Bounty* story, was more fretful than ever at this news, but he had a great deal to hold over Gable and managed to force him into an acceptance. However, there would be a delay since the shooting on Gable's Fox picture, *Call of the Wild*, had been held up.

When Gable won the Academy Award on February 27, it became more imperative than ever that he move on directly to a vehicle as important as *Bounty*. He returned, after many dragged-out weeks on *Call of the Wild*, deciding firmly to part with his wife. He went straight into *China Seas*, a raucous and rowdy story of adventure aboard a steamer sailing in Oriental waters, directed with great style and attack by Tay Garnett. Mayer tolerated his occasional tantrums on the picture, and even the fact that he chose to risk his life by refusing a double in a sequence in which he assisted numerous Chinese extras in roping in a runaway steamroller that crashed up and down the decks of the cantilevered studio ship.

Mayer launched the first of an important series of two-reelers, used in supporting programs. The title of the series was *Crime Does Not Pay*; in fashioning the mini-dramas, the studio had the cooperation of J. Edgar Hoover and the FBI. The short subjects, which would prove to be the breeding ground of directors of talent, stemmed directly from such early M.G.M. crime pictures as *Beast of the City*, for which Herbert Hoover had supplied the belligerent introduction. The series pointed to the evils of gangsterism during the Depression.

In the spring, Mayer launched an elaborate musical, *Broadway Melody of 1936*, to be released the following year. He was hitting his stride now; there would be no stopping him as he let go with his passionate love of musicals. He hadn't liked the rather cramped, impoverished look and vulgar, sexy toughness of Warner Brothers' Gold Diggers series, despite the fact that Busby Berkeley had illuminated them with exotic and surrealistic dance routines. For his *Broadway Melodies*, which would be far advanced from the semi-amateurish first picture of that name, he would shoot the bankroll, providing magnificent sets and costumes, glittering mirrored floors and sumptuous musical arrangements played by a sixty-piece orchestra.

As the star of *Broadway Melody of 1936*, he cast Robert Taylor, who was already showing improvement as an actor and was receiving heavy fan mail from women. Mayer was, Taylor later testified, "kind, fatherly, understanding and protective" toward him. Opposite Taylor, Mayer cast the actress, singer and dancer Eleanor Powell. With her rather horsy but appealing face, exquisite legs and remarkable coordination, Miss Powell was a virtuoso who never faltered as she danced all over Cedric Gibbons's gigantic, glittering nightclub set. In the romantic scenes, she played with an affecting naturalness, underacting in a manner which today makes her seem entirely modern.

Mayer was very attracted to Eleanor Powell. But he found her formidably strong-willed, uninterested in becoming his mistress. He invited her to the Mayfair Ball one Saturday night; she said she would first have to ask her mother. Mayer was pleased. Then Miss Powell announced she had nothing to wear. Mayer at once took her down to wardrobe and found a dress for her, and a white fox fur.

That night, at the ball, he said to her, "Aren't you going to ask me to dance?" She replied, "Mr. Mayer, where I come from, the man asks the lady to dance." He told her that Shearer and Crawford had begged him to dance with them. She shrugged. He swept a low bow, like a courtier, and said, tongue in cheek, "Miss Powell, may I have the honor of this tango?" She laughed and accepted.

They went on at 1:30 to the Clover Club to gamble. She was astonished to see Mayer mix a fiery sauce and pour it on everyone's steaks— they were eating colossally at this hour of the morning. Finally, hours later, he stood up and told her he was taking her home. She hesitated; then he talked her into it. As soon as she got into the car, he embraced her passionately. Primly, she drew back and said, "Now you just sit over there and I'll sit over here and when I get out there's no need to open the door!" He was furious, but he kept her on the payroll. He never dated her again.

Plans were advanced that spring for two pictures to be made in England, both of which were somewhat delayed: *Goodbye, Mr. Chips*, from the novel by James Hilton, and *A Yank at Oxford*, from a story by John Considine, Jr., and John Monk Saunders. Jean Harlow's divorce from Harold Rosson was expected and did not create much of a stir. Mayer was more preoccupied with assisting Thalberg in a series of communications with Frank Lloyd, hired from Fox to direct *Mutiny on the Bounty*, and presently in Tahiti shooting background material.

Rudolph Mayer surfaced again. In February, he had entered a sanitarium in Shanghai, suffering from gastroenteritis and a localized abscess and fistula. He was in a nervous condition, exhausted and desperate for money; the local consulate sent a message to the secretary of state in Washington, who forwarded it to Mayer, who did nothing.

That spring, a very serious matter came up concerning Franz Werfel's best-seller *The Forty Days of Musa Dagh*, which condemned the Turkish government's perpetration of the Armenian massacres. The inflammatory work was owned originally by Paramount. Mehmet Munir, the ambassador for Turkey in Washington, D.C., succeeded in having Paramount's Barney Balaban postpone its making. The Turkish embassy in Berlin also complained, in November 1934, on the interesting ground that "[it] is . . . a novel written by a German anti-Nazi, who is using the treatment of the Armenians by the Turks to excite sympathies for minorities in general." By January 1935, the U.S. Division of European Affairs, stimulated by Secretary of State Cordell Hull's disapproval of the project, stopped the picture being made.

It was therefore bold of Thalberg, with Mayer's approval, to buy the property from Paramount for the record sum of $100,000. Carey Wilson was scheduled to write the script, and William Wellman to direct, with William Powell as the star. Once Ambassador Munir got wind of this, he again complained to the government, and Frederick Herron, foreign manager of the Motion Picture Producers and Directors Association, informed Arthur Loew in New York that there would be difficulties ahead.

On May 13, Herron had an audience with Munir, advising him that the script would be carefully vetted to see that it would give no offense and would be submitted to Istanbul for approval. Munir advised that the picture would not only be unacceptable in any form, but could result in Hollywood pictures being prohibited in the Near East.

On June 4, the *Musa Dagh* matter blew up into a full-scale political incident. Robert P. Skinner, U.S. chargé d'affaires in Turkey, wrote to Cordell Hull urging him to have M.G.M. drop the idea. Munir cornered J. Robert Rubin at his office. While Mayer and Thalberg hesitated, and with them Nicholas Schenck and Arthur Loew, Armenian groups demanded that the studio not yield to Turkish pressure. Letters poured into M.G.M.'s various offices, and meetings were arranged with Armenian leaders. Samuel Marx, who had found the novel and recommended it be bought, was under continual pressure. Finally, on July 15, Mayer and Thalberg yielded. It was decided to bury the matter right where it stood. When it resurfaced two years later, there was little interest left in it and it was dropped again.

The spring also brought threats from Sacramento of heavily increased taxes in the industry, and Mayer began talking with Governor Ehringaus of North Carolina about moving the studio there. This was absurd; nothing could come of such plans. The question of taxes much possessed the Motion Picture Producers' Association (the word Directors had been dropped), of which Mayer was appointed the head for the fifth successive year in April; a most prominent member of the board of the MPPA was Winfield Sheehan. But again, Mayer could rise above personal hatreds when it came to industrial matters.

Not always; he was very upset, even more so than Thalberg, by the attacks on him at meetings of the Screen Writers' Guild that spring. The Communist John Howard Lawson, who had been pleased to receive from him payment for an adaptation of one of Mayer's favorite books, *Treasure Island*, and for the Joan Crawford vehicle *Our Blushing Brides*, trounced him and Thalberg for treating writers like newspaper copy boys. This charge was false and unwarranted. Mayer was so angered by the Communist belligerents in the union that he backed to the hilt an M.G.M. writer of a different color, James K. McGuinness (*Hell Divers, Tarzan and His Mate*), in his plans to form a separate union that in effect was M.G.M.-owned, lock, stock and barrel. McGuinness was backed by the ultra-rightist, anti-Semitic John Lee Mahin (*Beast of the City; Bombshell*) and by Howard Emmett Rogers (*Hold Your Man; Mystery of Mr. X*), among others.

In June, the Marx Brothers, much to Mayer's annoyance, moved into M.G.M. They began grabbing people as they entered the executive building, stripping them of their pants or skirts. When Thalberg came into his office, he found it full of smoke; the brothers had been cooking in his fireplace.

They were uncontrollable, infuriating, as they made their first M.G.M. movie, *A Night at the Opera*, but the crew's laughter and the similar response of executives at the rushes may have weakened Mayer slightly in his opposition. There was no way he would ever like Groucho Marx, a sourpuss who lacked the grinding appeal of his presence on the screen. When he met Groucho in a studio corridor, Groucho snubbed him.[1] Mayer never forgave the slight. He complained that Groucho smelled like an unwashed dachshund. The relationship did not improve, even when *Opera* earned $3 million in profits.

Selznick made *Reckless*, written under a pseudonym by himself, based on the life of singer Libby Holman. The script in many ways also mirrored Jean Harlow's life. As the tormented carnival showgirl-cum-Broadway star, married to a weak, dissolute and drunken husband (a part

---

[1] Mayer: How is the picture? Groucho: What business is that of yours?

abandoned by Joan Crawford), she was memorably strong. It is hard to understand why she accepted another role in which a husband (Franchot Tone) shoots himself; in a last scene, in a Broadway theater, she silences the booing, hissing, slow hand-clapping audience that accuses her of being a murderess by explaining how she tried to help her hapless mate. They cheer her to the echo. It was like Jean Harlow herself trying to silence the gossip that she might have killed Paul Bern. In one extraordinary sequence, the grand jury is actually seen bringing in a reluctant verdict of suicide. Is it possible that Mayer engineered this casting of Harlow in order to protect his embattled star?

On June 27, 1935, Selznick resigned from M.G.M. to set up his own production company, the resignation to be effective after he finished another Dickens adaptation, A Tale of Two Cities.

Shooting at last began on Mutiny on the Bounty that summer. Frank Lloyd handled it magnificently, despite the opposition to him of both Charles Laughton, cast as Captain Bligh, and Clark Gable. Gable's homophobia made the homosexual Laughton constantly miserable. Heavy seas rocked the imitation Bounty, and Laughton was seasick. Gable took off shark hunting while Laughton sulked in his Catalina bungalow. Thalberg flew in regularly by seaplane, screaming at Lloyd, who screamed back. Thalberg was endangering his health; his hysterical outbursts were in defiance of doctors' orders.

In one incident, Gable charged Laughton with treating him like an extra. Frank Lloyd canceled work for the day. Thalberg had to fly in for a midnight conference, insisting that Lloyd's instructions be carried out. Laughton was forced to obey.

Laughton imported a youth from the mainland as his masseur-lover, and this annoyed Gable even more. Back at the studio, Bligh's heroic longboat voyage to Timor was recreated in a tank; the actors were tossed around by wires which rocked the boat, and roasted under arc lights of several hundred watts until the makeup ran down their faces. After ten days of shooting, Frank Lloyd discovered that the actor Eddie Quillan should not have been on board the longboat at all, since he was among the crewmen loyal to Captain Bligh and had refused to leave the Bounty. Because of this error, another week was spent reshooting the sequence.

The results were splendid; Mutiny on the Bounty was one of M.G.M.'s finest achievements. Such sequences as the departure of the Bounty from Portsmouth and the voyage of the Pandora in search of the Bounty mutineers were superbly shot (by Arthur Edeson), directed and edited (the cutter was the indispensable Margaret Booth).

The great appeal of the picture for the public was that it was presented as a simple conflict between good and evil, between the champion of the underdog, Fletcher Christian, and the oppressive martinet, Captain Bligh. In the Depression, many people felt forced into virtual servitude by ruthless bosses, reminded constantly that others were waiting in line for their positions. Strikes were in the air; millions could identify with this story of rebellion against tyranny. The genius of Laughton and Gable was never more strikingly displayed, and the writers even risked sympathy for Bligh, effectively humanizing him, when he undertook the epic voyage to Timor. His exclamation when, bearded, starved and desperate, the survivors at last saw land ("We have beaten the sea itself!") was one of the greatest moments of the cinema, and moved many in the audience to tears.

The picture owed its dynamic, electric drive and momentum to Frank Lloyd, who mysteriously never worked at M.G.M. again. Taught in the hard school of the silent film, he had learned the necessity for fluid, thrusting movement, and he guided his willing cast with powerful intelligence and skill from the early press gang sequences in London to the final release as the mutineers discover their erotic paradise.

During the shooting, Norma Shearer gave birth to her second child, a daughter, Barbara, on June 15. Mayer was the first to give Thalberg his congratulations. Always sentimental over births, deaths and marriages, he sent Miss Shearer a magnificent bouquet of yellow roses and cheered her still further by authorizing Thalberg to select George Cukor to direct her in *Romeo and Juliet*, which would be an ambitious version of the Shakespeare play.

Early that fall, Mayer put together a very fine version of Eugene O'Neill's masterpiece, *Ah, Wilderness!*, adapted by Frances Goodrich and Albert Hackett, directed by Clarence Brown. This was a specific Mayer project, owing nothing to Irving Thalberg. The play appealed to Mayer deeply. The tale of a young boy growing to manhood, discovering women for the first time, struggling with his beloved parents, was everything Mayer could love in a subject. He very much wanted Will Rogers, America's patron saint, to play the role of the father. Rogers suddenly backed out to embark on a world flight with the celebrated pilot Wiley Post. The decision cost him his life; Rogers and Post died in a plane crash.

For the picture, Mayer chose the gifted young Eric Linden as the youthful protagonist and, in another significant role, Mickey Rooney. Rooney, pushing fifteen, was a product of vaudeville, tiny but beautifully built and coordinated. He was manic, fiercely energetic, already chasing every nubile girl on the lot, and capable of imitating anybody from Mayer down with impeccable skill. He had started his movie career with six pictures in 1933, including *Broadway to Hollywood*, in which he acted the grandson of veteran vaudevillians. Name any sport, he could play it; name any part, he could act it. He even carried off a dazzling Puck, on loan-out to Warner Brothers, in A Midsummer Night's Dream. By the time he embarked on Ah, Wilderness!, he had jumped around as a newsboy in Reckless, played Harlow's kid brother in Riffraff and fooled around on loan-out in The Healer. Mayer saw his star quality, and even put up with his youthful rudeness, impertinence and cocksure attitude. Not everyone at the studio adored Mickey Rooney, but few could deny a talent that amounted to genius.

That September, Mayer received the Mussolini Cup for Anna Karenina as Best Picture of the Year shown at the Venice Film Festival. The Italian ambassador presented the award to Mayer; actually, it should have gone to David O. Selznick. Like so many of his generation, Mayer believed that Mussolini, the hero of Henry Luce's Time magazine and Fortune, was a Good Thing; whereas M.G.M.'s Berlin office was temporarily closed (for six weeks!) because the Hitler government was troubling the Jews who were employed in it, the Italians displayed no serious symptoms of anti-Semitism.

One of the pleasures of that fall was the shooting of Rose Marie, with Jeanette MacDonald and Nelson Eddy. A memorable scene took place in which Allan Jones sang a major aria from Tosca. In every way, he showed up Nelson Eddy as inferior, both in voice and in physical presence. At the preview in Pasadena, Eddy came up to Mayer and said, "If you don't take Allan Jones out of the picture, I'm going on strike." Mayer had no alternative but to placate the popular star, and Allan Jones's scene wound up on the cutting room floor. Many people who had attended the preview wrote in protest. This was a rare example of Mayer yielding to an egotistical demand from a performer.

Another event was the discovery of the German-Austrian actress Luise Rainer. Born in Vienna in 1910, she had emerged in theater under the direction of Max Reinhardt and had made an impression in Pirandello's Six Characters in Search of an Author. She had also made three motion pictures, none of them distinguished. Hypersensitive, fastidious, demanding of herself and others, she had a delicately balanced temperament that could sometimes tilt into rages. Her special capacity as an actress was to work her way into the mind and spirit of the characters she played, becoming one with them.

It was Mayer's custom, particularly in view of the slowly deteriorating situation in Europe, to seek European performers who might be imported to Hollywood. He was mindful of the fact that after permitting the reopening of the M.G.M. offices in Berlin, the German government was restricting movie imports, and it might be useful to attract more of a foreign audience by adding up-and-coming players who could enact their roles in the German or French versions.

Some footage arrived from Mayer's wandering talent scout, Bob Ritchie, whom Mayer had so carefully exiled from Jeanette MacDonald. Mayer ran it in the company of his continuing story editor, Samuel Marx. He liked what he saw: Luise Rainer had looks, charm, a certain tender vulnerability he admired in women and the potential to be a star. Clarence Brown, still one of Mayer's favorite directors in the wake of *Ah, Wilderness!*, was about to leave for London, Paris and Berlin, and Mayer asked him to alter his itinerary to include Vienna, where he and Bob Ritchie could discuss a contract with Miss Rainer. They caught her at a difficult time: she had fallen in love with an aviator, who had been on an expedition to Africa and whose plane had crashed, killing him instantly, just before they were due to meet in Rome. She needed an escape from places where they had spent their love affair and, with qualms, agreed to come to Hollywood. Mayer made sure that flowers greeted her as she stepped into her suite on the ship, and that she was met by a contingent off the train in California.

He quickly learned that Miss Rainer had a rather shaky command of English. He instructed the ever-reliable Constance Collier to train her, not only in correct speech, but also in dramatic modulation. Miss Collier, as always, did a splendid job, and Miss Rainer improved rapidly.

Luise Rainer befriended Samuel Marx. There was no romantic attraction between them, and Miss Rainer was not over her bereavement. Mayer benignly encouraged the friendship; Miss Rainer was constantly in Marx's office, suggesting story ideas for herself. One day, she arrived wearing a strange patchwork dress and announced that it was made up out of pieces of the couch cover on which she and the aviator had made love.

She took a small beach house at Malibu, and Marx would go down there in the evening. She gave him a complete description of all the stars in heaven; next night, she seemed, he said, to know nothing of astronomy. She said she was a pianist and tinkled away at an expert "Liebestraum" with the skill of a concert artist; he insisted that was the only piece she knew.

Mayer found a place for her. Myrna Loy had walked off the set of *Escapade*, a remake of Paula Wesseley's vehicle *Maskerade*. Mayer was left without a female star. He put a call through to Marx's office, where he knew he was sure to find Miss Rainer, and summoned her to the set. She ran gleefully to her assignment, and Marx hardly ever saw her again.

Marx had introduced her to Clifford Odets, then at the height of his fame as a dramatist. Pleased with Miss Rainer's excellent performance in *Escapade* opposite William Powell, Mayer did not approve of her having an affair with a left-wing writer, and made his feelings known. No sooner had he given Luise Rainer her big break than he began to weary of her. She proved all too opinionated, if impeccably correct, in pointing out errors in the "Viennese" sets and costumes of *Escapade*. Her advice was resented by the art director Cedric Gibbons and by Adrian, who designed her clothes. Actors were not supposed to speak their minds; even Garbo tended to accept the clothes designed for her. Nor were actresses supposed to have an intellect, be well read or display willfulness and strength of character. Nevertheless, Thalberg firmly decided that only she could play the turn-of-the-century French star Anna Held in *The Great Ziegfeld*, with William Powell in the title role, that November; her round, pretty face, huge, dewy eyes, perfect hourglass figure, astonishingly resembled Held's. Although she can scarcely have had time to have found out anything about Held, who was once the toast of Broadway, she managed to carry off Miss Held's coquettishness, wide-eyed charm and vulnerability. The performance won her an Oscar. Myrna Loy, whom she had so abruptly replaced in *Escapade*, ironically played Billie Burke, the second Mrs. Ziegfeld; Anna Held was the first. It was still wearying for Mayer that Miss Rainer was supporting Odets in political statements against Hitler and fascist Spain.

That October, Selznick's tenure at M.G.M. came close to the end. He made the mistake of writing a long and frantic letter to Nicholas Schenck on October 3, grumbling about the way his pictures were treated. Schenck was furious and wrote an angry letter back. In another letter, never sent but apparently written in October, the angry young man explained what was in sum a disastrous misadventure on his part— *David Copperfield* and *Dinner at Eight* notwithstanding. He blamed Mayer for *Vanessa, Her Love Story*, which, he said, he had inherited from Walter Wanger; also for *Meet the Baron*, with radio stars; he was opposed to the casting of Wallace Beery in *Night Flight*, obviously a Mayer choice; he was against Mayer's substitution of Harlow for Crawford in *Reckless* (we have hazarded the reasons); he listed the successes. He kvetched about unnamed M.G.M. executives who went around lying (he changed it to saying) that he had been given a fabulous salary by Mayer; he charged that he had received no praise for *David Copperfield* or for *A Tale of Two Cities*. He also poured out a long, grumbling letter to Mayer on October 24. Nobody cared; he was battling against granite.

*   *   *

The new year, 1936, brought more disturbing news from Europe, and both Mayer and Irving Thalberg (again) appeared at the Hillcrest Country Club to give speeches warning of the imminent danger of Nazism and major anti-Semitic activity in Germany.

Mickey Rooney was a handful that year. At fifteen, when he was not allowed a driver's license, he bought himself a new Cadillac and acquired a chauffeur. He would brag about it to the press, irritating everyone at the studio. And even more than ever, now that he was in puberty, he couldn't keep his hands off any girl. The complaints over this were constant. Because he was tiny, some women found him unattractive, and he bought lifts to bring his height up. The tall girls occasionally laughed at him or ran away. This gave him an inferiority complex, which he overcompensated for by talking nonstop, bragging about everything he did, and announcing this, that and the other picture he would be making in the future. Many people were left exhausted. But Mayer adored this brilliant contemporary version of Peck's Bad Boy.

The new year brought an exchange of greetings with ex-President Hoover, of whom Mayer continued to be deeply fond. His loyalty to old friends, regardless of whether they had fallen from positions of power, was admirable.

An enemy died on January 9, 1936. John Gilbert, still only thirty-eight, was stricken with a fatal heart attack at his house in Beverly Hills. Washed up, hopelessly alcoholic, he had been having a prolonged affair with Marlene Dietrich, following the collapse of his marriage to Virginia Bruce. At the funeral, Miss Dietrich made a hysterical scene, walking in tears up the aisle to the flower-bedecked open coffin and then, rather spectacularly, fainting in front of everyone. Miss Bruce sold almost all of Gilbert's property after he died; Miss Dietrich managed to rescue the bed sheets on which she and Gilbert had made love.

In late February, producer Bernie Hyman's and director W. S. Van Dyke's San Francisco, with Clark Gable and Jeanette MacDonald, was energetically in progress. Mayer went to a dinner dance at the Metro Studio Club of the Ambassador Hotel, attended by seven hundred producers, stars and directors. The master of ceremonies was Pete Smith, former publicist turned short-film maker, while the popular comedian Ted Healy introduced individual acts. Healy sang a clever parody of Allan Jones. Mayer was furious. Without warning, he ran to the stage, pushing Healy aside. Healy laughed, thinking it was a gag, and the audience burst into loud applause for five minutes. Mayer began to scream that Healy should not make fun of Jones's voice.

The audience, to Mayer's fury, ignored him and urged Healy to continue. In Hollywood, this was equivalent to the Russian Revolution. Healy took the microphone and said:

> I don't feel I have done anything wrong. Mr. Mayer is the one in the wrong. I know Metro is the biggest company and that Mr. Mayer is a power. I'm not afraid of anyone. I don't have to be. I can still make a dollar singing in barrooms. I don't fear anyone in this business. But, if you folks feel I owe an apology, I apologize. Come on, L.B., give me a smile, doggone you.

Mayer walked on the floor and shook hands with Healy. He said:

> When I hear a voice as great as . . . Allan Jones's . . . I'm as much a fan as anyone and don't feel that such artists should be ridiculed even as an act.

Despite his laughing off Mayer's assault, Healy was severely affected by the incident. He developed major stress symptoms. Two years later, he died of a heart attack at forty-five.

It was known around the studio that Irving Thalberg's marriage to Norma Shearer was in ruins. Rosabelle Laemmle had returned from his past, and he had entered into a romantic relationship with her. This was devastating to Miss Shearer; in complete secrecy, Sam Marx reported, Thalberg began a divorce.

The Academy Awards took place on March 5, 1936. Mayer had called for a heavy push for Clarence Brown's *Ah, Wilderness!*, his favorite of the year because of its warm emphasis on family, over Thalberg's *Mutiny on the Bounty*, and had done the unthinkable: he had authorized advertisements in the trade papers featuring Leo the Lion with a card announcing AH WILDERNESS! hanging around its neck. The caption read, "Leo, you've given so much, get ready to receive." As it turned out, *Mutiny* got the award; Harry Cohn gave it to Irving Thalberg. Mayer had to smile.

On March 8, Mabel Walker Willebrandt called Mayer and told him that Rudolph was still laid up in a Shanghai hospital, very ill and penniless. Mayer reminded her that he had published notices he would do nothing further to help Rudy. He told her that, if it were really necessary, he would pay the hospital fees, but reminded her that on a previous occasion Rudy had entered into collusion with a doctor, pretending illness, and had gotten money out of him. He would only pay the hospital bills if a third party could be used as the go-between, and it would not be known that Mayer was responsible. Mrs. Willebrandt told him that her brother-in-law lived in Shanghai; the brother-in-law would pay the money, making it seem as if it had come from an American charitable fund. The arrangements were made.

*San Francisco* turned out to be splendid; Mayer was fascinated by Jeanette MacDonald's performance as a minister's daughter who becomes a nightclub star in the raffish city just before the great quake of 1906. Spencer Tracy emerged here as a major actor, playing a priest with a depth of conviction aided by the intelligent writing of Anita Loos. It was obvious he was marked for major stardom, more than holding his own with Clark Gable, who gave a vibrant performance as the nightclub owner, Blackie Norton. The cataclysm itself was magnificently staged.

Again, the great virtue of *San Francisco*, reflecting, as always, Irving Thalberg's impeccable taste and style, was that it appealed to the mass public on the basis of a very reliable principle. It was the thinly disguised story of Beauty and the Beast; Gable's Blackie was primitive, crass, brash, irreverent. Jeanette MacDonald's singer was pure, virginal and coy —a part written from beginning to end with the actress in mind. Spencer Tracy was a representative of the Deity; the picture became a struggle between the forces of nature and man's higher self. It was this shrewdly devised theme that made the picture work, along with the marvelous driving rhythm that marked the work of editor Margaret Booth. Gripping, irresistible, the picture conquered all but the most skeptical critics and became a colossal box office success.

The title song, composed by Walter Jurmann and Bronislau Kaper, set the seal of success on the picture. Mayer had kept Jurmann and Kaper doing little after he signed them in Paris, but now he wanted a profoundly American, expressive song and had thrown open the opportunity to several different composers. The winning team created a rousing melody, with lyrics by Gus Kahn, that Jeanette MacDonald sang unforgettably. Today, it is the official anthem of San Francisco.

After what seemed to Mayer and Thalberg interminable delays, *The Good Earth* was at last in production under the direction of Sidney Franklin that spring and summer. Following all the tortuous months in China, almost nothing of Frank Messinger's footage was used: a few shots of a crowd outside a public building, distant glimpses of an army on the march, pieces of a market scene. A colossal waste of money and time was hidden from the press by Howard Strickling and Howard Dietz, and instead rapturous press releases, announcing commencement of production, repeated the earlier canard that Pearl Buck was the idol of the Chinese people.

General Tu was a constant nuisance, trying to sell the studio stories and insisting, without results, on putting in a Chinese producer to work with Albert Lewin, who was supervising the production. Not getting anywhere in Hollywood, he tried unsuccessfully to see Will Hays in New York and beseeched Hays's foreign manager Frederick L. Herron with all kinds of nonsensical suggestions. He returned to Los Angeles as a fuss-budget on the set.

Lewin nursed the project along carefully, his good taste, romantic sensibility and insistence on accuracy shown in every frame. He had demanded that cinematographer Karl Freund shoot the picture. To play the heroic farmer Li (Wang Lung), he borrowed Paul Muni from Warner Brothers in exchange for Clark Gable, whom Warner's needed for the Marion Davies vehicle *Cain and Mabel*. Luise Rainer was the ideal choice as the farmer's wife, O-lan. Often silent, bowed, humble yet courageous, her treasuring of two pearls found during a revolutionary riot adding a touchingly feminine element to her characterization, she gave the performance of a lifetime. Thalberg's emphasis on a powerful story line that resembled in miniature the obstacle course of life itself gave the entire production a striking momentum. After storm, riot, adultery, drought and locust plague, when O-lan dies, her husband walks to the tree she planted long ago and utters the words, "You are the earth." It was the same theme of love of the land that animated *Gone With the Wind* and that appealed deeply to millions of people.

The masterwork was at last ready for editing on July 23. Thalberg began to panic that the Chinese government might protest that the original agreement signed with George Hill had not been met; they might embroil the studio in a major lawsuit.

Once again, the State Department came to the rescue. U.S. Counsul Willys Peck stepped in, and there were no further major problems. Apart from a two-day seizure by local censors in Peking in 1937, and some interferences by the Japanese puppet governments in the northern provinces, the picture achieved wide distribution in China. It was not until 1938 that it was banned in Japan for its favorable portrait of that nation's traditional enemy.

*The Good Earth* became a commercial and, for the most part, critical success, and can be called a lasting monument to a great studio at its peak. The spectacular sequences still overwhelm over half a century later, but above all, the true, sincere feeling for family life, no doubt stemming from Mayer's influence via Thalberg, surmounts any cynical response to the picture and brings the movie to at least the threshold of greatness.

The difficulties between M.G.M. and the unions increased in April. James K. McGuinness and John Lee Mahin, among the studio's leading right-wing writers, finally met with Mayer and Irving Thalberg to form the company union. Mayer got behind the McGuinness group, allowing them to use all studio facilities. McGuinness was rewarded with several choice subjects, including, not insignificantly, Winfield Sheehan's *Florian*, set in Vienna, which would bring that renegade temporarily back into the M.G.M. orbit. Mahin was given *Love on the Run*, *Wife vs. Secretary* and *Captains Courageous*. The splinter group became known as the Screen Playwrights, Inc. Bess Meredyth was a charter member. They invaded Guild meetings and sought the removal of such liberals as Doro- thy Parker, Sheridan Gibney, Dudley Nichols and Francis Faragoh. The Motion Picture Producers' Association, whose leadership Mayer would soon relinquish, supported the new union.

At the same time, the gangster William Bioff (alias Henry Martin) and George E. Browne, international president of the International Alli- ance of Theatrical Stage Employees (IATSE), were dominant in Holly- wood. According to a report prepared by Lieutenant LeRoy Sanderson of the Los Angeles Police Department, Bioff had operated with other mob- sters on the West Side of Chicago from 1921 to 1935, and had been arrested several times by members of the Chicago Police Department and held on suspicion of burglary, pimping and vagrancy. On February 2, 1939, he was charged with being involved in the murder of a man named Tommy Malloy, whom George Browne replaced as union busi- ness agent. Browne hired Bioff as a bodyguard. Soon after, another friend of Tommy Malloy was murdered by gangsters. Again, the Chicago police suspected Bioff.

George Browne was made international president of IATSE late in 1934. In January 1936, Bioff was sent to Hollywood, where he was placed in charge of the motion picture unions, Locals 37, 883 and 695.

On April 14, 1936, Browne and Bioff approached Nicholas Schenck at his offices in New York and demanded $2 million not to bring off a major industry strike. Schenck told Bioff he was crazy, and Bioff replied, "You know you'll have to pay. You'll have to pay more in the end if you don't pay now." Schenck called Mayer and Thalberg for an anxious discussion. The two labor leaders left.

Two days later, they returned for a meeting with Schenck and Sidney R. Kent, president of 20th Century Fox. Bioff said he had thought the matter over and decided to accept $1 million. He was turned down again. Finally, he agreed to accept $50,000 a year from each of the major companies and $25,000 a year from the smaller ones. Schenck again refused. But by April 21, after further conferences with Thalberg and Mayer, Schenck decided to go ahead. On April 24, David Bernstein, Loew's treasurer, issued a check for $50,000; Sidney R. Kent brought brown paper packages of cash to the office from each of the industry leaders. In addition, a contract was signed for future payments, and Bioff's new conditions were that he would get the $50,000 a year *after income tax*. Nicholas Schenck was at a loss to correct this arrangement.

David Bernstein had to pad expense accounts "like," as he said later, "a Hollywood hero's shoulders." He had to take the extortion money from the firm's funds and contrive a way of covering up its use on the books. In addition to the agreed-upon $50,000 a year, he had to produce certain out-of-pocket sums, taken from his own account at the National City Bank of New York and reimbursed as expenses from the company. At a hearing in New York in October 1941, Mayer would testify that he was well aware of the arrangements but was never told the finer points. It was not revealed until that year that Joe Schenck had been behind these deals, receiving a dozen deliveries of cash from Bioff between August 1935 and February 1937. Bioff was, in effect, Joe Schenck's bag man, to the detriment of Joe's brother Nicholas; soon, Joe Schenck would take over from Mayer as head of the MPPA.

Jean Harlow was in trouble in April. Viona Hessler, John A. Hartranft and other heirs of Dorothy Millette were suing her, claiming that they were entitled to portions of the Paul Bern estate. Miss Harlow was forced to settle with them, but only for a modest $2,000.

Later in April, Mayer, Irving Thalberg, Dorothy Parker, James Cagney and Fredric March jointly supported an anti-Nazi banquet in honor of Hitler's prominent critic, Prince Hubertus zu Lowenstein. The $20-a-head cover was used for relief for Jewish sufferers from Nazism. Immediately after the banquet, Mayer left with Edie and her husband William Goetz, Frank Orsatti and Howard Strickling for New York. He had grown closer to Edie in the past three years. He very much approved of Goetz's running, along with Darryl F. Zanuck, 20th Century-Fox, and was impressed by the Goetzes' splendid house and burgeoning collection of art.

He returned to spoiling Edie, giving her splendid gifts, which her husband tolerated. Simultaneously, he was drawing away from Irene and David O. Selznick. He disliked the fact that they had shown their independence by leaving M.G.M. He was not foolish enough to regard this as betrayal exactly, but this difficult pair had left the family, and that was painful for Mayer. With the financial support of the millionaire Jock Whitney, Selznick had embarked on a strong new career. He also became the proud father of Daniel Mayer Selznick on May 18, 1936. Mayer barely returned from the trip to New York in time for the birth; the Selznicks soon took off for Honolulu with Mr. and Mrs. Averell Harriman.

According to Irene, there were differences between her and her husband over Mayer's grandchildren, three-year-old Jeffrey and now Danny. Always manically involved in his latest projects, obsessed with work, gambling late into the night, Selznick hardly gave any attention to the boys. He yielded only at Christmas and Thanksgiving.

Oddities slipped into the studio schedule, direct contradictions of Mayer's policy of family pictures. *The Devil Doll* was a story of human beings shrunk down to tiny size; *Mad Love* showed a murderer's hands being grafted onto the stumps of an accident-mangled pianist. Presumably, as with *Kongo* and *The Mask of Fu Manchu* three years earlier, these pictures were rushed through to fill Nicholas Schenck's demands for more theater product. More to Mayer's liking was *Born to Dance*, shot that summer with Jimmy Stewart and Eleanor Powell, both at their best. Cleverly made, filled with electrifying dance routines, the picture contained one unforgettable sequence: Virginia Bruce singing "I've Got You Under My Skin" to a bemused Stewart. Beautiful, stylish and sophisticated, Miss Bruce epitomized, in that one song, the essence of the thirties as few others ever did.[2]

*The Devil Is a Sissy* was in production that June, a deeply affecting story of underprivileged kids in New York City, with a remarkable performance by Mickey Rooney. Mayer was pushing a new contract player, Frances Gumm, now known as Judy Garland. Ida Koverman had discovered the fourteen-year-old, forcing her on Mayer, convinced that she had great potential. Judy was conceived under a dark star: her father was bisexual, which caused her mother endless misery, and she was supposed to have been aborted. She discovered this fact early in her life and it affected her deeply.

Born in Grand Rapids, Michigan, on June 10, 1922, Judy Garland had suffered from an inferiority complex as she struggled up through the boondocks of vaudeville with her sisters. Seen by studio musical arranger Roger Edens at the Wilshire-Ebell Theater, she had sung "Dinah" to Ida Koverman; Mayer liked her rendition very well and took her around the studio, having her sing for the employees. He arranged for her to be featured in a twenty-minute short entitled *Every Sunday*, in which she appeared with Deanna Durbin. Both singers made a strong impression in this artless concoction, which was set in and around a park bandstand reminiscent of that which Mayer had enjoyed as a child in St. John, New Brunswick. Not even Mayer could have foreseen for this awkward, unhappy girl the extraordinary career which she would soon embark

---

[2] Miss Bruce was not always popular at the studio. In the last sequence of *The Great Ziegfeld*, she was seen seated in a large hoop skirt on top of a giant wedding cake. At lunchtime, the cast and crew left the cake, deserting her; unable to move because of her cumbersome costume, she had to sit up there for over an hour under hot lights, until at last they relented and rescued her.

upon. He kept her under contract. He did not, to his lasting regret, renew Deanna Durbin's; she went on to a vivid career at Universal.

Mayer's health, robust for several years, had begun to falter. He suffered from ulcers, not surprisingly in view of his schedule, and while in New York, had checked into Mount Sinai Hospital for two days of tests. Since his wife had been afflicted by cancer, he dreaded that he, too, would be stricken with the disease. Because of this fear, he began having far too frequent X rays.

On June 22, Frank Orsatti announced his engagement to beauty-contest winner Jean Chatburn. She had a contract at the studio. Mayer was overjoyed, and immediately gave his blessing. He attended the couple's Arizona wedding later that year. He was pleased that Robert Taylor was having an affair with Barbara Stanwyck, an actress he had very much admired in such pictures as *So Big* and *Ladies They Talk About*. The couple persistently denied their engagement. Mayer cast them both in *His Brother's Wife*.

Mayer embarked on a plan that May to break down Nazi domination of Austria's motion picture industry by making pictures in Vienna under the guidance of Dr. Eugen Lanske, head of the Austrian State Film Board. Lanske gave a speech at the Biltmore Hotel, announcing that unless the Nazi stranglehold were eased, he and other leading figures of the Austrian industry would have to move to Budapest. Although nothing came of the M.G.M. plan, Mayer gave his full support to Lanske over the next two years.

In July 1936, a question came up of whether Mayer would take vigorous action against President Roosevelt in the upcoming electoral campaign. J. F. T. O'Connor, comptroller of the currency and a helpful friend of Mayer's in government, lunched at the studio on July 3 with Mayer and the producer John Considine, a devoted Democrat, to discuss the matter. Mayer, unimpressed by the Republican candidate Alf Landon and always mindful of the main chance, betrayed his own party as completely as William Randolph Hearst had done, to his great annoyance, four years earlier. Mayer assured O'Connor that he would secretly support Roosevelt, or at least not oppose him; he said that, although the picture industry had planned to back Landon, that plan was now changed; and he felt confident, it seemed, in speaking for the industry as a whole.

Mayer was true to his word; as a reward, he and Joe Schenck, who was entirely with him in the matter, and had been, after him, the largest contributor to the 1932 Hoover campaign, were received by the re-elected president at the White House the following year. Such were the customary prizes for expediency.

On July 23, Walter Wanger came to see Mayer to discuss a contract for Charles Feldman's client Charles Boyer. Boyer was to be made available to Mayer for *Conquest,* in which he would play Napoleon to Garbo's Marie Walewska. Mayer asked Wanger point-blank if the rumors were true that Wanger, who would come on the picture as line producer, had an under-the-table profit-sharing deal with Boyer, who was asking the staggering sum of $12,000 a week. Wanger denied the charge; Mayer remained skeptical. After some careful sleuthing (and, it seems, persistent pressure on Feldman's fellow agent Jack Gordean) Mayer found out that Wanger was lying. Wanger called up and asked Mayer if he would lend Jean Harlow to him for another picture, to be made for Wanger's independent company. Mayer called him to the office to discuss the matter. "Do you get a share of Harlow as well when you borrow her from us?" Mayer asked. Wanger denied it; Mayer had already established with Gordean what Wanger was up to. At that moment, Mayer, for the second time in his life, hauled back and struck Wanger so hard on the jaw that the producer crashed to the floor. But this time Mayer had overdone it. He broke his right hand and the two men walked out in a daze to get first aid from an astonished Ida Koverman.

A picture which didn't get off the ground was *It Can't Happen Here,* based on the novel by Sinclair Lewis, about a dictator who assumes a Hitlerian role in American politics and the small-town editor who sets out to expose him. Will Hays was nervous about the movie because official government policy was to avoid direct public criticism of Hitler. Samuel Marx said that the real reason the project was dropped was that the script proved unfilmable. Mayer's official reason was that the budget would be prohibitive, and indeed, to stage mass rallies and scenes of the equivalent of a Nazi army would have been difficult. Mayer cannot have forgotten *Gabriel Over the White House;* he must have seen the anti-Hooverish elements in even a story summary. Had he read the novel itself, which in the first few pages provides a satirical portrait of a middle-aged female Hooverite, he would certainly never have embarked on the picture at all.

Mayer stepped up plans to import Jewish writers from Austria, Hungary and Romania, in part to enhance the qualities of his productions, in part to give them sanctuary from the Nazi menace. One of the most notable of these was Walter Reisch, who had written *Maskerade.* The general belief that Mayer had no interest in writers except as slaves of the lamp is contradicted by his special concern for Reisch. He would meet with Reisch in 1937, when he came to London.

Shooting began that July on *Camille.* Irving Thalberg not only admired the popular romantic play by Alexandre Dumas *fils,* but he also identified with it. It was the story of a courtesan who is stricken from the outset by tuberculosis. The theme of a remarkable creature doomed could only be close to his heart. As reworked by the writers Zoe Akins, Frances Marion and James Hilton, the character of Marguerite Gautier was seen as a frivolous, detached and self-indulgent beauty, sweeping all before her in the Paris of 1847, but threatened constantly by her creditors, who stalk her through the elaborate salons, waiting for a chance to spring. Sold out to the unattractive and villainous Baron de Varville, she is forced to play a double game, desperately flirting with a besotted youth, Armand Duval. Finally, the courtesan is ruined by the only true emotion she has felt: she makes the mistake of falling in love, which ultimately destroys her. In a finale that would have female audiences sobbing from Norway to Australia, Marguerite dies in her lover's arms.

Only Garbo could carry off so operatic a concept; only she would render believable the overperfumed situations and make the audience accept her duplicitous nature. George Cukor was shrewdly chosen by Thalberg to direct the picture; a certain feminine streak in his sensibility would be ideally valuable here. But life kept intruding into grand designs: while the picture was in preproduction, and just after Robert Taylor was cast as the hapless Armand, Cukor was arrested for propositioning a young man on the street. It took all of Mayer's and Thalberg's powerful connections through District Attorney Buron Fitts to spring Cukor from prison and put him back on the set.

The results were refined and impressive. Through the deliberate artificiality of the concept, the reminder of approaching death struck a chilling note of realism. Aside from one dreadful scene in which Lionel Barrymore as Armand's father presses Marguerite Gautier to an act of sacrifice, the picture was intelligently written, and it permanently enshrines Garbo's most mesmerizing performance. Her own duplicitousness and her teasing, insecure relationships with men, exemplified in her disastrous relationship with John Gilbert, were fully brought out by the director, who knew her intimately.

In August, Mayer traveled to New York for meetings with Nicholas Schenck, then proceeded to St. John, New Brunswick, in good spirits. It was his first visit there in twenty years. Accompanied by Howard Strickling and by his old friend, the Boston lawyer David Stoneman, partner of Bernard Berenson, he was honored at a lavish luncheon, seated between Chief Justice Baxter and St. John's Mayor MacLaren. Swallowing his feelings, he gave credit for the success of M.G.M. to Nicholas Schenck's leadership, and he characteristically selected *Naughty Marietta*, *Rose Marie*, *David Copperfield* and *Romeo and Juliet*, the premiere of which he had just attended in New York, as examples of quality productions that represented the studio at its best.

He said, "M.G.M. has been trying nicer, better, finer things, gradually to raise the taste of the public . . . We want to encourage other companies to take chances, to improve quality in every possible way." He spoke of the threat to world peace, mentioning the necessity for Great Britain and the United States to serve notice on Germany and "all those mad people who didn't get a lesson from the last war that we will give them hell if they start it up again." He added, "If those people over there had the money, they would be at war with us now." He went on to visit the Main Street district where he had grown up, found his former teachers at Elm Street School and an old classmate, who had become a hotel porter. He cried as he laid flowers upon his mother's grave. He told friends at a dinner that night that his lifelong motto was, "When you get to the end of your rope, tie a knot in it and hold on." They laughed and applauded loudly.

## Chapter Seventeen

# 1936–1937

During his stay in St. John, Mayer received disquieting news. Irving Thalberg was ailing; he was worn out by work on the screenplay of *Marie Antoinette* for Norma Shearer, plagued by trouble in the cutting of *The Good Earth*. He was having some awkward meetings with the writers of the schmaltzy Jeanette MacDonald–Nelson Eddy operetta *Maytime*, and was dissatisfied with the first days of work by Edmund Goulding, seriously thinking of replacing him with Robert Z. Leonard. By July, he had been so exhausted that he even decided against buying Margaret Mitchell's triumphant best-seller, *Gone With the Wind*, which David O. Selznick snapped up on the thirtieth of that month.

He was disappointed by the respectful, lukewarm reviews of *Romeo and Juliet*, which opened in New York on August 26. But he had managed to rally the strength to appear at the lavish California opening of *The Great Ziegfeld* in Los Angeles four days later.

During a visit to Del Monte Lodge, in Northern California, over the Labor Day weekend, Thalberg caught cold. He was seen shivering and pale at the Hollywood Bowl on the night of September 8, when Max Reinhardt's *Everyman* was presented. He came down with a sore throat, a fever, then a bad cough. He was found to be suffering from pneumonia. Thalberg told his intimate circle, as well as Norma, that he didn't expect to live.

Mayer went almost directly from the train to Thalberg's bedside in Santa Monica, to find the thirty-seven-year-old man weak, almost delirious. Discreetly, Rosabelle Laemmle had stayed away, and Norma, everything forgiven, was in anguish. So was Mayer, who was tormented by the thought of losing a beloved, if devious and prodigal, son.

Doctors forbade any visitors to Thalberg on the night of September 13. Mayer returned to his beach house after a gallant, strained appearance at the annual M.G.M. picnic given by Clarence Brown. By dawn,

Thalberg's temperature was at danger point. He died at 10:15 A.M. on September 14. Norma Shearer, her sister Edith, Thalberg's parents, William and Henrietta, the Lawrence Weingartens (his brother-in-law and sister Sylvia) and Bernie Hyman were at the bedside. It must have been distressing to Mayer to learn that Miss Shearer had kept him firmly away from those last moments, even though he had made an unprecedented departure from custom and stayed at home that morning to be on hand if needed.[1]

Mayer acted promptly. He closed production on *Camille, Maytime* and *A Day at the Races*, with the Marx Brothers, in honor of the departed leader. Only Garbo, utterly selfish as always, failed to convey her condolences or agree to attend the funeral. She did not even send flowers. Nelson Eddy and Jeanette MacDonald were deeply saddened; and as for the Marx Brothers, they were devastated. Groucho Marx adored Thalberg, regarding him as the only genius in Hollywood and the rescuer of the brothers from professional ruin. Against Nicholas Schenck's advice, Mayer ordered that *Romeo and Juliet* should have its Los Angeles premiere at the Carthay Circle on September 30, as, he believed, Thalberg would have wished.

Thalberg's funeral took place on September 16 at the B'nai B'rith Temple on Wilshire Boulevard at 10:00 A.M. Howard Strickling had sent out requests to all newspaper owners that there should be no unseemly spectacles of cameramen mobbing the stars or reporters demanding comments. The crowd was advised, through special requests from the press, that it would be appreciated if there would be silent respect rather than noisy demonstrations. Mayer helped Norma Shearer supervise the guest list, which was limited to the temple's capacity of 1,200. Displays of Mayer's gardenias decorated the apse; Thalberg's casket was decorated with simple bouquets and wreaths.

Rabbi Edgar Magnin conducted the service, reading the prayers in both Hebrew and English. President Roosevelt had sent a subdued, deeply felt message, which Magnin read. Grace Moore exquisitely sang the Twenty-third Psalm ("The Lord is my Shepherd, I shall not want").

Miss Shearer had decided on private services at the Sanctuary of the Benediction at Forest Lawn. The honorary pallbearers included Clark Gable, Douglas Fairbanks, Fredric March, Sidney Franklin, W. S. Van Dyke, Sam Wood, Robert Z. Leonard and Carey Wilson. Mayer's exclusion from the list indicates the differences between him and Shearer. He attended, with Margaret, the private services, in the company of Mr. and Mrs. Eddie Mannix, Jack and Virginia Conway, and Mr. and Mrs. Harry

[1] In some versions, Mayer was at the studio when he heard the news, and drove to the house to give his condolences to the widow.

Rapf. Howard Strickling, Howard Dietz and Edwin Loeb followed Nicholas Schenck and his wife into the chapel. Wallace Beery scattered flowers from his private plane.

Immediately after the funeral, the producer Albert Lewin, as devoted as ever to Thalberg, and with *The Good Earth*'s editing completed, left the studio. He would return years later as one of Mayer's most accomplished craftsmen.

Many stars remained so grief-stricken at the Carthay Circle opening of *Romeo and Juliet* that publicist Frank Whitbeck, standing in front of the theater, abandoned the usual policy of interviewing the stars as they entered, because he was afraid that they might break down. Instead, he simply announced them one by one.

Mayer insisted that a special panel be added to the credits of *The Good Earth*, reading: TO THE MEMORY OF IRVING THALBERG, WE DEDICATE THIS PICTURE, HIS LAST GREAT ACHIEVEMENT.

On October 5, unable to attend the premiere of *Romeo and Juliet*, Norma Shearer, exhausted and sleepless, came down with bronchial pneumonia almost identical to that suffered by her husband. She lay ill for twelve days. At one point she was given up for lost, and she called in Edwin J. Loeb to write a new will. But her physician, Dr. Verne R. Mason, tended to her magnificently, and she rallied suddenly; by midday on the seventeenth she was able to sit up and take nourishment.

In the meantime, Mayer had to continue his daily schedules. He was unable to persuade the Marx Brothers to return to *A Day at the Races* for another month, but *Maytime* was resumed with major rewrites.

Mayer asserted himself at once. He fired Goulding, as he had always wanted Thalberg to do. He scrapped the original script and all the Technicolor footage that had been shot. In a new, ninety-nine percent black-and-white version, Paul Lukas, who had played Jeanette MacDonald's husband, was removed and replaced by John Barrymore. In the original story, Nelson Eddy was married. Mayer detested this element; it meant that Eddy's character was an adulterer. He had the wife written out and Julie Haydon, who had played the role, sent back to New York. He also insisted on a sentimental epilogue shot in color. Robert Z. Leonard expertly handled this revamped musical romance, making it another M.G.M. commercial triumph.

Garbo returned to work on *Camille*. Despite the schedule that faced him, Mayer managed to squeeze in a visit to San Francisco, where he was greeted off the train by forty singing firemen as he spoke, on the platform, of his support of Fire Prevention Week. Mayor Angelo J. Rossi gave him a golden key to the city. He was accompanied by Margaret, Durand Howes of the Los Angeles Chamber of Commerce, Harry Rapf,

Ben Goetz, who was visiting from England, and Frank Orsatti. Mayer addressed a luncheon in his honor given by his friend, the prominent local financier and theater owner Louis R. Lurie. He chose the occasion to make his first public onslaught on Communism. He spoke of "Communists in Hollywood drawing down $2,500 a week . . . Some of them are great writers, who are demanding free expression in their work for pictures. The industry knows who they are and knows, too, that they are financed and supported by the Third Internationale."

Mayer went on to speak of how the industry had stopped them from spreading their "pernicious propaganda" through motion pictures, "the greatest molder of public opinion that ever existed." He was careful not to mention specific names, but one can only speculate on who they were.

As soon as Thalberg was buried, his partners in Title Guarantee and Trust and in the under-the-table partnership deal that included Mayer and Harry Rapf, and J. Robert Rubin, sought to prevent his widow from inheriting. The real estate share was willed to her; nothing could be done about that. But the little over seven percent of studio profits which she would normally be due was denied her by Nicholas Schenck, whose word on the matter was law. She engaged Mayer's own former lawyer, Edwin Loeb, to fight Schenck. Charles Feldman, her agent, also had little reason to like Mayer; he secured her a new contract, valid from July 14, 1937, but Schenck still failed to honor the profit-sharing terms.

With the advent of the Spanish Civil War, Hollywood was a hotbed of political controversy. Luise Rainer headed the anti-Nazi group, which was opposed to General Francisco Franco's backing by Hitler. Clifford Odets undoubtedly was her inspiration in taking this stand. Fredric March and his wife, Florence Eldridge, were pro-Loyalist liberals unfairly accused of Communist sympathies. On the opposite side of the political spectrum, the guest and contact lists of Georg Gyssling, Nazi consul general in Los Angeles, make interesting reading. Boycotted by most of the industry for obvious reasons, he numbered in his special manifesto, seized by American military agents at the end of World War II, Mayer's old friend Lewis Stone (shortly to become Judge Hardy in the Andy Hardy series), Walt Disney, Gary Cooper, Winfield Sheehan and Sheehan's wife, the opera star Maria Jeritza. What Mayer would have done if he had known of Stone's particular contact in this instance can only be guessed at.

By November, after the necessary interruptions and problems following Thalberg's death, the studio was once again humming with activity. A version of Rudyard Kipling's *Captains Courageous* was getting underway, directed by Victor Fleming and starring Spencer Tracy and Freddie

Bartholomew. Mayer had hired his old colleague John M. Stahl, from the Selig Zoo days, to direct *Parnell*, with Clark Gable as the troubled Irish patriot. Mayer lavished considerable personal attention on the film, ensuring a high degree of craftsmanship. From the opening of Parnell's departure from New York City in a snowstorm, to the debates in the House of Commons in London, his emphasis on quality could be seen in every frame. But Gable's unease in the central performance undermined the production, and it turned out to be a box office disaster.

A troublesome matter had to be dealt with in San Francisco. There was local objection to the M.G.M. film of that name, because of its portrayal of the violent and squalid Barbary Coast era; also, the staging of the earthquake, with citizens being swallowed up in giant cracks in the streets, was considered by many to be exaggerated. The Chamber of Commerce was nervous because this might deter tourism. Through his friend, the Bay Area banker John Francis Neylan, Mayer secured sufficient support to prevent a boycott and added, on Neylan's suggestion, a triumphant finale in which it was announced that a new San Francisco would be built following the quake of 1906. Shots of the city were prepared and introduced by a second-unit team to show that the present metropolis was not only magnificent, but safe.

Mayer's concern, as a former British subject, continued to be securing a foothold in England. With Nicholas Schenck, he arranged to obtain a fourteen percent Loew's shareholding in Gaumont-British, the major theater chain–studio complex in the British Isles. He began reshuffling his staff, putting the indispensable J. J. Cohn in charge of B-picture production. He was pleased to confirm Samuel Marx's role also as producer of low-budget films.

Marx had made an interesting discovery: in New York, he had seen a play, *Skidding*, by Aurania Rouverol, who had cowritten the Joan Crawford vehicle *Dance, Fools, Dance*. Marx was impressed with this warm and sentimental work, which dealt with the North Carolinian Judge James Hardy, the judge's wife and their wholesome, rapidly growing, all-American family. Marx foresaw the property's potential, and Mayer authorized him to hire Kay Van Riper to do the script. Miss Van Riper was confined to a wheelchair, suffering from arthritis, sciatica and other medical problems. But she brought off a good script, which would soon be enacted by Lionel Barrymore, Spring Byington, Sara Haden, Julie Haydon and Eric Linden, with Mickey Rooney as the young and ebullient Andy Hardy. Mayer liked the concept, and took a keen personal interest in the making of the film, directed by George B. Seitz.

\*    \*    \*

Irving Thalberg's will was probated that winter. Most of his fortune went to Norma Shearer; it was whittled down after heavy estate taxes and other deductions to a little over $2 million. He had managed to hide to the end the secret settlement in the Fox deal of 1929 which had earned him $325,000. Years later, Samuel Marx discovered the $75,000 settlement Thalberg had officially received and informed Norma Shearer, who doubted that her husband would have hidden money from her. Her business manager confirmed the truth, but neither she nor Marx found out about the remaining sum.

On January 1, 1937, Mayer, instead of giving his customary New Year's Day party, was aboard a train for a three-week visit to New York and Florida for meetings with Nicholas Schenck, with whom he enjoyed an armed truce for the good of the studio. He fell ill with a cold in Manhattan; visited daily by Howard Strickling, he insisted on continuing telephone discussions with Schenck from his suite at the Sherry Netherland. He was in touch with London, where Ben Goetz and Bob Ritchie were hard at work setting up production of feature films at M.G.M.'s Elstree Studios near London. Benny Thau was due to sail two weeks later. On January 22, Mayer left to stay with the Schencks at Miami Beach for ten days. While there, he was in touch with the West Coast, where much argument went on over the title of the Andy Hardy picture; finally, publicist Frank Whitbeck came up with A Family Affair.

On February 15, Selznick International Pictures assumed a shareholding in the RKO-Pathé Studio, with its sixty acres of property in Culver City. Mayer invested money in this arrangement, another shrewd way of increasing his power, in addition to his interests, via the Chase Bank, in 20th Century-Fox and United Artists. The new plant would call itself Selznick International Pictures Studio. Mayer had a celebration dinner at his house for Irene and David, for whom his respect had much increased.

The Academy Awards took place at the Biltmore Bowl on March 4, 1937. Mayer learned the results of the ballot at 6:00 P.M.; in those days, the information was customarily announced at a press conference. He was pleased (despite her politics) to learn that Luise Rainer was chosen as Best Actress for The Great Ziegfeld, but he was dismayed to discover later that she was not in the audience. Howard Strickling was dispatched from the Bowl to her home in Brentwood. After a hair-raising drive, he burst in and told her the news.

Clifford Odets said she shouldn't go; the business of Oscars was a capitalistic mistake. Strickling insisted. In tears, she put on a smart gown; Odets accompanied her, though she asked him not to. When they arrived at the Biltmore, they drove around arguing as to whether they would go in or not, until, at last, they walked in at ten-thirty.

George Jessel, as master of ceremonies, made a major mistake: Bette Davis, as previous award winner, was supposed to introduce Miss Rainer; Jessel introduced her instead. Miss Davis was furious; she stormed into the press room afterward, berating Jessel. Miss Rainer complained that she had to repeat her acceptance speech for the reporters. Turning, sweetly annoyed, to director Frank Capra, she said, "Why don't you direct this?"

There were gratifying moments that evening. Mayer insisted that Robert Z. Leonard, who had not been given an award as director of *The Great Ziegfeld*, should take a bow when Mayer was given the Academy Award for Best Picture. He summoned its producer, Hunt Stromberg, to the stage; Stromberg, in turn, told the audience that Mayer had ordered $250,000 added to the budget to allow for the splendid and elaborate dance sequences. Frank Capra introduced, for the first time, the Irving Thalberg Award to "encourage the pride, the fortitude, the good taste and tolerance that Thalberg put into pictures." He added movingly, "[The award] is to keep permanent [Thalberg's] message: the stars brighten the night; the laughter of children is a message to the ear."

A few nights later, Mayer hosted a *Great Ziegfeld* party, at which he, with great consideration, gave his Oscar to Hunt Stromberg and awarded the guests with miniature Oscars of their own.

In April, Mayer was able to persuade the still-depressed Norma Shearer to sign a four-picture contract, starting with *Marie Antoinette*. On May 7, he hosted over a thousand guests at a national sales convention at the Ambassador Hotel. That evening, on an M.G.M. studio sound stage, he personally emceed with Sophie Tucker, a fifteen-act vaudeville and musical floor show, studded with stars. Judy Garland sang "Dear Mr. Gable," dedicating the song to her idol; Ronald Colman, Elizabeth Allan and Reginald Owen were applauded as representatives of England, and could hardly restrain their giggles; "Let the Lion Roar" was sung, vigorously, by the studio choir, which gave a rendition of "Yankee Doodle Dandy," rewritten as "Yankee Doodle L.B."

Next day, Mayer hired Louis K. Sidney, director of Loew's radio station WHN, New York, to come to the coast and start a house radio program including all the M.G.M. stars except for Garbo and Shearer.

A striking new presence at the studio that year was the imposing Lillian Burns. Mayer imported her from the poverty row studio Republic to train inexperienced actors and actresses in the art of playing for the cameras, with a particular emphasis on preparing them for screen tests. He had first met her at Edie's wedding in 1930. Tiny, forceful, with a dynamic, somewhat exaggerated theatrical presence and mannerisms that occasionally reminded people of Bette Davis, she was in her thirties at the time and destined to become a Power.

With remarkable chutzpah, this daughter of Hungarian immigrants, born Lillian Sultzar, had based her entire knowledge of acting on nothing more than going to the theater and studying performances. She had asserted herself in an audience as a young woman, in 1923, when she had seen the great Judith Anderson in her American stage debut of "Peter Weston." In the play Miss Anderson portrayed the daughter of a factory owner; she learns that the man who has impregnated her has been shot dead by her brother. When, at the end of the second act, Miss Anderson screamed as only she could scream, Lillian Sultzar screamed with her. Shaken by the incident, Dame Judith never forgot it.

Arriving in Hollywood, Miss Burns, as she was then known, turned up at Republic's casting office. Asked if she intended to act, she replied, without blinking, "No. I will teach acting." The will became the deed: she did just that. Now Mayer let her take charge of his fledgling flock. He instinctively felt she could do what she claimed. "Get Burns!" became the rallying cry when a performer was in trouble. She sometimes would even usurp a director's prerogatives by taking performers aside and giving them advice. This special training had a mixed response from the studio.

At the time of this writing, in 1992, Lillian Burns remains friend, teacher, supporter, detractor and admirer of many M.G.M. alumni. Her technique was more effective than anything else in improving deportment, the use of significant gesture, the weight with which an eyelash flickered or a hand picked up a glass.

Mayer's first meeting with her was appropriately dramatic. He decided to use his protégé Betty Jaynes as a test case. He asked Lillian Burns, "When will she be ready to do a picture?" Lillian Burns replied, "Never." "What do you mean, 'Never'?" Mayer said sharply. "She's working with you, isn't she?" Miss Burns replied, "Yes. And she's very nice and her voice is lovely, but she's never going to be an actress."

Mayer expostulated. And then Lillian Burns said, "You'd better be careful of the director you choose for her, because he will have to have all the patience in the world!" Mayer flipped the switch on his dictaphone and snapped at his secretary, Jeanette Spooner, "Tell the barber I'll be down in five minutes!" That was Miss Burns's dismissal. Ida Koverman warned Miss Burns that she had better get her things together as she would be taken off by security at any minute. As it turned out, Mayer was impressed by her courage, realized finally she was right about Betty Jaynes and kept her on for the rest of his career at the studio.

Then, in the third week of May, Mayer fell ill. He apparently had a double hernia. To avoid local publicity and adverse industry comment, he was taken by car to San Francisco for an operation. He recovered quickly, and continued plans to travel to London in the late summer.

In June, Jean Harlow also fell ill, at her Beverly Hills home, with the same sickness that had preceded Mayer's mother's death: cholecystitis, or acute inflammation of the gall bladder. There was much gossip that the real cause of her condition was that she had become pregnant by William Powell and that her mother, a Christian Scientist, had refused to allow her to go to one of the reliable Hollywood abortionists; instead, Mrs. Bello had used knitting needles on her.

Whatever the cause, Jean Harlow was unable to return to work on her new picture, Saratoga, and another actress had to be brought in to double for her. Mayer is not on record as having been to see her, which may indicate that he believed the stories about the abortion and was furious.

On June 7, the actress began to fail. She had two blood transfusions and an intravenous injection; the fire department arrived with an inhalator, but it was too late. With no antibiotics available in those days, there was nothing that could help her, and at 11:37 A.M., at the Good Samaritan Hospital, she died. The Bellos, William Powell and her two doctors were at her bedside. The official cause was given as acute circulatory collapse following nephritis and uremic poisoning. She was only twenty-six years old. Saratoga was finished with a double in Harlow's place.

Just ten days later, Jeanette MacDonald married the actor Gene Raymond in the best-attended wedding in a decade. The Mayers were there. Staged at the Wilshire Episcopal Church, the nuptials took place amid dazzling displays of flowers and were followed by an elaborate party at the Beverly Wilshire Hotel. Nelson Eddy sang "I Love You Truly" and "Oh, Perfect Love."

That month, Mayer was in conference with the leading British producer Michael Balcon, who had been head of Gaumont-British for five years and whom Mayer now put in charge of British M.G.M.

The reason Mayer decided to make pictures in England is clear. Under the terms of the 1928 Cinematograph Films Act, the United Kingdom Board of Trade called for foreign film companies to make, or subsidize the production of, a quota of pictures using British staff and certain players. Meetings took place in London through the summer months of 1937, between officials of the U.S. embassy and representatives of the Foreign Office, the Motion Picture Producers and Distributors Association, and Sir William Brown, permanent under-secretary of the Board of

Trade. Pressure on Whitehall from M.G.M.'s reliable servant, U.S. Secretary of State Cordell Hull, resulted in a slacking of demands for M.G.M. to finance a full twenty percent of local production. Now, M.G.M. would have to make only a small handful of British-American movies over the next few years.

Michael Balcon was a difficult, tense man, fussy and irritable, but Mayer felt he was the best for the job and, typically, was prepared to overlook every disadvantage, including Balcon's dislike of him, in the interests of M.G.M. Balcon discussed with Mayer a treatment, written by Sidney Gilliat, for the first M.G.M. British picture, *A Yank at Oxford*, which would star Robert Taylor. Several writers, including Hugh Walpole, had tried to lick the subject: it was the story of a brash, small-town American runner who invades the sacred precincts of the British university and infuriates everybody by his overweening pride and capacity to win race after race. It was a good idea for a picture, designed to illustrate the friendly competition that existed between Britain and the United States and the necessity for a transatlantic brotherhood. Mayer was warm, courteous and hospitable to Balcon, asking him, at length, about possible subjects for future use in England. But the relationship was never comfortable; Balcon resented the fact that when Mayer asked him to dinner, it was a royal command. When Balcon scheduled dinner with Frances Marion, Mayer instructed him to come to his house at Santa Monica instead, called Miss Marion and said that Balcon would not be coming to her home. Balcon was furious; he escaped toward midnight by explaining that he had no ability at cards, so was unable to join the traditional after-dinner bridge game.

Mayer compelled him to come to the combined July 4 Independence Day and birthday party, given each year by Clarence Brown at Brown's San Fernando Valley ranch. Clark Gable was first to arrive with Carole Lombard, with whom he was deeply involved. Over 150 guests cheered as a naval escort ceremonially piped in the arrival of a giant birthday cake mounted on an imitation yacht, surrounded by gardenias. Mayer threw another party for Hunt Stromberg, who, exhausted from overwork, was now rapidly becoming a drug addict.

Balcon was astonished when he received a letter asking him to subscribe, along with all other studio associates, not only to the cost of the party, but to a vacation for Stromberg in Europe. He had to write a check, which was added to several dozen others given to Stromberg at the festivities in the Irving Thalberg bungalow. Mayer was ill that day; when he reached the bungalow, he was about to pick up a bundle of checks and hand them over to Stromberg when he suddenly fainted. Frank Orsatti ran to find Dr. Edward B. Jones. But he had forgotten that his appearance at the door was supposed to be a signal that Herbert Stothart's studio orchestra, which was waiting outside, would play "For He's a Jolly Good Fellow." The music echoed through the bungalow as Mayer lay unconscious on the floor.

The days were crowded that month. Mayer was busy having Cedric Gibbons design a new office in the soon-to-be-built executive building, with an all-white decor and a semicircular desk in emulation of Mussolini. He saw a polished cut of *The Firefly*, Hunt Stromberg's handsome production of the Rudolph Friml operetta, with Jeanette MacDonald, freed from Nelson Eddy, visibly enjoying herself as a Spanish spy during the Napoleonic wars. Allan Jones was her handsome costar, provoking Eddy's jealousy and fury at being replaced. Even though Jones's days at the studio were numbered, Mayer was delighted with his performance, especially his rendition of "The Donkey Serenade," which would soon be high on record charts.

Mayer was delighted with preliminary work on *Captains Courageous*. He was even able to tolerate the presence in the cast of a recent studio acquisition, Melvyn Douglas. He disapproved of Douglas who, along with Fredric March, was leading the left-wing faction in the Screen Actors' Guild, against the powerful right-wing faction headed by the president, Robert Montgomery. Montgomery was about to appear in Mayer's uncharacteristic production of *Night Must Fall*, from the play by Emlyn Williams, in which he would play a murderous psychopath. It had been a sensation with Williams a star on the stage. This was still further evidence that, when box office considerations were being weighed, Mayer would certainly make any picture, regardless of subject matter. It turned out to be one of the finest movies of the year.

In addition to the schism in the Screen Actors' Guild, there were perpetual problems for Mayer in the matter of the Screen Writers' Guild. With the Spanish Civil War in progress, the political conflicts within that organization were major. Before Thalberg died, the splinter group headed by Jim McGuinness was in trouble, overwhelmed by the sheer numbers of writers who were opposed to Franco and Hitler.[2]

On July 9, Mayer received a telephone call at his office. His older sister Yetta, with whom he had had only the slightest contact in recent years, had arrived at the downtown depot with her daughter Irene. They were on their way to San Jose for a conference on Rosicrucianism. Mayer sent a car for them; due to a misunderstanding, the driver didn't find them for several hours. Although Mayer was scheduled to leave the following morning for New York, he instantly found a place for them.

[2] Samuel Marx, under contract to Samuel Goldwyn, had found himself in an awkward middle position in these conflicts.

They stayed with his sister Ida, for one miserable night. She was too tidy for them; when they got up to go to the bathroom she made the beds behind them, and when they got up from the couch she fixed the pillows. They moved to a hotel. Later, they returned and settled in Los Angeles.

With Howard Strickling and Joe Schenck, Mayer took off in good spirits on the tenth. For the first time he had the kitchen of the Santa Fe Chief stocked with his own selection of prime beef and fresh produce, though he still did not indulge in the luxury, enjoyed by many millionaires in those days, of a private car. In his briefcase he had a record of the studio's net profits for the past seven months: almost $12 million.

He went directly to Nicholas and Pansy Schenck's home at Great Neck, New York, for a week's stay before his ship, the Italian vessel *Rex*, sailed for Naples. Joe Schenck, Benny Thau, who had joined him in Manhattan, and Howard Strickling sailed with him on the eighteenth. It was a rough crossing, which Mayer weathered with his customary good seamanship. Arriving in Naples, he took a train to Rome, where he had meetings at which he discussed the producer Hal Roach, who released pictures through M.G.M., with Vittorio Mussolini, the Italian dictator's twenty-one-year-old son. For some time, Mayer and Nicholas Schenck had been plagued by difficulties with fascist Italy.

In an effort to build up his own industry, Mussolini's film controllers were exercising severe sanctions against foreign pictures. Secretary of State Cordell Hull himself sent an anguished letter on the subject to his ambassador in Rome on October 9, 1936. Only sixteen million lire could be exported to Hollywood in a given year. The MPPA and M.G.M.'s Laudy Lawrence in Paris fought hard against these confiscatory restrictions. Will Hays telephoned the State Department in November of that year, painfully, even drastically, concerned; he went to Rome and saw Mussolini and the Pope. There were meetings of film company representatives with the commercial attaché of the U.S. embassy in Rome; there was talk of all Hollywood closing up shop. The State Department was involved to the hilt; then, as always, it was the servant of the film industry. In a last-ditch effort to save the day, on November 27, 1936, the acting secretary of state, David Moor, cabled the Rome embassy: CONGRATULATIONS ON BRINGING ABOUT A SATISFACTORY CONCLUSION TO THE MATTER; NO MORE TARIFFS, NO MORE CURRENCY CONTROL. But red tape delayed matters, until Hal Roach made his move.

Roach and Vittorio Mussolini had formed a company known as RAM (Roach-and-Mussolini) to make a series of five movies based on grand opera to be released by M.G.M. At that time, as has been noted, it was not uncommon for American business leaders, including the heads of movie studios, to express an unabashed admiration for Mussolini. Unlike Hitler, he was not taking a strong line on Jews; he was considered to be a bulwark against Communism; his efficiency provoked envy and admiration. Mayer was pleased to secure the deal, on behalf of Nicholas Schenck, and then proceeded to Bucharest, Budapest and Vienna, to Carlsbad for the cure, and to Berlin, seeking out opera stars whom Roach and Mussolini would find valuable. He would link up with the two men when they arrived in Hollywood in the fall.

Mayer had another purpose in his European expedition. He had reconnected with Ad Schulberg, who had agency offices in Hollywood, New York and London. Of a strong liberal persuasion, Mrs. Schulberg now represented as agent a number of significant European Jewish and non-Jewish writers and actors. She saw Mayer, who was always looking for talent, as a way of rescuing those artists who might be threatened by Hitler in the future. She was careful not to emphasize to Mayer the liberal leanings which some of them showed; by stressing that they were Jewish, or sympathetic to Jews, she ingeniously ensured his support.

In Vienna, he got wind from Bob Ritchie of the beautiful Austrian actress Hedwig (Hedy) Kiesler, who had made a stir playing nude scenes in the film *Ecstasy*. She had been charming in two intelligently written comedies, both in German. He made a note to see her films when he got to London. He also noted, on Mrs. Schulberg's suggestion, the name of one of her clients, the director Reinhold Schunzel, who had directed the charming cross-dressing comedy *Viktor und Viktoria*. Its star, Renata Muller, was under investigation by the Nazi propagandist Joseph Goebbels for having a Jewish lover; later, he had her murdered, announcing her death as a suicide. Among others Mayer found on his travels were Ilona Hajmassy (Massey), a sultry, skillful Hungarian singer; and the Warsaw-born Estonian soprano Miliza Korjus.

When Mayer arrived in London from Germany on August 25, he had much to discuss with Ad Schulberg. He also braced himself for meetings with Michael Balcon; production had begun on *A Yank at Oxford*, and Balcon was proving as recalcitrant as ever. Mayer engaged him in a screaming match, deliberately standing at a window of Balcon's office so that everyone outside would hear. He was not happy with Balcon's casting of Vivien Leigh as a flighty, flirtatious married woman who shows a romantic interest in the American athlete played by Robert Taylor. But it was too late to change the casting, and it turned out that Balcon was right anyway.

Mayer, at the suggestion of Ad Schulberg, went to see a modest costume drama entitled *Old Music*, by Keith Winter, showing at the St. James's Theater. The star was the attractive twenty-eight-year-old Scottish-Irish actress Greer Garson, who was a graduate with honors of both British and French universities. She had risen from the ranks of the Birmingham Repertory Theater to appear in a succession of West End plays, most of which were unsuccessful but did not tarnish her career. In 1933 she had made a disastrous marriage with a British civil servant on leave from India; they lived together less than thirty days, then separated.

Mayer was fascinated by her. She had poise, a musical speaking voice and a striking air of composure and dignity. Her red hair was exquisitely coiffed; she wore her clothes magnificently. Always an anglophile from his early years as a British subject in Canada, he knew that it was important to have a major British performer added to his studio roster.

In addition to these considerations, he was attracted to Miss Garson, who was very much his type; but he was sensible enough not to indicate this, at least for the time being. After the performance, he sat in his car outside while Bob Ritchie went to her dressing room to ask her if she would come to dinner. This was a very odd approach; it was customary to contact an actor or actress through the theater management. The stage door keeper wouldn't admit Ritchie and told Miss Garson, in his cockney accent, "Mr. Myer is waitin'." She thought it was a man selling silk stockings; she said he was to come back after the matinee the next day.

The doorkeeper corrected himself: it was Louis B. Mayer and his party. Miss Garson asked demurely if Mr. Mayer and those of his party had ladies with them. The doorkeeper said, "Yes." Then Bob Ritchie came in. "Where would you like to go?" "The Savoy Grill." Miss Garson remembers the conversation to this day.

At the Grill, Mayer was present with Ben and Goldie Goetz, the Michael Balcons and others. He asked Miss Garson if she had an agent. She said she did not. A manager? She had none. Mayer announced he would go to her apartment in Conduit Street next day to meet with her mother, Nina, who handled her career. He was always, since Anita Stewart days, great with mothers. That arrangement made, he danced with Greer Garson. He took out a ten-dollar bill to tip the waiter; she had never seen one. She asked if she could have one as a souvenir; tightfisted as ever, he gave her a single dollar bill instead.

Next day, Mayer arrived at her apartment for a late morning sherry; he sipped it gingerly and hated it. He succeeded in captivating both mother and daughter during that brief and happy visit. He straightforwardly offered Greer Garson an M.G.M. contract, and told Nina that he would be very happy to give her a job as a script consultant. She was delighted, but Garson was still unsure whether she would go ahead. It was very rare in Mayer's experience for an actress to hesitate at such an opportunity. There was a reason.

The year before, Douglas Fairbanks, Jr., had arranged for her to have a test for another picture, in which Fairbanks planned to appear. She had hated the way she looked in the test, and had become convinced she wasn't photogenic.

Mayer was certain the test had been badly done, and that, given the correct treatment of his own special test directors and cinematographers, she would emerge beautifully. He finally overcame Miss Garson's objections, but it was mid-October before she actually signed the contract. With his customary instinct for great talent, he did not hesitate for a moment to sign her. But it was a disappointment to Ad Schulberg, who had encouraged him to see her, that Mike Levee, not Mrs. Schulberg, became Greer Garson's agent.

He spent as much time as possible on location with *A Yank at Oxford;* wherever he went, his chauffeur had to fight through crowds of screaming women, who tried to clutch at Robert Taylor. Taylor complained to Mayer; conservative and reserved, very much in love with Barbara Stanwyck, who was back in Hollywood, he did not take advantage of the female fans who made themselves available to him. Mayer respected him for that.

Ad Schulberg reminded Mayer of Hedy Kiesler's presence in London. Bob Ritchie also mentioned Miss Kiesler. The Austrian actress had fled her husband, the Jewish munitions tycoon Fritz Mandl, who had become an Honorary Aryan and supported Hitler. (Honorary Aryan was a special status created by Goebbels for Jewish people who served Hitler personally.) She told the writer Roy Moseley that, on one occasion, she was horrified to hear Hitler talking to her husband in the dining room. This shock, following other revelations of Mandl's political involvement and his all-consuming possessiveness, drove her to a drastic step. She escaped, cramming her jewelry into a small suitcase. When she arrived in London, she was forced to sell much of it. She met Bob Ritchie, who encouraged her to meet with Mayer. She went to Claridge's Hotel, where Mayer was staying; he told her he had seen *Ecstasy,* but that she would have to make decent films in America. Struggling with an inadequate command of English, she replied that she had been coerced into the movie and that she wanted to prove herself as an actress.

Pressed by Ritchie, Mayer saw her potential. Her looks were exquisite; she had perfect breasts. He seems not to have been convinced that she had acting ability; instead of testing her, which would have been the normal procedure, he suggested to her that she should pay her own fare to Hollywood, at which time he would start her at $125 a week for six months. If she proved herself, her option would be exercised at a higher salary. Already famous in Europe, and of a strong character, Miss Kiesler knew her value and rejected the suggestion at once. Mayer was impressed by her spirit but did not revise the offer. He left the matter at that.

Another significant meeting in London was with the genial and suave, if sometimes arrogant, director Victor Saville, who, by the age of forty, had established a reputation for making movies of quality. Mayer asked Saville to breakfast at Claridge's; Saville impressed him immediately. Disaffected after leaving Gaumont-British, in which M.G.M. still had a fourteen percent share, and after that United Artists, Saville had decided to strike out on his own and had just bought, outbidding M.G.M., the A. J. Cronin novel *The Citadel*, about the rise of an idealistic doctor from a mining town to London. Mayer was impressed by the fact that Saville had found sufficient money, and had sufficient vision, to buy this property.

The contract with Saville was one of the most important of Mayer's career, and worth all the travail that preceded it. Saville not only brought *The Citadel* with him, but Enid Bagnold's *National Velvet*, a story after Mayer's own heart, strongly resembling his early success *In Old Kentucky*, about a teenage girl who wins the Derby disguised as a male jockey.

In the meantime, Saville was approached by Sir John Pratt, brother of Boris Karloff and high official of the Ministry of Information, and Alexander Korda, famous producer and agent of the British Secret Intelligence Service, MI6, to undertake a particular task. Knowing that he was going to Hollywood, the two men sought his support in infiltrating the Hollywood establishment. Saville was to determine who was pro- or anti-British; he was to seek to influence Mayer and other executives at the studio to make pro-British, anti-Hitler pictures, he was to disrupt the policy which still led to supplying private prints to Hitler and Mussolini, and to maintaining the M.G.M. offices in Berlin; and he was to develop projects that would in effect be anti-German propaganda. This secret mission Saville would carry out under Mayer's nose and without Mayer's slightest suspicion. Even when the assignment was exposed by the isolationist Senator Nye in a Senate committee hearing on moving picture and radio propaganda on September 5, 1941, the press buried the matter.

While in London, Mayer signed a new contract which made him, at well over $1 million a year, the highest-paid executive in the United States. At the same time, he met with his former enemy Adolph Zukor and other Hollywood representatives to fight the new quota system that would restrict the importing of American product. After numerous further meetings, Mayer, still in a good frame of mind, went to Paris to receive the Légion d'Honneur from the president of France.

On September 30, Mayer sailed from New York aboard the *Normandie*; Margaret had joined him from a sanitarium in France. To complicate matters, Ad Schulberg was also in his party. With him were Benny Thau, Howard Strickling and the writer Walter Reisch, whom he had also signed. Hedy Kiesler, with little or no luggage, had changed her mind about coming to Hollywood at her own expense. Using the name Hedwig Mandl, she boarded the vessel with Grisha Goluboff, whom Mayer told the press was her personal Russian protégé. Miss Kiesler's beauty captivated everyone; many were familiar with her from *Ecstasy*.

In an unpublished diary entry, Cecil Beaton gave a vivid account of the people aboard—the people that counted, that is: Cole Porter ("Tired, aging, snobbish Puck"), Danielle Darrieux ("Pretty but insipid"), Sonja Henie ("Top heavy suety blonde, wears huge, overpowering hats") and "a dark woman who was naked in a film called *Ecstasy* dancing with Louis B. Mayer—porpoise—nanny."

Just out from Le Havre, the vessel lost a propeller and had to return for repairs. Mayer gave a party to assuage his entourage, and Hedy Kiesler, with her "protégé," was included. Mayer was impressed with the effect she had on the male passengers and decided to sign her to a contract. He offered her seven years with options, with the proviso that she learn to speak English.

Two days out of Southampton, the ship ran into a storm. Mayer summoned Walter Reisch to his cabin, quite ignoring Reisch's state of seasickness, and discussed Hedy Kiesler, who, he felt, needed to be rechristened. He asked Reisch to come up with something. Next day, Reisch, Strickling, Benny Thau and Bob Ritchie met around the Ping-Pong table on A-deck, conferring while the regular players were forced to quit. After much discussion, Mayer remembered the most beautiful of the actresses he had employed: the now dead Barbara La Marr, from the old Selig Zoo days. He would rename Hedy Kiesler Hedy Lamarr. It was obvious she would have to have a proper wardrobe if he was going to announce her as a major discovery on arrival in New York. She had boarded the vessel with only one gray tailored suit and one pair of gloves, and had almost no money in her handbag. Mayer sent her to E-deck, where Dior and Chanel had boutiques. She was allowed to charge her clothes to the studio; she was also permitted to buy a matching set of expensive suitcases.

When the *Normandie* docked in New York, the press was dazzled by

Hedy Lamarr, and Howard Dietz, head of publicity, was there to promote her to the limit. Mayer gave a press conference on deck, mentioning all of the prominent figures he had hired. He already had rechristened Ilona Hajmassy Ilona Massey. He had cabled Bob Ritchie to clinch deals on Miliza Korjus and the Austrian actress Rosa Stradner.

Mayer arrived in Hollywood by plane on October 2. Due to a misunderstanding of which airport he would appear at, only Robert Vogel, of M.G.M.'s foreign division, was there to greet him. He returned to Santa Monica, and thence to the studio, to find a very difficult situation on his hands. Hal Roach and Vittorio Mussolini had turned up—just after the Italian dictator made a triumphal visit to Hitler in Berlin. Mussolini was staying with Roach at his house in Beverly Hills. Neighbors protested; letters, postcards and phone calls poured in from prominent Jewish citizens threatening to boycott RAM (and Roach/M.G.M.) pictures. The Anti-Nazi League, headed by Fredric March and James Cagney, held a meeting on the night of the Roach–Mussolini arrival, stating that every effort must be made to have the Italian dictator's son expelled. A handful of right-wing, pro-fascist Hollywood figures received the young Mussolini. These included Walt Disney, Gary Cooper, Winfield Sheehan, Will Hays and William Randolph Hearst. C. L. Willard, special representative of the State Department, turned up to report on the matter to the head office in Washington, D.C.

Fredric March, James Cagney, Luise Rainer and other anti-fascist members of the Screen Actors' Guild (much to the pretended annoyance of Robert Montgomery) staged a protest demonstration at Roach's studio, which bordered on M.G.M. Jimmie Fidler, popular Hollywood gossip on the CBS Radio network, had denounced Vittorio Mussolini. Jewish newspapers called for movie people to boycott Roach. They headlined the fact that Vittorio had written a book on his bombing of citizens of Ethiopia during his father's invasion of that country, and the fact that his brother was flying for Franco in Spain. The Fredric March faction took a full-page advertisement in *Variety*, quoting statements by Vittorio glorifying war and denouncing Roach for inviting him. Vittorio was hissed in a neighborhood theater when his face appeared in a newsreel. Black political figures shouted against him in meetings in downtown Los Angeles.

On October 5, three days after Mayer arrived, the controversy reached a peak. C. L. Willard wrote to the State Department:

> The whole thing seems to be the noisy anti-Nazi Jewish outfit [in action] and Roach is plenty frightened . . . Personally, I don't think it looks so good, and I'm afraid that [Benito] Mussolini will be pretty sore about

having his son stampeded out of the country. [Vittorio will] leave Los Angeles by plane tomorrow a.m.

Mayer's position was intolerable. The deal with Roach had been sealed. There was no question: M.G.M. was behind it. The hatred and vilification descending on Roach and Mussolini could only reflect on him. He laid low, concentrating only on pictures in production and on signing the few remaining contracts with European refugee artists that were needed.

He was forced to a decision. Supported by Nicholas Schenck, he canceled the deal with Roach, just after Vittorio Mussolini left town. With the cooperation of Howard Dietz and Howard Strickling, Mayer played up his encouragement of Jewish immigrant artists, ungenerously failing to mention Ad Schulberg.

Mayer was involved in meetings with his executive staff, which resulted in the cancellation of an invitation by the MPPA to the Duke and Duchess of Windsor, who were to have stayed with William Randolph Hearst and were to have been given an M.G.M. studio tour. In view of the Windsors' Nazi connections, the visit was no longer desirable. But, in secret, Mayer had meetings with Georg Gyssling, Nazi consul general in Los Angeles, to discuss how best certain pictures with an anti-German bias might be presented without offense to the Nazi government. Both Nicholas and Joseph Schenck were present at these discussions, held at an office that would soon be replaced by Cedric Gibbons's Mussolini imitation.

There was much weighing of the possibility that David O. Selznick might rejoin the studio. Jock Whitney, Selznick's financial partner, seemed to be in favor of the move, but Selznick, tense as always over charges of nepotism, finally broke the arrangement. Mayer contracted with Warner Brothers' director Mervyn LeRoy. LeRoy would move into M.G.M. on February 15 with his own unit, a unique arrangement in which he would be responsible only to Mayer. LeRoy was married to Harry Warner's daughter Doris, and was therefore hesitant in signing the deal; he would bring with him a number of artists under personal contract, including the young and promising Lana Turner. LeRoy had been loaned out to Metro to direct *Tugboat Annie* with Marie Dressler and Wallace Beery, and ever since Mayer had wanted him. Despite the fact that LeRoy's *They Won't Forget*, a searing study of prejudice in a Southern town, was no more Mayer's cup of tea than M.G.M.'s own *Fury*, Mayer saw potential in LeRoy. He had deeply admired LeRoy's picture *The World Changes*, a powerful story of the rise of a Chicago meat baron; Paul Muni and Mary Astor had been outstanding in it. The dynamic

director, known, with his stubby physique and permanent cigar, as Little
Caesar, from the title of his own gangster picture with Edward G. Robin-
son, soon proved to be one of the finest of all Mayer's resident craftsmen.
His talent would flower irresistibly in the years ahead.

## CHAPTER EIGHTEEN

# 1938-1939

IT IS TIME NOW to pause again and consider Louis B. Mayer as a presence and a man. He is fifty-two now, a little plumper.

He has recently overseen the building of a colossal, Italianate white structure, which will become known as the Irving Thalberg Building. His office is enormous, far removed from the modest rooms which William Randolph Hearst had complained about. An imitation of Mussolini's headquarters, with wall-to-wall white carpeting, it has a raised, semicircular desk, decorated with buttons and filled with numerous secret drawers, so positioned on its carpeted dais that the visitor is placed conveniently below eye level.[1] There are also a private elevator, a conference room and an elaborate bathroom.

Mayer's eyes are more intense than ever, concentrating, in still brilliant darkness, the full force of his personality. As he stares directly at you, his face is normally sallow, but flushes rapidly when he is angry or excited. He has two secretaries, Jeanette Spooner and the recently hired Sue Ream, who later will become the wife of the director Norman Taurog; both are inferior in position to Ida Koverman, who has a handsome outer office of her own. Not only are they always, by his requirement, to be impeccably dressed, but the stars who visit him must be as well: a crooked tie or creased jacket irritates him; and when Joan Crawford comes to the office to join him for a private conference office lunch in a swimsuit and bathrobe, he will send her home to change.

His routine seldom varies. In the morning, at 7:30, he rides horseback with Howard Strickling in Culver City, at the Dupuy Stables, or at the beach with his old friend, lawyer Lester Roth. He walks briskly for thirty minutes, his chauffeur following him. He arrives at the studio in his

---

[1] One haughty actress from New York walked into that office on an afternoon and said to its imposing occupant, "Don't you usually stand when a lady enters the room?" "Madam, I am standing," the diminutive executive replied.

riding clothes, takes the private elevator to his office, showers and changes into one of several impeccably tailored suits hanging in the closet. He always talks to Nicholas Schenck, when Schenck is in New York, in those early hours.

Jeanette and Sue have his appointment calendar laid out on his immaculate desk. He looks at his mother's picture and says a silent prayer to her; he believes she is looking down on him. He has a little book, *The Daily Word*, published by Unity, of St. Louis, Missouri, before him. It has a thought for the day; he follows that thought.

He makes phone calls and notes until 10:30, when his secretaries come in; they will work with him until 8:30 P.M., or even later.

His energy is overwhelming; his secretaries will never see its equal in anyone. They can't keep up as, impatiently, he throws off political comments, criticisms, praise, tears, laughter, in a series of explosions. His temper can still terrorize and defeat.

If anyone wants a raise, he will weep; if a salary cut is called for, he will bemoan the problems of the studio.

He insists on absolute punctuality in visitors—to the second. God help them if they are late.

And what of his movie family, that troublesome brood of stars with their giant egos, their tantrums, their love affairs? Clark Gable has at last found a measure of happiness, with the antic Carole Lombard; her joking, irritating, challenging presence in his life puts Gable in his place, makes him acknowledge an equal. Joan Crawford is in conflict with Franchot Tone, whose cultivated intelligence is too much for her, now that the attraction of his looks and charm and famous sexual skill have worn off. Garbo is still in transit, and is as distant, rude, pathologically afraid of people as ever; she is between affairs in 1938. Wallace Beery still flies his own plane with reckless courage, driving the studio front office into transports of despair.

Nelson Eddy and Jeanette MacDonald sing at each other in love duets. Hedy Lamarr has arrived in town with no project ready for her; Walter Wanger will borrow her for *Algiers*, which earns Mayer $1,000 a week over the $500 he is paying her. Mayer is prepared to overlook the fact that *Algiers* is written by a Communist, John Howard Lawson, whom he let go after *Treasure Island*. He has found a place for Ilona Massey in *Rosalie*; his French discovery, Jacqueline Laurent, turns up in *Judge Hardy's Children*, then goes home. Maureen O'Sullivan is lovely in *A Yank at Oxford* and *The Crowd Roars*, and still plays the only possible Jane to Weissmuller's Tarzan. Her marriage to John Farrow is rocky; he is a bully, a sadist, a fascist.

Mayer's executives—the skirt-chasing, insatiable Benny Thau; the bulldoggy Eddie Mannix; the smooth, secretive Howard Strickling; tough J. J. Cohn—all are firmly in place. Hunt Stromberg is suffering from drug addiction; Bernie Hyman is more expert and energetic than ever. And the directors, W. S. Van Dyke, Clarence Brown, Sidney Franklin and the rest, are as busy as stevedores.

Mayer's relationship with his family is still tense but warily respectful. He is almost never seen at David and Irene Selznick's mansion, and their Sunday lunch parties conflict with his own. He remains encouraging to the witty William and plaintive, sweet Edie Goetz and is pleased by the increasing excellence of 20th Century-Fox, and the exile of the hated (and now blatantly anti-Semitic and pro-Nazi) Winfield Sheehan. He is happy to see his nieces Mitzi and Ruth doing well as magazine writers and Jack a bright producer (*Yellow Jack*) at the studio; Yetta's daughter Irene is soon to be a stylist for Adrian. Although he can scarcely be said to approve of Hitler's increasingly anti-Jewish policies, he, as always, puts the interests of the studio ahead of any moral or political considerations and does not object to Schenck retaining, with an Aryan staff, the M.G.M. offices in Berlin. He authorizes the supply of personal prints of M.G.M. movies to Hitler and Mussolini, discontinuing this practice at the outset of World War II in Europe, and only because the dictators will fail to return the prints.[2]

In 1938, Mayer was more in charge of the production end of the studio than he had ever been. Following Thalberg's death, he had been delegating much of the responsibility to individual producers running units under the nominal supervision of Eddie Mannix. But increasingly, having sloughed off the residue of pictures that Thalberg had already authorized to be made, he had begun to set in motion projects of his own.

The studio was making sixty features a year, sixty percent of which were A pictures; Mayer was not fond of low-budget B pictures. An exception was the Andy Hardy series, reworked from the original platitudinous effort starring Lionel Barrymore. Late that fall of 1937, Mayer took an interest in George B. Seitz's *You're Only Young Once*, the sequel to *A Family Affair*, in which Lewis Stone, to whom he was still loyal, took over as Judge Hardy, Fay Holden, a British actress, became Mrs. Hardy and Mickey Rooney stayed on as Andy. The formula was continued, and Mayer insisted it be adhered to thenceforth. The benign but severe Judge Hardy would still punish an erring son or daughter with such treatments as going to bed at six at night or shoveling snow. His wife was patient, understanding and kitchen-bound. Young Andy was always

[2] Ironically, many pictures that Hitler saw and admired were banned officially by Goebbels.

in heat, but never asked more than a kiss of his girlfriends, and then with a degree of bashfulness. His pranks were innocent; if Mayer caught a scriptwriter introducing a scene in which Andy was rude to his mother, or refused to eat his dinner, he slashed a blue pencil through the lines.

He wanted to recapture the provincial, proper world he remembered, or misremembered, from his own childhood in St. John, New Brunswick. Jacob Mayer, strict, his word law, was not far removed from the correct Judge Hardy; Fay Holden came as close to Mayer's image of his mother as was possible for a gentile. He was reworking a nineteenth-century Jewish Family in twentieth-century WASP terms. Mayer was always impatient to see the rushes, whereas he would only watch finished footage on the other pictures. He would correct, suppress or irritate George P. Seitz and the producer, Carey Wilson.

Yet Mayer was not the model of rectitude he required the Hardys to be. He had found a new romantic interest: Beatrice Roberts. Brown-haired, blue-eyed, thirty-one, slender and pretty, Miss Roberts was of British descent. She was born in Belton, Texas, where she emerged as a promising dancer. She became a model in New York, her face so frequently seen on billboards that she was called "the most photographed girl in the world." She was Miss New York of 1925. She was in the musical *Oh, Please*, with Beatrice Lillie, moving to Hollywood in 1931. Mayer had noticed her when she appeared as a guest in a party scene in *San Francisco*; soon afterward, he began dating her. He fell in love with her; for years, she was the love of his life. She shared with him a passion for operettas and Viennese waltzes; she was an accomplished pianist, which, of course, appealed to him. He would like to have built her as a star, but his executive staff refused to believe she had acting ability and would not agree to her being cast in anything. Not even Mayer could force a producer to take on an actress. Miss Roberts accepted the situation, and Mayer insisted on keeping her under contract, loaning her out for picture after picture; when his old friend Conrad Nagel directed a feature picture, Mayer made sure that Beatrice Roberts was in it. He had an under-the-table arrangement with Universal to have her placed on semipermanent loan-out, and for years she appeared in Universal films as maids, nurses or secretaries, glimpsed for an instant; an attractive, fascinating dark presence, living out a ghostly career on the sidelines.

Much of January 1938 was occupied in trying to find a solution to script problems on *Three Comrades*, a version by F. Scott Fitzgerald and Edward Paramore of Erich Maria Remarque's celebrated novel of three young men in Germany in the wake of World War I. The movie starred Robert Taylor and Margaret Sullivan. Georg Gyssling was in frequent meetings with Joseph Breen, movie censor, insisting on a toning down of any and all inferences that the rabble of unemployed workers portrayed in the film could possibly be interpreted as nascent Nazis. In a memorandum dated January 22, Breen urged Mayer to give serious thought as to whether M.G.M. should make the picture at all, mentioning the company's distribution of movies in Germany; protests would surely come from Berlin. Gyssling wanted the script rewritten, and also for the good of the industry as a whole—that is, its dealings with the Nazis.

On January 27, Breen, prodded by Gyssling, held a meeting with Mayer, Eddie Mannix, executive Sam Katz, Benny Thau and producer Joe Mankiewicz, the result of which was that everyone (with, apparently, some protests from Mankiewicz) crumbled before Germany's wishes. Just to be sure, Breen sent a memo to Mayer that same night, reminding him of the agreement reached: there would be no suggestion of Nazi violence and terrorism; the burning of the books scene would be cut; all mention of Jews would be removed; the name Blumenthal would be changed; not one uniform would suggest the Nazis. As a result, the screenplay, rewritten by Mankiewicz, became mealymouthed, implying that the army of riffraff roaming the German city streets were Communists. Mayer, always mindful of the necessity not to aggravate foreign governments, yielded to this egregious pressure. Even after Joe Mankiewicz had done his worst, Georg Gyssling wasn't satisfied. He ran the picture with Breen on May 16, and insisted Breen have Mayer cut out part of a military parade and also a scene of troops on horseback. Again, Mayer gave in. Business—the studio—came first, before all moral or political or personal considerations, as always.

*Idiot's Delight*, a successful play by Robert Sherwood, presented a number of hurdles before it could be brought to the screen. In the theater, it was an effective indictment of fascism. The author skillfully evoked the lives of a handful of people of different nationalities staying in an Italian hotel on the brink of war; Sherwood predicted a full-scale Mussolini air attack on Paris. Joseph Breen tried to prevent M.G.M. from buying the property, but Mayer authorized Hunt Stromberg to go ahead and acquire the rights. The Italian consul general interfered to such an extent that when Sherwood came to Hollywood to write the adaptation, Stromberg was compelled to give him the choice of seeing the picture canceled or removing much of the serious political comment from it.

It is sad to report that Robert Sherwood crumbled; he cut out all references to Italy and Mussolini, based the story in some no-man's-land, turned the Italian dialogue into Esperanto and then, most shamefully of all, allowed Breen to forward the script to Rome for the approval of the fascist government. The result was that a cogent and penetrating drama was reduced to a mindless romantic-comic diversion, relieved only by a bombing raid at the end. But emasculated though it was, *Idiot's Delight* was banned in fascist Spain and in France and Switzerland, and was severely cut in Germany. It could only seem poetic justice that its market was reduced in this manner.

Mayer was busy with *Marie Antoinette*, which also presented substantial hurdles. Cedric Gibbons had recreated the French queen's court, the streets of Paris, the prison and the square where the guillotine blade fell. Sidney Franklin had been scheduled to make the picture, but Mayer became uneasy over Franklin's preparatory slowness and replaced him with W. S. Van Dyke. It was no problem to borrow Tyrone Power from the secretly affiliated 20th Century-Fox; William Goetz could fix the deal. Power made a handsome foil for Norma Shearer's performance in the title role. But the weight of work made it impossible for one director to handle the film. Julien Duvivier took up the reins for night shooting, bringing off such good scenes as John Barrymore's Louis XV announcing, "After me, the deluge." *Marie Antoinette* would prove to be a studio masterpiece, and it offered Norma Shearer's finest performance. The final scenes, in which the doomed queen parts from her children and makes her way to the guillotine, were proof positive of Van Dyke's continuing excellence, and the firm guiding hand of producer Hunt Stromberg.

That Mayer was still maintaining a comfortable relationship with his supposed enemies, the Democrats, was revealed on February 23, 1938, when Roosevelt sent him the warmest of greetings, welcoming the advent of the annual meeting of the Motion Picture Producers and Distributors Association, praising his chairmanship. Mayer responded appreciatively on March 2.

In May, Mayer made one of his favorite movies, *Love Finds Andy Hardy*. The picture introduced to the series a new favorite, Lana Turner, as well as Judy Garland. Mayer had become fascinated with Ann Rutherford, who had played the flirtatious Polly Benedict in the last two of the series. She took the bus to the studio, didn't have money enough to buy a car and was the very picture of pretty, girl-next-door innocence. Mayer was impressed with her from the beginning. Shooting a scene in *Love Finds Andy Hardy*, the actress received a note that she was required to visit Mayer in his office. He met her halfway to his door, telling her the plans he had for her future; he went into his usual shtick about not being able to give her a raise, because theater attendance was down. He was astonished when she pulled out her bankbook and showed it to him. She told him her life story: she described how she was saving to buy a house, because she wanted a proper home for her mother and grandmother.

Touched, he began to cry. She told him that if she couldn't get any more money, she would have to freelance. Moonlighting was forbidden at the studio: Mayer had not forgiven *Andy Hardy*'s producer Carey Wilson for doing so. But when he saw a tender, trembling young actress with her savings book, he melted. He granted her a raise without further demur. "God love him," Miss Rutherford says. He nurtured her scrupulously from then on.

His problem was Judy Garland. She was nervous and self-conscious. She worked extremely hard, but unlike Mickey Rooney, she didn't have a bottomless well of energy and inventiveness to draw from. Her extraordinary talent was based on driving emotion; Rooney's was based on manic, cheerful dynamism.

Dr. Edward B. Jones filled Judy Garland with benzedrine and other prescribed drugs, which he apparently did not know were addictive. Soon, she was hooked. She couldn't sleep without one drug, or wake without another. Hating to diet, she would take still other medications to burn off fat. Her thyroid glands were constantly under assault. The drugs made her nervous, either giggly or ill-tempered, overjoyed or depressed. The hunger for studio product influenced Mayer to the point that he overworked her. He fed her into the studio fire.

A picture dear to his heart was shot that spring. *The Great Waltz*, directed by Julien Duvivier, was a dazzling virtuoso work, handicapped only by the glum Fernand Gravet in the leading role of Johann Strauss. Luise Rainer made an effectively tearful heroine, and Miliza Korjus, Mayer's European discovery, was flamboyantly effective as a Viennese opera star.[3]

That spring, Mayer concluded his deal with Warner Brothers' director Mervyn LeRoy. Mayer asked LeRoy what he wanted to do first; LeRoy replied without hesitation: *The Wizard of Oz*. Mayer knew the famous Frank Baum children's story. He agreed even though the material was not appealing to him; he would have to pay the hated Samuel Goldwyn $50,000 for the rights. He allowed LeRoy a free hand to produce the picture, and for the next months of script rewrites, casting changes, with Judy Garland instead of Shirley Temple in the role of Dorothy, and switches of director, he never lost faith in LeRoy's ability to pull the project together.

The Academy Awards took place on March 10, again at the Biltmore Bowl. Spencer Tracy was unable to be present to accept his award as Best

---

[3] Miliza Korjus's career was ruined following an automobile accident in which she broke her feet; she became heavy. Later, she was mistaken for a German agent of almost identical appearance and was exiled to Mexico. Still on the FBI watch lists, she did not return to Hollywood until after World War II.

Actor for *Captains Courageous*, and Mayer was delighted to accept it for him. But he made an unfortunate speech, saying, "Tracy is a fine actor, but he is most important because he understands why it is necessary to take orders from the front office." He ameliorated this ill-advised statement by graciously inviting Mrs. Tracy to the stage.

Luise Rainer scored another victory for M.G.M. by winning for *The Good Earth*. Once again, she had been compelled by Howard Strickling, against the protests of Clifford Odets, to come to the ceremony. The rebellious pair arrived late. Afterward, Mayer thanked the Academy in an advertising spread in *Variety* and *The Hollywood Reporter*, but he remained displeased with Rainer.

That spring saw battle with Norma Shearer, who had long been complaining of attempts by Mayer and Schenck to eliminate the share of studio profits that Irving Thalberg had left her. Halfway through *Marie Antoinette*, with about $800,000 invested, Miss Shearer threw a temperamental fit and announced that unless she started getting a promised 7.3 percent profit share, she would leave the picture. Mayer called Schenck immediately. They agreed it would be cheaper in the long run to meet her demands, since if they did not do so, they would have to scrap the existing footage and yield to Samuel Goldwyn, who was offering her $250,000 a picture and 50 percent of the profits. Mayer agreed to carry out an earlier promise of a new three-year deal, with two pictures a year at $150,000 each. Miss Shearer still complained, until Nicholas Schenck called and told her that she would realize almost $2 million on the new deal. She would also be given held-up profit payments due on January 1, 1938. Mayer revealed, during the course of a stockholders versus Loew's, Inc. suit on December 13 of that year, that he would have given her $250,000 a picture if she had asked for it, because of the spot he was in. The episode did not make him feel any warmer toward the star, who seemed to be confusing her role as queen of France with real life. But in fact she was in the right.

All through that spring, there were renewed discussions on the power of the guilds. Mayer took charge of the industry's labor relations, annoying the anti-reactionary forces. The political polarizing of the unions was more marked than ever, and Mayer was charged with being pro-Hitler. This may have driven him to an appearance, on St. Patrick's Day, at the Islam Temple Shrine luncheon in San Francisco. For the first time in his career, he indirectly denounced the German dictator. He began by talking of the need for another St. Patrick, referring to the saint's driving out of snakes, and to serpents present in the world, "poisonous creatures, swollen with their own venom, so deadly they threaten all humanity, vipers who would destroy civilization itself to satisfy monstrous greed and lust to rule." He said, "I am a Jew and I try to be a good one." He added:

In some lands, in an increasing number, you are persecuted if you are a Jew. You cannot own anything, may not vote, may be driven from your home. If you are a Catholic you will find persecution in other lands. You will be imprisoned for daring to worship. Your priests will be humiliated. I never believed that in my lifetime men of the Cross, [or] sisters of mercy, would be imprisoned, ridiculed.

That week, he confirmed a contract that would make his brother Jerry studio manager and head of the purchasing department. Robert Montgomery stepped down as head of the Screen Actors Guild; Mayer felt that he had insufficiently controlled the increasingly left-wing elements in the group.

On May 26, Mayer was awarded the 1938 diploma for distinguished contribution to the advancement of motion pictures by the American Institute of Cinematography. Whatever his differences might be with his producers and directors, he had the almost unequivocal support of cinematographers, who liked him because he appreciated fine photography— the glamorous, rich look that such M.G.M. artists as Joseph Ruttenberg, Oliver T. Marsh, Harold Rosson and George Folsey gave to productions.

An important picture of that summer was *Boys Town*, written by John Meehan and Dore Schary from a story cowritten by Schary himself with Eleanore Griffin. Norman Taurog was the director. Spencer Tracy hadn't wanted the role of Father Flanagan, the stubborn, relentlessly pious priest who had formed the self-governing Omaha community of runaway delinquent kids on the thesis that "there is no such thing as a bad boy." A Catholic, Tracy felt he was unworthy to play the role because he had been involved in an adulterous affair with an actress.

It is lucky that he accepted the part, because otherwise the piety disclosed in it might have been insufferable. Radiant with sanctimonious self-confidence, Flanagan solves every problem presented by his flock, and the portrait of Boys Town is as sentimentalized as any picture of a community in Hollywood history.

But the picture was revolutionary in one sense: Schary had insinuated a Jewish character into the story, a young boy teased for his big nose, who speaks a Hebrew prayer while the other boys utter Protestant or Catholic grace before lunch. The script, of course, could not stretch at the time to include a black student: when the boys smear the rebellious Mickey Rooney with black shoe polish, he objects (in a line that would not be allowed today) to being turned into a " 'Mammy' singer." The true star of *Boys Town* was neither Tracy nor Rooney, but the eight-year-old child actor Bobs Watson. Playing the Town mascot Pee Wee, he left not a dry eye in the house as he rummaged for precious candies in Father Flanagan's desk, burst into tears as Mickey Rooney was flattened in the boxing ring or ran headlong after him, only to be hit by a car.

Mayer was captivated by Watson and wanted to sign him to a seven-year contract. He invited the boy to his office, where he showed him a model of the Santa Fe Chief mounted on silver tracks and then astonished his visitor by presenting him with the toy. He even did magic tricks for him. But Tracy and Bobs Watson's father jointly decided against signing the contract; they didn't want the boy to become M.G.M.'s property. Mayer was furious, but settled for a picture-to-picture arrangement because he needed Watson for the sequel, *Men of Boys Town*, and for Paul Osborn's whimsical *On Borrowed Time*.

The Boys Town children, like the little girls on the studio payroll, were taught at the M.G.M. Little Red School House, a quaintly charming, imitation early New England structure with a gabled roof and plantings of trees. The education laws called for pupils to go there three hours a day, and it wasn't enough: the classes had to be rushed and compressed, and very few pupils wound up with the equivalent of a decent grade-school education.

There was no one there to teach the kids to act, nor indeed did these brilliant children need teaching. Mickey Rooney beat the band: he could cry on cue, his face screwed up like Lionel Barrymore's, real tears streaming down his cheeks. He could snarl defiance better than anyone. (In the opening of *Boys Town* he was shown playing poker, smoking a cigarette, his feet up, his hat on the back of his head.) But Bobs Watson gave him competition in the 20th Century-Fox's *In Old Chicago*, when he saw his father dragged to death by runaway horses; he astonished Norman Taurog during Boys Town by saying, "Do you want all-the-way-down, or just halfway tears?" Informed that all-the-way-down tears were required, he sobbed till the tears splashed on his shoes.

When Spencer Tracy won the Academy Award as Father Flanagan, the following year, he sent Bobs Watson a telegram: THANK YOU BOBBY DEAR. HALF OF THIS STATUE BELONGS TO YOU. And indeed it was the truth.

Victor Saville's *The Citadel* began shooting in London on schedule in June. Mayer sensibly assigned King Vidor, who had a continuing sense of moral purpose in making fine motion pictures, as director. The problem was the casting of the female lead; a sympathetic actress was needed to match Robert Donat's sensitive country doctor. Mayer had contracted Elizabeth Allan to play the role; King Vidor felt she lacked star quality and decided to cast Rosalind Russell. Mayer and Schenck dropped Miss

Allan, who sued them; even though Mayer insisted she be given full compensation, she would not yield, her contract was canceled and her Hollywood career was ruined. She won her case in London, only to see the judgment reversed at the appeals court level. She was dropped from a subsequent picture, *Goodbye, Mr. Chips*.

Filled with good British actors, sensitively written by Ian Dalrymple, Emlyn Williams and others from a first draft by John Van Druten, *The Citadel* turned out to be a powerful and moving work. So, too, did Clarence Brown's coincidentally made *Of Human Hearts*, a project dear to Mayer, about a young boy's ambitions in a small town after the Civil War, acted to perfection by James Stewart and Walter Huston. It was an authentic piece of Americana: tender, evocative of a lost era, alive with the values Mayer held sacred.

That summer, Mayer became involved in a new hobby: horses. He bought a 600-acre property near Saratoga Springs, and he drew up plans for a training stable and a six-furlong track. It is uncertain how he first got the idea of this; it is possible that Hunt Stromberg, who was frequently at the various tracks, may have interested him in the Sport of Kings. He was friendly with Cecil B. DeMille's attorney, Neil S. McCarthy, who had become a breeder. He bought Saratoga yearlings, sons and daughters of Man-O-War, Blue Larkspur and Sir Galahad III, for a total of $78,000. He purchased War Woman, dam of Mata Hari, and Notley Abbey from Newmarket, the British stable. Notley Abbey would foal King's Abbey, which would win Mayer the 1942 Jerome Handicap. He bought Main Man, which would prove to be a high-performance stallion. He sent agents to Australia and New Zealand, but it would be two years before he would find the pride of Australasia: Beau Pere, a sire that would cost him $100,000.

It seems incredible that Mayer had sufficient time to cram in horse breeding along with his other work. He included in his customary visit to New York a journey to Saratoga Springs for the August races, with Frank Orsatti and Dr. Edward B. Jones. He was there when Sam and Harry Fox, of the Sam Fox Music Publishing Company, sued Loew's, Inc. and Metro for $1 million damages, charging that the defendants conspired to deprive their company of a publishing and promotional contract concerning all 20th Century-Fox music compositions. Settled out of court, the case again drew insiders' attention to the fact that Schenck and Mayer were still part of the Fox Studios through the Chase Bank and that Mayer's planting there of William Goetz was an extraordinary example of nepotism.

That summer he concluded a deal in which, in return for supplying a beleaguered David O. Selznick with the public's choice of Clark Gable as star of *Gone With the Wind*, M.G.M. would have the distribution rights and would in effect, and following further negotiations, have fifty percent of the picture's profits in some markets and seventy percent in others for seven years; after that, Selznick would resume control. Nicholas Schenck testified almost three years later, at a Senate committee hearing, that he had talked Selznick into the deal at the Saratoga Springs track. Schenck knew that Mayer was getting nowhere with Selznick, who was talking with Jack Warner in the hope of closing a deal with Warner Brothers. Schenck walked up to Jock Whitney, Selznick's financial backer, in his box, and told him that he would like to settle a deal immediately. He told Whitney, "If you are interested in a contract, the proper thing for you to do is make a deal with Mr. Warner, because the terms are better than ours. But if you are interested in real results, you ought to make a contract with us." Whitney agreed, if his partners would concur. They, including Selznick, did. As a result, M.G.M. got the world distribution rights and ownership of *Gone With the Wind*; Selznick always felt afterwards that he had sold his soul, along with his favorite project, to his father-in-law. (David Thomson, authorized Selznick biographer, feels that Schenck exaggerated the role he played. But he was under oath.)

Mayer suffered a blow on September 28. His favorite storyteller, Kate Corbaley, died suddenly at the age of sixty. He would never find another Scheherezade to equal her. Neither Lillie Messenger, whom he finally lured away from RKO, and who was to stay with him for seven years, nor Harriet Frank, who joined the staff later, could match Mrs. Corbaley's skill in telling a tale. At her funeral, on the thirtieth, Mayer turned to Samuel Marx, who was sitting next to him, and said, "I would sooner have lost one of my biggest stars than have lost that wonderful woman."

By October, Mayer was ready to run his horses at Santa Anita Park in the winter contests; he had streaked ahead of Harry M. Warner, Harry Cohn, William Goetz, Spencer Tracy, Al Jolson and even Bing Crosby as he acquired more and more runners. He took pleasure in noting the successful first runs of *Boys Town*.

That early fall saw Mayer releasing Luise Rainer, Oscars or not, from her studio contract, thus effectively terminating her career. According to Lana Turner, who appeared with her in *Dramatic School*, which Mervyn LeRoy was directing while involved in preproduction on *The Wizard of Oz*, Miss Rainer behaved badly on the set, quarreling with the New York director Robert B. Sinclair; at one stage she affected a fainting fit that held up the production. Her agent, Ad Schulberg, told her son Budd that it was not only Miss Rainer's misbehavior, but her marriage to

Odets, still anathema to Mayer, and her political views that destroyed her.

According to Rainer, in an interview with Dr. Margaret Brenman-Gibson, author of the authorized Odets biography, she herself had made the decision to leave, but there are several who differ with this. She described to Dr. Brenman-Gibson a somewhat theatrical encounter with Mayer in which he is supposed to have said, "Luise, we've made you, and now we're going to kill you." She claims she replied, "God made me, not you . . . In twenty years you will be dead . . . That is when I'm [sic] starting to live."

On November 2, 1938, she engineered a letter to President Roosevelt from the Hollywood Anti-Nazi League seeking his support as cosponsor of Talent in Exile, a mass meeting to be held at the Los Angeles Philharmonic Auditorium on December 3. Sponsors included Miss Rainer herself; Ring Lardner, Jr.; Bruno Frank, the writer, who was working on a script for RKO's *The Hunchback of Notre Dame*; Salka Viertel; and the directors Ernst Lubitsch and Fritz Lang.

Meanwhile, Greer Garson, a strong anti-German who kept out of radical politics, was back in England after months of tedious waiting and (according to Victor Saville) careful grooming, dieting and massage, shooting Saville's production of *Goodbye, Mr. Chips*. Mayer saw the rushes as they were flown in from London and was delighted with them, realizing that his and Saville's decision to replace Elizabeth Allan was justified. The exteriors shot at the public school Repton, the picture was faithful to the James Hilton novel on which it was based and gave fine opportunities, not only to Robert Donat as Hilton's disciplinarian schoolmaster rendered unselfish through the love of a good woman, but also to Miss Garson, as his savior who dies in childbirth. It was a story after Mayer's own heart; again, it took up his favorite theme: misguided human beings converted to decent behavior. It is easy to laugh cynically at such uplifting material today; but in the 1930s, millions were willing to accept sermons of this sort, and *Goodbye, Mr. Chips* was a hit and overnight made Miss Garson an international star.

While the picture was in progress, Mayer was distracted by yet another court case. He traveled to Sacramento on October 19 for a labor relations hearing. He charged that a lawyer, William H. Neblitt, had asked him to take up cudgels against IATSE. He neglected to mention during his testimony that the reason he had refused was because he was privy to the deal that Nicholas and Joe Schenck, and the other industry leaders, had made with Browne and Bioff in 1936. The moment Mayer lost the case, Neblitt sued him for half a million dollars for slander; Mayer was at Perris, in the California desert, making arrangements to set

up a training stable there bought from Frank and Jean Orsatti, when he
was served the subpoena. The case was settled out of court. Mayer could
take consolation from the fact that he was again the highest-paid individual in the United States, his income, presently, $1,296,503.

*The Wizard of Oz* ran into production delays. Richard Thorpe, who
began the picture, fell ill; George Cukor took over for a time and Victor
Fleming assumed the directorial reins. Mervyn LeRoy kept a firm, experienced hand on the fantasy, and the M.G.M. studio commissary was
overrun with obstreperous, bottom-pinching Munchkins. There were
mishaps: Buddy Ebsen, just cast as the Tin Man, collapsed, his lungs
coated with aluminum dust; he was replaced with Jack Haley. Margaret
Hamilton, as the Wicked Witch of the West, was badly burned at one
stage, and a stand-in was injured when the broomstick exploded.

Simultaneously, Hitler's idol and favorite moviemaker, Helene (Leni)
Riefenstahl, was embarking from Germany aboard the *Europa*, accompanied by Ernst Jaeger, M.G.M.'s talent-hunting stringer in Berlin, and
Werner Klingeberg, the Olympic Games secretary, for a visit to New
York and Hollywood. Her purpose was to introduce into America her
movie of the Olympic Games of 1936, staged in Berlin and designed
ultimately as a glorification of Hitler. It was also to appease M.G.M. and
other studios that were being roughly handled by the Berlin authorities.
Despite the constant efforts of Douglas Miller, commercial attaché to
the U.S. embassy in Berlin, from 1936 it had been an uphill struggle to
find open market arrangements for pictures, and Warner's, Universal,
RKO and Columbia closed down. But M.G.M., Paramount and 20th
Century-Fox continued; they avoided using Jewish stars, defeated the
revoking of their foreign exchange permits and made pictures that would
appeal locally. *Broadway Melody of 1938* ran for months in Berlin to
standing-room-only crowds and wild applause. Hitler loved Garbo and
Jeanette MacDonald and ran their pictures over and over again.

Raymond H. Geist, American consul in Berlin, calmly informed Secretary of State Cordell Hull, "Miss Riefenstahl is a leading figure in
national Socialist circles in Germany," adding a comment on the status
of her filmmaking career.

She announced that among those she intended to see in Hollywood
was Louis B. Mayer. It is unknown whether he had given her any indication that he might be prepared to receive her; certainly, no such invitation can have been issued through official channels. Heckled by protesters, Miss Riefenstahl continued on a journey which included meetings at
the Museum of Modern Art with Iris Barry, film curator, and her husband, John F. Abbott; a visit to Detroit to meet the pro-Nazi Henry
Ford, in the company of the local German consul Fritz Hailer; dinner

with Olympic Games chairman Avery Brundage in Chicago; and show-ings of the Olympic Games film in that city. She had friendly discussions with the ice-skating star Sonja Henie, whose manager offered to buy the film.

Miss Riefenstahl arrived in Hollywood on November 24 with a letter of introduction to Basil Rathbone. The sky was red with the blaze of forest fires. Unfortunately for her, there had been widespread publicity following the pogrom known as Kristallnacht. When Miss Riefenstahl and Jaeger got off the train, there were banners, engineered by the Anti-Nazi League, protesting her arrival. But she boldly continued with her visit, hosted by Georg Gyssling; he changed her reservations from the Garden of Allah Hotel, whose management had received death threats, to the Beverly Hills Hotel, where she stayed for three weeks. She an-nounced once more that she wanted to meet Louis B. Mayer—mindful, she told Ernst Jaeger, of Loew's powerful interests in Germany.

Mayer and Robert Vogel, head of his foreign division since 1930, paced up and down Mayer's office, discussing whether they would invite her to the studio. Vogel pointed out to Mayer that he was damned if he did and damned if he didn't. If Mayer let her in, the Jews would call him a traitor. If he kept her out, the Loew's shareholders would say he was letting his personal feelings interfere with his dividends. Mayer reached a decision. He called Miss Riefenstahl and told her that he would like to be friendly with her, to meet with her, but that the feeling was strong against Germans, and if she should happen to walk onto a sound stage and an electrician accidentally on purpose dropped a lamp on her head and killed her, M.G.M. would be legally liable. He offered to visit her instead. But, furious, she refused to see him. One can only assume that Mayer's admiration of her genius overcame his misgivings about her politics.

All except the hard-core of pro-Nazis predictably shunned Miss Riefenstahl. Gary Cooper, who had recently been a guest of Albert Goering, industrialist brother of Hermann Goering and of Hitler's close friend, Karl Ritter, of UFA Studios, in Berlin, called Miss Riefenstahl to tell her he had been impressed by his German trip and would arrange to pick her up from the Beverly Hills Hotel. Then he rang again to say he was sorry that he had to cancel, because he had been transferred to Mexico for a picture.

Walt Disney made no such excuses. He gave Miss Riefenstahl a three-hour tour of the Disney studios. Over lunch, he talked with her about the fact that his *Snow White* and her *Olympiad* were in competition for the Mussolini Prize in Venice. He said he would love to run her picture, but, since his projectionist belonged to IATSE, that organization might strike in protest, and he could be boycotted by the theater chains. Later, he lied that he didn't know who Leni Riefenstahl was when he gave her the tour. Landowners Edwin and Harold Janss feted her; Harrison Chandler of the Los Angeles *Times* renewed a Berlin friendship. The California Club showed her films, swearing the press to secrecy; Johnny Weissmuller was present. She was also feted by old-time actors Vilma Banky and Rod La Rocque.

Another who didn't hesitate to receive her was the inescapable Winfield Sheehan. Gyssling had told her Sheehan was "a friend of Germany." The Sheehans made no bones about giving her a full-scale reception with a hundred guests on December 28. Gyssling was there. Two of Miss Riefenstahl's pictures were shown that evening; Maria Jeritza announced that she would call Louis B. Mayer and Joseph Schenck to urge them to change their minds. Miss Riefenstahl wasn't interested. Will Hays agreed to meet her, canceling only at the last minute. Later, her partner Jaeger defected from the German government and wrote a series of articles on the visit in the Hollywood *Tribune,* a remarkable, short-lived anti-Nazi publication, financed by the prominent Warner Brothers director William Dieterle and edited by director E. A. DuPont.

The Berlin office at the time was in charge of a pure Aryan named Fritz Strengholt. He did such tremendous business, his reward was a visit to the studio. He arrived and told Robert Vogel he wanted to call his wife, to tell her he had arrived safely. When he finished the call in Vogel's office he was pale with fear. She was Jewish. His call had been monitored; he could hear that it had been. She told him she had been arrested; he refused to help. When he got back to Berlin he dropped her completely. She was sent to a concentration camp, while he stayed on as head of the Berlin office.

At the time, Robert Vogel was faced with some odd complications. Mayer had revived the idea of making Franz Werfel's pro-Armenian, anti-Turkish *The Forty Days of Musa Dagh.* On December 15, 1938, G. V. Allen of the State Department met with John Golden of the Bureau of Foreign Domestic Commerce and warned him that not only would all Hollywood pictures be banned in the Near and Middle East if the film were made, but there could be bans in that region on imports from Ford, General Motors and Socony-Vacuum. Two days later, Wallace Murray, representative of the U.S. government in Istanbul, advised Under Secretary of State Sumner Welles that "there appear to be indications that the motion picture industry intends to disregard, during the coming year, the sensibilities of totalitarian powers which have so often objected, without success, to the producing of certain types of films." *Musa Dagh,* he felt, would be an example of this kind of provocation. On the twentieth, George Messersmith of the State Department called John Golden, expressing concern that M.G.M. might aggravate not only Turkey, but also Germany and Italy. In view of this official policy of appeasement, there was nothing further Mayer could do, and again the project was dropped.

That winter, Mayer suffered from ill health; the pressures of two years of work following Thalberg's death had worn him down considerably. Eddie Mannix was also ill, laid up for weeks in the Cedars of Lebanon Hospital, and the executive Sam Katz, added to the studio just over a year earlier and not very popular, had to assume many responsibilities. Hunt Stromberg was in declining health, due to his increasing addiction to drugs. And of the studio stars, Judy Garland proved to be most consistently sick.

Surprisingly, in view of his appeasing (for business purposes) situation vis-à-vis Germany, Mayer signed the German-Jewish Ernst Lubitsch as director of the next Garbo picture, *Ninotchka*, a gentle satire on the Soviets. Lubitsch's refusal to return to Germany, with Honorary Aryan status, to head up UFA, the great Berlin studio, had aggravated the Führer, and *The Merry Widow*, his previous picture for M.G.M., had been banned outright in Germany.[4] For Mayer to engage him at this time was as deliberate an act of defiance as Mayer's speech to the Hibernians against Hitler. He was pursuing a dangerous double course: he was preparing the groundwork for Jewish immigration from Germany to Cuba, a plan stumbled on by the State Department. Paradoxically, he was also busy with other movie leaders, trying to maintain a foothold in Mussolini's Italy. There was talk of no further American pictures being distributed in that country, where Hal Roach's M.G.M. release, *Merrily We Live*, had been a hit. Vittorio Mussolini published an article in the magazine *Popolo d'Italia* on December 22, stating that it was not surprising that many Hollywood movies carried on Communist propaganda, because "Hollywood is as full of Jews as Tel Aviv." He charged that Hollywood was supplying its Italian earnings to the Reds in Spain; Vittorio's father, of course, was supplying General Franco with arms and money. The result of this threat to American interests in Italy was a decision to authorize an industry representative to go to Rome and meet with the Italian dictator to "correct the misunderstanding" existing between Hollywood and the Italian government. In June, Mayer's old friend from his first trip to Hollywood, Martin Quigley, editor and publisher of motion picture industry journals, supported by the MPPA, would set off, with Will Hays's blessing, to Rome. Quigley had strong

[4] *The Prizefighter and the Lady* was banned because Max Baer was Jewish. Amazingly, despite Paul Muni, who was Jewish, *The Good Earth* was not.

Vatican connections and guaranteed to say that he was not an official representative of the Hays organization but simply an editor and publisher.

After meetings with Nicholas Schenck in New York, Quigley would succeed in his mission. The Will Hays papers at the Indianapolis Public Library support, with ample documentation, the continuing association between Hollywood and Rome, even after the outbreak of World War II.

Since we are in a realm of paradoxes here, it is not surprising that, in December, the Nazi government of Austria seized certain M.G.M. prints of films and transferred them, without authorization, into the vaults of the Viennese archives. Arthur Loew protested, through the Gestapo in Berlin, using the U.S. embassy as a mail drop. The prints were released.

One who was not happy with M.G.M.'s continuing associations with Germany and Italy was Greta Garbo. Shortly to join British Security Coordination, which would be set up in 1940 by the London film executive Sir William Stephenson, as a special branch of the Secret Intelligence Service, Garbo was sent by Stephenson and Alexander Korda, also of SIS, to investigate the Swedish industrialist Axel Wenner-Gren. With her companion, the dietitian Gayelord Hauser, she set sail as a guest of Wenner-Gren aboard his yacht, *The Southern Cross*, from Nassau to Miami on February 28, 1939. She had grown increasingly disaffected with M.G.M., mollified only by the appointment of Lubitsch, a strong anti-Nazi, as her director on *Ninotchka*. For the rest of the war, she would devote herself to the allied cause; according to Sir William Stephenson, she was "a great heroine." She would risk her life involving herself in the mass rescue of Jews from Denmark, and would bring to bear a strong influence upon King Gustav of Sweden, who, at least until the Germans were defeated at Stalingrad, would maintain an uneasy secret alliance with Nazi Germany.

In early February, M.G.M.'s pressure on the Gestapo apparently resulted in the returning of at least some of the prints that had been seized in Vienna; the correspondence between George Messersmith, now assistant secretary of state, and the U.S. consul general in Berlin makes the matter clear. Once again, moral considerations had to be shaded in view of business necessities, and, of course, the world was still not at war.

At the Academy Awards at the Biltmore Bowl on February 23, there was, predictably, no mention of politics. Miliza Korjus, not yet stricken with dietary problems and pursued by accusations of being a Nazi, sang "The Star-Spangled Banner." Fred Zinnemann, an anti-Nazi émigré from Berlin, won an Oscar for an M.G.M. two-reel short; Walt Disney, to continue this political mix, won two awards, one for *Snow White and the Seven Dwarfs*. Mickey Rooney was given a special Oscar for being one of the two most profitable movie juveniles, the other being Deanna Durbin, whom Mayer had so unwisely let go. Above all, Spencer Tracy won for *Boys Town;* his statuette was inscribed, by mistake or not, DICK TRACY.

On March 29, Clark Gable and Carole Lombard were married in San Diego. Mayer was delighted; he admired Miss Lombard enormously, despite her use of language which he considered "unbecoming in a woman."

In May, Mayer left, with Howard Strickling, for New Brunswick, Canada, where he made a nostalgic visit to St. John, and to nearby Fredericton, where he received an honorary doctorate from the local university. He was greeted by fanfares, flags and bunting; at a luncheon on May 17, at the Queen Hotel in Fredericton, attended by over a hundred guests, he expressed a warm nostalgia, talking of "coming home to mother," and reminding the audience that she was buried in St. John. He spoke of the political menace in Europe, once again directly attacking the subject of Nazism ("The world's democracies can be depended on to come to the rescue of Mother England, if she is threatened with defeat by the two madmen of Europe and their dictatorial rule.").

Following the presentation of his doctorate, Mayer continued to his mother's grave site, where he broke into tears. Together with his cousin Nathan Cummings, a Chicago food executive, he dedicated a special plaque to Sarah Mayer, and confirmed with the local authorities that it would be maintained at his expense in perpetuity. He had a moving meeting with his former schoolteacher, Alice Maud Wilson, discussing his favorite childhood reading, including *Treasure Island* and *The Swiss Family Robinson*.

In May 1939, Mayer was advised by W. H. Beane, M.G.M. Police Chief Whitey Hendry's second in command, that Communist influences were powerful in the unions. On May 7, a rank-and-file Labor Committee representative was arrested by Los Angeles police detective LeRoy Sanderson. The man was found to have in his possession a quantity of Communist literature, including pamphlets, penciled notes and printed materials. Sanderson reported on May 6 that there was evidence to prove the suspect a dangerous agent working secretly in a subversive and un-American manner and a traitor to his fellow workers.

Correspondence obtained by Sanderson shows that many union leaders were corresponding as Communists, addressing each other as Comrade. All of this helped to effect the overwhelming feeling in the industry that the nest must be cleaned, and led directly to the first indications of government investigation into Hollywood.

Meanwhile, on June 17, Martin Quigley, to buttress his credentials in discussing the matter with Secretary of State Cordell Hull, told Hull, in connection with his trip to Italy, that he had "aided the present Government's [of Spain's] successful prosecution of the war against the Loyalists." In Rome, he conferred directly with Mussolini himself; conditions for Hollywood were improved in Italy.

That same month, Myrna Loy was on a tour of Norway and the Netherlands with her husband, the producer Arthur Hornblow, Jr., who would soon move from Paramount to M.G.M. While in Amsterdam, she was warned by a Hollywood representative (probably Laudy Lawrence) that she had been far too outspoken in criticizing publicly Hitler and his treatment of the Jews. When she returned to Hollywood to make the picture *I Love You Again*, she was appalled to receive a note from Arthur Loew severely advising her not to mix politics with her career, as Loew's had substantial investments in Germany. She wrote in her memoirs:

> Oh, Lord, this still makes me so mad I could spit. Here I was [fighting] for the Jews and they're telling me to lay off because there's still money to be made in Germany. Loew and many of the company's executives were Jewish, but they condoned this horror. I know it's incredible, but it happened.

During his journey to Canada, Mayer was pursued in a stockholders' suit, filed in Wilmington, Delaware, by the Loew's stockholder Arnold Hermann. Hermann brought up the painful fact that Darryl Zanuck had been used as an instrument in M.G.M.'s taking over the Fox studios through a Chase Bank–20th Century Pictures maneuver. Hermann charged that the deal, involving raising capital funds, in effect created a powerful competitor for Loew's/M.G.M. and defrauded the Loew's stockholders. It was settled out of court.

While Mayer was traveling, Robert Taylor married Barbara Stanwyck in San Diego. Taylor was appearing in *Lady of the Tropics* with Hedy Lamarr, whom Mayer was still determined to build as a major star. Taylor and Stanwyck had recently made *His Brother's Wife*, an underrated, entertaining comedy-drama in which the couple's passion for each other was displayed with an intensity precedented only by Garbo and Gilbert in *Love*. Mayer telegrammed his best wishes; he remained devoted to Taylor, who, politically and in every other way on Mayer's wavelength, never said a bad word about him for the rest of his days.[5]

[5] A year or two after the marriage, there was a party at the Taylors' house. Their friends hid in the darkness, with Miss Stanwyck's conspiratorial approval, ready to jump out and issue birthday greet-

Mayer returned to Hollywood to supervise, along with King Vidor, one of the most ambitious productions of the studio to date: *Northwest Passage*, from the popular novel by Kenneth Roberts about an expedition of Rogers' Rangers, to be shot in McCall, Idaho, and nearby Sylvan Beach. In mid-July, a specially chartered train, with Spencer Tracy, Robert Young, Walter Brennan and a hundred cast and crew members, chugged out of Los Angeles Union Depot for its destination. It would turn out to be an unpleasant shoot, with Spencer Tracy grumbling incessantly about the conditions. A strong, confident he-man in pictures, Tracy was, in truth, a constant worrywart, making working with him a struggle. Why he took on this picture, which called for him to wade through swamps in severe heat, is a mystery; he had sufficient clout to get out of it. As usual, he drank heavily, an additional burden on King Vidor. When the rushes came back to Hollywood, there were problems with the variable system of Technicolor; the producer, Hunt Stromberg, and the art director, Cedric Gibbons, were displeased with the look of the film. Yet it turned out to be a strong production, replete with vivid action sequences; it was only the difficulty of working with Tracy that prevented Mayer authorizing Part Two, which would have carried the story into the discovery of the Northwest Passage itself.

On July 14, Mayer hosted a luncheon at the studio for two hundred motion picture executives, stars, and lesser actors and actresses in honor of Dr. Frank Buchman, founder of the Oxford Group, also known as the Moral Rearmament Movement. Will Hays introduced Dr. Buchman. The event, following upon Mayer's previous expressions of admiration for Buchman, attracted the interest of the Hollywood left wing. George Seldes, in his liberal journal *In Fact*, would, in 1940, attack Mayer for this, charging that Buchman had expressed the sentiment, "Thank heaven for Hitler," in 1936. There was said to be considerable anti-Semitism in the Buchmanite movement. Buchman was a friend and house guest of Hitler's Gestapo chief, Heinrich Himmler.

There was talk that season of Norma Shearer's affair with George Raft, a star with extensive gangland connections. When they sailed to England on the *Normandie*, they were discussed more frequently among the passengers than Eleanor Roosevelt, Charles Boyer, Edward G. Robinson, Bob Hope and Roland Young, who were also on the passenger list. They conducted their affair openly as they were mobbed by crowds

---

ings when Taylor came through the front door. A key turned in the lock; from the faint light issuing from a not-fully-curtained window, the guests could see Taylor's form. Suddenly, he was heard to say, "Okay, Barbara, I'm feeling horny and I'm coming right upstairs." With that, they were astonished to see him remove his clothes and start, naked, toward the staircase. Somebody who apparently did not see him, and had been scheduled to turn on the lights at the crucial moment, did so. The most embarrassed individual in Hollywood fled the room.

in London, Paris and Cannes. Since neither was married, Mayer could only welcome the publicity; and particularly since Miss Shearer, despite Mayer's prolonged legal struggle with her over Irving Thalberg's will, was still an actress he admired. She needed this new fillip to her career; there were indications that the public was tiring of her.

On September 3, 1939, following Britain's final ultimatum to Germany, war broke out in Europe. Mayer received word in the early morning hours at his Santa Monica home. There is no calculating what he must have thought at that hour: the necessity to maintain links to Britain; the danger of losing foreign markets; his Jewishness; the need to bring Jews out of Europe with Ad Schulberg's aid; his position as the world's leading film executive. Several pictures were shooting that week, including *Broadway Melody of 1940* and *Fast and Furious*. He ordered no suspension of work on any of them. Business continued as usual, also in Berlin and Rome, but it was hard for many of the players to concentrate on their work. Right afterward, the British ship *Athenia* was sunk off the coast of Ireland. Ernst Lubitsch begged Mayer to do something; his baby daughter was on board. Mayer called a friend, Secretary of the Navy Frank Knox, who made sure she was identified as saved—and then advised what rescue boat she was on. Lubitsch remained grateful to Mayer for the rest of his life.

Meantime, *Gone With the Wind* was being completed after three years under David O. Selznick's inspired guidance. Mayer had nothing to do with the production itself, and he avoided asking to see rushes. Reports from the set were disturbing: at the outset, the original footage shot by George Cukor was considered, according to Selznick's executive assistant, Marcella Rabwin, insufficiently vigorous—too subdued, gentle and soft—and Clark Gable, as Rhett Butler, could not relate to Cukor because Cukor was a homosexual. In a scene described to this author by one of *Gone With the Wind*'s cinematographers, the late Lee Garmes, Gable announced to company and crew, "I want to be directed by a man!" Mortified, Cukor left the set. Victor Fleming took over.

Mayer made one of his mistakes that August. Instead of casting Greer Garson in a picture worthy to succeed *Goodbye, Mr. Chips*, he put her into a lesser movie, *Remember?* A star to her fingertips, she made the best of a bad job.

Victor Saville was still on orders from British Intelligence, shooting *The Earl of Chicago* in Hollywood, with Robert Montgomery. Jeanette MacDonald and Nelson Eddy were trilling or booming their way through the elegantly produced *New Moon*. Clark Gable and Joan Crawford were involved in the steamy mysticism of *Strange Cargo*. Mayer, anxiously protecting Hedy Lamarr, kept switching directors on her next vehicle, *I*

*Take This Woman,* jokingly called, "I Retake This Woman." In *Ninotchka,* Garbo gave a brilliant comedy performance in one of M.G.M.'s best pictures to date.[6] Another movie destined for praise was *The Women,* in which George Cukor, more at ease than he was on *Gone With the Wind,* expertly directed an all-female cast through a series of bitchy, amusing encounters and confrontations.

One M.G.M. project was certainly ill-advised. With the war on, while Mayer was fending off charges of pro-Nazism circulated by Luise Rainer and enemies on the Left, he embarked upon *Florian,* produced by Winfield Sheehan. Cowritten by the ultra-right-wing, union-busting James K. McGuinness, it was the story of the Lipizzaner horses, during the period of Imperial Austria. Sheehan was importing Lipizzaners for his Hidden Valley Ranch, negotiating with the Gestapo in Vienna to shoot on the spot.

*Florian* was a picture that could have been made by Dr. Goebbels. In the opening scene, the producer's philosophy is made clear. Discussing the future of Europe, a Dr. Josephus Hofer (Charles Coburn), seated in an *echt-Austrischen* cafe to the tune of a Strauss waltz, says:

> Dealing as I do with the elemental secrets of birth and death, I have devised this remedy. Czechs shall marry Austrians. Serbs shall marry Mohammedans. Slovaks Hungarians, Bosnians Croatians. And in a hundred years who would know whose mother was a Serb, a Hungarian, a Mohammedan . . . or care?

It was the unification that Hitler desired. A young horse owner says: "I planned the blending of his blood lines. Conformation, substance, disposition."

Later, the protagonists, royalist Austrians all, are embroiled in World War I; there is no mention that the British and Americans are fighting on the opposite side. In the treatment of the postwar era, the makers do not conceal their hatred of the socialist regime which Hitler overthrew. It is shown as government by the rabble. In the end, the pure-blood white horse (everyone is relieved that, although it was born black, the correct genetics will make it white in the third year) is retrieved from a corrupt and vicious America, where animals are ill-treated, to a pure and reborn Germany in the 1920s—the time when Nazism began.

Presumably, Mayer's new interest in horses, plus a wish to overcome Nazi intervention against Hollywood product in Germany, led him into this disastrous venture. During the preparations for the movie, Sheehan

---

[6] According to Walter Reisch, Mayer sent her a huge bunch of flowers on the first day of shooting; she returned it without a word.

had succeeded in reimporting his wife, Maria Jeritza, despite her notorious Nazi leanings, through Mexico, with the aid of Alva Warren, chief
of the U.S. Department of State Visa Division, and the normally more
sensible and wary George Messersmith. It is to be noted that then, as
later, immigration forms called only for a statement that the applicant
was not, and had never been, a Communist; no requirement was made as
to Nazi sympathies.

In order to obtain German and Austrian backgrounds, Mayer sent the
second unit director Richard Rosson over to Europe. To clear Rosson,
Sheehan had to make arrangements with the Gestapo, but an ill-advised
Vienna official accused Rosson of spying and imprisoned him. He languished in jail before Mayer, via Georg Gyssling, approached Hitler and
he was released. Rosson was replaced by a British cameraman—in time
of war with Britain.

## CHAPTER NINETEEN

# 1939–1941

ON OCTOBER 17, 1939, Mayer made his first serious move toward com-
mitting the studio to an anti-Nazi motion picture. Outbidding all other
studios, he and Nicholas Schenck authorized the purchase, for a potential total of $70,000 (a record for those days), of Ethel Vance's novel
*Escape*. Ethel Vance was a pen name for the American writer Grace
Zaring Stone, who used a pseudonym because of fear that her daughter,
who was traveling in Nazi Germany, would be caught and punished in
revenge.

It was the story of a young man, Mark Preysing, who searches for his
mother, a victim of Nazi persecution. Mayer chose Mervyn LeRoy, still
one of his favorites, to produce the picture; in turn, LeRoy selected Arch
Oboler, who had attacked Nazism boldly in his popular radio dramas, to
adapt the novel with Marguerite Roberts, another anti-fascist. In order
to avoid charges of pro-communism, usually flung at anyone in Hollywood who dared to criticize Hitler, LeRoy did not use one of the studio's
several Communist writers for the assignment. Times had changed: Joe
Breen did not submit the material to Georg Gyssling; he just insisted
that the relationship between a countess and a German general avoid
any hint of sexuality.

Mayer and LeRoy wanted the part-Jewish Reinhold Schunzel to direct
the picture. He had made a richly entertaining film in *Balalaika*, with
Ilona Massey, Mayer's Budapest discovery.[1] Schunzel turned it down; he
was terrified that his family in Germany would be sent to concentration
camps once his name was seen on the picture's credits. The anti-Nazi
composer Franz Waxman, who, ironically, was at the time recording the
music for *Florian*, falsely denounced Schunzel as a Nazi, saying that

---

[1] She was pushed out of M.G.M. because her lover, Sam Katz, found out, by the presence of a hat in
her front hall, that she was having an affair with the actor Alan Curtis. She married Curtis soon
afterward.

Schunzel's reason for declining was fear of getting into disfavor in Berlin. As a result, Mayer summoned the unhappy Schunzel to his office, kicked him out for good and blacklisted him as a director. [2]

That week, pushed by Victor Saville, Mayer authorized Sidney Franklin to conclude negotiations with Phyllis Forbes Dennis (Phyllis Bottome) in Cornwall, England, to buy her successful novel, *The Mortal Storm*. Married to a British consular official stationed in Munich, and herself a British secret agent controlled by the author John Buchan (Lord Tweedsmuir), she saw the rise of Nazism firsthand. *The Mortal Storm*, the story of the Nazification of the family of a prominent doctor, based on her friend and idol, Alfred Adler, was published in New York and London in 1938 and became an overnight hit.

Sidney Franklin assigned the British writer Claudine West, who was much opposed to Hitler, to write the script with another Britisher, Andersen Ellis, and the German author George Froeschel, former editor of a Berlin newspaper, who had fled Hitler. Breen did not submit the screenplay to Gyssling. Oddly, though, when it came to casting the picture, Franklin made no concession to "Germanism" in the accents of the all-too-American cast. Frank Borzage would direct; again, not a good choice because his sentimentalism would work against the necessary toughness of the material.

A week later, Mayer was in negotiations with Katharine Hepburn to buy Philip Barry's *The Philadelphia Story*, in which she was appearing at the Shubert Theater on Broadway. Howard Hughes had bought the screen rights to the hit comedy. He was having an affair with Miss Hepburn at the time, and neither she nor Hughes would agree to part with the rights unless she were to play the leading role of Tracy Lord on the screen. She had been declared box office poison in Hollywood following a series of ill-advised pictures at RKO and had bought up her contract from that studio at a bargain price in 1938.

Although most studios bid strongly, Mayer beat out the competition with an offer of $150,000. Miss Hepburn was a fan of M.G.M., and she wanted to meet Spencer Tracy. She had fallen in love with him in a movie theater when he "drowned" in *Captains Courageous;* once the tears began streaming down her cheeks, she knew she had been hooked. But she had never plucked up the courage to so much as write to him. Mayer was a fan of hers; asked, years later, what it was like to have kissed her (discreetly, on the cheek), he replied: "It was like kissing the Blarney Stone."

Unfortunately for Mayer, Miss Hepburn, who was decidedly liberal in

[2] Schunzel came back to the screen as an actor; he was particularly memorable as Von Ludendorff in John Farrow's *The Hitler Gang*.

politics, selected, of all people, Donald Ogden Stewart to adapt the play —Stewart took a handsome sum for adding a few lines and opening out the action. Although Stewart had been working on and off at the studio since 1930, his pro-Communist politics were anathema to Mayer. But Miss Hepburn's word was law; Mayer acceded to everything, and earned Miss Hepburn's admiration and respect forever. In her recent book *Me*, she wrote what was virtually a love letter to his memory.

An excitement of December was the completion of editing on *Gone With the Wind*. Marcella Rabwin, Selznick's executive assistant, ran a four-and-a-half-hour cut for Mayer at the Selznick screening room; Miss Rabwin recalls that he watched in complete silence, never once went to the bathroom and did not even stir at the intermission. He left without a word, visibly awestruck. If he had any lingering doubts about his son-in-law's gifts, they were dispelled as the splendid epic unfurled. He at once made sure that plans were advanced for Mervyn LeRoy to cast Vivien Leigh in a new version of *Waterloo Bridge*, a sentimental love story of World War I, with a subtle anti-German message in it.

At the outset of 1940, Mayer backed to the limit his old friend Herbert Hoover's Finnish War Relief fund, set up for the victims of Russian oppression. Robert Vogel, of M.G.M.'s foreign division, was in charge. Garbo separately gave $5,000 to Hoover for the Finns.

Both *Escape* and *The Mortal Storm* were in production in the first months of the year. *Escape* went through without a hitch; Robert Taylor played the role of the distracted son with passion and conviction, and Mayer could see parallels with his own mother in the tortured playing of Alla Nazimova as the captive Emmy Ritter. Only Norma Shearer seemed to be excessively mannered and far too "American" for the role of the German Countess Von Treck; the correct casting would have been Luise Rainer, but she was gone.

*The Mortal Storm* ran into trouble from the beginning. The director, Sidney Franklin, became ill from years of overwork and strain, and Victor Saville took over. Saville hated the work that had been done; in his unpublished memoir he wrote that "both cast and director seemed to have approached the subject as though it were a strong political disagreement between the Republicans and the Democrats." He was annoyed that the script had softened the bold intentions with which M.G.M. had embarked upon it.

The chief players, Frank Morgan, as the professor patriarch, James Stewart, Robert Young and Robert Stack, were hopelessly American and could never have been part Jewish, but it was too late to correct their accents or, better still, recast the roles. Saville did have the advantage of

Margaret Sullavan, who looked convincingly German as the ill-fated
Freya.[3]

On St. Patrick's Day, as a lifetime member of the Hibernians and a
member of Mecca Temple No. 1, Mayer was again rapturously received
by eight thousand members when he appeared at the Municipal Auditorium of the Islam temple in San Francisco. He delivered a patriotic
speech, calling for peace in the world. He spoke of

> a world in chaos . . . a hemisphere in flames . . . unoffending nations
> crushed beneath the engines of destruction and murdered by ruthless lead-
> ers who know of no law of man or God. There is a striking contrast
> between this holy man [St. Patrick] and these modern dictators, be they
> Communists or Nazis. St. Patrick's code protected the weak. But the dicta-
> tor crushes the weak. St. Patrick preached love. The dictator preaches
> hate—the dictator destroys.

Pro-Nazism was continuously present in Los Angeles as *Escape* and
*The Mortal Storm* were in production. In secrecy, Charles, duke of Saxe-
Coburg-Gotha, Hitler's personal representative, cousin of the Duke of
Windsor and an SS general, arrived in Hollywood seven months after
the European war had broken out, and when President Roosevelt was
committed to lend-lease. To have been named at such a meeting would
have played at once into the hands of the liberals, in particular W. R.
Wilkerson, editor and publisher of *The Hollywood Reporter*, who headed
up a ring of anti-Nazi informants in cooperation with the FBI's Richard
Hood and Frank Angell.

On April 5, 1940, Georg Gyssling gave a party for the duke, not at his
residence but at a rented bungalow of the Beverly Hills Hotel. The
Gyssling guest list, seized by U.S. Army Intelligence after the war, included, in alphabetical order, Los Angeles Sheriff Eugene Biscaluiz; Harrison Chandler of the Los Angeles *Times*; Gary Cooper; Marion Davies;
Walt Disney; Mr. and Mrs. William Randolph Hearst; Will Hays; Dr.
Rufus von Kleinsmid, president of the University of Southern California; actress Leopoldine Konstantin (without her writer husband Geza
Herczeg); Mr. and Mrs. Winfield Sheehan; the sugar king Adolf Spreck-
els and his wife; and Mr. and Mrs. Lewis Stone (alas for Mayer's dreams
of Judge Hardy). Friendly nations were represented by the ambassadors
of Argentina, Chile, Hungary, Italy, Russia (in an official alliance with

---

[3] One disturbing feature of this finely made picture is that the word "Jewish" is never mentioned
once; the term "non-Aryan" is applied. That was a quirk of the industry as a whole. The Directors'
Guild objected to Saville handling the picture without being a member; despite his anti-fascism, or,
perhaps, where some DGA members were concerned, because of it, he was not made a member
until 1944.

Germany), Switzerland, Belgium and Holland. Needless to say, no British, French, Norwegian, Yugoslavian or other anti-Hitler countries were seen there. No newspaper or magazine covered the party; even if it leaked, it would probably have been too dangerous to announce the guest list.

In May, economic conditions called for extensive M.G.M. staff (150 members) and salary cuts. In Washington, a government antitrust action took place, seeking unsuccessfully to disrupt the monopolistic holdings of the major studios. Mayer was not called on to testify; Nicholas Schenck expertly made mincemeat of Assistant Attorney General John F. Claggett, who proved to be ignorant of film industry matters.

Mayer flew to New York for two days, on May 23 and May 24, to give a secret statement to the government on the matter of Browne-Bioff and Joe Schenck, who was now firmly indicted for tax evasion—an easier charge to prove than extortion and filial blackmail. Actually, Schenck took the rap for his brother and all others who bribed the union leaders.

By early June, Nicholas Schenck, anticipating a German invasion of Britain and all too aware of the bombing of London, withdrew Ben Goetz and Bob Ritchie and closed down production at Denham following the filming of a new M.G.M.-British production, the excellent thriller *Busman's Honeymoon* (later retitled *Haunted Honeymoon*). Its star, Robert Montgomery, stayed on to become an ambulance driver in France. "I can't stand it, I've got to do something!" he exclaimed, as he heard that Hitler had invaded Holland and Belgium.

On June 28, J. Edgar Hoover, head of the FBI, reported to President Roosevelt that George Darrell, an alleged confidential agent to successive Mexican presidents, had contacted Mayer, the Los Angeles *Times'* owners and the heads of the Douglas Aircraft Corporation to assist in taking photographs in Mexico to prove his contention that Nazi infiltration had reached alarming proportions in that country. Mayer, so far as can be determined, volunteered to send down a photographic team, ostensibly to prepare backgrounds for a possible feature film, but in fact to seek the location of a secret Nazi airfield. But, until after Pearl Harbor, nothing was done; in early 1942, the threat was resumed, and it was believed that there might be a second Pearl Harbor–like attack against Los Angeles.

On June 10, 1940, soon after the German invasion of France and just a few daylight hours before *The Mortal Storm* got its first preview, anti-fascist M.G.M. employees gathered around a radio in producer Gottfried Reinhardt's office to hear President Roosevelt make his famous speech accusing Italy, which had just invaded France, of stabbing that nation in the back. Victor Saville, Sidney Franklin and Walter Reisch were present. Suddenly Garbo walked in; the men rose but she said, "Please, sit down. I just want to listen to the broadcast." When the speech was over, Garbo burst into tears. Now she would be still further devoted to the war effort.

On July 16, Axel Wenner-Gren, now under the gravest suspicion of Nazi sympathies, arrived in Los Angeles aboard the *Southern Cross* with his wife and sister-in-law. Garbo met them at the docks and took them with her in her Buick sedan, Wenner-Gren sitting in front with the driver, FBI agent Frank Angell following them, to Paramount Studios. Garbo's only contact there was Walter Wanger, who was working in the Korda–Saville network (but still had Mussolini's picture in his office). She was keeping an eye on Wenner-Gren, as she had on the previous yacht voyage, looking for indications of admiration for Hitler. Those loyalties became obvious very quickly. Garbo would soon wind up her contract and head for New York and neutral Sweden.

A curious incident occurred on July 25. Loew's had shipped *Gone With the Wind* to Paris three months earlier for subtitling, and in June the Germans had marched into that city. On the twenty-fifth, a high-ranking Nazi official marched into the head office of M.G.M. and, at gunpoint, forced the local manager to accompany him to the Bureau of Customs. He made the manager pay duty on the film, saw it released, then summarily seized it and shipped it off to Berlin for viewing by high-ranking figures of the German government.

On September 19, Arthur Loew wrote to Secretary of State Cordell Hull, demanding that something be done about this illegal seizure. Breckinridge Long, assistant secretary of state, wrote to the U.S. embassy in Berlin, which in turn applied to the propaganda ministry. Applications were also made through Vichy. It is likely that Hitler and Goering wanted to own the movie exclusively, and it was neither returned nor shown to the German public.

Mayer ordered work begun that summer on *The Yearling*, a version, by Paul Osborn, of Marjorie Kinnan Rawlings's story about a boy growing up with a pet deer in nineteenth-century Florida. The art directors, Cedric Gibbons and Urie McCleary, prepared a series of paintings of the Florida everglades and backwoods as they were in the 1870s. Richard Rosson, not yet recovered from the privations of an Austrian prison, was put in charge of the second unit, with assistant director Wallace Worsley as his right-hand man. Rosson's job was to find unspoiled parts of Florida that could match the seven full boxes of paintings; he was not to shoot anything unless the actual light matched what Gibbons and McCleary had envisioned.

They even had to match the look of trees and shrubs, based on old sketches of the scenery. This took six months, the company rising at 4:00 A.M. for sunrise shots, but the results, shot by Leonard Smith, were magnificent. On the St. Agnes River, they waited for hours to combine the images of fluttering egrets and moving clouds. For a bear fight scene complete with snarling hounds, they rehearsed with a stunt man in a bear suit, in temperatures of over a hundred degrees with ninety-eight percent humidity. Finally, after many delays, Rosson was ready to shoot the hunt, but the stunt man fainted and had to be replaced.

At last, at Ocana, the first unit arrived with Spencer Tracy, who was to star, and Victor Fleming, who was to direct. A chain gang of prisoners had fixed up the road for them to drive into town. The director and star were taken to a ramshackle clubhouse. Worsley gave Fleming and Tracy a tour. He recalled that Tracy and Fleming looked at each other and said in unison, "Let's go home." Actually, they stayed on for several weeks. Tracy was not only constantly complaining about the heat and humidity, he detested Richard (Gene) Eckman, the young Southerner who was cast as Jody, the deer-loving boy in the story. Millicent Bell, biographer of J. P. Marquand, recorded a small scene as witnessed by Marquand at the time:

> Tracy . . . the big, strong, kindly man whom you see so often giving up his last drop of water for a pal, took one look at little Jody and balked. He said he was goddamned if he would work with any little boy with an accent like that and that it was too hot anyway, and the whole thing was corny and would ruin his reputation.

For Eckman, this was a terrible blow, and he left the picture business. *The Yearling* was canceled. It was seven years before it was finally made, with a different director and cast, but incorporating the seven months of location work that had previously been done.

Katharine Hepburn had arrived at M.G.M. in late May. Not only had she succeeded in obtaining her chosen adapter for *The Philadelphia Story*, Donald Ogden Stewart, but she had persuaded Mayer to hire the director George Cukor, despite Mayer's continuing dislike and contempt for him as a homosexual. Mayer knew instinctively that Miss Hepburn was right; Cukor, who had made a hit with Philip Barry's earlier play *Holiday*, would be ideal for this antic, charming diversion. However, Miss Hepburn was unable to get the two stars she wanted most: Spencer Tracy and Clark Gable.

Mayer approached them, but Tracy was worn out by *The Yearling* and couldn't face any more work, and Gable felt that he was unsuitable for high comedy. Mayer suggested Jimmy Stewart instead; Miss Hepburn was delighted, because she had been captivated by Stewart in Mr. *Smith Goes to Washington*. Then she hit the jackpot: Cary Grant would costar with her on condition he got first billing. He gave his salary to the Free French, concealing the nature of his intelligence connections to France and England by announcing that the money had gone to the Red Cross.

Katharine Hepburn was even able to choose her cameraman (Joseph Ruttenberg), a privilege previously extended only to Garbo and Greer Garson. She and Ruttenberg got together on a practical joke. George Cukor had a flaring temper. On one occasion, he snapped at her, calling her "a goddamned amateur," and walked outside the sound stage to take a breather. On a prearranged signal, Hepburn and Ruttenberg guided actors, crew, everyone up into the flies. When Cukor returned, the sound stage was seemingly empty. He stood for a moment, scratching his head and chewing his glasses, wondering if he had gone mad and had wandered onto a wrong stage. He turned on his heel to walk out when, flagged by Hepburn, the entire company up above screamed in unison, "QUIET!!!" Cukor didn't appreciate the joke.

For all his admiration for Miss Hepburn, Mayer also found her irritating. Not only was she politically unacceptable to him, she kept peppering everyone with her radical opinions, which some at the studio, including James K. McGuinness, regarded as subversive. Her tousle-haired, freckled, angular, trousered presence was seemingly everywhere, as she ran but did not walk, gabbled but did not converse and laughed but seldom smiled. When she could not defeat by charm, of which she had an abundance, she conquered by sustained, nerve-wearing argument. There was no middle ground: people loved her or hated her. Those in the latter camp were fewer than in the former.

She also irritated Mayer by flying off with James Stewart on weekends in his single-engine Fairchild. She made Stewart so nervous with her constant stream of questions about the equipment that he very nearly crashed the plane in an attempt to silence her with a sudden, pancake landing. She got out of the plane unshaken and continued her opinionated talk without a break.

Mayer's faith in Katharine Hepburn was more than justified. He gave her a tremendous seven year contract even before *The Philadelphia Story* became a hit and put her back on the top of the movie pile. The picture grossed $594,000 in its first six weeks at Radio City Music Hall, a record; James Stewart went on to win the Academy Award for the part that Clark Gable had turned down.

Mayer was restless and troubled that summer over the Orson Welles production of *Citizen Kane*, which began shooting on July 29. Rashly, Welles, who had previously kept details of Herman Mankiewicz's script, cowritten by Welles, a dark secret, invited Louella Parsons and Hedda Hopper onto the set. The dazzling film was a satire on William Randolph Hearst, with Marion Davies cruelly portrayed as a clumsy, inept singer forced into a career by her master. Mayer heard rumors of this; he needed evidence, but already it was too late to change the schedule of the premiere of *Boom Town*, and Louella had to attend that instead. When Louella did finally go on the set, Welles bamboozled her into thinking that the movie was harmless. Perhaps because he did not want to draw too much attention to the picture by attacking it publicly, Mayer let the matter rest for months, returning to the subject after the first screenings.

Summer brought the conclusion of a drawn-out three-year court battle in which Edward Sheldon and Margaret Ayer Barnes, coauthors of the play *Dishonored Lady*, sued M.G.M. successfully for plagiarizing material in the 1932 Joan Crawford picture, *Letty Lynton*. Another event was the signing of Pandro S. Berman, gifted RKO vice president in charge of production, as leading M.G.M. producer. He had known Mayer as a teenager in Boston; his father, Harvey Berman, was Universal Studios general manager and was handled by Mayer through the Nate Gordon circuit. Berman had become famous through the Astaire–Rogers dance pictures at RKO, and Mayer launched him, appropriately, with *Ziegfeld Girl*, a concoction in which Lana Turner, Judy Garland and Hedy Lamarr were destined to make strong impressions.

Mayer put all of the studio's resources behind Secretary of the Navy Frank Knox in fashioning *Flight Command*, set at the San Diego Naval Base, a stirring drama of young men and their girls preparing for war; it was as bold a venture in its way as *Escape* and *The Mortal Storm*. Robert Taylor again played Mayer's favorite recurring character, a proud and arrogant male brought low by the contempt of his fellow enlistees and his basic sense of decency: *A Yank at Oxford* in the air.

In August, David O. Selznick Productions was incorporated, and David and Irene moved to Connecticut for several months to have a complete rest in view of David's exhaustion; Selznick International, the previous company, was dissolved. Mayer was kept informed of the changes. While in New York, Selznick worked closely with other movie industry leaders to bring to an end the government's prolonged antitrust suit. With the approval of Attorney General Robert H. Jackson, an agreement was reached on August 22, 1940, whereby theater owners would be able to see pictures before booking them, would not be forced to succumb to studio influence and pressure and would be able to set up arbitration boards to deal with disputes between producers and exhibitors. Pictures would be rented in blocks of five, instead of fifty-two (one for each week of the year). Exhibitors would not be forced to take on all manner of short subjects and unwanted B pictures in order to get quality productions. This would keep the industry in balance for another twelve years, but eventually the Department of Justice would bring about a severance of movie companies and their theaters that would effectively cripple the industry.

On October 24, Mayer was advised by Mabel Walker Willebrandt that Rudolph had been arrested for fraud in Shanghai; he had obtained $10,000 in Chinese currency from a French citizen, Jacques Hymendiger, on false pretenses and was now out on bail. There was nothing Mayer could do. Rudy was "saved" by the arrival of the Japanese, who arrested him at the time of Pearl Harbor and interned him in the notorious Bridge House.

A storm blew up in New York. Robert Montgomery, on leave from ambulance duty, flew in to attend the New York *Herald Tribune*'s forum on the film industry and charged Hollywood with failing to meet its wartime obligations. He was referring especially to Paramount, which had so far done virtually nothing to criticize Hitler. Montgomery was stimulated in his views by Alfred Hitchcock, one of the Korda–Saville group in British Intelligence, who was about to direct him in *Mr. and Mrs. Smith*. In a topsy-turvy political situation in Hollywood, one can only note the fact that, with the German-Soviet pact going on, the ultra-left-wing Dalton Trumbo joined the M.G.M. studio payroll, with Mayer's approval, to write *We Who Are Young*, a story of working-class life, for Lana Turner. M.G.M. had become a corral for all sorts of political animals.

And for all sorts of temperamental stars. One of Mayer's protégés and favorites, though he never attained the first rank, was the handsome and electric young John Carroll, who was making his mark as both singer and actor. He was on loan-out to M.G.M. for a couple of pictures, and Mayer was trying to buy his contract. Carroll was irritated by the fact that the wardrobe mistress wouldn't take care of his laundry. It began to build into a huge pile in his dressing room. He finally picked it all up, marched up to Mayer's office, swept past Ida Koverman as she screamed at him to stop, flung open the door and went directly to Mayer's desk, heaping it up in a mountain of shirts, dirty underwear and socks, until Mayer could barely be seen. He screamed, "Here! I can't get this done! You're the head of the studio. Maybe you can get it washed!" And he marched out. He didn't become an M.G.M. contract star.

Allan Jones's wife, the attractive Irene Hervey, made an almost equally unwelcome visit to Mayer's office. He liked her acting, and her pretty presence in his movies. Realizing this, and knowing that an option on her services was due, she went to see him and asked him for a raise above the $400 a week she was getting. He listened to her carefully, and then, instead of responding, said, "I have the best mouthwash in Hollywood." She thought, "Oh my God, do I have bad breath?" He stood up, led her to the bathroom, poured the mouthwash into a glass, tossed back his head and gargled with it. Then he handed it to her. She tried it, nodded her approval, and he led her back into his office. He said, "Now go out and buy that gargle!" All thought of getting a raise defeated, Irene Hervey left and didn't try again.

Mayer also had to deal with the bad manners of his less tutored players. Ava Gardner was particularly crude: a hillbilly. Mayer's chief dramatic coach, Lillian Burns, worked hard on her, and Howard Strickling begged Allan Jones and Irene Hervey to have Miss Gardner to their home so that at least she would know how people entertained. They had three servants at the time, a butler, a maid and a cook. Miss Gardner asked each in turn what they did. They were horrified. Then she sat at the table in front of numerous distinguished guests, and before her hostess could stop her, no sooner had she finished her main course than she picked up her napkin and wiped the knife and fork on it.


The export of motion pictures was perilous in those days. In December 1940, Arthur Loew was using Garcia and Diaz, a Nazi entrepôt, for shipping prints. It was located at the same address as the German consulate general in New York, 17 Battery Place, and was the headquarters of the ultra-fascist Spanish Falange movement. One very large batch of movies was sent by Loew via Garcia and Diaz on December 15, headed for Piraeus, the port of Athens, Greece. An Italian vessel, whose captain had apparently not been advised that the prints were aimed for Germany and Mussolini's Italy, captured the freighter bearing the prints at sea and impounded the movies as contraband. Arthur Loew swore out several complaints; the matter continued until 1941, when it turned out that the films were in the possession of Italy's Prize Court, which presided over foreign vessels seized at sea. Enrico Bitta of Loew's office in Rome took the matter up at the highest level, but it remained unresolved and the prints continued to be in the possession of the Italian government.

Toward the end of 1940, Pandro S. Berman was busy putting together *Ziegfeld Girl*. He was appalled to learn that producer Lawrence Weingarten and the executive Sam Katz had been making changes in the script over his head. He stormed into Mayer's office and said that, unless this nonsense stopped, he would resign. Mayer called off the watchdogs, but no sooner was *Ziegfeld Girl* finished than Berman found the studio's chief editor, Margaret Booth, in the cutting room with Bernie Hyman watching scenes and talking about making changes. Berman again said he was leaving the studio; Mayer again removed the interferers. After that, Berman had the same freedom that Mervyn LeRoy enjoyed. "It proved that Mayer was a great man," Berman said to this author years later. "Not nice, but great."

One thing Berman could not interfere with was Mayer's "Secret Service" (Berman's term), headed by James K. McGuinness, which examined every script for Communist propaganda with the zeal of the Gestapo. McGuinness was ever anxious to "find out" Dalton Trumbo or Donald Ogden Stewart, but even he could discover nothing subversive in their work. Mayer was troubled by the health problems of his inner circle: Eddie Mannix was depressed by the indictment of his closest friend, Joe Schenck; Benny Thau was becoming indiscreet in his affairs with stars and starlets, and was linked in studio gossip with Greer Garson; Bernie Hyman was experiencing heart trouble.

That November, Mayer was happy to hire a new studio Scheherezade, Lillie Messenger, whom Pandro Berman had used at RKO. She could not equal Kate Corbaley as a storyteller, but she could still hold Mayer enthralled. Later he added Harriet Frank to the payroll in an identical capacity.

Much of the winter of 1940–1941 provided the irritation of a plagiarism suit: Al Rosen was suing Mayer and Loew's, Inc., for taking much material from an old script, *Mad Men of Europe*, in making *The Mortal Storm*. Nothing came of this. Yet another irritation was supplied by Robert Montgomery, who was still unpopular with Mayer after his attack on the industry. He was cast as a psychopath in W. S. Van Dyke's *Rage in Heaven*, an intriguing story of a suicide staged as murder. Annoyed at being held to his contract when he wanted to be in Europe driving ambulances, Montgomery walked through the part with a deadpan expression. With Mayer's agreement, Gottfried Reinhardt, the producer, added an opening scene written by Christopher Isherwood in which it is mentioned that Montgomery's character has escaped from a Paris insane asylum and is suffering from a form of schizophrenia that causes expressionlessness. Montgomery didn't appreciate the joke.

One of Mayer's favorite projects of that year was *Honky Tonk*, a rousing story of a mischievous con man who invades a Nevada township in the late nineteenth century and sets everybody on their ears. The movie offered one of Clark Gable's most irresistible performances; he had seldom been better cast than as Candy Johnson, the magician, cardsharp and troublemaker whose fascination for Lana Turner as the daughter of the local justice of the peace cannot be suppressed. Pandro Berman and the writers Marguerite Roberts and John Sanford pulled a confidence trick on Mayer as audacious as any carried off by Gable's character. It was a strict Motion Picture Code rule that no couple could be seen even close to a double bed if they were not married in the story. The writers contrived an episode in which Lana Turner piles Gable into a double bed, and when he wakes up in the morning announces they are wed. But the ceremony is never shown, nor is there ever any real evidence that it took place, nor is there a sign of a wedding ring. It was the most outrageous example of defiance of the Motion Picture Code until Berman's and Marguerite Roberts's *The Sea of Grass*, five years later. Jack Conway spiritedly directed the antic comedy-drama.

Nineteen forty-one began painfully for Mayer with the launching of Orson Welles's *Citizen Kane*. Whatever his differences with Hearst, Mayer was still fond of him and of Marion Davies; he was appalled when Louella Parsons learned beyond a doubt that the picture satirized them. It rubbed salt in his wounds that his former employee, the film's writer, Herman Mankiewicz, who was presently locked in litigation with the studio against Al Rosen in the *Mortal Storm* case, should have so arrogantly pilloried his friends. Mayer promised Hearst to do what he could to have the picture banned. Not satisfied with this, Miss Parsons threatened him with the words, "Mr. Hearst says if [the public] wants private lives, I'll give [them] private lives." In other words, she would expose Mayer's secrets: the girls at the studio he allegedly slept with, probably his romance with Beatrice Roberts. It was an unnecessary and stupid maneuver of the columnist; she was preaching to the converted.

Mayer called Nicholas Schenck on January 10 and suggested that the M.G.M. chairman offer George Schaefer, head of RKO, the cost of making *Citizen Kane* if RKO would destroy the negative and all prints. Schenck went ahead; Schaefer refused. Mayer pulled a string and had W. G. Van Schmus, of Radio City Music Hall in New York, cancel the opening. But *Citizen Kane* (Mayer apparently never saw it, then or later) opened uncut at another theater in April, to acclaim as the greatest of American films.

Above all, Mayer was concerned with the radical elements in the picture; yet, ironically, he still went on employing the liberal writers Donald Ogden Stewart and Dalton Trumbo.

There was some blackly comic relief that winter, in an incident that was the talk of the studio. Jerry Mayer, still studio manager, had begun collecting rare birds; by using influence through the M.G.M. offices in Shanghai, he managed to order two white-crested Chinese pheasants of great rarity. A pair of these birds arrived and were sent to the prop department.

That day, at lunch, the commissary manager, Frances Edwards, said that a most delicious dish would be served Jerry by special request. He enjoyed it; she refused to tell him what it was until he had finished the last bite. He had eaten the Chinese pheasants. Frances Edwards was fired. She later opened a restaurant across the street that did better business than the commissary.

In March 1941, much to Mayer's distress, Joe Schenck, and his associate, Joseph H. Moskowitz, stood trial in New York on charges of tax evasion, including concealing gambling winnings, claiming fake stock losses and deducting absurd business expenses (for example, his sister-in-law's $53 mattress). Among the issues raised was Schenck's involvement with William Bioff in the labor union scam of 1936. The malfeasances included Schenck's failure to record his accounts in one set of books; only a hidden set contained the true facts.

A few much-needed laughs occurred when Harpo and Chico Marx testified. Captain Victor Johnson, one-time skipper of Schenck's yacht *Caroline*, described expensive and reckless voyages, in which Harpo, Irving Berlin and Douglas Fairbanks acted as ordinary seamen, and Mrs. Marx, Mrs. Berlin and Lady Sylvia Ashley were the stewardesses. It was shown that Schenck had an enormous gambling saloon in his Hollywood mansion. Riotous nights were described at the roulette, baccarat and blackjack tables. Not since the Fatty Arbuckle and William Desmond Taylor cases of the early 1920s had the public been so vividly regaled with an account of luxury, heavy drinking, beautiful women stashed in expensive apartments and mink coats handed out like taffy. It certainly took a degree of boldness on Will Hays's part (or enormous pressure from the industry) for him to appear on the witness stand and rather frailly seek to clean up Schenck's damaged reputation. On April 17, Schenck, who was still chairman of the board of directors of 20th Century-Fox, was found guilty on two counts of income tax fraud; Joseph H. Moskowitz was found guilty on one charge. Schenck was sent to the comparatively comfortable, minimum-security prison of Danbury, Connecticut, later the temporary home of certain members of the so-called Unfriendly Ten during the postwar blacklist era. As it turned out, a presidential pardon, possibly prearranged, had him freed after only four months.

That month, Mayer added a very important figure to the M.G.M. payroll: twenty-eight-year-old Red Skelton. The orphaned son of a circus clown, Skelton was raised in an attic room, sold newspapers at age ten, joined a medicine show and became a knockabout comedy artist aboard the *Cotton Blossom*, the original of Edna Ferber's *Show Boat*. He became a marathon walker and vaudeville artist; his favorite shtick was dunking doughnuts in a comic routine.

Mayer caught Skelton's act on one of his trips back east and, with his instant grasp of potential ability in the movies, hired him for a small part in *Flight Command*. He then had a vehicle built around him, *Whistling in the Dark*. That picture and its sequels made Skelton enormously popular. Millions of Americans responded to this bashful, dumb klutz, forever mugging and taking pratfalls, a simpleton's hat with turned-up brim pushed to the back of his head, his typical expression one of bemused befuddlement, eyes popping, mouth tightening into a thin-lipped, rubbery grin, his jaws slackening as he faced some new setback from a smart and hostile world.

In April, Mayer decided to place Dore Schary, whose career he had fostered since *Boys Town*, in joint charge of a quality B-picture unit. Schary had induced Mayer to embark on a controversial anti-Nazi picture, *Joe Smith, American*, a Paul Gallico subject about a factory worker tortured by Nazis in an unsuccessful attempt to have him reveal the secrets of a new bomb site. It was a daring movie, following as it did *Escape* and *The Mortal Storm*. Whatever misgivings Mayer may have had about it, they were overcome by the picture itself, written by Allen Rivkin, which he liked very much. He offered Schary the job of jointly taking over the unit with Harry Rapf, and gave them carte blanche to choose producers, stars and stories; as it turned out, the unit was not set up until August. Schary and Rapf would be in conflict from the outset.


Mayer was busy with his horse-breeding activities that spring. He had recently (October 1940) bought Beau Pere, the great Australian stallion, for $100,000, importing him from Melbourne by ship. He housed Beau Pere at breeder Daniel Midhoff's facility in Kentucky for six weeks, then brought him back to California, fretting that he had to board him locally while the work at his farm in Perris dragged on. The task was finished on May 15: six large stables, a barn, a splendid training track—it was the biggest and best-equipped of its kind in the West. How he found time to run the studio, give his Sunday brunch parties and drive for hours out to the Perris stables and back three times a week is beyond comprehension. Yet his manic energy drove him on and on.

On May 4, 1941, he was pleased to learn that his niece Mitzi Cummings, who had recently produced *Broadway Melody of 1940*, was engaged to the charming and artistically gifted painter and illustrator Sol Baer Fielding of Denver. The wedding took place just ten days later at her brother Jack Cummings's house. The same day, Greer Garson se-

cured her divorce from Alec Abbot Snelson. Also that same week, much
to Mayer's annoyance, Judy Garland tarnished her public innocence by
announcing she would marry the composer and conductor David Rose,
ex-husband of Martha Raye. Mayer strongly opposed the match, but
Miss Garland went ahead.

Mayer cast in all directions for subject matter. He had been told of the
excellence of the author William Saroyan, and decided to bring him into
the studio. Saroyan put together a screenplay for his own *The Human
Comedy*, a touching story of life in a small town, which Mayer felt would
be ideal as a starring vehicle for Mickey Rooney. At first, Saroyan got
along reasonably well with Mayer, but soon Mayer became uneasy about
him, and with good reason: Saroyan had little or no idea of screen
construction, made excessive demands and refused to be disciplined.
Howard Estabrook, who had done an excellent job of adapting *David
Copperfield* for Selznick, was brought in to produce a new screenplay, and
instead of William Wyler, whom Saroyan wanted, Mayer chose Clarence
Brown to direct. Saroyan never ceased to vilify Mayer, writing a play
called *Get Away, Old Man*, in which Mayer was the villain, then having
the impertinence to offer it to M.G.M. for a purchase price of a quarter
of a million dollars. Inevitably, it was sent back by return mail.

On June 24, Joe Pasternak moved from Universal to M.G.M. to become another powerful addition to the producing team headed by Hunt
Stromberg, Bernie Hyman, Pandro S. Berman and Victor Saville. He
again specialized in the kind of lush, schmaltzy musicals that he had
made with Deanna Durbin at Universal, and he became an FBI informer
on Errol Flynn's Nazi activities. Also in June, Victor Saville found another anti-Nazi subject: *Keeper of the Flame*, by the Australian novelist I.
A. R. Wylie, the story of a reporter investigating the death of a boys'
club idol, Robert Forrest, who in fact was a fascist, planning a coup
d'état against the government. The model was General Douglas MacArthur, an idol of Mayer's, and the reference was to an incident that had
actually taken place in 1934, when MacArthur was approached to bring
off such a coup, a fact that Saville kept carefully from Mayer.

Saville asked Lillie Messenger to cooperate with him in telling the
story to Mayer deceitfully, hiding its true message. Thinking it was a tale
of a patriot whose political purpose was misunderstood, Mayer approved
it. Totally bamboozled, he was tricked by Saville into using, once again,
Donald Ogden Stewart to rub in the film's liberal message. Katharine
Hepburn and Spencer Tracy agreed to star—also deceiving Mayer by
pretending not to know the film's purpose.

While Donald Ogden Stewart was writing *Keeper of the Flame*, Tracy
and Hepburn appeared in the sparkling political comedy *Woman of the*

*Year*, based on an idea by Garson Kanin and on a script cowritten by Kanin's brother Michael and the left-wing Ring Lardner, Jr. (who would one day go to jail for his beliefs). Hepburn's character was based on the anti-Hitler Dorothy Thompson.

The stars fell in love during the shooting of the picture, making the director, George Stevens, feel like a voyeur. Tracy and Hepburn bumped into each other in a corridor before they started shooting. Kate said, "So at last we're working together. I'm afraid I may photograph a little tall for you." And the producer, Joseph L. Mankiewicz, said, "Don't worry, Kate. He'll cut you down to size!"

The first day the actors worked together was in a scene in a New York bar. No sooner had the cameras started to roll than Hepburn knocked over a glass. Stevens kept the camera rolling; Tracy was determined not to be upstaged. Improvising rapidly, he handed Hepburn a handkerchief to mop up the drink. How was she going to hold her own in the scene against such formidable competition? She saw her opportunity when some of the liquor dripped onto the floor. She got on her hands and knees and began cleaning it up. George Stevens had to follow the movement, and nobody could see Tracy.

This psychological boxing match continued through the whole picture. The ending was changed. According to Hepburn, when she saw it at the preview, she disliked the final sequence in which she and Tracy were seen at a prizefight. She told Mayer it needed redoing and, although he liked it, he instantly agreed. In the new version, he humanized Hepburn, showing her making a desperate effort to cook a meal for Tracy in her self-appointed role of housewife, and, in a moment that brought gales of laughter all over the world, dropping an egg on her elegant shoe. Mayer felt that audiences would sympathize with Hepburn if she were shown helpless in a kitchen (her own marriage had lasted only six weeks because she had refused to wash dishes or mop the floor). Mayer was right: the idea of a smart woman journalist brought low by trying to behave like any other woman was an idea that had universal appeal . . . in 1941.

At the same time as Mayer indulged this liberal movie, he was forming a friendship with Archbishop Francis Spellman, the leader of the Legion of Decency, who had a pipeline to the Hitler appeaser Pope Pius XII.

Following the release of *The Mortal Storm* and *Escape*, the German government closed Loew's Berlin office. Arthur Loew, using the State Department as mail drop and go-between, applied for permission to ship from Berlin all M.G.M. negatives and destroy all positive prints. Permission was refused; Loew's was to surrender all movies to the German

archives for a nominal figure of one mark per kilogram. Arthur Loew contacted U.S. Secretary of State Cordell Hull to have this order rescinded, but it was not, and he was forced to yield.

By July 1941, M.G.M. A.G., as the company was known in Germany, was still firmly in place almost two years after war had broken out, its stockholdings of 500,000 marks, and one million marks in cash, retained by the Berlin branch of the Guaranty Trust Bank of Manhattan. Laudy Lawrence, recently returned from Paris as head of Loew's European operation, sought, through Cordell Hull, to shift the Berlin moneys to Amsterdam, under German occupation, to bail out the troubled Dutch branch. The Federal Reserve Bank approved the transfer on June 19, but the Berlin treasury did not. The funds were frozen.

The situation was different in Denmark, Hungary and occupied France. Loew's retained its holdings there, and until well after Pearl Harbor. In German-occupied Denmark, *Babes in Arms*, *Balalaika*, *Fast and Furious* and *Maisie* were especially popular. The Copenhagen branch was only closed on July 1, 1942; the Hungarian branch remained open until even later. *Ninotchka* was shown in Budapest in the summer of that year with Ernst Lubitsch's name removed. On September 7, 1941, the U.S. chargé d'affaires office in Vichy, France, reported:

> It appears that the permission granted Metro-Goldwyn and Paramount to continue to distribute [in occupied France] the films that they have been distributing in Germany in the southwest area [is] based upon the fact that these two companies [have] maintained their activity in Germany during the past years.

As for Mayer, he turned such questionable corporate activities to decent advantage, and in the greatest secrecy. Using the convenient cover of Loew's continuing cooperation with the Axis, he and Robert Vogel brought in twenty-seven Jewish employees and associates of the corporation, providing them with work and accommodations at Culver City. When two brothers, a doctor and a lawyer, needed to make an immediate escape, he and Vogel provided a guarantee of employment for them as screenplay writers. He did not concern himself with these importees' politics.

Mayer continued to keep left-wing writers on his payroll along with the reactionaries.

That July, Winfield Sheehan, leaving the studio after the completion of *Florian*, was scheming behind the scenes to provoke a senatorial inquiry into the anti-Nazi pictures Mayer had made. His position was (and one can detect the fine hand of Georg Gyssling in this) that such movies were produced in order to provoke anger and hostility in the public toward the Nazis. He and a fascist associate, G. Allison Phelps, a pro-Nazi broadcaster, found a willing ear on Capitol Hill. Senators Burton K. Wheeler of Montana and Gerald P. Nye (who, in the Chicago *Daily News* for September 1, would blame "foreign-born magnates of the Jewish faith" for anti-Nazi propaganda in pictures, at a time when both senators were in the direct pay of the German government) instigated the proceedings.

Starting at the outset of September, the Subcommittee of the Committee on Interstate Commerce called for an unpleasant and exhausting cross-examination of Nicholas Schenck, M.G.M. publicity chief Howard Dietz, Paramount president Barney Balaban,[4] Darryl F. Zanuck and Harry M. Warner. Senator Charles W. Tobey of New Hampshire was in charge of the Schenck investigation. Not one of the senators bothered even to see *Three Comrades*, *Escape* or *The Mortal Storm*. During the opening discussion between the senators, Nye, with German dollars in his pocket, said:

> I should like very much for the Committee to determine whether or not there are British agents operating in any capacity in the American moving-picture industry. To this end I would suggest the Committee summon Victor Saville . . . there is a rumor . . . that Saville is a British agent operating here in the motion-picture lots. Certainly he should be questioned as to what orders, if any, he received when he last left Great Britain . . . and especially about the kind of visa he possesses. Persistent is the report that the Ministry of Information arranged his visa to the end that he might work in Hollywood and represent the interest of this British ministry. From within the industry comes word that Saville entertains lavishly, and that each of his guests is served a full course of British propaganda.

Such "rumors" can only have emanated from James K. McGuinness.

Under questioning by Senators Clark of Idaho and Tobey of New Hampshire, Nicholas Schenck put up a strong show of defiance. He began with a survey of the history of Loew's—supplemented by reminders from the floor by J. Robert Rubin—which provides the historian with a unique account from the horse's mouth. The committee's purpose was to show the range of monopolizing and nepotism that could lead the

---

[4] Paramount's record at the time was lamentable. Balaban told the committee he had "not the manpower" to make anti-Nazi pictures, this from the head of a studio that had Ray Milland, a British patriot, Claudette Colbert, a supporter of the Free French, and Cecil B. DeMille, working underground for the British, under contract.

head of the motion picture industry to foist hate-breeding propaganda on an unsuspecting public when America was neutral.

Schenck revealed, correctly, that he had nothing to do with buying *The Mortal Storm*, but he did say he had read *Escape* on a train and urged the studio to buy it (he was a step behind Victor Saville). He took the position that, since the newspapers were full of Hitler's activities, a studio seeking to entertain the public would have to deal with that subject. This evaded the charge that the studio was being used as a propaganda instrument. Surprisingly, Victor Saville's name was never brought up again; were the senators advised that they would be in breach of security arrangements if they did so? Thus, the whole issue of British influence, no doubt to the chagrin of Winfield Sheehan, was sidestepped most expertly. The hearing was rendered pointless two and a half months later by Pearl Harbor, and the results of the subcommittee's deliberations were never published.

Following a temporary suspension by Mayer of all anti-Nazi projects, Howard Strickling (prodded secretly by Victor Saville) announced the studio's purchase of the British writer Helen MacInnes's thriller *Above Suspicion*, based on her travels through Nazi Germany with her husband, the Oxford professor and author Gilbert Highet. Saville first engineered it so that Lillie Messenger would soften the anti-Nazi elements in the story, as she read it to Mayer; then he suggested and was given *Old Music*'s author Keith Winter, whom Mayer respected, to write the first draft script. On top of that, Saville was allowed to have yet another British associate, Leon Gordon, to produce it.

A storm blew up when Joseph Breen read the script. He objected to a British agent killing a Nazi officer; the agent must be punished for his "sin." On October 20, 1942, after the information leaked and following the picture's completion, Elliot Paul, M.G.M. screenwriter and author, headed up a Screen Writers' Guild protest meeting. But the Hays office stood firm, upset only that M.G.M. had allowed the leak. No comment on Hays's and Breen's continuing political position seems necessary. This was almost a year after Pearl Harbor.

## CHAPTER TWENTY

# 1941-1944

IN OCTOBER 1941, pre-production work began at M.G.M. on one of Mayer's favorite projects, *Mrs. Miniver*, directed by William Wyler. The charming novella by Jan Struther was reworked by a battery of four writers, including James Hilton, as a romantic drama of an English-woman fighting the war on the home front.

When Mayer offered the role to Greer Garson, she refused it; Norma Shearer and Ann Harding had already turned it down, because the part called for Kay Miniver to be the mother of a grown daughter. Miss Garson also wanted to go to London and help the war effort by driving ambulances and appearing in British movies. But the producer of the film, Sidney Franklin (prodded, of course, by Victor Saville), persuaded her to take it on. He pointed out (and so did the British ambassador, Lord Halifax, who came to Hollywood to see Saville and all British directors and actors) that she would be more valuable as a propaganda weapon than as an ambulance driver.

*Mrs. Miniver* proved to be an overwhelming success. The script shrewdly established the heroine, the classic British upper-middle-class housewife, as touchingly human. Millions of women identified with the opening scene, in which she saw a silly but charming hat in a shop window, boarded a bus and then, with a look of bliss on her face, told the driver to stop, got off the bus and walked rapidly through crowded streets back to the store, where, in a burst of extravagance, she bought the desired headgear. Millions shared her sense of suspense when she tried to muster up the courage to tell her husband the truth. When she went to sleep with the hat hanging from her bedpost, there were sighs all over the free world.

Once hooked, the audiences that loved the film were never let go. As Mrs. Miniver proudly received the prize-winning, cross-pollinated rose from the local station master, as she faced her son going off to war and nights in an air raid shelter, and experienced the death of her daughter from German bullets, there were few dry eyes left. It was Greer Garson's firm, clear-cut, unsentimental playing, aided by an ideal tweedy, pipe-smoking foil in Walter Pidgeon, that ensured the movie's emotional veracity.[1]

The Japanese made their bombing raid on Pearl Harbor almost exactly a month after *Mrs. Miniver* began shooting. The day after, the cast assembled for work as usual, and their acting achieved an increased intensity under Wyler's inspired guidance. *Tortilla Flat* was also shooting that day; its star, Hedy Lamarr, already distressed by the loss of all she held dear in Europe, could not restrain her tears. On *The Courtship of Andy Hardy*, there was an equal sense of stress. Mickey Rooney at once decided to enlist in the Army; he was rejected 4F. But he did finally manage to enlist in 1944. Consternation was caused when Lew Ayres, the brave young physician of the *Dr. Kildare* series, announced that, as a pacifist, he would not join the service. The matter was publicly argued about until he was called up for the draft the following year. Let go by Mayer, he would later join an ambulance brigade.

One great star, married to Mayer's greatest, lost her life while on duty. On January 16, 1942, Carole Lombard was returning to Los Angeles from a bond-selling tour when the pilot flying the DC3 mysteriously went off-course and crashed into the Nevada mountains. Clark Gable was shooting *Somewhere I'll Find You* at the time. Devastated, he told Mayer he would not be able to go on working. Mayer closed the picture down for over a month; there could be no substitute for Gable. Immediately, General H. H. ("Hap") Arnold telegrammed Gable that he was wanted for service in the Army Air Force. Somebody at the studio, however, stopped the wire from reaching him until he had finished *Somewhere I'll Find You*. Gable, who was furious when he found out, enlisted soon afterward.

By May 1942, M.G.M. pictures were not only being shown in Nazi-controlled Hungary, but in Nazi-controlled Finland as well. Shipped through Stockholm, despite the fact that the Swedish government pre-cluded the slightest criticism of Nazis in Hollywood pictures, six features were sent over from New York that month. It was not until July 1, almost seven months after Pearl Harbor, that the German authorities in Helsinki forbade any further imports on pain of the prohibition of raw film stock to that city.

---

[1] Pidgeon, who had made his mark in early musicals and had been under contract to M.G.M. for years, only now coming into his own, was also from Mayer's place of upbringing, St. John, New Brunswick. One of his brothers had joined the young Louis Mayer in a local choir, and Pidgeon's family was close to both the Mayers and the Komienskys.

As it turned out, despite the fact that Finland was a launching base for German attacks on Russia, America never declared war on that country, even though Great Britain did. For America, Finland assumed a situation very much like Vichy, France, which also had U.S. diplomatic recognition.

In 1942, Norma Shearer, who had been supplanted as monarch of M.G.M. by Greer Garson, retired from the screen. In her last pictures, *We Were Dancing* and *Her Cardboard Lover*, her weaknesses as an actress were exposed. She played the parts with extreme artificiality, forced laughter and strained attempts at coquetry. Sadly, she was suffering eye problems that would later cost her most of her sight. She was still unpopular at the studio; according to Mayer's niece, Irene Mayer Holt, she still expected everyone in wardrobe to be her slave. She married her skiing instructor, the handsome Martin Arrougé. She was involved in litigation with the studio for her money due under the Thalberg will.

The circumstances of Miss Shearer's departure from the studio that had made her a great star were unhappy. She had foolishly allowed her agent, Charles Feldman, to go behind Mayer's back and negotiate with Jack Warner and Harry Cohn, boss of Columbia, to see if she could join one of them under contract. This was a typical Feldman maneuver, which she should never have permitted. Worse, she demanded $150,000 a picture, which her present box office status didn't justify. Feldman wouldn't budge on the price, and both Warner and Cohn turned her down humiliatingly.

In the spring of 1942, escapist fare was the order of the day. Greer Garson and Ronald Colman costarred in a gentle story of an amnesiac, *Random Harvest*; Hedy Lamarr was sultry and teasing in *White Cargo*. By now, Mayer had set in motion the ultimate WASP family fantasy, *The Human Comedy*, despite William Saroyan's numerous objections. Directed lyrically by Clarence Brown, it was the apotheosis of the escapist, World War II M.G.M. picture and was beloved of Mayer: the whimsical and tender story of the Macauley family in semi-rural Ithaca, California, narrated by a deceased father looking down from heaven.[2] Mickey Rooney gave one of his best performances as the mail boy Homer Macauley. Mayer handed a major opportunity to Van Johnson, whom he had been grooming from *Somewhere I'll Find You* through *A Guy Named Joe*. Blond, freckled, blue-eyed, muscular, with a bashful but brazen charm, Johnson was soon to be the idol of bobby-soxers and the biggest male star in the country. His rise was swift; there was a shortage of

---

[2] It was often said that the opening scene, of the five-year-old Jackie "Butch" Jenkins watching a gopher crawling out of his hole, was Mayer's favorite in pictures.

manpower at M.G.M., and a car accident, which called for a graft in his
head, had left him 4F.

An unrequited love of Mayer's at the time was Esther Williams. The
beautiful, skillful model and champion swimmer was his discovery; soon
she would be one of his biggest stars, her free-style strokes across the
studio swimming pool, surrounded by palm trees and beefy males (often
Van Johnson), treated as elaborately as any ballet. As so often before,
Mayer decided that, if she passed her screen test, he would put her in an
Andy Hardy picture; she wasn't very anxious for the opportunity.

Mayer told Louella Parsons in a radio broadcast in 1948:

> [Esther Williams] wasn't happy. I saw she was in no state to be argued
> with, so I asked her to step outside my office while I took care of other
> matters. I called Clark Gable, who had been asking me for new leading
> women. He came over after I said to him that he should be a discoverer of
> women as certain stage stars had been. I suggested he go into my adjoining
> office and look at the girl sitting there. He went in, looked her over, and I
> heard him wolf-whistling. He directed the test with her, and it was a great
> success.

Soon, she became a pinup of millions of male college students, servicemen and 4Fs: the epitome of cool, silky glamour, of whom it was said,
"Wet, she was a star."

On June 1, 1942, Victor Saville and George Cukor's *Keeper of the Flame*,
with Hepburn and Tracy, began shooting after many delays. Though
handicapped by some melodramatic scenes, the picture was fine—except
for the intervention of Georg Gyssling's old friend Joseph Breen. In the
picture, Hepburn plays a woman who has allowed her fascist husband to
die by not informing him that a bridge is down in a storm. Breen decreed
that, like the English agent who killed the Nazi in *Above Suspicion*,
Hepburn's character must not emerge as a national heroine at the end of
the picture but must be killed. This edict almost ruined the film. That
the Motion Picture Code was not altered to make murdering fascists and
Nazis acceptable on the screen was a lasting blot on the Code administration.

Mayer was restlessly seeking new performers, and he needed a five-
year-old child to star in *Journey for Margaret*, a fable by William L.
White of the London blitz and the orphan who survives it. He found a
tiny rival to Greer Garson as the best actress on the lot: Margaret
O'Brien, who had appeared in a bit in *Babes on Broadway*. Her attractive

mother, Gladys, was Mayer's physical type. She was also, of course, Roman Catholic; and in his own timeworn tradition, going back to Anita Stewart's mother, he set out to woo her. He fell in love with Gladys's dark, glossy hair, dark eyes and high cheekbones, and he almost certainly had an affair with her. According to Margaret O'Brien, he offered her mother one million dollars to marry him. This was a fatal mistake, undermining the attraction she had to his power and self-confidence; he lacked feelings of security when it came to women, and he always realized, painfully, that he was not handsome. As it turned out, Miss O'Brien scored a major personal triumph in *Journey for Margaret*, a picture that was admirably directed by W. S. Van Dyke and featured Robert Young's most deeply felt performance in pictures.

During that first year of the war, a certain informality, seldom found in the Thalberg era, crept into Mayer's studio, just as it did into American life. The patriotism of the age, in the wake of the Depression, brought a sparkling energy and vitality to the nation. Men's ties grew more exuberant, alive with flowers and animal motifs and faces; women's clothes reached extremes—purple or mauve costumes, enormous pillbox hats, or hats in the form of birds, lamp shades, fruit bowls—and the music that blared from radios and jukeboxes was brassy, cheerful, confident: the swing music of Benny Goodman, Glenn Miller, Tommy and Jimmy Dorsey; the belting strains of Sinatra, Helen O'Connell, Frances Langford and Ginny Simms.

Greer Garson was queen of M.G.M.; she remained immaculately British, maintaining tea breaks at 4:00 P.M. with silver and china. She tried to alter the working schedule to a civilized 10:00 A.M. to 7:00 P.M., but failed in that endeavor; time and sunlight were pillars of the studio operation. Joan Crawford intensified an ill-fated competition with this Great Lady ("I wouldn't like to be up against me," Miss Garson says) by knowing the birthday of every member of her crew and even their wives and children. At the end of her pictures, Crawford gave the entire production team gifts fashioned of sterling silver, with their own individual inscription. When someone was heard saying, "Who the fuck does she think she's kidding?" she burst into tears. She had already been ousted by Garson's greater popularity.

A scene of merriment in those days was the composer David Snell's bungalow; all the composers had bungalows, and the noise that emanated from them was often deafening. Snell would hold open house in the middle of a busy schedule, produce a bottle of Scotch from a desk drawer, or Coke, or orange juice. Lennie Hayton, husband of Lena

Horne, would noodle at the piano, the youthful André Previn would join in at four-handed piano and, with the composers Bronislau Kaper and Franz Waxman and actress Marsha Hunt (musicians' mascot and friend), everyone would make up songs. One effort (on Mayer) was composed to the Lord's Prayer and went:

> Our Father who art in the executive building, horrid be thy name. Thy profits come, thy will be done on earth as it is at M.G.M., for thine is the kingdom, and the power, and the glory, forever and ever . . . Amen.

Earl Brent, writer, composer and voice coach, composed a song to the melody of David Rose's *Holiday for Strings* that referred to Judy's marriage to Rose (Marsha Hunt sang it for this book):

> Judy Garland doesn't care / About her mansion in Bel Air / That she spent forty thousand for / When they were wed but now her ma / Insists that something should be done / To see that Judy gets her holiday / From Rose . . .

The Christmas parties were riotous, though not as orgiastic as in the old days, when Irving Thalberg was likely to find an executive humping a girl on his desk. There were neckings in shadowy areas behind sound stages, skirts lifted and condoms whipped from wallets, but much of the fun, in the holly-bedecked commissary and elsewhere, was as sweetly innocent as any in the M.G.M. dream movie Never-Never Land, cheek kissing and gentle hand holding and funny stories told and bets on races announced and the latest gossip spread and funny anecdotes spilled against The Boss, who would, with his customary terrifying charm, descend to spread a patriarch's grim good cheer.

The war years! On the home front, despite the bereavements, few who lived through that period would fail to think of it with nostalgia—a mixture of pain and pleasure; the movies themselves still cast a glow. The stars took off (with Mayer's blessing, and sometimes with staged farewells at the Santa Fe depot) on immense and exhausting—but deeply exhilarating—tours to perform for the boys, or to sell war bonds. At night, at the Hollywood or Stage Door Canteen, or in dance halls from San Francisco to New York, with blacked-out windows and couples, GIs and sometimes movie actresses swaying under the ceiling lamps, the atmosphere was sexy, joyful, patriotic. Mayer, in his booming studio, had reason for rejoicing.

But some did not.

On September 6, the Los Angeles *Examiner*, which appeared every morning on Mayer's breakfast table, contained an extraordinary story in its Sunday supplement. J. B. Powell, former editor of *The China Weekly Review*, reported from Shanghai in a smuggled telegram that he was a prisoner of the Japanese in the compound of the dreaded Bridge House Apartment Jail. He described a room crowded to suffocation, with no place left to sit on, even the floor. But a certain Rudolph Mayer, he wrote, "brother of the Hollywood movie magnate," had actually managed to find a seat in these appalling conditions, and succeeded in having two Chinese prisoners move aside to fit Powell in.

Powell wrote:

> Mayer laughingly told me he had saved the place because a Korean had died there of blood poisoning the night before. This did not increase my peace of mind, but nevertheless I was glad to get a corner.

Mayer immediately began to investigate the matter through the usual channels. It emerged that Rudolph had managed to escape.

Two days after this report appeared, William Goetz was appointed production chief for 20th Century-Fox, a matter of great rejoicing to Mayer, who continued to admire his son-in-law. Colonel Darryl F. Zanuck was now on duty with the Signal Corps, and in his absence Goetz would remain in charge. During his brief stay in office, he maintained the superb quality of 20th Century-Fox pictures.

On the night of October 6, 1942, Mayer learned that his trusted executive, Bernie Hyman, who had so splendidly produced *San Francisco* and other great pictures, had suffered a heart attack at his home in Mandeville Canyon. When Mayer arrived for a poker game, the rooms were filled with people; he made his way upstairs and pushed open the bedroom door, where a woman he didn't recognize was wiping the vomit from the dead man's face. Next to her stood Lawrence Weingarten, producer brother-in-law of Irving Thalberg. Mayer asked if there was anything he could do to help. Furious, the woman turned on him and snapped angrily, "Yes, you can leave us alone!" "Do you know who I am?" he screamed. "I don't care who you are, I told you to get out!" she shouted back.

Mayer was impressed. According to Howard Strickling, Mayer had met the lady in New York, but he had no recollection of that. Her name was Dr. Jessie Marmorston. Like him, she had immigrated from the Kiev region, albeit some ten years later, in 1897. Her father, like his, was a scholar whose only employment was pushing a cart. Like him, she was uncomfortable with her Jewishness and had changed her name from Marmorstein. And they also had in common an amazing capacity to self-create. She had worked her way through college, obtained a degree and married two doctors, the second of whom was Dr. David Perla, a childhood friend of Irving Thalberg's and a fellow sufferer from rheumatic fever and a rheumatic heart. Perla had died in 1940. Charismatic, forceful, attractive, she went through years of poverty and struggle, emerging, like her husband, as an expert on endocrinology. At the time of Bernie Hyman's death, she was visiting the M.G.M. producer Weingarten, who was divorcing Sylvia Thalberg. She soon would marry Weingarten. Dr. Marmorston returned to New York after Hyman's funeral, then came back to Los Angeles, rapidly becoming one of the most important people in Mayer's life: his trusted physician and friend.

It was not a physical affair but it was on his side a deep love nonetheless; on her side, Dr. Marmorston felt a wary respect, tempered by the fact that she did not find Mayer physically attractive. She was acutely embarrassed when, on one occasion, and before she could stop him, he took off her shoe and stocking and kissed her bare foot. Years later, asked if she went to bed with him, she slammed her fist to the table in anger and said, "Did you ever see a picture of him?" Why then did she remain his friend and physician for fifteen years? "Because he needed me," she replied. No other comment seems necessary. He was always good to her, and she never sent him a bill; he made sure the studio wardrobe department fashioned her clothes.

On July 12, while Mayer was out at his ranch, a letter arrived at the beach house calling for immediate payment of $250,000 or he would be killed. Margaret Mayer had the note handed over to the FBI; Mayer could not be reached as there was no telephone at the ranch. J. Edgar Hoover took charge personally; he had his local agents Richard Hood and Frank Angell arrange for a package of blank paper to be wrapped and taken to the appropriate address. Two young men, former gas station hand Channing Lipton and former boxer Meyer Philip Grace, were arrested in the act of collecting it.

At the trial before Judge Yankwich, on January 6, 1943, Lipton stated that his father, Lew Lipton, who had worked on the scripts of Mayer's remake of In Old Kentucky and two Buster Keaton features, The Cameraman and Spite Marriage, had been blacklisted for criticizing Mayer. There was no basis for the assertion: Mayer had hired Lipton to cowrite the script for Broadway Serenade, costarring Jeanette MacDonald and Lew Ayres, in 1939. Psychiatrists testified that Channing Lipton had been under a strain and had experienced a mental breakdown; he had not seriously intended to threaten Mayer's life or to extort money from him.

Francis X. Bushman, still smarting from Mayer's blacklisting of him, sent a letter to the judge in the middle of the trial charging Mayer with having ruined him also. Yankwich condemned Bushman roundly from the bench.

After three days of deliberation, the jury found the defendants not guilty; presumably, the members felt that the episode was no more to be taken seriously than a practical joke. Mayer was furious over the verdict.

Manpower was needed by the forces: Arthur Loew, still head of foreign distribution, tried, at forty-eight, to become a major in the U.S. Army, and Clark Gable took his physical in Washington and joined the Army Air Corps as a private, serving in Florida. James Stewart was already earning medals; Melvyn Douglas was working in the Office of Civil Defense in Washington.

Mayer decided that families at home desperately needed escape, and he authorized Joe Pasternak, Jack Cummings and Arthur Freed to shoot the bankroll in obtaining properties that could be turned into lavish musical entertainments. The unfortunate Pandro S. Berman was even compelled to produce an Abbott and Costello free-for-all, *Rio Rita*; Abbott dumb and dismayed, Costello roundly bumbling, brought riots of much-needed laughter from coast to coast.

A major worry of the fall of 1943 was that M.G.M. would not be able to cast pictures with male stars; with Clark Gable serving in Florida, Robert Taylor, Robert Montgomery and Van Heflin were all enlisting. A consolation was that the producer Albert Lewin, who had worked with Arthur Loew's twin brother David on *The Moon and Sixpence* and had left M.G.M. so abruptly after the death of Thalberg, changed his mind about Mayer and rejoined him, becoming one of the finest members of his team and perhaps (apart from Vincente Minnelli) the most original artist at M.G.M. For artist he was, one of the tiny handful of creative and cultivated producers in Hollywood.

Mayer had drawn apart from his daughters in the past years. He was impatient with Irene's harshness toward David Selznick, whose poor physique and problems with his feet had kept him out of the Army. Irene Selznick wrote cruelly about her husband in her memoirs, describing examples of his clumsiness, including a ghastly scene in New York, in which he caught his genitals in a drawer. She failed to appreciate the ability that would soon bring about a beautifully made if sappy picture of the home front, *Since You Went Away*.

Mayer was proud of William Goetz for acting in a dignified manner at 20th Century-Fox during Joe Schenck's disgrace. Yet he was almost never seen at William and Edie's elegant parties; the presence in his life of Beatrice Roberts and other occasional women (which Irene, with commendable loyalty, covered up in her memoirs) estranged both daughters, who adored the miserable, mentally disturbed Margaret, much of whose tortured existence was still spent in sanitariums. Margaret retreated into a dream world; Marsha Hunt would never forget going up to her bedroom during one of Mayer's still compulsory Sunday brunches and seeing Margaret's secret: an arrangement of funhouse mirrors in a closet that reflected her image to infinity. As Marsha watched, Margaret made a small, pathetic dance in the mirrors; all that she had in her life was the vision of herself repeated forever.

Given his conventional background and his feelings that mothers were sacred, it takes no feat of the imagination to see that Mayer must have felt much guilt over his family situation. Yet, it is likely that, like all successful men, he could tuck his guilt away as neatly as the perfectly folded handkerchief in his vest pocket. There was always work to be done; controversy and struggle; the daily handling of stars.

Of these, Lana Turner was increasingly popular. Expertly trained by Lillian Burns, she was a much better actress than she was given credit for; she had been excellent in *Honky Tonk*, so sexually expressive in her love scenes with Clark Gable that she had excited the jealousy of Carole Lombard. She was also strong in the gangster picture *Johnny Eager*, which made a star of Van Heflin. During the picture, her costar, Robert Taylor, fell in love with Miss Turner and told Barbara Stanwyck he wanted to marry her. Miss Stanwyck hid in her maid's house for days, depressed and angry that Taylor had betrayed her. Lana Turner told Taylor nothing could come of their relationship, and he went back to Stanwyck; but Stanwyck never forgave. In July 1942, Lana eloped to Las Vegas with the good-looking Steve Crane. Pregnant by December, she (and the studio) found out that Crane's divorce from his first wife was not legal. Crane asked her to pay his first wife to release him. She was furious; the quarrels were intense and protracted. Mayer pulled strings, and Miss Turner was granted an annulment. Crane went berserk. Headline after headline infuriated Mayer, who liked the image of his stars' spurious chastity and happiness preserved at all costs. First, Crane crashed his car off a cliff; then he took an overdose of pills and almost died. Finally, for the sake of their child, Cheryl Crane, Miss Turner took him back.

In 1943, Mayer had to go on dealing with the fights between Dore Schary and Harry Rapf of the A-minus or B picture unit. He had to struggle with the still rampant anti-Semitism of James K. McGuinness, who called Schary's unit the Yeshiva, or Jewish place of learning. Finally, Mayer resolved the problem by elevating Schary to take care of certain A-quality pictures while Rapf was placed in charge of the budgets.

With Mayer's blessing, Schary embarked on a picture entitled *Storm in the West*, to be set in the period after the Civil War, with thinly disguised characters resembling Hitler, Mussolini, Goering and Goebbels shown as bandits who have escaped from prison and are marauding the Wild West. Sinclair Lewis wrote the screenplay, which was illustrated by the accomplished drawings of Mayer's nephew Sol Fielding, as guidelines to Cedric Gibbons and whoever should be the associate art director on the picture.

No sooner was the script completed than McGuinness declared that the project was Communist propaganda (and this was the middle of the war, with Russia as an ally). Mayer was unnerved by the charge, especially when Nicholas Schenck supported it. He sent Lillie Messenger to New York to confer with Schenck, who was adamant. The picture was canceled; Dore Schary resigned. He joined David O. Selznick's RKO operation.

A curious note was struck at the studio that year. Desperate for money, William Dieterle, who had denounced Mayer again and again through his personally financed *Hollywood Tribune* in 1939, came to M.G.M. to direct *The Man on America's Conscience*, later retitled *Tennessee Johnson*.

The screenplay for *Tennessee Johnson* was written by John L. Balderston on Mayer's specific instructions. It leaked that Balderston would not only be glorifying the film's central figure, President Andrew Johnson, who had fought against black civil rights, but would excoriate Johnson's opponent, the pro-black Pennsylvania representative Thaddeus Stevens. While the script was being finished, Mayer attended a dinner party at the home of Walter Wanger and Wanger's wife, Joan Bennett; David and Irene Selznick were among the guests. Walter White, secretary of the NAACP, was present and managed to establish by subtle means that in fact the movie was under way. When he returned to Washington, he insisted on seeing the script. Nelson A. Poynter, Hollywood coordinator of government films, contacted Lowell Mellett, presidential aide and secretary of the Office of War Information, who also pressed Mayer for the screenplay, indicating in correspondence that there must be nothing which could disrupt national unity in time of war; the picture, both felt, might cause a political incident.

At the outset of August, the Communist *Daily Worker* declared that the picture being planned would arouse widespread resentment "among negroes." Mayer called White in person, assuring him he had nothing to worry about. He didn't get around to sending him the finished draft until the second week of August, and White, when he read it, was shocked. His report to Mellett was unequivocally damning; he charged that the picture would exacerbate already dangerous rifts in the body politic in Georgia and Alabama.

On August 19, Mellett telephoned Mayer, who, by coincidence, had just dashed off another letter to White, recalling their meeting at the Wangers' dinner and glowing with further reassurances. He told White he would never make a picture that would be anti-black or anti any other race. He wrote, "I live and breathe the air of freedom and I want it for others as well as myself." He had, as it happened, actually begun to shoot the picture, with Van Heflin as President Johnson and Lionel Barrymore as Thaddeus Stevens.

The correspondence grew more and more high-powered during the production. White continued to regard the film as a dangerous distortion of American history. Then, right in the middle of the shooting, the producer, J. Walter Rubin, died. It is possible that the stress surrounding the film's making, and the knowledge of what a disaster it might cause in racial relations, contributed to his fatal heart attack. His widow, Virginia Bruce, told the present author, many years later, that the problem of making this picture was the most crushing that had beset Rubin, following as it did Mayer's decision that he was no good as a director and could only serve as a producer. Apparently persuaded by James K. McGuinness that Communist elements were behind the black interference from Washington, Mayer hired him to take over from Rubin. This remained a secret until 1947, when McGuinness so testified before the House Un-American Activities Committee.

The picture was finished, and Lowell Mellett and Walter White saw it. They were furious. They demanded radical changes and retakes, which McGuinness was compelled to make. Stevens was no longer shown deliberately making Andrew Johnson drunk before the inauguration (Johnson was seen merely to be drinking on an empty stomach). The character of Stevens's black housekeeper, who was shown prodding him to support her people, was eliminated as equally offensive. Scene after scene was retaken by Dieterle, displaying Stevens in a more favorable light. He came off less as a raging, villainous monster than as a crusty, misguided curmudgeon. Even so, liberal groups protested against the picture after the first previews. Vincent Price, the black actor Canada Lee, Zero Mostel, Ben Hecht and many others jointly sent a petition to the Office of War Information demanding that the picture be destroyed. Mayer decided not to. But the good he had done with the all-black musical *Cabin in the Sky* was wiped out, and the "fascist" whispers Dieterle had fostered were heard again.[3]

In the version we can see on the screen, *Tennessee Johnson* is a simplistic story of the illiterate runaway apprentice who, taught to read and write by a librarian who becomes his wife, rises to the White House. Determined, as the only Southern senator to join the Union, to forgive his fellow Southerners, he fights against Thaddeus Stevens, who wants to destroy the rebels financially through a scorched earth policy.

The result remains a whitewash of Johnson, no doubt of it; but the persuasive acting of Van Heflin, who stepped into a new class as an actor, and of Lionel Barrymore, supported by Dieterle's exemplary direction, make this picture a worthy, if politically dubious, addition to the roll call of 1943. The trial that almost led to an impeachment in an 1860s Senate chamber was recreated masterfully by the director and staged by the art director Malcolm Brown.

Nineteen forty-three began, sadly, with yet another executive's death: W. S. Van Dyke, age fifty-three, his heart and liver ruined by heavy drinking, died on February 5. Mayer had reason to mourn him; he was never a critic's favorite, but he was certainly a very good director. Work was starting on an epic story, *America*, that would reflect Mayer's own experiences as a penniless immigrant rising to the top; King Vidor planned it as the third part of a trilogy of war (*The Big Parade*), wheat (*Our Daily Bread*) and now steel. James Cagney was first choice for the male lead, but Warner Brothers wouldn't let him go. Joel McCrea was busy working for the Department of Agriculture; Mayer tried to persuade President Roosevelt to release him, but got nowhere. Gary Cooper was getting ready to shoot *Saratoga Trunk*. Spencer Tracy was chosen now and went off to Detroit to look at factories, but, fretful as ever, he hated the locations and backed out. Soon, Brian Donlevy would replace him. The picture began shooting in April across the length and breadth of the country. Artificial and clumsy, it did not succeed: a Mayer dream unfulfilled.

And another picture was begun: of all things, *Song of Russia*, a hymn of praise to the Soviet Union. Paul Jarrico, the coscenarist, is the first to admit his affiliation to communism. Told of it, Mayer, according to Jarrico, said, "I know he's a Communist; I wouldn't have had him here for a minute if he wasn't a good writer."

With Richard Collins, Jarrico put together the story of John Meredith,

[3] It is peculiarly ironic to note that William Dieterle was under serious investigation as a Nazi agent at the time and nearly went to prison. This was one of numerous FBI false leads.

an orchestra conductor of the Leonard Bernstein mold, who is on a tour of the Soviet Union; he falls in love with Nadya Stepanova, a peasant girl and expert pianist. In one scene, Stalin appears in a glow of approval. Mayer got the anti-Communist Hungarian Joe Pasternak and the White Russian Gregory Ratoff, borrowed from William Goetz, to produce and direct, as well as a reluctant, hostile Robert Taylor, the arch-conservative anti-Communist, to star. Secretary of the Navy Frank Knox, Mayer's good friend, gave Taylor the first of two deferments from the draft in order to undertake the role.

Mayer wanted Ingrid Bergman to play Nadya Stepanova. He called Selznick, who had her under contract, to ask him if she might be available. Selznick asked to see the script; he hated it. He told Mayer it was pure Communist propaganda. Shocked by his reaction, Mayer asked Lawrence Weingarten what he thought; Weingarten agreed. Pasternak passed the word on to Collins and Jarrico. Mayer called a meeting. He began by complimenting Jarrico and Collins on the script; Pasternak glowed: God had smiled on him. Then Mayer said (Jarrico will never forget it): "There are certain problems. The word 'community' is too close to 'communism.' I want that taken out." He went on, "When the couple gets married they go to the girl's father's farm. It's called a collective farm. I want it to be a *private* farm." Jarrico said: "They don't have private farms in the Soviet Union. They only have collective farms and the critics will laugh at us if we say this is a private farm." Mayer said, "We won't say what kind of a farm it is. We'll allow the people who think it belongs to the girl's mother and father to think it's a private farm, and to those in the know it will be a collective farm." Jarrico says, "It was the perfect solution; we adjourned in triumph." A famous Communist, Anna Louise Strong, became technical adviser on the picture. With an office on the third floor of the Thalberg Building, her presence was very much felt down the executive corridors; it is a certainty that James McGuinness and his fanatical right-wing supporters protested her presence there. At the end of Song of Russia, Shostakovich's "United Nations on the March," a favorite of Stalin's, was played.

At the same time, Mayer's hymn to the British, The White Cliffs of Dover, was being shot. The film, magnificently made, if sentimental and heavy-handed, was produced by Clarence Brown and laced through with the best-selling doggerel of Alice Duer Miller.

The studio's patriotic efforts were stepped up. With the aid of armed services chiefs, propaganda picture after propaganda picture was launched. In Bataan, the twice-deferred Robert Taylor, grim and unshaven, played Sergeant Bill Dane, who leads a detachment ordered by General MacArthur to hold onto that Philippine peninsula at all costs.

Thirteen men die; at the finale, Dane is shown at his machine-gun post, his death a certainty, firing directly into the camera. Admired by such prominent critics as James Agee, *Bataan* is a picture virtually without women, and written without sentimentality. Mayer's influence was felt in only one scene, when the greenhorn GI Leonard Prickett (Robert Walker) writes a letter to his mother which he knows she will never receive.

And *Cry Havoc*, written by the always admirable Paul Osborn, dealt with even greater effectiveness with an all-female cast. Richard Thorpe directed, with great skill, several M.G.M. contract actresses, and others on loan, as nurses marooned in a bombproof hut attached to a hospital only a few miles from the setting of *Bataan*. Margaret Sullavan was persuasive and moving as Smithy, the malaria-stricken second-in-command of the medical unit under Fay Bainter; Joan Blondell, as a former burlesque queen, Ann Sothern, Ella Raines, Marsha Hunt and the rest of the cast acted to perfection a gallery of sympathetic and carefully drawn characters. Osborn brought out the tensions and strains of women of different walks of life drawn together only by fear, hunger and thirst, and by the desire to fight a common enemy. It was a daring touch in 1943 to add to these compulsive concerns a shared or competitive sexual desire for men. Even more than *Bataan*, this was a picture unsullied by false romanticism, and a credit to the studio. A third 1943 war picture, *Salute to the Marines*, also set in the Philippines, was less persuasive; a prison-camp melodrama, *The Cross of Lorraine*, was handicapped fatally by the fact that only one member of the starring cast, Jean-Pierre Aumont, was French, and the rest were unable to suggest convincingly that they were Gallic.

After a disappointing previous year, the March 4, 1943, Academy Awards, held at the Cocoanut Grove, were a triumph for Mayer. He had Greer Garson, her mother Nina (he had kept all his promises to employ her), Ronald Colman and Walter Pidgeon at his table. Jeanette Mac-Donald began by singing the national anthem, while the uniformed Tyrone Power and Alan Ladd walked in carrying the Stars and Stripes. Frank Capra announced William Wyler the winner as Best Director for *Mrs. Miniver* (Wyler was flying over Germany). Mayer received a special award for the Andy Hardy series. *Woman of the Year* and *Mrs. Miniver* won screenplay awards, and there was a proud moment when William Goetz gave Mayer the Best Picture Oscar for *Miniver*. Once again, as with Hunt Stromberg, Mayer announced that Sidney Franklin deserved the award—but Franklin was ill in bed. He gave Franklin the award later. Van Heflin won as best supporting actor for M.G.M.'s *Johnny Eager*; when Greer Garson and Teresa Wright won for *Miniver*, Mayer's eyes were filled with tears of joy. Greer Garson didn't speak for forty minutes (as has been claimed), but for about eight. Viciously misrepresented, hers was a moving and deeply felt address. The anti-British element in Hollywood crucified her.

Alexander Korda, the Hungarian-British producer who was head, through London films, of the Saville secret intelligence network in Hollywood, made a deal with Mayer that month. Korda hated Mayer; the feeling was mutual. But Korda knew that a merger of his outfit with M.G.M. was advantageous; and Mayer needed someone to revive, with Ben Goetz, a policy of coproduction. With Mayer's blessing, Korda set up an opulent headquarters at Claridge's, with Goetz flying to and fro by bomber to cement the deal. Thus, Mayer was woven into the web of the British Secret Intelligence Service, and the Claridge's suite was a hub of wartime activities. Not satisfied with the old M.G.M. studio at Denham, Korda set one up at Elstree; but he turned out to be extraordinarily lax at the job.

Mayer was in New York on March 16, 1943, to cement the arrangement with Korda and Nicholas Schenck; he was also in Washington that week to confer with House and Senate leaders on the film industry's position as a propaganda instrument. Mayer powerfully addressed the Oklahoma delegation; afterward, Oklahoma Senator Lyle H. Boren, a Democrat, was moved to read a full-scale speech of praise of Hollywood's war effort into the Congressional Record.

Mayer returned to pursue his racing interests, which had taken a back seat for months. He was delighted with the fact that Beau Pere had fathered no fewer than seventeen foals, and that fifteen more had been born, totaling twenty colts and twelve fillies. The Perris Ranch, expertly managed, boasted almost a thousand head of Hereford cattle and a hundred thoroughbreds, the finest in the state.

On October 6, Mayer flew to New York for meetings with Korda, who had just been knighted for his propaganda films and for his work (with his wife, Merle Oberon) in the Secret Intelligence Service. Ben Goetz and Sam Eckman of the London office flew in for the discussions. As usual, Korda was full of extravagant schemes; the least welcome to Mayer was his old bête noire Orson Welles's *War and Peace*. Korda would have announced the filming of the Egyptian Book of the Dead if he could—just to go on living off M.G.M. He caused everyone headaches, with nothing to show in return. Adopting an old anti-Hungarian cliché, Mayer was heard to say to Nicholas Schenck (Howard Strickling overheard him), "What's Korda's recipe for an omelet? First, steal two eggs."

At the time, William Goetz, who had seemed to be destined to run

20th Century-Fox for the duration, suddenly resigned and was replaced by the former jailbird Joseph M. Schenck, who seemed to have been forgiven everything. Goetz had decided to form an independent company, International Pictures, in which Mayer had a secret, under-the-table investment role. Just as 20th Century Pictures had been formed to absorb and take over Fox, so Mayer helped see to it that International Pictures would meld with Universal, and Universal International would be the result.

On November 8, Mayer was declared to be still the highest paid executive in the nation, at $949,765—less than at his peak in 1938. Mayer fought hard against a threatened departure by the great Clarence Brown. He managed to pull Brown back from International Pictures and offered him a plum: *National Velvet*, the story of the girl who won the Derby disguised as a jockey, which echoed Mayer's first success, *In Old Kentucky*. As it turned out, the picture was not made for another year; several script problems had to be ironed out. It would make a star of Elizabeth Taylor.

And now, Mayer fell in love again; he seems to have lost interest in Beatrice Roberts; Gladys O'Brien was entirely out of the picture. The agent Victor Orsatti, brother of Frank, introduced him to a client, Ginny Simms, who was under contract to Universal. Orsatti had a purpose: he wanted Ginny Simms to go to M.G.M. as a leading lady.

Dark, attractive, good-natured, popular with the GIs and a favorite of veterans' hospitals, Ginny Simms, at twenty-six, was a big radio star in 1943. She had a natural voice, with two octaves, and a magical glissando; she was perfectly suited to the 1940s, with that era's emphasis on energy, pizzazz, the razzle-dazzle of swing and bebop. Like Jean Howard and Beatrice Roberts, she was Texas-born. The daughter of a movie theater owner, she was at the Fresno, California, Teacher's College when she formed an Andrews Sisters–like trio, the Triads and Blue. She made her first hits with Kay Kyser, mortar-boarded and gowned band leader and "Professor" of swing; there was talk of Kyser being romantically involved with her. When they broke up, Kyser replaced her with the vocalist Georgia Carroll.

She started in B pictures; David Butler directed her in the fast-moving *That's Right, You're Wrong*, in which Kay Kyser, with her in tow, arrived in a topsy-turvy Hollywood. In *You'll Find Out*, the band was stranded in a mysterious mansion in a storm, with Boris Karloff, Bela Lugosi and Peter Lorre on the loose. Belting out "You've Got Me This Way," she was terrific.

When Victor Orsatti introduced her to Mayer, she was rich; she had nearly 18.5 million listeners a week, and tons of fan mail; she had a sprawling San Fernando Valley ranch, with twenty-five shorthorns, pigs, chickens and dogs. Her affluence pleased Mayer; it would look less like a case of patronage if he took her out. There was a handicap, though: he was always delighted if an actress he was interested in had a mother as a chaperone, but Ginny Simms also had a father, so he had to take the father out as well. And her father wasn't very impressed with him.

He took all three to the Mocambo and Ciro's nightclubs, where the stars came to dance before the plate glass windows over the pintable of lights that was Los Angeles. Sometimes a spotlight would swing to the table and Ginny Simms, just as in a movie, would stand up and deliver a song.

As was his custom, Mayer courted her with champagne and jewelry and flowers; when she went to New York and played the St. Regis Roof and the Waldorf, he was in front, applauding; and soon, as Victor Orsatti had wanted, he gave her an M.G.M. contract (just before, she had made *Hit the Ice*, with Abbott and Costello). He set about building a substantial musical for her, *Broadway Rhythm*, drawn from no less a source than *Very Warm for May*, by Jerome Kern and Oscar Hammerstein II, and had it rewritten from start to finish so that she would be the center of it. And one song, the classic "All the Things You Are" (done in the theater by Frances Mercer), would, for good measure, be sung by her.

As if all this were not enough, he gave his favorite nephew, Jack Cummings, the job of producing the movie, and signed Roy Del Ruth, who had done well with several musicals, to direct; star performers, led by Lena Horne, were put in as supporting attractions for what became, in effect, a musical revue. It was a handsome picture, beginning with Ginny Simms, radiant in white furs, descending a nightclub staircase: a star entrance if ever there was one. Mayer instructed his favorite color cameraman, Leonard Smith, to match the lighting that Darryl F. Zanuck specified for Betty Grable; he had Smith call 20th Century-Fox cinematographer Ernest Palmer to check on the technique used in Grable's *Coney Island*, his favorite movie.

At the time *Broadway Rhythm* was shooting, Mayer made the same mistake he had made with Jean Howard and Gladys O'Brien. He offered Ginny Simms a million dollars if she would marry him; she had sensibly held out against marriage, or even a physical affair, because she didn't want it to be thought she had obtained *Broadway Rhythm* on anything else but her talent. She was proud and decent, and when Mayer offered the money she was shocked. As for her father, who had money anyway, he delivered a remark for the books: "My little baby isn't for sale!" That said it all; the romance was over.

\*   \*   \*

In the summer, after a prolonged wait, Mayer received word that his brother Rudolph was in a Japanese internment camp in Manila. Robert Vogel and other staff members came to Mayer to tell him that every effort to obtain an exchange with a Japanese internee in Los Angeles had failed. Mayer said briskly, "Leave it to me!" He picked up the telephone and called Archbishop Spellman. According to Howard Strickling:

> Spellman, of course, had a direct line to the Pope; the Pope to Hitler; Hitler to General Tojo in Tokyo. Within days, Rudy was on a Swedish repatriation ship, on his way to Los Angeles. To tell you this is to give you the true meaning of L.B.'s power.

By the time Rudolph Mayer returned, Mabel Walker Willebrandt had quashed each and every residual criminal charge against this wayward member of the clan. By March 1944 (we see from Rudolph's application —his first ever—for Social Security) he would be working in New York City, for Loew's radio station WHN. Soon, he would be back to his old antics.

Mayer made a new contribution to the war effort with *Thirty Seconds Over Tokyo*, written by the Communist Dalton Trumbo, whose politics still did not trouble him, and directed, with his customary skill, by Mervyn LeRoy. In preparing this important picture, an account of the famous Doolittle air attack on Tokyo in 1942, Mayer had the coopera- tion of General "Hap" Arnold, as well as of Jimmy Doolittle himself. He was also in correspondence with General Douglas MacArthur, planning a picture about the heroic U.S. PT boat crews, with John Ford, who was now in intelligence, and Robert Montgomery, with whom he had at last made his peace, as liaison.[4]

On the evening of July 24, 1943, Greer Garson married Navy Lieuten- ant Richard Ney, who had played her son in *Mrs. Miniver*, at the Santa Monica Presbyterian Church. Their relationship had been hidden until *Mrs. Miniver* was released because of fear of public criticism that might reflect on the character she played; such were the connections in the public mind at the time between screen fantasy and human reality. Her divorce decree from Alec Snelson had come through on June 7. She was

---

[4] Made the following year, it became *They Were Expendable*, one of the finest of M.G.M. pictures and perhaps the most accurate portrayal of naval warfare achieved in Hollywood.

working on *Madame Curie* at the time; Ney had been given leave from Alaskan waters, but she had been ill in bed with influenza, which had delayed the wedding. The only witness was Miss Garson's mother.

*Madame Curie* was a courageous venture: a serious movie about science. Paul Osborn's screenplay, checked for accuracy by Eve Curie, Madame Curie's daughter, was of an extraordinary complexity; the Curies (he was acted by Walter Pidgeon) were shown as excited over separating radium from pitchblende as they were over the birth of their children. The picture was yet another example of M.G.M.'s greatness; Mervyn Leroy's direction, Osborn's writing, the acting of the stars, the art direction of the grim Curie laboratory hut and the somber photography of Joseph Ruttenberg were of a very high order.

It was for pictures of this caliber that, on August 26, the Mexican government, expunging the disgrace of Lee Tracy on *Viva Villa*, bestowed the Order of the Aztec Eagle, its highest award for a civilian, on Mayer at the Foreign Office in Mexico City. Foreign Minister Padilla pinned the medal on him. Others honored that evening were Walt Disney and James A. FitzPatrick, of the M.G.M. travelogues. John Loder and his wife, Hedy Lamarr, as well as Walter Pidgeon, were there, with Robert Vogel in charge of arrangements. After the reception, there was a showing of travel films on Mexico, led by FitzPatrick's latest, and an official dinner, at which Mayer spoke warmly of the importance of Mexican pictures. Guy W. Wray of the U.S. embassy wrote to Cordell Hull on September 15: "The entire visit took place without any untoward incidents and appears to have created an excellent impression."

Late in 1943, work began on *Meet Me in St. Louis*, the most important musical made at the studio in that period, a movie that was destined to become legendary. Mayer's favorite reader, Lillie Messenger, had come across the stories by Sally Benson in *The New Yorker*, evoking the charm of St. Louis at the time of the 1904 World's Fair. Nobody at the studio had wanted to do the picture; producer after producer had turned it down. Finally, Mayer said to Miss Messenger, "You want to do it? We'll give it to Arthur Freed to produce. He should be allowed at least one failure!" Mayer had Sally Benson approached for the rights—although Freed forever after claimed the credit. Miss Benson didn't want to work in Hollywood, so, after Mayer bought the material, he assigned Irving Brecher and Fred Finkelhoffe to adapt it, and Vincente Minnelli (the ideal choice) to direct it. The score, by various hands old and new (the title song was by Andrew B. Sterling and Kerry Mills), emerged impressively, played by Roger Edens to Mayer on a piano in his office. Judy Garland was cast as Esther Smith, Margaret O'Brien as her sister Tootie; Lucille Bremer, Leon Ames and Mary Astor were also cast.

From the beginning, this production, destined to be one of the studio's biggest hits, was plagued with difficulties that proved deeply frustrating to Mayer. Judy Garland was the chief problem. Her neuroses had by now assumed Garboish proportions. Just over two weeks into production, she said she felt ill; Eddie Mannix had to drive her home. She couldn't come to work for several successive days. Two days after Christmas, she was in the hospital; the schedule had to be reworked to have other people's scenes shot first. Mary Astor came down with a fever. Tom Drake also took sick; he had to leave the set after only three hours' work on December 30. Finally, on New Year's Eve, with Garland still absent, the picture was closed down. On January 8, she reported back late, announcing she could not begin work until noon. On the eleventh she called in to say she had an earache; she didn't report until 10:30. No sooner had Minnelli started the first take than she felt ill again and took to her dressing room with an ice bag on her head. She was thirty-five minutes late after lunch.

By now, Mary Astor had pneumonia. On the eighteenth and nineteenth, Garland was away and the picture closed down again. Mary Astor was out for the rest of the month, and Garland was sick once more. Then, on January 31, came the worst blow of all.

Margaret O'Brien's aunt Marissa called up and said she was taking her niece off to Arizona! And only because she had a bad cold! The picture closed down for a week while Miss O'Brien went on vacation, an astonishing circumstance. Then, while work was suspended, on February 3, the actress Joan Carroll was rushed to a hospital for an appendectomy and Mayer was told she would not be available for two weeks. Mary Astor had a relapse on February 7; Margaret O'Brien lingered on in Arizona; the picture closed down again. At last, on February 14, Mary Astor returned to work, and shooting recommenced. Next day, Margaret O'Brien was back in town and two days later returned to work. But no sooner was she in harness than Judy Garland again fell ill. The actor Harry Davenport was sick . . . Garland was ill through much of March. And so the picture dragged on.

Not only was Mayer consumed by the problems of *Meet Me in St. Louis*, he was still depressed by the fact that Ginny Simms had turned him down. He would put his head in his hands at his desk and sob like a child. Victor Orsatti struck again. He found a substitute: another actress he was handling. Like Ginny Simms, she was working in B pictures—at Columbia, the salt mine of Hollywood.

Her name was Ann Miller. She was yet another Texan, a dark, high-cheekboned beauty possessed of enormous energy. She had an earthy, uncomplicated, primitive sensuality and energy on the screen, though in private she was virginal, cool, highly moral and devoted to her mother.

She was in her twenties when Mayer met her. Born Lucille Ann Collier in Chireno, she was the daughter of a criminal lawyer. Afflicted with rickets as a child, she trained her legs in dancing school; she soon had a perfect body. Her showbiz mother, Clara, ditched a husband and carried Ann off to Hollywood, where, at age twelve, she was already dancing up a storm in front of Rotary and Lions' Club audiences. Lucille Ball spotted her in a San Francisco nightclub and a talent scout had her signed up at RKO; she was loaned out to Columbia, and was witty and charming in *You Can't Take It With You*. When Mayer got to know her, she was tapping her way through such brisk but forgettable programmers as *Time Out for Rhythm* and *Reveille for Beverly*.

She was warm, adorable, amusing; she played birdbrains on the screen with good-natured charm. Frank and Victor Orsatti gave a joint dinner party for her to meet Mayer, at Frank's house in Bel Air; Miss Miller kept up the tradition of all Mayer's women by bringing her mother along as a chaperone. Again, following tradition, Mayer worked on Clara first; he set out to dazzle her, and he succeeded. Ann Miller was fascinated by him and found him very attractive. After dinner, he came up to her in the orchid-filled living room and said, his eyes boring into hers—she will never forget his exact words—"I have enjoyed your dancing so much, Miss Miller. Perhaps you would give me the pleasure of permitting me to take you out to dinner—and dancing?"

Ann Miller, again, like Mayer's other women, made it clear she would bring her mother along. Mayer instantly agreed; he crossed the room and spoke to Clara. The result was that the three of them went out together; this didn't quell the gossips, but it did maintain an illusion of propriety for the nightclubbing public. He was so excellent on the dance floor he even managed to equal Ann Miller. He didn't tap-dance, of course.

She liked the fact that he never swore, never told dirty stories, and had a certain gentle innocence behind the tough exterior. His power and forcefulness excited her, even though he was almost sixty. She liked his constant emphasis on the sanctity of motherhood.

He would come to dinner with Clara and Ann; they always kept a bottle of Rock and Rye for him (he drank a little now). Mrs. Collier would cook; he loved her roast chicken and spinach soufflé, and chocolate soufflé for dessert. Sometimes they would listen to the radio together.

Mayer had recently rented a new house, at 910 Benedict Canyon Drive, from Warner Brothers, the Spanish bungalow once occupied at M.G.M. by Marion Davies; he moved there early in June 1944. He abandoned Margaret after forty years of marriage; according to most family members, he chose the date of their wedding anniversary, June 14, 1944, but Daniel Selznick, Mayer's grandson, insists that, out of consideration, he let the date pass. In view of the fact that he was in love with Ann Miller, and, family man though he was, had become wearied by Margaret, this decision could not be avoided. According to Mayer's close friend, the caterer Louisa di Salvio, Margaret, in those last weeks before Mayer left, was suffering from very severe mental and emotional disturbances. She told Louisa that she had everything she wanted, a famous and decent husband, a beautiful home, money and all they could buy, but she wasn't happy with herself: she hated her own being. For years, she had been struggling against an overwhelming inferiority complex because she was a simple housewife who was totally overshadowed by Mayer. Now, the years of suffering following her hysterectomy and Mayer's interest in other women pushed her over the edge. She tried to commit suicide several times with overdoses of pills and alcohol, but each time she was rescued with a stomach pump. Finally, she told Louisa, she had urged Mayer to leave her for good, and not to look back; all she wanted to do was to die. Other sources confirm that Margaret's condition was recurrent and extreme. According to Louisa di Salvio, Mayer was always kind and considerate to his wife on his visits to her, which were increasingly painful.

Daniel Selznick vividly recalls his grandmother during those dark hours, even though he was only six at the time. He was not, of course, told about the suicide attempts. He said that, although Margaret did her best to hide her wounds, the scars were all too visible; that she was poignantly protective toward her husband and his reputation, wishing only that he would be happy, even with another woman, and even though her heart was breaking; that she was without jealous and vengeful feelings. In future years, when Daniel was very close to her, he saw her clinging to her home as a refuge, seldom going out. She was fiercely loving of her possessions, her china and glassware; she poured her energy into paintings, emerging as a Sunday painter reminiscent of Cezanne; her talents were moderate, but the paintings were appealing, and working on them provided excellent therapy.

Often, as he grew older, Daniel would find her sitting on the patio at Santa Monica, staring over the Pacific Ocean, like some forlorn figure from the pages of a Russian novel. Filled with forgiveness for the man she had loved and who had betrayed her, bleeding in deep secrecy in her spirit, nursing and hiding her open sores, quietly she lived on.

Mayer introduced Sunday night dinner parties at his new home, catered by Luisa di Salvio, with food obtained from Chasen's Restaurant, and with many stars present; Ann Miller will never forget the superb cuisine. Famous singers and dancers would perform; the atmosphere was jolly and exciting. When the parties were over, even though he would have to be at the studio by 10:00 A.M. and would probably go riding before that, and even though he had been playing golf all day (he got through a game in forty minutes), he would still dismiss everyone and drive, through red lights, at breakneck speed to the late-night Mocambo to dance into the early morning hours with Clara and Ann, always in that order. Or sometimes he would ask everyone to pour into the screening room to see the latest M.G.M. movie. Even when he had a screening, he would ask Clara and Ann to stay on; very often, the phone would ring, and mother and daughter would listen in on the other line as a prominent actress would call him, saying if he would cast her in a certain picture she would be happy to spend the night with him. Miss Miller wrote in her memoirs: "I'm sure Mr. Mayer had many of his star lady-friends over to spend the night with him or vice versa. He may have enjoyed them but he did not respect them."

He liked to walk with Ann Miller through Beverly Hills in the middle of the night; once he gave her a ruby-and-diamond bracelet and a topaz ring. He begged Clara repeatedly, on his knees, to let him marry Ann. Miss Miller was willing; but there was always the question of divorcing Margaret, and Clara felt that Mayer was much too old. He tried to buy up Ann's contract from Harry Cohn of Columbia, to keep her in his "house." Cohn, to his frustration and fury, refused. He enlisted Victor Orsatti to plead his cause with Clara; nothing happened.

Following the completion of Meet Me in St. Louis in March 1944, Mayer announced plans for Uncle Tom's Cabin, to be produced by Arthur Hornblow, Jr., with Lena Horne as Eliza and Margaret O'Brien as Little Eva. Nothing came of this. He was heroically at work developing the Loew's pension plan, guaranteeing executives $50,000 a year on retirement and similar benefits for all performers, directors and crews. Mabel Walker Willebrandt worked overtime solving the concomitant tax problems in Washington.

Following a disappointing Academy Awards, in which only William Saroyan's original story of The Human Comedy and a Tom and Jerry animated cartoon were honored, Mayer left for New York for several weeks in April and May, much of it wasted in meetings with Alexander Korda.

That spring, Mayer embarked on two pictures that were far removed from the sort of family movies he wanted to symbolize M.G.M. policy.

*Gaslight,* based on Patrick Hamilton's play and an earlier British picture and directed by George Cukor, was the story of a fortune hunter (Charles Boyer, cast cleverly by producer Arthur Hornblow, Jr., against type) who terrorizes his wife (Ingrid Bergman) in order to unearth the jewels of the woman he has murdered. The picture was a harsh and uncompromising work, strikingly filmed, and Cukor's most cinematic achievement.

Another fine picture, even further away from the M.G.M. standard schmaltz, was Albert Lewin's *The Picture of Dorian Gray.* According to its star, Hurd Hatfield, Mayer was determined to make this picture against every obstacle. Albert Lewin went to him with the idea and everyone else thought it bizarre. Oscar Wilde on the screen? It wouldn't sell a ticket. Lewin told Mayer, "I have the money to make it independently if you don't want to do it." And Mayer replied, "Let's do it here."

Lewin wanted Hurd Hatfield, who was unknown, to play the diabolical Dorian Gray, whose portrait in the attic reflects his corrupt soul while his face retains an ageless youth. Wilde had conceived a homosexual pipedream of a blond Apollo; Hatfield was handsome, but dark-haired, gloomy, mysterious, opaque. That was exactly the deadpan quality Lewin wanted: a man whose squalid experiences are unreflected in his countenance. Mayer agreed; Hatfield will always be grateful to him for his fatherly, loving encouragement. Preparations went on for months, for the most exquisitely fashioned work of art in the studio's history, with the artist Gordon Wiles recreating nineteenth-century London in ink and wash sketches of great skill and beauty. Mayer kept Hatfield busy by casting him in *Dragon Seed,* a hymn to Chinese peasants, with Katharine Hepburn in a coolie hat and with a Bryn Mawr accent poisoning Japanese soldiers' soup.

Mayer approved Lewin's decision to have Ivan Albright paint the attic portrait of Dorian Gray—a horrifying picture of a face swollen with corruption—and for once, Herbert Stothart supplied a haunting musical score. Angela Lansbury was cast (discovered wrapping parcels at a department store, she had been a predatory maid in *Gaslight)* as Sybil Vane, the tragic barroom singer whom Dorian murders; she made a remarkable impression: a star in the making. The design of Hans Peters, working with Gordon Wiles, was impeccable: the London house with the checkerboard marble hall floor; the crowded Dickensian public house; the sinister, shadowy back streets of Blue Gate Fields. Hatfield's performance was also flawless: few other actors could have conveyed depravity and murderous cruelty with no more than the suggestion of a smile or a glance. Sir Cedric Hardwicke was the uncredited off-screen narrator, gently underlining the script's audacious inklings. Not only was the picture a triumph of Mayer and M.G.M., it was a triumph over Will Hays' successor, Joseph Breen.

But it brought disappointment to one prominent person. Just before it was due to be finally cast, a photograph arrived on Mayer's desk of a woman he recognized dressed as Dorian Gray. He turned the picture over. On the back, in a large, round, childlike hand were inscribed the words, "This is the part I was born to play." The signature was Garbo's.[5]

Almost as though he were guilty or uneasy over this extraordinary work (Hurd Hatfield was so nervous about the picture that he crept into the preview disguised as an old man in a gray wig and granny glasses), Mayer, in August, had in full swing several pictures weighted toward heavy escapism.

Van Johnson and Esther Williams were afloat in *Thrill of a Romance;* Frank Sinatra crooned, Gene Kelly danced and Kathryn Grayson trilled in *Anchors Aweigh,* George Sidney's gala musical of the Navy; Greer Garson and Walter Pidgeon were at their best in *Mrs. Parkington,* a Louis Bromfield story of a wealthy New York dynasty, powerfully directed by Tay Garnett. Thirty-three directors and as many stars were under contract.

During those years, Mayer was extraordinarily kind to his grandsons, Jeffrey and Daniel. Daniel remembers Mayer finding time to go shopping during a crowded schedule. He would take Daniel to a little store near the studio in Culver City, where five different kinds of corn were stocked; he was always anxious that the boys eat only the finest corn with their meals, and he also made sure he picked out the best kosher chicken for them. Nothing could be good enough for his grandsons. He applied to them the same principles that he did to his studio staff: just as his employees always went first-class, so Jeffrey and Daniel must go first-class through life. And his respect for their father, David, increasing gradually over the years, had now firmed into actual liking and warmth. Soon, unlike his daughter Irene, Mayer would forgive David for deserting Irene for the actress Jennifer Jones. After all, who was he to throw the first stone?

Through the summer of 1944, Mayer continued to court Ann Miller. She was constantly working, through *Carolina Blues, Hey, Rookie* and *Jam Session,* belting out songs, dancing excitingly in these movies that were on the bottom half of movie bills; Mayer saw all of her pictures. He kept begging, weeping, cajoling Harry Cohn to allow him to sign her;

---

[5] At about the same time, Aldous Huxley was asked to visit a house in Beverly Hills. He arrived, puzzled but intrigued by the anonymous invitation. He sat for a long time until at last a figure in a brown cassock, robe and rope sandals, with a beard, walked slowly toward him down a long corridor. A voice he recognized said, "This is the picture you must write for me, 'St. Francis of Assisi'!" It was Garbo.

then Cohn began to weaken. Prodded by Victor Orsatti, Cohn decided to cast her in an expensive picture entitled *The Petty Girl,* about the leggy beauties who appeared in *Esquire* magazine illustrations. It would be made on so large a budget that it would make it possible for Miss Miller to become a major star; Mayer would be forced to pay hundreds of thousands for her services.

Ann Miller wrote in her memoirs that she discovered she was a victim of this Orsatti horse-trading maneuver and decided she must break with Mayer. Like Ginny Simms, she was convinced that if she married him she would never be recognized as having talent of her own, only as Mayer's woman. And she suspected that he would want her to leave pictures, to become a housewife and a hostess. She saw a brighter prospect ahead; she was nobody's fool. But she didn't break off the relationship.

Mayer invited Miss Miller to a moment sacred to all horse owners: the birth of a foal. She wrote in her memoirs:

> He wouldn't leave the mother's side even for one minute. He just sat there with tears streaming down his face as he watched the . . . the bag of water breaking, and the little horse staggering to its feet . . .

He was with Ann Miller when he had a serious accident at Perris on August 27. A spirited horse reared, throwing him, and in the fall he crushed his pelvis. Dr. Jessie Marmorston was present. She immediately had the paramedics take him to Cedars of Lebanon Hospital in Los Angeles, where he underwent a serious operation. Herbert Hoover sent a note of sympathy on August 29:

> I see in the papers that you and your horse got reckless. We cannot have good men like yourself laid up in times like these . . .

Mayer's secretary, Jeanette Spooner, replied on September 13, saying that Mayer was well on the road to recovery.

During Mayer's weeks in Cedars of Lebanon Hospital, the most frequent visitor, apart from Ann Miller and Dr. Marmorston, was the celebrated Beverly Hills psychiatrist Dr. May Romm. Dr. Romm, like Mayer and Dr. Marmorston, was a Russian. Born in Vitebsk, on the Polish border, in the 1890s, she was also the daughter of an unskilled scholar; and the family also came to New York. Trained in medicine at Mount Vernon, she married an advertising man named Lippe Colodny and had a daughter, Dorothy. Later, she moved to California and married the wealthy Alexis Romm. He died, leaving her money; in New York, she became an expert in radium poisoning.

Encouraged by Dr. Abraham Abrill, a proselytizer of Freud, Dr. Romm became a psychiatrist in the 1930s. She was a resident at the New York State Psychiatric Institute, then moved to California, marrying Samuel Golding, an attorney. She set up practice on North Camden Drive in Beverly Hills in 1938 and took on Margaret, Irene and Edie Mayer as patients; Louis B. Mayer soon became one also. She managed to provide solace for all the tortured Mayers—another strong woman Mayer leaned upon.

She and Jessie Marmorston, formidable opponents, began to struggle for mental and emotional possession of Mayer. "They pulled and tugged at him; they dragged him limb from limb," Dorothy Colodny, May Romm's daughter, says. "There was *tremendous* competition between them to see who would be first into the hospital room." If Dr. Marmorston arrived at the same time, one would push ahead of the other; they refused to enter the room simultaneously. Dr. Marmorston was stronger; for all her fame as a shrink, Dr. Romm was always sorry for herself, frightened of everything, unable to be alone, oversensitive: a neurotic easily defeated by her remarkable adversary.

Mayer was cheered in the hospital by a synopsis given him of a novel, *Green Dolphin Street*, written by Elizabeth Goudge, which had won a newly established M.G.M. fiction prize, and which he saw as a suitable vehicle for Lana Turner. It was the story of a man who sent for the wrong mail-order bride from New Zealand; Australia was a good market for American pictures, with Europe (apart from England) virtually closed.

From his bed, he authorized the purchase of *The Green Years*, A. J. Cronin's novel of a Scottish family. And he weathered the crisis when, in mid-October, in a dispute between unions, IATSE employees at M.G.M. walked out for several days.

In those weeks, even while wracked with pain, Mayer had to make a difficult executive decision. Fred Zinnemann, a German director he had been building up from the B picture level, had started work on the Judy Garland–Robert Walker vehicle *The Clock*, a characteristic fantasy by Paul Gallico, author of *The Snow Goose*, about a young couple meeting in New York, falling in love and overcoming obstacles to obtain a marriage license. Mayer had authorized producer Arthur Freed to hire another romantic fantasist, Robert Nathan, to write the screenplay. In this daydream, New York was seen as a benign city, filled with helpful people. A justice of the peace would miss his homebound train to marry a couple; a milkman would take strangers aboard to deliver his rounds.

The real-life problems of Judy Garland intruded: she was more difficult than ever, hated Zinnemann's cool, detached treatment of her and
insisted he be fired. Mayer yielded; her present lover, Vincente Minnelli,
took over, and she responded well. But her perpetual lateness for trysts
in the picture, under the Astor Hotel clock, had its parallels in her
lateness on the set, and Robert Walker, cast as the Indiana hick GI who
has never seen a skyscraper, was going through torments at losing his
wife, Jennifer Jones, to David O. Selznick and was drinking heavily.
Seldom, even at M.G.M., had a movie fairy tale been more ironically
contrasted with the painful truths experienced by its principals. The
fantasy succeeded; it was another hit for Judy Garland, and by now *Meet
Me in St. Louis* was the biggest M.G.M. picture since *Gone With the
Wind*.

Mayer was away from the studio for eight weeks, in great distress—not
least when he had to read in *Variety*, on October 4, that Nicholas
Schenck, ostensibly in town to cheer him up, was, in fact, talking with
Eddie Mannix and his enemy, production executive Sam Katz, to see
which one would take over the studio. It was stated in *Variety* that he
might retire; he was furious, and called the editor demanding a retrac-
tion. It was not supplied; he had made the mistake of referring, at a sales
meeting in September, to the fact that he "hoped to have the benefit" of
the M.G.M. pension plan he had done much to promote.

Meanwhile, he received the mildly pleasant news that, after wasting a
fortune of M.G.M. money, Alexander Korda was at last making a picture
for the studio in England. *Perfect Strangers* starred Robert Donat and a
twenty-three-year-old Scottish actress Mayer would soon admire almost
as much as Greer Garson: the charming Deborah Kerr. He decided she
must come to Hollywood; she had made a mark in *Major Barbara*, *Hat-
ter's Castle* and *The Life and Death of Colonel Blimp*. She had much of the
dignity, poise and presence of Greer Garson; but she also offered strong
suggestions of sensuality, of banked fires, that the cool Miss Garson did
not. Mayer was fascinated, but it would be three years before he summoned her to Hollywood.

On Christmas Eve, Mayer returned for a big welcome-home party at
which Margaret O'Brien kissed him under the mistletoe and every producer, director and star was present. It was a happy moment at the end
of a painful year.

Arthur Freed and George Sidney's *The Harvey Girls* was shooting that
winter. Once again, Judy Garland misbehaved, arriving on set only to
announce she wouldn't be ready until after lunch, turning up late day
after day. And once again, the cast seemed to be jinxed by various
accidents and afflicted by a contagious malady of some sort. Lucille

Bremer and Janet Bean were in automobile crashes. Mayer was furious
when he discovered that Miss Garland would not speak to anyone at the
studio directly, that her phone was cut off and that only her secretary,
Evelyn Powers, could be reached. Her sicknesses continued; Miss Powers
was on the phone for hours each day with feeble explanations—and
then everyone threw up their hands. Leading man John Hodiak got a sty
in his eye, and Miss Garland announced she was too tired to work
because she was making Decca records until close to midnight. Even
when a crowd of extras had lined up for the "Atchison, Topeka and the
Santa Fe" number, Judy Garland said she wasn't sure if she would be well
enough to go ahead. She wasn't, the scene was canceled, thousands were
lost; at last she did it—perfectly, of course.

Anything to do with Judy Garland was the talk of the studio. Adela
Rogers St. Johns was always first in with the information, but neither she
nor Louella Parsons nor Hedda Hopper would dare print it. According to
Miss St. Johns, a studio executive used to make Miss Garland and a
publicity girl give lesbian displays for him; Drug Enforcement Administration officials arrived to investigate the star. They found that there was
a woman, head of a drug ring and connected to gangster Lucky Luciano,
who was peddling narcotics to performers. Eddie Mannix decided she
had to be gotten rid of. Mayer said, "Whatever has to be done, do it."
Mannix, of course, had been the bouncer at the New Jersey Palisades
Amusement Park. He arranged for a gangster to take the woman there
for a Sunday outing. They were in a cage hanging from the top of the
huge ferris wheel when the man told her he would throw her off unless
she stopped feeding drugs to Judy Garland. She stopped.

## CHAPTER TWENTY-ONE

# 1945–1948

BEFORE THE WAR WAS OVER, the enlisted male stars began to return to Hollywood from the fronts. Clark Gable arrived to make *Adventure*, an ill-conceived vehicle in which he costarred with Greer Garson. The story of a librarian and a roughneck seaman, heavy with mystical overtones, *Adventure* was neither a critical nor a commercial success; it became known as *Misadventure* in the motion picture trade.

It was unfortunate that Mayer's choice for Clark Gable's comeback was so inauspicious, since the star had done good service both in the United States and Belgium, and Field Marshal Goering had done him the honor of offering a million marks for his head. Gable had shot some 50,000 feet of film of German installations for U.S. Army Intelligence and had been given an Air Medal for that service; Mayer placed the studio laboratories at his disposal for development of the film.

Gable's attitude toward Mayer was not softened by the gesture. The star's incipient anti-Semitism, more or less suppressed in the 1930s, now became more marked, and his dissatisfaction with *Adventure*, as well as his dislike of Miss Garson and her tea breaks, was very intense. He had been affected by his war experiences; the postwar Gable was weary, disillusioned, all of the insolent cockiness of his prewar self knocked out of him. This change of character showed on the screen and had a certain lowering effect on all but his most devoted fans.

Robert Taylor returned from the Navy; soon, Pandro S. Berman would cast him in *Undercurrent*, with Katharine Hepburn, but audiences were not pleased to see him cast as a psychopath. In his preparation of vehicles for his stars, Mayer was slipping; always uncertainly in control of his pictures, increasingly leaving responsibility to others, he was slowly but surely seeing the ground slide from under his feet.

He clashed with his production team. Because so many had begun to slam his office door, quite unsettling the aging Ida Koverman, who still sat in the outer room, he hit upon a device that proved useful. He needed the producer Edwin H. Knopf, brother of the publisher Alfred Knopf, for a discussion. Knopf was on vacation at a lake in the mountains, fishing, when an M.G.M. messenger drew up in a speedboat with a request that he return to Mayer's office at once. Furious, Knopf arrived as bidden only to find that he had been summoned on a foolish pretext. He walked out angrily and tried to slam the door, but couldn't. Mayer had seen to it that it was on a newly installed vacuum hinge.

The 1944 Academy Awards were held at Grauman's Chinese Theater on March 15. Ingrid Bergman won for her performance in *Gaslight*, and Cedric Gibbons's art department was rewarded: a Special Effects award went to that department for *Thirty Seconds Over Tokyo*, for a harrowing re-creation of the Doolittle raid. To Mayer's delight, Margaret O'Brien received a special juvenile Oscar for her luminous acting. It was the last Awards ceremony of the war.

Every day brought exciting news to Mayer's office. On April 30, 1945, eighteen days after President Roosevelt's death and two days after Mussolini's, Hitler committed suicide and Soviet troops captured Berlin; on May 8, Germany surrendered. But Japan was still in the war, and it was not until August 6 that the atomic bomb fell on Hiroshima. Three days later, Nagasaki was leveled, and, on August 14, Japan surrendered. There was no suspension of shooting at M.G.M. on any of these days, but the commissary and studio back streets were alive with rejoicing.

Within days of victory, Arthur Loew was hard at work retrieving M.G.M. funds from formerly occupied Europe. The Germans had not confiscated Loew's, Inc., moneys in Berlin; 987,151.79 marks had lain there all through the war, untouched; the same money that Loew had tried, unsuccessfully, to transfer to Amsterdam in 1941. Similar sums were found intact in Tokyo, Rome, Budapest, Bucharest and other capitals.

There were well-founded fears that Great Britain would provide a new anti-American quota or tariff system in 1945 (it did) that could severely cut the $18.5 million-a-year British market for M.G.M. pictures. So sensitive was M.G.M. about Britain that when the London critic E. Arnot Robertson attacked *The Green Years* on the BBC, Arthur Loew threatened her bosses with retaliatory action. She was fired and sued M.G.M. She won the suit but lost on appeal, and her career never recovered. She died in exile.

Along with the national victories in Europe, there were victories for Mayer on the home front. In October 1944, Neil McCarthy, Hollywood attorney and friend of Mayer's, had bought for him, in Melbourne, Australia, the champion filly Busher and had imported the horse through submarine-haunted waters to the Perris ranch. Mayer was as delighted with Busher as he was with The Pye, the gelding ridden to victory in the British Derby by Elizabeth Taylor in *National Velvet*. Busher romped ahead again and again, winning the Santa Margarita Handicap, the Washington Park Handicap and the Hollywood Park Derby. At a party attended by Greer Garson, Mayer was heard to say, "She's gorgeous! Her red hair! Her perfect legs! What a beauty!" "Oh, thank you, Mr. Mayer," Miss Garson said sweetly. He was forced to tell her he was talking about Busher.

There was a painful incident that year, which haunted Mayer for the rest of his life. His horses came in first, second and third at Santa Anita; just as he rose in glory, the crowd turned on him and booed him. He lost all composure and hid his face in his hands.

Mayer wasn't feeling well; his fainting spells had grown more frequent. As he approached his sixtieth birthday, Dr. Marmorston and her rival, Dr. Romm, noted that he was very much afraid of death. As he had done for years, he made the serious mistake of skipping out of town for X rays and barium treatments. He flew to New York and checked into Mount Sinai Hospital for an entire week of tests. Mayer evidently was reminded of his mother's passing, at sixty-two, from cholecystitis. He was afraid that the results of his tests might be mixed up with someone else's and trusted only Drs. Marmorston and Romm; he had dispensed with Dr. Edward B. Jones.

Mayer's generosity was extraordinary. He took a cut in his salary to make possible retirement benefit funds for his workers. His driver, Slickum Garrison, turned out to be broke; Mayer gave him money to support his growing family. Louisa di Salvio, his caterer, told him she needed $7,500 deposit on a house or her beloved mother would be homeless. He called her to his office after a party; she was petrified that she might have displeased him with her selection of food, crockery and silver. But to her amazement, he not only praised her pheasant under glass, supplied for fifty people, but told her that he had something for her. He took an envelope from a desk drawer and handed it to her, telling her not to open it until after midnight the next night. Returning from a party at 1:30 A.M., she opened it and found a check for the full amount of the deposit. She burst into tears; later, Mayer told her to take her mother out to the best dress shop in town and spend $1,000 of his money (an enormous sum in those days) to buy her mother a brand new outfit.

He began to take clumsy executive actions, reshuffling staff, giving too much power to Sam Katz, whom he disliked, pushing others out. He sent Frank Orsatti, who wasn't even on the studio payroll, to Italy to make deals with the Puccini family for the rights to the composer's operas, as ill-fated a venture as the similar 1937 expedition of himself and Hal Roach to Rome, since opera-on-film had no interest for the mass audience.

He hesitated over a decision that Sidney Franklin called upon him to make: Franklin had decided to revive his own plan, dating from 1941, to make *The Yearling*; the producer had run the old footage shot in Florida and was impressed by it again. Maybe the bad behavior of Spencer Tracy and Victor Fleming in abandoning the picture (there had been a brief attempt to revive it with King Vidor) could now be expunged and the studio could turn out an Academy Award–winning prestige picture.

Mayer wasn't entirely comfortable, but Harriet Frank, one of his trusted tellers of tales, and Franklin, whose taste and skill he never ceased to recognize, talked him into going ahead with a lavish budget when costs of Technicolor and location shooting were formidably increased. It was one of the wisest decisions he ever made.

Franklin chose Clarence Brown to direct. As a Southerner himself and a lover of the wild, Brown, a poet flourishing in the commercial jungle, was entirely suited to the material. Paul Osborn was the ideal choice as adapter.

For the part of the farmer Penny Baxter, fighting with the problems of a growing, deer-obsessed youngster, Franklin went against Marjorie Kinnan Rawlings's original type (Lew Ayres would have been physically correct) and cast Gregory Peck, who had costarred with Greer Garson in *The Valley of Decision* and who had the rugged, rangy outdoor look of a pioneer farmer. As Ma Baxter, the producer daringly chose Jane Wyman, chiefly known as a lightweight comedienne at Warner Brothers.

The problem was that both stars had to be borrowed from difficult people. Gregory Peck was available only because Selznick, restless and dissatisfied as ever, had suspended work on *Duel in the Sun* and had temporarily let Peck go. But Selznick fretted that he shouldn't have. For Jane Wyman, Mayer had to go to Jack Warner, never Mayer's favorite. Warner struck a hard bargain. But there was no actress under contract to M.G.M. who could have played the part as well.

There was a much-publicized talent hunt for the part of Jody, the farmer's boy. Mayer wanted a tough, nut-brown Florida kid, but producer and director settled on a pale, spindly, rather overcivilized Tennessee schoolboy named Claude Jarman, Jr., who had no acting experience. It was an improbably but lucky choice, as Jarman managed the one expression of feeling without which the picture would never have worked: a sense of innocent wonder.

Brown went to the locations Richard Rosson and Wallace Worsley

had found in 1941, shot much footage with the cameraman, Charles
Rosher, and matched it to the existing material. Then Peck, Wyman,
Jarman, the crew and several deer were shifted to Ocala, Florida, and the
St. John's River for months of steamy, exhausting shooting in a reconstructed slab cabin and corncob and back house later copied and
matched in the studio's own version of the actual farming settlement
known locally as Baxter's Island.

Shooting the picture was often a burden on the players. During one
scene, in record heat, the deer kept breaking loose from Jarman and
wandering off camera. After numerous takes, the actors were streaming
with sweat; the makeup men had to plaster ice-cold chamois skins over
their faces. Crew members managed to lure the errant animal back with
lollipops and raisins, until at last the scene was completed.

The result of all this effort was a triumph of craftsmanship. Osborn
constructed the screenplay as a series of crises overcome, as numerous as
the hurdles built to contain the plant-eating deer. Blending old and new
film, Brown captured the rich green of the Everglades, the shallows and
jungle grass blades of the river, the thrust and surprise of the bear hunt,
the agony when a hunting rifle backfires and a rattlesnake bites Pa Baxter's hand. Above all, the writer caught, and the director conveyed, the
painful, loving and awkward relationship between parents and growing
boy as few motion pictures had done. Mayer was overjoyed with the
results.

While the picture was still unfinished, David Selznick called Mayer
and announced that he expected Gregory Peck to return to work immediately on *Duel in the Sun*. Mayer was furious at his son-in-law's lack of
consideration and pointed out that Peck was not going to be available
for an indefinite period. Sleepless and exasperated, Selznick simply had
to wait.

At the time, Robert Sisk produced, and Mayer's nephew by marriage,
Roy Rowland, sensitively directed, a Dalton Trumbo screenplay, *Our
Vines Have Tender Grapes*, about an immigrant Norwegian family in a
Wisconsin town. Mayer never admired Trumbo more than in this series
of rural episodes, involving a storm, two children lost in a floating bathtub in flood waters, a barn that catches fire, the excitement of Christmas
gifts opened at night. But one scene troubled this stickler for familial
propriety: when a neighborhood boy (Jackie "Butch" Jenkins) wants to
use the roller skates of one of the daughters (played by Margaret
O'Brien), she angrily refuses and her father suggests the mother smack
the child. Mayer, romantically unrealistic as ever, could not believe such

a suggestion and insisted Trumbo remove, and Rowland reshoot, the scene. It remains in the picture.

Mayer was always at home in the Never-Never Land of musicals. In June 1945, producer Joe Pasternak and director Henry Koster, inspired by a witty and inventive script by Myles Connolly and others, fashioned a movie that became one of Mayer's favorites. *Two Sisters from Boston* displayed all of the M.G.M. qualities in abundance: a strong period sense, fine art direction, a tuneful score and dances, correct for 1900, choreographed by Jack Donohue. The stars, newcomer June Allyson and Kathryn Grayson, were seen at their best; Mayer was building them carefully toward the top of their profession.

During the movie's shooting, Winfield Sheehan died. He had completed *Captain Eddie*, a screen biography of Captain Eddie Rickenbacker, the colorful American hero had shared Sheehan's defeatist, neutralist views in 1940 but had, unlike Sheehan, seen the error of his ways. The press raved about Sheehan's achievements; all of his criminal and pro-Nazi activities were predictably forgotten. Mayer was among the pallbearers, he who had moved mountains to oust Sheehan from the Fox Studios. As always in Hollywood, where power and money and fame were concerned, the ranks closed, the critics were silenced; all was forgiven and forgotten so that graves should not be sullied.

The gaudiest M.G.M. celebration of the new era, the Truman Age, was to be found in *Till the Clouds Roll By*, a travesty of the uneventful life of Jerome Kern, with a crowd-pleasing collection of musical sequences, the best of which starred Lena Horne. Also shooting were *The Lady in the Lake*, a revolutionary picture in which Robert Montgomery, directing as well as starring, told the story from the first-person point of view of the detective Philip Marlowe, his face seen only in mirrors, and Henry Koster's delicately fashioned *The Unfinished Dance*. All three pictures were made with the impressive craftsmanship that remained M.G.M.'s trademark. Pandro S. Berman, Sidney Franklin, Jack Cummings and Arthur Freed were still the most distinguished of Mayer's production team. The times were so rich and prodigal that Mayer could even risk an unsavory story of double cross, adultery and murder in James M. Cain's *The Postman Always Rings Twice*, expertly played by Lana Turner and John Garfield and directed by Tay Garnett.

That year saw the shooting of a picture that was close to Mayer's heart, one of the few made at the studio that dealt directly with his favorite theme of Roman Catholicism. *The Green Years*, produced by Leon Gordon and directed by Victor Saville, was M.G.M.'s newest version of an A. J. Cronin novel, adapted, in a model of screen construction, by Robert Ardrey and Sonya Levien. Set in Scotland, circa 1900–1911, the story centered on the coming to manhood of Robert Shannon, an orphaned half–Irish Catholic who has been set uneasily in the heart of a divided family, the Leckies. His impulse, as with so many of Cronin's heroes, is toward a medical career, but he stumbles repeatedly on his path. At the end, after he has almost become a priest, his friend, the drunken patriarch Alexander Gow, secures him an education through a will.

Victor Saville's direction of the picture amply justified Mayer's faith in him. Aided by the screenplay, by the sturdy performances of Charles Coburn as Grandfather Gow, Hume Cronyn as the tightfisted Papa Leckie, Jessica Tandy as Kate Leckie, Richard Haydn, perfection itself as the schoolmaster Jason Reid, and the modestly affecting Dean Stockwell and Tom Drake as Robbie, child and adult, the director achieved his masterwork. It is a sadness that the picture did not enjoy the critical response it deserved.

On July 27, Ginny Simms married the hotel heir Hyatt R. Dehn in Beverly Hills. This was painful enough, but now Mayer found that Ann Miller was drifting out of his life. She had fallen in love with the handsome elevator multimillionaire Reese Milner, a hard-bitten and brutal womanizer who deceived her into thinking he was gentle and good-natured. The first inkling of Milner's character emerged when Miss Miller began questioning him on various affairs that her boss, Harry Cohn of Columbia, had described to her. Mistaking the source of the information, Milner screamed, "That fat old Jew, Louis Mayer, is behind this! How can you love a man like that?"

At the same time, the manufacturer Harry Karl, who later married Debbie Reynolds, was also proposing to Ann Miller—and was also jealous of Mayer. She returned Karl's gifts of a fox coat and diamond bracelet and made up her mind to marry Reese Milner. Mayer was told of these events but, blinded by his addiction to Ann Miller, didn't believe them. It would have been too appalling that a third woman had turned him down.

Just before Christmas, Miss Miller called Mayer at his Beverly Hills house and told him of her decision. It came at the worst possible moment. Ann Miller recalls that Mayer's doctors had just taken a new set of X rays of his lungs and had found indications of severe effects of cigar smoking; he feared (though the diagnosis did not confirm it) that he had lung cancer. When she told him she was going to leave him, he burst into tears. "I heard this terrible sobbing, choking," she says; she will never forget it. He brooded over her decision, alone at the house except for his chauffeur, Frank, then took a large bottle of sleeping tablets and took them one by one. Frank found him as he lay close to death; paramedics rushed in with a stomach pump; Dr. Marmorston was at his side. Ann Miller, in tears, distraught with guilt, went with him and Marmorston to the hospital. Howard Strickling managed to keep the story out of the newspapers. Mayer recovered slowly; the shock remained with him for the rest of his life. Ann Miller married Reese Milner on February 16, 1946.

Mayer pulled himself together to allow Samuel Marx, who had been a very successful producer starting with *Lassie Come Home*, and had long thought of the project, to make what he hoped would turn out to be an interesting picture, *The Beginning or the End?*, the story of the making of the atomic bomb. Paramount's Hal Wallis was planning a similar project; Nicholas Schenck bought him out.

The idea for the movie came from Donna Reed's husband, Tony Owen, an agent for Charles Feldman. A former professor of Miss Reed's had worked at Oak Ridge on the bomb, and Owen had called Marx just two days after Hiroshima and Nagasaki to suggest the story. He was paid $40,000 for the idea.

Marx and Owen went to see Mayer, who said it was the most exciting subject for a picture that M.G.M. could ever make. He would put every top star under contract into it if Marx could bring him a good script.

Cleared at all levels of security, for such was the power of Loew's, Inc.'s man in Washington, D.C., Carter Barron, Marx and Owen went to Oak Ridge. They were met off the airplane by several scientists, who said they were scared stiff of what they had unleashed.

The pair proceeded to Washington, where they were received by President Harry Truman. He suggested the picture's title. Mayer wanted Marx to fly to Japan to see General MacArthur; Mayer himself would call MacArthur and arrange for MacArthur to give Marx film footage of the bombings. But there was no footage.

Marx and Owen went to see Albert Einstein at Princeton. The great scientist was very helpful and refused to take money for his cooperation. In New York, Marx met with Robert Oppenheimer, who wanted as his fee six pairs of nylon stockings, which were in very short supply, for his wife. The fee was supplied. Several scientists demanded money and in some cases were paid. They fought jealously for attention and positioning in the script. When it turned out that two of them had contributed much the same ingredient for the bomb, Marx had to promise to represent both of them on the screen.

Marx had a script written by Frank Wead. It was not good, and eventually, Mayer, influenced against the project by James McGuinness, gave Marx a second-string cast. McGuinness's insistence on the lightweight Norman Taurog as director was another mistake, though Taurog did his best. What could have been a megaton movie turned out to be a damp squib.

The 1945 Academy Awards were a thin harvest: Anne Revere won for her role in National Velvet, Harry Stradling for the cinematography of The Picture of Dorian Gray and Georgie Stoll for the best scoring of a musical picture for Anchors Aweigh. National Velvet got an editing award; The Yearling was not yet eligible.

On March 26, 1946, the Department of the Treasury presented Mayer with a scroll in honor of the studio's unrivaled purchase of war bonds. The following week, Mayer was again forced to announce that studio overheads were excessive and there must be immediate cost cutting. He sent his brother Jerry, who was ailing with stomach trouble, Sam Katz and Lawrence Weingarten to New York, for discussions with Nicholas Schenck. But it proved impossible to make any cuts.

On April 19, Mayer almost lost his favorite star. Greer Garson was shooting the picture A Woman of My Own, later retitled Desire Me, directed by George Cukor, at a rocky beach in Carmel, with her costar, Richard Hart, when a seven-foot wave swept in and carried her out to sea. Hart, who had a cardiac condition, was unable to swim powerfully enough to rescue her, but Vincente Sollesito, a deep-sea fisherman working as an extra on the picture, managed to drag her back to safety. Miss Garson suffered only shock, bruises and abrasions. The bigger injuries were caused to her career—the picture was a disaster, and began her gradual slide into near-oblivion.

In July 1946, an increasingly restless and angry IATSE labor force, including carpenters, painters, set designers and screen story analysts, struck against all the studios. Among M.G.M. pictures that had to close down were Rouben Mamoulian's Summer Holiday, a nostalgic musical version of Ah, Wilderness! On July 2, police squads aimed hoses at the picketers and arrested several demonstrators. Mayer ordered everything at M.G.M. brought to a standstill. The strike was settled after a few days.

On the same day of the strike, Margaret Mayer arrived in Reno to obtain her divorce. Meanwhile, Mayer had found a new love: Lorena Jones Danker, a former Busby Berkeley showgirl and bit player, who had been in Gold Diggers of 1933. She had made a small but definite impression as a darkly attractive maid in I Loved a Woman, an outstanding Warner Brothers picture about the meat business with Edward G. Robinson and Kay Francis; she had also appeared briefly in A Lost Lady, with

Barbara Stanwyck, *Jimmy the Gent*, with James Cagney, *Kansas City Princess* and *42nd Street*. Born in Georgia, she was a warm and appealing brunette in a direct line with Mayer's other loves, most all of whom were Southerners also. Her second husband, Danny Danker, an advertising executive, had died at the age of forty-two; he had worked with J. Walter Thompson, in whose offices she would find herself in later life. Danker had left her with a young daughter, Suzanne. Lorena was in her forties when Mayer met her.

Daniel Selznick, among others, found Lorena "the most charming woman who ever walked the earth." He said that she was adorable to Mayer, very much in love with him, and acted with him like a young girl on her first date. She would joke with him, fuss over him, laugh with him, tickle him, hug him; she would try to soothe him when he was depressed and angry; she was the joy of joys of his life.

There are some, including Samuel Marx, who doubt the sincerity of her feelings for Mayer; they wonder if she was not merely looking for social position and money: a gold digger of 1933 in real life. But Danny Danker had been extremely popular in the film community, and she had never suffered from financial want. Like many before her, she was captivated by Mayer's strength, physical sturdiness (she apparently wasn't aware of his imaginary or actual health problems) and display of power. Part of the movie world herself, she cannot have failed to have been excited that this greatest of all moviemaking executives was in love with her.

On his side, Mayer no longer needed to go out with an older woman or parent as chaperone, and he at last felt free. To find, at his age, an attractive woman who was adoring of him went to his head completely. The fact that Lorena was an expert dancer was the clincher. Still loving to go out to Ciro's and the Mocambo nightclubs, he found in Lorena an outgoing, party-loving, spirited companion. She was the one bright spot in his increasingly troublesome life.

He decided he would marry her. He became a romantic schoolboy again; still smarting from Ginny Simms' and Ann Miller's rejections, he was determined that she would not turn him down. He kept calling people she knew, asking them to put in a good word for him. She was fascinated by this show of insecurity; the last thing she would have expected, she told her close friend, the Hearst columnist Dorothy Manners, was that he would seem so innocent, childlike and inexperienced; he was sixty, after all. Despite her fondness for Mayer, Lorena held back from any commitment, and she had her daughter to consider; Suzanne missed her father painfully, and children were often reluctant to accept another parent.

There was an odd episode at his house that summer of 1946. Mayer had a mania for turning off the lights when he left a room, to save on electricity bills, sometimes forgetting that there were people in there. One night, during the projection of a movie, held in complete darkness because he had not allowed even a single glimmer from a lamp, there was a crash. Everybody ran to see what had happened; Rosalind Russell was lying pinned under one of his imitation Tudor armchairs. She had risen to go to the powder room and had tripped in the darkness. She screamed, "If my face is injured I'll sue you for the house, L.B.! The studio as well! Goddammit, why do you keep turning off the lights?" Abashed, Mayer helped her to her feet; she was not, in fact, disfigured, and she didn't sue him. He still went for the lights at future screenings and other people tripped and fell.

On September 30, nonmembers of IATSE struck, charging that IATSE and the studio bosses had entered into a collective bargaining conspiracy when the first strike was ended in July. Several M.G.M. pictures closed down. There was a riot at the studio, with the police aiming hoses at the picketers; next day, there was another fight on the lot, with IATSE and studio union conference members clashing and thirty-seven left badly injured. Thirteen picketers were arrested. Mayer called the district attorney, and the studio was surrounded by a supplementary police force as he and his staff drove in and out under armed guard. The strike spread to the Technicolor laboratories, forcing Mayer to delay plans for a nationwide release of *Till the Clouds Roll By* and compelling him to have picture after picture changed to black and white.

Soon, the strike spread through the industry, with IATSE members fighting their way through against cries—reminiscent of charges made in the Browne–Bioff era—of IATSE being "bought" by the studios. The idea that the strike was inspired by Communists spread, and Mayer may well have believed it. On November 11, police at M.G.M. seized thirty-six picketers and marched them off to jail. IATSE members' homes were bombed and children injured. On the nineteenth, union leader H. K. Sorrell surrendered to marshals and was arraigned before a grand jury.

Declared illegal, the strike was at last called off. But, at a time when the studio was in grave difficulties and every cent needed, it cost countless millions. There can be no doubt that the frenzy and paranoia of the blacklisting era that was just around the corner was, to an extent, sparked by the fear that communism in labor circles might prove the downfall of Hollywood.

\*   \*   \*

Irene Selznick was in New York at the end of 1946, beginning a distinguished career as a theatrical producer. Possessed of her father's irrepressible ego, she had never been suited to marriage, as her cruel and belittling account in her memoirs of her relationship with her husband makes clear. Selznick devoted himself now to planning pipe-dream vehicles for Jennifer Jones to follow the steamy excesses of *Duel in the Sun*, all of them confounded by his constant waffling. He devoted his life to Miss Jones, to the continuing mortification of Robert Walker and to the continuing distress of Irene, who began her producing career in summer stock, then embarked on Arthur Laurents's disappointing *Heartsong*, with Shirley Booth. During a break in rehearsals at New Haven in February 1947, a hysterical Jennifer Jones called her up in New York, pretending to be Dorothy Paley, wife of the CBS chairman. As they drove around in a cab she said Irene should take David back; that he refused to father her children. She tried to throw herself out of the taxi. Irene saved her. Irene told her, characteristically: "David is bad for himself and nothing you can do will change that."

The beginning of 1947 saw Mayer in an even darker mood. He decided, without warning, to dispose of many of his beloved racehorses, though he would keep the Perris farm and stables for almost two more years. The horses had become a burden; at sixty-one, he was feeling his age; the pressure of managing all of the problems connected with breeding, raising and racing them were weighing him down. His financial adviser, Myron S. Fox, suggested he liquidate and capitalize for the future. Lorena was concerned about the strain on his health. It was characteristic of him that he made a clean break, and in a spectacular fashion, by staging the biggest horse sale in California history.

The black-tie auction took place on February 27, 1947, with a society crowd of some five thousand people, including over two hundred millionaires, and a battery of reporters and photographers and newsreel cameramen. Stepfather fetched the highest price; the stallion was bought by Harry M. Warner, who had flown in from New York, for a record $200,000. Honeymoon went for $135,000 and Mayer's beloved Busher—prancing in multicolored ribbons under the arc lights—went for the same amount to Mayer's close friend, the lawyer Neil McCarthy, who wanted Mayer to enjoy unlimited access to the filly. McCarthy also bought Flaming Beau, a colt by Beau Pere, Mayer's much admired Australian sire, for $35,000, and two other horses. Director Raoul Walsh bought an Argentinean filly for $37,000, and George Brent and Harry James pitched in. At the end of the day, Mayer netted $1,553,500. Later,

William Goetz also bought horses, in part to enable Mayer to have access to them.

News from the Loew's accountants was gloomy: Paramount, Warner and 20th Century-Fox were outgrossing M.G.M.; the studio's slipping to fourth place worried Nicholas Schenck. The new M.G.M. pictures, showing the result of budget cuts, were disappointing, despite the best efforts of the production team of Joe Pasternak, Jack Cummings, Arthur Hornblow, Jr., and Arthur Freed. Pasternak's *This Time for Keeps* and Freed's *Good News* were lightweight, the latter picture anachronistically dressed for a 1920s subject and outclassed by 20th Century-Fox's *Margie*, which was correctly in period and a much better picture. Clarence Brown was out of his element in the musical collective biography *Song of Love*, with Katharine Hepburn as an improbable Clara Schumann and Robert Walker miscast as Brahms; Margaret O'Brien made her worst picture in *Tenth Avenue Angel*, and *Green Dolphin Street*, for all of its director Victor Saville's high-powered technical prowess, proved to be a disappointment. As for *The Kissing Bandit*, with Frank Sinatra—the best policy is silence.

*The Sea of Grass* was more interesting. It was directed by the young Elia Kazan. He was furious that the studio would not let him shoot the story on location, in the grasslands of New Mexico, and that the wardrobe called for by Mayer for Katharine Hepburn as costar was improbably lavish. He has since disowned the picture, instructing the readers of his memoirs not to see it. It was a contradictory example of a film that defied the censorship codes and the prevailing right-wing climate. Cowritten by the liberal Marguerite Roberts, with three liberals in the leading roles (Hepburn, Tracy, Melvyn Douglas) and a decidedly left-wing director, it took a critical approach to capitalist land ownership in the New Mexico of the 1880s, even denouncing its own supposed hero, Colonel Jim Brewton, for driving free settlers off his land. How Mayer got involved in this politically overt project is a mystery, but even more extraordinary is the fact that the script showed Brewton's wife becoming pregnant out of wedlock and giving birth to an illegitimate son without dying as a moral punishment. This was extremely rare for the period. From the beginning Mayer had forbidden any such theme to be used at the studio. It seemed that, once again, Hepburn could get away with anything—and it seemed also that Mayer was losing his grip.

It was a year of ill-health for Mayer, worry over failing revenues, and a deep-seated fear for what the future would bring. There were no excuses or safety valves in Hollywood. Lorena Danker was, of course, still a consolation, cheering him up, dancing with him in nightclubs, trying to take the edge off things.

His sister Ida had lately begun a lifelong campaign for a Jewish Home for the Aged. Using, with his blessing, the illustrious Mayer name, she joined forces with Mary Pickford and began raising what would finally amount to millions, with five secretaries working long hours, in a crowded office where the phones rang constantly. She was tirelessly energetic and vital: a woman obsessed. His elder sister Yetta had little to do with the rest of the family, though her daughter Irene continued with her namesake, the reigning M.G.M. designer Irene, as an excellent stylist. Jerry Mayer, already stricken with cancer in his fifties, was still in place as studio manager. Jerry's son Gerald, who had been an outstanding officer in amphibious forces in the Navy and had returned with seven battle stars, was working as a tests and shorts director at M.G.M. and would prove to be a sensitive and thoughtful director of features.

Ida's children, Ruth and Mitzi, flourished as magazine writers; Ruth's husband, Roy Rowland, was doing well as a director; Mitzi's husband, Sol Fielding, was an accomplished artist, part of Cedric Gibbons's art department.

As for Rudolph Mayer, he was back in town, and Mayer could only groan at the thought. Rudolph had moved from his radio job in New York to the M.G.M. offices. He took up residence at the Gaylord Hotel on Wilshire Boulevard, as elegant, stylish and improbable as ever, sporting a long cigarette holder and fine clothes acquired by some mysterious means.

For all his many faults and his criminal record, the family remained captivated by him and his colorful schemes; he was a glorious rogue, a sport, a black sheep returned. It was this fatal charm that embroiled the decent and kindhearted Sol Fielding in a venture that would cost him dearly, and that would cause a severe rift in the family, affecting Mayer himself.

The story, still a painful one to several Mayers, began in mid-1947, when Rudolph, always looking for promotional schemes, drove around the still largely undeveloped Palos Verdes peninsula on the California coast and found splendid potentialities for real estate there. He took his favorite nieces, most frequently Yetta's daughter Irene, to see the gray-green scrub and rolling sandhills. He sought Sol Fielding's aid; Fielding had some experience with real estate. Rudolph decided to buy 250 acres, which was owned at the time by a corporation known as Ocean View Properties, and rename it the Sunview Estates. In order to buy the land, he needed $25,000 as a down payment; irresistible as always, he somehow talked Sam Friedman, a former silent partner in his old Canadian Company, Dominion Iron and Wrecking, into advancing him the cash in return for a share in the property. Fielding came in as a partner.

Arriving at the Carthay Theatre for the premiere of *Strangers May Kiss;* from left: Nicholas Schenck, Mayer, Norma Shearer and Thalberg, 1931. *(Marc Wanamaker: The Bison Archives)*

Robert Taylor with Mayer, circa 1936. *(Marc Wanamaker: The Bison Archives)*

To Howard —
With our affectionate regards always

Thalberg and Shearer, circa 1932. *(The Howard Strickling Collection)*

M.G.M.'s keeper of secrets, Howard
Strickling, with John Gilbert, circa 1928.
*(The Howard Strickling Collection)*

Marie Dressler with Howard Strickling, circa
1932. *(The Howard Strickling Collection)*

Celebrating Lionel Barrymore's twenty-fifth anniversary in films with a new contract, 1935;
from left: Mayer, Barrymore, Nicholas Schenck. *(Marc Wanamaker: The Bison Archives)*

At the M.G.M. sales conference, May, 1937; from left: Bill Koenig, Harry Rapf, Sam Katz, Jerry Mayer, E. J. Mannix, Mayer, Al Littman, Bill Rogers. *(Marc Wanamaker: The Bison Archives)*

Greer Garson accepting the Picturegoer's Cup, Britain's Oscar, for her work in *Adventure*; from left: Nina Garson, C. Aubrey Smith; Mrs. Henry B. Livingston, Mayer, Garson, Henry Livingston, Dame May Whitty, 1944. *(Marc Wanamaker: The Bison Archives)*

A birthday party for Clark Gable, 1938; from left: Ed Sullivan, Spencer Tracy, Mayer, Myrna Loy and Gable. (*Marc Wanamaker: The Bison Archives*)

Clark Gable with Carole Lombard and Mayer, 1938. (*Marc Wanamaker: The Bison Archives*)

A rare photo of Clark Gable with Thalberg (left) and Frank Capra, circa 1938. (*The Howard Strickling Collection*)

Judy Garland's birthday party, June 11, 1939; from left: Ann Rutherford, Betty Jaynes, Mayer, Garland, Mickey Rooney, Leni Lynn, June Preisser. (*The Howard Strickling Collection*)

Mayer on visit to FBI headquarters in Washington in the 1940s; from left: Howard Strickling, J. Edgar Hoover, Mayer. (*The Howard Strickling Collection*)

Louis B. Mayer, circa 1948. (*The Howard Strickling Collection*)

Key M.G.M. staff, from left: Eddie Mannix, Arthur Loew, Mayer, William Rogers, Dore Schary, February 8, 1949. (*Marc Wanamaker: The Bison Collection*)

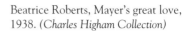

Beatrice Roberts, Mayer's great love, 1938. *(Charles Higham Collection)*

Ida Koverman, Mayer's legendary assistant, possibly the most important person at the studio besides Mayer and Thalberg, 1950. *(The Howard Strickling Collection)*

On the set of *Plymouth Adventure*, from left: Dore Schary, Clarence Brown, Spencer Tracy, Francis Cardinal Spellman, Van Johnson, 1951. *(The Howard Strickling Collection)*

Mayer with his great friends Cardinal
Spellman and Eric Johnson, early 1950s.
(*The Howard Strickling Collection*)

Mayer and Lorena attend the Keeneland
Yearling Sales in Lexington, Kentucky, July
16, 1954. (*AP/Wide World Photos*)

Mayer with new bride and stars; from left: Lorena Mayer, Mayer, Ava Gardner, Mickey
Rooney, December 1948. (*The Howard Strickling Collection*)

Before he actually made the down payment to Ocean View Properties through the title office, Rudolph sold one-fifth of the 250 acres of the land he didn't own yet for $500,000 to the real estate investor Charles E. Kenner. He arranged to meet Kenner in the title office. The papers were drawn up; Rudolph signed them. At that moment, Kenner produced a cashier's check for $500,000 and Rudolph handed it to the clerk. Kenner had bought 50 acres for the price of 250; he shouted, "You son of a bitch, I could have bought the whole property for the half million!" Rudolph put the $25,000 back in his pocket.

Fielding had the idea of using Sunview Properties for Federal Housing Authority developments. He was stumbled because Kenner put an earth mover on it and wouldn't budge; it took a court order to make the man move. Fielding got hold of an engineering and architectural firm to survey the property and give an estimate on what it would take to install a development. This was costly and slow; the FHA authorities raised questions about what plans they had for a supermarket, a police precinct, a fire department, even a bus line. Mayer and Fielding were given an exact time limit in which to come up with the specifications and blueprints; Fielding arrived at the FHA on the appointed day with minutes to spare.

But when all of the approvals were in, Rudolph could not produce the cash; all of his money was gone in a botched deal involving the takeover of the popular Piggly-Wiggly restaurant chain, and he could not raise additional capital. In 1948, Mayer would have to bail Rudolph out of bankruptcy and take over the property. But more of this later.

On April 25, in absolute secrecy, Mayer had a major operation, details of which are unknown, at the Stanford-Lane Hospital in Palo Alto, California. Only a tiny note in the Hearst collection of the Bancroft Library at Stanford reveals this; he told only an old friend, J. F. T. O'Connor, about it. The operation was successful, but it left him tired and weakened. He wasn't helped by the news, received three days later, that Margaret Mayer, who was suffering from a paralytic stroke at age sixty-two, complicated by high blood pressure and (again) severe mental disturbances, even including hallucinations, had won her divorce. Of a total property and shares paid her of $3.25 million, Mayer had to provide her with $1.25 million at once and the rest in installments ending on March 25, 1950. The beach house, valued at $250,000, was hers for life, though it was agreed she would lend it to him for large parties. Since Mayer was still the highest paid U.S. executive, even though his income was way down—to about $500,000—the settlement was not unreasonable. But he fretted and brooded over it.

To his woes could be added the niggling away of the government in an antitrust suit against M.G.M. that spring. At the first national sales convention since 1941, held, as of yore, at Manhattan's Hotel Astor, William F. Rodgers, vice president in charge of sales, urged the employees not to be disheartened—the very fact that this was mentioned was ominous. Would the government invoke the Sherman Act to sever Loew's theaters from M.G.M.? Would even the grand old Capitol Theater in New York be threatened? There was a brief reprieve; the dreaded disaster did not occur quite yet.

On May 19, Mayer suffered another blow. Frank Orsatti, still his close friend—the closest, apart from Major John Zanft, his business manager Myron Fox, Arthur Freed and Howard Strickling—died of a heart attack at his Santa Monica home. Because of his fear of death, Mayer did not attend the funeral, a considerable shock to Orsatti's widow and brothers. He was in court that week, and much of the next weeks, suing the City of Beverly Hills and the county for levying excess taxes on his properties, which included a bank building on Wilshire Boulevard; he lost. Court costs were higher than the amount sued for—in the region of a mere $14,000.

Reports were gloomier than ever at the various sales department meetings in New York. George Murphy flew to Manhattan with a compilation movie of M.G.M.'s past achievements, but it didn't help. Nicholas Schenck began thinking of ways to either replace Mayer (difficult, in view of his carefully fashioned contract) or find a new executive to take over many of his duties.

One bright moment was supplied when, on May 28, Jack Cummings married Betty, the attractive daughter of Jerome Kern. Cummings's divorce from Marjorie Straus had just become final; Betty Kern had been married to Artie Shaw. The couple eloped to Las Vegas; no family member was present.

Mayer started plans to revise M.G.M.'s British production—always something in which he took a strong personal interest. *Young Bess*, the story of Princess Elizabeth I, would star Deborah Kerr; *The Secret Garden* would star Margaret O'Brien. He and Nicholas Schenck put Ben Goetz back in charge there, and Victor Saville returned to London. At the same time, there was talk of setting up a studio in Mexico City. Also, $250,000 was paid for the rights to Ruth Gordon's play *Seasons Ago*, about her early years; it eventually became *The Actress*, with Spencer Tracy and Jean Simmons. But these were scattered efforts to shore up a collapsing studio, rather than signs of bold executive policy. Such pictures as *Song of the Thin Man*, a futile attempt to recapture the charm and excitement of the old, surefire series, *The Arnelo Affair* and *Merton of the Movies* were dismal prospects for the fall release lists.

Already in trouble, Mayer sanctioned an action that caused anger in the industry. He had Carole Brandt of the story department offer several leading New York literary agents $5,000 a year each to let the studio see every property they handled before anyone else. All turned down the suggestion, one of them in language that no newspaper could print.


Throughout the spring and early summer of 1947, the most persistent topic of conversation at M.G.M. was communism. Not since 1939 had there been so much political talk, often escalating into high-powered arguments, in the commissary at lunchtime. The studio executives, directors and players were polarized again. Eddie Mannix, head of the studio under Mayer, kept telling everyone that General George Patton should have been given his head and gone in and got the Russian Commies, even if it meant World War III. Sam Katz was with him in that view. James K. McGuinness, inexhaustible as ever, looking for Communists under every desk, agreed. Joe Pasternak, Jack Cummings and Samuel Marx were neutral. Robert Taylor was leader of the right-wing among the stars; Gene Kelly was bell-ringer of the liberals.

Of the studio's writers, at least two, Dalton Trumbo and Lester Cole, were Communists. Ironically, they were Mayer's favorite writers. Lester Cole he treated like a son. Blacklisted in the 1930s for militant Writers' Guild activities, the sharply intelligent Cole had come back in 1944 to write *None Shall Escape*, a prophetic movie that looked forward to the end of the war and the trial of the Nazi war criminals at Nuremberg. Jack Cummings had asked him to do *Fiesta*, a musical set in Mexico; he had written the powerful thriller *High Wall*, which, by a peculiar irony, its ultra-right-wing star, Robert Taylor, considered the best script he had read. And Cole had brought off a picture that reduced Mayer to tears at its first screening: *The Romance of Rosy Ridge*, produced by Cummings and directed by Roy Rowland—a Mayer family affair, and a story for all families—based on MacKinlay Kantor's novella.

*The Romance of Rosy Ridge* was the story of a Confederate farming family in 1865; the stubborn father (Thomas Mitchell) is still fighting the Union and the black-masked night riders. A Union soldier (Van Johnson), anxious to see the burying of old conflicts, wanders onto the property and falls in love with the farmer's daughter. The picture ends with a plea for nonsectarian Americanism. The script was richly composed, and Roy Rowland's evocation of farm life, the wheat rushed in before a storm, the barn dance, the sudden news that a beloved son may have returned, with the family running happily through the fields, had the lyrical intensity of his own *Our Vines Have Tender Grapes*.

Mayer burst into tears in the final sequence, overwhelmed, especially, by the fine-hewn acting of Selena Royle as the farmer's wife. He had Jack Cummings, who watched it with him, tell Cole that it was the best picture he had seen since *Over the Hill to the Poorhouse*, with Mary Carr, in 1920.

Mayer even did the unthinkable—writers were always very low on the totem pole—and actually befriended Cole. He encouraged Cole to develop another movie: it was *The Mercer Girls*, a true story of the 1860s, of three hundred Seattle men who shipped mail-order brides west. He wanted Katharine Hepburn for the part of the bride, one of the first American women doctors; her character would revolt against the cattle-market conditions and would lead the emancipated women to freedom in Washington State. Mayer liked the story, and so did Jack Cummings; but Sam Katz—whose attitude to women was contemptuous and chauvinistic—tore the treatment to shreds, screaming, "Communist crap! All this shit about women's rights! In the kitchen, in the bed, that's their place!" Cummings was barely able to stop Cole from striking Katz to the ground.

Knowing that Mayer hated Katz, Cummings decided to approach him. But Katz, by an ingenious ruse, had made Mayer beholden to him. Katz had taken Mayer to San Francisco to undergo shots extracted from monkey testicles for loss of virility—not uncommon in a man over sixty who was under exhausting pressure. Lester Cole wrote in his memoirs:

> L.B.'s transplants were no more successful than Katz's and though he hated Katz for talking him into it, he still feared Katz would publicize his mortification. Katz had him by his proverbial—and impotent—balls.

This must have been an exaggeration: the truth probably was that Mayer was unable to climax as often as he had in the past; temporary ejaculatory incompetence is often misunderstood for impotence in older men. Decline of male vigor required a psychological adjustment, an acceptance of waning powers. This was, of course, something Mayer would not have dealt with easily or would have liked to discuss with Dr. Jessie Marmorston or Dr. May Romm.

Mayer next assigned Cole to write a version of the life of the Mexican revolutionary Emiliano Zapata, which Jack Cummings would produce, with all of its echoes of Selznick's *Viva Villa*.

Mayer took a strong interest in the prospective movie; he liked the fact that his nephew, Cummings, would at last be making an important political picture, and the theme—of a rebel against a corrupt demagogue—surprisingly intrigued him. He rejected outright Katz's repeated charges of a Communist conspiracy in making the film, and, risking revelation of the trip to San Francisco, dismissed him from the project and gave Cummings carte blanche. Cole and Cummings flew to Mexico, and Robert Vogel cleared every obstacle for them there.

But when they returned, Eddie Mannix axed the project. "How did this Commie son of a bitch get in here?" he screamed. "It's a picture about a revolution!" "Didn't America start with one?" Cummings snapped. "You comparing us to goddamned Bolsheviks and lousy spics?" Mannix yelled.

Cummings got President Alemán of Mexico on the telephone. Aleman told Mannix he had approved the script. Mannix delivered the immortal remark: "Okay, so this son of a bitch Zapata was a revolutionary! So was Jesus Fucking Christ!" All Mayer heard from Mannix was that the picture was going to be made. But two days after the meeting, September 23, 1947, marshals arrived and served Lester Cole with a subpoena. Cole was charged with refusing to admit to his membership in the Communist party; it is reasonable to suspect that Sam Katz, Eddie Mannix and James K. McGuinness were responsible. Mayer was in a quandary: one of his favorite writers was being charged with communism, official government policy was anti-Communist and he hated communism with all his soul. Yet Cole was one of his favorites among the writers; he would fight to the death for any member of his M.G.M. family. While he brooded, several of his stars, including Gene Kelly, Judy Garland and Myrna Loy, joined the Committee for the First Amendment, supporting Cole and nine others, the so-called Unfriendly Ten, all of whom sheltered behind that amendment in responding.

On September 21, 1947, Mayer made a very serious mistake that could have proved injurious to any lesser career. Anxious to avoid testifying at the House Un-American Activities Committee hearings, he sent one Mickey Rosner to intercede with that committee to have him excused. Later, Westbrook Pegler, the dreaded King Features Syndicate columnist, published a statement that Rosner was an "underworld character." Rosner, Pegler alleged, had taken $2,500 on false pretenses from Charles Lindbergh and his wife to find out details of their kidnapped baby. He had been arrested and acquitted several times on grounds of attempted extortion or fraud; he had been at the center of controversy as chief of police of Long Beach, California, starting in 1936. Pegler called him "Ambassador Extraordinary to the Underworld." Rosner pleaded to allow Mayer off the hook on the ground that his brother Jerry was desperately ill. Rosner was dismissed at once.

On September 29, Jerry died of cancer at the Cedars of Lebanon Hospital in Los Angeles. He had undergone two operations in San Fran-

cisco and a third had proved unsuccessful. Gerald Mayer recalls that his
Uncle Louis was devoted to Jerry, that he constantly turned up at the
house and the hospital with words of encouragement and good will. But,
given his own terror of cancer, Jerry's death can only have increased his
fears. Was the disease a strain in the family genes?

After much consultation with Nicholas Schenck, Mannix, his lawyers
and various stringers of the House committee, Mayer reached a painful
decision. He was due in Washington on October 18 to testify at the
House Un-American Activities hearings. On October 11, he summoned
Lester Cole to his office. He told Cole that he regarded him and Trumbo
as two of his best writers; he didn't want to lose them.

He said that if Cole would break with the Communist party, and
publicly, he would guarantee him a magnificent future with M.G.M.
Cole could direct his own scripts; he could have Jack Cummings as his
permanent and exclusive producer; his salary would be doubled. Cole
refused. Mayer stood up, shaking with rage and pointing to the door.
"Goddam crazy Commie!" he screamed. "Get out!"

Just before Mayer left Hollywood, he accepted an invitation from Eric
Johnston, head of the Motion Picture Producers' Association, to set up a
committee of five, known as the Motion Picture Industry Council. Other
members were Walter Wanger, executive Henry Ginsberg, Joseph
Schenck and Dore Schary. The first meeting was held in the executive
dining room at M.G.M. on October 13; the council agreed it would
protect any and all industry members who might be falsely charged with
being Communists.


When Mayer walked into the caucus chambers of the Old House Office
Building in Washington, D.C., on the morning of October 20, 1947, he
saw an impressive spectacle: from two cut-glass chandeliers, klieg lights
hung in clusters, providing a dazzle of illumination for the batteries of
newsreel cameras. Four hundred spectators filled the brown leather seats,
watching intently as he was led, looking very pale, by uniformed attendants, to the polished mahogany table bristling with microphones and
flanked by cameras on tripods, the reporters packed so tightly on the
floor in front of the desk that one of them sat on his foot.

Tiny, rotund and bald, House Committee Chairman J. Parnell
Thomas sat on a high dais behind a long desk like a Spanish inquisitor.
In order to be seen over the desk top, he had propped his small body on
a fat, white Washington business telephone directory. Mayer looked at
him impassively, then folded his hands, his face a mask. He glanced at
the director Sam Wood, so long under contract to him in the 1930s,

who testified first. The head of the ultra-rightist Motion Picture Alliance for the Preservation of American Ideals, Wood denounced David O. Selznick's favorite director, John Cromwell, as an agent of a foreign power, and among others, Mayer's former employee John Howard Lawson, Dalton Trumbo and Donald Ogden Stewart as men with "Communist leanings." He even dared imply that Katharine Hepburn . . . but that brought laughter.

Mayer appeared next. Questioned by Chief Investigator Robert E. Stripling, he delivered a long, impassioned speech, probably put together for him by Howard Strickling. He denounced communism, called for legislation that would prevent employment of its adherents, mentioned that *Song of Russia* was "an opportunity for a pat on the back of our then ally, Russia," noted that Secretary of the Navy Frank Knox had recalled Robert Taylor for the film, mentioned the U.S. Signal Corps' pro-Soviet *The Battle for Stalingrad* and expressed pride in the picture. This was entirely the correct approach by any standard and should have humiliated the committee.

He said, under further questioning, that no Communist propaganda had been inserted into the pictures written by Trumbo and Cole and that he had "as much contempt for Communists as for anybody living in this world." Asked whether he had engaged American Bund members, he said, "Probably"; but unfortunately, he did not elaborate on this intriguing response. Asked again about *Song of Russia*, he said that he had never been in Russia, conveniently forgetting he had been born there. He mentioned his censorship of collective farming as a theme. He said he would soon be embarking on an anti-Communist picture.[1] He recalled the fight over *Tennessee Johnson*. Asked by Congressman Richard B. Vail of Illinois what made highly paid writers Communists, Mayer said, "I think they are cracked!"

He was about to step down when Stripling started up again. He asked if Mayer had had government authorization to make *Song of Russia*. Mayer confirmed that he liaised with the government in the matter and that there were no political implications in the picture. ("If I met my God I would repeat the same thing.")

He whipped out a number of reviews of the film and read them aloud. All were favorable. They weren't what the committee wanted to hear. Mayer was forced to step down for Ayn Rand, author of the novel *The Fountainhead*. She had just seen *Song of Russia* in Hollywood. She spoke with contempt of the picture's glowing picture of Moscow, with clean streets, no food lines, sumptuous restaurants and happy children in white

[1] *The Red Danube.*

blouses. She described the beautiful village in the picture, far removed from the filthy, squalid hamlets she remembered from her years there (she had not been back since 1926). Mayer said later, at a hearing on *Lester Cole v. Loew's, Inc.*, and under oath:

> I felt I had been kicked aside [in favor of Ayn Rand] at the House Committee and hadn't been allowed to finish. I was disgusted; the whole conduct of the Committee was a disgrace.

He left immediately. He was unwilling, as a dismissed witness, even to listen to certain of his colleagues testify.

Robert Taylor appeared on October 22. He described meeting Lowell Mellett, presidential aide, in Mayer's office to discuss *Song of Russia* and the changes he had wanted in the script. He stated that he would never work with a Communist and that he looked forward to anti-Communist pictures. He was never asked if he had known Lester Cole was a Communist—a bad slip by the committee.

James K. McGuinness, called the same day, was in his element. He stated he had refused to join the Anti-Nazi League in the 1930s because he saw it as a "Communist front." He charged Communists with trying to suppress *Tennessee Johnson*. He mentioned that protests against its original (he didn't say antiblack) bias were received from five "Communists": Donald Ogden Stewart, writer Hy Kraft, writer Richard Collins, director Jules Dassin and writer Ring Lardner, Jr.

He stumbled when he called the radical Republican from Philadelphia, Thaddeus Stevens, a patron saint of communism; that was too much for Pennsylvania Congressman John M. McDowall, who said, "(Our state) is very proud of . . . Stevens." McGuinness said of M.G.M., "I don't think we have the whitest condition in the industry. I think we have a share of Communists in our employ." Committee member Richard Nixon drew more from him on the alleged Communist thought control of Hollywood.

Lester Cole asked at the hearing if he could read a prepared statement, and J. Parnell Thomas ruled that he could not. The statement, issued to the press afterward, read, in condensed form:

> After years of failure by James K. McGuinness and others to disrupt the Screen Writers' Guild, a desperate appeal was made to [former House Un-American Activities investigator] Martin Dies. When he and Browne and Bioff failed to disrupt the Guild, this new committee was formed. It is out for one thing: to rule or ruin the Industry.

Again fearful of cancer, Mayer went to New York immediately after the hearing and checked into Mount Sinai Hospital for a further week of tests. He traveled to New Haven to see Irene successfully launch an out-of-town opening of Tennessee Williams's A *Streetcar Named Desire*; though the play was scarcely his cup of tea, he admired Irene's production. As he had during the making of *The Sea of Grass*, he chose to overlook the alleged Communist leanings of her director, Elia Kazan; admired Jessica Tandy, whom he had had under contract, and who had acted so well in *The Valley of Decision* and *The Green Years*, as Blanche; and noted the vibrant presence of the young Marlon Brando as Stanley Kowalski. He beamed joyfully at Irene's after-the-show party.

He returned to New York, where he issued a statement on November 17 to his Hollywood team by cable:

> Forget politicalisms and get down to business or resign. If anybody feels he is determined to espouse the Communist cause, let him be courageous enough to leave now and stop taking our money and wasting our time.

On November 24 he attended, at the Waldorf-Astoria Hotel, the so-called Waldorf Conference, with Harry Warner; Barney Balaban and Y. Frank Freeman of Paramount; Harry Cohn; Sam Goldwyn; Darryl F. Zanuck; William Goetz; Dore Schary, Mayer's former employee, now vice president in charge of production at RKO Pictures, and other studio heads. The group discussed pressure from the boards of directors of the various companies, as well as threats from American Legion posts for the boycott of certain pictures. Schary said that precipitate action might be unwise; Mayer said he was afraid of public opinion and that people had thrown stones at the screen when *The Sea of Grass* was playing because of its "left-wing" director and stars.

Mayer spoke of the need for a law against communism. He added, "There is an awful pressure on the industry and on me; we are in a terrible jam. Exhibitors will protest. It's frightful the way these things develop. We must do something at once." Darryl F. Zanuck announced that he had decided on a policy of not employing Communists and that he had discharged the writer Ring Lardner, Jr. Schary was asked if he agreed with his executive board (he meant Howard Hughes) in "their" firing producer Adrian Scott and director Edward Dmytryk for communism. He replied that he had hoped they would only be suspended, but the decision had been made. The upshot was that all present would, despite individual differences, hold together "for the good of the industry," and that all and any known Communists would be discharged.

It is clear that the real, deep-seated fear shared by all concerned was not that they had employed or might still be employing Communists, but that the mass audience, and in particular the American Legion, felt that everyone who was a Communist was a paid and subversive agent of an enemy power. It was the *public* these executives were afraid of; they took no genuine ideological stand on the matter.

On the train back to California, Mayer ran into, of all people, Lester Cole. He spoke to Cole like a father, telling the young man that they both had to remember they were servants of the public, and must say what the public expected to hear. He told Cole:

> It isn't a crime to belong to the Communist party. You shouldn't have sheltered behind the First Amendment. You should have said if you were or were not a Communist. The FBI knows you were, anyway.

Cole replied, "I have to stick to the gang that says they won't admit it." Mayer threw up his hands.

A rather desperate show of good will occurred when Mayer ordered *Ninotchka* and *Comrade* X reissued immediately to remind the public that Metro had once satirized communism. *Variety* published the following statement on December 3, 1947; it resembled a proclamation of an execution in the Middle Ages:

> [Trumbo and Cole] slated for axing at Metro in connection with the Red Purge, still hold their jobs due to legal obstacles. E. J. Mannix . . . huddled all day [on the first] trying to figure out angle to jump or bypass legal hurdles presented by Trumbo's contract . . . the studio is withholding firing [Cole] in order to axe both together.[2]

A few days later, the Unfriendly Ten, including Trumbo and Cole, surrendered to marshals, following an indictment for contempt of Congress for refusing to testify whether they were or were not Communists. All went to prison.

The year 1948 started off on another sour note. On New Year's Eve, Benny Thau, whom Mayer still regarded as one of his finest executives, and his girlfriend, the beautiful actress Frances Gifford, whom Mayer was nursing toward stardom, were driving from Los Angeles to Arrowhead Springs when a driver ran into them head-on. The car was demolished; Thau almost lost a leg, and Frances Gifford had several head injuries. Mayer rushed to the Good Samaritan Hospital to see them. Once again, as doctors told him that Thau almost died, he was reminded of the fragility of the human condition.

[2] This happened a week later.

In March, Lester Cole filed suit against M.G.M. on the ground of wrongful dismissal; the case would not be heard until November. As if to rub salt in the wounds of the various unions and guilds, Nicholas Schenck fired dozens of employees, cut pension plans and fringe benefits for lesser employees, yet at the same time upgraded Mayer's salary along with those of Howard Dietz, Marvin Schenck (his nephew), Leopold Friedman and others.

In the meantime, Mayer was building a new star, his first discovery in several years, the remarkable twenty-six-year-old tenor Mario Lanza. Under six feet, but weighing more than 200 pounds, Lanza was a body-builder with enormous muscles; his addiction to food, however, con-stantly dragged him down, out of condition. He was a child, emotional and often crazy. Mayer had first seen him in August 1947, when he attended Lanza's memorable concert at the Hollywood Bowl. Ida Koverman, always on the lookout for new talent, had insisted that he go. He had been so impressed that he had gone backstage to give Lanza his personal congratulations. Then he had everybody available at the studio turn up on a sound stage to hear Lanza sing his heart out for over an hour. He signed the temperamental performer to a seven-year contract beginning at $750 a week; if Lanza proved himself in pictures, he would elevate him in stages to $10,000 a week.

Mayer had asked Joe Pasternak, the ideal choice, to produce the Lanza pictures. A script was commissioned immediately from Bruce Manning, who had written, for Pasternak, some of the brightest Deanna Durbin musical comedies. Manning concocted a preposterous fantasy entitled *That Midnight Kiss*, which told the story of an obscure truck driver who, auditioning for José Iturbi (as himself) in a humble garage, overwhelms the genial pianist-conductor and secures a contract under the aegis of a wealthy patroness of the arts (Mayer's old friend, Ethel Barrymore). In this contrivance, Lanza, with barely a moment of rehearsal, would ap-pear as the star, replacing a prominent performer (Thomas Gomez) in a newly invented opera, *The Princess*, composed of various out-of-copy-right symphonic works. Kathryn Grayson would be the love interest.

Lanza was originally tested for camera in black and white because there was a shortage of color stock at the studio and it wasn't certain that the picture could be made in Technicolor. The film's director, Nor-man Taurog, obtained color stock under the table. But he didn't tell Mayer right away. He ran the test for Mayer in black and white, as agreed. Mayer was appalled. Lanza's dark hair and dark face against a dark background made him almost disappear. He turned to Taurog in despair. Taurog pressed a button and uttered a code word to the projec-tionist. Suddenly, Lanza came on the screen in magnificent color, singing full out. Mayer leaped from his seat with excitement, expressed his amazement that Taurog had found the color stock and pumped his hand ecstatically.

While the picture was being prepared that spring, Lanza proved to be a handful. His sudden success went to his head completely. Still unable to read a score despite the fact that he could sing D-flat over high C with strenuous mastery, he was rude, brusque and vain much of the time. He was filthy in his personal habits, urinating whenever he felt like it, in corridors or on his dressing room floor; the studio staff significantly put a pig trough outside his room, and on another day a pail. He would disappear during rehearsals and eat five-, six- and seven-course meals, his waistline swelling to over forty-two inches and making it impossible for his clothes to fit. On one occasion, while working with his singing trainer, he fainted, like a heroine in a Victorian novel, because the corset he was wearing at the time was too tight.

On one occasion, in front of José Iturbi, Lanza urinated on a plant. Iturbi was furious; indeed, his dislike of Lanza is visible on the screen. Lanza forgot his lines, gobbled some spaghetti and, when the plant was taken away, used a pail. At one sound stage, he relieved himself while Kathryn Grayson was rehearsing there. Mayer summoned Lanza to his office and screamed at him to learn to use a bathroom. As Lanza left, workmen on a ladder emptied a pail of urine on Lanza's head.

Mayer almost lost him completely in those preparatory days for *That Midnight Kiss*. Mayer liked to have his stars perform from a balcony overlooking the dining room at his Beverly Hills house. Judy Garland had once sung for his guests. Howard Strickling told Lanza that Mayer wanted him to give such a performance. Lanza arrived, puffed up with pride at being asked to such an exclusive social occasion as a Mayer dinner party. He was in black tie. Two maids opened the door and took him through part of a hallway and up a staircase to the balcony. "There must be some mistake," Lanza said. "Why are they serving dinner on the second floor?" At that moment, one of the maids flung open the door and there was the balcony, with Mayer and his large party seated below at the table. Lanza was horrified. It was obvious to him now that he had not been invited to the meal. He stormed out. It was a long time before he was sufficiently pacified to return to work.

Mayer was back in New York in May 1948 for further meetings with Nicholas Schenck, and to complete arrangements to buy, as a personal investment and in defiance of the antitrust laws, the Rivoli Theater. He paid $1.5 million for it to the estate of the late Charles E. Barney; the result was that he also made a deal with the United Artists theater chain, which was subleasing it to Spyros S. Skouras, head of 20th Century-Fox. Strings were pulled and Mayer escaped investigation in the matter—Joe Schenck also avoided prosecution that spring when he bought a theater chain.

Nicholas Schenck put two M.G.M. pictures into release, made just before the Washington hearings. They both had a political slant: *State of the Union*, made by Frank Capra and Liberty Films, with Hepburn, Tracy and Van Johnson, and *B. F.'s Daughter*. Paradoxically, the former movie, based on a stage play, denounced corruption in the Republican party. Bolstered by the presence of Hepburn, typecast as a liberal heroine, and with the right-wing Adolphe Menjou as the villainous campaign manager (Menjou had testified against communism in movies to the House committee), the picture, shot at the height of the anti-Red hysteria, was a poke in the eye for opportunistic and exploitative campaign management and criticized the extreme right wing. Yet again, a need for product surmounted any fear that the studio might be branded for releasing a "Communist" picture.

Even more surprisingly, Robert Z. Leonard's *B.F.'s Daughter* actually provided a sympathetic portrait of a man of the left. Written by Luther Davis, based on a novel by J. P. Marquand, it dealt boldly with the subject of socialism versus capitalism. Thomas W. Brett, played by Van Heflin, is a liberal assistant professor on economics at Columbia (an intellectual hero in a Hollywood movie was in itself revolutionary) who marries Polly Fulton (Barbara Stanwyck), the daughter of a construction multimillionaire (Charles Coburn). Brett is disgusted when he finds out that his wife has financed his lecturing career, but in the end he is mollified by her declaration that she really loves him. By now he has emerged as a Roosevelt Brain Truster and is willing to let dirty money be turned to good work. The script's only concession to the present political trend was in the sequence when Martin Ainsley, a hotshot socialist radio commentator based on Drew Pearson, who enjoys big money while attacking it, learns the errors of his ways and stops attacking Fulton and his capitalist friends. It is true that at the end of the picture Thomas Brett is effectively wealthy and powerful, but he has never sacrificed his ideals, and even helps, platonically, a beautiful concentration camp refugee who has been blinded by the Nazis. For Mayer to have approved this picture was courageous and surprising; it was made by impeccably right-wing figures.

The adapter's purpose in the picture was to show that much can be learned from both capitalism and intellectual anticapitalism. The former economics professor realizes he has been blinded by prejudice even as the radio commentator pays grudging tribute to the quiet heroics of a patrician attorney. In this amazing film, everyone changes through the years, and for the better. No more graphic example can be seen than the rich, formerly empty-headed friend of B. F.'s daughter who is seen at the end as serious and much more in touch with her feelings and closer to her fellow men. The war is shown as having much to do with the metamorphoses experienced by everybody in the film. Besides demonstrating the spirit of patriotic dedication that prevailed during World War II, B.F.'s Daughter also suggests that the warring factions demonstrated at the beginning of the story and stemming from the Depression had been overcome in the uniting of classes toward victory. The script is saying that now, with the blacklist darkening Hollywood, differences must be reconciled for the greater good; ideology is too strong for the real world. B.F.'s Daughter, underrated and even maligned by critics, and disowned by J. P. Marquand, was the most important picture M.G.M. had made in many years.

Although the studio provided escapist fare in The Pirate, with Gene Kelly and Judy Garland, On an Island with You, A Date with Judy and Summer Holiday, which suffered from studio cuts and failed dismally, these two political pictures got the most attention, but no critic pointed to the anomaly of their existing at all.

At the beginning of May 1948, Mayer again took a train to Washington, D.C. He was summoned, interestingly enough, as a defense witness in the Dalton Trumbo trial; Lester Cole had waived the right to a jury hearing. Restless and irritable, with nothing to do, Mayer cooled his heels at the Mayflower Hotel for a week, until at last he was summoned to court.

Trumbo's attorney, the able Robert W. Kenny, was in the peculiar position of seeking supportive statements from the very man he was attacking in Lester Cole's suit against M.G.M. for wrongful dismissal. He began by asking Mayer to enumerate the pictures he had made with Trumbo, the next question being whether there was any evidence that they contained Communist propaganda. Obviously, Mayer's response would have been in the negative. But the judge overruled the question as irrelevant. Kenny risked contempt by asking if two of the movies were Thirty Seconds Over Tokyo and Our Vines Have Tender Grapes. He was forbidden to continue.

Mayer returned in a disgruntled mood, his time wasted, to Hollywood. There, he signed approvals for a picture of a different color: Conspirator, an all-out attack on communism, which would be written by Sally Benson and Gerald Fairlie and directed by Victor Saville, who had turned his Secret Intelligence Service attentions from Nazism to anti-Sovietism. It was as much a propaganda picture as Saville's early World War II films: the story of a Russian spy (played by Robert Taylor, doing his bit in the cold war), acting as a British Army officer, who is driven ultimately to suicide.

There were a few consolations that summer, as Mayer returned yet again to New York in an effort to find a way out of the present studio doldrums. At a fund-raising testimonial dinner at the Hotel Astor for the United Jewish Appeal, he was given an illuminated scroll in appreciation of his public services and philanthropic activities; he had been giving money to the Appeal for many years. It was a disappointment that Herbert Hoover, because of another engagement, was unable to be there, but the cheers, led by Emil Friedlander of the Appeal and Paramount's Barney Balaban, were encouraging in a bleak hour. It was depressing to think that fifteen sound stages at Metro were dark, with only one picture starting up, *The Barkleys of Broadway*, with Judy Garland (whom Mayer was forced to fire for even worse behavior than usual and replace with Ginger Rogers) and Fred Astaire.

On July 1, Dore Schary resigned from RKO and Nicholas Schenck decided to offer him the job of associate vice president in charge of production at M.G.M., a blow to Mayer.

## CHAPTER TWENTY-TWO

# 1948-1950

LIKE MAYER, the forty-two-year-old Schary was the child of impoverished Russian immigrants; the elder Scharys had settled in New York just a few years after the Meirs. Tall, with enormous horn-rim glasses, mild-mannered, Schary was a Reader's Digest version of an intellectual. He was intelligent and charming, and his jointly written, Academy Award–winning screenplay for *Boys Town* was always one of Mayer's favorites. Although Schary had been in and out of M.G.M., largely because of internal political intrigues, Mayer had never ceased to respect him and had observed his career at RKO, where he had been associated with David O. Selznick, with considerable interest. Schary's chief ability was bringing in quality pictures on a budget. Given the stinginess of its then-owner, Howard Hughes, and its perennial losses, RKO had at least achieved considerable prestige by 1948, and such pictures as *The Set-Up* (a melodrama about boxing), *The Window, They Lived By Night* and *Crossfire* (a persuasive account of anti-Semitism reworked from a novel about homosexuality) had received very strong critical approval.

Schary's appearance before the House committee had been cautious, neatly avoiding charges of communism that Mayer only later began to consider seriously. Such charges were, of course, without foundation. However, many on the Left felt that Schary had betrayed them, and that his post–House committee address to the Writers' Guild was a notable example of trying to have one's cake and eat it.

Mayer could not fail to note that Schary was a direct appointee of Nicholas Schenck; that Schenck was known to be gunning for him; and that it would be a typical Schenck maneuver to put in charge of production an individual who had, many years before, obtained at least tacit support from the studio rank and file and at least some (Harry Rapf was a notable exception) of the top echelon of executives. Moreover, it is clear that Schenck, always shrewd and far-seeing, would realize that even Mayer's own family, including Jack Cummings, would not necessarily leave M.G.M. if Schary took over. They might, indeed, have more in common with him than with their own formidable relative.

Schary could trim budgets, introduce more modern pictures, with a contemporary, newsworthy slant, increase the emphasis on violence, which audiences were now demanding, and bring in certain writers and directors from RKO who had established a reputation for forceful craftsmanship and a dislike of the kind of schmaltz that, in those tougher post–World War II days, had begun to exhaust audiences' patience.

Mayer was never less than cunning, and he must have known that it would not be in his best interest to fight against Schary's appointment. The clever move would be to appear to have in part instigated the idea of hiring Schary, and to approach that prickly but able younger executive with a paternal air.

He invited Schary to his house on a Sunday morning in mid-July, to discuss with him the immediate future. He offered him a mid-morning refreshment, but Schary very coolly declined it, saying that he had had a late breakfast. Mayer tried to assert his power by outlining Schary's duties, a miscalculation since Schary could be relied upon to know what those duties would be. Schary cut him short in the middle of a sentence with a sharp, uncompromising statement: "I'm coming here on one condition, and one only. Autonomy." Mayer said that his contract would not contain any such guarantee. Schary rose from his chair, saying, "Then there's no point . . ." Mayer said, wrongly, "Irving Thalberg didn't have anything like such an arrangement." Schary said, "I know, and I know what he went through."

The meeting ended uncomfortably for both men. Nicholas Schenck arrived in Los Angeles, anonymously to escape a summons. He stayed with his brother Joe. The following Saturday, Mayer drove up to Joe Schenck's house with two attorneys. It was a difficult encounter. Schary repeated his statement to Nicholas Schenck: he would have autonomy and nothing else. He also told a lie: he said he had had carte blanche with Howard Hughes at RKO.

Schenck agreed that Schary would have the right to buy properties, provided the cost did not exceed $100,000; he would have the choice of casting, and of assigning producers and directors. But he would have to refer to Mayer, once he had made these decisions, and if Mayer should disapprove, the matter should be referred to Schenck. Schary went cold. He said, "I will consult with L.B. I'll be happy to. But if I have to wait for decisions on my own decisions, I'm not head of production. I left RKO because of this. I won't be an office boy." Mayer shruggingly said, "That's okay with me. We'll get along all right."

At the end of the meeting, there were some minor points to be ironed out: Schary's precise title (it later became vice president in charge of production, identical with Thalberg's), permission to travel first-class with his wife and so forth. These details were to be settled the next day, at Mayer's house. But, just beforehand, Mayer made a serious miscalculation. That morning, early, Mayer drove to Schary's home and, rather transparently trying to make sure he was safe, a pathetic power ploy for a man in his position, said to Schary, "Hold out for whatever you want. Nick Schenck's a hustler. You and I will work together." Schary was a Schenck man, not by reason of any personal admiration, but because of common sense; Mayer's smarter move would have been not to have gone to see Schary, and to have done nothing but praise Schenck then and later. Didn't he realize that Schary was as much a jungle fighter as he was and might leak his statement back to Schenck?

It seems that Mayer undertook another move in that crowded twenty-four hours; subsequent events show that he must have reminded Schenck that he had a cast-iron contract as (still) the highest-paid executive in America, with over seven percent of the studio's net profits, and that, were he to be dislodged by Schary and paid off with a golden handshake, it could cost Schenck millions. At Mayer's house that afternoon, Schenck compelled Schary to agree that he would defer to Mayer on the right of final decision on all projects. Schary was visibly shaken and this time didn't fight the decision. He may have felt that he had overstepped the mark at the previous meeting. He expressed unease that Eddie Mannix might intervene between him and Mayer in executive decisions, swaying those decisions against him. Schenck and Mayer reassured him on that score.

Schary confirmed an earlier promise to double the studio's production line up from the eighteen slated for release to thirty-five by the fall of 1949. In order to achieve this increase, he would guarantee that he would bring in a number of low-budget pictures, each one of which would cost no more than $1.2 million to produce. As it happened, Mayer had already embarked on such a policy and had recently completed production on two excellent low-budget pictures, Act of Violence, for which Schary was later given credit, and Stars in My Crown.[1]

It was agreed that Schary should take the scripts for several pictures that were about to be produced with him on vacation in Colorado, where he was to address a writers' conference in Denver. Among these scripts were The Great Sinner, a version of Dostoyevsky's The Gambler; The Secret Garden, based on the children's novel; Neptune's Daughter, a

[1] The main pictures just completed, or about to be, were typical Mayer fare: Julia Misbehaves, Command Decision and The Three Musketeers.

musical starring Esther Williams; and versions of *Madame Bovary* and *The Forsyte Saga*.

Just before Schary left, Mayer hosted a luncheon for him in the executive dining room. It was a clever tactic, since Schary was sitting down with men who had, in the past, been his bosses. Few could fail to resent his importance; several froze when he emphasized the importance of writers, always low on the totem pole, and insisted they be included in production conferences. One of the few who were happy to see him back was Samuel Marx, who respected his expertise.

Schary acted tactlessly. Addressing the writers' conference at the University of Colorado in Denver on August 3, he took an unwarranted slap at Mayer without mentioning him by name, referring to the mindlessness of Hollywood productions and demanding a new, more intellectual policy: "If every other medium has a right to make us think, why doesn't the motion picture?" He was ignoring the fact that, like a quality publisher interlarding popular novels and biographies with serious literature, Mayer had put in motion, along with Thalberg or after Thalberg's demise, such serious movies as *The Big House, The Secret Six, Beast of the City, The Wet Parade, The Good Earth, Fury, Yellow Jack, The Picture of Dorian Gray, Madame Curie, The Valley of Decision, High Wall* and *B. F.'s Daughter*, to mention only a few.

Schary unwisely delivered a gratuitous attack on his fellow writers, who, he said, came out to Hollywood in "plaid coats, sports shirts, fancy cars, and contributed to the extravagance, waste and screwball character of the industry . . ." But then, he added, came the writers with a social conscience. This uncalled-for critique of the colorful and raffish craftspeople who created so many M.G.M. pictures in a previous era was another slap at Mayer and a pat on the back for Schary himself.

Schary turned up for a press conference in New York on August 10. He dared to say that while Thalberg was a fine moviemaker, "in the past few years [the studio] has been playing it safe." Showing his essential weakness, that of a middlebrow "intellectual," who also wanted to appear to be a powerhouse executive, he betrayed the values he had praised in Denver by saying, "I don't like sordid or morbid pictures . . . I think some longhair critics are all wrong when they confuse art with adultery and obscenity."

In an answer to a question, he said: "I have supervision of all Metro production, domestically and abroad, subject only to the command [sic] of Mr. Louis B. Mayer. My contract is for fourteen years."

When Schary returned, Mayer, maintaining his dignity, was coolly receptive of the new production chief. They managed a truce and got off on fairly good footing when Schary, with Nicholas Schenck breathing down his neck, hesitated to pay $100,000 for the rights to Edward Streeter's popular comic novel *Father of the Bride*. Mayer told Schary never to hesitate to pay top dollar if he loved a property. Schary respected him for that advice.

But they had their differences. Although Mayer did not introduce his perennial ghastly favorite, *The Rosary*, to Schary, he did produce another bee from his bonnet: the story of a window cleaner who wipes a different window on each floor of an office building, and each time he cleans the glass, the audience looks in and sees a different story emerge. Schary dismissed the idea.

Hedging his bets with the House committee, Schary put in motion a project that Mayer had prepared: the long-delayed *The Red Danube*, which would be directed by George Sidney and would be given a lavish budget and a strong cast headed by Walter Pidgeon, Angela Lansbury, the newcomer Peter Lawford and Janet Leigh. This would turn out to be M.G.M.'s first outright propaganda picture since the war.

After Schary was settled in, Sam Katz walked out with a $1 million cash settlement. Al Lichtman was similarly dislodged. There was much discussion of a renewed venture, long on the studio shelf: Henryk Sienkiewicz's *Quo Vadis?*, "adapted" by Cecil B. DeMille in the 1932 *The Sign of the Cross*. It was the story of the Roman emperor Nero and the early Christian martyrs.

Schary and Mayer had a screenplay, written in 1942 by S. N. Behrman, brought out of cold storage, and producer Arthur Hornblow, Jr., was asked to come up with a new script. After talking with Sam Wood as possible director, Mayer yielded to Schary's suggestion that John Huston should handle the picture. Although Huston's movies were not to Mayer's taste, since they emphasized untoward aspects of American society, he agreed. After all, Huston was a name to conjure with. Mayer had apparently forgotten or forgiven Huston's act of manslaughter some twenty-five years earlier, and he had, of course, always been fond of Huston's father, Walter. Hugh Gray, a British classical scholar, was asked to prepare the groundwork for a new script, which Huston would write.

At the same time, there was discussion of another potential epic, *King Solomon's Mines*. Although the mishaps surrounding *Trader Horn* in 1929–1930 still haunted M.G.M., the appeal of making an African adventure in those troublesome days of the cold war was strong. The British had brought off a version of Rider Haggard's classic in 1937, but it had made little impression. M.G.M. had bought the rights from the Haggard estate in 1946. Producer Sam Zimbalist, always enamored of the book, pushed it through.

Helen Deutsch, widely admired for her work on *National Velvet*, was engaged as writer. In November, unit production manager Walter Strohm would leave for Africa to scout locations.

Other developments were afoot: David Loew, twin brother of Arthur Loew and son of Marcus, and his partner Charles Einfeld had embarked upon an independent outfit, releasing through M.G.M., entitled Enterprise Productions. Unwisely backed by the Bank of America, this proved to be a shaky company. A deal was struck with General Aniline and Film to use the Agfa color system, originally developed under Hitler and seized by the Soviet government.

Mayer was opposed to the studio entering into television production, and M.G.M. was the last of the major studios to take the plunge. He disliked television, partly because of its cheapness and shabbiness, and partly because he doubted its commercial future. But Schary foresaw what it could become.

A point of difference occurred in October, when Schary purchased his own project, *Battleground*, from RKO. It was the story of a battalion during the Battle of the Bulge. Mayer felt that audiences were weary of war subjects; Schary maintained that human dramas on any subject were always box office. Schary appealed to Nicholas Schenck and won. Robert Pirosh had already drafted the script; Schary chose William Wellman to direct. Starring John Hodiak and Van Johnson, the picture would turn out to be well made and a box office success.

Mayer maintained his grip on the lives of the stars; as before, though he had to yield to Schary in the matter of day-to-day production, he was able to sustain, albeit awkwardly, his position as patriarch. One of his "sons" was in trouble: while Mayer was in New York, Robert Walker was arrested on drunk and disorderly charges. Lana Turner was involved in a stormy marriage with the millionaire Bob Topping. Greer Garson was recovering from an earlier, and painful, divorce from Richard Ney. Mayer remained loving and kind to Judy Garland, whose *Easter Parade*, in which she costarred with Fred Astaire, enchanted him. But he still remained distant from Clark Gable, whose career was slipping as badly as Greer Garson's.

Mayer's relationship with Lorena Danker deepened. Like the figures in an M.G.M. romantic comedy, they eloped to Yuma, Arizona, on December 3, with Lorena's eleven-year-old daughter, Suzanne, in tow. They checked in to the humble Coronado Auto Court. Early the following morning, they pulled city clerk Willard Daniel out of bed, piled him into their rented car and had him scribble out the marriage license on the backseat, whereupon he joined them for breakfast at a drive-in. At 9:00 A.M., they joined Howard Strickling and M.G.M. police chief Whitey

Hendry at the offices of Sheriff J. A. Beard, where Justice of the Peace R. H. Lutes conducted the two-minute civil ceremony.

The newlyweds ran a gauntlet of reporters and photographers, nimbly jumping into Sheriff Beard's car. Beard drove the group, with siren wailing and lights flashing, through the downtown streets, the press in headlong pursuit. Once the Mayers reached the California border, Beard dropped them off, and they ran to a prearranged Yellow Cab. Just yards behind them, a Chevrolet carrying Los Angeles *Times* ace reporter Edward Meagher and crack photographer Red Humphries drew up with a jolt. The cab driver led Meagher and Humphries on a wild chase down the windswept highway, until suddenly the Meagher vehicle caught fire and ran into a ditch. Laughing loudly, Mayer and his entourage whizzed off to Palm Springs.

The joyous event was shadowed. Ominous sounds were being heard from New York, as the protracted antitrust hearings, in which the Justice Department was fighting Loew's, in an attempt to enforce the division of Loew's Theaters from M.G.M., continued at full pitch. Also that week, Lester Cole's suit against M.G.M. for reinstatement of his contract and damages for alleged losses amounting to $70,200 was in progress (it had begun on November 30) in the Los Angeles Federal District Court before Judge Yankwich. Three days after his wedding, Mayer appeared as a witness for the defense. His testimony was honest and fair, even to the detriment of Loew's case. He said he had known Cole for two years; that Cole had written three fine films for the studio; that Cole was on good terms with everyone at M.G.M.; that his morals were above reproach. An earlier deposition by Mayer was read. In it, Mayer had stated that the motion picture industry was wrong in allowing a witch-hunt; that such an inquisition was a shoddy way of getting publicity for the House committee, and that he didn't give a damn whether Cole and Dalton Trumbo were Communists; that his only responsibility as studio chief had been to see that no ideology ("Communist, Democrat or Republican") was ever put on the screen.

Judge Yankwich used, under judicial privilege, the opportunity to attack Eric Johnston, head of the MPAA, saying:

> Mr. Cole was made to suffer a penalty, not for what his employers thought of him, but for Johnston's dogmatic attitude; Johnston insisted his own doxy was orthodoxy and everyone else's was heterodoxy.

Cole won. *Variety* said on December 17: "Cole has a debt of gratitude to Louis B. Mayer. Mayer won the case for Cole even before Cole took the witness stand."

Nicholas Schenck was furious at the trial's outcome. He had his lawyers threaten Cole (and Trumbo) that Loew's, Inc., could take their
cases all the way up to the Supreme Court, which would ruin them
because of the legal costs involved. The two men settled for half of what
they were owed and exited into the wilderness.

Immediately after the trial, Mayer left, with Lorena and Howard
Strickling, for New York. He combined the delayed honeymoon, at the
Sherry Netherland, with meetings with Nicholas Schenck, who was on
the verge of his annual Christmas vacation in Florida. He met with
Arthur Hornblow, Jr., who was concluding preliminary arrangements
with John Huston to shoot *Quo Vadis?* in Rome.

During Mayer's ten days in the city, Stanley Donen and Gene Kelly
arrived for preparations on the big musical *On the Town,* in which
M.G.M. had invested when it was presented on Broadway.

Schary had enthusiastically backed it, again displaying his love of
realism; instead of the customary M.G.M. picture, lushly upholstered
and romantic, *On the Town* was the fulfillment of Gene Kelly's long-held
dream of situating a picture of this kind in a real city, featuring recogniz-
able contemporary people. Mayer, inspired by friends such as Lillie Messenger, had been admiring of the project from the beginning, despite
statements to the contrary, and in fact had agreed with Nicholas
Schenck that the stage original should receive financial backing from
Loew's, Inc. In direct contrast with the white-tie-and-tails, sophisticated
image presented by Fred Astaire, Kelly had firmly established the working man as the hero of dance. *On the Town* would be staged in part in a
living, breathing New York, its songs (lyrics by Betty Comden and
Adolph Green, music by Leonard Bernstein) would be filled with nostalgic or contemporary references to Manhattan. To the cast would soon be
added Mayer's former flame, Ann Miller, Vera-Ellen, and Jules Munshin.
Above all, Frank Sinatra would lend his skinny, haggard, irresistible
presence to the story, ably matched by Betty Garrett, who would play a
sex-starved lady cab driver.

Miss Garrett went into the Mussolini office to discuss her role with
Mayer. He said to her, "It's not enough to have things in your head"
(and he poked her in the head), "but in the heart," and he poked her
breast. He put his hands on her shoulders and shouted, "To have a good
career in pictures, you need lots of weight above you," and he pushed
her clean off the chair to the floor. As she rose unsteadily to her feet, he
yelled, "I can see you're a girl with your feet on the ground!" And he
stamped on her feet till he almost broke them. As she limped out, he
warned her, "Don't have babies." She was in too much pain to reply.

Betty Garrett was brilliant in *On the Town;* her manic energy and attack in performance are still enjoyably watchable today. But Mayer never forgave her for not agreeing to join him for the indefinite future.

When Mayer returned to Hollywood, Pandro Berman and Vincent Minnelli's *Madame Bovary*, adapted from Flaubert by Robert Ardrey, was in production. It was the antithesis of everything Mayer liked in pictures: in Ardrey's version, the audience was asked to sympathize with an adulteress on the ground that she was locked in romantic daydreams. Minnelli romanticized the story by applying his special touch; at times, the picture resembled an operetta without lyrics or a score.

Nevertheless, there was no undercutting the amoral character of the story, the special pleading represented by showing the author's trial, in which James Mason as Flaubert asked for mercy and forgiveness for his heroine, or the grim finality of the ending, in which Emma Bovary is shown taking arsenic and dying in agony. It is probably fortunate that Mayer's comments on the picture have not been recorded.

And other movies were afoot that would never have been launched upon when he was in charge. *Any Number Can Play* was a nonjudgmental picture of compulsive gamblers; Anthony Mann's *Border Incident* was a violent and acrid account of the trade in illegal Mexican immigrants; the gentle Roy Rowland was switched from the lyricism of the Margaret O'Brien pictures to the urban toughness of *Scene of the Crime*. Schary's *Battleground* would be in production by April. These were not good times for Mayer.

One picture in particular made him unhappy; ironically it was being produced and directed by his favorite, Clarence Brown. The project was *Intruder in the Dust*, adapted by Ben Maddow from the novel by William Faulkner. Brown, partly because of his integrity and strength of character, and partly because, like Faulkner, he was from the South, persuaded the difficult author to let him go ahead. In December, he had been on location at Faulkner's hometown of Oxford, Mississippi, overcoming numerous local objections to the picture being filmed there. The story was a harrowing account of mob violence: when a male member of a locally powerful family is found shot, an innocent black bystander is accused of the crime. A lawyer takes the case reluctantly, fighting against local prejudice and the stubborn, self-serving behavior of the black prisoner. A young boy and an old lady jointly assist the cause of justice, until the true villain, the leader of the lynch mob, is exposed.

Faulkner assisted Brown by driving him around the country, putting him in touch with local farmers and helping him to prepare for a spring shoot. The picture would turn out to be one of the finest in the history of M.G.M., some scenes of it rewritten by Faulkner (an episode in a jail cell, and another in a sheriff's kitchen) to assure the maximum degree of authenticity. For Mayer, it was an unpleasant thought that this excoriation of the typical small-town Southern mentality could be delivered by "his" studio. He was no more in tune with *Intruder in the Dust* than he had been with Fritz Lang's *Fury*, some fourteen years before.[2]

The atmosphere at M.G.M. grew more tense in the early months of 1949. Mayer's mood was a combination of indifference and depression. He was troubled by such personal burdens as the fact that David O. Selznick was divorcing Irene to marry Jennifer Jones, as well as by his differences with Schary. When Mayer came into the executive dining room and sat down at the head of the table, a pall fell over it; those present didn't talk freely, and he no longer could inspire their friendship.

Mayer dislodged his nephew Sol Fielding from the Palos Verdes properties. On June 20, Fielding would actually be forced by Mayer and Myron Fox, in the presence of Fielding's brother-in-law Jack Cummings, to sign a quit claim releasing the valuable real estate holdings; and so would Rudolph Mayer, in October. Mayer handed over the running of the properties to Jack Cummings, in return for bailing Rudolph out of bankruptcy. For years, Fielding and his wife, Mitzi, were in court, struggling desperately to retrieve the money owed to them. They would receive only a miserably inadequate settlement after Mayer was dead. To the end of his life, Sol Fielding refuses to blame Mayer for the final decision, stating that Myron Fox influenced him against them.

There was much stress between Mayer and his stepdaughter, Suzanne. According to Lorena's intimate friend, Hearst journalist Dorothy Manners, Mayer's attitude to the child was inflexibly Victorian: she should be seen and not heard; she should not speak to her elders as an equal; she should be demure, quiet and respectful. Her father, Danny Danker, had spoiled her lovingly; he had allowed her to sit up late with the adults at the dinner table; he had encouraged her to express her opinions; he had given her the finest clothing and dolls, and made her feel like a princess. Now, she had to eat her meals separately from her parents, go to bed before parties, and at an early hour. She wasn't allowed to fool around and giggle and scream and run up and down stairs like any normal child. As a result, she became sullen, withdrawn and remote; sometimes she would go to her room and refuse to come out.

Mayer's friend Louisa di Salvio still catered to him, from time to time,

---

[2] According to Clarence Brown, Mayer insisted that he have the proud, falsely accused black man, played by Juano Fernandez, doff his hat to the white lawyer, played by David Brian. Brown, with the full support of Faulkner, who understood deeply the victim's belligerent character, refused. And Schary stood with him in the decision.

mostly Chasen's or Italian food. She found Lorena a demanding and
difficult employer. According to her, Lorena was so extreme a perfectionist that if she saw a waiter's black tie was crooked, he was sent back
to the kitchen to straighten it and never employed again. If Lorena came
into the kitchen and saw a waiter or chef with a spot on his apron, he
had to remove it at once, and in front of her. Food had to be served at
the precise moment appointed; if the clock had stopped striking as the
guests entered the room, she was furious. Lorena's favorite chefs, Albert
Joya and Frank Baradzo, were petrified of displeasing her, and were kept
under her rigid supervision.

Though tough with her staff (and very tight with tips), Lorena was, as
always, an excellent hostess, charming and considerate to her guests, but
even she could not avoid occasional conflicts between those present or
certain unfortunate incidents. One evening, William and Edie Goetz
were present when somebody said, talking about her own honeymoon
and glancing at the Goetzes, "Where did you two go for your post-
wedding trip?" "Honolulu," Edie replied. The woman continued, "I
don't understand the appeal of that place. So many people go there; but
unless you're a beach bum there's nothing to do." "But there was plenty
to do!" Goetz replied with a laugh. "What?" the woman asked challeng-
ingly. There was a pause, while everyone looked at Goetz. "We fucked!"
Goetz explained. Mayer was furious; he detested language of that sort.
He stood up and left his own table and didn't return.

One night, the writer William Ludwig accepted the Mayers' invitation
to the house but said he would have to have dinner early because he had
TB and must be in bed by ten o'clock. Lorena, in sending out the
invitations, instructed the guests to arrive at 6:30 P.M. The ferocious
Columbia Pictures boss Harry Cohn arrived forty minutes late, explaining that he had been looking at rushes and had lost track of the time.
Mayer screamed at him. Cohn said he would be leaving early to return
to his rushes. Mayer yelled, "You'll go when I want you to go!" Ludwig
said later, "I never saw such fear in a human face as I saw in Harry
Cohn's that night." Mayer behaved similarly to other studio chiefs when
they displeased him: he never let anyone doubt who was king of the
Hollywood jungle—even now.

There was another episode on Good Friday. Almost everyone at the
dinner that night was Jewish. The guests, gossiping and talking business,
assembled at the table. Suddenly, a prominent Hollywood figure said,
"We should all bow our heads in grace and think of the suffering of our
Lord Jesus Christ! He is here to save us from our sins!" The Jewish guests
were shocked into silence. Mayer's face was black with anger, even

though he was still flirting with Catholicism. Again, he left his own table and went upstairs.[3]

Stimulated by the inescapable James K. McGuinness, the manic search for possible Communists at M.G.M. went on in 1949. Armand Deutsch, heir to the Sears, Roebuck fortune, joined Schary's team as a producer. Marvin Schenck, Nicholas Schenck's nephew, who was acting as his uncle's liaison and source of information at the studio,[4] called Deutsch into his office and asked him to sign a paper stating that he had never been, and was not now, a Communist. Deutsch refused. Marvin Schenck asked him the reason for his refusal. "I hate communism," Deutsch replied. "I didn't beat my mother, either. But I'm not going to sign a document to say that I didn't." Many others at the studio were asked to sign; only a few did.

According to Armand Deutsch, Mayer began to believe that Schary might himself be a Communist. To reveal this unwarranted suspicion was a mistake; it made him seem paranoid, insecure and hysterical.

Schary's visits to his office were increasingly uncomfortable for Mayer, who began to suspect palace plots to dislodge him. The filmmaker Kenneth Anger recalls a visit to one of the executives at M.G.M. at the time. They were talking when suddenly Anger became aware of another presence in the room. He turned around and a gray-headed, gray-suited figure disappeared silently through the half-open door. It was Mayer spying on the conversation. He would, no doubt, have bugged the entire studio if he could.

Mayer covered his fears and uncertainties during the times when Schary discussed future projects with him. He wouldn't listen to them in full, but would stop Schary after some half-dozen story ideas and buzz Ida Koverman to come in with refreshments. Then, while Schary sat there, he would begin discussing his struggles with Irving Thalberg and other reminiscences of the early days, until Schary's eyes glazed over. Sometimes, with matters pressing at his office, Schary would stop to say, after the tenth hearing of an anecdote, and hoping to get back to work, "Oh, yes, L.B., you told me that bef—" and Mayer wouldn't hear him and would go on and on. Then, without warning, Mayer would jump up and

---

[3] A similar problem occurred each Christmas of Mayer's second marriage. Lorena and Suzanne wanted a proper Christmas, so an uneasy compromise was reached: the wreath was not put on the front door but on a side door, and the Christmas tree and mistletoe were in a side room. Next day, all trace of trees, holly, mistletoe and decorations were removed and sent out to the garbage. December 26 became the regular date of a Jewish party.

[4] Marvin Schenck was known as the glacier watcher; his job was said to be looking out of a window of his office in Culver City every few days to see if a glacier had formed and was moving rapidly toward the studio.

say, "And be careful of Mr. Schenck, the gentleman from New York. He will give you a little bit of caviar, but he will also give you a knife in the back." Schary would protest. He would say that Schenck didn't talk about Mayer in this manner; that Schenck was reasonable and decent to him, Schary. And Mayer would say, "That's because he's trying to get something out of you. He may give you a jar of caviar when he gets on a train, but he's fiddling with the table knife, figuring how to use it." Schary would squirm as this conversation was repeated over and over again.

Again, Mayer was using the wrong approach. It would have been smarter of him not to have attacked Schenck to Schary, so that word of his false praise would get back to New York; he could have retained a link with Schenck, criticizing certain of Schary's policies over Schary's head. He could have seen the danger in the constant emphasis on low-budget pictures of violence, made by Schary, and have predicted that they would not make money. At least, by taking up that line, he would have sufficiently unsettled Schenck to make Schenck doubt Schary's abilities. Instead, he set about unwittingly sawing the planks for his own scaffold.

He was equally off the beam following the Academy Awards at the Academy Theater in Hollywood on March 24. Since he had approved John Huston to write and direct *Quo Vadis?*, he should have kept any adverse opinions of Huston to himself, if only to support what was one of his last executive choices at the studio. Instead, he railed to Schary about the fact that Huston's *The Treasure of the Sierra Madre* received Oscars for Best Supporting Actor (Walter Huston), as well as Director and Screenplay (John Huston). He told Schary he was disgusted with the picture, and that it was a shock that John should have allowed Walter, his own father, to appear throughout as a toothless, unshaven, filthy gold prospector. He shouted at Schary, "This great director has his father take his teeth out in front of millions of people? He makes a fool of his dad? We in Hollywood know that Walter doesn't have any teeth, but not everybody in the world knows that! How could he do this to his dad?"

Schary was dumbfounded. The realist in him could not accept the father-loving romantic in Mayer, nor, since Mayer had a good dentist, may he have suspected Mayer's own toothless condition. It was as though William Goetz or David Selznick, in collusion with his daughters, had shown him, the great Louis B. Mayer, without his teeth in a close-up.

Mayer did something that was unconstitutional according to studio procedure. Before Schary saw the pages, he managed to sneak into his office part of the Huston screenplay for *Quo Vadis?* and detested it on sight. It was a grim, realistic drama in which Nero was seen as a dictator like Hitler, running a city through terror. The elements of the saintly Christians sacrificing their lives to the emperor's lions, singing hymns as they entered the arena, was anathema to Huston and virtually eliminated from his adaptation of the novel. Mayer wanted to reject the whole concept and start again. The writers John Lee Mahin, S. N. Behrman (who had begun the script in 1942) and Sonya Levien, whom he especially admired, were brought in to eliminate the political parallels and turn the movie into a virtual remake of Cecil B. DeMille's *The Sign of the Cross*. Gregory Peck and Elizabeth Taylor remained the stars. Soon, John Huston would walk off the picture. Schary was furious at Mayer's interference.

*On the Town* began shooting in April. The original plan to shoot the entire movie in Manhattan proved to be impossible, though many newspaper stories appeared asserting that the policy had not been discontinued. In fact, only the sequences of the sailors wandering around the city were done in the actual streets and on top of the buildings. The Empire State Building, the thoroughfares filled with Yellow Cabs and screeching traffic, the apartment buildings, all of these were duplicated at Culver City. Throughout the shooting, Betty Garrett, who played the lady cab driver, and her husband, Larry Parks, who had starred in *The Jolson Story*, were being investigated for alleged Communist sympathies.

To make sure that the studio was unequivocally anti-Soviet, Schary, with Mayer's rubber-stamp approval, at last embarked on *The Red Danube*. Shrewdly, he chose Gina Kaus, an Austrian novelist who knew Vienna intimately, to do the script, with the English writer Arthur Wimperis brought in to help with scenes that involved British military officers. The story of the awkward relationship between the Allied powers, which still included the Russians in early 1946, centered on the efforts made by Colonel Piniev to recapture a defecting Bolshoi ballerina, Maria Buhlen. Far from being the crude propaganda work it was described as at the time, *The Red Danube* presented its Russian colonel as an intelligent and respectable, if rigid and ruthless, proponent of Soviet policy, following his duties as religiously as the British commandant played by Walter Pidgeon. The performance of Louis Calhern, complete with flawless Russian accent, as Piniev, and the worthy playing of Pidgeon, Angela Lansbury and Janet Leigh (as the ballerina) added stature to the writing, and to the accomplished direction of George Sidney. A small scene of refugees aboard a train, shot by the great Charles Rosher, had a Dostoyevskyan intensity.

Schary tackled the issue of conflicts in the medical profession in the

wretchedly titled *The Doctor and the Girl;* Theodore Reeves based the
screenplay on *Bodies and Souls,* a current best-seller by Maxene van der
Meersch. The story of Dr. Michael Corday, son of a wealthy Park Avenue doctor, who, eager, ambitious and callous, is plunged into the inferno of Bellevue Hospital in Manhattan, was the antithesis of the Kildare series that Mayer held dear.

Curtis Bernhardt, borrowed from Warner Brothers, was the correct
choice as director. Glenn Ford, a new addition to the M.G.M. stable of
stars and a realistic, hardheaded actor of the kind Schary liked best,
played the young doctor to the life. The picture was uncompromising
and stark. Operations were shown as bloody and gruesome; the father's
attitude to his son marrying a sickly girl was cruel in a way Mayer would
never have tolerated. It was a daring, original, overlooked picture: not
only does Corday's sister become pregnant out of wedlock, always allow-
able by the Breen office but seldom permitted at M.G.M., but she is seen
to cause her own abortion, unheard of in pictures up to that time. Furthermore, the doctor who is Corday's father's best friend loses the patient on the operating table. Wasn't it time for Mayer to think about
retiring?

He managed to hang on to a few projects, in which he was superfi-
cially involved: the musicals. His nephew Jack Cummings's *Lovely to
Look At,* a version of Jerome Kern's *Roberta,* resulted in part from the
fact that Cummings was married to Kern's daughter and managed to
wrest the rights from RKO. *Three Little Words,* based on the lives of
composer and lyricist Bert Kalmar and Harry Ruby, was also put into the
works. Budgets, however, were clamped down to $1.5 million a picture;
the trims called for a cancellation of Greer Garson as Catherine of
Aragon and Jean Simmons as Anne Boleyn in *Anne of the Thousand
Days* and of *The Pickwick Papers,* both to be shot in England. Scott
Fitzgerald's *Tender Is the Night* was sold to Zanuck at 20th Century-Fox;
*Li'l Abner* was abandoned.

*Annie Get Your Gun,* arranged in cooperation with Irving Berlin, was
top of the list of productions and was given an additional million dollars
above the normal ceiling. Judy Garland was the obvious choice for the
title role. But she was suffering from a nervous breakdown, and finally
even Mayer was compelled to admit he could do nothing with her.
Nicholas Schenck wanted to drop her permanently. Schary was indifferent. But Mayer felt that Miss Garland needed hospitalization. By offering to pay her hospital fees out of his own pocket, he shamed Schary
into having the studio put up the money. (Why she could not have paid
the fees herself remains a mystery.) Later on, Miss Garland would do
nothing but denounce Mayer cruelly and falsely, charging him with

feeding her drugs and ruining her health and career. Doctors Marmorston and Romm recommended the Peter Bent Brigham Hospital in Boston, run by Dr. Augustus Rose, which Mayer recalled because his wife, Margaret, had also been treated there. Miss Garland left for Boston in April.

The question arose of who was to replace her in *Annie*. Schary suggested Betty Garrett, and Mayer was not averse to the idea. But Miss Garrett was again told she would have to sign a new seven-year contract; three and a half years of her old contract still stood. She was annoyed by this, particularly that she was supposed to take a salary cut on the new deal, even though she would be starring in the M.G.M. picture of the year. Her husband, Larry Parks, had fought a similar struggle at Columbia against an immensely long, exclusive contract, and she decided to stand with him. She told Schary, "You've got three and a half years of my life you can do what you want with. Why should I sign more time away?" As a result, she lost the role that might have made her a major star—at least until she and Parks were blacklisted for their politics.

Betty Hutton played Annie and gave the performance of her career. For once in a long time, Mayer could find a picture he liked; George Sidney directed *Annie* with tremendous verve, exactly matching the energy and dash of the stage production.

The realistic pictures went on and on. *Devil's Doorway* was as sympathetic a picture of anti-Indian prejudice as *Intruder in the Dust* was of antiblack; Schary smartly trumped Robert Taylor's right-wing ace by casting him as a noble Indian. *East Side, West Side* was a firm and unsentimental picture of life among the New York rich, in which a mother (played by Gale Sondergaard) was shown, for the first time in an M.G.M. picture since *Another Language*, as cynical and unaffectionate. The left-wing John Barry (he would face blacklisting) was chosen to direct a hard-nosed thriller, *Tension*, about a meek pharmacy clerk plotting his wife's murder. Schary embarked on plans, not realized immediately, to make Dostoyevsky's *The Brothers Karamazov*, with its un-Mayerish themes of madness, epilepsy and illicit sex. And *Black Hand*, with Gene Kelly, of all people, as its star, was a dark, harrowing story of Italian gangs, set in a bleak earlier New York.

Simultaneously with these ventures, Greer Garson's latest picture, *That Forsyte Woman*, did not cause much excitement, and her career continued in decline. Margaret O'Brien retired, as expected, at the age of twelve; Mayer wept buckets at her farewell party.

Mayer went to New York, then continued on to Boston to visit with Judy Garland at the Peter Bent Brigham Hospital. He brought gifts and flowers, and was a tender and loving friend to his ungrateful star. In consultation with Schenck back in New York, Mayer discovered that his contract would be renewed for another year, and he agreed with Schenck that the studio's present policy and competitive bidding between exhibitors for product was acceptable as a temporary compromise with the increasingly aggressive Department of Justice antitrust investigations.

At the same time, problems arose in Rome on *Quo Vadis?*. Eddie Mannix was there, struggling with an unfavorable union situation, interference from the government and threats of Communist infiltration and disruption of the shooting. State Department reports indicate that the reason for a decision that was made to postpone the production for a year was precipitated by these issues, rather than by a temporary eye infection suffered by Gregory Peck while he was shooting *Twelve O'Clock High* at 20th Century-Fox. The infection was given as the real reason for the postponement.


On April 12, 1950 the Jewish War Veterans of America gave a fifty-fifth anniversary dinner in Mayer's honor at the Waldorf-Astoria Hotel in New York. At that dinner, he was presented with the Gold Medal of Merit. The evening began with a Massing of Colors, the national anthem sung by NBC baritone Maurice Finnell and an invocation. Among the speakers were Cardinal Francis Spellman, Eric Johnston and Brigadier General Julius Klein. Telegrams of congratulations came from General Omar Bradley, Fleet Admiral C. W. Nimitz and, to Mayer, the most welcome of all, Douglas MacArthur from Tokyo ("When you acclaim Louis Mayer, please add my voice. The great of the earth come and go—some recognized as such—some not. I am glad your distinguished organization did not fail in its judgment tonight.").

Among the guests on the dais were Henry Ford II, New York State Attorney General Nathaniel Goldstein and Mayer's good friend Kaufman Keller, chairman of Chrysler.

On his return to Hollywood, Mayer was embroiled in a lawsuit in which he fought an earlier judgment by the Riverside County jury awarding a Perris real estate dealer $20,000 as a broker's fee in connection with the sale of the ranch. At the same time, on June 13, Jack Cummings and his cousin Nathan C. Cummings, the Chicago foods tycoon, were present in St. John, New Brunswick, with Mayer's blessing, to dedicate a handsome chapel in the presence of Lieutenant Governor D. L. MacLaren and St. John's mayor E. W. Patterson, in honor of Sarah Mayer and Nathan Cummings's mother. Mayer regretted deeply that he could not be present.

In those months, Mayer's friendship with Kaufman T. Keller, chairman of Chrysler, deepened considerably. For years, they had met in New York, Chicago and Washington, but now Keller used every excuse to come to Los Angeles to join Mayer. Vigorous, dynamic, exactly the same age as Mayer, Keller exemplified for him the American dream, the real-life hero of a success story in automobiles that resembled the theme of King Vidor's *An American Romance.*

Bedrock Pennsylvania Dutch, Keller had begun as a secretary to a temperance lecturer; he worked his way up on the engineering side at Buick, joining Walter Chrysler's crack executive team at the age of forty-one. By 1928, he was president of Dodge.

When Walter Chrysler died in 1940, Keller became the most successful leader in the automobile industry, Chrysler outstripping General Motors and Ford in performance and profit two to one. He did magnificently in World War II, but faltered badly with the coming of peace, gradually losing his leadership. His graphic speech (referring to his desire for a high chassis, he said, "We like to build cars to sit in, not piss over") was much criticized. In 1949, he was consoled by a close relationship with Mayer and Cardinal Spellman; Sue Taurog recalled later that these three improbable partners, Protestant, Catholic and Jew, would often take long drives together over weekends when Mayer was in New York.

The spring of 1950 saw a recommencement of work on *Quo Vadis?*. Sam Zimbalist replaced Arthur Hornblow, Jr., as producer; Mervyn LeRoy replaced John Huston as director and was, undoubtedly, Mayer's choice; Schary preferred Anthony Mann, who did some night scenes for the picture. Stewart Granger would have been ideal as Marcus Vinicius, the romantic pagan centurion who falls in love with the Christian girl Lygia. But he refused to sign a long-term contract, and Mayer was forced to let him go. Granger had reason to regret this decision.

Though pushing forty and a chain-smoker, Robert Taylor looked remarkably vigorous and handsome still, and was selected to play Vinicius. Deborah Kerr took over as Lygia when both Elizabeth Taylor and Jean Simmons were ruled out. Peter Ustinov had been tested for Nero as early as 1949 but had been dropped as a prospect because Sam Zimbalist decided he was too young. Actually, as he wired Zimbalist, he was too old; Nero had died at twenty-six; Ustinov was twenty-nine. Amused, Zimbalist gave in.

Mayer's close friend and favorite writer John Lee Mahin worked out an authentic final draft screenplay, drawing from Professor Hugh Gray's exhaustive research in the original Latin texts.[5] Schary was furious be-

[5] Peter Ustinov, one of the most learned of actors, has confirmed this.

cause Mayer had private meetings with Mahin on the script without referring to Schary. Yet Schary had no business to grumble: he despised the project from the beginning, had no taste for epics or indeed any picture in the grand manner and hadn't bothered to go over the previous drafts put together by Sonya Levien and S. N. Behrman. His only adjective for the entire project was "lumpy."

Mayer's decision to shoot *Quo Vadis?* in high summer was daring in view of conditions of record heat, but no doubt he remembered the disastrous winter filming of *Ben-Hur* in 1924, when, following his near-death and precipitate departure, icy rains deluged Rome and winds damaged the reconstructed Joppa Gate. Furthermore, he must have felt that the heat would add to the authenticity of the picture's barbaric spectacle, since the games and gladiatorial contests and chariot races of ancient Rome were normally held in the hot season.

Mayer personally instructed Robert Surtees, who had so magnificently photographed *King Solomon's Mines*, to take over as cinematographer. Onto Mayer's desk came copies of unit manager Henry Henigson's detailed reports; he had completed, in a remarkably short time, a reduced replica in wood of the original massive stone structure of the Circus Maximus, begun and abandoned a year earlier, and with seats to accommodate seven thousand extras. Henigson had also, within the dilapidated confines of a patched-up, postwar Cinecitta Studio, created a whole Roman world: Nero's palace, the Christians' humble homes, underground cellars, catacombs and council chambers. The great art director William Horning, liaising closely with Cedric Gibbons in Hollywood, brought off a magnificence of design unparalleled in any other movie reconstruction of the place and time.

A thousand seamstresses were employed to make ten times that many costumes, from elaborate court robes to simple tunics. It was decided to use actual chain mail, which caused extreme stress to many of the performers. But Mayer had never forgotten Irving Thalberg's desire for authenticity.

The shooting began on May 25, 1950. Despite every effort, it proved impossible to install air conditioning at Cinecitta. The temperature on the sound stages often exceeded 100 degrees, and, between shots, Robert Taylor, Leo Genn and other players had to strip down and be hosed off. The exteriors were even more harrowing to shoot than the interiors. Forty-nine-year-old Mervyn LeRoy had to scale eighty-foot wooden towers to shoot scenes in a broiling midday sun until, at last, even Little Caesar faltered and called for a specially constructed electric chair lift. He had to direct his fourteen assistants, on other towers and on the ground, through interpreters, since he spoke scarcely a word of Italian.

Staging the gladiatorial fights in the arena was especially grueling. Led by Max Baer's wrestler brother Buddy, the most powerfully built men available had been trained for weeks in the use of spears, swords and nets. But even so, several were badly cut across their shoulders and chests and had to be rushed to first-aid units.

The lions were the worst problem. Stunt doubles were dressed as the Christian martyrs, and were to lie down in the sawdust while the lions appeared to be nibbling them. Unfortunately, the lions had been well fed, despite Sam Zimbalist's orders to the contrary; they wandered out into the sunlight, yawned and wandered back again. LeRoy screamed furiously to "bring out some hungry lions!" None could be found. For two weeks, while the sequence was delayed, the lions were deprived of all but the most minimal food. Then, LeRoy had dummies matching the small-part players set down in the arena with large slices of bleeding, raw meat attached to them under their robes. Once the lions smelled the blood, they tore at the dummies with a will. LeRoy threw his hands up in joy.

Robert Taylor was restive, irritable and nervous throughout the shooting. He missed his wife, Barbara Stanwyck, who was making a picture in Hollywood. When she arrived in July, she was horrified to find that he was having an affair with an Italian actress; she returned to America and began divorce proceedings.

As the shooting wore on, there were several major conflicts in the crew. The enormous unit generally had been assembled locally. A proportion of these were *generici*, members of the local craft union earning four dollars a day. But most of the unit were members of the *comparse*, earning only one dollar a day. In an effort to meld these two conflicting groups, Zimbalist had arranged that the *generici* would select and control the comparse. But every day the *generici* brought in their selection, hundreds more *comparse* would turn up for work and a fight would ensue, as the unemployed fought desperately to be given preferment. In one battle, staged in the arena itself, four men were hospitalized and one was seriously injured. Several were sent to jail. Another fight erupted over water; only twenty-five cans a day were delegated by the generici for use by the workers. On one occasion, when the last drop was exhausted, there was a riot and twenty-five more cans had to be brought in.

Zimbalist tried to bring in the *carabinieri* (the local police) and even the army, but the Italian government refused to allow this. The budget escalated colossally, but Mayer didn't complain: he was excited by the rushes as they came in, overpowered by the spectacle and delighted that LeRoy had not changed the religious theme. Furthermore, not a dollar of

American money needed to be spent; the equivalent of $6 million in frozen lire from 1941 was being used for the production.

*Quo Vadis?*, excoriated by almost all reviewers, was beloved of the public. It was, as Mayer predicted and Schary did not, a colossal box office success. And it was an intelligent, sober, extremely authentic narrative of a lost world, in which at least two performances achieved the highest level: Ustinov's childish, petulant, pathetic Nero, and Leo Genn's exquisitely ironical, coolly accurate Petronius.

More frozen lire found an equally worthy purpose: the motion picture *Teresa*, personally produced by Arthur Loew, still the inexhaustible head of his late father's international organization. Fred Zinnemann was the director of this new picture.

Stewart Stern, who would become famous for *Rebel Without a Cause*, was the movie's sensitive author. He had been in the infantry in World War II and drew from his experiences to delineate the sufferings of the neurotic central figure, played by John Ericson, whose mind has been affected by the tensions of a campaign. It is extraordinary that Mayer authorized the project: like *The Red Badge of Courage*, the film portrayed an insecure, hapless coward; and, quite against Mayer's canon of values, Mrs. Kass, as played with intense brilliance by Patricia Collinge, was portrayed by Stern as a selfish monster who shudders and cries when she finds by accident the wedding picture of a son who has been too frightened to tell her he has an Italian war bride. When the bride (played by Pier Angeli) arrives in Manhattan, this monster mother forces her to sleep in a room separate from her husband, and in every way makes her life impossible. It must have been intolerable for Mayer to have let this picture through.

He was more comfortable with Vincente Minnelli's *Father of the Bride*, starring Spencer Tracy and Joan Bennett, a comedy about a male parent's sufferings when his daughter gets married; it was released that summer to critical and commercial success. He identified with the theme, recalling his own daughters' expensive weddings, and his own nervous state, some twenty years earlier.

That summer, Mayer bought from Mervyn LeRoy, under gentle pressure from Lorena, a large and opulent house at the prime address of 332 St. Cloud Road. Busy with affairs at the studio, Mayer left the move to his wife. Ironically, Lorena hired William Haines, the homosexual actor Mayer had banished from the studio in 1935, and who hated Mayer with all his heart, to redo the house. Mayer said nothing, and Haines, swallowing his pride, did the job and took the money. The result was commonplace California modern: desert beige carpets, creamy walls, masses of gold-threaded chairs, a sort of Hiltonian antiseptic palace with not much more charm than the furniture department of an expensive store. Almost from the outset, Lorena began entertaining even more lavishly than she had in Beverly Hills. Still no cook herself, she always had the finest caterers, and the rooms were decorated by the most expensive florists. Suzanne was a little older now and was given slightly more latitude, but Mayer retained his disciplinary attitude toward her. It must have been hard for her, when so many girls (and boys) her age were having a good time and were freewheeling through life.

With the postponement of *Quo Vadis?*, it was clear that M.G.M. needed a box office winner. As early as 1946, there had been discussion of filming *King Solomon's Mines*, Rider Haggard's famous novel of African adventure, first published in 1885, the year of Mayer's birth. It had been filmed once before, in England, directed by Robert Stevenson and starring Paul Robeson, Cedric Hardwicke and Anna Lee. It was the story of three explorers searching Africa for the legendary mines of King Solomon. The novel was dominated by a strong sense of magic, of the eerie and unexplained, and offered a marvelous villainess in Gagool, the ancient witch-woman of a tribe who, in a spectacularly grisly finale, is crushed to death between two grinding stones in a treasure chamber.

Helen Deutsch had been at work on a script since October 1948, and, while she was still writing, unit manager Walter Strohm had taken off for Africa that fall. Many of Strohm's discoveries on location influenced Miss Deutsch in her writing. She dropped the character of Gagool completely, and also the splendid figure of Captain Good, whose monocle, catching the sun, dazzled a threatening group of Africans. The finest episode in the book, when, using a pocket diary, the explorers correctly predict an eclipse, thus seeming to be possessed of supernatural powers, was also jettisoned. Miss Deutsch, with the approval of Mayer and Schary, settled upon a simple adventure story in which the hunter Allan Quatermain assists a young woman in finding her husband. Haggard, a typical Victorian, would never have tolerated the presence of any woman on such a safari, even though there were precedents of female explorers in the period.

Mayer and Schary settled on producer Sam Zimbalist to handle the complex project. Through Mayer's friendship with Kaufman Keller, a deal was made to have Dodge trucks built for the unit. Deborah Kerr was hired to play the leading woman's role. She had wanted to act in *The African Queen*, but Mayer had long since decided against this project, as it portrayed a suggestion of sex between a woman missionary and a boat captain, and he feared giving offense to religious groups. When Miss

Kerr mentioned her wish to do *The African Queen* at dinner at Schary's house, he handed her the part in *King Solomon's Mines* instead. She would go to Africa, after all.

Schary decided to hire a British director, Compton Bennett, who had a success with *The Seventh Veil*. Bennett wanted Errol Flynn to star as Allan Quatermain; but Mayer preferred the idea of Stewart Granger, who had emerged as a romantic star of British films. Zimbalist hired the documentary filmmaker Armand Denis as technical adviser. Richard Carlson would play Deborah Kerr's younger brother.

Director, leading players and a scratch crew left for Nairobi, Kenya, in October. Reports came weekly onto Mayer's desk, telling of the harrowing shoot. Compton Bennett clashed with Stewart Granger from the beginning. When they met, he infuriated the fiery star by saying, "I wanted Flynn." The rushes looked slow and dull, and Schary telegrammed Bennett urging him to increase the pace. Granger took over, refused to work with Bennett and laid out scenes with his fellow players.

Difficult sequences were shot in December at Murchison Falls, where the temperature was 150 degrees. Despite everybody's caution in using Vichy water, ginger ale or wine to drink and brush their teeth with, crew members were stricken with dysentery and had to be evacuated.

Much of the picture's quality was due to Robert Surtees's photography, and to the *Perils of Pauline*–like character of Helen Deutsch's script, which showed Deborah Kerr threatened by every kind of dangerous creature, from a tarantula crawling on her skirt to a python hissing at her. Protected by air-conditioned trucks, makeup persons and hairdressers, she looked far less ruffled than she would have been on an actual journey of this kind. Star glamour had to be preserved in those days, and she arrived, after a safari of thousands of miles and endurance tests that would have leveled most people, looking as if she had just stepped out of a beauty parlor in Beverly Hills. She proved to be remarkably resilient, flying a thousand miles from one location to another, climbing escarpments and thrusting through heavily jungled valleys. She was the only cast member who proved illness-free and untouched by stress. It was only when she returned to England that she would come down with a viral influenza that put her in bed for weeks.

Even she was shocked when a wounded cape buffalo unexpectedly charged Stewart Granger, and when a tribe of Masai natives, misunderstanding a director's order, threw spears at her, Granger and Carlson, missing them by inches.

When the shooting got under way in October, Mayer was in Miami with Lorena to visit her parents, and in New York for meetings with Nicholas Schenck. There was still no serious inkling, at least to the uninitiated, that he might be on his way out. He affirmed his contract for another year and made public that he still had over 11,000 shares of Loew's stock.

He returned to Hollywood in November to provide warm and gentle support to Judy Garland, following her long and painful sojourn at the hospital in Boston. During her absence from Hollywood, he and Schary had agreed on a project for her. This was *Summer Stock*, a nostalgic attempt to revive the innocent charm of *Babes in Arms* and *Babes on Broadway*, the plot of which it virtually recapitulated: it was the story of a troupe of players who take over an impoverished girl's barn to rehearse in, then enlist her as their star when they lose their leading actress.

Neither Judy Garland nor Gene Kelly, who was the best possible choice to appear opposite her, cared for the material, correctly feeling that the time for this type of subject had long since passed. With the spectacular success of his masterpiece, *On the Town*, Kelly had advanced the musical form by twenty years; he dreaded the thought of turning the clock back. The sympathetic and thoughtful Charles Walters was chosen to direct. But from the beginning, despite Mayer's and producer Joe Pasternak's support, Judy Garland was again in so bad a condition that making the film was an ordeal. Her neuroses were so severe that Dr. Rose, her Boston physician, had to be flown in to take care of her. She would turn up, often late, for a sequence, burst into tears, announce she could not continue, then run to her dressing room and lock the door. She fought with Charles Walters; she screamed at Gene Kelly; she mercilessly ill-treated her husband, Vincente Minnelli, and even her infant daughter, Liza; then she would be an angel.

She entertained departing minor cast members at parties, kidding, laughing, camping it up. She played ball on the sound stage, fell over giggling, cracked jokes that had everyone in gales of laughter. Then she would develop headaches and have to go home, where she would cry hopelessly for hours.

Pasternak, already a martyr to Mario Lanza, suggested to Mayer that he should fire Miss Garland and cancel the picture. Mayer was as loyal and generous as always to the star. He said she had never had a failure and that she must be given another chance. "If you stop production now, it will finish her," he told Pasternak.

As the picture went on, Judy Garland's weight went up and down; for days, the production was closed while she went on a crash diet, then would collapse with weakness from lack of food. She began to imagine cast and crew attacking her, shouting abuse at her, laughing at her. She was so addicted to the drug paraldehyde that her breath stank, and even when Gene Kelly complained that kissing her was an endurance test, she refused to use a spray. She took off to Carmel with a hypnotist and everybody threw up their hands.

Nobody was happy with the rough cut. It was agreed that the picture needed a new production number. In the spring of 1950, Garland returned to the studio, slim, apparently in good health, filled with energy and vitality. She carried off a big number, "Get Happy," surrounded by male dancers in black tie. It was the best sequence in an uneven picture that has improved with time.

In the early months of 1950, while *Summer Stock* dragged on, Mayer had to deal with Mario Lanza on his latest vehicle, *The Toast of New Orleans*. Once more, Lanza's weight fluctuated as drastically as Miss Garland's. He argued violently with Kathryn Grayson; he was on drugs, starving, sickly. Sometimes, he missed days of work. His trainer tried to get him into shape, forcing him to go for early-morning runs, compelling him to use weights to tighten his muscles, keeping him to salads and boiled eggs. Like Judy Garland, he was capable of pulling himself together when the occasion demanded: his version of "Be My Love" became a hit, the biggest for a single artist on RCA Red Seal. The song alone made the picture a success. He began planning *The Great Caruso*, the story of his idol; he begged Mayer to allow him to play the role, offering him passionate support in his long struggle with Schary. Schary shrugged; the material was of no interest to him, but so long as Lanza was box office he wouldn't argue. Lanza traveled to Oregon to stay at Ginger Rogers's Rogue River Ranch for extensive workouts.


Mayer always knew Americans wanted heroes; they wanted to identify with success and personal glory; they hated movies about failures, defeated, questionable people or (how times have changed!) antiheroes. When Schary brought a project to him, *The Red Badge of Courage*, he was opposed. Stephen Crane's classic novel, written when the author was only twenty-two, was based on Matthew Brady's illustrations of the American Civil War. Slight in content, no more than a vivid, intensely visualized sketch, the book was unsuitable for filming. It portrayed a man's cowardice: the central figure, a fledgling Union recruit, flees before the Confederate guns, only turning around through humiliation and discovering his manhood in the line of fire. Mayer knew that whatever the hero's regeneration, few would accept a male protagonist turning yellow in an extremity.

The idea had come from the producer Gottfried Reinhardt; he had mentioned it to John Huston, who had wanted to tackle a classic American novel in the wake of his disappointment over *Quo Vadis?*. Huston tried to talk Mayer into undertaking the picture. Mayer did his melodramatic best to dissuade him, sinking to his knees as he protested that Americans wanted warm sentiment, singing "Mammy," Al Jolson's hit song, and kissing the disgusted Huston's hands. It was a theatrical display that backfired, leaving Huston with a dinner table story for the next several years.

On June 8, 1950, Schary sent Mayer a memorandum indicating that to make *Red Badge* would bring M.G.M. prestige; knowing the fatality of the decision, and perhaps realizing that Schary would be blamed for it, Mayer called in Reinhardt and Huston to his office, flourished the letter at them and told them they could go ahead. Meanwhile, Nicholas Schenck approved; Dore Schary's *Battleground* had become a box office hit, and if Schary wanted to make another war picture, that was all right with him.

Huston took off to Mexico to work on revisions of a script that Albert Band, his production assistant, had drafted. It was agreed that Lillian Ross, of *The New Yorker*, would be present throughout preproduction and the actual shooting, a decision that almost everybody connected with the picture would soon have reason to regret.

Miss Ross obtained an early audience with Mayer. He told her he was against *The Red Badge of Courage*. For anyone in his position to cast aspersions on a studio project to a journalist was unthinkable; it broke the code. He apparently wanted to show that Schary was a bad executive, making decisions that could not be justified commercially. He complained about the recently released Darryl F. Zanuck picture, *Kiss of Death*, in which Richard Widmark, as a sniggering villain, pushed an old lady in her wheelchair down a steep flight of stairs to her death. He used it as a stick to beat an increasingly violent Hollywood. "Step on the mother! Kick her!" he shouted. "That is art, they say?" She wrote down his words and used them to make fun of him.

Gottfried Reinhardt took his director, actors and crew, and Miss Ross, to Chico and Calabasas, where Huston had a ranch, for many suffocating weeks of shooting. Huston effectively staged four big battle scenes, and Audie Murphy, America's most decorated war hero, acquitted himself well, against type, as the coward-turned-hero. Huston mixed a professional and nonprofessional cast, believing that his talent would meld them successfully. The results were uneven and awkward. Huston and Band's script was not so much reconceived in movie terms as a slavish following of the original casual narrative line; shorn of Crane's literary context, the dialogue seemed awkward and unconvincing emerging from the mouths of contemporary actors.

Though there was no denying Huston's skill and artistry, Reinhardt knew, when he saw the rushes, that the picture was a potential box office disaster. Within the studio, self-protecting executives, knowing this was a Schary project, could be relied on to utter sycophantic praise. But there would be no avoiding the public.

Mayer refused to attend the first-time private studio screenings. Instead, as always, he preferred to wait for the first public preview.

In February 1951, Mayer saw the picture for the first time at the Picwood Theater in Westwood. Lorena came with him. He sat through the sequences of the young recruits being trained, the preparations for battle, Audie Murphy's panic-stricken flight, the death of certain soldiers, the violent and unrelieved struggle of men at war. It was the antithesis of everything he liked in a movie: brilliant but cold and heartless, the opposite of Clarence Brown's evocation of the Civil War in *Of Human Hearts* or Victor Fleming's in *Gone With the Wind*. He might have forgiven Huston if the public had disagreed, if they had wept and laughed in the right places. But instead, the audience reacted against the director's intellectual approach; they sensed a lack of warmth in the picture. They laughed at scenes of death and dying, probably because they were presented with cinematic flashiness and second-rate actors. Murphy's headlong run brought the house down; here was America's hero fleeing before the rifles of a long-ago army. What could be more ridiculous? When one harrowing military encounter had the audience rocking, Mayer turned to his wife and said, "That's Huston for you!" Lillian Ross scribbled his words down; they were audible across the aisle.

For a senior movie executive to make a public criticism of a leading director in a public theater was unheard of in the history of Hollywood. By this time, Mayer had thrown away the rule book and didn't care what anyone thought of it. He and Lorena, who agreed with him, marched out of the lobby, where Benny Thau joined them. Then the Mayers took off in Kaufman Keller's studio Chrysler.

Mayer wanted to shelve the picture. Schary talked about an art-house release. Reinhardt got permission to hold the film to general distribution, but would add an explanatory narrative advising the public that this was an important subject. It was a killer suggestion. If there was anything the public didn't want, it was a lecture. Reinhardt castrated the picture, then Dore Schary cut its arms and legs off. He sliced two of the four battle scenes, reduced sequences that had brought laughs. The result was a sixty-eight-minute picture oddity, which became a critic's favorite, cited as an example of the crassness of Hollywood tycoons in failing to recognize art. What remains is a handsome fragment, a broken mural from a derelict building.

In the movie's wake, Lillian Ross published, in 1952, *Picture*, amalgamating her articles in *The New Yorker*. Praised by everyone who relished the worst possible accounts of Hollywood, the book was poor reward for Mayer's and Schary's generosity to the author in opening their doors to her. Theirs was a mistake that wouldn't be made again.

In the meantime, Judy Garland was as much of a problem as ever. Mayer had given her the picture *Royal Wedding*, which was framed around the 1947 nuptials of Prince Philip and Princess Elizabeth in London. She had failed to turn up for work, and Mayer was forced to admit he could do no more with her. On June 20, Vincente Minnelli was talking with Judy at their home in Beverly Hills, when she suddenly walked to the bathroom. Minnelli heard her scream, "I want to die!" He broke the door down. She was standing there, with a broken glass in one hand, her neck streaming blood.

She hadn't severed an artery; the wound was superficial. On September 29, 1950, Mayer issued a statement announcing her permanent departure from M.G.M.: "Judy has been with us since childhood, and our devotion to her will always remain."

## CHAPTER TWENTY-THREE

# 1950–1954

A SEVERE BLOW came on November 16, 1950. The indispensable Carter Barron, always one of Mayer's best friends on the East Coast and the invaluable head of the Loew's operation in Washington, D.C., died after a prolonged struggle with brain cancer at the age of forty-five. It seemed incredible that the handsome, muscular, red-haired Barron, whom everyone liked for his cheerful disposition, should have been taken away so painfully and so cruelly. Mayer agreed at once to be honorary pallbearer; President Truman sent a wreath and a sorrowful statement to the family; Nicholas Schenck and Howard Dietz flew to Washington for the funeral.

In November, a movie that was destined to be one of Mayer's favorites began shooting on the studio backlot. Again, the subject matter was of no interest to Dore Schary; Mayer was essentially in charge. *Show Boat*, originally a stage triumph of Florenz Ziegfeld, had been filmed twice before, both by Universal, which ceded the rights; again, it helped that Jack Cummings was married to Jerome Kern's daughter. Mayer gave the job of directing the musical to George Sidney; Howard Keel was cast as the riverboat gambler Gaylord Ravenal, Kathryn Grayson as his wife, and William Warfield was brought from an Australian tour to play the part of the black laborer Joe who sings "Ol' Man River." Joe E. Brown, always a favorite of Mayer's, and Agnes Moorehead were cast as the riverboat captain Andy and his wife. Ava Gardner replaced Lena Horne as the tragic Julie. She gave her best performance in the part.

Sumptuously produced, splendidly recorded, the picture lacked the intimate charm of James Whale's 1937 version. But there was no suppressing the magnificence of the score and lyrics, and the awkwardly constructed final act, always a bugbear of Ziegfeld's, was reworked more effectively in this version. Mayer saw the picture eleven times, relishing the fact that at least something of his dream vision of America was sustained in these dark hours at the studio. He was pleased also with the recently completed *Royal Wedding* and *The Great Caruso*, both of which were successful at the box office.

The new year of 1951 brought a sudden, shocking tragedy. Rudolph Mayer, bailed out of bankruptcy by his brother, and following the relentless shafting of Sol Fielding and other family members, was living at the comfortable, if not opulent, Gaylord Hotel on Wilshire Boulevard. The family, despite all he had done to them, still found this mysterious charmer irresistible.

On the evening of February 27, he was in bed smoking a cigar when he fell asleep. The cigar fell into the bedclothes and set fire to the bed. Within minutes, the room was ablaze and he was unable to escape. The entire floor was wiped out, and although all the inhabitants managed to flee, several were affected by smoke inhalation. Death was attributed to heart failure. Rudolph left only debts, most of which his sister Ida managed to settle.

Soon afterward, Mayer made a trip to New York to see Schenck. It was not encouraging. Worst of all, Schenck accorded lavish stock options, the ability to buy stocks at a discount, to Dore Schary and five other executives, including Arthur Loew and Eddie Mannix, but not (a pointed insult) to Mayer. Schenck also granted warrants to purchase shares in return for contract extensions to Loew, Benny Thau, Joseph Vogel, Charles C. Moskowitz and Louis K. Sidney. Mayer hit the roof when he heard about this.

An appalling incident occurred on March 3. Mayer, who was beginning to show an interest in retrieving his abandoned racehorse career, was in his box at the Santa Anita Handicap when a wildly gesticulating, frenzied madman hurtled toward him screaming that he was wearing twelve dynamite sticks and was armed with a gun; he would blow Mayer to pieces and "the whole damn joint" as well. Somebody standing in the adjoining box picked up some folded chairs that were stacked together and flung them at the man, bringing him to the ground. Mayer was badly shaken, but, with his characteristic courage, stood up and reassured everyone that he was all right. The man was identified as Paul Salzburg, fifty, of El Centro and Calexico, and was armed only with a useless cigarette package equipped with a battery that would cause no injury to his victim. Mayer sent an award to his rescuer, automobile dealer S. T. Stone of Temple City.

There was a major consolation on March 29. At the Academy Awards ceremony at the Pantages Theater in Hollywood, hosted by Fred Astaire, Mayer was given an honorary award for "distinguished service to the motion picture industry." The writer-producer Charles Brackett was chosen to make the introduction, an astonishing gaffe since Brackett's script (with Billy Wilder) for *Sunset Boulevard*, and his coproduction thereof, had exasperated Mayer the previous summer. Mayer had called for his and Wilder's horsewhipping for portraying Gloria Swanson as a fading female star reduced to hiring a gigolo writer to service her.

Thus, a devastating satirist of the Hollywood Mayer represented was chosen to give the award to a grand old exemplar. Could tastelessness go further?

According to Mason Wiley and Damien Bona, coauthors of *Inside Oscar: The Unofficial History of the Academy Awards*, "Rumors were already circulating [that] night that Mayer's departure [from M.G.M.] was imminent." It seems probable that that indeed was the case. And Mayer's state of mind cannot have been improved by the fact that Brackett and Wilder won the Oscar for Best Screenplay for *Sunset Boulevard*, or that the hated picture obtained two other awards. *Father of the Bride* and *King Solomon's Mines*, both nominated for Best Picture, lost out to *All About Eve*; at least, the great Robert Surtees won for *King Solomon's Mines*, and the picture also gleaned an award for editing.

It would have been sensible for Mayer to have used the occasion of his honor from the Academy to act in a dignified manner and announce that he was quitting M.G.M. to embark on other fields. But his restless, tormented nature broke loose in a series of awkward confrontations with Dore Schary, who, as always, maintained a mealymouthed middle ground. When an announcement was made in the motion picture trade papers that Schary had been granted a brand new contract (actually, it had been confirmed in January), Mayer was irritable. He accused Schary of betrayal and Nicholas Schenck of ignorance and arrogance. It was as though he were staging a melodramatic background for a precipitate departure. He again flew east for meetings with Schenck, who was still, all too clearly, on Schary's side.

He even made the mistake of giving interviews to the press in which he criticized Loew's, Inc. When Thomas Brady of the New York *Times* published an interview with him, he summoned Brady back to his office and, despite the intercession of Howard Strickling, made the serious mistake of trying to correct Brady for his presentation of his accurately quoted remarks.

At the same time, Schenck was becoming increasingly annoyed with Mayer, even over the most petty matters. The actress Jayne Meadows had made a strong impression in two M.G.M. pictures, *Undercurrent* and *The Lady in the Lake*. Marvin Schenck had seen her in the play *Kiss Them for Me* on Broadway, had become fascinated with her and had encouraged her; so had M.G.M. producer Pandro Berman. Mayer was impressed by her work, but didn't actually meet her.

In 1951, her option came up; Mayer did not see star potential in her
and declined to renew her contract. Marvin Schenck was disappointed,
and reported that disappointment to Uncle Nicholas, who felt strongly
that Mayer had acted wrongly in failing to support Miss Meadows's
career. Although Schenck could have overruled Mayer and renewed her
contract, he apparently preferred to use her departure as an excuse to
show up Mayer as lacking his previous ability to select and develop stars.
On his deathbed, six years later, Mayer picked up a photograph of Jayne
Meadows and told a physiotherapist, "That young lady cost me my studio."

On a visit to Schary's office, Mayer, in a rare mood of conciliation,
asked what he would do if he retired. Schary admitted he didn't have
sufficient money to do so. But he said that if he were Louis B. Mayer, he
would travel, author books and provide a motion picture relief fund.
Mayer replied:

> You say that because you're a *kobtzen* [Yiddish for pauper] . . . I don't
> owe this industry or Loew's, Inc., a goddamn cent . . . Screw the com-
> pany and screw the stockholders! I've been everywhere. Why should I
> want to travel?

This irrational response to a reasonable if somewhat smarmy question
was illustrative of Mayer's state of mind. He said, "I spoke to Westbrook
Pegler, who had an item in his column about your being a Communist
spy. I told Westbrook that I would never have a Communist working for
me." Schary replied, "Some friends of mine say, 'How can you be working for a Jewish fascist?' I tell them L. B. Mayer is *not* a Nazi!" "Well,
many people think I'm a Catholic," Mayer, with unconscious humor,
said.

Schary suggested that Mayer might give his money to the Academy of
Motion Picture Arts and Sciences. Mayer replied, "I created the Acad-
emy Awards and they're ruining the industry." His face flushed violently.
Schary cleared out.

Mayer began complaining to friends and family about Schary's alleged
betrayal of him, even though Schary was far too insecure behind his
mask of bespectacled, scholarly charm to risk a *coup d'état* against his
ferocious boss.

A ghastly meeting took place in the spring of 1951. Schary walked in
to Mayer's office and the phone rang. J. Robert Rubin was on the line
from New York. Mayer told Rubin that he would no longer confer with
Nicholas Schenck. Then, looking meaningfully at Schary, he snapped
out the fatal words, "Bob, you can tell your friend Mr. Schenck that he

and Mr. Schary can take the studio and choke on it." He slammed the
telephone down and, glaring at Schary, folded his arms and waited for a
response. Schary was silent. "What do you have to say?" Mayer snarled.

Schary replied weakly, "L.B., is something wrong?"

"You bet there is," Mayer said. "And don't pull that look on me. You
and Schenck have plotted this all along. Sit down and I'll tell you
everything, you little kike!"[1]

Schary said he wasn't afraid of Mayer and didn't want to fight with
him. ("I'm leaving you and that's all.") He started out of the room,
followed by Mayer's curses.

Schary called his lawyer, David Tannenbaum. Tannenbaum advised
him to call Schenck in New York. Schenck advised Schary to reason
with Mayer. Schary declined. Schenck said, "Wait till tomorrow."

Benny Thau, Eddie Mannix and Louis K. Sidney begged Schary to
apologize. Schary refused.

Next morning, Schenck called Schary again. Schary was again adamant he would not see Mayer, but instead would leave the studio. "You
can't leave, because I am responsible for your being here," Schenck said.
Finally, Schary yielded and returned to Mayer's office. He apologized if
he was at fault, and said he couldn't imagine what had caused the argument. Mayer screamed at him. Schary walked out and called Tannenbaum. Tannenbaum urged him to call Schenck. He declined, said he was
going home. He wouldn't stay in the studio one minute longer.

Later in the day, Schenck called Schary at home. Schary declined to
discuss the matter any further. He again stated that it would be better if
he resigned. Schenck said, "Just go about your duties and you won't have
to see Mayer." Mayer stormed into the studio gym, where Marvin
Schenck was working out, and told him he was leaving M.G.M.

Mayer resigned the following afternoon. According to Samuel Marx,
Mayer was driven by his chauffeur, Frank, to the studio gate, in one of
Kaufman Keller's Town and Country Chrysler station wagons. A guard
stopped the automobile at the gate. He informed Frank that Mr. Schary
expected the car back, and that Mr. Mayer was no longer entitled to use
it. Mayer had to get out, stand in humiliation at the entrance of the
great studio he had founded and built to supremacy, while one of his
personal Chrysler fleet of five was brought from the house.

Mayer's departure was so abrupt that almost none of his surviving
executives can remember exactly what took place. One minute he was
in the studio, the next minute he was gone. There was no time for his
supporters to arrange a farewell party, to offer him support, to announce

---

[1] In another version, Schary told Don Knotts of the American Film Institute that Mayer said: "You
no-good Jew, son of a bitch!"

that they might leave with him or to protest to Schenck. It seemed on the surface as though Mayer had followed his suicidal pattern of previous years and that, in a metaphorical sense, overwhelmed with suspicion, anger, jealousy, hostility and uncontrollable rage, cut his own throat. But the truth was different: Mayer thought he had an ace in the hole. Mayer's San Francisco associate Louis R. Lurie had planned for weeks to buy Warner Brothers from its owners, Harry, Jack and Albert, and put Mayer in charge. But the day Mayer left the studio, at the eleventh hour of negotiations, Harry Warner changed his mind, leaving Mayer high and dry.

Almost as though Schenck feared a mass walkout, he, with great cunning, called an emergency summit meeting in Chicago of Schary, Mannix, Thau, J. J. Cohn, Louis Sidney and Marvin Schenck. Even Mayer's old friend J. Robert Rubin was enlisted for the meeting. To rub salt in Mayer's wounds, Schenck had Howard Dietz of the New York publicity office announce the Chicago conference in all the newspapers.

The executive group from Hollywood flew together; if the plane had crashed, it would have been the virtual end of M.G.M. An emergency luncheon was held at the Ambassador East Hotel. Schenck, who had flown in with Rubin from New York, instructed his executive staff in the new studio operation that would be set up in Mayer's wake. Schary would not be in complete charge: Mannix and Thau would divide responsibilities with him. Mannix would assign directors, replace performers and add new scenes. Thau would be in complete charge of talent. Sidney would be custodian of the studio's anti-Communist policing, and would take care of budgets. Cohn would be chief of the studio operation.

At the end of the meeting, Schary drew Schenck into another room and said that he didn't want Mannix, Thau, Cohn and the rest to run the studio with him. He needed autonomy; his January contract promised it. He would be responsible only to Schenck. Schenck was dismayed. But he knew he would lose Schary, and he could be sued for breach of contract, if he disagreed.

Schenck walked into the suite and told Mannix, Thau and the others that he had forgotten the terms of Schary's contract. Mannix was upset. He suggested that there might be some way he could work with Schary on such matters as retakes of pictures. Schary said he would be glad to discuss any question of production decisions, but he would have to make the final choices. Schenck said he would honor Schary's contract to the letter. The meeting broke up.

Back in Los Angeles, Mayer was left to fret and fume at home. His resignation had been announced in all the newspapers on June 26. Many articles that appeared had the flavor of obituaries, summarizing his career and attainments as though he were dead.

In those terrible months of exile, according to Daniel Selznick, Mayer's life became a torment. His family's nerves, especially Lorena's, were stretched to the limit to deal with his screams of unbridled anger, grumbles against Schary and Nicholas Schenck, outbursts at the disloyalty of his immediate circle at the studio, shouts of desperation and slammings of the fist on tables or loud shutting of doors. Danny remembers him pacing like a caged lion, up and down the opulent living room at St. Cloud Road.

Sometimes even the impeccably gracious Lorena, much as she adored him, carefully though she sustained her role as consort to a Hollywood monarch banished from his throne, would scream back at him or burst into tears and run into her bedroom. Suzanne, whom Mayer had adopted by now, was equally affected by these scenes, and the other members of the family, Jeffrey and Daniel Selznick and Edie's daughters Barbara and Judy, were similarly dragged through the inferno. Such old, well-worn pleasures as dinners in fine restaurants or a box at the Hollywood Bowl, especially for the John Philip Sousa brass band concerts, no longer held their savor. Dr. Romm did what she could to console, and Dr. Marmorston was an incessant presence, somewhat irritating the family by her air of absolute command, of owning Louis B. Mayer lock, stock and barrel, and her not infrequent mentions that she had supplied her medical services free of charge. Mayer clung to her as much as he did to his own wife and daughters for consolation in the grip of a nightmare.

It cost Nicholas Schenck a fortune to settle Mayer's contract. Mayer was guaranteed ten percent profits on all M.G.M. pictures made or re-released since 1924. The figures ran into millions, the exact amount varying according to different sources.

Mayer wasted no time in making his next move. He decided to join Louis Lurie in attempting to acquire RKO Pictures and its entire, government-threatened theater circuit from Howard Hughes. This was an astonishing switch: if it worked, it would put him in charge of the studio that Schary had departed. Mayer would attempt to turn RKO into a smaller version of M.G.M. in terms of quality, large-scale productions, would try to lure his former executive staff to his new operation and would change RKO's policy of low-budget, strong action pictures in the same way that Schary had sought to alter M.G.M.'s own policy. At the same time, Mayer retained, ironically, all but 1,500 of his former 12,000 shares of Loew's common stock.

Mayer busied himself with renewing his racehorse interests. He negotiated with his son-in-law William Goetz, who had extended himself by building a fine collection of French Impressionist paintings, to buy Goetz's horses, including a number that Goetz had bought from Mayer. In the auction at Hollywood Park, Mayer paid a total of $206,600 for seven head, including $37,000 for the successful Grantor, $27,000 for Miss Barbara and her foal and $26,000 for Your Hostess, whose management by Goetz had intensely annoyed Mayer. Mayer also bought from Joe Schenck, with a syndicate including rancher Tom Peppers, millionaire philanthropist Alfred Hart, and stable owners Harry Curland and Jay Paley, a controlling interest in the Del Mar Racetrack. He traveled to Lexington, Kentucky, where he bought the winning two-year-old filly Princess Lygia, named for the character played by Deborah Kerr in *Quo Vadis?*, for $100,000.

Mayer renewed an earlier friendship with Republican Senator Robert A. Taft; he attended a Taft-for-President rally in Rockland, Maine, and conferred closely with Senator Owen Brewster of that state.

He began discussions with Herbert J. Yates, president of Republic Pictures, toward buying that studio as well as RKO. Yates controlled over fifty percent of Republic's stock and 20,885 shares of Associated Motion Picture Industries, which Mayer was also seeking to buy.

On September 12, Mayer received sad news. His old and devoted friend Lewis Stone died of a heart attack at the age of seventy-three, in circumstances that seemed appropriately heroic for the man who had played Judge Hardy. Stone heard some hooligans throwing rocks into his swimming pool and ran after them to apprehend them. He collapsed as he left his front gate and died within a few moments.

On September 18, Mayer signed up Lillie Messenger's husband, Alexis Thurn-und-Taxis, as his assistant. Thurn-und-Taxis, a member of the wealthy German family that had owned the pre–World War II Taxi Telegram monopoly, the European equivalent of Western Union, had been working at CBS as screenwriter and director. Sophisticated, elegant and charming, Thurn-und-Taxis was involved in his wife's recently formed actors' agency, which handled, among many other prominent clients, a close friend, Marlene Dietrich. Mayer formed an association with CBS board member and shareholder I. B. (Ike) Levy, who was involved with Official Films, Inc.

The tireless retiree was in New York in December, dealing with a stockholders' suit led by businessman Gustave Garfield in which it was claimed that he had an improper degree of equity in Loew's, Inc. In meetings with J. Robert Rubin, Mayer agreed to sell out his interests in the corporation for approximately $2.5 million.

Garfield objected, stating that such a sellout was improper according to corporate procedure and that Mayer should return the money. Mayer,

Garfield said, should not receive his ten percent participation in studio profits since he had surrendered that right with the voluntary termination of his contract.

Mayer attacked Loew's with a cross-claim, warning Schenck not to proceed with any conciliatory measures toward Garfield, and refusing to return any payment. Mayer charged that he was due further monies from his last two years of employment, ending on August 31, 1951. He demanded $1 million. The suits were settled out of court.

Mayer snapped up properties, including Thomas Mann's novel *Joseph and His Brethren*, the musical *Paint Your Wagon* and Graham Greene's novel *The End of the Affair*.

Throughout April, Mayer, who had dropped the idea of buying Republic, possibly because Herbert Yates declined to yield his personal control of the studio, continued negotiations with Howard Hughes at RKO. Louis Lurie met with Mayer in Florida and New York in April for further discussions. Hughes was seldom available for a meeting; shifting between various hotels in Las Vegas, pursuing nubile men and women and up to his eyes in work on his airplane and petroleum interests, he was unable to deal with much else, remaining an elusive and maddening negotiator.

Even when Mayer was backed by Henry Ford II and Kaufman Keller of Chrysler, Hughes hesitated. This was maddening for Mayer, who longed to take over the studio and still smarted from losing Warner Brothers.

In mid-April, Mayer talked with Hughes at the home of attorney Neil McCarthy. Hughes promised him that the arrangements would go through, and that he would be able to have his own Louis B. Mayer Productions, the title appearing on the movie credits, with RKO existing only as a releasing organization. He would have autonomy, both at the RKO studio on Gower Street in Hollywood and at the Culver City RKO Pathé facility. He would have Jerry Wald, a dynamo in the Mayer mold, as his production executive. In return, Mayer would put up between five and ten million dollars of revolving credit.

McCarthy, telling Hughes that Mayer's name would enhance RKO's prestige, common stock values and production qualities, said he would require that Mayer be paid twenty percent of all profits, the same arrangement Samuel Goldwyn had. Hughes was amenable to this arrangement, but the negotiators were unable to reach an agreement on the purchase of RKO stock, for which Hughes wanted $11.50 per share, a profit of $2.50 per share on Hughes's payment for his controlling interest to the tycoon Floyd Odlum.

Talks continued through May. Mayer continued to give his support to

Robert Taft, and he and Ida Koverman, who had stayed on at M.G.M. instead of going to work for him, were in constant touch with Herbert Hoover, who was also lending his weight to Taft.

Mayer's dream of having his own RKO studio evaporated. Mercurial and unreliable, Hughes sold out to the Chicago tycoon Ralph E. Stolkin, head of a specially formed syndicate that included Los Angeles theater chain owner Sherill C. Corwin and two oil men. The deal did not go through until September, when Stolkin finally put a deposit down on a final purchase price of $7,345,940. But later, Stolkin and his partners would pull out. Meanwhile, Mayer and Louis Lurie, irritated by Hughes's duplicity and slovenly business dealings, lost all interest in RKO.

Mayer turned to other plans. He investigated the possibilities of a promising new cinematic form, Cinerama. Realizing that television, which he had so long opposed and refused to take seriously, was already absorbing the mass audience, he felt that a new gimmick might attract them back again.

Cinerama, a system using several projectors and three screens to give a powerful but unstable image, was the invention of the shy and gangling Fred Waller, who formed the Cinerama Corporation in 1946. Lowell Thomas, the famous broadcaster, traveler and author, was a partner in it. Another partner, *King Kong* producer Merriam C. Cooper, met with Mayer in the late spring of 1952 at Mayer's offices in Beverly Hills and convinced him that he should lend money and prestige to Cinerama.

For several weeks, Mayer brooded over the potential of the new wide-screen system, and at last, at the end of July, he took off for New York to see Cinerama demonstrated. With him, as he traveled out to Fred Waller's Oyster Bay house and screening room, was the amiable financier Dudley Roberts, Jr., who had obtained a substantial number of shares in the invention. Among those present at the screening were the producer Mike Todd, who would promote Cinerama, and Lowell Thomas. It was an exciting evening; Mayer was enthralled by the excitement of seeing the three huge panels melding together, sometimes perfectly, sometimes not, plunging the viewer into many spectacular scenes. Among these were an aerial tour of the Grand Canyon, a ride on the Venice canals in a gondola, a ripsnorting ride on the Big Dipper at an amusement park, a front-row seat at a performance of the Vienna Boys Choir and stirring patriotic scenes of American traditional sites, accompanied by a choir singing the national anthem. Mayer felt that he was in the presence of an astonishing revolution in filmmaking, which would counteract utterly the small, gray, flickering images of television. Shaking the hands of all concerned as the screening ended, he expressed his warm enthusiasm and agreed to support the system to the limit. He invested substantially

in it, and also agreed to become chairman. This was a great coup for Fred
Waller and for Lowell Thomas, and they were ecstatic at his decision.

In late August, as Adlai Stevenson's campaign for president intensified, Mayer, who had been forced to admit that Robert Taft was no
longer a viable candidate even before Taft was eliminated from the race
at the Republican Convention, was throwing his weight behind Dwight
D. Eisenhower (he would much have preferred General MacArthur).
William Goetz was still resolutely behind Stevenson. Knowing that Stevenson was due shortly in California, Goetz decided to hold a lavish
fund-raising benefit at his and Edie's house. But Goetz had a twinge of
conscience and decided he could not give offense to his father-in-law.
Dore Schary then stepped in and suggested that the party should be at
his own home. Under pressure from Schary, Goetz weakened and allowed Schary to send out invitations in which Schary and Goetz jointly
invited the guests. It was a tremendous occasion, crowded with the elite
of Hollywood Democrats. Mayer was horrified when he got wind of the
event. Reading of it in the newspapers the following morning was insup-
portable for him. And there was another blow: a few days earlier, Mayer
had asked Goetz to leave his commanding position at Universal–International Studios and join the nucleus of a production company Mayer
was beginning to organize. Goetz had turned him down coldly; remembering the fact that Mayer had set Goetz up, first with 20th Century
Pictures and later with International Pictures, Mayer was bitterly disillusioned with his son-in-law.

Edie's action in supporting Schary's reception for Stevenson was, at
the very least, an act of outright tastelessness, and could be interpreted
fairly as an act of betrayal. Mayer called Edie, screaming at her in anger.
She replied (she remembered thirty-two years later), "What do you want
me to do, divorce Bill? I've lived with him longer than I lived with you,
and get it through your head, I love him!" Mayer said, "When I see your
husband, I'll turn my head away." And then he added, "On second
thought, when I see either one of you, I'll turn my head away." Edie
slammed the phone down.

They never spoke to each other again. Edie's defection shattered him.
She had the effrontery to say to the present author, "All he had to do
was call up and apologize to my husband." The only person who should
have apologized was William Goetz.

From then on, Mayer cut off all interest in the Goetzes' daughters.
When Judy married in 1954, he failed to answer her invitation. When
he saw the couple in New York in 1956 with their young baby, they
called out to him, but he walked furiously past them and jumped into his

waiting limousine. For some reason, Judy Goetz's husband, Richard Shepherd, found this surprising.

Mayer could forgive Irene for supporting Stevenson, but he could not forgive Edie for joining with her husband and Schary. And Irene, always full of hatred for Edie, did nothing to try to mend the rift.

On November 19, at a dinner at the Biltmore Hotel Bowl in Los Angeles, Mayer became the second recipient of the Screen Producers Guild's Milestone Award (the first recipient was Jesse L. Lasky). Introducing Mayer, the group's president, Sol C. Siegel, announced that Mayer was, above and beyond any other industry leader, responsible for the establishment of the creative producer system as it existed then. Tactlessly, Siegel credited Mayer with shaping the career of Dore Schary (Siegel would soon replace Schary—another irony). Mayer retained a poker face at the mention of Schary's name. Siegel also cited Arthur Freed, Sidney Franklin, Pandro Berman and Lawrence Weingarten among those Mayer had helped. The award was just: Mayer had indeed given a rare degree of autonomy to these figures.

Joe Schenck was called to the podium. Schenck, in direct defiance of his brother, who had continued to bad-mouth Mayer at every opportunity, praised Mayer to the limit. Norma Shearer spoke of her long working relationship with Mayer, avoiding the fact that she had intermittently over the years fought him over their several shares in M.G.M. players and profits. "Through L.B., I met my Prince Charming," she said, and added, rather oddly in view of her husband's early death, "I have danced happily ever after." Bob Hope said:

When Mayer began making pictures, Vine Street and Hollywood Boulevard were practically just cow paths. If L.B. had gone into the real estate business we wouldn't have to be giving him this dinner tonight. He came to California twenty-five years ago with nothing but a box camera, thirty-eight dollars and an old lion. He parlayed these into a monument known throughout the world as . . . the Bank of America.

Presented with a silver plaque, Mayer talked earnestly of his early days in Haverhill, skipped over his entire M.G.M. career in a matter of seconds, then seized the occasion to promote Cinerama. He said:

This is a tremendously thrilling screen entertainment. It has a ceiling: not a ceiling in quality or imagination, but in where and how it can be used. No one knows for sure, but my guess is that no more than two hundred theaters will have Cinerama within the next two or three years. It is for selective theaters, for selective stories, for selective audiences.

At the end of the evening, Lena Horne, who had little good to say for
Mayer in her numerous public appearances of the next forty years, sang
three numbers with her husband Lennie Hayton at the piano, and Ethel
Merman belted out "There's No Business Like Show Business."

There was a poignancy in the occasion, because nobody present, including Mayer's own nephew Jack Cummings, either then or later, gave
the slightest indication that they would come in with Mayer were he to
form his own independent studio or successfully take over another.


Eisenhower's victory in the 1952 election was a consolation for Mayer's
many torments. Gustave Garfield's stockholder suit against Mayer and
Loew's dragged on, forcing Mayer, on May 11, 1953, to agree to return
$150,000 as part of the out-of-court settlement. Cinerama was proving a
great success. Its original showings at the Broadway Theater in New
York, starting on September 30, 1952, had proved to be a sensation, and
the Los Angeles opening in early 1953 was equally impressive. Jack
Warner, never Mayer's favorite, had meetings with him to discuss producing two Cinerama features a year, but this proved to be impractical.
By April 26, Cinerama had grossed more than $1 million in profits; this
figure would grow to $10 million by December. But the problem of
limited screenings was always a handicap, and it was because of this that
Spyros Skouras, the chairman of 20th Century-Fox, began to consult
with experts on developing CinemaScope.

When Skouras saw the new system demonstrated in Paris, a system
that the movie tycoon J. Arthur Rank in England had just let slip
through his fingers, Skouras was ecstatic. Seeing the Arc de Triomphe
and the Eiffel Tower glowing magnificently on the wide screen, Skouras
grabbed a telephone and called New York.

Al Lichtman, of all people, was the first to agree with Skouras about
CinemaScope's potential; he handled 20th Century-Fox theaters. Skouras snapped up the original Henri Chrétienne lenses, and a sample reel
was pulled together. CinemaScope was superior to Cinerama, chiefly
because there were no dividing lines in the image.

For its first CinemaScope film, 20th Century-Fox chose The Robe,
based on a novel by Lloyd C. Douglas. It was rushed into production at
record speed from a long-existing script. The announcement of The Robe
was a crushing blow to Mayer. It was the kind of picture, the story of the
soldier who won Christ's robe in a dice game, that he would love to have
made himself. And one of his favorite M.G.M. writers, Gina Kaus, had
written the script (with Philip Dunne).

Nineteen fifty-three turned out to be the year of CinemaScope; despite harsh reviews (critics said that looking at a movie was now like staring through the world's largest mailbox slit), the public endorsed the system. When the newly huge 20th Century-Fox logo, with its blazing searchlights, came up on the screen, accompanied by a revamped fanfare composed by Alfred Newman, audiences broke into applause; a moment later, the immense vistas and sprawling crowd scenes of *The Robe* brought gasps and cheers.

Mayer concluded negotiations with theater tycoon Stanley Warner (no relation to the Warner Brothers) to purchase the rights to Cinerama. It was less than a year since Mayer had first taken over.

Mayer retained ownership of *Joseph and His Brethren.* But he had considerable difficulty in overcoming the problems of the script for Thomas Mann's immense epic novel. John Lee Mahin, closer to Mayer than ever, and sharing his offices on Charleville Drive in Beverly Hills, had worked for much of the year on the screenplay. Mayer had in mind casting Jennifer Jones in the leading female role; he sent it to her and her husband, David Selznick, whom he now regarded as an ally. Selznick had reservations about Mahin's work, feeling it wasn't ready for filming. On September 16, 1953, he sent a memorandum to Mayer and Mahin, discussing not only the shortcomings of the material, but the correct way to present it. He indicated, tactlessly, that it would need the touch of a Cecil B. DeMille to carry off *Joseph and His Brethren* successfully; no one else, he felt, could match DeMille's combination of sex and religion. He warned against falling between two schools of an "artistic" movie and a broad, crude effort. In view of the fact that Mayer had initiated and pushed through *Quo Vadis?*, and that he had brought off previous epics with equal skill, and in view of the fact that Selznick made derogatory remarks about *Quo Vadis?* in his note, it is surprising that Mayer remained friendly with him afterward. Mayer sold the property to producer Jerry Wald, who hired Clifford Odets, still Mayer's bête noire, to adapt it.

Schenck and Schary took up CinemaScope that year. Though Schary went on making realistic pictures, among them *Take the High Ground*, an Army training story, Mayer's nephew Gerald's all-black *Bright Road* and a western, *Escape From Fort Bravo*, he began to imitate Mayer's policies in an attempt to rescue the studio from a drop in profits. Mayer would have been proud to have made *The Story of Three Loves*, an exquisitely fashioned trilogy directed by Gottfried Reinhardt and Vincente Minnelli; *Mogambo*, a remake of *Red Dust*, with the potent combination of Clark Gable, Ava Gardner and Grace Kelly; Esther Williams's vehicle *Easy to Love*, with a stunningly shot climax by Busby Berkeley set in Florida's Cypress Gardens; *Young Bess*, a vivid evocation of the Tudor era; the long-planned *The Actress*, based on Ruth Gordon's autobiographical play *Years Ago*, with Spencer Tracy and Jean Simmons, magically directed by George Cukor; and the rousing *Kiss Me Kate*. There was no loss of craftsmanship at M.G.M.; the spirit of Mayer hung on, conveyed by his former producers Jack Cummings, Sidney Franklin and Arthur Freed. It can only have been painful for Mayer to realize that Schary was gleaning praise, and substantial commercial value, from traditional movies of the sort that Mayer himself had initiated.

Lorena remained beautiful, charming, a fine hostess, supplying a cool, soothing hand to Mayer's fevered brow. Suzanne was an attractive young lady; she had made an impression at Marymount, Los Angeles's most exclusive Roman Catholic girls' school (later, she would enter a convent as a novice, but would drop out of it and marry). In January 1954, Mayer wrote to Herbert Hoover, who was living at the Waldorf Towers in New York, and to Hoover's secretary, Bernice Miller, on the matter of Suzanne's entering Stanford University. Hoover used his influence in that direction; as a graduate and benefactor of that institution, he was placed, better than anyone, to assist her.

Mayer suffered a great annoyance in February. On the fourteenth, Ed Sullivan's Sunday television show, "Toast of the Town," featured a thirtieth-birthday salute to M.G.M., with Dore Schary as guest of honor. In giving a pocket history of the studio, with an emphasis on *Gone With the Wind*, Schary omitted any mention of Mayer or David Selznick; Schary took credit for thirty years of M.G.M.'s achievements, and there was no reference to the fact that Selznick was creator of *Gone With the Wind*. Mayer, seeing the telecast at home, called Selznick in New York in a transport of fury, screaming that he had "never seen such an outrageous scandal." He attacked Nicholas Schenck and Dore Schary, charging them with conspiracy. Selznick told *Variety* that the program was "disgraceful and inexcusable." Asked by the *Variety* reporter if he would sue the network, Mayer said, "What kind of a suit could I file? Can I say I'm the great Louis B. Mayer? This is impossible!" Selznick called a press conference to express his anger and dismay. M.G.M. producers, led by Arthur Freed, were asked for their opinions, but remained mealymouthed, protecting their jobs. Selznick issued a statement, giving a complete history of his experiences at M.G.M. It was not until three weeks later that the controversy died down.

Mayer plunged into yet another one: in April, he traveled to Haverhill with Clarence Brown to be honored at a celebratory luncheon. He made the mistake of attacking CinemaScope and *The Robe* (it was doubtful if he actually saw the film), thus giving enormous publicity to Cinerama's rival system. He annoyed many by giving a speech praising

Senator Joseph R. McCarthy, whose anti-Communist campaign he applauded, and he had to weather further criticism when it was discovered that he had acted as an adviser to McCarthy in the preparation of a promotional film, paradoxically made by CinemaScope's owners, 20th Century-Fox, through its Movietone News Division. He irritated friends and admirers by seemingly undermining his continuing support of Cinerama by investing in Mike Todd's Todd-AO, yet another wide-screen process that in many ways was superior to its competitors. Although *This Is Cinerama* was, by October 26, in its 109th week on Broadway, Mayer was reexperiencing earlier doubts about its future. Even though the Stanley Warner Theaters effectively controlled Cinerama, Mayer remained an investor and, at least nominally, chairman.

A blow came in November. Mayer's friend and loyal, long-term colleague Ida Koverman died on the twenty-fourth. She left an estate of only $20,789, surprisingly little for an elderly woman who had been thrifty all her life. Much of the money was accounted for in household furnishings, a car and Bank of America stocks. The reason for her not leaving M.G.M. with Mayer and remaining his secretary is inexplicable to this day. She left him nothing; some small memento would surely have been in order. Had there been a rift between them?

Her funeral was an event. Among the stars present were George Murphy, Jimmy Stewart and Edward G. Robinson; among the studio executives were Eddie Mannix, Benny Thau, Robert Z. Leonard, Howard Strickling and agent Billy Grady. Mayer and Schary sat in the same pew, staring straight ahead, not even glancing toward each other. Following Lionel Barrymore's recent demise, Ida Koverman's departure reminded Mayer all too painfully of his own mortality. He resumed medical tests to make sure that his own health was secure.

The results were encouraging, but Mayer was still very afraid of imminent sickness and death. He took instruction from Fulton J. Sheen, the leading exponent of popular Catholicism, as a postulant to convert to Catholicism. His daughter Irene talked him out of it. She told him that if this short, fat Jew should pretend to be a Catholic, people would scream in laughter at him. He admitted reluctantly that she was right.

## CHAPTER TWENTY-FOUR

# 1954–1957

MAYER NEVER CEASED to keep a sharp eye on the goings-on at Loew's, Inc. and M.G.M. He never ceased to dream of returning to glory at Culver City. He can only have rejoiced that the Department of Justice at last left no alternative to Nicholas Schenck in implementing the consent decree whereby the Loew's Theater empire, from the high and mighty Capital Theater in New York City down, was forced to separate from the studio. He could see a wide chink emerging in the corporate armor. And then there was the welcome news that Dore Schary was found to be ailing, first with stomach trouble, then with gallstones. Soon it would be announced that M.G.M.'s profits were down another million, and the number of pictures the studio was making was greatly reduced. Such ineffectual pictures as *Scandal at Scourie*, the nadir of Garson and Pidgeon, Red Skelton's fade-out *The Great Diamond Robbery*, Mickey Rooney's pathetic *A Slight Case of Larceny* and Cary Grant's stinker *Dream Wife* were all failures. Even the reliable Lana Turner faltered badly in *The Flame and the Flesh*; *Betrayed* did just that to Clark Gable, and ended his career at the studio; and *Jupiter's Darling* sank Esther Williams without so much as a bubble.

Nineteen fifty-four was a dark year at M.G.M.,[1] and Mayer began planning, at the end of it, to seize the occasion to rescue the sinking Titanic he had launched almost thirty-one years before. He had yet another advantage, learned through the grapevine as well as through the trade papers, in that Nicholas Schenck was growing increasingly weary of Schary. Schenck had opposed Schary's *Bad Day at Black Rock*, a powerful story of a war veteran who brings a medal to the father of the

---

[1] A few movies of that year were good: *Rhapsody*, an observant, lushly handsome study of musicians and the very rich; the splendid *Beau Brummell*, staged in England; *Executive Suite*; and the Sigmund Romberg musical biography, *Deep in My Heart*.

nisei soldier who saved his life in combat; an entire Western desert town becomes bent on destroying this stranger in its midst.

In the early months of 1955, a palace revolution began at Loew's, similar to that in *Executive Suite* and in Schary's later story of corporate struggle, *The Power and the Prize*. Arthur Loew, survivor of plane wreck and corporate change, still master of the foreign side of the company, was being backed by several powerful board members to supplant the aging Schenck. Loew, Mayer must have felt, would be an easier target than Schenck; Schenck's sudden "resignation" as president and elevation to the meaningless position of chairman of the board came just at a time when Schenck's latest executive action, against *Bad Day at Black Rock*, was being proven misguided by the strong critical and commercial response to the picture. With Loew in office, the jittery Schary was given a temporary reprieve. It was understood that Schenck, at seventy-four, well past retirement age, would be put out to pasture the following year.

Mayer's position as Cinerama chairman still made him viable as a potential studio leader. He kept up his friendship with Herbert Hoover, always a name to conjure with; every thirty days, he sent Hoover a Fruit of the Month at the Waldorf Towers, and Hoover responded joyfully to the series of welcome gifts. His eternal fondness for Hoover, his continuing friendships with Arthur Freed, Howard Strickling, Clarence Brown and Kaufman Keller, sustained Mayer during his sojourn in the wilderness.

He stumbled at a banquet of the American Cinema Editors in his honor, held at the Los Angeles Ambassador Hotel on March 23, when he predicted that the effects of color television on the movie industry would be of short duration:

> In the old days, all you had to do was shoot any western in Technicolor and you had a box-office hit. But the novelty soon wore off, and as always, it was learned that nothing ever takes the place of top entertainment values, no matter how you dress up the material.

On May 21, Margaret Mayer died of heart failure at Cedars of Lebanon Hospital in Los Angeles. Irene used as an excuse her involvement in a British stage production of Enid Bagnold's *The Chalk Garden* and refused to fly to her mother's bedside. Edie was in attendance in the last days. Margaret left an estate of approximately $2 million; in an unwise decision, she made her two warring daughters, who hated each other more than ever, joint executors with the California Trust Company, and divided her house and other physical property between them. She left legacies to her granddaughters; Edie's daughter Judy Shepherd was given the choice of $100,000 in cash or her grandmother's platinum ring set with an 18.4-carat emerald-cut diamond. When Judy chose the ring, Irene was furious; according to Edie, she had wanted the ring herself, and the moment she heard the news, she sent Edie an angry letter, insulting Judy cruelly. Irene and Edie fought over the disposition of the house at Santa Monica, which was sold to Peter Lawford. Irene failed to attend her mother's funeral. Mayer was not present either.

On June 6, attorney Raymond C. Sandler and his wife Helen, Margaret Mayer's niece, sued the estate in Superior Court of Los Angeles on behalf of their son, nine-year-old Michael. The plaintiffs claimed that Michael had been left $25,000 in a 1947 will, and that the reduction of this sum to $1,250 in the present document was improper and the result of Margaret Mayer's "great and unnatural fear" of displeasing her daughters and William Goetz. It was pointed out that Helen Sandler had been left $500,000 in the earlier will but now received only $25,000. In the complaint, the Sandlers charged that Mrs. Mayer was kept under sedation during the last months of her life and was terrified of her family; Mrs. Selznick and the Goetzes, the Sandlers stated, had seized control over the ailing woman's mind. How Irene Selznick, who had been absent in Europe, could have exercised any influence was unexplained.

Meanwhile, Mayer took off to London that same week with Lorena and with Mr. and Mrs. Clarence Brown. They were in Paris on June 16, where he began negotiating for the rights to Agatha Christie's stage success, *Witness for the Prosecution*, which he would produce independently and which Clarence Brown would direct. But Mrs. Christie didn't want Mayer to have the property, and the negotiations collapsed around the $325,000 mark.

Back in London, Mayer criticized much of the present motion picture scene and talked of making *Paint Your Wagon* as the first Cinerama production with a continuing, coherent story. Clarence Brown recalled later that Mayer was like a child when it came to traveling. He left everything, packing and unpacking, train and boat tickets, hotel and meal reservations, to Lorena and the Browns. He was terrified of being left alone at any time, especially in railroad depots or airports, and he could never be put to his own devices. He even left magazine and book purchases to his companions. This childlike aspect of his nature was characteristic and known only to those closest to him. The contrast with his dominance at home scarcely needs stressing.

After almost four months of litigation, with little evidence of any sinister influences exerted on Mrs. Mayer, the Sandlers dropped their suit against Irene Selznick and the Goetzes.

In New York on his way home in July, Mayer had meetings with the former movie actress and millionairess Hope Hampton, one of Orson Welles's models for the unhappy wife of Charles Foster Kane in *Citizen Kane*. She was the widow of the Kodak tycoon Jules Brulatour, and was interested in investing in motion pictures. Richly bejeweled, heavily made up, a staple of every first-night party and charity event, Mrs. Brulatour fascinated the Mayers. But she failed to come up with any cash, and Mayer's negotiations with her came to nothing.

That spring, Mayer, full of bitterness, gave a sharp and startling interview, the longest of his career, to Gitta Parker and William Woodfield of the *American Weekly*. It did not appear until after his death. On the subject of acting, he screamed:

> What in hell does acting have to do with being a star? We can teach anyone to act. Haven't you been to a flea circus? They can learn fleas to act. I've never met a star as stupid as a flea. Maybe almost as stupid, but not stupider. I only had three great actors: Tracy, Garbo and Dressler . . . Robert Montgomery was a good actor, but cold, cold as ice . . . If I give [fleas] awards, they'll do anything I want. That's why I started the Academy Awards! The best pictures ever were the Andy Hardy series.

Not even Mayer's worst enemies, of whom Samuel Goldwyn remained the leader, had accused him of running a flea circus. He exaggerated his first encounter with Garbo, describing her as a horse weighing 200 pounds, with a face he had to buy ("I had to take Stiller as well, but it was worth it"). He declared that when he showed pictures of her to Thalberg, Thalberg said, "You're crazy!" It is impossible to believe that. He also said that when he suggested Robert Taylor, whose real name was Spangler Arlington Brugh, Thalberg said, "You can have half of him." By now, Mayer was obviously pulling his interviewer's leg. He was hard on Mickey Rooney, saying that Rooney's misbehaviors and divorces had resulted in the cancellation of the Andy Hardy series.

Turning in another direction, Mayer, in March 1956, bought the disused Lincoln Hotel on Eighth Avenue and Forty-fourth Street in New York. He still owned the Rivoli Theater on Broadway and much other real estate in midtown Manhattan. He planned to build a shopping arcade from the Astor Hotel west to Eighth Avenue, crossing Shubert Alley. On June 4, Mayer's friend and colleague J. Robert Rubin resigned from the Board of Loew's, Inc., thus snapping the last connection of the corporation with the Mayer epoch. Rubin hadn't been happy on the board since Mayer left.

In July, Mayer fell ill in Manhattan, arriving back in Hollywood on July 13 with pneumonia. He lay in Good Samaritan Hospital for two weeks, and his blood count was found to be low. There was fear that he might have pernicious anemia, but his beloved Dr. Jessie Marmorston did not convey this to him. Thanks to antibiotics, the pneumonia was brought under control, but there was a small spot left on one lung, and this also gave rise to concern. Mayer managed to rally sufficiently to send a warm letter to Herbert Hoover on July 31, thanking him for his anxiety, and he wrote again on August 31, to express his joy at Hoover's televised appearance at the Republican Convention.

He was stimulated by news that fall that Arthur Loew was wearying of his job as president of Loew's, Inc., and, with four months still to go on his contract, resigned in early November. Loew was replaced by the board with Joseph Vogel, whom Mayer had known since the early 1930s. Mayer saw in him far less of a rival than Loew. Vogel was a mediocre, widely-liked company man. He had begun his career at the age of fourteen as an usher at Major Bowes' Capital Theater; three years later, he had risen to become treasurer, and a year after that manager of all the New York Loew's cinemas. A few years after that, he was general manager of the entire theater operation.

Vogel was no more happy with Dore Schary than Arthur Loew had been. Schary had made the mistake of redoing several of Mayer's biggest hits in an effort to show he could improve on the master's products. Among these efforts were a feeble new version of *The Barretts of Wimpole Street*; *Gaby*, a frail remake of *Waterloo Bridge*; and *The Opposite Sex*, a garish, if spirited, reworking of *The Women*, with men included and much of the wit left out. Even *High Society*, with the megawatt cast of Grace Kelly, Bing Crosby and Frank Sinatra, was not the equal of its original, *The Philadelphia Story*. It seems incredible that Schary would risk showing up his own weaknesses by trying to improve on perfection.

Joseph Vogel had the unenviable task of snatching victory from disaster. Schary had to go. Vogel summoned him to New York and dismissed him. Schary's removal cost Loew's heavily: he would receive $100,000 a year, less insurance charges, for the rest of the term of his contract and beyond. And Vogel had no one to put in his place. Sol C. Siegel, an unimpressive producer, was his choice for a replacement, a selection that was scarcely inspiring to the shareholders.

It was time for Mayer, the aging lion, to show that he still had teeth. But his health had not recovered from the pneumonia attack that followed his return to Los Angeles. He felt alarming drops of energy, and would telephone Dr. Marmorston in the middle of the night; while Lorena sat by patiently, the good doctor would drive over to Bel Air and give him shots of vitamin $B_{12}$, the popular panacea of that era. Not content with these treatments, Mayer would take off with increasing frequency to San Francisco for an excessive number of tests that were made by his old friend and respected physician Dr. Arthur Bloomfield.

During one of those tests in December 1956, Dr. Bloomfield noticed the first serious irregularity: a proliferation of white cells beyond those discovered following the pneumonia. The cells indicated, at the least, very severe anemia; and there were signs of enlargement of liver and spleen that suggested the onset of leukemia.

It was too early to be sure. Mayer was told little; certainly, the dreaded word "leukemia" was never mentioned; Dr. Marmorston could put down Mayer's feelings of weakness and tiredness to his being over seventy, and he was content with that explanation. He found comfort in a treatment Dr. Marmorston had used earlier and now revived: giving him adrenal cortical extracts obtained from horse urine.

Mayer needed to concentrate on something other than his health, and by early December, with Schary and Loew out of the way, he set about a campaign to seize power at Loew's, Inc. He needed a man who was fearless and not subject to pressure to push his cause; were he to buy up large blocks of shares himself (he still owned 11,500), he would be exposed to too much adverse publicity.

Always going for the top, he settled on the majority shareholder Joseph Tomlinson, Canadian president of Consolidated Truck Lines, who had a trucker's build and voice. Over six feet three inches tall, and 250 pounds of solid muscle, Tomlinson could knock over a quarterback with a slap of his hand. This booming giant owned, with his wife and in-laws, 250,000 shares of Loew's common stock. Insufficiently well to make the trip to Manhattan or Toronto to see Tomlinson, Mayer selected an emissary: the smooth, darkly handsome young Stanley Meyer, a recent friend, who had launched the successful television series "Dragnet," starring Jack Webb.

Stanley Meyer proved to be an effective go-between. His personable charm soothed Tomlinson's savage breast. A lifelong movie fan, Tomlinson was bewitched by the thought that the great Louis B. Mayer was coming to him, hat in hand, seeking his support. Saying nothing to Joseph Vogel, Tomlinson flew out to California, where the Mayers threw an exquisitely catered and flower-decked dinner party in his honor. The elite of Hollywood were present; Tomlinson yielded to Mayer's charm, to his picture of a golden future in which the two men would bring back the great days of a vanished Hollywood.

Inspired by the visit, Tomlinson returned to Manhattan and arranged appointments with the presidents of the Loew's banking companies Lazard Freres and Lehman Brothers. He found support in those elevated circles; encouraged, he sent a lengthy memorandum, in which Mayer's fine hand could be seen, on December 14, 1956, calling for Vogel's immediate resignation; Vogel had been in office just over a month. Vogel naturally declined, and instead, afraid of a palace revolution, made a compromise arrangement with Tomlinson. The executive board would be reconstructed, made up half of Tomlinson's appointees, half of Vogel's. Tomlinson brought in Kaufman Keller and other friends of Mayer's court, including the former secretary of defense Louis Johnson. Vogel retaliated by bringing in his own group of six community leaders. A thirteenth, neutral board member was chosen: Ogden Reid, president and managing editor of the New York *Herald Tribune*.

Tomlinson set out on a campaign designed to unsettle Vogel and his and Mayer's enemy on the board. He harassed Vogel day after day, week after week, with countless telephone calls and written messages, demanding what amounted to a complete documented history of Loew's for the past twenty years. He called for contracts with stars, producers and directors; minutes of meetings; briefs, responding briefs and depositions from innumerable stockholders' suits; minutiae of accounting; mountains of ledgers; heaps of correspondence. Moving into offices and a board room on the eleventh floor of the Loew's headquarters on Broadway, Tomlinson was swamped with documentation.

But he was unable to find any evidence of malfeasance in the corporation's operation, succeeding only in giving an impression of pettiness, which reflected, by extension, on Mayer.

Loew's, Inc. had a specially appointed executive committee that acted when the board of directors was not in session. Tomlinson, inspired by Mayer, sought to have Mayer placed on this committee, but failed.

During the war of attrition, Vogel was barely able to run the company, and the Culver City operation floundered without leadership until Sol C. Siegel took over. Ben Javits, a lawyer representing Tomlinson, resigned because he objected to his client's methods of harassment. Vogel brought out an opposing trump card: the distinguished trial lawyer Louis Nizer. And Vogel strengthened his hand by removing from the corporation all of Nicholas Schenck's and Mayer's associates, canceling deals with Schenck-related contractors and firing treasurer Charles Moskowitz, who had maintained a neutral position between Mayer and Schenck.

But then he stumbled: as inept in Hollywood matters as he was expert in theater affairs (and he was about to lose his theaters because of the Department of Justice's consent decree), he proved stubborn in trying to force his board, through Sol C. Siegel, to accept the moviemaking team of Harold Hecht, James Hill and Burt Lancaster as special contractees to M.G.M., with Lancaster guaranteed the title role in a remake of *Ben-*

*Hur.* The board rejected Hecht–Hill–Lancaster, chiefly because the three men wanted autonomy and their kind of up-to-date filmmaking didn't jibe with some board members' conservatism.

This failure of Vogel's seemed to strengthen Mayer's hand, and Stanley Meyer telephoned Vogel and Louis Nizer, suggesting that a compromise might be reached. If Tomlinson were to cease his belligerent action and the warring board members could find a common ground, might not Louis B. Mayer be let in as an adviser only, not a president or chairman, and might Stanley Meyer not be made his special assistant? The ploy failed instantly. Vogel lost respect for Stanley Meyer and dismissed the idea out of hand.

Vogel stumbled again. He decided to have his next major board meeting, in July, held at the M.G.M. studios, presumably because he thought that he might influence the dissenting board members by showing how Mayer's former executives were in support of him. However, he had neglected to note that certain of his own group would be too busy with other matters to undertake the journey to California. The former secretaries of the Army and Navy were tied up in New York and Washington; thus, Tomlinson obtained an 8–4 majority on the board. Mayer entertained his eight supporters (Ogden Reid was in Manhattan) at the Bel Air house, and once again the hard-working Lorena pulled out all the stops as hostess. The talk went on in a cloud of cigar smoke until the small hours.

The studio meeting exposed Vogel's weaknesses. True, he could summon, along with his four remaining board members, such egregious figures as Eddie Mannix and Benny Thau, who had long since sold Mayer down the river, to acclaim him at the private dining room luncheon. But he could persuade nobody, even his most loyal adherents, when he unwisely dragged out the Hecht–Hill–Lancaster proposal again. He had no real understanding of movies, no real policy; his lack of dynamism was all too obvious, and Sol C. Siegel still pleased few as his appointee. Tomlinson called for Vogel's resignation at the meeting. Once more, Vogel refused to go.

On July 23, 1957, while still in Hollywood, Vogel made another mistake. He issued an angry statement to the shareholders, circulated widely to the press, singling out Mayer for his "conspiratorial tactics." His statement read, in part:

> During his tenure of twenty-seven years, [Mayer] received over twenty million dollars in compensation. In the last three years of his authority as studio head [Vogel inaccurately cited 1947, 1948 and 1949], the pictures we released lost nine million dollars. [This statement was also wrong.] This

is the man who, at age seventy-two, is attempting to recapture his position through the Tomlinson and Stanley Meyer machinations.

Even Vogel's adherents in the picture business knew that this statement, featured on the front page of the New York *Times*, was misleading. Quite apart from its errors of fact, Mayer had brought in millions in profits during his lifetime, and, in his last years at M.G.M., the studio had not shown a loss.

Meanwhile, the business consultants Heller and Company, headed by Charles MacBride, had prepared an independent report, called for by Joseph Vogel, on the matter of the conflict at Loew's and the corporation's present situation. The report was issued on July 25. To Vogel's dismay, it called for his resignation as president. Joseph Tomlinson was to replace him, Mayer was to become chairman and Louis Nizer was to be discharged. Nizer went to work on MacBride. His powers of persuasion were such, and his picture of the Loew's situation so gloomy, that MacBride reversed his position, declared his own report invalid and wrote a new judgment backing Vogel to the hilt. Tomlinson charged Vogel and Nizer with improperly influencing MacBride. Nizer tried to wean away from Louis B. Mayer one of Mayer's keenest supporters on the board, the Dallas banker Fred Florence. Florence failed to yield to Nizer's hypnotic powers of oratory, but he weakened Mayer's position by resigning.

Tomlinson took a rash step. Holding a 6–4 majority, he called for a rump meeting of the board on July 30 in New York. He knew that three members of the Vogel group would be unable to attend; Vogel himself was stranded in Hollywood. Vogel decided to sit still: his ploy here was to allow the Tomlinson group, unopposed, to elect Tomlinson and Louis B. Mayer and Stanley Meyer as directors; this would be proven to be illegal and could easily be found so in court, thus wrecking Mayer for good.

Increasingly weakened by anemia, with the word "leukemia" bandied around, without his knowledge, by his inner circle of doctors, Mayer had to brace himself for a trip to New York. At an executive meeting in Culver City, on July 26, Vogel advised the staff that he would be calling a September 12 stockholders' meeting to quash Mayer and Tomlinson for good. He was applauded by several of those Mayer had raised to the top of their profession.

Mayer arrived at the Hampshire House on Central Park South on July 29. The flight had tired him, but he was buoyed by the vigorous presence of a recent friend, former Hollywood producer Samuel Briskin, whom he had decided to bring to the Loew's board when he returned to glory.

Reporters swarmed around the hotel as Mayer walked to his limousine, which would carry him to the Loew's offices on the morning of the thirtieth. He answered every question and posed patiently for photographs. As he entered the Loew's Building, he was greeted by more press men. He said, smiling, and showing much of his old fire, "I am hungry to get back in business with Leo the Lion. I will bring back M.G.M.; I will restore the corporation to the top."

Pausing before he entered the eleventh-floor board room, Mayer told the reporters, "Mr. Vogel is, everyone agrees, a very nice man, but he is not competent to run Loew's, Inc."

His friends and supporters rose at the board room table to applaud him as he walked in. Louis A. Johnson was the chair. Present also were Kaufman Keller; Ray Lawson, managing director of the Royal Bank of Canada; Joseph Tomlinson and Stanley Meyer. Mayer and Briskin were elected to the board in a matter of minutes. They walked out in triumph to applause from their supporters.

That afternoon, Joseph Vogel issued a statement from Culver City declaring the meeting illegal; he maintained that a quorum of seven other than the chairman was required by the New York and Delaware bylaws, and that only five people were in attendance. He called the meeting "a brazen and revealing attempt by a small faction to prevent the stockholders from deciding whether Tomlinson and Mayer should be declined as directors." He went on to state that Mayer was now out in the open as a conspirator ("This program has simply been shifted from obstruction to usurpation").

Mayer laughed when the statement was quoted to him by reporters. On August 2, he was enjoying a late-morning coffee at Rumpelmayer's Coffee Shop in the St. Moritz Hotel near the Hampshire House when a process server handed him a summons. It came from two Loew's stockholders, Louis and Helen Brandt, brother and sister-in-law of the independent theater chain owner Harry Brandt, demanding that he pay back $3 million to the corporation because the clause in his contract calling for Mayer and his heirs to receive profits in perpetuity was illegal. The Brandts stated that he should not be receiving a retirement income of $36,000 a year, and that his receipt of $2.7 million as a severance payment was entirely out of order.

Two days later, Louis Nizer obtained an injunction against Mayer and Tomlinson serving as directors on the ground that they had not been elected by a proper majority of an approved board. Judge Herbert Spector of the New York Supreme Court issued the injunction on the basis that seven members were needed for a quorum. Tomlinson failed on appeal.

Mayer received this news on August 10. He had arrived in San Francisco on the seventh by air, and was taken directly from the plane in a very weakened condition to Stanford Hospital, where he was cared for by Drs. Arthur Bloomfield and William P. Creger. He had frequent blood transfusions starting on the eighth, every day for four days, and after that every six days. On August 11, Joseph Vogel sent out a letter to all shareholders and the press, again attacking Mayer. Feeling terrible, Mayer learned that Harry Brandt, brother of the two litigants whose summons had been served on him in New York, was forming a stockholders' protective committee to fight him. On August 16, Harry T. Arthur, chairman of the Southern California Theater Owners' Association, agreed to join Brandt in his attack. This was grievous news; Mayer had always believed he had Southern California theater managers in his pocket. The blood transfusions continued.

Mayer was still in the hospital on August 26, when, following a brilliant example of oratory from Louis Nizer, Chancellor Collins J. Sikes, of the Court of Chancellory at Delaware, declared that the July 30 rump committee had acted improperly and that Mayer and Briskin were to be removed at once from the board. This was a crushing blow to Mayer, who still managed, four days later, to show his customary good manners in sending a warm note to Herbert Hoover at the Waldorf Towers, regretting that he could not attend Hoover's birthday luncheon.

On September 16, Mayer was removed to Bel Air, where his favorite doctor, Oscar Magidson, visited him twice, ordering his removal to UCLA Medical Hospital on the morning of the eighteenth. At the hospital, Dr. John S. Lawrence was in charge. Dr. Magidson also visited the patient twice daily, with extraordinary devotion. Frantic, Mayer called on physicians from Boston and elsewhere, which was not easy for the resident physicians or for Dr. Magidson.

Mayer languished at UCLA for weeks. He was testy, fretful and bitter. He gave his nurses a difficult time. When an elderly nurse came to attend him, he climbed out of bed and screamed angrily at her, "You need this bed more than I do!" She fled in tears; an attractive young nurse replaced her.

Dr. Marmorston was with him during transfusion after transfusion. He still was not told that he had leukemia. Irene flew in from New York, acting, according to Jessie Marmorston's official biographer William Pashong, abominably. She played one doctor against the other, fought with the nurses and reduced everyone to exasperation. It was claimed by Dr. Marmorston that in that period Irene persuaded Mayer to alter his will, cutting out Dr. Marmorston's legacy of $250,000. Dr. Marmorston alleged that Irene told Mayer that if he left money to the doctor it might be thought, by Lawrence Weingarten and the public, that he had been Jessie's lover. There is no truth in the story; Mayer did not alter the will, which had remained in existence, unchanged, since 1955.

Mayer's physical condition deteriorated seriously. His system was unable to accept whole blood transfusions, a technique discontinued by the 1990s; he rejected the infusions violently. He suffered from very severe abdominal pain, which even morphine could not entirely suppress. He began bleeding from the gastrointestinal tract and suffered from heart rhythm problems. His transfusions came, of course, from male and female donors, who were paid $80 per person. One potential donor, a woman, claimed that he found out she was giving blood and refused to receive it on the ground that female blood would not mingle with male. Assuming the story is true, it would mean that he had not previously been informed of the sources of the blood he was receiving.

Often he would cry out, apparently referring to Edie, "Is she here yet? Is she outside?" Irene never told Edie this; according to Dr. Marmorston, she pretended her father was calling for her. Mayer began to hallucinate; Clarence Brown recalls that Mayer fancied that someone had come in in the night and turned off the blood plasma dripping from a bottle down a tube into his veins. He refused to sleep, telling Brown that "some son of a bitch might try to do it again." He told Dr. Marmorston the doctor had hung him upside down so the blood would remain in his brain. He screamed that his enemies had stolen his beautiful double bed and put him in this miserable single one. He yelled that there was no furniture in the hospital room (it was beautifully furnished, and filled with flowers) because his enemies had stolen the chairs and tables.

He refused to listen when his friends unwisely tried to tell him that the final decision of the Delaware Supreme Court on October 11 had been against him and that he was now irrevocably removed from the Loew's board. A kidney infection set in; he was so depressed that he even hid his face when he was told of the great hit of *Cinerama Paradise* in New York and Los Angeles. Nobody had the courage to tell him that Joseph Vogel was restored by an overwhelming majority at the October 12 stockholders' meeting. For him, anyway, it was all over.

Louis B. Mayer slipped into a coma in the late evening of October 28; there was no sign of recognition when his devoted wife came to his bedside. At 12:35 A.M., on October 29, he died.

# EPILOGUE

THE MEMORIAL SERVICE TOOK PLACE, with Rabbi Edgar Magnin presiding, at the Wilshire Boulevard Temple on October 31. Five thousand people gathered outside; only two thousand could be admitted. It has wrongly been claimed that Samuel Goldwyn, asked why so many attended, said, "They wanted to be sure he was dead." It was alleged with equal viciousness that many places in the synagogue were empty, but in fact a very few seats were being held for important persons who might arrive at the last minute.

Jeanette MacDonald sweetly sang "Ah, Sweet Mystery of Life." Cantor Samuel Browder intoned two Hebrew prayers.

The pallbearers were Myron Fox, Mendel Silberberg, Howard Strickling, Benjamin Swig, a San Francisco friend, and Louis Johnson. The honorary pallbearers included Herbert Hoover, Cardinal Spellman and Cardinal James Francis McIntire. Spencer Tracy was chosen to deliver the oration. It is said to have been worked on by Carey Wilson, John Lee Mahin and Howard Strickling, among others. It reflected Tracy and Katharine Hepburn's passionate admiration for Mayer. Among other things, Tracy said:

> The merchandise he handled was completely intangible. He couldn't weigh it with a scale or measure it with a yardstick. For it was a magical merchandise of laughter and tears, of enlightenment and education. It was nothing more than gossamer . . .

The will was probated. The exact amount of money in the estate was not made clear; at first, it was stated to be between $7 million and $8 million, but later this was corrected to a figure of $11.5 million. In order to avoid heavy taxes, much of the cash had already been disbursed, a substantial sum of it set up to form the Louis B. Mayer Foundation, which would make grants to universities, and to hospitals, for medical research. Mayer left Lorena the Bel Air house and its contents; five automobiles, including four surviving Chryslers, and $750,000 and interests in oils and minerals. He left $500,000 to Irene and nothing to Edie, her husband or her children, since "I have given them extremely substantial assistance during my lifetime through gifts and financial aid to William Goetz, and to the advancement of his career (as distinguished from that of my former son-in-law, David O. Selznick, who never requested nor accepted assistance from me) in the motion picture industry." Mayer set up a half-million-dollar trust for Suzanne, and another for his grandsons Jeffrey and Daniel Selznick. He left $100,000 to Jack Cummings; a meager $400 a month for life to his sister Ida; $25,000 to Ruth and Jack's sister Mitzi, Mrs. Sol Fielding; $50,000 to Myron Fox; $50,000 to Howard Strickling; $5,000 to his secretary, Jeanette Spooner; and, in a special codicil, $10,000 to a more recent secretary, Helene Stebbins Delson. His wife's relatives received decent legacies, but Mayer's other relatives, including his sister Yetta, were ignored.

The will made no mention of Mayer's ownership of the Rivoli Theater in New York, hotels in Manhattan and elsewhere, his office building at 197 N. Canon Drive, other buildings at 9401 and 9441 Wilshire Boulevard, property at 910 Hartford Way, Beverly Hills, a restaurant at 3520 Wilshire, land in Riverside County and in San Bernardino, legacies of the former Title Guaranty and Trust. His numerous horses also went unmentioned; Daniel Selznick, who became head of the Louis B. Mayer Foundation, cannot explain how they were disposed of, or who got the money. They may have been deeded separately to Lorena.

So poorly was the will worded by Myron Fox that no provision was made for payment to Mayer's numerous physicians, all of whom had to send demand letters to Fox in order to be reimbursed. As late as 1958 and 1959, the demands continued. Not even refuse collection services, groceries, veterinary services for the horses and stock transfer fees were paid until Fox was compelled to settle. Fox also moved in on various loans Mayer had made to his family: close to $40,000 to Sol Fielding, who was suing the estate for $750,000 restitution in the Palos Verdes Estates matter, and was forced by Fox into another humiliating settlement; $10,000 to Victor Orsatti and $5,000 to Orsatti's wife, Marie MacDonald; $10,000 to Adela Rogers St. Johns; and more modest amounts to Alfred E. Green, who had been with Mayer on *In Old Kentucky*; M.G.M. costume designer Irene (Gibbons), who was perpetually and mysteriously broke; and, oddly, Dr. Marmorston, who proceeded to take action against the estate for some $200,000 she was owed in many years of unpaid medical service. (Later, Myron Fox disgracefully settled with her for a mere $27,400.)

Because of Fox's inadequate preparation of the necessary documents, Lorena, who acted honestly, was forced to put up with a constant stream of dunning documents and letters. She herself had to apply to Fox for a living income of some $9,000 a month based on the substantial costs of running the Bel Air estate, and she also had to apply for funds in order to continue and complete Suzanne's education. This cannot have been pleasant for her, nor can Fox's relentless pursuit of Mayer's family for repayment of sums that surely could have been waived in view of Mayer's death.

Inventory after inventory was drawn up, as the threats of litigation, actual suits and countersuits dragged on. Some of the facts that emerged were intriguing: Lorena had been spending $51,000 a year on clothes, a very large sum for 1958, and she had not owned outright, it is astonishing to learn, the magnificent collection of jewelry that she kept in the house, including one $37,000 emerald-cut diamond ring (the gems were itemized among Mayer's legacies to her). Another revelation in the probate files was that Mayer had shares in Columbia Pictures and had retained a substantial holding in Loew's, Inc. The sheer number of his ownerships of horses was amazing. He had evidently built up his stable almost to the point it was at when he had his spectacular sale in 1947. Lorena sold the Bel Air house to Jerry Lewis in 1958 and remarried.

Today, Mayer's remains rest in a vault wall of the Home of Peace Cemetery, not far from the former site of the Selig Zoo. Above him sleeps his sister Ida. She was always said to be an even more powerful personality than he; it seems appropriate that, in death, she should still have first billing.

# ACKNOWLEDGMENTS

MY FIRST AND GREATEST DEBT is to the members of the Louis B. Mayer family, who, with unstinting generosity, and without restriction, granted, for this unauthorized biography, many hours of interviews and informal conversations, which collectively illuminated the history of their great relative. Daniel Mayer and Jeffrey Selznick, Ruth and Roy Rowland, Mitzi and Sol Fielding, Gerald and Irene Mayer and Irene Mayer Holt were mines of information. Throughout, my wonderful editor, Sarah Gallick, at Donald I. Fine, was an inspiration, an unstinting support and a guide; my copy editor Laura Daly was deeply appreciated and my agent, Daniel A. Strone, was always there when needed. The authorities Marc Wanamaker, David Thomson, Tony Slide and Robert Birchard read the book for accuracy.

Jeffrey Hearn in Washington, D.C., performed miracles in locating previously untapped government files, including the all-important Record Group 59: 8–4061: Motion Pictures: State Department files in the National Archives, which contained the entire foreign history of M.G.M. and Loew's, Inc.; Christopher Ely in San Francisco pored, undaunted, through thousands of uncataloged and unindexed William Randolph Hearst papers housed at the Bancroft Library, the University of California at Berkeley, and later, with his colleague Bill Lutton, did sterling work in Boston, Massachusetts, finding Mayer's homes, unearthing obscure documentation; David Bafumo combed through the collection of papers in the Franklin D. Roosevelt Memorial Library at Hyde Park, New York; and Matthew Parris diligently explored the Upton Sinclair collection at the Lilly Library of the University of Indiana at Bloomington, and opened the doors to the Will Hays collection at the Indianapolis Public Library.

Robert C. McKay went through thousands of Dore Schary papers at the University of Wisconsin at Madison; Paul Stewart searched the files of the Public Records Office at Kew, near London, England, and the files of the British Film Institute and the large collection of magazine holdings at Colindale, London; Dan Johnson, genealogist, found many treasures in the files of the Provincial Archives in Fredericton, New Brunswick, Canada; Marcia Koven of the Jewish Historical Society of St. John, N.B., did fine work in her special field; Julio Vera, Sherry Harris and Gerry Wineman searched faded cards, Soundex records, passenger lists and passport files at the Temple of the Latter Day Saints in West Los Angeles.

Jade Belyea undertook field work in Montreal, Quebec; in Los Angeles, a large and vigorous team worked for countless hours. They include Nile Coates, Richard Goetz, Caroline Yeh, Paul Sheifer, Richard Dreyfuss, Peter Stonier and Dino Pinto. Nile, Paul and Peter together copied some fifty-eight years of articles on the subject in hand in *Variety*, not a task for the fainthearted, since *Variety* has no index. In all, this splendid team uncovered a total of almost 55,000 pages of documents, almost all of them untouched by the scholar.

They received help from good people in archives and university libraries. Of these, I must single out Ned Comstock of the Doheny Library of the University of Southern California Special Collections; Howard Prouty and Barbara Hall of the Academy of Motion Picture Arts and Sciences Library in Los Angeles; the staffs of the Hearst collection at the Bancroft and the Library of the Yivo Institute for Jewish Research in New York (especially Mrs. Abramowicz, librarian); Dwight Miller and his associates at the Hoover Presidential Library at West Branch, Iowa; Dane Hartgrove, Kathie Nicastro and John Vandereit of the Civil Reference Branch of the National Archives in Washington, D.C.; John E. Taylor and Edward Reese of the Military Reference Branch; Robert W. Coren of the Center for Legislative Archives; David Pfeiffer of the National Records Center at Suitland, Maryland; Ronald C. Davis and Thomas Culpepper of the Institute for American Studies, Southern Methodist University, Dallas, Texas; Linda Davis of the National Security Archive; Joyce Muncie and Mattie George of the Maryland State Archives at Annapolis, Maryland; Randy Goss of the Delaware State Archives; Charles Bell of the University of Texas Library of the Performing Arts at Austin; Professor Douglas Gomery of the University of Maryland at College Park; Dr. Robert Gotlieb of the Mughar Memorial Library of the University of Boston; Robert Parks of the Roosevelt Memorial Library at Hyde Park; Joe Samora of the San Quentin Prison Archives; the staff of the Public Record Office, and the British Film Institute, London; the Provincial Archives of Canada at Fredericton; the Citizenship Records Office of Sydney, Nova Scotia; and the staffs of the

Los Angeles, San Francisco, Boston, Washington and New York Public Libraries, and the Lincoln Center Library of the Performing Arts.

I owe a tremendous debt to a grand trio of M.G.M. veterans, and close friends of Louis B. Mayer, the ever-loyal (and now, sadly deceased) Samuel Marx (I wish I had agreed with him on the Paul Bern case!), J. J. Cohn and Robert Vogel. I am especially grateful to Gerald Turbow and to those experts on the history of movies, including Marc Wanamaker, whose Bison Archive is a treasure trove for the historian; Robert Birchard, expert on the early days of film making; Professor Doyce Nunis, authority on Los Angeles history; Anthony Slide, fine chronicler of Hollywood's pioneers; and Miles Kreuger, friend and expert on the musical cinema and theater, whose Institute of the American Musical is a diamond mine. John Cooper of Starlight Roof, Pasadena, California, and Mary Reaves, and Eddie, Donovan, Heidi and all the Brandts of Eddie Brandt Video have been very helpful. Werner Pockart helped me to correspond with Leni Riefenstahl. The following are listed, not in any order, as having contributed indispensably to the chronicle: those deceased are itemized at the end.

Kirk Crivello; Wendy Cooper; Leatrice Gilbert Fountain, daughter of John Gilbert; Pierre Camus; Pierre Sauvage; Norma Pisar and Elizabeth Horowitz, daughters of Dr. Jessie Marmorston; Bill Pashong; Alice Garber; Philip Loewe; Gregg Mitchell; Ruth Spencer; Barbara Biane, niece of Howard Strickling; Mildred Nesselroth; Sharon Dobbs; David Bradley; Ken Du Maine; Howard Holtzman; Dorothy Colodny, daughter of Dr. May Romm; Dr. Brian Miller; Cathy Henderson; Bob Tabian; Clay Marquardt; Gerald Clarke; Tim de Grood; Mimi Henry; Sylvia Mazurki; Anthony Slide; Robert Gitt; Rich Finnegan; Rod Perla of All Systems Go, electronics genius; Betsy Maclain; Betty Lasky; Robert Board, Marion Davies expert, and his magic screening room; Harriet Frank, Jr., and Irving Ravetch, in their serendipity house; John Ernst; Kenneth Anger; Edward and Renée Torres Ashley; Vera Burnett, friend and stand-in of Marion Davies; Dr. Scott Christianson, studio dentist; Lisl Cade (wise New Yorker, great counselor); Michael Harris, ace attorney; Dr. Joseph Choi, retired Chief Autopsy Surgeon, Los Angeles; Amy Schiffman; Cooper C. Graham; Stephen Farber; Jay Garon; Patrick McGilligan; Dr. Michael Stefan, king of physicians; Mrs. Edwin H. Knopf.

And Paul Jarrico; Albert Hackett; Katharine Hepburn; Greer Garson; Aljean Harmetz; Charles Hooper; John Meredyth Lucas, son of Bess Meredyth; David Hahn; Ring Lardner, Jr.; Betty Comden and Adolph Green; Anita Page; Booth Woodruff, brother of Edwina Booth; Charles Hooper; Henry Rogers; Dean Strickling; Leni Riefenstahl; Sgt. Louis

Danoff, Hollywood Homicide Division, Los Angeles; William Tuttle; Marsha Hunt; Betty Garrett; Ted Arno and Susan Fraine of Loew's, Inc.; Donald Knox (where are you?), invaluable historian, interviewer for the American Film Institute Oral History Program; Joel Robinson; Joel Greenberg; Leonard Brener; Lillian Tall; Kevin Thomas; Judd Marmor; Michael Grace; Richard Renaldo; Harry and Maurice Rapf; Dorothy Manners; Jayne Meadows; Virginia O'Brien.

*And* Margaret O'Brien; Hurd Hatfield; George Sidney; Lillian Burns Sidney; Gregory Peck; Allan Jones; Walt Odets (who supplied the valuable correspondence between his father, Clifford Odets, and Luise Rainer); Gloria Stuart, gallant fighter of Nazism in the Los Angeles of the 1930s; Ann Rutherford; Rupert Allason, Member of Parliament (Nigel West); David Jenkins; Nick Oldsborough; Albert Regoso; Cecilia Callejo; Gloria Luckinbill; Armand Deutsch; Ruth Miller, daughter of ace detective LeRoy Sanderson; Sidney Kirkpatrick; Steve Robinson, Marie Dressler authority; Tessa Williams, Jeanette MacDonald authority, and her colleagues of the evergreen Jeanette MacDonald Fan Club; Scott Carrier and Robert Dambacher of the Coroner's Office of Los Angeles; Judge Lester Roth; Tondra Abrams of Sotheby's; Rospo and Barbara Pallenberg; Budd Schulberg; Sue Worsley; Mrs. Vincente (Lee) Minnelli; Marcella Rabwin, David O. Selznick's right hand for many years; Marianne Dirkson, daughter of Reinhold Schünzel; Cliff Jahr; Judy Lowman; Mrs. Walter Jurmann; Mrs. Emmerich Kalman; Louisa di Salvio, princess of caterers; Edward Turk; Albert Band; Hal Elias; Mrs. Ernst Jaeger; Dr. Martha Mierendorf; Jerry Berg, guardian of the Rabbi Magnin papers; Nick Beck, devoted historian; Dorothy M. Brown, helpful biographer of the late Mabel Walker Willebrandt; Pandro S. Berman; Herbert Nusbaum, former M.G.M. legal counsel and good friend to film scholars; Bobs Watson; Richard Ney; Ann Miller; Ginny Simms; Robert Young; Martin Kosleck, friend and confidant of the late Mercedes de Acosta; and Victoria Shellin, *sine qua non* of my working life, who undertook the fearsome task of typing this book.

Of those no longer living, I would like to name my beloved friend, King Vidor; Howard Strickling, devoted friend of Louis B. Mayer, master publicist; Frank Whitbeck, his inspired associate; Douglas Shearer; Clarence Brown; William Daniels; Norman Foster; Raquel Torres; Phil Berg and Leila Hyams; Nick Grinde; Lee Garmes; Leatrice Joy; James Wong Howe; Victor Saville (whose unpublished memoirs proved to be a valuable source); Ina Claire; Duncan Renaldo; Mrs. Olive Carey; Nelson Eddy; Rouben Mamoulian; Elsa Lanchester; Walter Reisch; George Cukor; Herman G. Weinberg; Mervyn LeRoy; Miliza Korjus; Sir William

Stephenson; Joe Pasternak; Wallace Worsley; Barbara Stanwyck; Robert Surtees; and Spyros Skouras.

## ARCHIVES, LIBRARIES AND OFFICES CONSULTED

Yivo Institute for Jewish Research; St. John, New Brunswick; Jewish Historical Society, Citizenship Registration Office, Sydney, Nova Scotia; Provincial Archives, Fredericton, New Brunswick; National Library, Ottawa; Land Registry Office, Montreal; Boston Historical Society; Boston Census Archives; Haverhill Historical Society; Boston Superior Court Archives; Bison Archives; Los Angeles Central Library City Directory Archives; California State University, Northridge, Map Room; Los Angeles Hall of Records; Los Angeles City and County Archives; Lincoln Center Library of the Performing Arts: New York Public Library; National Archives and Records Service, Washington, D.C.; and the branches in Suitland, Maryland; Laguna Niguel, California; St. Louis, Missouri; Bayonne, New Jersey; Hearst Archives, Bancroft Library, University of California at Berkeley; Doheny Library, University of Southern California; UCLA Research Library, Los Angeles; M.G.M. legal files, then at Culver City, now sadly unavailable to scholars in Atlantic City; the Louis B. Mayer Library of the American Film Institute, Los Angeles; Academy of Motion Picture Arts and Sciences; Hearst Newspaper Archives, USC; Loew's, Inc., papers; Hoover Presidential Library, West Branch, Iowa; Howard Strickling Archives, Upland, California; Indianapolis Public Library; Lillie Library, University of Indiana, Bloomington; Library of the Performing Arts, University of Texas, Austin; American Film Institute, Los Angeles; Von Kleinsmid Library, USC; Public Record Office, London; Library of Congress, Washington, D.C.; Franklin D. Roosevelt Memorial Library, Hyde Park, New York; University of Wisconsin, Madison; Northwestern University; Chicago Public Library; Georgetown University Library.

## SPECIAL ACKNOWLEDGMENT

Roger Mayer of Turner Entertainment made available over four hundred important motion pictures, including many from TNT's unique Warner Brothers collection. Not only was I able to see scores of important films not yet available on videocassette or laser disc, which provided an important picture of the fine craftsmanship of a great studio, but comparisons were invaluable. Thus, I could see how a director like William Dieterle made a certain kind of rich, heavy, opulently mounted biography at Warner's, for example, *The Life of Emile Zola* and *Juarez*, while at M.G.M., in *Tennessee Johnson*, he worked in a more sober, conservative and even more accomplished mode. It was possible through that lost Warner classic *I Loved a Woman* to see how Alfred E. Green, Mayer's director of the old Selig Zoo days, developed into a refined craftsman and directed (very well) the second Mrs. Mayer, Lorena Jones Danker, in a small part in the picture. It was possible to observe Barbara Stanwyck, free, fierce and exciting in Warner's *The Gay Sisters* and *My Reputation*, as the controlled, reserved star of M.G.M.'s equally splendid *East Side, West Side* and the extraordinary, unknown *B. F.'s Daughter*. Such Warner's social dramas as *They Won't Forget* and *Dust by My Destiny* could be compared with M.G.M.'s *Fury* and *Intruder in the Dust*; the restraint and severity of the M.G.M. pictures contrasted with the all-out passion and vibrant attack of the Warner films. In addition, comparisons with 20th Century-Fox pictures were instructive; far too few of these have been released and I had to lean heavily on friends who had taped Fox pictures off television, but the comparison with the Warner product was, I found, more meaningful. Jerry Solowitz and Marianne Goldson and Dick May of Turner were other stalwarts who made this enterprise of comparison possible; my debt to them can never be repaid.

# SELECTED
# BIBLIOGRAPHY

Astor, Mary. *Mary Astor: A Life on Film*. New York: Delacorte Press, 1971.

Baedeker, Karl. *Central Italy and Rome*. New York: Charles Scribner's Sons, 1909.

———. *Northern Germany*. Leipzig: Karl Baedeker, Publisher, 1913.

———. *Berlin and Its Environs*. New York: Charles Scribner's Sons, 1923.

———. *Italy from the Alps to Naples*. Leipzig: Karl Baedeker, Publisher, 1928.

Bainbridge, John. *Garbo*. New York: Holt, Rinehart and Winston, 1971.

Barlett, Donald L., and James B. Steele. *Empire—The Life, Legend and Madness of Howard Hughes*. New York: W. W. Norton, 1979.

Behlmer, Rudy. *Memo From David O. Selznick*. New York: The Viking Press, 1972.

Berg, A. Scott. *Goldwyn: A Biography*. New York: Alfred A. Knopf, 1989.

Berg-Pan, Renata. *Leni Riefenstahl*. Boston: Twayne Publishers, 1980.

Bowen, Norman R., comp. *Lowell Thomas, the Stranger Everyone Knows*. New York: Doubleday & Company, Inc., 1968.

Brenman-Gibson, Margaret. *Clifford Odets: American Playwright*. Volume One. New York: Atheneum, 1982.

Brown, Dorothy M. *Mabel Walker Willebrandt: A Study of Power, Loyalty, and Law*. Knoxville: University of Tennessee Press, 1984.

Callinicos, Constantine, with Ray Robinson. *The Mario Lanza Story*. New York: Coward-McCann, Inc., 1960.

Cameron, Evan William. *Sound and the Cinema—The Coming of Sound to American Film*. New York: Redgrave Publishing Company, 1980.

Cazemajou, Jean. *Stephen Crane, 1871–1900, Écrivain Journaliste*. Paris: Librairie Didier, 1969.

Coffee, Lenore. *Storyline—Reflections of a Hollywood Screenwriter*. London: Cassell, 1973.

Cole, Lester. *Hollywood Red*. Palo Alto, Calif.: Ramparts Press, 1981.

Conway, Michael, Dion McGregor, and Mark Ricci, comps. *The Films of Greta Garbo*. New York: Cadillac Publishing Company, Inc., ND.

Crane, Stephen. *Stephen Crane: Letters*. New York: New York University Press, 1960.

Danischewsky, M., ed. *Michael Balcon's 25 Years in Films*. London: World Film Publications, Ltd., 1947.

de Acosta, Mercedes. *Here Lies the Heart*. New York: Arno Press, 1975.

deMille, Agnes. *Dance to the Piper*. Boston: Little, Brown, 1952.

Deutsch, Armand. *Me and Bogie*. New York: G. P. Putnam's Sons, 1991.

Dressler, Marie. *The Life Story of an Ugly Duckling*. New York: Robert M. McBride and Company, 1924.

———. *My Own Story*. Boston: Little, Brown, 1934.

Drosnin, Michael. *Citizen Hughes*. New York: Holt, Rinehart and Winston, 1985.

Eames, John Douglas. *The M.G.M. Story*. New York: Crown, 1975.

Erté. *Things I Remember*. New York: Quadrangle/New York Times Book Company, 1975.

Fairbanks, Douglas, Jr. *The Salad Days*. New York: Doubleday, 1988.

Forslund, Bengt. *Victor Sjostrom*. New York: Zoetrope, 1988.

Fountain, Leatrice Gilbert. *Dark Star*. New York: St. Martin's Press, 1985.

Frank, Gerold. *Judy*. New York: Harper & Row, 1975.

Gabler, Neil. *An Empire of Their Own*. New York: Doubleday, 1987.

Geist, Kenneth L. *Pictures Will Talk*. New York: Charles Scribner's Sons, 1978.

Gerber, Albert B. *Bashful Billionaire: The Story of Howard Hughes*. New York: Lyle Stuart, Inc., 1967.

Gilbert, Martin. *Winston S. Churchill: The Wilderness Years (1929–1935)*. London: Heinemann, 1981.

Glyn, Anthony. *Elinor Glyn*. London: Hutchinson, 1955.

Glyn, Elinor. *Romantic Adventure*. London: Ivor Nicholson and Watson, Ltd., 1936.

Granger, Stewart. *Sparks Fly Upward*. New York: G. P. Putnam's Sons, 1981.

Grobel, Lawrence. *The Hustons*. New York: Charles Scribner's Sons, 1989.

Guttmann, Allen. *The Games Must Go On: Avery Brundage and the Olympic Movement*. New York: Columbia University Press, 1984.

Hepburn, Katharine. *Me*. New York: Alfred A. Knopf, 1991.

Hoover, Irwin Hood. *42 Years in the White House*. Boston: Houghton Mifflin Company, 1934.

Hopper, Hedda. *From Under My Hat*. New York: Doubleday, 1952.

Hunt, Frazier. *The Untold Story of Douglas MacArthur*. New York: Devin-Adair Co., 1954.

Huston, John. *An Open Book*. New York: Alfred A. Knopf, 1980.

Infield, Glenn B. *Leni Riefenstahl*. New York: Thomas Y. Crowell, 1976.

Karl, Frederick R. *William Faulkner: American Writer*. New York, Weidenfeld and Nicholson, 1989.

Kirkpatrick, Sidney D. *A Cast of Killers*. New York: E. P. Dutton, 1986.

Kotsibilas-Davis, James. *The Barrymores*. New York: Crown, 1981.

Kotsibilas-Davis, James, and Myrna Loy. *Myrna Loy: Being and Becoming*. New York: Alfred A. Knopf, 1987.

Lambert, Gavin. *Norma Shearer*. New York: Alfred A. Knopf, 1990.

Lewis, Sinclair. *It Can't Happen Here*. New York: Doubleday, Doran, 1935.

Loos, Anita. *A Girl Like I*. New York: The Viking Press, 1966.

———. *Kiss Hollywood Good-bye*. New York: Viking, 1974.

MacArthur, Douglas. *Reminiscences—General of the Army*. New York: McGraw Hill Book Company, 1964.

Marion, Frances. *Off With Their Heads!* New York: Macmillan, 1972.

———. *Spiders in a Bottle* (unpublished), circa 1972.

Napley, Sir David. *Rasputin in Hollywood*. New York: Weidenfeld and Nicholson, 1990.

Nash, Jay Robert, and Stanley Ralph Ross. *The Motion Picture Guide*. Chicago, IL: Cinebooks, 1986.

Oates, Stephen D. *William Faulkner: The Man and the Artist*. New York: Harper & Row, 1987.

Odets, Clifford. *The Time Is Ripe*. Edited by Walt Odets. New York: Grove Press, 1988.

O'Leary, Liam. *Rex Ingram*. Dublin, Ireland: The Academy Press, 1980.

Parish, J. R., and R. L. Bowers. *The M.G.M. Stock Company*. New York: Bonanza, 1972.

Pensel, Hans. *Seastrom and Stiller in Hollywood*. New York: Vantage Press, 1969.

Peters, Margot. *The House of Barrymore*. New York: Alfred A. Knopf, 1990.

Prindle, David F. *The Politics of Glamour*. Madison: The University of Wisconsin Press, 1988.

Robinson, David. *Chaplin*. New York: McGraw Hill, 1985.

Ross, Irwin. *The Image Merchants*. New York: Doubleday, 1959.

Ross, Lillian. *Picture*. New York: Holt, Rinehart and Winston, 1961.

Ross, Murray. *Stars and Stripes*. New York: Columbia University Press, 1941.

Sarlot, Raymond, and Fred E. Basten. *Life at the Marmont*. Santa Monica, Calif.: Roundtable, 1987.

Schary, Dore. *Heyday*. Boston, Toronto: Little Brown, 1979.

Schulberg, Budd A. *Moving Pictures: Memories of a Hollywood Prince*. New York: Stein and Day, 1981.

Selznick, Irene Mayer. *A Private View*. New York: Alfred A. Knopf, 1983.

Shearer, Norma. *Autobiography*. Unpublished; worked on by Howard Strickling.

Shulman, Irving. *Harlow, an Intimate Biography*. New York: Dell Publishing Company, Inc., 1964.

Sinclair, Upton. *Upton Sinclair Presents William Fox*. Published by the author, 1933.

———. *The Autobiography of Upton Sinclair*. New York: Harcourt Brace and World, 1962.

Slide, Anthony. *The Idols of Silence*. Cranbury, N.J.: A. S. Barnes, 1976.

———. *Early Women Directors*. Cranbury, N.J.: A. S. Barnes, 1977.

————. *The American Film Industry: A Historical Dictionary*. New York: Limelight Editions, 1990.

Stewart, Donald Ogden. *By a Stroke of Luck!* New York: Paddington Press, Ltd., 1975.

Strait, Raymond. *Lanza, His Tragic Life*. Englewood Cliffs, N.J.: Prentice-Hall, Inc., 1980.

Tornabene, Lyn. *Long Live the King: A Biography of Clark Gable*. New York, G. P. Putnam's Sons, 1976.

Turner, Lana. *Lana: The Lady, the Legend, the Truth*. New York: G. P. Putnam's Sons, 1976.

Vance, Ethel. *Escape*. New York: Grosset and Dunlap, 1939.

Van Dyke, W. S. *Horning into Africa*. Los Angeles: California Graphic Press, 1931.

Veiller, Bayard. *The Fun I've Had*. New York: Reynal and Hitchcock, 1941.

Vickers, Hugo. *Cecil Beaton*. London: Weidenfeld and Nicholson, 1985.

# NOTES ON SOURCES

## CHAPTER ONE

BIRTHPLACE: Louis B. Mayer naturalization papers; spellings: Yivo Institute for Jewish Research, New York. BIRTHDATES: Yetta Mayer papers, courtesy Irene Mayer Holt. GRAVESTONES: Probate files. ADDRESSES: City directories: Brooklyn, New York; St. John, New Brunswick. DETAILS OF ST. JOHN: Interview: Marcia Koven, St. John Jewish Historical Society files; clippings; photographs. MAYER'S SCHOOLING: Grade school records: Provincial Archives, Fredericton, New Brunswick; interview: Mrs. E. MacCready. ECHO STORY: Interview: Allan Jones. RESTAURANT STORY: Conversation with Adela Rogers St. Johns. CITIZENSHIP OF JACOB MAYER: Provincial Immigration Archives, Sydney, Nova Scotia. BAR MITZVAH: Description based on photograph courtesy Mr. and Mrs. Sol Fielding. DETAILS OF KOMIENSKYS: Interviews: Mrs. Roy Rowland, Mrs. Sol Fielding, Irene Mayer Holt. MARRIAGE: Interviews: Mrs. Mildred Nesselroth, Mrs. Roy Rowland. SCHENBERG AND MAYER HOUSEHOLDS: Census report supplied by Boston Historical Society. BROOKLYN: City directories.

## CHAPTER TWO

YOUNG EXHIBITOR: Screen Producers' Guild speech cited. ADDRESSES IN HAVERHILL: Haverhill city directories. DESCRIPTION OF HOUSES: Haverhill Historical Society, photographs and clippings. ORPHEUM THEATER: Programs courtesy Haverhill Historical Society; *Evening Gazette* files. DIVORCE OF KOMIENSKYS: St. John; Boston Superior Court records. SARAH MAYER'S DEATH: Death certificate; interview: Mrs. Roy Rowland.

## CHAPTER THREE

AMERICAN FEATURE FILM CORPORATION: Corporate records: Boston Archives. *THE SQUAW MAN*: Cecil B. DeMille papers. ALCO: *Variety*; *The*

*Moving Picture World.* MASON: Courtesy Herbert Goldman; records of St. Cecile Lodge. RECEIVERSHIP: New York Federal District Court dockets. RICHARD ROWLAND: *Variety; The Moving Picture World.* FRANCIS X. BUSHMAN: Interview: Mrs. Iva Bushman; *Wid* magazine, 1914–1917; *Photoplay,* 1914–1917. MARY MILES MINTER; Interview: Ruth Rowland OLGA PETROVA: *Motion Picture Story* magazine; *Shadowland; Wid; The Moving Picture World,* 1914–1917. ANITA STEWART: Interview: DeWitt Bodeen; *Photoplay,* 1914–1917. SMITH LITIGATION: New York Superior Court dockets; *The Moving Picture World.*

## CHAPTER FOUR

VITAGRAPH CASE: Boston Superior Court dockets. DRAFT EVASION: National Archives files, St. Louis. MONTREAL SALVAGE BUSINESSES: Montreal city directories; corporate records; interview: Gerald Mayer. YETTA MAYER STORE: Interview: Irene Mayer Holt. JULIUS MEYER: Interview: Mrs. Roy Rowland; Boston Superior Court dockets. SELZNICKS: Irene Selznick memoirs. ADDRESSES IN BOSTON: Boston city directories; local research photographs by Chris and Lesley Ely and Bill Lutton. *VIRTUOUS WIVES* ACCOUNT: Hedda Hopper memoirs. *IN OLD KENTUCKY: The Moving Picture World; Variety, Wid,* 1917–1918. SELIG ZOO: Selig papers, Academy of Motion Picture Arts and Sciences, Los Angeles; interview: Professor Doyce Nunis. TRAIN JOURNEY: interview: Edith Goetz; Martin Quigley Collection, Georgetown University, Washington, D.C.

## CHAPTER FIVE

ARRIVAL IN LOS ANGELES: Description from photographs courtesy the Bison Archive and Marc Wanamaker; interview: Professor Doyce Nunis; Los Angeles guide books; city directories. EARLY STUDIOS: Interviews: Marc Wanamaker, Robert Birchard, Doyce Nunis, Anthony Slide. LOIS WEBER: Interview: Anthony Slide; *Motion Picture Story* magazine; *Variety; The Moving Picture World; Wid.* CHAPLIN/HARRIS: David Robinson authorized biography. NEW YORK TRIP: Irene Selznick memoirs. TRUCKEE SHOOT: *Variety; The Moving Picture World.* CLAUSON, KATTERJOHN CASES: Los Angeles Superior Court records. TRANSIT DOCUMENTS: Jerry and Rheba Mayer, St. Alban's Records, Mormon Temple, Los Angeles.

## CHAPTER SIX

FAILURE OF COMPANY: Interview: Gerald Mayer. TRIP TO PALM SPRINGS: Interview: Mrs. Roy Rowland; her papers. BESS MEREDYTH: Interview: John Meredyth Lucas (son). FRANCES MARION: Interviews: Frances Marion; her unpublished manuscript, *Spiders in a Bottle.* KENMORE HOUSE: Grantor/Grantee real estate documents, Los Angeles Hall of Records.

WILL HAYS: Will Hays papers, Indianapolis Public Library. LEROY SAN-
DERSON REPORTS: LeRoy Sanderson papers, courtesy Ruth Miller (daugh-
ter). B. P. SCHULBERG: Interview: Budd Schulberg. NEW YORK, SAN
FRANCISCO VISITS: *Variety*; *The Moving Picture World*; San Francisco
*Chronicle*. HARRIS LAWSUIT: *Variety*; Los Angeles Superior Court dockets.

## CHAPTER SEVEN

IRVING THALBERG: Interviews: J. J. Cohn, Samuel Marx, Robert Vogel,
Howard Strickling; Strickling papers courtesy Beverly Biane (niece). REAL
ESTATE COMPANIES: Grantor/grantee records, Los Angeles. PAUL BERN:
Interviews: Samuel Marx, Leatrice Gilbert Fountain, Leatrice Joy, DeWitt
Bodeen, King Vidor, J. J. Cohn. BARBARA LA MARR: Interview: Leatrice
Gilbert Fountain; *Photoplay*. NORMA SHEARER: Howard Strickling papers;
interviews: Douglas Shearer, Irene Mayer Holt, J. J. Cohn, Samuel Marx; Gavin
Lambert biography; portions of unfinished memoir by Norma Shearer with
Howard Strickling, courtesy Beverly Biane. MARCUS LOEW: Marcus Loew
Collection, Lincoln Center Library of the Performing Arts, New York.
SCHENCK BIRTHDATES: Immigration application forms, National Archives,
Bayonne, New Jersey. CONEY ISLAND PARTY: *Variety*. RAMON
NAVARRO: Interviews: DeWitt Bodeen, Howard Strickling, J. J. Cohn, Sam-
uel Marx.

## CHAPTER EIGHT

STUDIO PROBLEMS: Testimony under oath: Nicholas Schenck, 77th Con-
gress, First Session, September 7–10, 1941; interviews: Robert Birchard, Marc
Wanamaker, Anthony Slide, Doyce Nunis. WILLIAM RANDOLPH
HEARST: Hearst papers, Bancroft Library, University of California at Berkeley.
ELINOR GLYN: Interview: King Vidor. ERICH VON STROHEIM: Interview:
J.J. Cohn. *BEN-HUR*: Exhaustive files on production, Doheny Library, USC,
Los Angeles. MABEL WALKER WILLEBRANDT: Interview: Dorothy M.
Brown; her biography of Mabel Walker Willebrandt.

## CHAPTER NINE

GARBO: Garbo legal file supplied by Herbert Nusbaum, former M.G.M. legal
counsel, 1987. TOD BROWNING: Interview: Forrest J. Ackerman. ERTÉ:
Memoirs. DUELL CASE: Gish memoirs. BIRTHDAY OF STUDIO: *Variety*.
HAVERHILL HOMECOMING: Same. M.G.M. STUDIO TOUR MOVIE:
Courtesy Robert Birchard. *THE BIG PARADE*: Interview: King Vidor. CHAR-
IOT RACE: Interview: J. J. Cohn.

## CHAPTER TEN

SANTA MONICA, GLENDALE LAND: Grantor/grantee records, Los Angeles. TITLE GUARANTEE AND TRUST: Same. SAN FRANCISCO VISIT: San Francisco *Chronicle*. JOHN GILBERT: Interviews: Leatrice Gilbert, King Vidor, J. J. Cohn. HOWARD STRICKLING: Interview: Barbara Biane. ZUKOR: *Variety*. BREWSTER: *Variety*. *ANNIE LAURIE*: Gish memoirs. PRITCHARD: Superior Court of Los Angeles records. WEDDING: Leatrice Gilbert Fountain: *Dark Star*. NORMA SHEARER: Howard Strickling papers; Shearer-Strickling unfinished memoir. EDITH GOETZ: Interview: Edith Goetz. RAPF: Interviews: Maurice and Harry Rapf. CUMMINGS FAMILY: Interviews: Mrs. Roy Rowland, Mrs. Sol Fielding. MOTLEY FLINT/JULIAN: Superior Court of Los Angeles records.

## CHAPTER ELEVEN

BANQUET: *Variety*. HANSON: Los Angeles *Times*. L. B. MAYER ARREST DOCUMENT: Superior Court of Los Angeles records. GILBERT ARREST: Same. MAYER TALKS TO DAUGHTERS: Interview: Edith Goetz; Irene Selznick memoirs. KING VIDOR: Interview: King Vidor. SELZNICK: M.G.M. files. ASA KEYES: Los Angeles Superior Court records. THALBERG–SHEARER: Howard Strickling files; memoir. PLAYA DEL REY: Grantor/ grantee records, Los Angeles. *THE WIND*: Lillian Gish memoirs. LONGWORTH: *Variety*. RADIO: *Variety*. *ROSE MARIE*: *Variety*. *CALLAHANS AND MURPHYS*: *Variety*. DRESSLER/MUSSOLINI: Dressler memoirs. LOEW DEATH: *Variety*; New York *Times*, Los Angeles *Times*. THE SCHENCKS: Interviews: King Vidor, J. J. Cohn, Samuel Marx. LION STUNT: *Variety*. LINDBERGH: Los Angeles *Examiner*. KOVERMAN TELEGRAM: Hoover Library, West Branch, Iowa. BALL: Los Angeles *Times*. NEW YORK TRIP: *Variety*. *JAZZ SINGER* OPENING: *Variety*; New York *World*. *THE TRAIL OF '98*: Interview: Clarence Brown. SELZNICK CHARACTER: Interview: Marcella Rabwin. THALBERG–SHEARER HONEYMOON: Howard Strickling papers; interview: Douglas Shearer; Norma Shearer memoir. *WHITE SHADOWS*: Interview: Raquel Torres. VAUDEVILLE SHORTS: Interview: Nick Grinde. MISHAPS: Interviews: William Haines, Phil Berg, Leila Hyams, Anita Page, Norman Foster, King Vidor, J. J. Cohn, Douglas Shearer.

## CHAPTER TWELVE

CECIL B. DeMILLE AT M.G.M.: DeMille papers seen at DeMille's estate. *THE BROADWAY MELODY*: Interview: Anita Page. KANSAS CITY TRIP: San Francisco *Chronicle*. HOOVER CAMPAIGN: Hoover papers. THE BELLAMY TRIAL: M.G.M. files. JOHN GILBERT: Interview: Ina Claire. JULIAN: Los Angeles Superior Court records. LOEW/FOX: Upton Sinclair correspondence with William Fox for an authorized biography; Sinclair papers, Indiana University at Bloomington. *HALLELUJAH*: Interview: King Vidor; M.G.M. files. *TRADER HORN*: This and all subsequent references: Interviews: Booth Woodruff (brother of Edwina Booth), Olive Carey, Duncan Renaldo, Richard Renaldo; Edwina Booth papers courtesy Booth Woodruff; State Department files; National Archives, Washington, D.C. WILLEBRANDT: Willebrandt papers. KOVERMAN LETTERS, STRING-PULLING: Hoover papers. *TRIAL OF MARY DUGAN*: Bayard Veiller memoirs; M.G.M. files; Shearer/ Strickling memoir. AMBASSADOR TO TURKEY: Hoover papers; State Department files. ACADEMY AWARDS: Academy of Motion Picture Arts and Sciences files. *MADAME X*: M.G.M. files. ROBERT MONTGOMERY: Interviews: Howard Strickling, Douglas Shearer, J. J. Cohn, Frank Whitbeck, Irene Mayer Holt. CLASH WITH IRENE: Irene Selznick memoirs. FOX STRUGGLES FOR CONTROL: Upton Sinclair/Fox correspondence, Bloomington; *Fortune* magazine. HEARST-WARNER'S NEGOTIATIONS: Hearst papers. EDITH GOETZ: Interview: Edith Goetz. ACCIDENT: New York *Times*; *Variety*; Sinclair papers. MUNDSZTUK: Hoover papers. SHAREHOLDER SUIT: *Variety*; *Wall Street Journal*. CHURCHILL: Los Angeles *Times*; Strickling papers. THALBERG MONEY SCAM: *Variety*; Interview: Samuel Marx.

## CHAPTER THIRTEEN

MAYER STATE OF MIND: Interviews: King Vidor, Ina Claire, William Haines, Howard Strickling, J. J. Cohn, Frances Marion, Samuel Marx. CULVER: Interview: Robert Vogel. KATE CORBALEY: Interview: Samuel Marx. ORSATTI: Los Angeles Superior Court records. ANTIQUES SCAM: Interview: Wallace Worsley. GOETZ WEDDING: Interview: Edith Goetz; Los Angeles *Times*; photograph of grave inscription: Nile Coates. RUDOLPH MAYER: Interviews: J. J. Cohn, Sol Fielding, Irene Mayer Holt; *Variety*; Federal Court files. BIG QUARREL: Irene Selznick memoirs. FOX/LOEW'S: Upton Sinclair papers. SUMMIT DRIVE HOUSE: Interview: Marcella Rabin. FLINT AND CHANEY DEATHS: Los Angeles *Times*. RICHIE LETTER: Hoover papers. *PHANTOM OF PARIS*/EDNA BEST: *Variety*. FIGHT WITH WRITERS: *Variety*. ROBERT YOUNG: Interview: Robert Young (for the New York *Times*). SUPREME COURT HEARING: Supreme Court files. JACKIE COOPER CONTRACT: Los Angeles Hall of Records. WALLACE BEERY: Los Angeles *Examiner*; M.G.M. files. GABLE: Lyn Tornabene: *Long Live the King*. MARGARET MAYER POSITION: *Variety*. STOCKHOLDER SUIT: *Variety*; *Wall Street Journal*. SALARY CUTS: *Variety*. GABLE WALKOUT: Tornabene. EXTORTION PLOT: Los Angeles *Times*; Los Angeles Superior Court records. *DESPERATE*: De Acosta memoirs. *GRAND HOTEL*: M.G.M. files.

## CHAPTER FOURTEEN

JERRY MAYER FIRED: Interview: Gerald Mayer. PARTY: Confidnetial source. BROTHEL: Confidential source. TRIP TO WASHINGTON: *Variety*; Washington *Post*. LAWSUIT: Los Angeles Superior Court records. CHICAGO: Hoover papers. BANK FAILURE: State Department files. PAYMENT DEFERRED: Interview: Margaret O'Sullivan. JOSEPH JACKSON: Los Angeles *Times*. HARLOW WEDDING: Anita Loos; Irene Selznick memoirs. AFFAIR WITH AD SCHULBERG: Interview: Budd Schulberg; Schulberg memoirs. SCHULBERG/FELDMAN AGENCY: Charles Feldman collection, American Film Institute, Los Angeles. GAMES: Los Angeles *Times*. BRUCE/GILBERT WEDDING: Los Angeles *Examiner*. SELZNICK: Irene Selznick memoirs; Selznick papers, Hoblitzelle Theater Collection, University of Texas at Austin, courtesy Jeffrey Selznick, Charles Bell. PAUL BERN DEATH: Coroner's files; probate files on Paul Bern; interview: Dr. Joseph Choi; inquest hearing transcription; Los Angeles *Times* and *Examiner*; interviews: Samuel Marx, Joyce Vanderveen, Howard Strickling, J. J. Cohn, King Vidor, Adela Rogers St. Johns. GOULDING: State Department files; Anita Loos letter to Cecil Beaton; Mabel Walker Willebrandt letters. LOEW EXPEDITION AND AIR CRASH: State Department files. RALLY: Hoover papers. THALBERG/SELZNICK: Selznick papers. THAU: Interviews: Howard Strickling, J. J. Cohn, Samuel Marx. DUNCAN RENALDO CASE: *Variety*. RUDOLPH MAYER SCAM: State Department files; *Variety*. RASPUTIN LAWSUIT: New York *Times*. GABRIEL: Walter Wanger collection, University of Wisconsin at Madison. SELZNICK AT M.G.M.: Selznick files. EARTHQUAKE: Los Angeles *Times*; Irene Selznick memoirs. CASH FLOWN IN: *Variety*. STRIKE PLANS, SALARY CUTS: *Variety*. DESCRIPTION OF MEETING/VAJDA/ROBSON, ETC: Interview: Samuel Marx. SCHENCK/EARLY: Early files, Franklin D. Roosevelt Memorial Library, Hyde Park, New York. QUESTIONABLE OPERATIONS: Irene Selznick memoirs; Upton Sinclair papers. MAYER/EARLY: Roosevelt Library. CRAWFORD/FAIRBANKS: Los Angeles *Examiner*; morgue clips: *Examiner* cross-files, annex, University of Southern California Libraries, Los Angeles. ILLNESS, COLLAPSE: Hearst papers.

## CHAPTER FIFTEEN

HOMECOMING: Hearst/Hoover papers. THALBERG TRIP: Howard Strickling papers; Shearer/Strickling memoirs; Interview: Samuel Marx; *Variety*; Gavin Lambert: *Norma Shearer*; interviews: Tessa Williams, Nelson Eddy. DRESSLER STORY: Dressler memoirs. MAYER/SELZNICK/EARLY: Roosevelt Library. BOLSTERING 20th: Tornabene; Interview: Mary Astor. HARLOW BEHAVIOR: *Variety*. CLASH WITH WARNER: *Variety*. MAUREEN O'SULLIVAN/MAYER: Interviw: Maureen O'Sullivan. CLOVER CLUB: Interview: Samuel Marx; Irene Selznick memoirs. SELZNICK PROB-

LEMS: Selznick papers, Austin, Texas. GABLE ILLNESS: Tornabene. KISS BREAKS TEETH: Interview: Dr. Scott Christianson, studio dentist. MacDON-ALD/MAYER: Interviews: Tessa Williams, Samuel Marx. SHEARER/ANTOI-NETTE: Gavin Lambert biography. TRAIN TRIP/LOEB: *Variety*. IRENE IN-FORMER: Irene Selznick memoirs. ESKIMO: W. S. Van Dyke memoirs. MYRNA LOY: Myrna Loy memoirs. MAYER/MacDONALD PROPOSAL: In-terview: Tessa Williams. *QUEEN CHRISTINA*: Interview: Samuel Marx; M.G.M. files; interview: Rouben Mamoulian; Walter Wanger papers, University of Wisconsin at Madison; Leatrice Gilbert Fountain: *Dark Star*. CRAWFORD SALARY: *Variety*. GABLE ACCIDENT, COVERUP, MILTON BEECHER: Interview: Samuel Marx. HARLOW: Selznick files. ARGUMENTS AT HO-TEL: Raymond Sarlot and Fred E. Baston: *The History of the Chateau Marmont*. HUSTON CRASH: Lawrence Grobel: *The Hustons*. PARTY: Los Angeles *Ex-aminer*. BUNGALOW: Interview: Samuel Marx; Ben Hecht papers, Northwest-ern University, Chicago. *VIVA VILLA* INCIDENT: State Department files; Selznick papers. TONE/CRAWFORD: Los Angeles *Examiner*. O'SULLIVAN/FARROW: Interview: Maureen O'Sullivan. HARLOW CASE: Los Angeles Superior Court records. HIBERNIANS: San Francisco *Chronicle*. GARBO/MAMOULIAN: Interview: Rouben Mamoulian. CODE: Lester Cole files: Academy of Motion Picture Arts and Sciences. YOUSSOUPOFF SUIT: Lon-don *Times*; interview: Harold Holtzmann. RALSTON: Interview: Esther Ral-ston. JEAN HOWARD: Conversations with Jean Howard before this book planned; *Vanity Fair; Interview* magazine; New York *Times* (variously on Ethel Borden); Ethel Borden obituaries; interviews: Samuel Marx, Mrs. Edward Ash-ley (Renée Torres); Charles Feldman papers. CAREY WILSON: Interview: Samuel Marx; Los Angeles *Times* and *Examiner*. MAYER RAIDS: *Variety*; Hearst/Hoover papers. BARRETTS: Interviews: Maureen O'Sullivan, Elsa Lanchester; Charles Laughton and William Randolph Hearst papers. GARBO/ELIZABETH ALLAN: Interview: Roy Moseley. LAWSUIT: Los Angeles Supe-rior Court records. SELZNICKS' RETURN: *Variety*; Los Angeles *Exam-iner*.PRACTICAL JOKE: Interview: Herman G. Weinberg. ROSSON'S PO-LIO: Los Angeles *Times* and *Examiner*; *Variety*. HOWARD BURGLARY: Los Angeles *Times*. RUDOLPH MAYER: State Department/Willebrandt files. TRACY: Interview: Bobs Watson; Katharine Hepburn memoirs; interview: Howard Strickling. *THE GOOD EARTH*: State Department files, including complete correspondence M.G.M./U.S. consuls in China. HARLOW/POW-ELL: standard Harlow biographies. BORDEN/SAND: *Variety*. DRESSLER DEATH: Interviews: Howard Strickling, Samuel Marx. KAPER/JURMANN: Interview: Mrs. Yvonne Jurmann. HYSTERECTOMY: Interviews: Samuel Marx, Mrs. Sol Fielding. JEAN HOWARD: See above. MARRIAGE: Los An-geles *Examiner*; Feldman papers. FELDMAN AGENCY: Feldman papers, American Film Institute. UPTON SINCLAIR: Upton Sinclair papers; news-reels courtesy UCLA film archive. LONDON VISIT: *Kinematograph* weekly; British Film Institute files.

## CHAPTER SIXTEEN

HEARST/WARNER: Hearst papers. DAVID COPPERFIELD: *Variety*. UNIONS: *Variety*. MacDONALD/RICHIE: Interviews: Samuel Marx, Tessa Williams. ALLAN JONES: Interview: Allan Jones. NELSON EDDY: Interview: Nelson Eddy. MARX BROTHERS: Interviews: Samuel Marx, J. J. Cohn, Robert Vogel. *MUTINY:* M.G.M. files; Charles Laughton papers (courtesy Elsa Lanchester); interview: Elsa Lanchester; *Variety*. GABLE: Interview: Tay Garnett. MUSICALS: Interview: Marvyn LeRoy. RUDOLPH MAYER: State Department/Willebrandt papers. WERFEL/*MUSA DAGH:* State Department files; interview: Robert Vogel. MAYER ARGUMENTS: *Variety*.MARX BROTHERS: As above. BOUNTY: As above. *AH, WILDERNESS:* Interview: Allan Jones. LUISE RAINER: Clifford Odets/Rainer letters, courtesy Walt Odets; interviews: Walter Reisch, Samuel Marx, Robert Vogel, Billie Burke. SELZNICK GRUMBLES: Selznick papers. GRADY/LICHTMAN: *Variety*. JOHN GILBERT: Interview: Leatrice Gilbert Fountain; *Dark Star;* interview: Marlene Dietrich. HEALY INCIDENT: *Variety*. ROSABELLE LAEMMLE RETURN: Interview: Samuel Marx. RUDOLPH: State Department/Willebrandt files. *SAN FRANCISCO* THEME SONG: Interview: Yvonne Jurmann. *THE GOOD EARTH:* State Department files. UNIONS: *Variety*; LeRoy Sanderson police files. BROWNE–BIOFF SCAM: New York *Times*; LeRoy Sanderson police files. BANQUET: Los Angeles *Times*. MAYER/SELZNICKS/GOETZES: Interview: Edith Goetz; Irene Selznick memoirs. JUDY GARLAND: Interview: John Graham; Gerold Frank biography. ORSATTI WEDDING: Los Angeles *Examiner*. LANSKE: *Variety*. ROOSEVELT SUPPORT IN SECRET: Roosevelt papers. WANGER/MAYER: Charles Feldman papers. *IT CAN'T HAPPEN HERE:* Interview: Samuel Marx. IMPORTING JEWS: Interview: Walter Reisch. CUKOR ARREST: Interview: Patrick McGilligan. ST. JOHN VISIT: Los Angeles *Times*, St. John papers.

## CHAPTER SEVENTEEN

THALBERG ILLNESS AND DEATH: Los Angeles *Times;* interview: Tessa Williams. PREMIERE: Interview: Frank Whitbeck. MAYTIME: Interview: Tessa Williams. SAN FRANCISCO: San Francisco *Chronicle*. SHEARER FIGHT: Los Angeles Superior Court records. HOLLYWOOD POLITICS: Interviews: Gloria Stuart, Dr. Martha Mierendorf; Georg Gyssling files, Department of Army, Intelligence and Security Command, Fort Meade, Maryland. PARNELL: Tournabene. SAN FRANCISCO: San Francisco *Chronicle*. ENGLAND: *Kinematograph Weekly*. HARDY SERIES: M.G.M. files, USC; interview: Samuel Marx. THALBERG WILL: Hall of Records, Los Angeles. EASTERN VISIT: *Variety*. ODETSES: Academy files. STROMBERG/MAYER: AMPAS files. PARTY: *Variety*. LILLIAN BURNS: Interview: Lillian Burns Sidney. HARLOW: Death records/probate files, Los Angeles Superior Court.

ABORTION RUMOR: Interview: Sidney Kirkpatrick (documents seen by him in LeRoy Sanderson papers are missing). BRITAIN: *Kinematograph Weekly; Variety*. BALCON: Victor Saville memoirs. DOUGLAS: Interview: Melvyn Douglas. YETTA VISIT: Interview: Irene Mayer Holt. TRIP TO ITALY: *Variety; Kinematograph Weekly;* State Department files. ROACH AND MUSSOLINI: State Department files. AD SCHULBERG: Interview: Budd Schulberg. STAR FINDS: Interview: Budd Schulberg; *Variety*. BRITAIN: Michael Balcon memoirs; Victor Saville unpublished memoirs. ALEXANDER KORDA SECRET AGENT: Interview: Rupert Allason, MP (Nigel West). VICTOR SAVILLE AS SECRET AGENT: Confidential family source. TRANSATLANTIC CROSSING: Cecil Beaton Diaries; Joel Greenberg Oral History with Walter Reisch, American Film Institute series; interview: Walter Reisch. ROACH/ MUSSOLINI/HOLLYWOOD: State Department files; C. L. Willard special reports. WINDSORS: State Department files. GYSSLING: Gyssling files. MERVYN LeROY: LeRoy memoirs; conversations with Mervyn LeRoy.

## CHAPTER EIGHTEEN

MAYER ROUTINE: Donald Knox interview with Sue Ream Taurog Oral History, American Film Institute. PRINTS TO HITLER AND MUSSOLINI: Interview: Samuel Marx. HARDY SERIES: Interview: Samuel Marx. BEATRICE ROBERTS: Pandro S. Berman Oral History, American Film Institute; interviews: Pandro S. Berman, Samuel Marx, Kirk Crivello. *THREE COMRADES:* Motion Picture Production Code files, Academy of Motion Picture Arts and Sciences, Los Angeles. *IDIOT'S DELIGHT:* Same. *MARIE ANTOINETTE:* M.G.M. files. RUTHERFORD: Interview: Ann Rutherford. GARLAND: Gerold Frank biography. MILIZA KORJUS: FBI main files on Hilda Kruger. SHEARER DEMANDS: *Variety.* SHRINE SPEECH: San Francisco *Chronicle.* JERRY MAYER: *Variety* interview: Gerald Mayer. CINEMATOGRAPHERS: *Variety.* BOYS TOWN: Schary memoirs; interview: Bobs Watson. *THE CITADEL:* Interview: King Vidor; Victor Saville memoirs. HORSES: Los Angeles *Examiner;* various racing magazines; interviews: Samuel Marx, J. J. Cohn. *GONE WITH THE WIND:* Nicholas Schenck statement, Senate committee, September 1941. CORBALEY DEATH: Interview: Samuel Marx. LUISE RAINER BEHAVIOR: Lana Turner memoirs; Dr. Margaret Brenman Gibson: *Clifford Odets, Volume 1* (unfinished). LETTER TO ROOSEVELT: Franklin D. Roosevelt Memorial Library, Hyde Park, New York. GARSON/ALLAN: Victor Saville memoirs. NEBLITT CASE: *Variety.* LENI RIEFENSTAHL: Riefenstahl memoirs; series by Ernst Jaeger, Hollywood *Tribune;* interviews: Mrs. Ernst Jaeger, Robert Vogel; Riefenstahl biographies; letter from Leni Riefenstahl to author; State Department files. STRENGHOLT: Interview: Robert Vogel. *MUSA DAGH:* State Department files. ROGERS: Interview: Robert Vogel. LUBITSCH: Interviews: Herbert Luft, Herman G. Weinberg. MUSSOLINI/ ROACH: As above. GARBO AS SPY: Interviews: Sir William Stephenson, Victor Saville. ST. JOHN VISIT: Marcia Koven, Jewish Historical Society; St.

John papers, Dan Johnson. KIBRE: LeRoy Sanderson police files. QUIGLEY: State Department files; Quigley papers, Georgetown University. LOY: Loy memoirs. SUIT: Chancery files, Wilmington, Delaware. NORTHWEST PAS-SAGE: Interview: King Vidor. BUCHMAN: Variety, Los Angeles Times; In Fact; interview: George Seldes. ATHENIA: Interview: Nicola Lubitsch (daughter). FLORIAN: State Department files; print courtesy Turner Entertainment; Immigration files. RICHARD ROSSON ARREST: State Department files.

## CHAPTER NINETEEN

ESCAPE: Variety. WILLIAM LeBARON: New York Herald Tribune. SCHUNZEL: Interview: Marianne Dirksen (daughter). PHYLLIS BOTTOME: Los Angeles Superior Court files. THE PHILADELPHIA STORY: Interview: Katharine Hepburn. GONE WITH THE WIND: Interview: Marcella Rabwin. FINNISH: Interview: Robert Vogel. THE MORTAL STORM: Victor Saville memoirs. HIBERNIANS: San Francisco Chronicle. SAXE-COBURG-GOTHA: Gyssling files, Department of Army. RUDOLPH MAYER: State Department/ Willebrandt papers. LONDON/WAR: Victor Saville memoirs; British Film Institute files. DARRELL/MEXICO/BOMBING OF L.A.: FBI files, Franklin D. Roosevelt Memorial Library, Hyde Park, New York. GARBO/WENNER-GREN: Wenner-Gren FBI main file, Charles Higham Collection, USC. GONE WITH THE WIND PRINTS SEIZURE: State Department files. THE YEAR-LING: Interview: Wallace Worsley. HEPBURN: Interviews: Katharine Hepburn, George Cukor, Pandrdo S. Berman, Lawrence Weingarten. CITIZEN KANE: Orson Welles papers, Indiana University, Bloomington; assistant, Michael Romary. PLAGIARISM/BERMAN: Interview: Pandro S. Berman. SELZ-NICK: Selznick papers. TRUST SUITS: Variety; Wall Street Journal. RU-DOLPH MAYER: State Department/Willebrandt papers. MONTGOMERY: Variety. JOHN CARROLL/LAUNDRY: Interview: Allan Jones. IRENE HER-VEY/SALARY: Same source. AVA GARDNER: Interview: Edith Goetz. SHIP-PING/DIAZ: State Department files. ZIEGFELD GIRL: Interview: Pandro S. Berman. LILLIE MESSENGER: Interview: Samuel Marx. SUIT: Los Angeles Superior Court files. DORE SCHARY: Dore Schary papers; interviews: Harry and Maurice Rapf. CITIZEN KANE: See above. BIRD STORY/JERRY MAYER: Interview: Robert Vogel. SCHENCK TRIAL: New York Times. SKEL-TON: Variety. HORSES: Los Angeles Examiner. FIELDING WEDDING: Los Angeles Times. DR. JEKYLL: Saville memoirs. SAROYAN: Interview: Samuel Marx; Saroyan biographies. PASTERNAK: Interview: Joe Pasternak. FBI/PAS-TERNAK: Errol Flynn FBI files, USC. KEEPER OF THE FLAME: Victor Saville memoirs. WOMAN OF THE YEAR: Interviews: Katharine Hepburn, George Stevens. SPELLMAN: Charles Higham, American Swastika. LOEW'S/ GERMANY: State Department files. SHEEHAN/NYE, ETC.: Drew Pearson reports, various. COMMITTEE: Hearings published 1942 (see bibliography for full details.) ABOVE SUSPICION: Motion Picture Code files.

## CHAPTER TWENTY

*MRS. MINIVER:* Interview: Greer Garson. DISTRIBUTION OF FILMS ABROAD: State Department files. NORMA SHEARER DEPARTURE: Interview: Irene Mayer Holt; Charles Feldman papers. ESTHER WILLIAMS: Broadcast transcript, USC, Doheny Library, courtesy Ned Comstock. KEEPER: Interview: Katharine Hepburn; Motion Picture Code files. MARGARET O'BRIEN: Interview: Margaret O'Brien. STUDIO MERRIMENT/COMPOSERS: Interview: Marsha Hunt. RUDOLPH MAYER: Los Angeles *Examiner.* HYMAN/MARMORSTON: Interviews: Elizabeth Horowitz (daughter), William Pashong, authorized biographer of Marmorston. THREAT: Los Angeles Superior Court files. GOETZ/MARGARET MAYER: Interviews: Edie Goetz, Marsha Hunt, Mrs. Edwin H. Knopf. LANA TURNER: Lana Turner memoirs. SCHARY: Interviews: Samuel Marx, Sol Fielding. TENNESSEE JOHNSON: Office of War Information files, Suitland, Maryland, branch of the National Archives; Roosevelt Memorial Library files; interview: Dr. Martha Mierendorf, Dieterle authority. PAUL JARRICO: Interview: Paul Jarrico. KORDA: *Variety.* GINNY SIMMS: Interview: Ginny Simms. RUDOLPH MAYER: Interviews: Howard Strickling, Robert Vogel, Gerald Mayer, Sol Fielding. TRUMBO: Interview: Dalton Trumbo. MEXICO AWARD: Interview: Robert Vogel. *MEET ME IN ST. LOUIS:* Arthur Freed papers, Doheny Library, USC. ANN MILLER: Interview: Ann Miller. LESCH: State Department files. LEAVING MARGARET MAYER: Interviews: Sol and Mitzi Fielding, Luisa di Salvio. *DORIAN GRAY:* Interview: Hurd Hatfield. GARLAND: Arthur Freed papers. DEBORAH KERR: M.G.M. files. *THE HARVEY GIRLS:* Interview: George Sidney; Arthur Freed papers.

## CHAPTER TWENTY-ONE

GABLE RETURN: Tornabene. VACUUM HINGE: Interview: Mrs. Edwin H. Knopf. LOEW/EUROPEAN FUNDS: State Department files. E. ARNOT ROBERTSON: London *Times.* GARSON/BUSHER: Interview: Samuel Marx. DR. MAY ROMM: Interview: Dorothy Colodny. LUISA DI SALVIO: Interview: Luisa di Salvio. *THE YEARLING:* Interview: Gregory Peck; Academy of Motion Picture Arts and Sciences files; interview: Clarence Brown. SELZNICK/JONES: Irene Selznick memoirs; interview: Edith Goetz. MILLER/MILNER: Ann Miller memoirs. *THE BEGINNING OR THE END?:* Interview: Samuel Marx. GARSON ACCIDENT: Los Angeles *Examiner.* LORENA DANKER: Interview: Dorothy Manners; AMPAS files; *I Loved a Woman* courtesy Turner Entertainment. RUSSELL STORY: Interview: Dorothy Manners. STRIKE: Los Angeles *Examiner.* IRENE SELZNICK IN THE THEATER: Irene Selznick memoirs. AUCTION OF HORSES: Los Angeles *Times.* FAMILY AFFAIRS: Interviews: all family members. RUDOLPH MAYER/PALOS VERDES ESTATES: Los Angeles Superior Court files; interviews: Sol Fielding, Irene

Mayer Holt. DIVORCE: Los Angeles Superior Court files; also DIVORCE
AND COURT CASES. CAROLE BRANDT: *Variety*. LESTER COLE: Lester
Cole memoirs. KATZ STORY: Lester Cole memoirs. MICKEY ROSNER:
Westbrook Pegler papers, Hoover Presidential Library, West Branch. JERRY'S
DEATH: Interview: Gerald Mayer. HOUSE COMMITTEE: HUAC transcripts,
U.S. Government Printing Office, 1948. WALDORF CONFERENCE: Dore
Schary papers. COLE/TRAIN: Lester Cole memoirs. THAU/GIFFORD: Los
Angeles *Times*. LANZA: Academy of Motion Picture Arts and Sciences; inter-
view: Joe Pasternak. SKOURAS: Interview: Spiro S. Skouras. *B. F.'s DAUGH-
TER*: Political comment supplemented by Dr. Gerald Turbow. UNITED JEW-
ISH APPEAL: Mayer collection, Doheny Library, USC.

## CHAPTER TWENTY-TWO

SCHARY: Dore Schary papers, including contracts, University of Wisconsin at
Madison; Dore Schary: *Heyday*; interviews: Armand Deutsch, George Sidney.
*QUO VADIS?*: Academy of Motion Picture Arts and Sciences files; State De-
partment files; Lawrence Grobel: *The Hustons*; interview: Hugh Gray. ELOPE-
MENT: Los Angeles *Times*; Academy files. COLE HEARING: Los Angeles
Superior Court files. *ON THE TOWN*: Interview: Gene Kelly, published in
part in Charles Higham: *Celebrity Circus*. BETTY GARRETT: Interview: Betty
Garrett. *INTRUDER IN THE DUST*: Faulkner biographies, various. FIEL-
DING MATTER: Interview: Sol Fielding; Grantor/grantee records. LUISA DI
SALVIO: Interview: Luisa di Salvio. WILLIAM LUDWIG: Don Knox: Oral
History with William Ludwig for the American Film Institute. COMMUNIST
HUNT AT STUDIO: Interview: Armand Deutsch. MAYER EAVESDROPS:
Interview: Kenneth Anger. SCHARY: See above. *QUO VADIS?*: See above.
*ON THE TOWN*: Interview: Gene Kelly, Ann Miller, Betty Garrett. *ANNIE
GET YOUR GUN*: Interview: Betty Garrett. JUDY GARLAND/BOSTON
HOSPITAL: Gerold Frank: *Judy*. JEWISH WAR VETERANS' DINNER: Louis
B. Mayer papers, USC. RIVERSIDE: Los Angeles Superior Court records.
CUMMINGS DEDICATIONS: St. John Jewish Historical Society. K.T. KEL-
LER: *Current Biography*. *QUO VADIS?* AMPAS files; conversations with
Mervyn LeRoy before book planned. TAYLOR ADULTERY: Conversations
with Rovert Surtees. UNIONS IN ROME: State Department files. BEL AIR
HOUSE/FAMILY: Interview: Dorothy Manners. *KING SOLOMON'S MINES*:
Academy files; Stewart Granger memoirs. LIZA MINNELLI: Don Knox: Oral
History with Charles Walters for American Film Institute. LANZA: Interview:
Joe Pasternak; Academy files. SCHARY AGAIN: As above. HUSTON/
MAMMY STORY: Huston memoirs. *RED BADGE*: Lillian Ross: *Picture*; inter-
view: Albert Band; Academy files; Schary papers; conversations with John Hus-
ton. GARLAND THROAT-CUTTING: Gerold Frank biography.

## CHAPTER TWENTY-THREE

CARTER BARRON DEATH: Washington *Post*. *SHOW BOAT*: Interview: George Sidney. RUDOLPH MAYER DEATH: Los Angeles *Times; Examiner* morgue; death certificate; interviews: Sol Fielding, Irene Mayer Holt. STOCK OPTIONS: Schary files; *Variety*. SANTA ANITA INCIDENT: Los Angeles *Examiner* morgue; numerous clips. HORSE WHIPPING: Interview: Billy Wilder. THOMAS BRADY INTERVIEW: New York *Times;* JAYNE MEADOWS: Interview: Jayne Meadows. MAYER ATTACK ON COMPANY: Don Knox Oral History with Dore Schary for American Film Institute; Schary papers and *Heyday;* Westbrook Pegler papers, Hoover Library. MAYER'S DEPARTURE: Knox Oral History; Schary papers; Schary: *Heyday;* Academy files; interviews: J. J. Cohn, Robert Vogel, Howard Strickling; Strickling papers. *Variety;* New York *Times;* Los Angeles *Times*. AMBASSADOR EAST, CHICAGO MEETING: Dore Schary: *Heyday;* Schary papers. LURIE/DEALS/WARNER'S, RKO RE-PUBLIC/PLANNED TAKEOVERS: *Variety*. HORSES: *Variety*. LEWIS STONE: Los Angeles *Times; Variety*. THURN-UND-TAXIS: *Variety*. GAR-FIELD: *Variety*. HUGHES DISCUSSIONS: *Variety*. CINERAMA: Academy files; Charles Higham: *Hollywood at Sunset;* interview: Spiro S. Skouras; Laurance Rockefeller; GOETZ/STEVENSON/SCHARY: Interviews: Edith Goetz, Mimi Henry (Goetz's niece); Schary papers; Dore Schary: *Heyday:* Adlai Stevenson papers. INDUSTRIAL AWARD: Louis B. Mayer papers, USC. MILE-STONE AWARD: *Variety*. CINEMASCOPE: Interview: Spiro S. Skouras; Academy files. RICHARD ROSSON, ETHEL BORDEN DEATHS: *Variety*. *JOSEPH AND HIS BRETHREN:* Interview: Jerry Wald (who later acquired rights). ED SULLIVAN SHOW: *Variety*. HAVERHILL VISIT: Haverhill Historical Society. IDA KOVERMAN WILL: Probate files, Los Angeles Hall of Records.

## CHAPTER TWENTY-FOUR

DARK DAYS AT M.G.M.: Schary papers. CINERAMA: Academy files. MAR-GARET MAYER DEATH: Probate files, Los Angeles Hall of Records; Interview: Edith Goetz. SANDLER SUIT: Los Angeles Superior Court files; *Variety*. MAYER/ENGLAND: Conversations with Clarence Brown before book planned. HAMPTON: *Variety;* interview. ATTACK ON STARS: *American Weekly*. LINCOLN HOTEL: *Variety*. ILLNESS: Interviews: Elizabeth Horowitz (Marmorston daughter), William Pashong. SCHARY FIRING: Schary papers; Dore Schary: *Heyday*. DR. BLOOMFIELD AND OTHER MEDICAL DATA: Louis B. Mayer probate files; numerous bills; details of treatments; letters to Myron S. Fox; interview: William Pashong. PROXY FIGHT: *Fortune* magazine; the New York *Times, The Wall Street Journal;* Louis Nizer memoirs. SUM-MONS: *Variety*. DEATH: Interviews: Clarence Brown, William Pashong.

MEDICAL CHARGES: Louis B. Mayer probate file; medical bills and reports by all doctors concerned.

## EPILOGUE

FUNERAL: Los Angeles *Times*. WILL: Louis B. Mayer probate files. PROP-ERTY OWNERSHIPS: Probate files; lawsuits from Sol Fielding, Yetta Mayer, et al., Los Angeles Superior Court files. VAULT: Visit to Home of Peace Cemetery with Gerald Mayer.

# INDEX

American support, 123, 239, 265, 270
death of, 348
M.G.M. films distributed to, 268, 275, 289
Mussolini, Vittorio, 264, 265, 270, 271, 289
Mussolini Prize, 239, 287
*Mutiny on the Bounty* (film), 232–33, 237–39, 243
Mutual Pictures, 26
Myers, Carmel, 90, 159
*Mystic, The* (film), 90, 93

Nagel, Conrad, 70, 90, 94, 117, 126, 150, 188, 199, 276
Nathan, Robert, 344
*National Velvet* (book and film), 268, 333, 349, 355, 381
*Naughty Marietta* (film), 230, 231, 232, 251
Nazimova, Alla, 299
Nazis
American film industry relations, 277, 302
American sympathizers, 256, 286–87, 295, 300, 301
Austrian film industry and, 249, 290
British support of, 271
films condemning, 297–98, 311, 312, 315, 316
Hearst meeting with, 226–27
Mayer and Thalberg speeches against, 208, 242, 280–81, 291
see also Anti-Nazi League; Hitler, Adolf; Jews
Neblitt, William H., 285
Neilan, Marshall (Mickey), 42–43, 46, 51, 71, 75, 90–91
*Neptune's Daughter* (film), 378–79
Nesselroth, Mildred, 12
*Never the Twain Shall Meet* (film), 87
New Brunswick. See St. John (New Brunswick)
*New Moon* (film), 170, 294
New Orpheum Theater, 17, 20, 21
Newsreels, 122, 143, 146, 148–49, 157, 227–28
Ney, Richard, 335, 336, 381
Neylan, John Francis, 257
Niblo, Fred, 55, 64, 70, 76, 77, 81, 82, 87, 88, 98, 102, 108, 117, 150
Nichols, Dudley, 246
Nielsen, Alice, 19–20
Nigh, William, 122
*Night at the Opera, A* (film), 232, 236
*Night Flight* (film), 206, 241
Nimitz, C. W., 392
*Ninotchka* (film), 289, 290, 295, 314, 370

Nixon, Richard, 368
Nizer, Louis, 426, 427, 428, 429, 430
Nolan, Mary, 137, 166
*None Shall Escape* (film), 363
Nordhoff, Charles, 233
Normand, Mabel, 49
Norris, Peter, 110
North, Wilfrid, 36
*Northwest Passage* (film), 293
Novarro, Ramon, 64, 67, 70, 76, 88, 151, 177
career decline, 171, 176
films, 94, 98, 102, 164, 207, 209
homosexuality, 64
"talkie" films, 130, 137, 152, 155
Nye, Gerald P., 268, 315

Oberon, Merle, 332
Oboler, Arch, 297
O'Brien, Gladys, 321, 333
O'Brien, Margaret, 320–21, 336, 337, 340, 345, 351, 359, 362
Academy Awards, 348
retirement, 391
O'Connor, J. F. T., 249, 361
Odets, Clifford, 241, 256, 258, 259, 280, 285, 417
Odlum, Floyd, 412
*Of Human Hearts* (film), 283
*Old Music* (play), 265
Olivier, Laurence, 210
*Olympiad* (film), 287
Olympic Games, 182, 286, 287
Omoolu, Mutya, 153
*On an Island with You* (film), 374
*On Borrowed Time* (film), 282
*One Clear Call* (film), 51, 53, 54
O'Neil, Nance, 20
O'Neill, Sally, 122
*On the Town* (play and film), 383–84, 389
*Operator Thirteen* (film), 220
Operetta films, 232
Oppenheimer, Robert, 354
*Opposite Sex, The* (film), 424
Orpheum Theater, 16–17
see also New Orpheum Theater
Orr, William A., 101
Orsatti, Frank, 46, 157, 158, 176, 181, 182, 217, 249, 256, 283, 349–50, 362
Orsatti, Morris, 157
Orsatti, Victor, 433
Osborn, Paul, 282, 302, 331, 336, 350, 351
Oscar awards. See Academy Awards
O'Sullivan, Maureen, 172, 205, 214–15, 230, 274